T0140259

IFIP Advances in Information and Communication Technology

568

Editor-in-Chief

Kai Rannenberg, Goethe University Frankfurt, Germany

IFIP – The International Federation for Information Processing

IFIP was founded in 1960 under the auspices of UNESCO, following the first World Computer Congress held in Paris the previous year. A federation for societies working in information processing, IFIP's aim is two-fold: to support information processing in the countries of its members and to encourage technology transfer to developing nations. As its mission statement clearly states:

IFIP is the global non-profit federation of societies of ICT professionals that aims at achieving a worldwide professional and socially responsible development and application of information and communication technologies.

IFIP is a non-profit-making organization, run almost solely by 2500 volunteers. It operates through a number of technical committees and working groups, which organize events and publications. IFIP's events range from large international open conferences to working conferences and local seminars.

The flagship event is the IFIP World Computer Congress, at which both invited and contributed papers are presented. Contributed papers are rigorously refereed and the rejection rate is high.

As with the Congress, participation in the open conferences is open to all and papers may be invited or submitted. Again, submitted papers are stringently refereed.

The working conferences are structured differently. They are usually run by a working group and attendance is generally smaller and occasionally by invitation only. Their purpose is to create an atmosphere conducive to innovation and development. Refereeing is also rigorous and papers are subjected to extensive group discussion.

Publications arising from IFIP events vary. The papers presented at the IFIP World Computer Congress and at open conferences are published as conference proceedings, while the results of the working conferences are often published as collections of selected and edited papers.

IFIP distinguishes three types of institutional membership: Country Representative Members, Members at Large, and Associate Members. The type of organization that can apply for membership is a wide variety and includes national or international societies of individual computer scientists/ICT professionals, associations or federations of such societies, government institutions/government related organizations, national or international research institutes or consortia, universities, academies of sciences, companies, national or international associations or federations of companies.

More information about this series at http://www.springer.com/series/6102

Luis M. Camarinha-Matos ·
Hamideh Afsarmanesh ·
Dario Antonelli (Eds.)

Collaborative Networks and Digital Transformation

20th IFIP WG 5.5 Working Conference
on Virtual Enterprises, PRO-VE 2019
Turin, Italy, September 23–25, 2019
Proceedings

 Springer

Editors
Luis M. Camarinha-Matos ⓘ
NOVA University of Lisbon
Monte Caparica, Portugal

Hamideh Afsarmanesh ⓘ
University of Amsterdam
Amsterdam, The Netherlands

Dario Antonelli ⓘ
Polytechnic University of Turin
Turin, Italy

ISSN 1868-4238   ISSN 1868-422X (electronic)
IFIP Advances in Information and Communication Technology
ISBN 978-3-030-28466-4   ISBN 978-3-030-28464-0 (eBook)
https://doi.org/10.1007/978-3-030-28464-0

This Springer imprint is published by the registered company Springer Nature Switzerland AG
The registered company address is: Gewerbestrasse 11, 6330 Cham, Switzerland

Preface

Collaborative Networks and Digital Transformation

Collaboration is a main enabler for organizations striving to achieve differentiated competitive advantage. The 4th Industrial Revolution and its wide variety of emerging dimensions are characterized both by their required extensive digitalization as well as strong interconnections among their composed systems, products, services, value chains, and business models, among others.

The increasing availability of sensors and the smart and mobile devices connected to the Internet, powered by the pervasiveness of Cyber-Physical Systems and Internet of Things equipped with distributed computational power and intelligence, have boosted hyper-connected organizations. The focal points of this revolution span over: vertical integration of smart production systems, horizontal integration of organizations through global value chain networks, adoption of through-engineering across the entire value chain, acceleration in manufacturing and service provision, and digitalization of provided products and services, giving rise to new business models that support customer intimacy. Next to Industry 4.0, the same trends increasingly surface in many other areas and sectors, including: Economy 4.0, Health 4.0, Agriculture 4.0, Transportation 4.0, Water 4.0, Tourism 4.0, Logistics 4.0, etc.

These emerging trends challenge the way collaborative networks and systems are designed and operate. Previously proposed solutions for the networks' organizational structures, applied algorithms and mechanisms, governance principles and models, among others, need to be revisited and redesigned in order to comply with the speed of evolving scenarios. Furthermore, the new proposed solutions shall converge a number of relevant advanced technologies, such as CPS, IoT, Linked Data, Data Privacy, Federated Systems, Big Data, Data Mining, Sensing Technologies, and many others. They shall additionally suggest a stronger focus on system dynamics, addressing the impact of several variables, such as the time, location, and population.

PRO-VE 2019 provides a forum for sharing experiences, discussing trends, identifying challenges, and introducing innovative solutions aimed at fulfilling the vision of goal-oriented collaboration in networks that support digital transformation. Understanding, modeling, and proposing solution approaches in this area require contributions from multiple and diverse areas of research and development, including computer science, industrial and electrical engineering, social sciences, economy, organizational science, and advanced technologies, among others. Comprising these areas is well tuned to the interdisciplinary spirit of the PRO-VE Working Conferences.

PRO-VE 2019, held in Turin, Italy, was the 20th event in this series of successful conferences, including:

PRO-VE 1999 (Porto, Portugal), PRO-VE 2000 (Florianopolis, Brazil), PRO-VE 2002 (Sesimbra, Portugal), PRO-VE 2003 (Lugano, Switzerland), PRO-VE 2004 (Toulouse, France), PRO-VE 2005 (Valencia, Spain), PRO-VE 2006 (Helsinki, Finland), PRO-VE 2007 (Guimaräes, Portugal), PRO-VE 2008 (Poznan, Poland), PRO-VE 2009 (Thessaloniki, Greece), PRO-VE 2010 (St. Etienne, France), PRO-VE 2011 (Säo Paulo, Brazil), PRO-VE 2012 (Bournemouth, UK), PRO-VE 2013 (Dresden, Germany), PRO-VE 2014 (Amsterdam, The Netherlands), PRO-VE 2015 (Albi, France), PRO-VE 2016 (Porto, Portugal), PRO-VE 2017 (Vicenza, Italy), and PRO-VE 2018 (Cardiff, UK).

This proceedings book includes selected papers from the PRO-VE 2019 Conference. It provides a comprehensive overview of major challenges that are being currently addressed, and specifically recent advances in various domains related to the digital transformation and collaborative networks and their applications. There was therefore a strong focus on the following areas related to the selected main theme for the 2019 Conference:

- Collaborative models, platforms, and systems for digital revolution
- Manufacturing ecosystem and collaboration in Industry 4.0
- Big data analytics and intelligence
- Risk, performance, and uncertainty in collaborative networked systems
- Semantic data/service discovery, retrieval, and composition in a collaborative networked world
- Trust and sustainability analysis in collaborative networks
- Value creation and social impact of collaborative networks to the digital revolution
- Technology development platforms supporting collaborative systems
- Collective intelligence and collaboration in advanced/emerging applications
- Collaborative manufacturing and factories of the future, e-health and care, food and agribusiness, and crisis/disaster management

We are thankful to all the authors from academia, research, and industry, for their contributions. We hope this collection of papers represents a valuable tool for those interested in research advances and emerging applications in collaborative networks, and in identifying future open challenges for research and development in this area. We very much appreciate the dedication, and the time and effort spent by the members of the PRO-VE international Program Committee who supported us with the selection of articles for this Conference and provided valuable and constructive comments to help authors with improving the quality of their papers.

July 2019   Luis M. Camarinha-Matos
                                                              Hamideh Afsarmanesh
                                                              Dario Antonelli

Organization

**PRO-VE 2019 – 20th IFIP Working Conference
on VIRTUAL ENTERPRISES**
Turin, Italy, 23–25, September, 2019

Conference Chair

Dario Antonelli, Italy

Program Committee Chair

Luis M. Camarinha-Matos, Portugal

Program Committee Co-chair

Hamideh Afsarmanesh, The Netherlands

Program Committee

Antonio Abreu, Portugal
Hamideh Afsarmanesh, The Netherlands
Dario Antonelli, Italy
Américo Azevedo, Portugal
Thomas Beach, UK
Frédérick Bénaben, France
Peter Bernus, Australia
Xavier Boucher, France
Jeremy Bryans, UK
Luis M. Camarinha-Matos, Portugal
Wojciech Cellary, Poland
Naoufel Cheikhrouhou, Switzerland
Eric Costa, UK
Rob Dekkers, UK
Filipa Ferrada, Portugal
Adriano Fiorese, Brazil
Rosanna Fornasiero, Italy
Gary Fragidis, Greece

Cesar Garita, Costa Rica
Ricardo Gonçalves, Portugal
Ted Goranson, USA
Paul Grefen. The Netherlands
Dmitri Ivanov, Germany
Tomasz Janowski, Portugal
Javad Jassbi, Portugal
Dimitris Karagiannis, Austria
Adamantios Koumpis, Germany
Matthieu Lauras, France
Leandro Loss, Brazil
António Lucas Soares, Portugal
Laura Macchion, Italy
Patricia Macedo, Portugal
Nikolay Mehandjiev, UK
Kyrill Meyer, Germany
Istvan Mezgar, Hungary
Paulo Miyagi, Brazil

Arturo Molina, Mexico
Paulo Novais, Portugal
Adegboyega Ojo, Ireland
Ana Inês Oliveira, Portugal
Eugenio Oliveira, Portugal
Martin Ollus, Finland
Angel Ortiz, Spain
A. Luis Osório, Portugal
Hervé Panetto, France
Iraklis Paraskakis, Greece
Adam Pawlak, Poland
Jorge Pinho Sousa, Portugal
Raul Poler, Spain
Ricardo Rabelo, Brazil
Yacine Rezgui, UK

João Rosas, Portugal
Hans Schaffers, The Netherlands
Jens Schütze, Germany
Weiming Shen, Canada
Volker Stich, Germany
Chrysostomos Stylios, Greece
Klaus-Dieter Thoben, Germany
Lorna Uden, UK
Paula Urze, Portugal
Katri Valkokari, Finland
Rolando Vallejos, Brazil
Antonio Volpentesta, Italy
Lai Xu, UK
Christian Zinke, Germany
Peter Weiß, Germany

Special Session Organizers

Special Session on Digital Transformation in Food and Agribusiness

Mareva Alemany, Spain
Angel Ortiz, Spain
Jorge Hernandez, UK

Special Session on Education and Enabling Tools of Industry 4.0

Dorota Stadnicka, Poland
Doriana D'Addona, Italy
Dario Antonelli, Italy

Special Session on Data Management to Support Collaboration in Value Creation Network

Dimitris Karagianis, Austria
Mario Lezoche, France

Special Session on Collaborative Decision-making for Value Creation Networks

Xavier Boucher, France
David Romero, Mexico

Special Session on Digital Transformation of the Supply Chains

Rosanna Fornasiero, Italy
Andrea Zangiacomi, Italy
Elena Pessot, Italy

Organizing Committee

Dario Antonelli (OC Chair), Italy
Giulia Bruno, Italy
Franco Lombardi, Italy
Teresa Taurino, Italy
Agostino Villa, Italy

Technical Sponsors

IFIP WG 5.5 COVE
Co-Operation infrastructure for Virtual Enterprises and
electronic business

Society of Collaborative Networks

Organizational Co-sponsors

Nova University of Lisbon

Contents

Industry 4.0 Challenges

Non-technical Challenges of Industry 4.0 3
  Wojciech Cellary

A Meta-Model of Cyber-Physical-Social System: The CPSS Paradigm
to Support Human-Machine Collaboration in Industry 4.0 11
  Bereket Abera Yilma, Hervé Panetto, and Yannick Naudet

Collaborative Networks and ICT Trends for Future CPPS and Beyond 21
  István Mezgár

Computational Creativity to Design Cyber-Physical Systems
in Industry 4.0 29
  Sanaz Nikghadam-Hojjati and José Barata

Advanced Cyber Physical Systems

Adaptive Integration of IoT with Informatics Systems for Collaborative
Industry: The SITL-IoT Case 43
  A. Luis Osório, Luis M. Camarinha-Matos, Tiago Dias,
  and José Tavares

Collaborative Softbots: Enhancing Operational Excellence in Systems
of Cyber-Physical Systems 55
  Ricardo J. Rabelo, Saulo Popov Zambiasi, and David Romero

A Systematic Review of Collaborative Networks: Implications for Sensing,
Smart and Sustainable Enterprises 69
  Fábio Müller Guerrini and Juliana Suemi Yamanari

Finding the Right Way Towards a CPS – A Methodology for Individually
Selecting Development Processes for Cyber-Physical Systems 81
  Günther Schuh, Violett Zeller, Max-Ferdinand Stroh,
  and Philipp Harder

Open Innovation

Crowd Engineering: Manage Crowd Contributions for Design
and Manufacture of Innovative Products 93
  Agostino Villa and Teresa Taurino

Open Innovation Practitioners Mindset on Risk.   103
  Paula Urze, João Rosas, Alexandra Tenera,
  and Luis M. Camarinha-Matos

Developing a Green Product-Based in an Open Innovation Environment.
Case Study: Electrical Vehicle   115
  Ricardo Santos, Antonio Abreu, and Vitor Anes

Commute Green! The Potential of Enterprise Social Networks
for Ecological Mobility Concepts   128
  Christian Zinke-Wehlmann and Julia Friedrich

Managing Disruption in Collaboration

Development of a Methodology for the Analysis and Evaluation
of Alternative Actions in Disruption Management in Production   143
  Ben Luetkehoff, Volker Stich, Moritz Schroeter, and Felix Steinlein

Actionable Collaborative Common Operational Picture in Crisis Situation:
A Comprehensive Architecture Powered with Social Media Data   151
  Julien Coche, Aurélie Montarnal, Andrea Tapia, and Frederick Benaben

A Knowledge-Based System for Collecting and Integrating
Production Information   163
  Giulia Bruno, Emiliano Traini, and Franco Lombardi

Big Data and Learning

Interactive Machine Learning: Managing Information Richness in Highly
Anonymized Conversation Data   173
  Ari Alamäki, Lili Aunimo, Harri Ketamo, and Lasse Parvinen

Methods of Data Mining for Quality Assurance in Glassworks   185
  Łukasz Paśko and Paweł Litwin

A Digital-Enabled Framework for Intelligent Collaboration
in Small Teams.   193
  Juanqiong Gou, Qinghua Liu, Wenxin Mu, Wenchi Ying,
  Hamideh Afsarmanesh, and Frederick Benaben

Collaborative Knowledge Management

Supporting Transparent Information/Knowledge Federation
in Collaborative Administrative Environments.   205
  Beibei Pang, Hamideh Afsarmanesh, Juanqiong Gou, and Wenxin Mu

A Method of Ontology Evolution and Concept Evaluation Based
on Knowledge Discovery in the Heavy Haul Railway Risk System 220
  *Tiancheng Cao, Wenxin Mu, Aurélie Montarnal,
  and Anne-Marie Barthe-Delanoë*

Designing a Trusted Data Brokerage Framework in the Aviation Domain . . . 234
  *Evmorfia Biliri, Minas Pertselakis, Marios Phinikettos,
  Marios Zacharias, Fenareti Lampathaki, and Dimitrios Alexandrou*

Collaborative Business Ecosystems and Processes

A Model of Evolution of a Collaborative Business Ecosystem Influenced
by Performance Indicators 245
  Paula Graça and Luis M. Camarinha-Matos

Verifying for Compliance to Data Constraints in Collaborative
Business Processes 259
  John Paul Kasse, Lai Xu, Paul de Vrieze, and Yuewei Bai

Collaborative Networks Management from a Theory
of Constraints Perspective 271
  Alexandra Tenera and João Rosas

Collaborative Government and Social Policies

Next Generation Government - Hyperconnected, Smart and Augmented 285
  Adegboyega Ojo

Inter-governmental Collaborative Networks for Digital Government
Innovation Transfer – Structure, Membership, Operations 295
  Magdalena Ciesielska and Tomasz Janowski

Where Are Females in OSS Projects? Socio Technical Interactions 308
  Ikram El Asri and Noureddine Kerzazi

Digital Transformation of Supply Chain

A Digital Platform Architecture to Support Multi-dimensional Surplus
Capacity Sharing 323
  *Henrique Diogo Silva, António Lucas Soares, Andrea Bettoni,
  Andrea Barni Francesco, and Serena Albertario*

Investigating Supply Chains Models and Enabling Technologies Towards
Collaborative Networks 335
  *Elena Pessot, Andrea Zangiacomi, Frank Berkers,
  David Hidalgo-Carvajal, Ron Weerdmeester, and Rosanna Fornasiero*

Toward an Agile Adaptation of Supply Chain Planning:
A Situational Use Case   344
   Sanaa Tiss, Caroline Thierry, Jacques Lamothe, and Christophe Rousse

Managing Logistics in Collaborative Manufacturing: The Integration
Services for an Automotive Application.   355
   Nicola Mincuzzi, Mohammadtaghi Falsafi, Gianfranco E. Modoni,
   Marco Sacco, and Rosanna Fornasiero

Collaborative Services for Digital Transformation

Evaluating the Applicability and Utility of an Elderly Care Ecosystem.   365
   Thais A. Baldissera and Luis M. Camarinha-Matos

Towards a Mobility Payment Service Based on Collaborative
Open Systems.   379
   A. Luis Osório, Luis M. Camarinha-Matos, Hamideh Afsarmanesh,
   and Adam Belloum

Value-Added Services, Virtual Enterprises and Data Spaces Inspired
Enterprise Architecture for Smart Cities   393
   Sobah Abbas Petersen, Zohreh Pourzolfaghar, Iyas Alloush,
   Dirk Ahlers, John Krogstie, and Markus Helfert

Collaborative Building Ecosystems

Outlining a New Collaborative Business Model as a Result of the Green
Building Information Modelling Impact in the AEC Supply Chain   405
   João Vilas-Boas, Vahid Mirnoori, Alim Razy, and Agostinho Silva

Development of a Conceptual Architecture for the Energy Management
of Building Ecosystems   418
   Filipa Ferrada, Ana Inês Oliveira, João Rosas, Patrícia Macedo,
   Ricardo Almeida, and Luis M. Camarinha-Matos

Collaborative Safe Escape in Digital Transformation   431
   Ana Inês Oliveira, Pedro Pereira, and Javad Jassbi

Data Semantics in Food and Agribusiness

Semantic Support for Scenarios to Improve Communication
in Agribusiness.   447
   Leandro Antonelli, Diego Torres, Mariángeles Hozikian,
   and Jorge E. Hernandez

Collaboration Networks for Information Empowerment
of Food Consumers... 457
    Antonio Palmiro Volpentesta, Alberto Michele Felicetti,
    and Nicola Frega

Big Data Transformation in Agriculture: From Precision Agriculture
Towards Smart Farming...................................... 467
    María Angeles Rodríguez, Llanos Cuenca, and Ángel Ortiz

Digital Transformation in Food and Agribusiness

Servitization of Biomass Processing for a Virtual Biorefinery:
Application to the Lignocellulosic Biomass in a French Local Territory..... 477
    Michelle Houngbé, Anne-Marie Barthe-Delanoë, and Stéphane Négny

Collaborative, Distributed Simulations of Agri-Food Supply Chains.
Analysis on How Linking Theory and Practice by Using
Multi-agent Structures 487
    Alejandro Fernandez, Jorge E. Hernandez, Shaofeng Liu,
    Hervé Panetto, Matías Nahuel Pankow, and Esteban Sanchez

Enhancing the Sustainability Performance of Agri-Food Supply Chains
by Implementing Industry 4.0................................. 496
    David Pérez Perales, María-José Verdecho,
    and Faustino Alarcón-Valero

Data Management for Collaboration in Value Creation Networks

Data-Driven Pattern-Based Constructs Definition for the Digital
Transformation Modelling of Collaborative Networked
Manufacturing Enterprises 507
    Concetta Semeraro, Mario Lezoche, Hervé Panetto, Michele Dassisti,
    and Stefano Cafagna

Data Privacy Concerns Throughout the Customer Journey and Different
Service Industries 516
    Marko Mäki and Ari Alamäki

Connected and Multimodal Passenger Transport Through Big Data
Analytics: Case Tampere City Region, Finland..................... 527
    Riku Viri, Lili Aunimo, and Heli Aramo-Immonen

Collaborative Decision-Making in Value Creation Networks

Framework to Model PSS Collaborative Value Networks and Assess
Uncertainty of Their Economic Models   541
    Xavier Boucher, Khaled Medini, and Camilo Murillo Coba

A Business Model Assessment and Evaluation Framework for City
Logistics Collaborative Strategic Decision Support   552
    Giovanni Zenezini, Jesus Gonzalez-Feliu, Giulio Mangano,
    and Laura Palacios-Arguello

Assessment of Failures in Collaborative Human-Robot
Assembly Workcells   562
    Domenico A. Maisano, Dario Antonelli, and Fiorenzo Franceschini

Discrete Event Simulation as a Support in the Decision Making to Improve
Product and Process in the Automotive Industry - A Fuel Pump Component
Case Study.   572
    Luis E. Villagomez, Daniel Cortés, José Ramírez, Alejandro Álvarez,
    Rafael Batres, Ivann Reyes, Germán Esparza, Nancy Cruz,
    and Arturo Molina

Virtual Reality in Education for Industry 4.0

Application of Virtual Reality in Designing and Programming
of Robotic Stations   585
    Dariusz Szybicki, Krzysztof Kurc, Piotr Gierlak, Andrzej Burghardt,
    Magdalena Muszyńska, and Marek Uliasz

Application of Virtual Reality in the Training of Operators and Servicing
of Robotic Stations   594
    Magdalena Muszyńska, Dariusz Szybicki, Piotr Gierlak, Krzysztof Kurc,
    Andrzej Burghardt, and Marek Uliasz

VR Training for Security Awareness in Industrial IoT   604
    Vasiliki Liagkou and Chrysostomos Stylios

Education and Enabling Tools for Industry 4.0

Simulations of Manufacturing Systems: Applications in Achieving
the Intended Learning Outcomes.   615
    Paweł Litwin, Maksymilian Mądziel, and Dorota Stadnicka

Influence of Trust Factors on Shared Laboratory Resources
in a Distributed Environment   624
    Jannicke Baalsrud Hauge, Valentin Kammerlohr, Barbara Göbl,
    and Heiko Duin

Key Performance Indicators Integrating Collaborative and Mobile Robots
in the Factory Networks. 635
Khurshid Aliev, Dario Antonelli, Ahmed Awouda, and Paolo Chiabert

Author Index 643

Industry 4.0 Challenges

Non-technical Challenges of Industry 4.0

Wojciech Cellary[(✉)]

Poznan University of Economics and Business,
Niepodleglosci 10, 61-875 Poznan, Poland
cellary@kti.ue.poznan.pl

Abstract. Cyber-physical systems, Industry 4.0, and Economy 4.0 are defined as current trends in industrial manufacturing and more broadly – in economy and society. Three non-technical challenges are distinguished: (1) a challenge to future employees requiring new educational methods; (2) a challenge to fixing errors in complex software and training datasets; and finally (3) a challenge to responsibility of complex software designers, developers and integrators. These challenges may be considered as directions of future research on Industry 4.0 and Economy 4.0. All these challenges have roots in technology, but they have far social consequences.

Keywords: Cyber-physical systems · Industry 4.0 · Economy 4.0 · Artificial intelligence · Human's role · Fixing errors · Responsibility

1 Introduction

Industry 4.0 is a concept that originates from the industrial community and is currently broadly discussed by both industrial and the scientific community. Industry 4.0 emerged in the aftermath of the rapid development of information technology and robotics that together has given birth to new kinds of integrated systems [9]. There are plenty of technical issues that must be solved to make such systems run efficiently, reliably and safely [11]. There are also some non-technical issues that must be solved to prepare societies to use such systems. In this paper, in Sects. 2, 3 and 4 we first define Cyber-physical systems, Industry 4.0, and Economy 4.0. Then, we describe three selected challenges that have roots in technology, but that have far social consequences. In Sect. 5, we describe a challenge to future employees who will need to cooperate with robots controlled by artificial intelligence. In Sect. 6, we deal with a challenge of fixing errors in complex software used in cyber-physical systems, especially ones that are driven by big data. In Sect. 7, we present a challenge to determination of responsibility for errors and their consequences that without a doubt will arise when cyber-physical systems will be massively deployed. Section 8 concludes this position paper stating that each of the above challenges requires new methods and approaches that are unknown as of now. Therefore, they may be considered as directions for future research.

© IFIP International Federation for Information Processing 2019
Published by Springer Nature Switzerland AG 2019
L. M. Camarinha-Matos et al. (Eds.): PRO-VE 2019, IFIP AICT 568, pp. 3–10, 2019.
https://doi.org/10.1007/978-3-030-28464-0_1

2   Cyber-Physical Systems

To understand the concept of Industry 4.0, it is necessary to start with contemporary information technology (IT). IT is currently – more than ever – focusing on data flow. The internet of people and internet of things (IoT) are mass data sources. Depending on a network usage scenario, the 5th generation of wireless telecommunications – 5G – will provide high data rates across a wide coverage area, or low latency and high reliability for mission critical applications, or sporadic communication for up to one million IoT devices per square kilometer. Data storage clouds provide essentially infinite storage for the big (i.e., massive) combined data sets generated by these devices and systems. Machine learning, neural networks and other techniques of artificial intelligence permit us to efficiently process collected big data to acquire new knowledge. Feedback is provided again by the internet of people and the internet of things influencing peoples' behavior either directly or indirectly through their environments. A characteristic of contemporary IT is the fact that the above data technologies depend on one another. Only when all are applied together, do they constitute a system that provides value for people.

A consequence of the data flow system is the convergence of the physical world with the digital world forming the cyber-physical world [4, 5]. Up to now, the physical world coexisted with the digital world. For example, a physical bank branch coexisted with an e-banking website. Almost all the banking operations were possible in both the physical and the digital bank. Only a few operations requiring a physical signature were not available in the e-banking web. In the near future, we can imagine a bank "robot" working in the cyber-world. For example, it is possible to imagine that a customer arrives at a gas station, refuels her car, and goes out without any explicit payment operations requiring physical objects like a credit card or a mobile phone. The sum due is paid automatically by the bank robot. This is possible because the car and the face of the customer are recognized by the system of the gas company cooperating with the bank, and the sum due is automatically deduced from her account using a direct debit scheme.

3   Industry 4.0

One may expect that such cyber-physical systems will emerge in different areas. The most natural area is factories, where these systems are called *smart factories* [11], or in the broader sense – industry, called *Industry 4.0* [7–10, 12, 13]. A factory is a good candidate for application of cyber-physical systems, because it is a closed environment precisely controlled by factory management. Therefore, cyber-physical systems may be deployed step by step in a controlled manner, mitigating the risk involved.

Industry 4.0 may be defined as the information-intensive transformation of manufacturing in a cyber-physical environment of:

- Data,
- People,
- Processes,

- Services,
- Systems, and
- IoT-enabled industrial assets

  due to:

- Generation,
- Leverage, and
- Utilization of actionable information

to improve innovativeness, efficiency, productivity and customization [8]. In [2] collaborative networks are considered to be a core enabler of Industry 4.0.

However, the above definition is not particularly revolutionary. Industry has always tried to improve its efficiency and productivity to reduce costs and increase profit, to modernize through innovations so as to get competitive advantage over competitors, and to better satisfy its customers with customization of its products. For a long time, these goals have been achieved by aligning the IT solutions responsible for generation, leverage, and utilization of information with business processes and services involving people. Thus, the revolutionary character of Industry 4.0 may be best expressed as follows:

The goal of Industry 4.0 is to provide mutually cooperating cyber-physical systems with decision-making autonomy.

It is the planned autonomy of cyber-physical systems that makes the difference between Industry 4.0 and former approaches. Former approaches required the human maker of operational decisions to take responsibility for the decision outcome. The autonomy of cyber-physical systems in Industry 4.0 is possible due to the intensive data flow mentioned above and the application of artificial intelligence techniques to process big data to extract knowledge leading to autonomous decisions.

4 Economy 4.0

The idea of Industry 4.0 may be extended to Economy 4.0 [6]. Economy 4.0 encompasses a full digital value chain from suppliers of materials and components required for production, through all the brokers and providers of necessary services, up to the final recipients of the entire production, i.e., end-customers, regardless of who they are:

- Entrepreneurs,
- Consumers,
- Owners of buildings,
- Owners of retail stores,
- Employees,
- Citizens,
- Passengers,
- Patients, etc.

Economy 4.0, on the one hand, encompasses Industry 4.0 with its cooperating smart factories, while simultaneously extending smart concepts to many other sectors such as: smart energy grid, smart mobility and transportation, smart buildings, smart healthcare, smart breeding, etc. The range of Economy 4.0 may be classified as follows:

- Technologies 4.0 applied within a smart factory;
- Technologies 4.0 applied for cooperation among factories (smart or not);
- Manufactured smart things deployed in smart end-user environments;
- Digital services provided to users of smart environments.

In Economy 4.0 logistics and supply chain management play a particular role. They may be seen as tools of integration: vertical – within a smart factory, and horizontal – between factories, and between factories and smart end-user environments [1].

Economy 4.0 constitutes a more challenging environment than Industry 4.0 for two main reasons. First, it is an open environment controlled by more or less vague rules obeyed or not by different independent objects. Second, people in this environment are not trained as smart factory employees about how to interact most effectively with autonomous cyber-physical systems. Both reasons increase the risk of malfunctioning, and inaccurate interpretations of the actions of cyber-physical systems.

5 Challenges to Future Employees

The main challenges to achieving Economy 4.0 are adding the proper level of autonomy and intelligence to systems. The goal here is not only to make the systems more intelligent, but also to make them more efficient, effective, communicating, agile and flexible, and thus well adapted to the global, inter-connected, real-time economy. A consequence of this challenge is the necessity to find a right balance between autonomous and self-organizing systems, and the planning role of humans (employees).

A future employee will have to demonstrate his/her knowledge level, and his/her ability to cooperate with machines, including robots, in real world scenarios containing fast-changing conditions, requirements, and goals. Adaptation of work methods to the requirements of Economy 4.0 requires an holistic, but agile management approach in real-time, within rapidly changing, distributed environments. This means moving from an approach based on centralized organization and planning to an approach based on ad-hoc planning and risk management.

We may then anticipate that the human's role will then be markedly transformed in Economy 4.0. The depth of the change can be illustrated by the following example showing two extremes. Currently, to provide transportation of goods, the trucks that are used are driven by truck drivers. A truck driver may be seen as an operator of systems of interconnected devices, both mechanical and electronic, that comprise the familiar vehicle called a truck. In the future, in Economy 4.0, autonomous trucks will replace human-driven trucks, so the truck driver's job will gradually disappear. A human will be required, however, to play the role of a manager of a fleet of autonomous trucks. In other words, a human will be a supervisor of autonomous systems of devices controlled by artificial intelligence. This job is much more challenging. Working in concert with artificial intelligence, an employee will need enhanced skills of thinking and reasoning to be able to supervise autonomous decisions made by the system controlled by artificial intelligence.

6   Challenge to Fixing Errors in Software

The ancient Romans said: "Errare humanum est" which means: "To err is human". This truth is particularly well known to programmers, who are constantly making, discovering, and fixing errors in software.

Information, being the basis of decisions may be:

- Retrieved from memory,
- Computed, or
- Assumed.

In case of erroneous data, it is possible to find the errors and correct them. In case of an erroneous program, it is possible to find wrong piece of code and correct it. But, in case of erroneous assumptions and specifications, the entire system may need to be rebuilt. Fixing errors in data or code is an operational IT activity. However, changing specifications and assumptions adopted before the system was developed is a strategic interdisciplinary activity, especially if a cyber-physical system is concerned. Re-designing the digital part of a cyber-physical system is a challenge, but re-designing the non-digital part of a cyber-physical system, e.g., mechanical one, is usually much harder. It is worth noting that specifications and assumptions may become erroneous during system exploitation due to changes in the environment the system is devoted to serve. In the case of the fast-evolving Economy 4.0, such situations may arise frequently. The problem of system reliability is even harder when we take into account the need to protect systems against cyberattacks that may be considered as a fast evolving part of (hostile) environment of cyber-physical systems.

Fixing errors in software is hard, but methods to do that have been elaborated within software engineering discipline. Fixing errors of artificial intelligence systems stemming from design specification errors or invalid assumptions will be an enormously complex challenge. If we are dealing with a neural network consisting of thousands of nodes and trained by peta-bytes of data, then finding out why it generates erroneous results may approach impossibility. Perhaps we will discover ways to allow other artificial intelligence methods to help us with that.

7   Challenge to Responsibility

An important aspect of human life is discovering who or what is responsible for any significant accident. Consequently, today, methods of determining who is responsible for an accident are well developed. In the case of Economy 4.0, however, the problems are much harder and methods for determining responsibility for errors and accidents are not yet set. Consider, for example, the above mentioned autonomous truck travelling without a human driver that is involved in a serious single vehicle accident without injuries to any person in the vicinity. There are several suspects who might be responsible for that accident. The first is the truck owner. However, the truck owner is a car rental company. If it maintained the truck properly as required by law, it would be difficult to say that it had responsibility for the accident. The second suspect is the person who rented the truck. However, the renter in this case is also a company whose warehouseman loaded some goods into the truck, carefully secured them, then entered the customer's address and clicked "go". Again, very likely this renter had nothing to do with the accident.

If the truck's mechanics were right, then the next suspect are computer systems, i.e., hardware, internet and software. In case of an autonomous truck, hardware is not only an on-board computer, but also a cloud in which programs, data, maps, etc. are stored. If the on-board computer has not been mechanically damaged, it can be checked if it worked correctly. However, the cloud cannot be easily checked. There are usually several million processors in each data center composing a cloud. Only advanced testing software may check if any of them is functioning incorrectly. It is also difficult to determine which particular processor was supporting the truck that had the accident. Moreover, each processor was allocated to serve the truck for a very short time-slot. Then, the service could be taken over by another processor, or even a different data center located in a different country.

The cause of the accident could also be a break in internet communication. The internet is a very complicated system consisting of gates, routers, cables, fiber optics, wireless communications, satellites, etc. Each data packet exchanged between the cloud and the truck can go a different way. Generally, the internet works very reliably due to error detection and repeating the transmission of incorrectly transmitted data packets, although not all packets reach their destination immediately. Occasionally, however, it fails. The impacts of such failures are often unnoticeable, but in an Industry 4.0 environment, this may change and internet failures may start resulting in actual damages.

The most suspect component for the autonomous truck accident described above is the software operating the autonomous vehicle. This does not mean, however, that assigning blame only requires us to find and charge a suspect programmer. Hundreds of programmers who do not even know each other are involved in creating such a complex software that is required to drive an autonomous truck. One team of programmers once wrote a program module solving a general problem and put it in a digital library. Another team of programmers used this module in their vehicle guidance program module. Yet another team of programmers assembled the whole software system to drive an autonomous truck from such modules developed independently. The system was thoroughly tested by independent testers. It is practically impossible to determine who is responsible for an error in a software system so large and complex that has been developed and validated by so many people.

As mentioned in Sect. 6, an even harder problem is finding a person responsible for errors generated by artificial intelligence. Neural networks recognize images by calculating probability based on millions of cases stored in the cloud, so the result depends not on a human, but on which cases have been recorded and used to train the neural network.

8   Conclusions

Current societies are more and more dependent on software systems controlling not only the digital world, but also the cyber-physical world [3]. With increasing deployments of autonomous cyber-physical systems, the risk of damages caused by decisions following from their malfunctioning or wrong interpretation of the situation around them increases. As we have indicated above, cyber-physical systems are controlled not only by very complex software, but also by the big data sets used to train systems of artificial intelligence. The complexity and size of programs and training data are so massive that they cannot be verified for correctness using traditional software engineering methods. On the other hand, society cannot allow the errors of such software to be dismissed as a "force majeure" (which traditionally refers to the forces of nature beyond human's control such as tornados, hurricanes, eruption of volcanos, earthquakes, tsunamis, etc.). Humankind cannot lose control over his own products. Therefore, one of the greatest challenges of modern computer science and engineering is to develop new methods of identifying the causes and fixing errors in complex information systems including artificial intelligence. The goal should not be to find and to punish a guilty programmer, but to ensure the error cannot reoccur.

Industry 4.0 and Economy 4.0 will maximally challenge our educational systems. The demand for routine cognitive and physical work will decrease, because computers and robots will do such work more precisely, effectively and cheaply. However, computers and robots controlled by artificial intelligence do not understand what they manage, they only count the probability of realizing possible scenarios that have already arisen in the past, and choose the one that optimizes a given criterion, in particular, the criterion that minimizes costs of production or service provision. Thus, Industry 4.0 and Economy 4.0 will need people who think, reason and understand how to control artificial intelligence to prevent terrible mistakes that may happen if the past is mindlessly repeated. Understanding and creativity will remain the exclusive domain of humankind. Therefore, the educational system will be required to transform itself to provide Industry 4.0 and Economy 4.0 with graduates who have capabilities attuned to 4.0 systems thinking, reasoning and creativity. These are the people we will depend on to be capable to cooperate with computer systems and robots controlled by artificial intelligence in conditions of distribution, diversity and uncertainty.

Acknowledgments. Many thanks to Louis E. Freund, Ph.D., Professor Emeritus in the Department of Industrial & Systems Engineering at San Jose State University, San Jose, CA, USA. Dr. Freund is founder and former Director of the SJSU Graduate Program in Human Factors/Ergonomics. The author is grateful for his participation in many thorough discussions and for his comments that greatly improved the manuscript.

References

1. Azevedo, A.: Collaborative transformation systems - path to address the challenges around the competitiveness of mature countries. In: Camarinha-Matos, L.M., Afsarmanesh, H., Rezgui, Y. (eds.) PRO-VE 2018. IAICT, vol. 534, pp. 21–32. Springer, Cham (2018). https://doi.org/10.1007/978-3-319-99127-6_2
2. Camarinha-Matos, L.M., Fornasiero, R., Afsarmanesh, H.: Collaborative networks as a core enabler of industry 4.0. In: Camarinha-Matos, L.M., Afsarmanesh, H., Fornasiero, R. (eds.) PRO-VE 2017. IAICT, vol. 506, pp. 3–17. Springer, Cham (2017). https://doi.org/10.1007/978-3-319-65151-4_1
3. Cellary, W., Freund, L.E., Kwan, S.K., Leitner, C., Spohrer, J.: The human-side of service engineering: advancing technologies impact on service innovation. In: Proceedings of 6th Naples Forum on Service (2019, to appear)
4. Cyber-Physical Systems: Enabling a Smart and Connected World. https://www.nsf.gov/news/special_reports/cyber-physical/
5. Cyber-Physical Systems. https://www.nist.gov/el/cyber-physical-systems
6. Economy 4.0 and its labour market and economic impacts. http://doku.iab.de/forschungsbericht/2016/fb1316_en.pdf
7. Industry 4.0: Definition, Design Principles, Challenges, and the Future of Employment. https://www.cleverism.com/industry-4-0/
8. Industry 4.0: Technologies Integrations, Security, People/Workers and Society. https://devisionx.com/fourth-industrial-revolution/
9. Industry 4.0: the Fourth Industrial Revolution – Guide to Industrie 4.0. https://www.i-scoop.eu/industry-4-0/
10. Plattform Industrie 4.0. https://www.plattform-i40.de/PI40/Navigation/EN/Home/home.html
11. Industry 4.0: Building the digital enterprise. https://www.pwc.com/gx/en/industries/industries-4.0/landing-page/industry-4.0-building-your-digital-enterprise-april-2016.pdf
12. Schweichhart, K.: Reference Architectural Model Industrie 4.0 (RAMI 4.0). An Introduction. https://ec.europa.eu/futurium/en/system/files/ged/a2-schweichhart-reference_architectural_model_industrie_4.0_rami_4.0.pdf
13. Stich, V., Gudergan, G., Zeller, V.: Need and solution to transform the manufacturing industry in the age of industry 4.0 – a capability maturity index approach. In: Camarinha-Matos, L.M., Afsarmanesh, H., Rezgui, Y. (eds.) PRO-VE 2018. IAICT, vol. 534, pp. 33–42. Springer, Cham (2018). https://doi.org/10.1007/978-3-319-99127-6_3

A Meta-Model of Cyber-Physical-Social System: The CPSS Paradigm to Support Human-Machine Collaboration in Industry 4.0

Bereket Abera Yilma[1,2(✉)], Hervé Panetto[2], and Yannick Naudet[1]

[1] Luxembourg Institute of Science and Technology (LIST),
Esch-sur-Alzette, Luxembourg
{bereket.yilma,yannick.naudet}@list.lu
[2] Universite de Lorraine, CNRS, CRAN, Nancy, France
herve.panetto@univ-lorraine.fr

Abstract. The 4th industrial revolution (Industry 4.0) heavily relying on the concept of Cyber-Physical Systems (CPS) has transformed the manufacturing industry into an intelligent environment. Advances in manufacturing and automation industries created hyper-connected industrial ecosystems that are not limited to smart production but also facilitate organizational integration. Hence, fostering the creation of collaborative, networked and intelligent industries. One of the emerging advances in the digital transformation of industries is the creation of environments where humans work in close collaboration with sensor enabled smart machines and robots. Particularly the close involvement of humans in such smart environments challenges system designed methodologies mainly because human aspects are not considered in CPS design frameworks. In this paper, we present an approach to support this aspect of Industry 4.0 taking a Cyber-Physical-Social System (CPSS) paradigm to incorporate human aspects with the existing notion of CPS. We propose a meta-model of CPSS that can serve as a framework to design systems involving human and CPS collaboration.

Keywords: Industry 4.0 · Cyber-Physical-Social system · Meta-model · Human-machine collaboration

1 Introduction

The introduction of Cyber-physical systems (CPS), together with advances in Information and communication technologies (ICT) has been the major driving force for the 4th industrial revolution [10]. These advances are empowering an era of digital transformation by offering connectedness and intelligent computation. Thus, promoting collaboration in production systems and organizational integration. Industry 4.0 particularly in manufacturing and automation fields forecasts promising solutions for the future of digitized industrial ecosystem. One of the major expected outcomes of this revolution is the allocation of tedious and repetitive tasks to intelligent machines and robots [8, 12]. According to [9] "CPS describes a broad range of network connected, multi-disciplinary, physically-aware engineered systems that integrate embedded computing (cyber) and technologies into the physical world. Such design approaches

L. M. Camarinha-Matos et al. (Eds.): PRO-VE 2019, IFIP AICT 568, pp. 11–20, 2019.
https://doi.org/10.1007/978-3-030-28464-0_2

mainly incorporate the orchestration of physical devices and phenomena with computational nodes". The era of digital transformation is evolving faster than expected. One aspect of this evolution is to enhance advanced collaboration mechanisms in industries; particularly collaborations involving humans and machines [6, 7, 11, 13]. In these industrial contexts, the nature of relations between humans and CPS is demanding not only task execution but also cognitive interaction. However, the current design approaches of industrial systems heavily rely on the core concept of CPS lacking efficient means to link technical and social prospects. This degrades the quality of collaboration and can compromise safety [5] resulting challenges to deliver and cope with the speed of evolution in Industry 4.0. Particularly the main challenge originates from the complexity of human nature, as people usually do not follow rules that are not matching with their way of thinking, preferences, needs and capabilities. Additionally each individual is unique and her behaviour under different circumstances is driven by a complex phenomenon, which has not yet been fully understood.

As Industry 4.0 is enhancing such collaborative industrial environments, the need for a design framework that goes beyond CPS is not far-fetched. Hence, a system design methodology that incorporates human aspects will be complementary to the future of digitized industrial ecosystem. In this work, we propose an approach to support this prospect by taking a Cyber-Physical-Social system (CPSS) paradigm. CPSS is an emerging concept developed by integrating a social aspect to the existing CPS notion. We first conceptualise the notion of CPSS through a definition that is grounded on a generic framework provided by the theory of systems. Then we illustrate all kinds of relationships that may occur between systems, subsystems and components in a system of CPSSs. Ultimately we present a meta-model of Cyber-Physical-Social systems, which can serve as a base framework for the designing of complex systems that involve close collaboration of humans and CPS for the future Industry 4.0 applications. Finally we provide a case study example to demonstrate how the extended meta-model can be used to obtain a compact model, which can then be used for further analysis.

2   Cyber-Physical-Social System (CPSS)

From a general perspective CPSS is the composition of Cyber-Physical System (CPS) and Social system. CPS refers to a generation of systems with integrated computational and physical capabilities strongly related to the 4-th Industrial Revolution [1]. The Social aspect refers to interacting individuals, having each their own cognition, preferences, motivation and behaviour [2, 4]. The development of CPSS is still in its infancy. Over the past decade, different researchers used different terminologies to refer to the integration of the human aspect into CPS projecting different conceptualizations. For instance in [16–18] Cyber-physical-human systems (CPHS) was used, being defined as *"a system of interconnected systems (computers, cyber-physical devices, and people) 'talking' to each other across space and time, and allowing other systems, devices, and data streams to connect and disconnect."* In [15] the concept of Cyber-Physical-Social-Thinking hyperspace (CPST) was introduced for geological information service system. This work defined CPSS as *"a system deployed with emphasis on humans, knowledge, society, and culture, in addition to Cyber space and Physical space. Hence, it can connect nature, cyber-space, and society with certain rules.",* where as for CPST, it is established through the mergence of a new dimension of thinking space into the CPS space. The thinking space is *a high-level thought or idea raised during the intellectual activities of people.* The work visualises the *Intellect* of humans separately from the *social aspect* of CPSS as *thinking space.* On the other hand the term Social-Cyber-Physical-Systems (SCPS) was also used in [19] and [20], being defined as *"a complex socio-technical system in which human and technical aspects (CPS) are massively intertwined."* According to this definition, the scope of SCPS extends to the intangibles of social context, which includes social culture and norms, personal beliefs and attitudes, and informal institutions of social interactions. The notion of CPSS is conceived in many works; however, the usage is not homogeneous. Furthermore, the perspective and way of defining also varies from domain to domain. In an effort to address this gap, recently a holistic definition and domain-independent conceptualisation of CPSS grounded on a generic framework provided by the theory of system was proposed by [2]. In our work, we adopt a perspective on CPSS represented by the following definition.

Definition 1: *CPSS is a system strictly composed of a Cyber-Physical System (CPS) and a Social System (SS), in which the system's components interact in a virtual and physical environment, where CPS and SS are defined respectively as follows.*

*A **CPS** is a system encompassing all the systems and subsystems of Cyber and Physical Systems, their components and the interaction between them, as well as integration of computation with physical processes.*

*A **Social System** is a system that comprises interacting individuals, having each their own cognition, preferences, motivation and behaviour.*

Digitized industrial ecosystems emerging as a result of rapid advances in Industry4.0 are environments where humans and sensor enabled smart devices cohabit a physical space of collaboration. Hence, can be seen as CPSS environments. Following this, we present a meta-model of CPSS that can support such collaborative system design approaches in Industry 4.0.

3 A Meta-Model of CPSS

In this section, we illustrate all kinds of relationships that may occur between CPSSs, CPSs, SSs and their components (cyber, physical, Social). Then we ultimately formalise the CPSS paradigm through a meta-model inspired by the one proposed by [1] for CPS.

3.1 Towards a Meta-Model for CPSSs

We define a CPSS as a set CPSS = $\{CS, PS, SS, R^P, R^C, R^S\}$, where *CS* (Cyber System)*, PS* (Physical System) and *SS* (Social System) are sets containing *Cyber components, Physical components and Social components* respectively. Atomic CPSS is one that is strictly composed of *one Cyber, one Physical and one Social component.*

A Composite CPSS is one that is formed by the combination of CPSSs or components from two or more CPSSs. Similarly, we define CPS as a set CPS = {*CS, PS* R^P, R^C}. Atomic CPS is one that is strictly composed of *one Cyber and one Physical component*. A Composite CPS is one that is formed by the combination of CPSs or components from two or more CPSSs. Finally, R^P, R^C, R^S represent respectively the sets of physical, cyber and social relationships that may exist between system's components or between systems parts and their environment as detailed below and illustrated in Fig. 1.

R^P (Physical Relations):- refers to the relation between systems, subsystems and components to be physically connected and the transmission of physical objects between components.

R^C (Cyber/Virtual Relation):- refers to the presence of an information flow/control or sharing of computational node between/within systems, subsystems and components.

R^S (Social Relation):- refers to the flow of information/ transfer of knowledge between social components (*i.e.* humans). It also reflects cognitive ties that govern human behaviour.

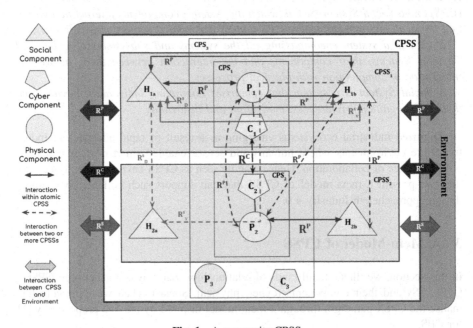

Fig. 1. A composite CPSS

Figure 1 is an example of a system of CPSS, which is composed of two CPSSs and one CPS. This example illustrates all types of relationships and forms of interactions that may exist within a system of CPSS. The top shaded box represents a single CPSS (CPSS$_1$), which is composed of a CPS (CPS$_1$, most inner box), and a Social System with two components (humans) H_{1a} and H_{1b}. CPS_1 is composed of a Physical component (P_1) and a Cyber component (C_1). $CPSS_2$ is another CPSS containing (CPS_2, H_{2a}, H_{2b}, P_2, C_2) for the corresponding components in $CPSS_1$. CPS_3 is a composite CPS containing CPS_1, CPS_2 and its own Cyber and Physical components P_3, C_3. The shaded boarder represents the external environment.

In a system of CPSS three forms of interaction can occur. *I. Interaction within a single CPSS (among subsystems and components), II. Interaction between two or more CPSSs, and III. Interaction between CPSS and its environment.*

I. **Interactions within a single CPSS:** - interactions within a single CPSS can be of Physical, Cyber or Social nature as illustrated on Fig. 1.

$\mathbf{R^P}$: - Physical relations within a single CPSS can exist between Human and Human (H_{1a} and H_{1b}), Human and Physical components (H_{1a} and P_1) and (H_{1b} and P_1) or between two or more physical components. This type of interaction is visually observable as it involves direct contact in the physical world.

$\mathbf{R^C}$: - Cyber relations within a single CPSS refer to the sharing of computational resources and the flow/control of information among the different components of the system.

$\mathbf{R^S}$: - A social relationship within a within a single CPSS takes two different forms.

   i. *A direct communication/ Conversation in the physical world (R_D^S)*

   ii. *Indirect communication through a CPS medium (R_V^S).*

II. **Interactions between different CPSSs:** - can be of Physical, Cyber or social relations represented by dotted lines on Fig. 1.

$\mathbf{R^P}$: - A direct physical contact between Humans (H_{1b} and H_{2b}), physical components (P_1 and P_2) or Human and Physical components (H_{1b} and P_2).

$\mathbf{R^C}$: - Is a virtual information flow/ control between cyber components of two or more CPSSs (C_1 and C2).

$\mathbf{R^S}$: - A social relationship between different CPSSs also takes two different forms as it is within a single CPSS (direct communication - R_D^S between (H_{1a} and H_{2a}) and through a CPS medium - R_V^S between (H_{1b} and H_{2a}).

III. **Interactions between CPSS and external environment:** - Physical, Cyber and Social relations represented by bold arrows connecting the CPSS to different systems, subsystems and components of the external environment.

3.2   CPSS Meta Model

In Fig. 2, we propose a meta-model for CPSS based on our definition of CPSS and the formulation of a system of CPSSs, using the UML 2.0 notation. The meta-model formalizes the minimum requirement for the emergence of a CPSS as an atomic unit and the modeling of a composite CPSS. The emergence of a CPSS requires a connection between at least one social component and one physical component that is linked to at least one cyber component.

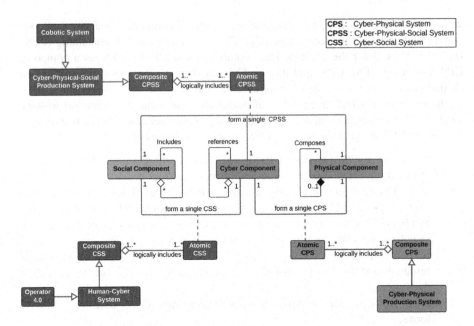

Fig. 2. Meta-model of CPSS: *The blue concepts depict concepts from* [1]

Atomic CPSS emerges when this minimum requirement is fulfilled. Accordingly, each atomic CPSS is given a single social component, a single physical component, which models its mechanical behaviour and a single cyber component for computational functionality. This is presented in the meta-model by the relationship *'form a single CPSS'* between the classes 'Social component', 'Cyber component' and 'Physical component'. As an extension to the composition of complex CPSS the aggregate relation *'logically includes'* is introduced to the model. An atomic CPSS *'is physically part of'* a composite CPSS and with inheritance relation it can lend its functionality. The class of *'Cyber-Physical-Social production system (CPSPS)'* can be viewed in the model as a subclass of composite CPSS and Cobotic system is a subclass of CPSPS. Whenever a system is in the relation *'is physically part of'* this also entails that it is being *'logically included'* in that system. A similar analogy was used in [1]. When the 'Social component' is not instantiated, an atomic CPS can emerge represented by the relationship *'form a single CPS'*.

The meta-model we presented in this work is a partial extension of [1] and is subject to further extension/modification in an effort to model complex properties and interdependence between components. Additionally we introduce the notion of Cyber-social system (CSS) in the model, which is not a concept developed currently but possibly in the future. Despite the terminology, CSS is currently being used to refer an online social network, in this context the future CSS could imply a system where human cognition is supported through cyber components. This concept is also partially shared by [3] automation aiding enhanced cognitive capabilities such as perception, memory, reasoning and decision (Operator 4.0), a subclass of Human-Cyber system. Once having a well-developed and operational CSS, there will be a different horizon and additional possibilities to the emergence of the future CPSS. This is introduced here with the goal of having a meta-model that is flexible and open to accommodate new concepts in the evolution of the domain. However as this is not the scope of this paper, it will not be discussed further. The concept of SPS (Social-Physical system) is not included in the model because it is the long existing standard manual system of operation with no actual relevance in this context. In the following section, we present a case study of Cyber-Physical-Social production system.

4   Case Study

Let us consider an abstract scenario of *aerospace engine systems plant* modified and adopted from [14]. This case study is chosen because it simulates the emerging advent in Industry 4.0, which is a collaborative production systems between human and CPS. This is a plant producing parts of engine system for the aerospace industry. The production system is organised as job shop. In the production line of the plant, there are manufacturing engineers, operators and maintenance technicians that are skilled and able to perform tasks on different machines. In order to improve efficiency robotic cells are introduced at job shops to collaborate with the workers. In this production system there are several machines designated for different tasks. Most of the activities require similar set of skills but there are few activities that require additional skills for which additional training is needed. However, the company's orientation for task identification and worker involvement follows socio-technical principles, which allows collaboration and knowledge sharing between the workers through live chat and virtual assistance. This highlights social interaction between the workers to support each other.

Figure 3 illustrates a simplified version of this sophisticated process of the plant in an effort to visualise with best possible detail the composition of such complex Cyber-Physical-Social Production System (CPSPS) and the interaction between different components. As it can be seen on the figure, one can assume a simplified version of the job shop with three different machines equipped with robotic cells to collaborate with the workers. The physical parts of each machine and robotic cells with their embedded computational capabilities form the three CPS units. However since human workers are present at the vicinity of these workstations to work in collaboration with the robotic cells, individual CPSSs can emerge at each workstation.

The current approaches of designing such systems rely on CPS frameworks, which limits the nature of collaboration to task execution leaving no room for possible cognitive interaction. In this particular case study, the introduced robotic cells are programmed to perform a predefined task and they execute it with maximum effectiveness in order to help the human workers. The collaboration in this case is only task execution or workload sharing with the humans for a global objective of improving performance.

However, this nature of collaboration is not able to handle human dynamics (unexpected human actions and changing needs due to a different state of mind). This is unknown to the CPS, which has no capabilities to reason on such kind of changes. Hence, it can significantly affect collaboration quality, work efficiency and can compromise worker's safety. We believe collaborations in such systems should evolve

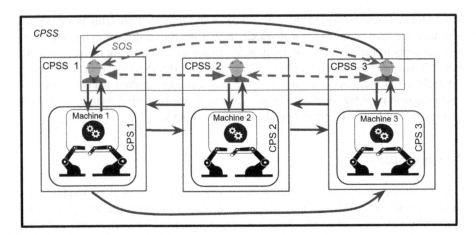

Fig. 3. Example of cyber-physical-social production system (CPSPS) *applied to a plant that produces parts of engines for aerospace industry. Dotted lines represent social relations and solid lines represent Cyber and physical relations.*

from task execution to cognitive interaction. Our Postulate is that taking the CPSS paradigm opens opportunities to reconfigure such systems and put human dynamics at the center of the interaction. Such systems should be designed taking into account not only cyber and physical components but also important social aspects of humans. We believe the CPSS paradigm with the support of artificial intelligence brings several opportunities for the future of Industry 4.0 facilitating seamless collaboration and support between human and CPS.

The field of artificial intelligence is revolutionising many domains empowering systems with the ability to learn from data, reason (predict/infer), make intelligent decisions and self-correct. Industry 4.0 has unexploited potential to benefit from artificial intelligence since current manufacturing environments are equipped with sensor enabled wearables and machines capable of collecting various types of data, high speed and real time computational power. Particularly in Cyber-Physical-Social Production Systems putting human as part of the system, AI can help in transforming industry of the future to a better collaborative working environment where collaborative robots and machines can learn and recognise complex human behaviour, response patterns, values and needs. Thus, pursue important human aspects, make decisions and perform predicted actions that humans would approve to become better companions. Additionally it makes it possible to customise and personalise workspaces matching physical and cognitive characteristics of workers to support special needs, disabilities, aging and other kinds of personal limitations and opportunities. In future studies we aim to further develop and extend the meta-model also validate proposed opportunities at design phase through experiment at execution phase in selected case studies.

5 Conclusion

In this paper, we proposed an approach to support human-machine collaboration in Industry 4.0 through a Cyber-Physical-Social systems (CPSS) paradigm. CPSS is an emerging concept that intertwines human aspects to the existing notion Cyber-Physical systems (CPS). Current system designs approaches in Industry 4.0 heavily rely on the core concept of CPS, which does not incorporate human aspects. Thus, degrading collaboration quality and leaving room for compromised safety. We believe the CPSS paradigm supports the future of Industry 4.0 in bridging this gap as it effectively integrates human aspects with CPS. In general, the emergence of such intelligent collaborative industrial environments together with the complexity of human dynamics make systems more complex. Nevertheless taking a CPSS paradigm offers opportunities to better understand and model complex interactions. We elaborated the emerging notion of CPSS by visualising all kinds of relationships and interactions that may occur within a system of CPSSs. Additionally the extended meta-model is a step towards having a generic framework. As it brings human dynamics closer to CPS, it jointly opens opportunities to benefit from artificial intelligence in learning complex human behaviours, values and needs to enable machines and robots in becoming better companions during collaboration. Future studies will investigate this further.

References

1. Lezoche, M., Panetto, H.: Cyber-Physical Systems, a new formal paradigm to model redundancy and resiliency. Enterp. Inf. Syst. 1–22 (2018). https://doi.org/10.1080/17517575. 2018.1536807
2. Yilma, B.A., Naudet, Y., Panetto, H.: Introduction to personalisation in cyber-physical-social systems. In: Debruyne, C., Panetto, H., Guédria, W., Bollen, P., Ciuciu, I., Meersman, R. (eds.) OTM 2018. LNCS, vol. 11231, pp. 25–35. Springer, Cham (2019). https://doi.org/ 10.1007/978-3-030-11683-5_3
3. Romero, D., Bernus, P., Noran, O., Stahre, J., Fast-Berglund, Å.: The operator 40: human cyber-physical systems & adaptive automation towards human-automation symbiosis work systems. In: Nääs, I., et al. (eds.) Advances in Production Management Systems. Initiatives for a Sustainable World. APMS 2016. IFIP Advances in Information and Communication Technology, vol. 488, pp. 677–686. Springer, Cham (2016). https://doi.org/10.1007/978-3-319-51133-7_80
4. Naudet, Y., Yilma, B.A., Panetto, H.: Personalisation in cyber physical and social systems: the case of recommendations in cultural heritage spaces. In: 2018 13th International Workshop on Semantic and Social Media Adaptation and Personalization (SMAP) (2018). https://doi.org/10.1109/smap.2018.8501890
5. Moulières-Seban, T., Bitonneau, D., Salotti, J.M., Thibault, J.F., Claverie, B.: Human factors issues for the design of a cobotic system. In: Savage-Knepshield, P., Chen, J. (eds.) Advances in Human Factors in Robots and Unmanned Systems. Advances in Intelligent Systems and Computing, vol. 499, pp. 375–385. Springer, Cham (2017). https://doi.org/10. 1007/978-3-319-41959-6_31

6. Hernoux, F., Nyiri, E., Gibaru, O.: Virtual reality for improving safety and collaborative control of industrial robots. In: Proceedings of the 2015 Virtual Reality International Conference on ZZZ - VRIC 2015 (2015)

7. Panetto, H., Iung, B., Ivanov, D., Weichhart, G., Wang, X.: Challenges for the cyber-physical manufacturing enterprises of the future. Ann. Rev. Control **47**, 200–213 (2019)

8. Mourtzis, D., Fotia, S., Boli, N., Vlachou, E.: Modelling and quantification of industry 4.0 manufacturing complexity based on information theory: a robotics case study. Int. J. Prod. Res. 1–14 (2019)

9. Derler, P., Lee, E.A., Tripakis, S., Törngren, M.: Cyber-physical system design contracts. In: Proceedings of the ACM/IEEE 4th International Conference on Cyber-Physical Systems - ICCPS 2013 (2013)

10. Arnold, C., Kiel, D., Voigt, K.-I.: How the industrial Internet of Things changes business models in different manufacturing industries. Int. J. Innov. Manag. **20**, 1640015 (2016)

11. Bouffaron, F., Dupont, J.-M., Frédérique, M., Morel, G.: Integrative construct for model-based human-system integration: a case study. IFAC Proc. Vol. **47**, 12317–12324 (2014)

12. Moeuf, A., Pellerin, R., Lamouri, S., Tamayo-Giraldo, S., Barbaray, R.: The industrial management of SMEs in the era of Industry 4.0. Int. J. Prod. Res. **56**, 1118–1136 (2017)

13. Zhang, F., Liu, M., Shen, W.: Operation modes of smart factory for high-end equipment manufacturing in the Internet and Big Data era. In: 2017 IEEE International Conference on Systems, Man, and Cybernetics (SMC) (2017)

14. Fantini, P., Pinzone, M., Taisch, M.: Placing the operator at the centre of Industry 4.0 design: Modelling and assessing human activities within cyber-physical systems. Comput. Ind. Eng. (2018)

15. Zhu, Y., Tan, Y., Li, R., Luo, X.: Cyber-physical-social thinking modeling and Computing for geological information service system. In: Proceedings of the 4th International Conference on Identification, Information, and Knowledge in the Internet of Things (IIKI 2015), Beijing, China, October 2015

16. Sowe, S.K., Simmon, E., Zettsu, K., Vaulx, F.D., Bojanova, I.: Cyber-physical-human systems: putting people in the loop. IT Prof. **18**, 10–13 (2016)

17. Smirnov, A., Shilov, N., Gusikhin, O.: Cyber-physical-human system for connected car-based e-tourism: approach and case study scenario. In: 2017 IEEE Conference on Cognitive and Computational Aspects of Situation Management (CogSIMA) (2017)

18. Kumar, S.A., Bhargava, B., Macedo, R., Mani, G.: Securing IoT-based cyber-physical human systems against collaborative attacks. In: 2017 IEEE International Congress on Internet of Things (ICIOT) (2017)

19. Kannisto, J., Makitalo, N., Aaltonen, T., Mikkonen, T.: Programming model perspective on security and privacy of social cyber-physical systems. In: 2016 IEEE International Conference on Mobile Services (MS) (2016)

20. Xu, Q., Su, Z., Yu, S.: Green social CPS based e-healthcare systems to control the spread of infectious diseases. In: 2018 IEEE International Conference on Communications (ICC) (2018)

Collaborative Networks and ICT Trends for Future CPPS and Beyond

István Mezgár[(✉)]

Research Laboratory on Engineering and Management Intelligence,
Institute for Computer Science and Control, Hungarian Academy of Sciences,
Budapest, Hungary
mezgar@sztaki.mta.hu

Abstract. Enterprises are forced to implement continuously new ICT architectures, devices and technologies to react in time to the demands of the market for high quality, individualized products. These demands can be fulfilled only by well-organized and operated networked production systems. Cyber Physical Production Systems (CPPS) represent this type of networks connecting their different components through collaborative networks (CN), using emerging technologies in a very flexible and efficient way. The paper gives a short overview on the trends of CN and CPPS as systems, than the Brain Computer Interface (BCI) is introduced as a new technology to control devices in CPPS. As a next step a new paradigm for future production systems, beyond the CPPS is presented; the biological transformation in manufacturing (BTM), where biology, IC and manufacturing technologies are merged. There are many open questions in reference to BTM that need to be answered by the manufacturing community.

Keywords: Cyber Physical Systems · Brain Computer Interface · Collaborative Networks · Biological Manufacturing Systems

1 Introduction

The fast evolution of information and communication technologies (ICT) have resulted a new digital economy that has reached a point from where this process can be called as the "fourth industrial revolution". In this environment Cyber Physical Systems (CPS) are interlinked through real and virtual objects and processes. This phase can be characterized with deep interdisciplinary integration of technologies in digital, physical and biological world [1]. Manufacturing industry also belongs to those sectors that are basically changing in most of their component systems as new paradigms are involved into the production.

Today Artificial Intelligent (AI) technologies are the most dominant technologies for most sectors of economies, Gartner states that AI will become the biggest megatrend of the next decade [2]. The key AI technologies, e.g. deep learning, deep reinforcement learning, artificial general intelligence, machine learning, and conversational user interfaces appear not only as single applications but in many cases in an embedded, integrated form with other emerging technologies (e.g. AI+IoT, AI+BigData, AI+5/6G).

Published by Springer Nature Switzerland AG 2019
L. M. Camarinha-Matos et al. (Eds.): PRO-VE 2019, IFIP AICT 568, pp. 21–28, 2019.
https://doi.org/10.1007/978-3-030-28464-0_3

AI research got a big push and it seems that the level of AI applications will define the overall technological level of a country, as AI appears in most sectors of the economy. USA is traditionally dominant in this market, but China is raising radically its investment level (both states invest billions of USD into research founds) [3]. These AI based technologies can be applied in CPPS as well.

The paper gives a short overview on the trends of CN and CPPS as systems, than the Brain Computer Interface (BCI) is introduced as a new technology to control devices in CPPS. New human-machine communication technologies are in the first line of emerging technologies.

In the next section a new paradigm for future production systems, beyond the CPPS is presented; the biological transformation in manufacturing (BTM), where biology, IC and manufacturing technologies are merged, and the goal is to explore the application possibilities of the knowledge of biological principles in manufacturing processes. According to the predictions of different institutions the realization of highest (third) level of biological manufacturing will be in real industrial use only about after 2030 [4].

The paper discuss the above technologies only from technical viewpoints, but it is important to mention that there are non- technical fields (e.g. society acceptation, ethical questions) too, that are influenced by these technologies in a great extent and have back-reaction on these technologies as well. The focus of the paper is on human centric technologies and the biologisaton of manufacturing, so some critical questions of these fields can be discussed for future developments:

- What are the main gaps between BTM and traditional manufacturing?
- In which fields of manufacturing could be involved additional biological methods, processes?
- What can be the main negative factors in the introduction of BTM?

2   Collaborative Networks and CPPS

2.1   Collaborative Networks and Their Challenges for Future Production

In this section the trends of Collaborative Networks and CPPS as a whole system will be presented in connection with Industry 4.0 concept based production systems.

The different collaboration issues in production systems based on the Industry 4.0 concept are analyzed, compared and summarized in a structured way in [5]. Based on this evaluation 13 main group of challenges have been defined for further research. The importance of humans in the systems (in group 4) and the application of nature related disciplines (in group 7) in CNs are defined as well.

In order to give a proper answer to these challenges emerging technologies should be applied: extensive application of AI in decision making and in organization of CNs, collaborative censor fusion, collaborative robot–human work (corobots), and new interfaces are needed (e.g. BCI).

2.2   Cyber-Physical Production Systems (CPPS)

CPSs can be applied in many fields of economy, in healthcare, different fields of industry, agriculture. In the field of production/manufacturing the specialized CPS is called CPPS and focus on operating highly effective, flexible production system. Cyber-Physical Production Systems (CPPS), relying on the newest and foreseeable further developments of computer science (CS), information and communication technologies (ICT), and manufacturing science and technology (MST) [6]. CPPS can be characterized by strong collaboration of systems both among machine and human agents that results intensive communication.

There are numerous surveys, studies and whitepapers published on the challenges, trends of future manufacturing systems and CPPS. In the most important fields the predictions are overlapping each other, only the accents are put in different points. A few word summaries of the results of two studies are introduced especially only those points of the works that can be connected to the topic of this position paper.

In the whitepaper of [7] the following main Research Priorities for Cyber-Physical Manufacturing have been defined (2 points are selected from 14 on the list): RP2. Worker at the center in manufacturing systems; RP7. Cyber Native Factories.

The Report of the ManuFUTURE – EU High-Level Group [8], contains 10 groups of trends for future manufacturing systems in Europe, in four of them are reference on humans and biology: "AI will support all human's activity in manufacturing", "Biotech transformation of products and processes", "Collaboration and integration between humans and technology", "New interfaces between humans and machines will enable new levels of collaboration".

In the "Implementation Roadmap" chapter the bio based eco-systems are mentioned that although biotechnology has already significant developments these concepts call for a significant R&D effort and the mass implementation of the results will be a mid to long term target (2030–2040 for the 3rd level biologisation).

3   Human Machine Cooperation and Interfaces (BCI)

In the operation of highly digitalized production systems humans have a central role. Besides the conventional interfaces (e.g. keyboard and touch-screen, voice and gesture based techniques) BCI can be applied as well. In the literature many experts define the human machine interfaces (HMI) as critical technology and BCI is the interface that is handled with great expectations [9]. In the past years BCI is used in a growing extend in applications for healthy people (e.g. gamers, AR/VR applications) and now it appeared in the manufacturing world too.

3.1   Definition, Main Characteristics

BCI is a technology that allows the direct communication between the brain and an external device. A BCI can be described on a lower technical level as an artificial intelligence system (pattern recognition, machine learning) that can recognize a certain set of patterns in brain signals following five consecutive stages; signal acquisition, preprocessing or signal enhancement, feature extraction, classification, and the control interface. The controlled device can then send feedback to the user either via normal sensory pathways (screens, sounds) or directly through brain stimulation, thereby establishing a closed control loop.

BCI systems can be divided into three groups according to the placement of the electrodes used to detect and measure neurons firing in the brain; invasive-, semi-invasive and non-invasive techniques. The most sophisticated BCIs are bi-directional that can both record signal from the device and stimulate the nervous system.

There are also new and potentially dangerous situations in connection with BCI security. In BCI a hacker is no longer limited in access to machines and systems, but rather has the potential, to access partially the minds of living individuals [10]. New methods, processes have to develop to avoid these critical and dangerous situations.

3.2   BCI Applications in Manufacturing

There are examples of BCI applications in the field of manufacturing control as well. In the field of human-robot collaborative assembly has been applied BCI described in [11]. The human thought is realized as the desired robot movement to assist the human. This solution is an extension of multimodal communications (e.g. voice, gesture, haptic) and can realize more effective assembly.

In the paper [12] two classification algorithms are proposed by the authors for Brain Computer interfaces. The two algorithms are the Restricted Boltzmann Machines and the Long Short time Memory. The classification accuracy obtained from the two proposed methods showed similar accuracy than for the common Artificial Neural Network, opening the possibility to be used in manufacturing systems.

3.3   Manufacturing Related Advantages, Disadvantages and Trends of BCI

The advantages of BCI in manufacturing are: (1) BCIs can create direct communication between a human brain and any external devices; (2) EEG technique and neurochips make easier building BCI applications; (3) BCI stimulates researchers by generating new challenges.

The following features can be listed as disadvantages: (1) EEG technique needs extensive training for the users, (2) BCI techniques are slow and high costs, (3) Security/privacy problems are unsolved, (4) Ethical issues can be raised that can prevent further intensive BCI development.

The trends of BCI represent the raising of the theme. Intensive researches have been started in BCI field in the last years that resulted new HW elements as well, e.g. a BCI chip specially designed for decoding brainwave information.

Taking into consideration the research trends industrial application of BCI is predicted by the Gartner in more than 10 years [2].

4 Beyond CPPS; Biologisation in Manufacturing

4.1 Biologisation

There are significant improvements in the digitalization of manufacturing, both in the field of products and production in all phases of their life cycles. But taking into consideration the problems in connection with the limited resources of energy and material, new solutions have to be found for the industry. In this way the increased usage of practical solutions generated by the nature, e.g. from the biology came to light and can be handled as templates. The new solutions require the convergence of advanced technologies; require the knowledge of biologically inspired processes and aspects of sustainability. Inter- and trans-disciplinarity will be the defining features of future economy and production systems and these can create in this way a new age, a new paradigm.

4.2 Definition of Biologicalisation

The basic term for involving biology to the production is "biological transformation" ("Biological Transformation in Manufacturing"-BTM) but there are several other terms for the same concept. The authors in [4] apply the expression "biologicalisation" and define "biologicalisation in manufacturing" as "The use and integration of biological and bio-inspired principles, materials, functions, structures and resources for intelligent and sustainable manufacturing technologies and systems with the aim of achieving their full potential." According to a simplified definition it can be given as "the systematic application of the knowledge of biological processes aiming at optimizing a production" [13].

4.3 Main Characteristics of Biologicalisation

Three levels of biological transformation can be distinguished starting with the inspiration-level which is followed by the integration-level and finally the level of interaction, [13]. The levels are defined according to the merge- rate of biological- and technological paradigms.

On the inspiration-level biological concepts are transferred to value creation networks, called bio - inspired manufacturing. Bio inspired concepts are well known in technology and have been applied for years (e.g. swarm/ant algorithms). The integration-level is the next layer, given as bio-integrated manufacturing. In this level biological systems are actually integrated into manufacturing systems, e.g. the substitution of chemical processes by biological processes [13]. The level of interaction is the last level towards a huge leap to biological transformation of manufacturing systems. This layer represents the final step towards a fully bio-intelligent value creation network (bio intelligent manufacturing) which is the result of a completely new production paradigm. On the interaction-level technological, biological and information systems converge and collaborate.

4.4   Examples of Biologicalisation in Manufacturing

Cyber-Physical Production Systems (CPPS) are a good example for the inspiration-level biological system as they have a similar structure to natural ecosystems with their sub-elements/systems with the connected specific tasks and system behavior and interconnection (complex communication, flexible exchange of resources) [14]. By an abstraction the characteristic of natural systems can be transferred to CPPSs to make use of their optimized way of performance.

The use of microorganisms in machining processes is a good example for the integration-level. In [15] and [16] possible utilizations of microorganisms for micro-machining has been introduced. A bacterium has been used that metabolize metal for their energy production. Another example is when microorganisms can be integrated into the metal working fluids (MWF) to replace mineral-oil-containing MWFs and thus reduce the pollution of the environment [17]. In the field of product development the virus-built batteries, protein-based water filters, cancer-detecting nanoparticles can be listed as examples [18].

An example on interaction-level is the EVOLOPRO project [19]. The goals of the project are to develop methods for increased productivity, more robust processes and the improvement of products by using biological principles of diversity of variants and the theory of facilitated variation for complex self-adapting technological processes.

4.5   Main Advantages of Disadvantages of Biological Manufacturing Systems

The advantages of BTM are as follows: environment friendly, energy saving, lower cost, more efficient.

The following characteristics can be listed as disadvantages: research/experiments have to be done, longer installation time, risk of introducing a system/process, alternative technologies exist, not the best solution is offered but a better one than the previous.

4.6   Future Trends for Biological Manufacturing Systems

Future trends cannot define exactly for Biological Manufacturing Systems as they are very complex systems, very diverse disciplines are involved. The trends of component technologies can be estimated and as a second step can be predicted the introduction of a BMS. Machine learning (ML) and artificial intelligence (AI) are fundamental techniques in many fields of BMSs.

Selecting some AI related technologies their estimated industrial application time by the Gartner are as follows: Deep Neural Nets – Deep Learning, 5G between 2–5 years, Digital twin, Quantum computing, Smart Fabric, IoT Platform, Edge AI - between 5–10 years, BCI, Smart Dust, Biotech - more than 10 years [2].

5 Conclusions

The CPPS will remain dominant production system type in the future as well. The IC technologies applied in CPPS operation will develop quickly and this can modify the structure, the architecture, the way of communication, their collaboration in a great extent. As human beings have central role in these production systems the communication between humans and different devices have special emphasis. The BCI can help humans in the field of manufacturing system as well and within a few years BCI can get higher role especially in collaborative robotics.

A new paradigm, the biologisation of manufacturing (biologicalisation) can be the next step beyond CPPS in the field of production. In the biologisation of manufacturing the applied technologies are the result of deep integration of fully different fields (biology, ICT, manufacturing). These high level interdisciplinary technologies can apply more efficient, energy saving, green technologies, but parallel can generate challenges that are not easy to answer. The acceptance of these new technologies from the side of individuals, companies and the society, solving the connected moral/ethical problems are the biggest challenges for the future. Some of these challenges have been introduced in the paper and these have to be discussed by the manufacturing community to give proper answers in time.

Acknowledgement. This research has been supported partially by the Ministry of National Economy of Hungary through the GINOP-2.3.2- 15-2016-00002 grant, realized by the "Industry 4.0 research and innovation centre of excellence" project.

References

1. Schwab, K.: The Fourth Industrial Revolution: What It Means and How to Respond (2015). https://www.foreignaffairs.com/articles/2015-12
2. Panetta, K.: 5 trends emerge in the gartner hype cycle for emerging technologies 2018 (2018). https://www.gartner.com/smarterwithgartner/5-trends-emerge-in-gartner-hype-cycle-for-emerging-technologies-2018/
3. EU: Communication Artificial Intelligence for Europe (2018). https://ec.europa.eu/digital-single-market/en/news/communication-artificial-intelligence-europe
4. Byrne, G., Dimitrov, D., Monostori, L., Teti, R., van Houten, F.: Biologicalisation: biological transformation in manufacturing. CIRP J. Manuf. Sci. Technol. **21**, 1–32 (2018). https://doi.org/10.1016/j.cirpj.2018.03.003. ISSN 1755-5817
5. Camarinha-Matos, Luis M., Fornasiero, R., Afsarmanesh, H.: Collaborative networks as a core enabler of industry 4.0. In: Camarinha-Matos, Luis M., Afsarmanesh, H., Fornasiero, R. (eds.) PRO-VE 2017. IAICT, vol. 506, pp. 3–17. Springer, Cham (2017). https://doi.org/10.1007/978-3-319-65151-4_1
6. Monostori, L.: Cyber-physical systems. In: Chatti, S., Tolio, T. (eds.) The International Academy for Production. CIRP Encyclopedia of Production Engineering, pp. 1–7. Springer, Heidelberg (2018). https://doi.org/10.1007/978-3-642-35950-7
7. Taisch, M., Tavola, G., De Carolis, A.: Future trends and research priorities for CPS in manufacturing, Whitepaper, sCorPiuS project (2017)

8. ManuFUTURE Vision 2030: A Competitive, Sustainable and Resilient European Manufacturing, Report of the ManuFUTURE – EU High-Level Group (2018)
9. Lazarou, I., Nikolopoulos, S., Petrantonakis, P.C., Kompatsiaris, I., Tsolaki, M.: EEG-based brain-computer interfaces for communication and rehabilitation of people with motor impairment: a novel approach of the 21st century. Front. Hum. Neurosci. **12**, 14 (2018). https://doi.org/10.3389/fnhum.2018.00014
10. Bonaci, T., Calo, R., Chizeck, H.J.: App stores for the brain: privacy & security in brain-computer interfaces. IEEE Technol. Soc. Mag. **34**(2), 32–39 (2015)
11. Wang, L., Mohammed, A.: Brainwaves driven human-robot collaborative assembly. CIRP Ann.-Manuf. Technol. **67**(1), 13–16 (2018). https://doi.org/10.1016/j.cirp.2018.04.048
12. Balderas, D., Molina, A., Ponce, P.: Alternative classification techniques for brain-computer interfaces for smart sensor manufacturing environments. In: Proceedings of the 15th IFAC Symposium on Information Control Problems in Manufacturing, Ottawa, Canada (2015). IFAC-PapersOnLine **48**(3), 680–685
13. Dieckhoff, P., Möhlmann, R., van Ackeren, J. (eds.): Biological Transformation and Bioeconomy, White paper, Fraunhofer-Gesellschaft zur Förderung der angewandten Forschung e.V., München (2018)
14. Neugebauer, R., Ihlendfeld, S., Schlissfeld, U., Hellmich, A., Noack, M.: A new generation of production with cyber-physical systems – enabling the biological transformation in manufacturing. J. Mach. Eng. **19**(1), 5–15 (2019)
15. Istiyanto, J., Kim, M.Y., Ko, T.J.: Profile characteristics of biomachined copper. Microelectr. Eng. **88**(8), 2614–2617 (2011)
16. Hocheng, H., Chang, J.H., Hsu, H.S., Han, H.J., Chang, Y.L., Jadhav, U.U.: Metal removal by Acidithiobacillus ferrooxidans through cells and extra-cellular culture supernatant in biomachining. CIRP J. Manuf. Sci. Technol. **5**(2), 137–141 (2012)
17. Meyer, D., Redeczky, M., Brinksmeyer, E.: Microbial-based metalworking fluids in milling operations. CIRP Ann. **66**(1), 129–132 (2017)
18. Hockfield, S.: The Age of Living Machines: How Biology Will Build the Next Technology Revolution. W. W. Norton & Company (2019). ISBN-13: 978-0393634747
19. Degen, F.: Evolutionäre Selbstanpassung von komplexen Produktionsprozessen und Produkten, EVOLOPRO, Projektantrag Fraunhofer Leitprojekt (2018). https://www.ipt.fraunhofer.de/de/trendthemen/biologische-transformation/evolopro.html

Computational Creativity to Design Cyber-Physical Systems in Industry 4.0

Sanaz Nikghadam-Hojjati[(✉)] and José Barata

Universidade Nova Lisboa - FCT – DEE Quinta Da Torre,
2829-516 Caparica, Portugal
{sanaznik, jab}@uninova.pt

Abstract. The Fourth industrial revolution to be successfully implemented requires higher levels of creativity and innovation in the collaboration, design and composition of its cyber-physical building blocks. Powering industry 4.0 by creativity and innovation triggers efforts for better understanding of human creativity concepts and its intersection with cyber-physical systems in industry 4.0. Since computational creativity is an emerging field of research within AI that focuses on theoretical and practical issues in the study of creativity, the goal of this paper is to motivate a discussion about the application of computational creativity to design cyber physical production systems, which are at the core of industry 4.0. The fundamental research question in the paper is about the applicability of computational creativity in an industry 4.0 context.

Keywords: Industry 4.0 · Computational creativity · Cyber-physical systems · Design · Collaborative network

1 Introduction

The fourth industrial revolution is the information-intensive transformation of industries in an connected environment of data, people, processes, services, systems and IoT-enabled industrial assets which is looking for a way and mean to realize smart industry ecosystems of industrial innovation and collaboration [1]. The term Industry 4.0 refers to the combination of several major innovations in digital technology which includes cyber-physical systems, internet of things, cloud computing, cognitive computing and collaborative networks as its core enabler that can lead businesses to differentiated competitive advantages [2, 3]. According to a survey from 1600 C-level executives in business and government across 19 countries, 87% of these business leaders believe Industry 4.0 will lead to more social and economic equality and stability [4]. Alongside collaboration as the nucleus for all dimensions of the 4th industrial revolution, creativity will be one of the top skills valued in 2020 [5] and collaboration definitely an important aspect [6, 7]. According to the Zion Market Research, the global computational creativity market, which is responsible for finding creative and innovative solutions across different fields, was approximately USD 205 million in 2018 and is expected to generate around USD 1,115 million by 2026 [8]. Collaboration has always functioned as the kernel of creative works [9], but it seems the future of industry and

© IFIP International Federation for Information Processing 2019
Published by Springer Nature Switzerland AG 2019
L. M. Camarinha-Matos et al. (Eds.): PRO-VE 2019, IFIP AICT 568, pp. 29–40, 2019.
https://doi.org/10.1007/978-3-030-28464-0_4

digital transformation without creative collaboration and creative collaborative networks will be ambiguous.

As more and more complex and adaptive industrial systems are required, better solutions to design these new systems are needed, that should go much further ahead than just the application of fancy IT solutions such as the cloud or simple IoT approaches. Regarding these systems in a new perspective might be the only way to effectively solve the challenges imposed by industry 4.0. Seeing these systems as collaborative networks of machinery and people and applying all the theoretical framework that has been developed in the last years [6, 10, 11] can be an important contribution, together with a new vision on the importance of applying computational creativity to generate creative solutions to complex problems.

Based on mentioned aspects, the goal of this paper is to motivate a discussion about the application of computational creativity to design cyber physical production systems, which are at the core of industry 4.0.

The paper discussion is centered around the following questions:

RQ1 – Can creativity be implemented by computers?
RQ2 – Is computational creativity appropriate and applicable in an industry 4.0 context?
RQ3 – Is computational creativity appropriate for collaborative tasks?

Hence, this study explores industry 4.0 and computational creativity existing research works to provide better and clearer understanding of their concepts, requirements, nature and processes to answer the mentioned research questions.

Section 2 briefly outlines industry 4.0 and Cyber Physical Systems (CPS). Section 3 discusses about what creativity is and elaborates on how creativity is being introduced to the computer world (computational creativity). Section 4 describes a simple industry 4.0 system that will be used to illustrate how creativity can used to support its design. The research challenges faced by the application of computational creativity to design industry 4.0 systems composed of cyber-physical systems are listed in Sect. 5. Finally, Sect. 6, presents the conclusions for this paper.

2   Industry 4.0 and Cyber-Physical Systems

Economic challenges driven by technological and social development in the twenty first century´s world is provoking industrial enterprises to improve their agility and responsiveness in other to gain ability to manage whole value chain. Hence, enterprises require assistance of virtual and physical technologies which provide collaboration and rapid adaptation for their business and operations [12]. The industrial revolution of the 21st century leads industries to be smarter in decision-making and more flexible in production volume and customization, extensive integration between customers, companies, and suppliers, and above all higher sustainability and better optimization based on environmental variables and available resources [13]. This movement allows much greater agility and mix in a factory without sacrificing quality, cost, or speed. That will allow the company to innovate more rapidly and gain greater revenues. In future manufacturing, enterprises must cope with the need of rapid product development, flexible production as well as complex environments [14], cyber-physical systems, and collaborative networks have to enable the communication/collaboration between humans, machines and products alike [3].

Cyber-Physical Systems (CPS) which has been perceived as the core foundation of industry 4.0 [15], are systems of collaborating computation entities, that have an intensive connection with the surrounding physical systems and their ongoing processes through collaborative networks is the core foundation of Industry 4.0 [16].

CPS in the 4th industrial revolution can pursue different goals under different industrial and manufacturing circumstances. New smart CPS can drive innovation and competition in different sectors such as agriculture, energy, transportation, building design and automation, healthcare, and manufacturing. Small and medium-sized enterprises (SMEs), particularly start-up companies in the IT industry, are key participants in the development of the innovation and value creation potential of cyber physical systems.

Even though CPS strongly rely on technological advancements, the creativity, flexibility and problem-solving competence of human stakeholders is strongly needed for their operation [17].

Since CPS involves transdisciplinary approaches, merging theory of cybernetics, mechatronics, collaboration, design and process science [18], creative computation might be crucial in the design of cyber physical production systems to reduce creativity dependency from human stakeholders. This type of CPSs based on creative computation can support agile creative production to increase customer satisfaction and improve extensive integration between customers, companies, and suppliers, and above all sustainable creative economy. Hence, computational creativity-based CPS support, generate and/or evaluate creative solutions.

To achieve its basic goals industry 4.0 production systems should be basically cyber physical production systems, whose inherent collaborative and complex nature calls for highly creative designs.

3 Computational Creativity

The intersection of artificial intelligence, cognitive psychology, philosophy, and the art fields is on the basis of a multidisciplinary endeavour that is known as Computational Creativity. Mechanical Creativity, Artificial Creativity and Creative Computing are other names for this fascinating new field [19]. It uses computer and artificial intelligence-based technologies to study, emulate, motivate and enhance human creativity to reach one of various aims [19]:

- to develop and design models, methods and computer-based programs that can stimulate and enhance human creativity without necessarily being creative themselves;
- to develop and design models, methods and computer-based programs that can generate human-level creative ideas;
- to better study and understand the nature and processes of human creativity and apply a computer perspective about the human creative behaviour.

In summary, Computational Creativity is the capacity of finding, creating and developing solutions that are novel, interesting and appropriate for computational technologies. These aspects should go beyond human-level intellectual and computational capacity, which is far above the current state of the art in Artificial Intelligence, especially in what respects the high level cognitive functions [20, 21]. One important issue is clearly identifying the two different approaches for computational creativity: (1) using computers to stimulate human creativity, and (2) using computers to generate creative works. In this paper we are focused on the second approach.

Computational creativity cannot be achieved without a clear understanding of human creativity. Therefore, it is needed to investigate the most important cognitive models of creativity developed by psychological and behavioural scientists: (1) Psychodynamic Models, (2) Personality Models, (3) Psychometric Models, (4) Problem-Solving Models, and (5) Constraints Model of Creativity.

Psychodynamic Models of Creativity: Psychodynamic Models consider creativity an unconscious process. The unconscious mind allows creativity because it is less rigid and less specialized than the conscious mind [22]. Some researchers find these models of creativity unsettling because they give very little credit to individual or self-creativity.

Personality Models of Creativity: Personality Models of Creativity recognised the role played by individuals during the creative process. Garlick states that differences in an individual's ability to process information depend on brain differences [22]. Based on this approach people with higher level of Neural plasticity can have higher level of creativity. Some find these models of creativity oppressive because they give little credit to the thought base creativity.

Psychometric Models of Creativity: Psychometric Models consider creativity as something that can be taught [23]. Divergent thinking and Free Association thinking empower creativity and creative idea generation that brainstorming, followed by convergent thinking transform into valuable and appropriate solutions for the problem. For Psychometric Models creativity involves three major phases: (1) Problem Consideration; (2) Thinking of possible solutions; (3) Testing or evaluation those solutions to determine whether they are useful or not [24].

Problem-Solving Models of Creativity: In these models, creativity is about finding new and original solutions for problems. All searches for these novel solutions take place in a problem space. The problem space consists of the: (1) Initial state; (2) Search space and (3) Goal state. According to Weisberg, creative problem solving is a gradual development from initial knowledge to a final goal state [24].

The Constraints Models of Creativity: Constraints models of creativity consider creativity as an activity in creative problem solving [25]. Reitman argues that incremental problem-solving technique is a matter of constraints. Externally imposed and self-imposed constraints help the individual to reach a creative solution by narrowing the search space and guiding him or her towards the goal state [26].

These models can be used to understand better how the cognitive process of creativity is developed. All this work can be used to support the development of computer models that can be the basis for the development of creating creative computer programs. Computational creativity researchers from the AI area have already developed important work in creating computer programs that produce creative work [27], although not to generate industry 4.0 creative designs.

Psychologists and artificial intelligence (AI) scientists such as Boden [28], believe that there are three different processes to generate creative ideas: combination, exploration, or transformation [28]. These processes, if properly applied can be the genesis for novel and valuable ideas. They may be differentiated by the sort of psychological and cognitive processes that are involved in generating the creative and useful ideas in the human brain [29].

Combinational Creativity: involves generating unknown, surprizing and valuable combinations of known and usual ideas. Sometimes, the combinational creative outcomes can be unexpectedly novel, and extremely appropriate. In short, startlingly creative. Combinational creativity relies on a shared conceptual foundation and it happens by creating recognizable associations between ideas that were formerly only indirectly linked together. Combinational creativity outcomes require a fraught and valuable store of knowledge in the person's mind, and numerous different paths to move between this knowledge. It is combinational creativity that is usually mentioned in the definitions of "creativity" and is studied by experimental psychologists and neuroscientists specialized in creativity [29]. Combinational creativity is the most difficult for AI to model. Computers do not have any problem in making new and novel combinations of familiar concepts that are already stored or even accessing them. But there are two important problems. The first one is that the process of combining familiar concepts can continue for ever. The second problem is how to make these new combinations valuable and significant, which requires deep world knowledge, such as cultural knowledge. Human brain has a treasure trove of world knowledge which includes cultural knowledge. This is the missing element in generating many novel and valuable combinations by computers. However, artificial intelligence has this ability to generate novel and significant combination within a stoutly constrained context. But currently AI systems, including CPS, has no access to a rich and tightly structured storage of concepts that normal adult human has made in his/her life [29].

Exploratory Creativity: it rests on using the existing stylistic rules or conventions to generate novel structures (ideas), whose possibility may or may not have been realized before the exploration took place. Usually, these rules are largely, or even wholly, implicit. Style-defining rules should not be confused with the associative rules that underlie combinational creativity. Style-defining rules are normally called "generative rules" by AI scientists. Every structure produced by following them will fit the style concerned. Most artists and scientists spend their working time engaged in exploratory creativity. It can produce higher valued structures, or ideas. This type of creativity can often offer surprises that are rather deeper than merely seeing the previously unseen. The premise of exploratory creativity is that the new idea is not in your head yet, but that ideas already in your head would only lead you to explore beyond them [28, 29]. AI can model the exploratory creativity by enough clarifying the rule of relevant thinking style for putting them into an artificial intelligence program. Experts in the different styles spending their lifetimes to immersion into one style and give a verbal description for them which is not suit for computer implementation. Nevertheless, modelling exploratory creativity is much more possible for AI experts then earlier processes [29]. In many exploratory models, the computer comes up with results that can be compared with even professional human results [30].

Transformational Creativity: Boden defined transformational creativity ideas as "impossibilist surprise". In transformational creativity, the space or style itself is transformed by altering (or dropping) one or more of its dimensions. As a result, ideas can now be generated that simply could not have been generated before the change. The resulting change is so marked that the new idea may be difficult to accept, or even to understand. Sometimes, many years will have to pass before it can be valued by anyone outside a small group of aficionados. Boden believes that transformational creativity generates the most radical ideas, the ones that have the likelihood of winning a Nobel prize. The premise of transformational creativity is assuming (or hypothesizing) that an idea (or a few) in your head are actually wrong, and exploring the possibilities that result from accepting it [29]. Some people believe previous processes of creativity can at least be simulated by computer, but no computer could ever achieve transformational creativity because this processes not just producing new and significant idea, it also involves in producing new way of thinking based on new generated rules. They believe computer performance is based on their specified and determined rules and cannot go beyond these rules. Boden [31] criticizes this issue and argues that what is ignored by other researcher in this matter is that the program may include rules for changing itself. She suggests programs that contain evolutionary algorithms such as genetic algorithms can make random changes in the programs own task-oriented rules [31]. Insofar as computer's performance is caused by its program, everything it does was somehow implicit in the instructions provided by its programmer. As soon as computer programs are affected by unforeseen internal or external events than genuinely new types of results can emerge [32].

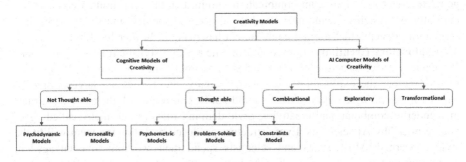

Fig. 1. Creativity models

Figure 1 classifies the different types of creativity models discussed in this section. The Cognitive Models of Creativity are those models developed by psychologists and behavioural scientists that explain how the creativity is processed in the brain, while AI Computer Models are those developed by computer scientists to support the implementation of creative based computer tools. So, computer scientists are developing new computer-based models that are inspired on the Cognitive Models of Creativity. Considering all that was discussed in this section the Research Question "RQ1 – Can creativity be implemented by computers?" is answered.

4   A Production System Illustrative Example

To answer RQ2, a simple assembly production system is described to illustrate how computational creativity can used to support its design. This example was previously used to demonstrate a different concept [33], but it is still very valid for the current case. The assembly of an adhesive tape roller dispenser (see Fig. 3) is the task to be considered. This product consists of the Part 1 and Part 3 joined together by a screw (Part 4), and Part 2 (tape roll). The assembly operation is going to take place on top of the work-piece carrier that are transported by the conveyors [33].

The choice of available system modules, for simplicity reasons, is limited to a small set (examples in Fig. 2) such as: a vertical and horizontal moving axis (Z and X), and a bulk feeder for screws. What is being considering here is the different digital twin modules following the RAMI 4.0 that may be available from different suppliers, and which can be considered as candidates for creating different possible layouts to answer a customer problem or order. Figure 4 illustrates how the two robotic axis (Z and X) are combined together with a 2-finger gripper to make a two axis pick and place robot. This created pick and place unit is used to execute all the required assembly operations for the Tape Roller Dispenser [33].

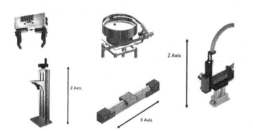

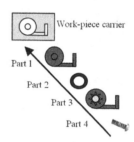

Fig. 2. Modules to be selected

Fig. 3. The adhesive tape roller dispenser. From [33]

Layout. The computational creativity-based design tool can generate many new and significant layouts and choose the one that best answers the end-user defined constraints and available modules.

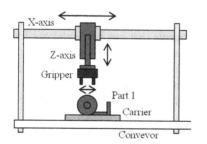

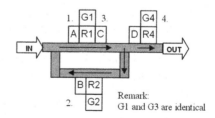

Fig. 4. Robot with one gripper and Part on a work-piece carrier. From [33]

Fig. 5. Circular layout with Robot 1 Part 1 and Part 3. From [33]

The layout shown on Fig. 5 is produced, which is characterized by having all robots with identical topology, as indicated in Fig. 4. The loop shown in the layout of Fig. 5 make the system more flexible and adaptable. Another interesting characteristic is the fact that work piece carriers are allowed to execute two differentiated tasks, any time they are visiting robot 1 (R1). In this especial example, Robot R1 works faster than Robots R2 and R4, and thus assembles Part 1 as well as Part 3. Empty work-piece carriers are input in the indicated 'IN' point, while 'OUT' represents the point where the finished product and its assigned carrier leaves the system. The letters A, B, C and D on Fig. 5 are the feeders for all Parts. Part 4, the screw, can be fed by any feeder type, for instance a bowl feeder as indicated in Fig. 2 that can be picked up by a magnetic screwdriver. The tape roll might be fed using a simple tubular gravitic feeder, and the main body parts can be store on pallets [33].

5 Computational Creativity Research Challenges in Designing Cyber Physical Production Systems

The problem described in the previous section is a typical manufacturing design problem which represents one type of industry 4.0 problem that could benefit from the application of computational creativity. In this type of problems, the goal is to autonomously and intelligently generate the best layout and configuration that answers the requirements by the application of computational creativity. Hence, computational creativity-based design tools can be a new generation of tools adequate to develop Cyber-Physical based Industry 4.0 systems in which collaboration between components are an important issue. Despite the application of computational creativity being not ended on design tools, this paper is focused on this class of problems as they are enough to illustrate its basic goals.

To motivate discussion and point out research directions in developing these new generation of computational creativity-based design tools (CCBDT) a sketch of a possible building blocks for such a tool is described in Fig. 6.

This proposed building blocks main goal is to support the development of a new generation of design tools whose main decision process is based on computational creativity, and therefore support the development and implementation of industry 4.0 based cyber physical systems. Novel and valuable creative layouts can then be generated by machines.

The most important components or parts of this building blocks are:

1. The digital twins of the manufacturing components that can be candidates for the possible generated layouts. Essentially, the most important characteristic to be considered here is the description of the operating parameters, and their functionality or basic skills that are relevant for the considered problem;
2. The objectives that are the products to be produced (for instance, the adhesive tape roller dispenser);
3. The basic operational modules, such as the Collaborative network module, User interface, Knowledge intelligence module, and the Supervision Module that orchestrates the functionality of the tool, interacting with all the main components;

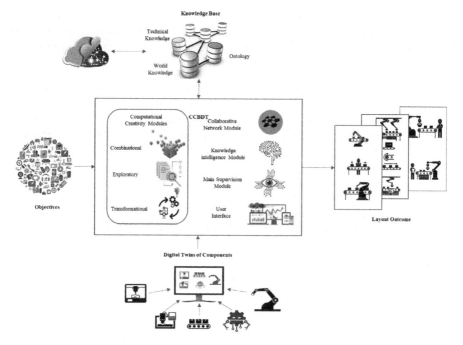

Fig. 6. Possible building blocks for a CCBDT

4. The knowledge management module that is responsible to manage and interact with all the different knowledge bases that are fundamental in a computational creativity process or system. As it was mentioned during the discussion of creativity and computational creativity, there is no creativity without different type of knowledge. So, technical knowledge is very relevant and fundamental, but common-sense knowledge (world knowledge) is also an important player to implement the different creative approaches (combinational, exploratory, and transformational). Ontology is included to indicate that concepts and their relations are fundamental. Of course, technical and world concepts will also be part of the ontologies. Technical and World KBs are more related to rules or set of rules that are important in the creative process. It must be noted that learning will be an important process to be included in the architecture to update the different knowledge bases;

5. Finally, the most novel part of this architecture the modules that will support the computational creative process. The idea is to have three different modules, each one responsible for one of the creative processes: combinational, exploratory, and transformational. The intention is to create a modular system that can accommodate a stepwise approach in which the system can be enriched with modules as they are being developed. If no modules to support transformational or combinational creativity are available, but exploratory modules are already available, then the system will only apply exploratory creativity. If all modules are available, then different solutions will be considered applying all the different three processes.

The proposed building blocks is much more to raise new questions than an answer to the problem. The authors' goal is much more to motivate discussion by raising some initial research challenges. Hence, the following research points might be considered as a starting point:

- Structure the work about creativity (non-computational). It involves working with psychologists, behavior scientists, cognitive scientists, artificial intelligence scientists, and neuro scientists and really understand what has been done until now and how it can be applied to computer-based systems. The study of the existing Cognitive Models of Creativity (Fig. 1) needs to be understand and better studied about how they can be adapted to computer models.
- Getting a good review and structure about all the computational creativity work. What Computer Models of Creativity exist, where they have been applied and how they can be used in our domain. Moreover, what new models are needed and what new field of applications in the Cyber Physical Production Systems computational creativity can be applied.
- Refine and work on a more elaborated architecture for CCBDT (Fig. 6).
- Understand and explore how computational creativity can be used and applied to facilitate collaboration in collaborative networks.

6 Conclusion

This paper is a very preliminary work but novel in terms of proposing a new approach for the application of computational creativity in the development of computer based supporting tools for the design of Cyber-physical based Industry 4.0 systems. The novelty is therefore proposing that creativity is not a magic but a type of Artificial Intelligence that can emulate the three basic types of human creativity: combinatorial, exploratory, and transformational. It is hoped that this work can motivate strong discussions and raise new research challenges based on what has been discussed and proposed on this paper.

The RQ1 was positively answered in Sect. 3, and the most important research question about the appropriateness of creativity to industry 4.0 (RQ2) is believed to be supported by what was described in Sects. 4 and 5. The answer to the research question 3, (RQ3) about the application of creativity in collaborative networks is also believed to be positively answered for two main reasons: (1) collaboration is an important part of the solution for industry 4.0, and (2) creative based computer tools are needed to implement and support collaborations.

A lot of work is still needed to be done in terms of implementing these three basic types of computational creativity processes, but what is important for now is that industry 4.0 can really get advantage from the application of computational creativity techniques, that have been essentially used in the areas of art, music, and literature generation. Its application in this domain, can be an important novelty and helping to bring the issue of creativity to different application areas rather than just design tools.

Another important conclusion is related to the implementation that the proposed building blocks left open. The most important challenge is how to really implement computer combinations, explorations, and transformations. A lot of work has been done in other areas (music, art, literature) that can be the starting point. Another implementational aspect is the learning that needs to be integrated in the architecture in order to keeping real time update of the knowledge bases, and all the knowledge modelling issues behind the representation of common knowledge.

The authors really look forward to having the possibility to continue proceeding this very challenging and innovative work of applying computational creativity in the world of industry 4.0 and integrate it with the collaborative networks work that has been done.

Acknowledgements. This work was supported in part by the FCT/MCTES (UNINOVA-CTS funding UID/EEA/00066/2019) and the FCT/MCTES project CESME - Collaborative & Evolvable Smart Manufacturing Ecosystem, funding PTDC/EEI-AUT/32410/2017.

References

1. Majstorovic, V.D., Mitrovic, R.: Industry 4.0 programs worldwide. In: Monostori, L., Majstorovic, V.D., Hu, S.J., Djurdjanovic, D. (eds.) AMP 2019. LNME, pp. 78–99. Springer, Cham (2019). https://doi.org/10.1007/978-3-030-18180-2_7
2. Geissbauer, R., Vedsø, J., Schrauf, S.: A strategist's guide to Industry 4.0. Strategy +Business, pp. 148–163 (2016)
3. Camarinha-Matos, L.M., Fornasiero, R., Afsarmanesh, H.: Collaborative networks as a core enabler of industry 4.0. In: Camarinha-Matos, L.M., Afsarmanesh, H., Fornasiero, R. (eds.) PRO-VE 2017. IAICT, vol. 506, pp. 3–17. Springer, Cham (2017). https://doi.org/10.1007/978-3-319-65151-4_1
4. The Fourth Industrial Revolution will change the world – but only 14% of execs are ready for it (2019)
5. Motyl, B., Baronio, G., Uberti, S., Speranza, D., Filippi, S.: How will Change the Future Engineers' Skills in the Industry 4.0 Framework? A questionnaire survey. Proc. Manuf. **11**, 1501–1509 (2017). https://doi.org/10.1016/j.promfg.2017.07.282
6. Camarinha-Matos, L.M., Scherer, R.J. (eds.): PRO-VE 2013. IAICT, vol. 408. Springer, Heidelberg (2013). https://doi.org/10.1007/978-3-642-40543-3
7. Camarinha-Matos, L.M., Afsarmanesh, H., Rezgui, Y. (eds.): PRO-VE 2018. IAICT, vol. 534. Springer, Cham (2018). https://doi.org/10.1007/978-3-319-99127-6
8. Computational Creativity Market by Deployment, by Operating System, and by Application : Global Industry Perspective, Comprehensive Analysis, and Forecast, 2018–2026 (2019)
9. Graham, J., Gandini, A.: Introduction: collaborative production in the creative industries. In: Collaborative Production in the Creative Industries, pp. 1–14. University of Westminster Press (2017). https://doi.org/10.16997/book4.a
10. Camarinha-Matos, L.M., Boucher, X., Afsarmanesh, H. (eds.): PRO-VE 2010. IAICT, vol. 336. Springer, Heidelberg (2010). https://doi.org/10.1007/978-3-642-15961-9
11. Afsarmanesh, H., Camarinha-Matos, L.M., Lucas Soares, A. (eds.): PRO-VE 2016. IAICT, vol. 480. Springer, Cham (2016). https://doi.org/10.1007/978-3-319-45390-3
12. Akdil, K.Y., Ustundag, A., Cevikcan, E.: Maturity and readiness model for industry 4.0 strategy. In: Akdil, K.Y., Ustundag, A., Cevikcan, E. (eds.) Industry 4.0: Managing The Digital Transformation. SSAM, pp. 61–94. Springer, Cham (2018). https://doi.org/10.1007/978-3-319-57870-5_4

13. Shrouf, F., Ordieres, J., Miragliotta, G.: Smart factories in Industry 4.0: a review of the concept and of energy management approached in production based on the Internet of Things paradigm. In: IEEE International Conference on Industrial Engineering and Engineering Management, pp. 697–701 (2014). https://doi.org/10.1109/IEEM.2014. 7058728

14. Vyatkin, V., Salcic, Z., Roop, P., Fitzgerald, J.: Now that's smart! IEEE Ind. Electron. Mag. **1**, 17–29 (2007). https://doi.org/10.1109/MIE.2007.909540

15. Xu, L.D., Xu, E.L., Li, L.: Industry 4.0: state of the art and future trends. Int. J. Prod. Res. **56**, 2941–2962 (2018)

16. Monostori, L.: cyber-physical production systems: roots, expectations and R&D challenges. Proc. CIRP **17**, 9–13 (2014). https://doi.org/10.1016/j.procir.2014.03.115

17. Frazzon, E.M., Hartmann, J., Makuschewitz, T., Scholz-Reiter, B.: Towards socio-cyber-physical systems in production networks. Proc. CIRP **7**, 49–54 (2013). https://doi.org/10. 1016/j.procir.2013.05.009

18. Lee, E.A., Seshia, S.A.: Introduction to Embedded Systems. A Cyber-Physical Systems Approach. MIT Press, Cambridge (2017)

19. Colton, S., Lopez de Mantaras, R., Stock, O.: Computational creativity: coming of age. AI Mag. **30**, 11 (2009). https://doi.org/10.1609/aimag.v30i3.2257

20. Duch, W.: Computational creativity. In: Dubitzky, W., Wolkenhauer, O., Cho, K.H., Yokota, H. (eds.) Encyclopedia of Systems Biology, pp. 464–468. Springer, New York (2013). https://doi.org/10.1007/978-1-4419-9863-7

21. Schmid, K.: Making AI systems more creative: the IPC-model. Knowl.-Based Syst. **9**, 385–397 (1996). https://doi.org/10.1016/S0950-7051(96)01049-0

22. Garlick, D.: Integrating brain science research with intelligence research. Curr. Dir. Psychol. Sci. **12**, 185–189 (2003). https://doi.org/10.1111/1467-8721.01257

23. Plucker, J.A., Renzulli, J.S.: Psychometric approaches to the study of human creativity. In: Handbook of creativity, pp. 35–61. Cambridge University Press, Cambridge (1999)

24. Weisberg, E.W.: Creativity: genius and other myths. W.H.Z. Freeman and Company, New York (1986)

25. Stokes, P.D.: Creativity From Constraints: The Psychology of Breakthrough. Springer, New York (2006)

26. Reitman, W.R.: Creative problem solving: notes from the autobiography of a fugue. In: Cognition and Thought: An Information Processing Approach, p. 168. Wiley, New York (1965)

27. Besold, T.R., Schorlemmer, M., Smaill, A. (eds.): Computational Creativity Research: Towards Creative Machines. Atlantis Press, Paris (2015). https://doi.org/10.2991/978-94-6239-085-0

28. Boden, M.A.: The Creative Mind: Myths and Mechanisms. Routledge, London (2004)

29. Boden, M.A.: Computer Models of Creativity. AI Mag. **30**, 23–34 (2009)

30. Cohen, H.: A million millennial medicis. In: Cohen, H. (ed.) Explorations in Art and Technology, pp. 91–104. Springer, London (2002). https://doi.org/10.1007/978-1-4471-0197-0_7

31. Boden, M.A.: Mind as Machine: A History of Cognitive Science. Oxford University Press, Oxford (2006)

32. Boden, M.A.: Creativity as a neuroscientific mystery. In: Vartanian, O., Bristol, A.S., Kaufman, J.C. (eds.) The Neuroscience of Creativity, pp. 3–18. The MIT Press, Cambridge (2013)

33. Frei, R., Serugendo, G.D.M., Barata, J.: Designing self-organization for evolvable assembly systems. In: 2008 Second IEEE International Conference on Self-Adaptive and Self-Organizing Systems, pp. 97–106. IEEE (2008). https://doi.org/10.1109/SASO.2008.20

Advanced Cyber Physical Systems

Adaptive Integration of IoT with Informatics Systems for Collaborative Industry: The SITL-IoT Case

A. Luis Osório[1(✉)], Luis M. Camarinha-Matos[2], Tiago Dias[1], and José Tavares[3]

[1] ISEL - Instituto Superior de Engenharia de Lisboa,
Instituto Politécnico de Lisboa and POLITEC&ID, Lisbon, Portugal
lo@isel.ipl.pt, tdias@cc.isel.ipl.pt
[2] Faculty of Sciences and Technology, NOVA University of Lisbon
and CTS-UNINOVA, Caparica, Portugal
cam@uninova.pt
[3] FORDESI, Informatics Systems, and Solutions Company, Lisbon, Portugal
jose.tavares@fordesi.pt

Abstract. Legacy industrial infrastructures are facing complex challenges to evolve to integrated solutions through the adoption of novel computing and business paradigms. The fast-growing collaborative businesses introduce the additional complexity of managing cooperative interactions among systems of business partners. The SITL-IoT research project aims to develop an open integrated and collaborative systems landscape for the silos agri-food industry. This case considers a silos' operator managing a maritime silos terminal in collaboration with the seaport administration, where trucks transfer bulk products to silos or bulk storages and distribute them to factories. The existing legacy management and supervision solutions are neither integrated nor properly prepared to cope with collaborative processes. Furthermore, the interactions with business partners are complex and follow dedicated integration solutions that pose difficult challenges in terms of management and evolution, since they do not follow open collaborative models or technology implementations. This paper discusses the problem domain and the approach to co-design and implement a technology-agnostic open integration infrastructure to support such collaborative network. The proposed approach considers a multi-supplier strategy for the adaptive integration of things on Internet of Things (IoT), considering the collaborative networks dimension.

Keywords: Collaborative networks · Internet of Things · Systems integration · Cyber-physical systems · Distributed systems

1 Introduction

Industrial companies are facing complex challenges to adapt their sensor/actuator and computing systems to new business models to maintain competitiveness. The fast move towards digital transformation, pulled by retail, social and media companies

L. M. Camarinha-Matos et al. (Eds.): PRO-VE 2019, IFIP AICT 568, pp. 43–54, 2019.
https://doi.org/10.1007/978-3-030-28464-0_5

(e.g., Amazon, Facebook, Netflix), as well as the objectives highlighted by Industry 4.0, put pressure on traditionally conservative industrial systems not only to adhere but also to evolve their technology landscapes to offer advanced management and operations intelligence. However, such trend is complex and difficult to make effective since current approaches still lack a clear systemic structuration. In fact, such traditional approaches consider the incorporation of software parts to improve specific features of a system or the development of independent applications to automate specific processes, without a well-founded systems' engineering approach. Hence, there is an urgent need to evolve towards a systems' thinking paradigm, in order to be able to effectively develop complex composites of collaborative components.

In this paper, we address the challenges faced by a maritime terminal silos operator when deciding about the strategy to integrate multi-supplier things following the Internet of Things (IoT) trends [4], owing both to the legacy of its current solutions and the expectations of an agri-industry silos concessionaire. Such legacy solutions lack an automatic procedure for the loading of trucks for the transport of bulk products from silos conveyor structures to factories or intermediary logistics infrastructures that is able to smoothly cope with complex collaborative interactions. The challenge is how to structure such cyber-physical components into manageable systems so that they can be part of more complex systems or system of systems (SoS) [19].

The main expectation of this project, named SITL-IoT, is to develop a technology strategy evolve to a higher integration level of legacy and new technical systems. An utmost challenge is how to organize such complex technology systems/elements into integrated vendor agnostic and reliable composites or aggregations. By composites, we mean elements of a system under the same responsibility domain (e.g., from a single vendor or integrator). By aggregation, we mean an agreement between responsibilities under different responsibility domains. Aggregation is important to reduce the governance risks of existing computing related technology landscapes [3]. As a contribution to modularity abstractions, we consider the concept of "informatics system" as a composite of computing centric elements, establishing a well-bounded responsibility. We consider a cyber-physical system as a composite of computing and physical interacting elements involving contributions from Informatics Engineering and Electrical Engineering [9].

In another dimension, the SITL-IoT project addresses the need to coordinate processes involving business stakeholders. The legacy processes involve truck drivers that need to interact with self-service kiosks to operate bulk product transports. These processes are expected to evolve to electronic interactions, making the transport more efficient based on automatic scheduling and authorizations of truck or train operations. The IoT perspective needs to consider a cross border scope, since we need to cope with a diversity of business stakeholders, including telecom operators, vehicle owners and manufacturers, manufacturers of the micro embedded connected devices, etc. On the other side there are organizations like the silos concessionaire, a user organization that needs such things framed to be reliable (responsibility), integrated (in system of systems and collaborative networks), cost-effective (vendor agnostic) and manageable, maintainable, and supported by integrated models. Integration is a complex endeavour, since the interdependence of responsibilities tends to be difficult to manage. In many cases, user organizations have independent 24 h/7 days support for each critical system even when they are under aggregation mechanisms.

The SITL-IoT is an integrating project joining: (1) an agri-food industry maritime terminal concessionaire SDL, aiming to evolve for integrated and collaborative operations and management of their supervision, control, and business processes; (2) a technology company FORDESI, already a supplier of a silos management system (SIGSIL product), which is committed to offering a vendor agnostic and advanced integrated and collaborative technology system and solutions; and (3) research organizations POLITEC&ID&ISEL and UNINOVA, which provide an open model driven systems engineering (MDEOS) framework.

The paper is organized in five main sections. Section 2 positions the problem and the main research questions. Section 3 summarizes and discusses research and industry contributions to the area. Section 4 presents and discusses the SITL-IoT project case and the proposed approach. The last section draws some conclusions and outlines open questions for further research.

2   Problem Domain and Main Research Questions

The SITL-IoT project aims to define an approach for agile integration of physical sensors and actuators under an IoT and cloud computing strategy, as depicted in Fig. 1.

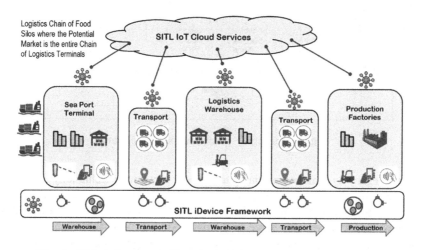

Fig. 1. SITL-IoT systems vision for logistics terminal and products flow

The agri-food silos operator company has a terminal concession of the port of Leixões/Porto Portugal, managing a complex network of technological systems and interacting with networked business partners. The aims of the project fit well with the industry 4.0 and digital transformation trends [7]. The Silo business ecosystem supervises and manages IoT/cyber-physical (mechanical, electrical, automation and computing) artefacts that need to be considered under a unified and single collaborative responsibility.

The agri-food silos ecosystem is under operation, and supported by five main systems (informatics or cyber-physical), as depicted in Fig. 2:

i. The Monitoring System, responsible for collecting events from temperature sensors and energy consumption instrumentation;
ii. The SCADA, which is a supervision and control system;
iii. The SIGSIL, a product and a central responsibility of FORDESI, which is composed of a customer portal, a mobile portal, and an operations portal, with interoperation to the WS Mobile and OPCS systems;
iv. The WS Mobile Portal System for managing the interaction of SDL's operators and truck drivers from ubiquitous user interface devices;
v. The OPCS system, which is responsible for the management of the domain processes control.

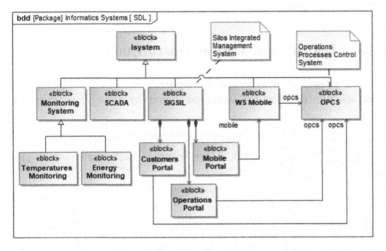

Fig. 2. The legacy systems at the silos operator

These legacy systems are not integrated under a common technology framework. For instance, the Monitoring System does not process events from the other systems. Moreover, the two systems on the left (Monitoring System, and SCADA) are from two competing suppliers, while the three on the right (SIGSIL, WS Mobile, and OPCS) are from FORDESI. It is interesting to note that no interactions exist between the two systems on the left; they are isolated "islands" [5].

Technically, suppliers agree on some interaction strategy, e.g., based on an enterprise integration bus. The difficulty lies in the fact that the new system responsible for establishing such an enterprise bus raises additional research questions, since another system needs to be managed. So, the question is if the right strategy to create higher integration levels should be delegating on current suppliers to agree on interoperation mechanisms or to adopt open and vendor-agnostic infrastructures.

To meet this later goal, the challenge is to find an approach for establishing a sustainable multi-supplier technology framework, where systems from different vendors interact under an integrated system-of-systems framework. One key problem is to find the right modularity division of responsibilities, considering that a sustainable technology solution is the one that gets advantage from market competition for each elementary responsibility [5, 16]. Another concern is the design and validation of an appropriate structuration of collaborative responsibilities.

3   Related Research

The SITL-IoT project is conceptually aligned with Industry 4.0 or smart manufacturing [7]. It does not involve a manufacturing execution system, but it considers systems responsible for the execution of the SDL processes and, at the base, it involves a distributed cyber-physical system. Such system comprehends multiple embedded devices positioned at different sites that operate as actuators or perform data acquisition through sensors, which we can consider as elements positioned at "Field Level" [2]. One example of such elements is a Truck Weighting physical infrastructure to obtain position and weight of trucks.

The smart city concept and the emergence of sensor data available under open data models have motivated research and industry contributions to make huge amounts of sensor data available through cloud services [1]. While the idea is interesting for a more "*citizen-centric and participatory mobility model*" [21], the authors point for a backbone leveraged by ICT and open data. In fact, in the smart-city concept, the IoT has been the driver for new services offered by computing elements, contributing to data to be analyzed based on cloud systems [13]. While emphasizing the value of IoT and cloud computing, the mentioned work adopts an open infrastructure for sharing data sets and understand the interdependencies in such complex dynamic systems. Interdependencies appear as one of the recurrent problems in constructing enhanced intelligent mobility and friendly cities. The Open Data maturity report from the European Commission [8] positions cities like Lisbon in a high ranking, as open data is concerned. However, from the presented list of recommendations, it seems that it is lacking a technology strategy in terms of infrastructure responsibilities. The question is whether we need a kind of "city operating system" (what in [12] is called Urban Operating System) to provide an integrated ICT technology strategy for the coordination and integration of the complex system of systems.

In [12], the authors establish a parallel with corporate enterprise resource planning (ERP) to question the need for structuring consistent concepts towards the idea of Urban Operating System. The work discusses experiences of smart-city architectures of IBM, Microsoft, and Hitachi, pointing the need to "*view the city as an experimental site for the transmutation of corporate integrated information systems into an urban context*" [12]. We find this discussion interesting because it corroborates our hypothesis for the need of a novel technology strategy for answering business requirements under complex evolving ubiquitous computing elements as composites or aggregations of things (IoT), crossing infrastructure elements to business or control process automation systems. As in the SITL-IoT case, the IoT sensors and actuators need to interoperate, not only as sources of open data but also as elements composed or aggregated into cyber-physical or informatics systems. Despite the number of available standards, e.g., internet engineering task force (IETF) CoAp/REST or MQTT messaging protocol on the application layer of a communication stack, the huge number of open and proprietary specifications makes interoperability an unsolved challenge [1].

The relevance of IoT for SITL-IoT deserves a discussion about relevant IoT platforms like OpenMTC, FIWARE, Site-Where, and Amazon Web Services IoT, as established in [10]. In that work, the authors proposed a reference architecture as an abstraction for the discussed platforms, depicted in Fig. 3.

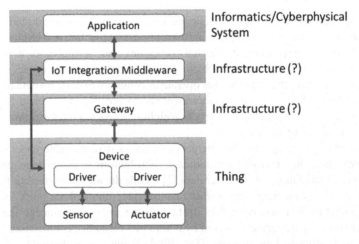

Fig. 3. IoT reference architecture (adapted from [10])

The proposed reference architecture raises a few questions related to how to frame the approach into a complex system of systems perspective. The Gateway seems to be necessary only if the "things" cannot cope with the proposed communication protocols and related stack layers (HTTP or MQTT, and JSON or XML for payload). It is suggested that IoT Integration Middleware "*may comprise all kinds of functionality that are required by a certain cyber-physical system, for instance, a rules engine or graphical dashboards,*" but the proposed architecture still includes an upper Application layer. Although the approach has some interesting features, we argue that dealing with all existing specific technologies and protocols is not realistic. Hence, in our perspective, an adaptive strategy is needed to plug the elements to the systems and to support the interactions between the systems [4].

The IoT is being materialized on a diversity of ecosystems (smart-cities, transports, mobility, home automation, healthcare), making possible the mobile ubiquity sensing and computing. The convergence of communication infrastructures, currently evolving fast to the 5G (fifth generation), also raises the need for a novel approach to the fast-upcoming Everything Integrated and Collaborative. The question is whether we need an IoT Manager, as proposed in [6], or a strategy to make IoT things pluggable to (aggregation) or into (composition) higher level constructors (systems and elements of systems), sourced from a diversity of technology and process cultures and under clear administrative boundaries.

4 The SITL-IoT Approach Under ISoS and ECoNet Frameworks

Given the initial problem formulation proposed by FORDESI, a decision was taken to adopt the MDEOS strategy [16] as a (co)-development effort based on the CEDE collaborative development environment [16] and the ISoS framework [11], towards an open technology landscape for SDL. Figure 4 depicts the ISoS framework and the collaborative business relations of SDL and FORDESI as a technology supplier under the ECoNet framework and platform.

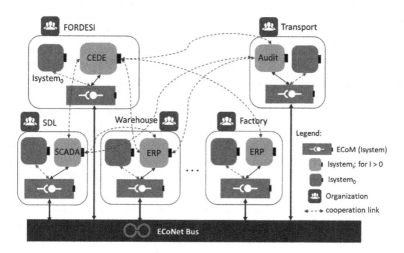

Fig. 4. The vision behind the SITL-IoT project

This research project gives an opportunity to rethink the legacy modularity, since both the Monitoring System and the SCADA functions are supposed not only to be maintained but also to evolve.

The adoption of the right modularity strategy is another issue, not only from the technical perspective but also from the vision and interests of the suppliers of the other legacy systems. The existing "things" and sub-systems provided by competing suppliers must evolve and be adapted to the ISoS framework. From our previous research [11, 15, 17], and considering the commitment of the SDL, we believe that other suppliers will adhere to the open specifications model, taking the advantage of being prepared to adopt open solutions.

4.1 The Isystem of Isystems (ISoS) and ECoNet Models

As depicted in Fig. 4, the extended SDL ecosystem comprehends warehouses, factories, and transport organizations and involves FORDESI as a supplier and support organization. The interactions flow through the Isystem ECoM [18], specialized in establishing collaborations and responsible for managing the data and coordination exchanges. Specialized collaboration contexts are to be designed and developed to establish short and long term collaboration relations [7]. Using ECoM to establish an ECoNet collaborative network has the advantage of following a unified technology approach. Based on the simple infrastructural mechanisms, each specific collaboration case, e.g., the exchanges with port authorities to access port community system, needs a specialized collaboration context to be installed [18]. The advantage is that the Isystems from all the organizations interacting in the context of a port community system share the same interchange mechanism.

ECoM is an Isystem integrated with the remaining Isystems of SDL through a new meta-Isystem that is designed and developed as the main entry point for the SDL technology landscape. The Isystem concept is part of the ISoS framework [11], where an $Isystem_0$ (the mentioned meta-Isystem) is the entry point to access and introspect about the installed Isystems. This entry point establishes a secure and authenticated access to a *self-awareness()* web service. It assumes that any Isystem developer can implement the access to the *selfAwareness()* service, since it follows web services standards. Through the $Isystem_0$ it should be possible to access the other Isystems, under the assumption that any computational responsibility is "wrapped" into an Isystem concept.

One important research item in the SITL-IoT project is the (re)construction of the modularity in SDL considering a revision of business processes, both internal and collaborative, in order to establish the Isystem structuration that better fits activity needs.

An Isystem is structured as a composite of Cooperation Enabled Services (CES) elements [14]. Access to the CES services follows a strategy like the one adopted for an Isystem. A CES is accessed and introspected through the *selfAwareness ()* web service, which is the entry point to obtain the implemented services and the information necessary to access them. A service can be implemented in any legacy or new technology. A Generic Modelling Entity object holds the necessary information encoded/decoded by a predefined MIME tag. This means that no restrictions are imposed to developers of CES elements, since they are free to adopt the technologies considered to be most appropriate. The ISoS approach aims to reduce the risks of having innovation hampered by vendor lock-in situations.

Also, the offered flexibility allows a single CES to answer under different technology implementations. The multi-technology CES approach enables the incorporation of innovative features, making the product competitive without compromising interoperability. In fact, interoperability is adaptive, since any peer can obtain information about the implementation and the necessary elements for each specific implementation, making it possible for peers to access the service.

The SITL-IoT project offers the opportunity to validate the ISoS framework under an open specifications and development initiative. An initial question is how to migrate the existing products supplied by FORDESI, since they were developed using a different technology. Considering the adopted mechanism to cope with technology diversity, the main problem would not be the "wrapping" of legacy implementations but rather the (re)design of the "would-be" architecture.

4.2   Integration of Legacy Systems and IoT Things

From our perspective, there are two main structuration lines for the "things". On the one hand, "things" can be in the WAN space, meaning that thing's data needs to be transported by global communication providers. On the other hand, "things" can be local to the bounded infrastructure and therefore the communication is exclusively based on the LAN. Still, there are other application domains, as the example of the vehicle-to-vehicle or vehicle-to-infrastructure communication (V2X), where the communication is hybrid [20]. The communication can use the cellular or the road operator's G5 infrastructure, depending on availability and on mechanisms to improve reliability. In the SITL-IoT case, it seems that a hybrid approach is appropriate, since trucks, drivers and the SDL's personal can use ubiquitous mobile devices as sensing devices, which contributes for a smarter and agile processes control.

Hence, a hybrid strategy can consider the following association cases:

i. The IoT "things" are elements of the organization's ISoS technology landscape, and therefore they are framed under the CES abstraction.
ii. The IoT "things" embed mobile elements, like trucks or nomadic devices held by a truck driver or a foreign person (from a different organization), in which case the access to the sensors is through the collaborative partners' Isystems.
iii. The IoT "thing" of a foreign person interacts with the physical "things" in the SDL's infrastructure. The smartcard to authenticate a foreign user is an example of such situation that requires a learning interaction phase between the Isystems of both organizations for the sharing of the necessary authentication data.

Therefore, an IoT "thing" can be the responsibility of either the ISoS [11] of SDL (a Local Thing), or a business partner interacting in the context of an operation (Collaborative Thing), as depicted in Fig. 5.

The hypothesis of an interaction between a truck and the silos terminal weighing infrastructure to make the weighing operation aware of truck characteristics like its tare can be considered. In this particular case, the Collaborative Thing is modelled as a service playing a surrogate role (digital twin) responsible for managing the interactions with a business partner; the owner of the IoT "thing" modelled by the ISoS service. It can be a truck IoT from different transport companies dynamically detected and associated with making the weighting process accurate. The approach needs further research and validation, owing to the difficulty to guarantee interoperation considering heterogeneous "things" embedded into trucks.

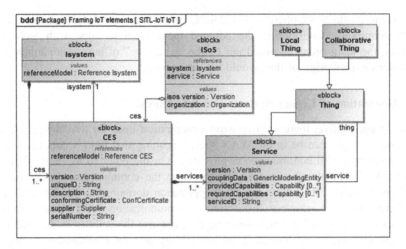

Fig. 5. The SysML model framing of the IoT "things" to the ISoS framework

5   Conclusions and Further Research

This paper presents and discusses the initial approach of the SITL-IoT project aiming at establishing a strategy for an open technology landscape for both the user organization and the associated collaborative network. The initial formulation of the SITL-IoT vision is presented and discussed. While considering the holistic vision for the collaborative network, the paper discusses the framing of IoT elements into the proposed holistic open integration strategy. The preliminary research, based on results from previous projects, suggests the IoT elements need to be under a clear governance model. The proposed approach, while not undervaluing public communication infrastructures (communication and internet service providers), assumes that the IoT devices are elements of cyber-physical or informatics systems. With such approach, we do not discard the access to IoT through public Internet/web services, whilst at the same time we uphold the responsibility integrity led by the system concept.

Nevertheless, the proposed strategy faces many obstacles requiring further research and validation. The so far theoretical CES model needs to be demonstrated in wrapping legacy implementations, and one main question encompasses the cost and the risks of such required changes. Beyond the migration problem, the SITL-IoT faces several other challenges, among which we consider:

- The cost of wrapping legacy systems needs to be clarified. This problem is related to decision making regarding the right Isystem or CES modularity, due to the related market competing issues. In other words, achieving the balance between the market/business interests and the openness strategies.
- The strategy to follow making local or just-in-time access to data critical for operation. A practical example can be the case of a planned truck that needs to be replaced after a breakdown, and the new tare weight need to be obtained.

- The design and management of both the operational processes and the collaborative processes already established based on long term contract agreements to their execution control and auditing. The collaboration contexts managed by the ECoNet/ECoM seem to be flexible enough to develop higher collaboration models of collaboration processes, but this needs to be verified.

This project is particularly relevant for this study, considering that a supplier, the FORDESI company, decided to invest on an open strategy to rethink the offered products and architecture for the integration of the overall automation solution of the agri-food silos industry.

Acknowledgments. Special thanks to Paulo Borges, as a research fellow leading the development of ISoS in a pre-stage for an open specifications and open source initiative under SOCOLNET scientific network and its ARCON-ACM initiative. This work has been partially supported by the PT2020 project SITL-IoT promoted by FORDESI company, BP Portugal through the research project HORUS, and the A-to-Be (Brisa Innovation and Technology) company with the project MOBICS/CITS. Partial support also from the Center of Technology and Systems – UNINOVA, and the Portuguese FCT-PEST program UID/EEA/00066/2019.

References

1. Ahlgren, B., Hidell, M., Ngai, E.: Internet of Things for smart cities: interoperability and open data. IEEE Internet Comput. **20**, 52–56 (2016)
2. Bagheri, B., Yang, S., Kao, H.-A., Lee, J.: Cyber-physical systems architecture for self-aware machines in industry 4.0 environment. IFAC-PapersOnLine **48**(3), 1622–1627 (2015). 15th IFAC Symposium on Information Control Problems in Manufacturing
3. Balalaie, A., Heydarnoori, A., Jamshidi, P.: Microservices architecture enables devops: migration to a cloud-native architecture. IEEE Softw. **33**(3), 42–52 (2016)
4. Calado, J.M.F., Osório, L.A., Prata, R.: An adaptive IoT management infrastructure for EcoTransport networks. In: Camarinha-Matos, L.M., Bénaben, F., Picard, W. (eds.) PRO-VE 2015. IAICT, vol. 463, pp. 285–296. Springer, Cham (2015). https://doi.org/10.1007/978-3-319-24141-8_26
5. Calado, J.M.F., Osório, A.L.: Dynamic Integration of Mould Industry Analytics and Design Forecasting. In: Camarinha-Matos, L.M., Afsarmanesh, H., Fornasiero, R. (eds.) PRO-VE 2017. IAICT, vol. 506, pp. 649–657. Springer, Cham (2017). https://doi.org/10.1007/978-3-319-65151-4_57
6. Calderoni, L., Magnani, A., Maio, D.: IoT manager: an open-source IoT framework for smart cities. J. Syst. Archit. (2019). https://doi.org/10.1016/j.sysarc.2019.04.003
7. Camarinha-Matos, L.M., Fornasiero, R., Afsarmanesh, H.: Collaborative networks as a core enabler of industry 4.0. In: Camarinha-Matos, L.M., Afsarmanesh, H., Fornasiero, R. (eds.) PRO-VE 2017. IAICT, vol. 506, pp. 3–17. Springer, Cham (2017). https://doi.org/10.1007/978-3-319-65151-4_1
8. Cecconi, G., Radu, C.: Open data maturity in Europe report 2018: new horizon for open data driven transformation. Technical report, European Data Portal - European Commission - Directorate General for Communications Networks, Content and Technology, By the European Commission, Directorate-General of Communications Networks, Content & Technology, November 2018

9. Derler, P., Lee, E.A., Vincentelli, A.S.: Modeling cyber; physical systems. Proc. IEEE **100** (1), 13–28 (2012)
10. Guth, J., Breitenbücher, U., Falkenthal, M., Leymann, F., Reinfurt, L.: Comparison of IoT platform architectures: a field study based on a reference architecture. In: 2016 Cloudification of the Internet of Things (CIoT), pp. 1–6. IEEE, November 2016
11. Osório, A.L., Belloum, A., Afsarmanesh, H., Camarinha-Matos, L.M.: Agnostic informatics system of systems: the open ISoS services framework. In: Camarinha-Matos, L.M., Afsarmanesh, H., Fornasiero, R. (eds.) PRO-VE 2017. IAICT, vol. 506, pp. 407–420. Springer, Cham (2017). https://doi.org/10.1007/978-3-319-65151-4_37
12. Marvin, S., Luque, A.: Urban operating systems: diagramming the city. Int. J. Urban Reg. Res. **41**, 01 (2016)
13. Nahrstedt, K., Cassandras, C.G., Catlett, C.: City-scale intelligent systems and platforms. CoRR, abs/1705.01990 (2017)
14. Osório, A.L., Camarinha-Matos, L.M., Afsarmanesh, H.: Cooperation enabled systems for collaborative networks. In: Camarinha-Matos, L.M., Pereira-Klen, A., Afsarmanesh, H. (eds.) PRO-VE 2011. IAICT, vol. 362, pp. 400–409. Springer, Heidelberg (2011). https://doi.org/10.1007/978-3-642-23330-2_44
15. Osório, A.L., et al.: Open multi-technology service oriented architectur for "its" business models: the ITSIBus etoll services. In: Camarinha-Matos, L.M., Afsarmanesh, H., Ortiz, A. (eds.) PRO-VE 2005. ITIFIP, vol. 186, pp. 439–446. Springer, Boston, MA (2005). https://doi.org/10.1007/0-387-29360-4_46
16. Osório, A.L.: Towards vendor-agnostic IT-system of IT-systems with the CEDE platform. In: Afsarmanesh, H., Camarinha-Matos, L.M., Lucas Soares, A. (eds.) PRO-VE 2016. IAICT, vol. 480, pp. 494–505. Springer, Cham (2016). https://doi.org/10.1007/978-3-319-45390-3_42
17. Osorio, L., Gonçalves, C., Pereira, A., Antunes, B., Barrocas, N., Amador, A.: ITSIBUS jini and RFID open service-oriented architecture for toll management. In: JavaONE - San Francisco; Session BOF (Birds-of-a-Feather)-9041 (2005)
18. Osório, L.A., Camarinha-Matos, L.M., Afsarmanesh, H.: ECoNet platform for collaborative logistics and transport. In: Camarinha-Matos, L.M., Bénaben, F., Picard, W. (eds.) PRO-VE 2015. IAICT, vol. 463, pp. 265–276. Springer, Cham (2015). https://doi.org/10.1007/978-3-319-24141-8_24
19. Vargas, I.G., Gottardi, T., Braga, R.T.V.: Approaches for integration in system of systems: a systematic review. In: Proceedings of the 4th International Workshop on Software Engineering for Systems-of-Systems, SESoS 2016, pp. 32–38. ACM, New York (2016)
20. Wang, X., Mao, S., Gong, M.: An overview of 3GPP cellular vehicle-to-everything standards. GetMobile: Mob. Comput. Commun. **21**, 19–25 (2017)
21. Yadav, P., Hasan, S., Ojo, A., Curry, E.: The of open data in driving sustainable mobility in nine smart cities. In: Proceedings of the 25th European Conference on Information Systems (ECIS) Guimaraes, Portugal, 5–10 June 2017, pp. 1248–1263 (2017)

Collaborative Softbots: Enhancing Operational Excellence in Systems of Cyber-Physical Systems

Ricardo J. Rabelo[1](✉), Saulo Popov Zambiasi[2], and David Romero[3]

[1] Federal University of Santa Catarina, Florianópolis, Brazil
ricardo.rabelo@ufsc.br
[2] University of Southern Santa Catarina, Florianópolis, Brazil
saulopz@gmail.com
[3] Tecnológico de Monterrey, Monterrey, Mexico
david.romero.diaz@gmail.com

Abstract. This paper outlines the use of Collaborative Networks foundations at the intra-organizational level, applying them in the support of systems of Cyber-Physical Systems (CPSs), and of collaborative softbots in more particular. Five use case scenarios have been implemented upon a didactic shopfloor as a proof of concept. In spite of the complexity related to the knowledge modeling of softbots, the achieved results demonstrated the potentials of better human-automation symbiosis when groups of CPSs, information systems and humans have to cooperate and collaborate using collaborative softbots to improve operational excellence and human satisfaction in smart, social factories.

Keywords: Collaborative softbots · Industry 4.0 · Cyber-Physical Systems · Social factories · Service Oriented Architecture · Collaborative Networks

1 Introduction

Industry 4.0 can be defined as a production model characterized by an increasing digitalization and interconnection of smart products, services, manufacturing systems, value chains/networks and business models [1]. One of the core elements of Industry 4.0 looking at the digital transformation of production systems are the *Cyber-Physical Systems (CPSs)* [2, 3]. In general, a CPS can be defined as "an integrated environment, with computational and physical capabilities, such as sensing, communication and actuation, with feedback-loops where physical processes affect computations and vice-versa" [2, 3].

Although such CPS *capabilities* can be considered as still very advanced for many manufacturing enterprises, particularly for manufacturing SMEs, Industry 4.0 brings up new technical requirements for enterprise information and operational systems and technologies [2, 4]. They include: distributed and decentralized autonomy; cognition and control; failures, faults and anomalies supervision and resilience; adaptation and plug-and-play capabilities; cybersecurity; emergent behavior and self-organization; (big) data integration and interoperability; sensing and cooperative data collection;

© IFIP International Federation for Information Processing 2019
Published by Springer Nature Switzerland AG 2019
L. M. Camarinha-Matos et al. (Eds.): PRO-VE 2019, IFIP AICT 568, pp. 55–68, 2019.
https://doi.org/10.1007/978-3-030-28464-0_6

virtualization/digitalization/simulation; data-driven control and optimization; collaboration in a system of CPSs; and symbiotic interaction of CPSs and humans [2, 4, 5]. These two last requirements are of particular interest in this paper.

Collaboration between CPSs involves many issues to handle [6]. *Collaborative Networks* [7] is the scientific area that offers a theoretical basis to study the collaboration phenomena including organizations and general entities. Camarinha et al. [1] have provided a long list of possible links between *Collaborative Networks* and *Industry 4.0,* including its application in networks of collaborative CPSs.

Despite the crucial importance the 'automation and control' part has in CPSs, many works in literature have underestimated the impact of the Industry 4.0 on the workers and, at the same, on the new systems' requirements needed to support the new types of *human-machine interactions* [8, 9]. Several authors (e.g. [9–11]) have pointed out the need for a shift in the way workers and machines interact when looking at boosting their cooperation and collaboration towards smarter symbioses, and hence, at enhancing their operational excellence and human satisfaction towards a cognitive, smart industry [10, 12].

Some approaches have been adopted for that, being *software robots* one of the most promising ones [13, 14]. A *software robot,* also called just as *softbot* [15], can be defined as a "virtual system deployed in a given computing environment that automates and helps humans in the execution of tasks by combining capabilities of conversation-like interaction, system intelligence, autonomy, and process automation". *Softbots* can be also seen as a powerful approach to facilitate the introduction of modern *digital lean manufacturing* and *Jidoka* concepts in terms of helping humans in quality control [16].

In this paper, we define *collaborative softbot* as "a software agent that reactively or proactively cooperates with other softbots, CPSs, information systems and humans helping its users to solve complex or unfamiliar problems, and/or to take care of distributed information requests".

In previous research [11] authors presented a work where a *single softbot* helped a single machine's operator in the execution of some tasks via a high-level and voice-enacted interaction. However, this showed to be not enough regarding collaborative CPSs [6] and Industry 4.0 systems requirements [2, 4, 5]. The works found out in the literature are either theoretical (e.g. in terms of issues or architectures to support CPSs human interactions [9]) or they implement simple scenarios, composed of one operator - one softbot - one CPS [11]. None of the works has tackled the problem of *collaborative softbots* in a system of CPSs.

This work presents a contribution to address this gap. A collaborative softbot's integrated environment has been implemented taking the Industry 4.0 design principles into account [2, 5] and deployed looking at an existing *FESTO didactic shopfloor* using a tool called *ARISA NEST* for deriving softbots.

This paper is organized as follows. Section 1 has introduced the problem and the objectives of the work. Section 2 summarizes the literature review. Section 3 depicts the Arisa NEST tool. Section 4 describes the implemented prototype and its results. Section 5 presents some preliminary conclusions and the next main steps of this work.

2   Basic Foundations and Related Work

In general, *softbots* in an Industry 4.0 scenario [e.g. 11] mean 'talking' to operators about their daily workflows, technical problems, and work-related topics [17].

Similar approaches to *softbots* were proposed in the past, mostly using "agents" [18] and "holonic" systems [19]. Although intelligence and autonomy had been a relevant motivation for their use, agents and holons were actually adopted to ease coordination, systems' architecture design, and integration or synthesis of disparate sources of information [20]. They are now being revisited thanks to their intrinsic features and potentials regarding Industry 4.0 technologies, such as Artificial Intelligence (AI) tools and Machine Learning techniques, which are more mature and robust to be used in real industrial environments, together with the advances on the Industrial Internet of Things (IIoT), Big Data Analytics, and Cloud Computing.

Some authors state that "agents" and "softbots" are equivalent concepts when considering their possible implementation capabilities, and that the difference in terminology just comes from the Schools where they were originated (distributed AI vs. software engineering) [11]. Another reading is that while "agents" and "holons" are more directed to provide some intelligence, autonomy and coordination to a system (usually via structured agent communication languages), "softbots" are more directed to help humans in automating user-customized actions and to intuitive chatting via natural-like language. As a matter of fact, agents can also have or implement such softbots properties and vice-versa.

Softbots do not aim at replacing the native user interfaces (i.e. human-machine/computer interfaces) between workers and machine tools, or of enterprise information systems, such as an ERP or MES. Instead, they simply represent a higher-level of human interaction with those systems, also skipping fixed and predefined menus that are typically accessed via keyboard and mouse. Depending on the way *softbots* are programmed and configured, and eventually learn and evolve, they can execute the actions that are actually defined in given business processes (e.g. Robotic Process Automation (RPA)) or in the functionalities of the CPS they represent (e.g. accessing information from IIoT devices and intelligent objects, or executing ad-hoc activities specifically designed to handle operators' needs).

A *softbot* can be exhibited as a simple icon in a computer's screen or as a sophisticated hologram elsewhere, for example. The information to be provided by the softbot to attend human requests or to interact with other systems can come from a direct invocation to the own systems' functionalities or from the access to cloud environments or local databases that store information generated by those systems.

Conceptually, a *softbot* can be associated to one single system (i.e. one CPS) or it can embrace many systems, becoming in this way a system of systems (i.e. one softbot representing many CPSs of e.g. a manufacturing cell).

Besides the more user-friendly way "softbots" represent in terms of human-machine/computer interaction, there are also some important potentials from the functional point of view. A compilation of this includes [11, 21]: (a) Automatic and/or autonomous execution of actions, from simple alarms to complex business processes, involving communication with diverse devices; (b) higher efficiency and execution correctness when compared to humans, especially in repetitive, hazardous, unsafe and/or unhealthy activities; (c) Filtering, reasoning and pre-selecting useful data to be used in different business contexts and problems; (d) More "quality time" for humans for more valuable activities, such as management and reasoning, instead of lower-value activities, like checking boring and repetitive tasks; (e) More intuitive and effective conversation, especially when compared to FAQs or text manuals in the Web; (f) Accurate, real-time, and up-to-date information as softbots can quickly have access to the right and authorized sources, also helping in the companies' ICT governance; (g) Automatic generation of operational data and dashboards for further performance evaluation as well as for assisted, interactive operators' decision-making and conflicts resolution (e.g. via automatic negotiation; interactive bargain, etc.); (h) "Standard" answers, which are important to guarantee that both experienced operators and the ones in training will receive the complete-enough and consolidated information needed; (i) Adaptive and more objective answers regarding operators' experience, emotions, technical profile, business context, and personal goals' status; (j) Learning and self-evolving behavior; and (k) Higher availability, being able to answer and process many actions simultaneously all the time.

Collaborative softbots in a system of CPSs does not mean only allowing CPSs to interact with each other, directly, but also 'collaborating' with companies' systems and actors to more properly attend specific human requests or handle general issues. It is also important to point out that collaboration is a result of a rational process that a *softbot* (in this case) can have and that ends up looking for 'external' help [22]. This happens when it realizes it has not enough or not trustworthy enough information and capacity or capability to accomplish a given task respecting given requirements, or when it has no interest to accomplish the task on its own regarding its future plans or execution costs [22]. Therefore, *collaboration* does not mean "forcing" interactions between CPSs just to account that, but rather to support it when needed.

In terms of related works, few ones have been found out in the literature about *softbots* on the shop floor.

Schwartz et al. [13] proposed a concept of "hybrid teams" to face the increasing need for higher-level collaboration between humans, industrial equipment and software. Several potential hypothetical cases are described and the requirements for a generic architecture are presented. May et al. [23] proposed a taxonomy identifying the many aspects to be considered for implementing worker-centric systems in manufacturing. Nazarenko and Camarinha-Matos [6] elicited general requirements for collaboration between CPSs, which included the so-called "human orientation". Kar et al. [17] identified various scenarios for softbots in IIoT environments and proposed a general system architecture, which is based on cloud computing and on a centralized chat platform to connect diverse chat channels. Caldarola et al. [24] proposed an architecture for a CPS with one chatbot, focusing on the problem of different semantic interpretation to better understand users' requests. None of these five works has implemented their proposals or has addressed "collaborative softbots". Similarly to [11], Kassner et al. [25] proposed a general architecture for what they called a "social factory", implementing a softbot to interact with one single machine. The goal was to illustrate the potential benefits of this in a smart factory environment. In the same line, Dersingh et al. [26] developed a chatbot to monitor and record issues of a production line and to notify corresponding workers for appropriate actions. Longo et al. [27] implemented a framework to support the interaction of humans with physical equipment and their digital twins in a cyber-physical environment. The novelty of this work mainly relies on making users interact with a softbot that represents a virtual entity (i.e. a digital twin). Chen et al. [28] developed an engine that captures the production plan, and transform and adapt it to the skills and experience of the involved users so as to improve factory effectiveness and efficiency as well as the satisfaction of factory staff. Gnewuch et al. [29] made some experiments to evaluate the effects of how pre-designed delays in the conversation between users and systems could positively shape users' perception of chatbots. They realized at the end that delays in some situations can create a more human-like environment, and hence a better symbiosis between human and chatbot.

Despite the importance of all these works, none have addressed collaboration between groups of softbots linked to CPSs.

3 The ARISA NEST Tool

ARISA NEST[1] is an academic tool developed as a PaaS-based environment to allow the derivation of both single and groups of softbots. Softbots can be accessed both via desktop PCs and mobile phones running the Android operating system.

It has a number of commonalities, differences, pros and cons when compared to some recent tools for chatbots or softbots, like *Cortana, Siri, Alexa,* and *Watson*[2]. The purpose of this paper is not to compare them, but rather using one through which the main Industry 4.0 systems' requirements can be implemented [4]: interoperability, modularity, virtualization, real-time information, service-orientation, decentralization and autonomy, which is the case of ARISA NEST, for example.

ARISA NEST supports not only conversations between different softbots, but also the coding in the LUA language[3] of any kind of functionalities, which can be implemented both as scripts of simple functions and as more complex object-oriented programs. Programs can comprise since simple direct invocations to services (e.g. web services and REST) and external and legacy systems' APIs, till more complex orchestrations and choreographies. A *softbot* is internally organized under a Service Oriented Architecture (SOA) style and was inspired in the Belief-Desire-Intention (BDI) agent's architecture [22]. It is open to support different communication languages running under HTTP, including proprietary protocols, agent communication languages (ACL) and AIML (Artificial Intelligence Modelling Language) [22].

---

[1] ARISA NEST tool for softbots derivation – https://arisa.com.br/, developed in Brazil, in Portuguese.

[2] Cortana https://developer.microsoft.com/en-us/cortana, Siri https://www.apple.com/ios/siri/, Alexa https://developer.amazon.com/alexa, Watson https://www.ibm.com/watson/how-to-build-a-chatbot.

[3] LUA programming language – https://www.lua.org/.

Broadly, a *derived softbot* has the following internal modules: (a) an *Interface,* involving possibilities to interact with other softbots via e-mail, instant messaging, social networks, text consoles, voice, etc.; (b) a *Toolbox,* as a general programming and configuration set of tools to customize and deploy softbots; (c) *Interoperability Services,* comprising a set of services to support the interoperability between the softbot and the systems it has to communicate with; and (d) a *Personal Assistant Manager,* responsible to define, configure, integrate, interoperate, and deploy a softbot as well as to manage the execution of all internal softbot's entities. Softbot's functionalities can be implemented as web services/SOAP protocol or REST.

A key element in the ARISA's model is the *context,* a concept got from AIML. All planned dialogues with users are modeled in XML and have to be carefully defined a priori. Messages are internally structured as forms. *Contexts* mean all the subjects (and the related key terms, including synonymous) users are supposed to talk about when asking things or ordering actions to the softbot. In other words, users can write (or say) a sentence whatever they want since the expected keywords are given. Regarding different idioms, ARISA NEST uses a Google library for automatic translations. New contexts, terms and flows can be added, removed or modified anytime during the softbot's lifecycle. It also uses Google APIs to support communication via voice.

Users are trained about the available contexts in the given softbot. Although all the contexts are organized as a tree (starting with the root node), any node can be directed reached by the internal engine so that the softbot can execute the request more effectively considering users' previous knowledge, and without having to go through fixed sequences of menus. However, in the case the user does not feel satisfied with the answer, he/she can keep asking to the softbot until he/she gets pleased with the provided content or receives a positive acknowledge about the requested action.

Figure 1 gives a broad view of ARISA environment. It has three main parts. Roughly, in the upper bar, *Search* option allows seeing all the derived softbots that are running as ARISA is a PaaS general environment; *Bots* lists the softbots derived by a given user so (s)he can edit them; *Help* provides general information about the ARISA platform, how to derive softbots, etc.; *Settings* refer to users' configurations (e.g. the softbot's name ['*Roy*'] and the icon); and *Exit* is to leave the environment.

In the left sidebar, by clicking on the softbot's icon, in the *Collaborators* option the user can remove or associate other users to the softbot; *Context* provides means to add and manage the subjects and key terms to be used in the conversations (as shown in Fig. 1); *Beliefs* allows to edit and manage the softbot's facts about the application environment it was derived for; *Behaviors* grants access to edit and manage the softbots' functionalities; *Web Services* allows registering the web services linked to the softbots' functionalities; *Chats* option shows all the messages exchanged with the softbot's 'friends' (other softbots and users). All this is exhibited in the central part of the screen. Finally, the *Close* option, which ends the session. The right sidebar is the chatting space, where the *language* to be used can be selected (this information is used to access the Google library, as explained before).

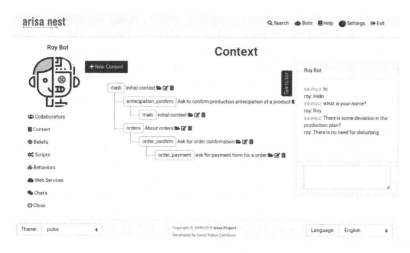

Fig. 1. ARISA NEST general user interface

ARISA NEST offers some basic computing security support. Being it a PaaS-based system, the first level is provided by the own server against cyber-attacks via firewalls. All the exchanged messages between softbots uses https with SSL connections meaning messages. The database where the facts which represent part of the knowledge used by the softbot to answer user questions is also protected from undesired injections. Users have a login and password as well as a valid e-mail address, guaranteeing users authentication.

4   Implementation Scenarios and Results

The implementation of this work has considered the FESTO didactic plant existing in our research lab. It is composed of seven CPSs that work as described below.

Basically, a *distribution station* receives components according to the production plan. This is further received by the *testing station*, which checks several aspects to guarantee assembly conformity. In the case the component is not OK, it is put out of the production line; otherwise, the component is separated/sorted according to its size, weight, color and material by the *separating station*. The *processing station* does the planned machining operations (if any) in the sorted component and stores it in a *buffer*. The *pick & place station* starts the first phase of the assembling, picking components from the buffer according to the orders' due date indicated in the production plan. The *muscle press station* completes the assembling process joining different components to compose the final product. Finally, the *sorting station* takes the different final products and sorts them according to their types for further packing and delivery. Although these stations are organized to work in sequence, they are conceptually treated in this work as decoupled, autonomous and distributed CPSs. Each station is equipped with a PLC Siemens S7-1200 full DC and a set of sensors and actuators, having a link to the outside via a Profinet network and the OPC protocol.

Regarding the softbot's architecture, a web services-based wrapper has been built on top of each station. Each station/wrapper works in tandem with its 'manager' module, which represents the CPS and that is designed to work as the CPS 'connector' within the manufacturing environment. The *softbot part* is one of the macro functionalities of the manager. In [30] the authors detail this architecture. In the implemented scenario, each CPS is associated with one single station and it was derived to have one respective softbot. Two operators can interact with more than one softbot in a 'one worker, multiple machines' philosophy (OWMM).

Softbots can be used in many scenarios in the context of Industry 4.0. BCG [21] has outlined ten general scenarios where software assistants could be helpful in leveraging operational excellence, inclusiveness, satisfaction and motivation, safety and continuous learning. Plenty of examples and situations can be created out of this [see 11]. Five 'use cases' have been derived from that in this proof of concept work. Each one is presented below, which shows some GUIs and how it is generally handled in the ARISA tool.

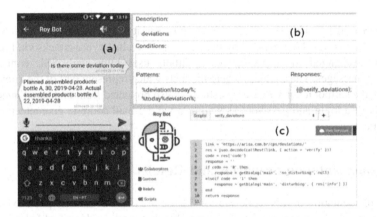

Fig. 2. Softbot querying the MES system about production plan deviations

Use Case I: Operator 1 asks, via voice, to the *separating station* CPS's softbot called *'Roy'* (which is a name similar to a friend instead of a formal system) about current deviations in the production plan considering the number of final assembled products - counted by a specific sensor in the *sorting station* – due to some problems occurred during the work shift (see Fig. 2a). *'Deviation'* word and *'today'* are the key terms the softbot is prepared to hear, which in turn is handled by one of the CPS's manager services (see Fig. 2b). The softbot understands that *'today'* means checking what is the day today and takes this date as the target. The *separating* CPS's softbot *reacts* to this request, accesses the MES's database directly (there is no need to broadcast messages to other CPSs to try to get this information as it is normally stored in the MES or ERP) and sends the information back to Operator 1, noticing him about the expected and actual assembled products amount.

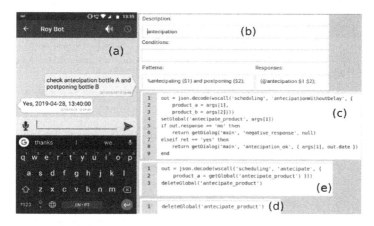

Fig. 3. Softbot querying the ERP system about the possibility of a production re-scheduling

Use Case II: Given the delays in the production plan (as fewer products have been assembled), Operator 1 asks, by typing in the keyboard, the *pick & place station's* softbot if it is possible to anticipate the production of *bottle A* without delaying *bottle B*'s due date (see Fig. 3a). Some typed words are taken by the softbot as key terms besides that fact that Operator 1 knows that such products' names are valid in the system. The softbot *reacts* to this, executing the proper CPS's manager service, and interacting with the ERP's scheduler module via its API (Fig. 3b and c). The scheduler can return two parameters after some calculations: 'NO', meaning this is not possible; 'YES' and *'date&time'* value, meaning it is possible, and that the activity linked to 'bottle A' at *pick & place* should start on the given date and time. This information is sent back to the Operator 1, together with a confirmation message 'YES' or 'NO' (Fig. 3d–e). (S)he evaluates that and, given the autonomy philosophy in Industry 4.0, (s)he takes the final decision in the case (s)he agrees on ('YES'). The softbot then invokes again the scheduler to update the production plan, which in turn should update the dispatcher's plan. The dispatcher updates the *pick & place's* PLC program so that the new production sequence can be performed. The operator also has the possibility to access the ERP database, stored in a cloud, to have a broader vision of the production via e.g. Gantt charts and performance indicators dashboards.

Use Case III: During the execution of the new schedule (previous case), the *pick & place's* softbot asks to the *distribution* softbot if there are bottle *caps* enough in stock to accomplish the task (see Fig. 4a). The distribution's softbot firstly asks Operator 2 (*'Rick'*) about it via voice. He answers *'I do not know'*, and then the softbot access the inventory information stored in the ERP database (see Fig. 4b). The distribution softbot sends the stock amount ('50') to the pick & place's softbot, which verifies that this is not enough and notifies Operator 2 (see Fig. 4c) about it. In parallel, the softbot sends an e-mail to the purchasing department to warn it about that too. This also aims to demonstrate that interactions in an Industry 4.0 environment can be non-hierarchical, crossing many and different company's layers/departments directly.

Fig. 4. Softbot querying the ERP system about raw materials inventory

Use Case IV: The *testing station's* softbot permanently and *pro-actively* checks the execution status of this station in the MES's database. In the case, it detects the station is currently stopped because the bottle's cap has been placed upside down, which was a fault detected by one of the testing's sensors. The softbot sends a message, via OPC, to the *testing's* PLC to go into alarm as well as sends an SMS message to operators 1 and 2's smartphones (see Fig. 5a). Operator 1 was nearer to the station, confirms the problem exists and asks, by typing in the *testing's* softbot how to solve the problem (see Fig. 5b). The softbot accesses the company's intranet and shows to him the exact part of the troubleshooting manual that explains the possible solutions (see Fig. 5c).

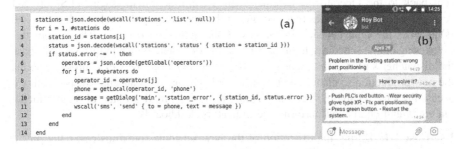

Fig. 5. Softbot querying the station's troubleshooting manual

Use Case V: All softbots *proactively* show a real-time log in the FESTO central PC with the list of the orders in place, their due date, and if they are in time or delayed. This information is obtained from the MES database, which has all data in English. However, the softbot realizes that the operator present in the work shift is Brazilian, so it automatically translates the data to Portuguese to turn the communication more pleasant to the operator (see Fig. 6). "*No horário*" means 'in time'; "*atrasado*" means 'delayed'; and "*planejado*" means 'planned'.

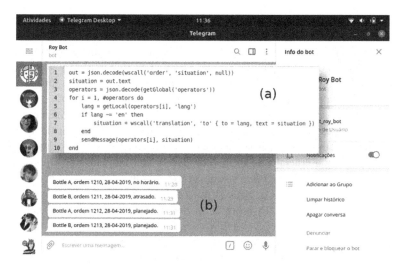

Fig. 6 Softbot translates to a different language the data

5 Conclusions and Further Work

This paper has outlined the use of Collaborative Networks foundations [6, 7] at the intra-organizational level, applying them in the support of *collaborative softbots*.

Five collaborative softbots' use cases have been implemented to show the potentials of better human-automation symbiosis when groups of autonomous, heterogeneous and distributed CPSs, humans, and information systems have to cooperate and collaborate to improve operational excellence and human satisfaction in smart, social factories (e.g. [9, 25]). Although it was implemented in a local environment, the used service-oriented, open and distributed architecture [30] could support the communication with CPSs from other companies as well as services from external providers (so creating virtual organizations and inter-organizational scenario) since some implementation and governance guidelines are set up.

The implementation tried to comprise usual scenarios where *collaborative softbots* might be helpful. The actions were performed as planned, assisting human operators in some tasks, both in terms of interacting and collaborating when needed, and by automating tasks execution on behalf of him/her.

A small group of students was generally trained to use the softbots but knowing very well the subjects in advance. The results were very promising, showing that softbots can be more effective and user-friendly when they asked for some information and actions. This includes the access to information an individual operator usually would not have (or not so easily or promptly) from ERP and MES systems as well as from other CPS/softbots. However, the way softbots' knowledge-base is modeled, populated and maintained is crucial to guarantee answers accuracy and requires a very experienced software engineer and domain expert working together in the designing phase. Besides that, although the way the implemented softbots' wrappers had facilitated integration with physical CPSs - and regarding that this is a proof-of-concept work - some simplifications were made to overcome some tough usual interoperability issues when dealing with industrial systems integration.

The ARISA NEST tool could support all the defined requirements. However, being an academic tool, it has some limitations and some levels of complexity when deriving particular softbots. One of the aspects refers to softbots' behavior programming, although this limitation is also present in the other tools in the market.

Regarding that *softbots* can collaborate directly via messages exchange with any system, and even considering that Industry 4.0 preconizes non-hierarchical interactions, it is important to emphasize that some enterprise information systems (like ERP and MES) keep playing a crucial role in the companies and they are not supposed to be replaced by softbots. Besides *ad-hoc* business processes that can be designed looking at particular needs of softbots (e.g. actions out of the scope of e.g. ERP systems), the chatting part of softbots basically represents a more natural way operators can interact with systems.

This is an on-going R&D work. Next main steps comprise the consideration of machine learning techniques to support softbots evolution and operators' profiles to improve symbiosis between them; the integration of a BPM-like component to help developers in the softbots programming, execution and coordination; and the use of ontologies to better support semantic interoperability between users and softbots as well as between softbots and systems.

Acknowledgements. This work has been partially supported by CAPES Brazilian Agency for Higher Education, project PrInt CAPES-UFSC "Automation 4.0".

References

1. Camarinha-Matos, L.M., Fornasiero, R., Afsarmanesh, H.: Collaborative networks as a core enabler of industry 4.0. In: Camarinha-Matos, L.M., Afsarmanesh, H., Fornasiero, R. (eds.) PRO-VE 2017. IAICT, vol. 506, pp. 3–17. Springer, Cham (2017). https://doi.org/10.1007/978-3-319-65151-4_1
2. Lee, J., Bagheri, B., Kao, H.A.: Recent advances and trends of cyber-physical systems and big data analytics in industrial informatics. In: Industrial Informatics. IEEE (2014)
3. Colombo, A., Karnouskos, S., Kaynak, O., Yin, S.: Industrial cyber-physical systems – a backbone of the fourth industrial revolution. IEEE Ind. Electron. Mag. **11**(1), 6–16 (2017)
4. Hermann, M., Pentek, T., Otto, B.: Design principles for industry 4.0 scenarios. In: Proceedings of 49th IEEE Hawaii International Conference on System Sciences, pp. 3928–3937 (2016)
5. Lamnabhi-Lagarrigue, F., et al.: Systems & control for the future of humanity, research agenda: current and future roles, impact and grand challenges. Annu. Rev. Control **43**, 1–64 (2017)
6. Nazarenko, A.A., Camarinha-Matos L.M.: Towards collaborative cyber-physical systems. In: IEEE 2017 International Young Engineers Forum (YEF-ECE), pp. 1–6 (2017). https://doi.org/10.1109/yef-ece.2017.7935633
7. Camarinha-Matos, L.M., Afsarmanesh, H.: Collaborative networks: a new scientific discipline. J. Intell. Manuf. **16**(4–5), 439–452 (2005)

8. Romero, D., et al.: Towards an operator 4.0 typology: a human-centric perspective on the fourth industrial revolution technologies. In: Proceedings International Conference on Computers & Industrial Engineering (CIE46), Tianjin/China, pp. 1–11 (2016)
9. Romero, D., Wuest, T., Stahre, J., Gorecky, D.: Social factory architecture: social networking services and production scenarios through the social internet of things, services and people for the social operator 4.0. In: Lödding, H., Riedel, R., Thoben, K.-D., von Cieminski, G., Kiritsis, D. (eds.) APMS 2017. IAICT, vol. 513, pp. 265–273. Springer, Cham (2017). https://doi.org/10.1007/978-3-319-66923-6_31
10. Jones, A.T., Romero, D., Wuest, T.: modeling agents as joint cognitive systems in smart manufacturing systems. Manuf. Lett. **17**, 6–8 (2018)
11. Rabelo, R.J., Romero, D., Zambiasi, S.P.: Softbots supporting the operator 4.0 at smart factory environments. In: Moon, I., Lee, G.M., Park, J., Kiritsis, D., von Cieminski, G. (eds.) APMS 2018. IAICT, vol. 536, pp. 456–464. Springer, Cham (2018). https://doi.org/10.1007/978-3-319-99707-0_57
12. Kumar, N., Kumar, J.: Efficiency for Industry 4.0. Hum. Technol. **15**(1), 55–78 (2019)
13. Schwartz, T., et al.: Hybrid teams: flexible collaboration between humans, robots and virtual agents. In: Klusch, M., Unland, R., Shehory, O., Pokahr, A., Ahrndt, S. (eds.) MATES 2016. LNCS (LNAI), vol. 9872, pp. 131–146. Springer, Cham (2016). https://doi.org/10.1007/978-3-319-45889-2_10
14. Kopec, W., et al.: Hybrid approach to automation, RPA and machine learning: a method for the human-centered design of software robots. arXiv:1811.02213v1 (2018)
15. Kim, J.H.: Ubiquitous robot. In: Reusch, B. (ed.) Computational Intelligence, Theory and Applications. Advances in Soft Computing, vol. 33, pp. 451–459. Springer, Heidelberg (2005). https://doi.org/10.1007/3-540-31182-3_41
16. Romero, D., Gaiardelli, P., Powell, D., Wuest, T., Thürer, M.: Rethinking Jidoka systems under automation & learning perspectives in the digital lean manufacturing system world. In: IFAC Conference on Manufacturing Modelling, Management and Control (2019)
17. Kar, R., Haldar, R.: Applying chatbots to the internet of things: opportunities and architectural elements. Int. J. Adv. Comput. Sci. Appl. **7**(11), 147–154 (2016)
18. Barata, J., Camarinha-Matos, L.M.: Coalitions of manufacturing components for shop floor agility. Int. J. Netw. Virtual Organ. **2**(1), 50–77 (2003)
19. Van Brussel, H., Wyns, J., Valckenaers, P., Bongaerts, L.: Reference architecture for holonic manufacturing systems. Comput. Ind. **37**(3), 255–274 (1998)
20. Lu, Y.: Industry 4.0: a survey on technologies, applications and open research issues. J. Ind. Inf. Integr. **6**, 1–10 (2017)
21. BCG Boston Consulting Group. https://www.bcg.com/ptbr/publications/2015/technology-business-transformation-engineered-productsinfrastructure-man-machine-industry-4.aspx
22. Ferber, J.: Multi-Agent Systems – An Introduction to Distributed Artificial Intelligence. Addison-Wesley, Boston (1999)
23. May G. et al.: A new huma-centric factory model. In: 12th Global Conference on Sustainable Manufacturing, pp. 22–24. Elsevier (2015)
24. Caldarola, E.G., Modoni, G.E., Sacco, M.: A Knowledge-based approach to enhance the workforce skills and competences within the industry 4.0. In: 10th International Conference on Information, Process, and Knowledge Management, pp. 56–61 (2018)
25. Kassner, L., Hirmer, P., Wieland, M., Steimle, F., Königsberger, J.K., Mitschang, B.: The social factory: connecting people, machines and data in manufacturing for context-aware exception escalation. In: 50th Hawaii International Conference on System Sciences (2017)
26. Dersingh, A., Srisakulpinyo, P., Rakkarn, S., Boonkanit, P.: Chatbot and visual management in production process. In: International Conference on Electronics, Information, and Communication, pp. 274–277 (2017)

27. Longo, F., Nicoletti, L., Padovano, A.: Smart operators in industry 4.0: a human-centered approach to enhance operators' capabilities and competencies within the new smart factory context. Comput. Ind. Eng. **113**, 144–159 (2017)
28. Chen, X., Bojko, M., Riedel, R., Apostolakis, K.C., Zarpalas, D., Daras, P.: Human-centred adaptation and task distribution utilizing levels of automation. In: 16th IFAC Symposium on Information Control Problems in Manufacturing, pp. 54–59 (2018)
29. Gnewuch, U., Morana, S., Adam, M., Maedche, A.: Faster is not always better: understanding the effect of dynamic response delays in human-chatbot interaction. In: 26th European Conference on Information Systems (2018)
30. Siller, H., Romero, D., Rabelo, R., Vazquez, E.: Advanced CPS service oriented architecture for smart injection molding and molds 4.0. In: IEEE 9th International Conference on Intelligent Systems, pp. 1–7 (2018)

A Systematic Review of Collaborative Networks: Implications for Sensing, Smart and Sustainable Enterprises

Fábio Müller Guerrini$^{(\boxtimes)}$ and Juliana Suemi Yamanari

São Carlos School of Engineering, University of São Paulo,
São Carlos, SP, Brazil
guerrini@sc.usp.br, jusuemi@usp.br

Abstract. The formation of collaborative networks advocates the efficient sharing of information and knowledge, agile and intelligent decision making for the improvement of operational, financial and organizational performance. Such configuration is motivated by the technological advances, increasing demand for customized products and dynamism characteristic of the digital era. Sensing, Intelligent, and Sustainable Enterprises (S ^ 3) address a new vision to be disseminated among organizations seeking competitive advantage. Based on the literature on Collaborative Networks and S ^ 3 Companies, the article proposes to systematically review the state-of-the-art of collaborative networks, identifying challenges and future research opportunities present at the intersection of these two approaches. As a contribution of the research, is presented a conceptual framework based on the main results of the review.

Keywords: Collaborative networks · S ^ 3 enterprises · Competitiveness

1 Introduction

Weichhart et al. [1] proposed the Sensing, Smart and Sustainable Enterprise, which characterizes a company's sensitive ability to understand its own environment and act in concern with the many collected information, making decisions faster, more efficient and more in order to become competitive and sustainable. Sensing enterprise indicates the ability to anticipate future decisions by capturing multidimensional information, enabling the company to reach and know the different scenarios [2]. Smart enterprise refers to the ability of companies to adapt rapidly to competitive market changes and challenges in an agile way to create and exploit knowledge in response to the opportunities [3]. Sustainable enterprise is associated with environmental, social, economic and ethical concerns [4]. Weichhart et al. [1] signaled challenges and developments for the S ^ 3 approach to become a reality. S ^ 3 Enterprises cover a number of domains of knowledge in, among them, business collaboration. The review seeks to answer the main question:

How has the discipline of collaborative networks addressed in recent years the advances of companies in relation to the new requirements of the competitive market?

© IFIP International Federation for Information Processing 2019
Published by Springer Nature Switzerland AG 2019
L. M. Camarinha-Matos et al. (Eds.): PRO-VE 2019, IFIP AICT 568, pp. 69–80, 2019.
https://doi.org/10.1007/978-3-030-28464-0_7

This review article intends to contribute to knowledge by identifying mechanisms in the context of collaborative networks that inspire companies that seek to become S^3, contributing by identifying the main domains of application, challenges and research approaches.

2 Methodological Procedures

According Fischl, Scherrer-Rathje and Friedli [5], the literature review aims to map, summarize and evaluate the relevant knowledge of a particular subject. The approach used in this research is based on three main steps [6]: planning, conduction and dissemination. In the planning stage, it was identified that $S \wedge 3$ Enterprise need studies on the characterization of the collaboration domain. It was decided to systematically review the concept of "collaborative networks" in search of evidence on the motivators of collaboration. Already in the stage of conducting the study, three databases were selected: Scopus, Web of Science and SciELO. In these databases, the keyword entered was "collabo * network *" with asterisks to contemplate the term and its plural and between quotation marks to search the two words together. The first filter applied in the systematic search was the keyword "collabo * network *" (for Scopus and Web of Science) and "collaborative networks" or "collaborative network" or "collaboration network" (for SciELO) in abstracts, keywords and document titles. The second filter refers to the time limitation, from 2012 to 2017. Because it is an incipient approach ($S \wedge 3$ Enterprises), it is considered that such a limitation does not negatively affect the quality of the research, since the last years are (1988), which is characterized by intense advances in information and communication technologies (ICTs), internet and social networks [7]. The third filter was the exclusive selection of papers in journals indexed and related to engineering. The 138 selected articles were read in full and the contributions acquired will be exposed in the sequence, in the stage of disclosure of the evidences found. After reading in full the 138 articles, fifteen articles were disregarded in the analysis because they did not present relevant contributions. Therefore, in total, 123 articles contributed to the research. Facing the necessity of synthesis, the paper presents the main results citing directly 75 papers.

In the next item the main motivators of collaboration are discussed, basing the construction of evidence on $S \wedge 3$ Enterprises and, consequently, the elaboration of a conceptual framework.

3 Results

The results are based on the identification of the main motivators of the collaboration, search approach and application field.

3.1 Motivators of Collaboration

The main factors that motivate organizations to collaborate are sharing information and knowledge, resources and skills, risks and benefits; growing demand for product variety and customization, dynamicity and market competitiveness, exploration and capture of new business opportunities, innovation, improving business performance, rapid advancement of Information and Communication Technologies (ICTs), costs reduction, economic, social and environmental sustainability.

Sharing Information and Knowledge: The ability to share information and knowledge motivates companies to create collaborative networks [8]. The tools to support sharing are based on information and communication technology (ICT), RFID systems [9], standards-based systems that allows computer-human interaction through a web service [10]. Knowledge management allows the aggregation of different factors used and people in order to improve decision making, adapt to new technologies and share knowledge through collaborative networks [11]. Collaboration with universities, and with suppliers, reflects on the efficiency of innovation through technical communication and knowledge transfer [12]. Technological frontier countries seek incentives to collaborate with other countries investing in research in order to create networks of excellence [13]. In this context, the European Union funds collaborative projects between organizations with the intention of disseminating and eventually creating new knowledge [14]. Clusters are more likely to receive research and development subsidies, benefiting from the ease of access to the knowledge disseminated in this concentration of companies seeking collaboration [15]. Scientists promote the exchange of knowledge in exchange for recognition in the scientific environment [16]. The process about knowledge requires adequate strategies, tools and methods, as well as definitions of the consequences and needs of collaborative partnerships [17].

Sharing of Resources and Skills: The manufacturing industry faces challenges and the principle of business collaboration helps to share resources and competences [18], reflecting the capture of business opportunities [19], profitability of the company [17], access to information and knowledge and the company's reputation [20]. An entrepreneur faces uncertainties such as resource capacity that can be viable through collaboration [21]. Resource sharing fosters the search for collaboration [22].

Risk and Benefit Sharing: The investment in capacity expansion is the uncertainty that motivates a decision maker to collaborate with other companies, since the technologies suffer a rapid obsolescence [23]. R&D projects are motivated to form partnerships to share risks and benefits [24], specifically the initial phase of product development. Online collaboration platform can encourage risk management more efficiently and effectively, especially in cases with diminished technical, financial and human resources [25].

Growing Demand for Product Variety and Customization: The customization of products enables aggregation of value, quality of service and increase in sales volume [26]. The growing demand for customized products generates the stakeholders need for knowledge [27]. Collaboration between companies is a mechanism to manage the growing demand for services associated with production processes [28]. The e-work encompasses computer-supported collaborative operations in distributed organizations can serve as a tool to assist traditional enterprises [29].

Dynamicity and Market Competitiveness: The complexity and dynamism of the market are a highly competitive business environment [30]. Intense changes such as rapid technological development, internationalization of the market and trade, as well as socioeconomic and political issues have affected society and business [31]. Collaborative networks improve the sociability and usability of ICTs [32], and are considered effective for geographic and social issues, as it enables a trust relationship between partners, establishing common policies, infrastructure and interoperability [33]. Market demands interfere with the harmonization and interoperability of collaborative networks [34]. The dynamic environment reflects in the growing number of publications, conferences, responsibilities and impact society as a whole [35]. It is necessary to renew, expand, adapt and modify products and processes [36]. Consumers demand quality products with agility and cost-effectiveness [37]. Collaboration networks allow the management of complex and dynamic systems [38]. During the management of these systems, the loss of knowledge during product development should be avoided [39]. Social capital as a key resource for collaborative practices [40].

Exploration and Capture of New Business Opportunities: Collaboration allows capturing new business opportunities. The collaborative networks provide conditions in new and unexpected business opportunity [41]. In the academic context, a collaborative can facilitate access to resources [42]. Collaboration allows the increase of visibility and the recognition of own competences [16]. The search for collaborative partners is an important channel for winning new clients [43].

Innovation: Collaborative networks have six times the capacity to develop innovation compared to organizations that operate individually [44]. Companies that collaborate technologically are more likely to generate product innovations and specifically radical innovations, and the larger the company, the more likely it is to generate innovations [36]. Public research funding facilitates the production of knowledge and is a key element to develop technology innovations [45]. Knowledge management, trust building and communication among partners in a collaborative network are essential factors for innovation [46]. The failure to harness the knowledge embedded in the collaborative network is detrimental to the innovation [39].

Improving Business Performance: Several organizations seek to stablish collaboration networks to gain agility, complement activities, competitiveness, and improve resources, gain innovation power, flexibility, efficiency and effectiveness of operational activities [47]. The collaborative scenario encompasses criteria, mechanisms, and decisions that improve business performance [18]. Collaboration is proven an effective strategy to improve service levels, process stability and the utilization of productive resources [48]. Collaboration among researchers aims to improve the quality of research, increase scientific productivity [49] and longevity [50]. In R&D projects, collaboration fosters the exchange of knowledge, sharing of resources and costs among employees, improving expected results, and industry performance [51]. In humanitarian projects, intergovernmental collaborative networks improve the quality of services provided to clients, as well as optimize the use of resources and reduce expenses [52]. Collaborative networks are motivated by the urgency to rescue lives, thus advocating for efficiency and interoperability in services [53]. In the academic and industrial contexts, the motivation is associated with the search for improvement of business performance and, consequently, competitiveness [54].

Rapid Advancement of ICTs: The organizations in collaborative networks aim to meet the needs of the market [55], such as virtual organizations and regional clusters [56]. ICTs support collaboration and the breakdown of geographical barriers of the global market [57]. ICTs accumulate knowledge from different domains to leverage the collaborative relationship [58]. ICTs are relevant to help manage the highly unpredictable nature of demand and the short lead times associated with the products [27]. Network technologies enable the harmonization of internal and external communications [58]. The demand for constant technological improvement and advances capable faces new challenges such as interoperability [37].

Costs Reduction: The importance of the efficient structuring of the collaborative network so that the costs of adopting this strategy do not exceed the desired benefits [59]. Uncertainties on the global stage drive collaboration to reduce costs, improve trust, and meet consumer demand [60]. The reduction of transportation costs through the formation of collaborative networks among suppliers [61].

Economic, Social and Environmental Sustainability: Global warming as a factor that motivates companies to improve their environmental and social reputation [62]. Managers have been attacking the question of environmental sustainability for the development of products, intensifying the collaborative partnerships [63]. There is a trend of international collaborative partnerships for mitigating climate change [64]. Collaborative efforts contribute to the reduction/minimization of environmental impacts. Network sustainability requires strategic planning as well as a common understanding of how partners collaborate, and interact with society and the physical environment [31].

3.2 Search Approaches

The first approach is conceptual. Durugbo and Riedel [65] proposed a conceptual model to assess the readiness of organizations in collaborative networks to service the product/service system, with multiple case study in four different sectors. Grilo et al. [66] proposed a model for business interoperability in the context of collaborative networks. Kumar [11] proposed a framework for knowledge management, which could serve as an early warning system to avoid excessive product recalls. This framework was approached in a practical study in the food sector. Lyons et al. [27] developed a knowledge-based framework to demonstrate how different collaborative networks can support product variety and customization.

The second approach is bibliographic review. Di Cagno, Fabrizi and Meliciani [13] conducted a study on R & D projects and concluded that participation in projects funded by the European Union is an important channel for knowledge transfer. Karimi and Khalilpour [64] developed a bibliometric review, considering the years 1980 to 2013, on the evolutionary trend of international carbon capture and storage collaborations, analyzing the collaborative network of the countries that publish on this subject. Kim and Perez [67] considered the years from 1997 to 2012 to carry out a bibliometric review of industrial ecology.

The third approach was the proposition of models, frameworks, prototypes, systems, architectures, etc., in a conceptual or mathematical way, without practical applications. Li and Du [68] proposed a framework to support the sharing of data among all the participants of a collaborative network, proposing the cloud as the main support tool. This framework is an intelligent intermediary system that helps companies to search, question and recommend potential collaborators.

Surveys and case studies were addressed in fewer investigations. Macke et al. [40] conducted a survey to identify the relationship between the elements of interorganizational social capital and the competitiveness of the collaborative network. Dias and Escoval [44] also used the survey to identify the main pillars of innovation in hospitals and concluded that external collaboration is the main driver of innovation, while technology behaves as a mechanism that facilitates innovation in hospitals. The case study was used in the research of Saetta, Tiacci and Cagnazzo [47], where they presented the first organization that adopted the model of Virtual Development Office. Boehm and Hogan [69], in turn, conducted a qualitative case study to analyze collaborative networks between universities and industries.

In summary, approximately 55% of the selected studies proposed models, architectures, prototype frameworks or systems, considering both the studies that applied in a real case and those that did not apply in a real case.

3.3   Fields Application

Fields application are diverse, however, the intention to systematize their occurrence is to elucidate possible applications within the scope of S^3 Enterprise. Approximately 34% of studies were performed without specifying a sector. These studies usually present problems and solutions without necessarily associating them to a given field. Chen et al. [70] proposed a collaborative network security management system that can identify and treat new distributed attacks more quickly and effectively. Huang et al. [12], in turn, studied how much regulatory pressure and customer pressure affect the organizations' environmental decisions.

The studies about collaborative networks in the academic context have been quite frequent. Boehm and Hogan [69] investigated the role of the lead researcher in collaborative research projects and empirically validated the entrepreneurial role in building collaborative networks. Chakraborty et al. [50] proposed two classification models to predict at the beginning of a researcher's career, how long the group to which it belongs will remain active and how productive it will be. Other studies focused on R & D, technology, virtual organization and other sectors. Arriagada and Alarcón [71] proposed a model to develop management strategies and maturation of knowledge applied to civil construction. Baek et al. [72] proposed a framework for the design of collaborative services in agricultural communities.

Seventeen publications have specified the field of study, however, were unique in addressing such a sector. Studies were carried out on start-ups in industry: auto parts, state environmental agencies, silk, malting, wine, bio-pharmaceutical, furniture, consultancies, and humanitarian organization, among others. This diversity of fields in the framework of collaborative networks motivates the conduction of studies on S^3 Enterprise. Regardless of the industry or focus of the research, companies and universities are generally looking for collaborative relationships to meet the new challenges imposed by current business models.

4 Results Systematization

The systematic review of a widespread and consolidated discipline (collaborative networks) sought to detect how much the researchers have directed, albeit indirectly, their respective research to the new vision mentioned above. It was possible to highlight the main motivators for the formation of collaborative networks: sharing of information and knowledge; resources and skills; risks and benefits; increasing demand for variety of products and customization; dynamism and competitiveness of the market; exploration and capture of new business opportunities; innovation; improving business performance; ICTs; cost reduction and economic, environmental and social sustainability. The main challenges identified by the researchers were: trust among partners; the interoperability of the information systems of the partners involved; the stage of selecting the collaborative partners; the alignment and clear definition of strategies and objectives; ensuring the security of data and information shared over the internet or other informational system.

Figure 1 presents a conceptual framework contemplating the challenges and opportunities identified in the systematic review with the objective of organizing and facilitating the understanding of the objectives intended in the work, as well as contribute with literature and future practical work on the theme. The study of collaborative networks was adopted through the intersections with the S ^ 3 approach.

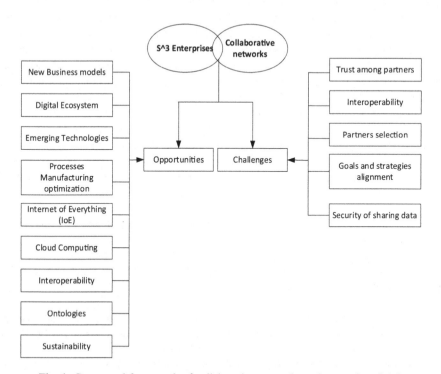

Fig. 1 Conceptual framework of collaborative networks and enterprises S ^ 3

5 Conclusions

The systematic review on collaborative networks was carried out because it is a consolidated subject in the literature and that meets the research gaps identified in the work of Weichhart et al. [1]. The approach of a mature discipline aims to guide the development of the new paradigm discussed in the present study, S ^ 3 Enterprise. The research sought to identify the main motivators, research approaches, most frequent application domains and the list of countries that published the most, for the construction of a conceptual framework with the main challenges and opportunities of collaborative networks and S ^ 3 Enterprise.

Motivators represented the reasons why companies seek collaboration, and consequently the benefits they seek are implicitly associated. It is worth mentioning that they are implied in the proposed framework, since they were essential for understanding the challenges and opportunities of the areas under study. The most common research approaches, application domains, and the list of countries that most published on the subject were complements that sought to reinforce the idea that collaborative networks are comprehensive and effective strategies for addressing aspects of the digital age.

However, although collaborative networks have advantages, they also have internal limitations such as the availability of resources (physical, human, organizational and financial) and the ability to coordinate them in an integrated way; external constraints expressed by institutional factors governed by rules and conduits in the network operating environment; and associated challenges such as developing trust between partners, interoperability of information systems, selection of collaborative partners, alignment and clear definition of strategies and objectives among all stakeholders, ensuring data security and information shared over the internet or other informational system.

The systematic review allowed us to identify some opportunities in the intersection of collaborative networks and S ^ 3 Enterprise, such as: the need to develop new business models; the fostering of a digital ecosystem; the development and/or adaptation of emerging technologies; the optimization of manufacturing processes; the exploration of the aspects brought by the internet of everything; the use of cloud computing; the development of interoperable systems; the elaboration of ontologies, architectures, models, frameworks that support the development of the disciplines in question; and sustainable development in the economic, social and environmental aspects of business.

References

1. Weichhart, G., Molina, A., Chen, D., Whitman, L.E., Vernadat, F.: Challenges and current developments for sensing, smart and sustainable enterprise systems. Comput. Ind **79**, 34–46 (2016)
2. Ferro-Beca, M.D., Sarraipa, J., Agostinho, C., Gigante, F., Jose-Nunez, M., Jardim-Gonçalves, R.: A framework for enterprise context analysis based on semantic principles. Comput. Sci. Inf. Syst. **12**(3), 931–960 (2015)

3. Filos, E.: Smart organizations in the digital age. In: Mezgar, I. (ed.) Integration of ICT in Smart Organizations. Idea Group Publishing, London (2006)
4. Mauricio-Moreno, H., Miranda, J., Chavarría, D., Ramírez-Cadena, M., Molina, A.: Design S3-RF (sustainable x smart x sensing - reference framework) for the future manufacturing enterprise. IFAC-PapersOnLine **48**(3), 58–63 (2015)
5. Fischl, M.C., Scherrer-Rathje, M., Friedli, T.: Digging deeper into supply risk: a systematic literature review on price risks. Supply Chain. Manag.: Int. J. **19**(5/6), 480–503 (2014)
6. Tranfield, D., Denyer, D., Smart, P.: Towards a methodology for developing evidence-informed management knowledge by means of systematic review. Br. J. Manag. **14**(3), 207–222 (2003)
7. Fornasiero, R., et al.: Implementation of customization strategies in collaborative networks through an innovative reference framework. Prod. Plan. Control **27**(14), 1158–1170 (2016)
8. Jayaram, J., Pathak, S.: A holistic view of knowledge integration in collaborative supply chains. Int. J. Prod. Res. **51**(7), 1958–1972 (2013)
9. Quetti, C., Pigni, F., Clerici, A.: Factors affecting RFId adoption in a vertical supply chain: the case of the silk industry in Italy. Prod. Plan. Control **23**(4), 315–331 (2012)
10. Lin, H.W., et al.: Design of a global decision support system for a manufacturing SME: towards participating in collaborative manufacturing. Int. J. Prod. Econ. **136**(1), 1–12 (2012)
11. Kumar, S.: A knowledge based reliability engineering approach to manage product safety and recalls. Expert Syst. Appl. **41**(11), 5323–5339 (2014)
12. Huang, X.-X., et al.: The relationships between regulatory and customer pressure, green organizational responses, and green innovation performance. J. Clean. Prod. **112**, 3423–3433 (2016)
13. Di Cagno, D., Fabrizi, A., Meliciani, V.: The impact of participation in European joint research projects on knowledge creation and economic growth. J. Technol. Transf. **39**(6), 836–858 (2014)
14. Protogerou, A., Caloghirou, Y., Siokas, E.: Twenty-five years of science-industry collaboration: the emergence and evolution of policy-driven research networks across Europe. J. Technol. Transf. **38**(6), 873–895 (2013)
15. Broekel, T., Fornahl, D., Morrison, A.: Another cluster premium: Innovation subsidies and R&D collaboration networks. Res. Policy **44**(8), 1431–1444 (2015)
16. Welch, E.W., Jha, Y.: Network and perceptual determinants of satisfaction among science and engineering faculty in US research universities. J. Technol. Transf. **41**(2), 290–328 (2016)
17. Swarnkar, R., et al.: A framework for collaboration moderator services to support knowledge based collaboration. J. Intell. Manuf. **23**(5), 2003–2023 (2012)
18. Liotta, G., Kaihara, T., Stecca, G.: Optimization and simulation of collaborative networks for sustainable production and transportation. IEEE Trans. Industr. Inf. **12**(1), 417–424 (2016)
19. Hsieh, F.S., Lin, J.B.: Context-aware workflow management for virtual enterprises based on coordination of agents. J. Intell. Manuf. **25**(3), 393–412 (2014)
20. Michaelides, R., et al.: Collaboration networks and collaboration tools: a match for SMEs? Int. J. Prod. Res. **51**(7), 2034–2048 (2013)
21. Leung, R.C.: Networks as sponges: international collaboration for developing nanomedicine in China. Res. Policy **42**(1), 211–219 (2013)
22. De Prato, G., Nepelski, D.: Global technological collaboration network: network analysis of international co-inventions. J. Technol. Transf. **39**(3), 358–375 (2014)
23. Renna, P.: Capacity investment decision by Monte Carlo approach in a cooperation network. Int. J. Prod. Res. **51**(21), 6455–6469 (2013)

24. Bojanowski, M., Corten, R., Westbrock, B.: The structure and dynamics of the global network of inter-firm R&D partnerships 1989–2002. J. Technol. Transf. **37**(6), 967–987 (2012)
25. Effio, D.G., et al.: A look at state-level risk assessment in the united states: making decisions in the absence of federal risk values. Risk Anal. **33**(1), 54–67 (2013)
26. Cheikhrouhou, N., Pouly, M., Madinabeitia, G.: Trust categories and their impacts on information exchange processes in vertical collaborative networked organisations. Int. J. Comput. Integr. Manuf. **26**(1–2), 87–100 (2013)
27. Lyons, A.C., et al.: The application of a knowledge-based reference framework to support the provision of requisite variety and customisation across collaborative networks. Int. J. Prod. Res. **51**(7), 2019–2033 (2013)
28. Zhang, H.K., et al.: Promoting efficient communications for high-speed railway using smart collaborative networking. IEEE Wirel. Commun. **22**(6), 92–97 (2015)
29. Zhong, H., Ozsoy, E., Nof, S.Y.: Co-insights framework for collaborative decision support and tacit knowledge transfer. Expert Syst. Appl. **45**, 85–96 (2016)
30. Cao, Q., Thompson, M.A., Triche, J.: Investigating the role of business processes and knowledge management systems on performance: a multi-case study approach. Int. J. Prod. Res. **51**(18), 5565–5575 (2013)
31. Maccarthy, B.L., Jayarathne, P.: Sustainable collaborative supply networks in the international clothing industry: a comparative analysis of two retailers. Prod. Plan. Control **23**(4), 252–268 (2012)
32. Durugbo, C.: Collaborative networks: a systematic review and multi-level framework. Int. J. Prod. Res. **54**(12), 3749–3776 (2016)
33. Noran, O.: Collaborative networks in the tertiary education industry sector: a case study. Int. J. Comput. Integr. Manuf. **26**(1–2), 29–40 (2013)
34. Jardim-Goncalves, R., et al.: Reference framework for enhanced interoperable collaborative networks in industrial organisations. Int. J. Comput. Integr. Manuf. **26**(1–2), 166–182 (2013)
35. Sochat, V.V.: AuthorSynth: a collaboration network and behaviorally-based visualization tool of activation reports from the neuroscience literature. Front. Neuroinformatics **9**, 6 (2015)
36. Minguela-Rata, B., Fernandez-Menendez, J., Fossas-Olalla, M.: Cooperation with suppliers, firm size and product innovation. Ind. Manag. Data Syst. **114**(3), 438–455 (2014)
37. Moghaddam, M., Nof, S.Y.: The collaborative factory of the future. Int. J. Comput. Integr. Manuf. **30**(1), 23–43 (2015)
38. Lelah, A., et al.: Collaborative network with SMEs providing a backbone for urban PSS: a model and initial sustainability analysis. Prod. Plan. Control **23**(4), 299–314 (2012)
39. Shankar, R., et al.: A collaborative framework to minimise knowledge loss in new product development. Int. J. Prod. Res. **51**(7), 2049–2059 (2013)
40. Macke, J., et al.: Social capital in collaborative networks competitiveness: the case of the Brazilian wine industry cluster. Int. J. Comput. Integr. Manuf. **26**(1–2), 117–124 (2013)
41. Taticchi, P., et al.: A management framework for organisational networks: a case study. J. Manuf. Technol. Manag. **23**(5), 593–614 (2012)
42. Sabatier, M., Chollet, B.: Is there a first mover advantage in science? Pioneering behavior and scientific production in nanotechnology. Res. Policy **46**(2), 522–533 (2017)
43. Jansson, K., Karvonen, I.: Using CNOs in international marketing and outbound logistics. Cogent Eng. **1**(1), 940667 (2014)
44. Dias, C., Escoval, A.: The open nature of innovation in the hospital sector: the role of external collaboration networks. Health Policy Technol. **1**(4), 181–186 (2012)
45. Beaudry, C., Allaoui, S.: Impact of public and private research funding on scientific production: the case of nanotechnology. Res. Policy **41**(9), 1589–1606 (2012)

46. Guan, J., Zhang, J., Yan, Y.: The impact of multilevel networks on innovation. Res. Policy **44**(3), 545–559 (2015)
47. Saetta, S., Tiacci, L., Cagnazzo, L.: The innovative model of the virtual development office for collaborative networked enterprises: the GPT network case study. Int. J. Comput. Integr. Manuf. **26**(1–2), 41–54 (2013)
48. Moghaddam, M., Nof, S.Y., Menipaz, E.: Design and administration of collaborative networked headquarters. Int. J. Prod. Res. **54**(23), 7074–7090 (2016)
49. Kim, H., Jung, W.S.: Bibliometric analysis of collaboration network and the role of research station in antarctic science. Ind. Eng. Manag. Syst. **15**(1), 92–98 (2016)
50. Chakraborty, T., Ganguly, N., Mukherjee, A.: An author is known by the context she keeps: significance of network motifs in scientific collaborations. Soc. Netw. Anal. Min. **5**(1), 1–21 (2015)
51. Guan, J., et al.: Does country-level R&D efficiency benefit from the collaboration network structure? Res. Policy **45**(4), 770–784 (2016)
52. Tchouakeu, L.M.N., et al.: Humanitarian inter-organisational collaboration network: investigating the impact of network structure and information and communication technology on organisation performance. Int. J. Serv. Technol. Manage. **19**(1–3), 19–42 (2013)
53. Noran, O.: Collaborative disaster management: an interdisciplinary approach. Comput. Ind. **65**(6), 1032–1040 (2014)
54. Zhang, F.Q., et al.: Modeling and analyzing of an enterprise collaboration network supported by service-oriented manufacturing. Proc. Inst. Mech. Eng. Part B-J. Eng. Manuf. **226**(B9), 1579–1593 (2012)
55. Andrés, B., Poler, R.: Relevant problems in collaborative processes of non-hierarchical manufacturing networks. J. Ind. Eng. Manag. **6**(3), 723–731 (2013)
56. Renna, P.: Decision model to support the SMEs' decision to participate or leave a collaborative network. Int. J. Prod. Res. **51**(7), 1973–1983 (2013)
57. Cardoso, T., Camarinha-Matos, L.M.: Pro-active service ecosystem framework. Int. J. Comput. Integr. Manuf. **26**(11), 1021–1041 (2013)
58. Durugbo, C.: Managing information for collaborative networks. Ind. Manag. Data Syst. **114** (8), 1207–1228 (2014)
59. Kandjani, H., Bernus, P., Wen, L.: Reducing the structural complexity and transaction cost of collaborative networks using extended axiomatic design theory and virtual brokerage. Concurr. Eng. Res. Appl. **22**(4), 320–332 (2014)
60. Andres, B., Sanchis, R., Poler, R.: A cloud platform to support collaboration in supply networks. Int. J. Prod. Manag. Eng. **4**(1), 5–13 (2016)
61. Paltriccia, C., Tiacci, L.: Supplying networks in the healthcare sector: a new outsourcing model for materials management. Ind. Manag. Data Syst. **116**(8), 1493–1519 (2016)
62. Jaegler, A., Burlat, P.: Carbon friendly supply chains: a simulation study of different scenarios. Prod. Plan. Control **23**(4), 269–278 (2012)
63. Dangelico, R.M., Pontrandolfo, P., Pujari, D.: Developing sustainable new products in the textile and upholstered furniture industries: role of external integrative capabilities. J. Prod. Innov. Manag. **30**(4), 642–658 (2013)
64. Karimi, F., Khalilpour, R.: Evolution of carbon capture and storage research: trends of international collaborations and knowledge maps. Int. J. Greenh. Gas Control **37**, 362–376 (2015)
65. Durugbo, C., Riedel, J.C.K.H.: Readiness assessment of collaborative networked organisations for integrated product and service delivery. Int. J. Prod. Res. **51**(2), 598–613 (2013)

66. Grilo, A., et al.: Construction collaborative networks: the case study of a building information modelling-based office building project. Int. J. Comput. Integr. Manuf. **26**(1–2), 152–165 (2013)
67. Kim, J., Perez, C.: Co-authorship network analysis in industrial ecology research community. J. Ind. Ecol. **19**(2), 222–235 (2015)
68. Li, K., Du, T.C.: Building a boundary-spanning service for coopetition. Expert Syst. Appl. **42**(22), 8413–8422 (2015)
69. Boehm, D.N., Hogan, T.: 'A jack of all trades': the role of PIs in the establishment and management of collaborative networks in scientific knowledge commercialisation. J. Technol. Transf. **39**(1), 134–149 (2014)
70. Chen, Y., et al.: Evolution of regional scientific collaboration networks: China-Europe emerging collaborations on nano-science. Int. J. Technol. Manag. **63**(3–4), 185–211 (2013)
71. Arriagada, D.R.E., Alarcón, C.L.F.: Knowledge management and maturation model in construction companies. J. Constr. Eng. Manag. **140**(4), B4013006 (2014)
72. Baek, J.S., Meroni, A., Manzini, E.: A socio-technical approach to design for community resilience: a framework for analysis and design goal forming. Des. Stud. **40**, 60–84 (2015)

Finding the Right Way Towards a CPS – A Methodology for Individually Selecting Development Processes for Cyber-Physical Systems

Günther Schuh, Violett Zeller, Max-Ferdinand Stroh$^{(\boxtimes)}$,
and Philipp Harder

Institute for Industrial Management, FIR, RWTH Aachen University,
Campus-Boulevard 55, 52064 Aachen, Germany
{Guenther.Schuh, Violett.Zeller, Max-Ferdinand.Stroh,
Philipp.Harder}@fir.rwth-aachen.de

Abstract. Numerous traditional, agile and hybrid development approaches have been proposed for the development of CPS. As the choice of development process is crucial to the success of development projects, it has become a major challenge to identify the best-suited process.

This paper introduces a methodology for identifying the best-suited CPS development process, based on the individual boundary conditions for a certain development project within a company. The authors used a set of eight indicators to assess a CPS-development project. The results of the assessment were matched with CPS-development approaches. Based on the matching results a best-suited development process was selected. The application is shown for a use case in the German manufacturing industry. The developed method aims to reduce the risk of project failure due to the wrong choice of development process.

Keywords: CPS · Development process · Agile development

1 Introduction

Industry 4.0 and digitalization are transforming our companies. In order to keep pace with this development, companies are forced to transform their products and systems from mecha(tro)nical into Cyber-Physical Systems (CPS) [1]. CPS connect the (real) physical world with the (virtual) cyber world. They are connected and consist of actuators and sensors, as well as a human machine interface to interact between the physical and the cyber world. They are empowered to assist humans in their decision making process and may even act autonomously. Therefore a CPS may span from a single machine to a whole (connected) production site [2].

Different development processes from *conventional*, *hybrid* to *agile* have been proposed in the past. However, there is no best suited process for the development for all types of CPS [3, 4]. It is more likely that for every development project one individual process will solve the trilemma of providing a solution with the best *quality* at the lowest *cost* with the shortest *time to market* [5].

Published by Springer Nature Switzerland AG 2019
L. M. Camarinha-Matos et al. (Eds.): PRO-VE 2019, IFIP AICT 568, pp. 81–90, 2019.
https://doi.org/10.1007/978-3-030-28464-0_8

CPS are the backbone of Collaborative Networks as well as the drivers for Digital Transformation. Thus, the choice of development process is a crucial aspect within the realization of Collaborative Networks and Digital Transformation. As the right choice of development processes is also crucial to the success of a development project, it is very important for a company to select a process that will fit to their individual boundary conditions [4]. Currently there is no methodology to select a development process for CPS based on the boundary conditions of the company. For this reason, the aim of this paper is to present a methodology to select the best-suited development process based on the individual boundary conditions in order to close the identified research gap.

To do so, a short introduction into the different development processes is given and a set of relevant CPS development processes is identified. Afterwards a set of indicators to define the level of agility for a project is selected. The set of indicators is used as a means of assessment for a development project in order to identify the best-suited development process. The application is demonstrated for a CPS-development use-case in the German manufacturing industry.

The overall goal of the paper is reflected in the research question: "How can the best-suited development process for a CPS development, based on the structured assessment of the individual boundary conditions, be selected".

For the overall research, case-study research by EISENHARDT [6] will be applied. The case-studies help selecting the relevant models for the development of CPS as well as determining the indicators for identifying the level of agility for the different models. Furthermore, they will be used to validate the results of the assessments. For this paper the focus was set on building a first prototype of the methodology in order to prove its relevance. Therefore the content of the methodology is based on literature research and own constructs. The methodology is applied to one case-study. Future research will then evaluate and enhance the indicators, the development processes and matching in detail, based on several case studies.

2   Background

Manufacturing companies generally use development processes in order to support their product development. The development processes describe the processes and activities within the development step by step. There is a variety of development processes, which are suitable for different purposes and boundary conditions [7].

In general, development processes can be divided into three groups: *conventional, agile* and *hybrid*. Figure 1 shows the direction of progress within the three approaches.

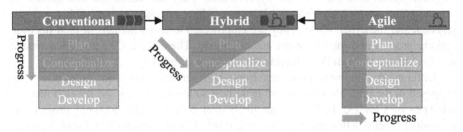

Fig. 1. Direction of progress in conventional, hybrid and agile projects [8]

In conventional development approaches, the product development process is split into different phases that strictly follow each other. Once a previous phase is completed, a subsequent phase begins. Hence, in conventional developments, the progress follows the four phases *plan, conceptualize, design* and *develop* sequentially, as shown in Fig. 1 [9].

However, using the strictly sequential approach of conventional development processes in flexible development environments with volatile requirements can be quite challenging. In order to control flexible processes, *agile* concepts were introduced in the field of software development and have partially been transferred to physical product developments by now [10]. Compared to conventional development processes, agile development processes are less structured and aim to respond flexibly to new requirements, insights and customer feedback that may arise in the course of the development [11]. Thus the development progress in agile projects runs parallel in the four development phases (Fig. 1) [8].

Besides conventional and agile approaches there is a third category called *hybrid*, which has evolved from combining these two [12]. By combining the concepts, advances from both approaches, such as stability and flexibility, can be used simultaneously, leading to promising development processes especially for highly complex products, e.g. for the development of *Cyber-Physical Systems* [13]. Combinations to form a hybrid development process are not limited, a wide variety of patterns can be created by combining any conventional with any agile process [14]. Several procedures can be varied within a project structure according to the situation in order to implement the project-specific requirements in the most suitable way [15]. The direction of progress in hybrid projects is neither strictly sequential as in conventional projects, nor entirely parallel in all four phases as in agile concepts (Fig. 1).

3   Description of the Methodology

The developed methodology for individually selecting development processes for *Cyber-Physical Systems* is shown in Fig. 2. It is divided into four phases, which are executed in the displayed order.

Fig. 2. The four steps of the developed methodology

In phase one the given project is subdivided into several subprojects. The division into subprojects is done in order to reduce the complexity of the overall CPS development. The number of subprojects is not fixed but should be chosen appropriate to the project's size.

Phase two is the assessment of the project which is conducted during a workshop with the participants of the project. In detail, each of the subprojects defined in the first step is assessed by using a profile as means of assessment. The profile consists of different indicators, which indicate agility or conventionality depending on the assessment. The set of indicators is presented in the following chapter (Table 1).

In phase three the developed matching algorithm is applied to the assessed subprojects. The algorithm counts the number of matches of each subproject with each of the development processes in the system.

In phase four, the matching results are presented. The most suited model for the overall project is selected by comparing the matching results of the different subprojects. Besides selecting a single model, it is also possible to combine different development processes into a comprehensive one. Thus, universal hybrid concepts can be designed which are well suited for the given boundary conditions of the project.

3.1 Indicators for the Choice of Development Process

There are already several approaches presenting indicators to identify the level of agility for development projects. Some of them offer a quantitative analysis but are derived from experience (e.g. [9]). Other indicators are of a qualitative form and do not fit the use as an assessment methodology (e.g. [16]). The set of indicators selected for this paper from DIELS were derived from a literature research, follow a quantifiable scale and cover internal and external indicators [17].

DIELS developed a set of eight indicators for determining agile product scopes. The identified project-relevant indicators stand either for or against the use of agile methods in the product development, depending on their characteristics (see Table 1). The indicators are divided into (five) internal and (three) external ones, depending on whether they can be controlled by the company or not. All of the indicators of DIELS have four different characteristics, graded in three-steps from plan-driven (value 0) to agile development (value 9), which are shown in Table 1 [17].

Table 1. Indicators for determining agile product scopes by Diels [18]

Indicators/rating		0 (plan-driven)	3	6	9 (agile)
Internal	(a) Solution space	*Parallel development*	*Focused development*	*Highly convergent dev.*	*Alternative oriented dev.*
	(b) Prototype manufacturability	*Technical model*	*Functional model*	*Design model*	*Concept model*
	(c) Resources	*Very low*	*Low*	*High*	*Very high*
	(d) Technology ability	*No knowledge about technology*	*Proof of functionality*	*Prototypical application*	*Technology in use*
	(e) Corporate culture	*Hierarchical*	*Disciplined*	*Clan*	*Democratic*
External	(f) Market relevance	*Minor features*	*Basic features*	*Performance features*	*Enthusiasm features*
	(g) Market accuracy	*Incremental change*	*Derivative change*	*Platform change*	*Breakthrough change*
	(h) Market volatility	*None*	*Low*	*Medium*	*High*

For the development of the methodology for individually selecting development processes for *Cyber-Physical Systems* the approach of DIELS was chosen as a basis. DIELS's indicators were identified during a comprehensive literature research and a following systematic consolidation, thus they fully meet the demand for project-specific boundary conditions. In addition, this approach distinguishes between plan-driven, agile (and hybrid) approaches and allows a quantifiable evaluation. Furthermore, DIELS's approach presents a set of indicators specifically designed for determining which product scopes can be developed using agile concepts. Transferring the agility indicators to characterize both development processes and subprojects can be accomplished without further modification.

3.2 Selected CPS-Development Processes

For developing the methodology a total of nine conventional, hybrid and agile development processes were selected, which are listed and categorized in Table 2. The selection was carried out on the basis of statistics on distribution of the models [19, 20]. The statistics on hybrid development processes were less clear, since in principle any combination of a conventional and an agile process would be possible. Hence, for the development of the methodology, hybrid models that have been described in literature or applied in practice were selected. Generally, further development processes can be added to the methodology independent of their nature (*agile, hybrid, conventional*).

For each development process the value of the characteristic, which describes it most accurately, was assigned according to the agility indicators of DIELS in Table 2. Low values represent plan-driven development (value 0), whereas high values represent agile development (value 9). The classification of the models was based on a literature research. As it is a first approach, the classification will be detailed and validated in future research. The sources used for classification are mentioned in brackets next to the respective process in Table 2.

Table 2. Categorized conventional, hybrid and agile development processes using the agility indicators of DIELS [17]

Dev. processes/indicators		(a)	(b)	(c)	(d)	(e)	(f)	(g)	(h)
Conv.	Waterfall model [21]	0	0	0	0	0	3	0	0
	Systems engineering [22]	6	0	3	0	0	3	9	3
	V-model (VDI 2206) [23]	6	0	0	0	3	3	3	0
Hybrid	Agile-stage-gate [24]	6	9	6	6	6	9	3	3
	Water-scrum-fall [25]	6	9	6	3	6	6	3	3
	Scrum-V-model [26]	6	9	3	3	6	6	3	3
Agile	Scrum [27]	9	9	9	9	9	9	9	9
	Extreme programming [28]	6	9	9	9	9	9	9	9
	Kanban [29]	9	9	6	9	6	6	9	9

3.3 Description of the Matching Process

During the matching process, the characteristics of the defined subprojects are matched with the characteristics of all development processes one after the other, as shown in the example in Table 3. The number of matches with each development process is counted and can be used as an indicator for the suitability for the subproject. In the displayed example the given development process would have a total of four out of eight possible matches with the subproject, leading to a suitability value of 50%.

Table 3. Example of the matching process of a subproject with a development process

Indicators / Rating	0	3	6	9
Solution space	⊗			
Prototype manuf.	X	O		
Resources		X	O	
Technology ability		⊗		
Corporate culture			X	O

(left table labelled *Internal*)

Indicators / Rating	0	3	6	9
Market relevance	⊗			
Market accuracy			O	X
Market volatility				⊗

(right table labelled *Extern*)

O = characteristic of the dev. process
X = characteristic of the subproject

4 Discussion of the Results for a Use-Case

The methodology was applied to a medium-sized technology company located in Germany. The overall goal of their development was to design and build an IoT factory. In this case, IoT Factory refers to a factory with connected assets, such as machines and transportation systems allowing data based production control and autonomous actions. This is in alignment with the definition of CPS given in Sect. 1 of this paper. Thus the "IoT Factory" can be considered a CPS (consisting of several sub-CPSs) in its entirety. The main benefits of this factory are to reduce lead times and realize batch size one. This will be reached by a high level of automation and connectivity for the different steps within the production line. The new factory will be implemented into a supply-chain of conventional "non-IoT" factories.

Due to a large number of undefined requirements and the future orientation of the project, the choice of development process was not obvious. At this point, the methodology presented in Sect. 3 was applied in order to individually select a development process for the project.

The first step was to divide the project into four subprojects: *Production Machine Design, IT Systems, Intralogistics,* and *Construction. IT Systems* refers to the relevant IT-Systems for controlling the production environment (e.g. ERP, MES). Usually the subprojects require competencies from different disciplines, such as IT, mechanical and electrical engineering for the *Production Machine Design.*

Every subproject was then assessed with the set of indicators presented earlier. Table 4 gives an overview of the assessment results.

Table 4. Assessment results of the four subprojects

Subprojects/indicators	(a)	(b)	(c)	(d)	(e)	(f)	(g)	(h)	Ø
01: Production machine design	6	3	3	6	6	6	3	3	**4.5**
02: IT-Systems	3	3	3	6	3	6	3	3	**3.75**
03: Intralogistics	3	6	3	9	6	6	3	3	**4.88**
04: Construction	3	6	0	9	0	9	0	3	**3.75**

On average, subproject 03 had the highest ranking on a scale from conventional to agile development. However, none of the projects were rated strongly towards agile approaches. Most of the ratings were within the range of the hybrid development processes. An interesting result in the assessment was that the subproject *IT-Systems* was rated less agile than the *Production Machine Design*. Hence showing that not only the development goal is relevant for the choice of the development process but also other boundary conditions such as corporate culture. As different departments may be involved in the subprojects, indicators may also differ between the different suprojects.

In General, CPS projects require interdisciplinary teams. That is why it is very important to have an assessment of every subproject, as the team composition may differ by discipline (Engineerg, IT, etc.) as well as the department involved (R&D, Prodcution Management, etc.). If the selected model does not support the team composition the project is likely to fail.

Figure 3 shows the matching results for the development processes for the assessed use-case. For all development processes selected in Sect. 3.2, the suitability value was calculated and all development processes were listed in descending order of suitability.

Subproject 01			Subproject 02			Subproject 03			Subproject 04		
Dev. Proc.	Σ	%	Dev. Proc.	Σ	%	Dev. Proc.	Σ	%	Dev. Proc.	Σ	%
Scrum-V-M	6	75	Scrum-V-M	4	50	Scrum-V-M	5	63	Waterfall	3	38
Agile-St-G	5	63	Agile-St-G	3	38	Wa-Scr-Fall	4	50	Agile-St-G	2	25
Wa-Scr-Fall	5	63	SE	3	38	Agile-St-G	3	38	XP	2	25
SE	4	50	Wa-Scr-Fall	3	38	Kanban	3	38	Scrum	2	25
Kanban	2	25	V-Model	2	25	SE	2	25	SE	2	25
V-Model	2	25	Kanban	1	13	XP	1	13	Kanban	1	13
XP	1	13	XP	0	0	Scrum	1	13	Scrum-V-M	1	13
Scrum	0	0	Scrum	0	0	V-Model	1	13	V-Model	1	13
Waterfall	0	0	Waterfall	0	0	Waterfall	0	0	Wa-Scr-Fall	1	13

Fig. 3. Matching results of the four subprojects with the development processes

For subproject one to three, the hybrid *Scrum-V-Model* shows the highest rate of suitability. Generally, the processes leaning towards strong agile or conventional development have a lower number of matches. Based on the average assessment results which were all between 3.75 and 4.88, which is mostly in the hybrid range, the result was expected and plausible.

For subproject four, the *Waterfall Model* has the highest number of matches. However, this subproject was not grasped by the methodology very well, as there were only three matches, resulting in an overlap of just 38%.

Based on the matching results for the individual subprojects a coherent development process for the overall project had to be defined (phase 4). Subproject one to three all showed the highest suitability for the hybrid *Scrum-V-Model*, combining an agile project phase in the beginning with a conventional project phase for final deployment of the results. The selected processes suit the use case quite well, as the development goal is an IoT Factory, which requires both, a high level of innovation (Scrum), as well as a high level of accuracy and stability in the deployment phase (V-Model).

For subproject four, which refers to the construction of the factory as well as the physical placement of the assets within the factory, a plan-driven process is also very well suited. Especially building projects require a high level of planning and accuracy as most of the steps taken in the processes may be irreversible in the end. Due to its strong focus on planning, a waterfall process can easily be integrated into the *V-Model* phases of subprojects one to three. The selected development processes were implemented in the project as proposed by the presented methodology.

In summary, a very well-suited development process for the presented use case could be identified with the presented methodology. This shows that the proposed methodology can be used in order to identify the best-suited development processes.

Future research will consider further case studies in order to enhance the proposed methodology. Based on that, the indicators, choice of development processes as well as the matching algorithm, can be further refined. As the selection of the development process currently requires a lot of detailed knowledge, future work will also focus on automatically finding and composing a development process along the different subprojects.

5   Conclusion

This paper introduces a methodology for selecting the best-suited CPS development process based on the individual boundary conditions at a company. In beginning conventional, hybrid and agile development processes are introduced. Afterwards a set of indicators for the choice of the development process on a scale from conventional over hybrid to agile are selected. A selection of CPS-development processes is then classified within the identified set of indicators. The same set of indicators is then used as a means of assessment for the boundary conditions of CPS development projects. Therefore the development processes, which were typed with the set of indicators, are matched with the results of the assessment of the development project. In order to reduce complexity, the assessed project is divided into subprojects that are assessed on their own. Based on the matching results an individual development process is selected for every subproject. The results are combined to an overall development process for the assessed development project. For this paper, the presented methodology was applied to a case-study from a German manufacturing company.

References

1. Schuh, G., Anderl, R., Gausemeier, J., ten Hompel, M., Wahlster, W.: Industrie 4.0 Maturity Index. Managing the Digital Transformation of Companies, Munich (2017)
2. Jordan, F., Bernardy, A., Stroh, M., Horeis, J., Stich, V.: Requirements-based matching approach to configurate cyber-physical systems for SMEs. In: Kocaoglu, D.F. (ed.) Technology Management for the Interconnected World, pp. 1–7. IEEE, Piscataway (2017)
3. Eigner, M., Koch, W., Muggeo, C.: Modellbasierter Entwicklungsprozess cybertronischer Systeme. Springer, Berlin (2017). https://doi.org/10.1007/978-3-662-55124-0
4. Reinhart, G. (ed.): Handbuch Industrie 4.0. Geschäftsmodelle, Prozesse, Technik. Hanser, München (2017)
5. Feldhusen, J., Grote, K.-H. (eds.): Pahl/Beitz Konstruktionslehre. Springer, Heidelberg (2013). https://doi.org/10.1007/978-3-642-29569-0
6. Eisenhardt, K.: Building theories from case study research. Acad. Manag. Rev. **14**, 532–550 (1989)
7. Lindemann, U. (ed.): Handbuch Produktentwicklung. Hanser, München (2016)
8. Feldhusen, J., Löwer, M., Bungert, F. (eds.): Agile methods for design to customer (2009)
9. Boehm, B.W., Turner, R.: Balancing Agility and Discipline. A Guide for the Perplexed. Addison-Wesley, Boston (2004)
10. Gloger, B.: Scrum in der Hardwareentwicklung (2014)
11. Engstler, M., Hanser, E., Mikusz, M., Herzwurm, G. (eds.): Projektmanagement und Vorgehensmodelle 2014. Gesellschaft für Informatik e.V. (GI), Bonn (2014)
12. Kuhrmann, M., et al.: Hybrid software development approaches in practice: a European perspective. IEEE Softw. **36**(4), 20–31 (2018)
13. Sandhaus, G., Knott, P., Berg, B. (eds.): Hybride Softwareentwicklung. Das Beste aus klassischen und agilen Methoden in einem Modell vereint. Springer, Berlin (2014). https://doi.org/10.1007/978-3-642-55064-5
14. Kuhrmann, M., et al.: Software and system development in practice: waterfall, scrum, and beyond (2017)
15. Engstler, M., Mikusz, M., Fazal-Baqaie, M.: Gesellschaft für Informatik e.V. Bonn, G.f.I.e. V., Hanser, E., Volland, A. (eds.) Projektmanagement und Vorgehensmodelle 2015, Bonn (2015)
16. Welge, M., Friedrich, C., Shair, A.: Integration von agilen Methoden in der Systementwicklung. In: Maurer, M., Schulze, S.-O. (eds.) Tag des Systems Engineering. Zusammenhänge erkennen und gestalten, pp. 341–350. Carl Hanser Fachbuchverlag, s.l. (2013)
17. Schuh, G., Dölle, C., Diels, F., Kuhn, M.: Methodology for determining agile product scopes in development projects. In: Kocaoglu, D.F., Anderson, T.R. (eds.) Managing Technological Entrepreneurship: The Engine for Economic Growth. PICMET 2018, pp. 1–9. IEEE, Piscataway (2018)
18. Diels, F.: Indikatoren für die Ermittlung agil zu entwickelnder Produktumfänge, Aachen (2018)
19. Komus, A., Kuberg, M.: Status Quo Agile. Studie zu Verbreitung und Nutzen agiler Methoden Eine empirische Untersuchung (2017)
20. Theocharis, G., Kuhrmann, M., Münch, J., Diebold, P.: Is water-scrum-fall reality? On the use of agile and traditional development practices. In: Abrahamsson, P., Corral, L., Oivo, M., Russo, B. (eds.) PROFES 2015. LNCS, vol. 9459, pp. 149–166. Springer, Cham (2015). https://doi.org/10.1007/978-3-319-26844-6_11

21. Royce, W. (ed.): Managing the Development of Large Software Systems: Concepts and Techniques. IEEE Computer Society Press, Washington, DC (1987)
22. Haberfellner, R., de Weck, O., Fricke, E., Vössner, S.: Systems Engineering. Grundlagen und Anwendung. Orell Füssli, Zürich (2012)
23. VDI 2206: Entwicklungsmethodik für mechatronische Systeme. Beuth, Berlin (2004)
24. Cooper, R.G., Sommer, A.F.: Agile–stage-gate for manufacturers. Res.-Technol. Manag. **61**, 17–26 (2018)
25. West, D.: Water-scrum-fall is the reality of agile for most organizations today (2011)
26. Timinger, H., Seel, C.: Ein Ordnungsrahmen für adaptives hybrides Projektmanagement. Projekt Manag. aktuell **4**, 55–61 (2016)
27. Schwaber, K.: Agile Project Management with Scrum. Microsoft Press, Redmond (2004)
28. Beck, K.: Embracing change with extreme programming. Computer **32**, 70–77 (1999)
29. Anderson, D.J.: Kanban: Successful Evolutionary Change for Your Technology Business. Blue Hole Press, Sequim (2010)

Open Innovation

Crowd Engineering: Manage Crowd Contributions for Design and Manufacture of Innovative Products

Agostino Villa and Teresa Taurino[(✉)]

DIGEP – Department of Management and Production Engineering,
Politecnico di Torino, Corso Duca Degli Abruzzi 24, 10129 Turin, Italy
{agostino.villa, teresa.taurino}@polito.it

Abstract. The increasing complexity of designing and manufacturing products as well as the growing speed required for their innovation is pushing large and medium-small companies to an ever-broader search for new ideas and for a wide availability of experts, able to provide timely contributions. Existing approaches mainly address the early phases of the product lifecycle in the frame of "open innovation". The crowd engineering approach is to organize an efficient and effective utilization of the "crowd", i.e. a wide set of persons, from students to private experts, and to start-ups and smart SMEs, which could be involved in the creation of innovative products. The first purpose of the paper is to give a presentation of Crowd Engineering in terms of a logical frame where crowd-workers will contribute into an informal collaborative network to fulfill technical and social needs. Then a schematic model based on an analogy between Crowd Engineering and Supply Relationship Management, will be outlined thus offering, on one hand, suggestions for a real implementation, on the other, some hints for a research agenda.

Keywords: Crowd Engineering · Combinatorial optimization model

1 Introduction

A collaborative network is a network consisting of a variety of entities (e.g. organizations and people) that are largely autonomous, geographically distributed, and heterogeneous in terms of their operating environment, culture, social capital and goals, but that collaborate to better achieve common or compatible goals, and whose interactions are supported by computer networks [1]. In the last decades, the growing complexity of the design of new products, the increasingly shorter time-to-market required to market new products, and the spread of the so-called "augmented products" [2], i.e. products with constantly increasing services, is pushing companies, both large and medium-small, to an ever-broader search for ideas and innovations, through a wide availability of experts, able to provide timely contributions.

Consequently, companies need to re-engineer the design and production process, since many experts, companies, interested persons, associations, etc., which provide them with the many contributions that are usable, form a real "crowd". The Crowd Engineering builds social solutions of design and production of innovative products, by

© IFIP International Federation for Information Processing 2019
Published by Springer Nature Switzerland AG 2019
L. M. Camarinha-Matos et al. (Eds.): PRO-VE 2019, IFIP AICT 568, pp. 93–102, 2019.
https://doi.org/10.1007/978-3-030-28464-0_9

"empowering companies to turn the force of their crowds (suppliers, customers, part-ners and also employees) into business advantage" (https://www.definitions.net/definition/crowdengineering).

It is evident that such a re-engineering problem involves a careful selection of both the "Contributors" and the contributions themselves for the new product creation or production. This problem has been tackled with multi-criteria decision analysis approaches (MCDA), such as Analytic Hierarchy Process [3, 4] Analytic Network Process [5], Goal and Mixed-Integer Programming [6], Data Envelopment Analysis [7], and the Fuzzy Set theory [8]. However, little information is given about some feedback from practitioners and from implementations of such approaches, which are still few. In practice, as recently observed in some particularly innovative Mid-Small Enterprises (SME) registered in the PMInnova Program [9], the ongoing trend toward the individualization and even personalization of products results in new additional challenges for industrial enterprises in the frame of "open innovation" [10], i.e. with wide supports from externals.

To this scope, Crowd Engineering must set the following objectives:

- Establish new design approaches, strategies, methods and tools for the co-creation of innovative, individualized products by opening the product creation to the "crowd";
- Enable crowd-based product creation by next generation product data exchange, based on standards and open source;
- Realize an efficient procedure to collect, select, integrate contributions, such to obtain a good overlapping of the set of collaborative selected contributions and the desired scheme of the innovative product.

These three objectives can be achieved by developing the Crowd Engineering approach in a user-centric way, i.e. with a strong direction of the multi-dimensional design process implemented by an institution, institute or company, having a clear idea of the innovative product to be obtained and a considerable ability to define a "call for innovation creation" to a set of potential contributors.

The organization of the paper will be as follows. Section 2 is dedicated to give a preliminary logical overview of the Crowd Engineering concept and an outline of its structure. Section 3.1 first describes a schematic model of Crowd Engineering, based on the analysis of its analogy with the Supplier Relationship Management. Sections 3.2 and 3.3 will discuss a schematic model of Crowd Engineering, by outlining the theoretical methods for supporting the multi-dimensional selection. Finally, Sect. 4 will present some hints of a research agenda, based on a Crowd Engineering work-flow scheme.

2 Preliminary Logical Overviews of Crowd Engineering

The Crowd Engineering procedure aims to focus, structure and translate into practice new ideas dedicated to collaborative co-creation. It is obtained from a process of collecting contributions from various sources (people, associations, SMEs, etc.), their selection and their integration for the purpose of conceptual and detailed design, the development of the necessary production operations, the production of new products oriented to the user. Crowd Engineering is based on the advancement of the well-known triple helix towards a quadruple helix for innovation systems (see Fig. 1). The classic triple-helix from 1995 knows only three actors. But emerging innovations do not necessarily match consumer demand, so the helix has to be extended by a by a »user« component, involving end users/consumers in the innovation process. Therefore, additional attention has to be paid to community-based approaches, originated by "collaborative network", that appears to be powerful social frames for value creation [1].

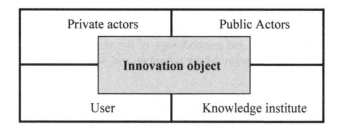

Fig. 1. Quadruple helix for innovation systems

Therefore, the Crowd Engineering project is stated by a "call for innovation creation" with the scope of searching and collecting contributions from many "Contributors" in order to integrate them so as to obtain a product (system or object) with characteristics of total novelty, structure and forms that allow production, all set by the Crowd Engineering Project Management (named in the following simply as "Manager"). The goal of the Crowd Engineering problem, as defined above, is advertised by the Manager in a broad way, in order to be able to receive contributions from many Contributors. Each Contributor proposes his own contribution, without knowing the contributions of the others or their participation in the research launched by the above mentioned "call". Therefore, the Contributors are potentially competitive. The Manager must have a "measure of usefulness" in order to verify if a contribution provided by an actor can be useful for the solution of the Crowd Engineering problem, in the sense that it can contribute to the achievement of the Crowd Engineering project objective. To this end, the Manager must evaluate each individual contribution obtained by each Contributors, and perform a multi-dimensional selection such as to collect only contributions with the following characters:

- A contribution must be "active" i.e. such to give rise to information/data that are coherent with some part of the innovative product or some operations that can contribute to the innovative product creation; this first attribute of a contribution can be evaluated according to the adopted measure of usefulness, above mentioned;
- Two or more contributions must be "collaborative", i.e. such to be usable in collaboration with other contributions, thus generating a more effective and active action in the design and production process; this further attribute of a pair of contributions can be evaluated by adopting a "measure of similarity" between the

two contributions, with respect to the result of the "problem", that is to some part of the innovative product or to some innovative operation necessary to produce it.

From a simplified point of view, the Manager, once evaluated as useful the contribution will be, could consider a second different contribution to understand if the two contributions are collaborative: their joint use facilitates the achievement of the Crowd Engineering goal in a more efficient and effective way with respect to the individual ones. Once recognized a pair of collaborative contributions, the Manager will evaluate to support the couple with a third contribution, by estimating the joint use of the three in terms of an increasing - if any - of the measure of collaborative utility. Progressively, the Manager can reach a complete set of contributions, all complementary, such as to express an admissible solution for the Crowd Engineering project. The logical Crowd Engineering overview briefly described above, has the sole purpose of illustrating in a simplified way the concepts and methodology of the problem. Indeed, it makes evidence of the combinatorial nature of the contributions' selection problem.

3   Schematic Model of Crowd Engineering

A schematic model of the Crowd Engineering approach can be obtained by the analogy between the Crowd Engineering and the Supply Relationship Management (Sect. 3.1). This first analogy suggests taking also into account the evident links between Crowd Engineering and Crowdsourcing, as well as with "Collaborative Networks" (Sect. 3.2).

3.1   Analogy Between Crowd Engineering and Supply Relationship Management

An enterprise performance, especially of small and medium-sized, largely depends on the relations with its suppliers, often belonging to different value chains, as in several industrial districts analyzed in [11, 12]. Then, a good enterprise-suppliers relationship is a necessity for any industrial organization, to be able to respond to dynamic and unpredictable chains of the final products demand [13, 14]. Therefore, a Supplier Relationship Management (SRM) is a methodology that organizes all the interactions of the enterprise with third-party organizations, which supply goods and services in order to allow the best possible product creation [15]. The evaluation of a supplier is then the process of measuring the performance of the suppliers itself, as well as of its capability to meet the buyer (i.e. the enterprise) demands. Tacking now into account the above logical description of the Crowd Engineering approach, it is possible to identify a strong analogy between the two processes, as shown in Table 1. Therefore, it is to use the SRM approach to give a schematic illustration of the Crowd Engineering procedure.

Table 1. Correspondences between crowd engineering and supply relationship management.

Phases and actors of crowd engineering	Phages and actors of supply relationship management
Actors:	*Actors*:
Contributors	Suppliers
Manager (with clear view of the innovation)	Producer (with clear view of the final product)
Phase1. Identify contributions	Phase 1. Specify the purchase strategy
Phase 2. Select the useful contributions	Phase 2. Evaluate the supplier performance
Phase 3. Integrate the selected contributions into the innovative product description	Phase 3. Make collaborative-integrated the Suppliers with respect to the final product
Phase 4. Evaluate the global set of contributions IF necessary, iterate	Phase 4. Evaluate the feedback from the producer IF necessary, iterate

3.2 Relations of Crowd Engineering with Crowd-Sourcing and Collaborative Networks

In order to make evidence of the strict relation between Crowd Engineering and Crowd-souring, the definition of the latter as reported in [16] is here referred to: "*Crowdsourcing is the act of taking a job traditionally performed by a designated agent (usually an employee) and outsourcing it to an undefined, generally large group of people in the form of an open call.*" [17].

In practice, Crowdsourcing is a powerful tool because it describes collaborations both in research and in design actions which can significantly enlarge both the group of (potential) scientific partners, and the team of designers. With regards to the scientific context, Crowd sourcing implies to fist clearly identify the problem to be solved by the crowd, and then to plan a reasonable balance between natural antagonisms of contributors. Therefore, Crowdsourcing makes evidence of some important, and also critical aspects, of Crowd Engineering that, with respect to the former, now it appears to be the operative practical version. Referring now to relations between Crowd Engineering and Collaborative networks, among the different variety that the latter assumes in industry and services (see [18]), its aspect of "collaborative engineering" is concerning teams of technicians and engineers belonging to different companies and cooperating together on a common significant project, thus sharing skills and experiences, thus moving towards the creation of a "virtual community".

Therefore, the existence of a collaborative network is a very useful prerequisite for a company intending to start a Crowd Engineering project. In fact, the Collaborative network can become the area of first and fundamental diffusion of the "call for innovation creation", providing the most favorable environmental conditions for the launch of the Crowd Engineering project itself. A verification of this occurs in the next Session, where the operational scheme of a Crowd Engineering project is outlined, especially in the selection phase of the contributions and acceptance of the new ideas, two key phases of such a project.

3.3   Crowd Engineering Operational Scheme

As for SRM, also in case of Crowd Engineering, for an effective collaboration, Manager and contributors (i.e., suppliers of contributions for the innovation required by the Manager) need to share profits in order to achieve a win-win situation. To come to an effective and profitable collaboration/integration of contributions, a Crowd Engineering operational scheme is mandatory [19–21]. Such a scheme is illustrated in Fig. 2. It is just the representation of the Table of correspondences, being derived by SRM scheme illustrated in [3], but specifically adapted to the Crowd Engineering concept.

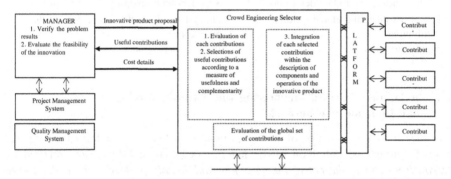

Fig. 2. The SRM-based scheme of the platform specifically adopted to the crowd engineering model.

The scheme is self-explanatory. The scheme inputs are the contributions sent by the "crowd", that is from the various types of suppliers of innovative ideas, in large numbers. The "heart" of the Crowd Engineering scheme is the Selector which, in accordance with the steps shown in the previous table, consists of the following parts:

(1) evaluation of each contribution and selection of each one useful among them by evaluating an associated *"measure of usefulness"* that represents the coherence of the contribution with the project goal and a *"measure of complementarity"* for each couple of contributions, as defined in Sect. 2;

(2) integration of each selected contribution within the description of the parts (components) and operations (of production) of the innovative product to be created;

(3) evaluation of the overall correspondence among the selected contributions and all the parts and all the operations of the innovative product.

The Manager is operating in the final block of the scheme, with the following aim:

(4) verifying the problem result, that is an admissible global correspondence among the selected contributions and all the parts and all the operations of the innovative product;

(5) evaluate the real feasibility of the hypothesis of an innovative product obtainable from the integration, bearing in mind that different additions (with different uses of the contributions) are possible even though they obtain the same final product.

(6) evaluate costs and revenues in each case produces an innovative product among the feasible ones;

(7) evaluate the usefulness and the cost of every useful contribution received, to offer a profit to those who have helpfully responded to his call.

To implement its functions, the Manager receives as input:

- selected useful contributions;
- proposals for innovative products developed by the Selector.

It also interacts with the Warehouse Management System, for the needs of components, and with the Quality Management System, to estimate the performance of the resulting innovative products.

4   Some Hints for a Research Agenda

The development of the Crowd Engineering approach to select the best possible set of contributions from the "crowd" for innovative products creation, is one of the more challenging lines of evolution for smart enterprises.

To offer some considerations that could be utilized by experts when the needs for innovation become so important and critical for the survival of the enterprise, some ideas for the application of the Crowd Engineering approach is now presented, as a sequence of Work Phases (i.e. a Work-flow), summarized in the following Table 2. Indeed, a Manager needs to have a detailed description of the sequence of phases to be applied, starting from the definition and description of the innovative product desired, up to the Crowd Engineering organization and use.

This simplified workflow suggests some hints for future research lines in which a comprehensive view of the Crowd Engineering, Crowd-sourcing and Collaborative network could contribute to a real innovation of the creation process of new products.

According to [16], some main research lines can be envisaged, for assuring a useful and significant development of Crowd Engineering and its practical implementation in industrial and service frames:

(a) identification of robust methods to identify and select fruitful contributions for a given innovation project goal, such to be clearly transferred to the crowd and understood by each potential contributors; this will characterize the communication power from the innovation project Manager and the wide range of individuals and entities that could give really new ideas, in a form to be recognized and integrated by the Manager itself;

(b) selection and clear communication of incentives (or earnings) for the individual contributors, clearly related to the usefulness of the contribution and its integration with the rest, and finalization to the goal of the project;

(c) promotion of healthy competition among contributors, while preserving the anonymity of contributions and guaranteeing their ownership, especially as the project takes shape and the integration of contributions will become increasingly evident (as is the exclusion of contributions of little value or not useful);

(d) the correct evaluation (above all in economic terms) of the theoretical contributions and their validation, especially in the case of particularly innovative contents; similar considerations apply to the evaluation of contributions with a rapid practical impact;

(e) Finally, the organization of a structure for managing the interactions of the Manager (or project team) with the crowd, through a structure that manages the center-contributor relations clearly but preserving the privacy of each one.

Table 2. Outline of the crowd engineering workflow.

N°	Scope	Description	Documentation
Work Phase 1	**Call-for-contributions**, referred to the a-priori selected consumer goods type	Definition of a descriptive **framework of the a-priori selected consumer goods type**, to be used as a reference by: potential contributors, i.e. people or organizations - as above - who intend to participate in the call, sending their contributions	Document with clear unambiguous presentation of the consumer goods type
Work Phase 2	**Strategies to manage the crowd of contributors**, by creating a "community of innovators"	Policies, strategies and initiatives in order to leverage the crowd, that means to **gradually create a "community of innovators".** Who will send their proposals (data, suggestions, project indications)?	(A)Communication protocols, managed by Crowd Engineering Manager (B) Rules to which participants must satisfy in defining and formulating contributions (C) Clear rules on the refusal of contributions.
Work Phase 3	**Methods for accepting and selecting contributions** depending on their usefulness	(a) Formulation and presentation of the structure of the "Crowd Engineering Selector" to guarantee an accurate, clear and unambiguous acceptance (or refusal) of the contributions	(A) Documentation of the structure of the "Crowd Engineering Selector"
Work Phase 4	Organizational **platform** denoted Crowd Engineering Selector, for the integrated management of all strategies, and initiatives and tool utilizations	*Development of the* **Platform dedicated to managing all the activities that will be done for selecting, evaluating and integrating contributions**	(A)Documentation of the Platform, functionality (B) Authorizations of all contributors to include their data, info's and contributions in the Platform
Work Phase 5	**Impact evaluation of the Crowd Engineering application**	Analysis of the Platform applications to pilot case, such as their correspondence with the product tree graph nodes and links	(A) Data and information gradually gathered and cataloged in order to describe the result

Acknowledgments. This research has been developed in the context of the PMInnova Program (www.pminnova.eu).

References

1. Camarinha-Matos, L.M., Afsarmanesh, H.: A comprehensive modeling framework for collaborative networked organizations. J. Intell. Manuf. **18**(5), 529–542 (2007)
2. Browne, J., et al.: RFID in product lifecycle management: a case in the automotive industry. Int. J. Comput. Integr. Manuf. **22**(7), 616–637 (2009)
3. Saminathan, M.V., Hemamala, K.: Analysis of Supplier Relationship Management Model using AHP. https://www.amrita.edu/sites/default/files/analysis-of-supplier-relationship-management-model-using-ahp.pdf
4. Schniederjans, M.J., Garvin, T.: Using the analytic hierarchy process and multi-objective programming for the selection of cost drivers in activity-based costing. Eur. J. Oper. Res. **100**(1), 72–80 (1997)
5. Meade, L.M., Presley, A.: R&D project selection using the analytic network process. IEEE Trans. Eng. Manag. **49**(1), 59–66 (2002)
6. Selen, W., Hott, D.: J Oper Res Soc **37**, 1121 (1986). https://doi.org/10.1057/jors.1986.197
7. Cooper, W.W., Seiford, L.M., Zhu, J.: Data envelopment analysis. In: Cooper, W.W., Seiford, L.M., Zhu, J. (eds.) Handbook on Data Envelopment Analysis. International Series in Operations Research & Management Science, vol. 71, pp. 1–39. Springer, Heidelberg (2004). https://doi.org/10.1007/1-4020-7798-X_1
8. Deschrijver G., Kerre, E.E.: On the relationship between some extensions of fuzzy set theory. Fuzzy Sets Syst. **133**(2), 227–235 (2003). ISSN 0165-0114. https://doi.org/10.1016/S0165-0114(02)00127-6
9. PMInnova Program, agremento Politecnico di Torino – Gruppo Bnca di Asti, A. Villa Responsible (2018). www.pminnova.eu
10. Gassmann, O., Enkel, E., Chesbrough, H.: The future of open innovation. R&D Manag. **40**(3), 213–221 (2010)
11. Taurino, T.: Using collaboration management in industrial clusters – case study of Italian energy cluster. Manag. Prod. Eng. Rev. **9**(4), 138–149 (2018)
12. Villa, A., Taurino, T.: From industrial districts to SME collaboration frames. Int. J. Prod. Res. **56**(1–2), 974–982 (2018). https://doi.org/10.1080/00207543.2017.1401244
13. Antonelli, D., Bruno, G., Taurino, T., Villa, A.: Conditions for effective collaboration in SME networks based on graph model. In: Camarinha-Matos, L.M., Scherer, R.J. (eds.) PRO-VE 2013. IAICT, vol. 408, pp. 129–136. Springer, Heidelberg (2013). https://doi.org/10.1007/978-3-642-40543-3_14
14. Antonelli, D., Bruno, G., Taurino, T., Villa, A.: Graph-based models to classify effective collaboration in SME networks. Int. J. Prod. Res. **53**(20), 6198–6209 (2015). https://doi.org/10.1080/00207543.2015.1038368
15. Chandra, C., Kumar, S.: Supply chain management in theory and practice: a passing fad or a fundamental change? Ind. Manag. Data Syst. **100**(3), 100–114 (2000)
16. Buecheler, T., Sieg, J.H., Fuckslin, R.M., Pfeifer, R.: Crowdsourcing, open innovation and collective intelligence in scientific method: a research agenda and operational framework. In: Proceedings of Alife XII Conference, Odesse, Denmark, pp. 679–686 (2010)
17. Howe, J.: Crowdsourcing. Why the power of the crowd is driving the future of business (2010). http://www.crowdsourcing.com/

18. Camarinha-Matos, L.M., Afsarmanesh H., Collaborative networks in industry and services: research scope and challenges. In: Symposium on Cost Oriented Automation, La Habana, Cuba (2007)
19. Viroli M., Beal, J., Damiani, F., Pianini, D.: Efficient engineering of complex self-organising systems by self-stabilising fields. In: IEEE 9th International Conference on Self-Adaptive and Self-Organizing Systems, Cambridge, MA, pp. 81–90 (2015). https://doi.org/10.1109/saso.2015.16
20. Groen, Eduard C., Doerr, J., Adam, S.: Towards crowd-based requirements engineering a research preview. In: Fricker, S., Schneider, K. (eds.) REFSQ 2015. LNCS, vol. 9013, pp. 247–253. Springer, Cham (2015). https://doi.org/10.1007/978-3-319-16101-3_16
21. Snijders R., Dalpiaz, F., Hosseini, M., Shahri, A., Ali, R.: Crowd-centric requirements engineering. In: IEEE/ACM 7th International Conference on Utility and Cloud Computing, London, pp. 614–615 (2014). https://doi.org/10.1109/ucc.2014.96

Open Innovation Practitioners Mindset on Risk

Paula Urze[1,2(✉)], João Rosas[1,3], Alexandra Tenera[1,4],
and Luis M. Camarinha-Matos[1,3]

[1] Faculty of Sciences and Technology,
NOVA University of Lisbon, Caparica, Portugal
{pcu,abt}@fct.unl.pt
[2] Interuniversity Center for the History of Science and Technology (CIUHCT),
Lisbon, Portugal
[3] Center of Technology and Systems (CTS), UNINOVA,
Caparica, Portugal
{jrosas,cam}@uninova.pt
[4] Research and Development Unit for Mechanical and Industrial Engineering
(UNIDEMI), Caparica, Portugal

Abstract. Open Innovation is a strategy used by organizations to more promptly comply with the continuous changing market needs and renew their income streams. But its effective achievement depends on the practitioners' ability to assume concrete mindset, like openness, acceptance of risk, talent to build trust and to learn from successes as well as from failures. Based on these assumptions, the paper explores the concept of mindset in open innovation. The approach is twofold combining sentiment analysis over interviews on web documents with semi-directive interviews conducted in IT companies. The results include a characterization of OI practitioners' mindset concerning risk and related elements.

Keywords: Open innovation · Risk mindset · Collaboration

1 Introduction

Open innovation (OI) is generally seen as a key collaborative strategy that organizations can use to evolve and keep up with the (emergent) market shifts and disruptive technological development. According to several studies, the advantages of OI over lesser open models of innovation have been proven [1, 2]. Despite the diversity of theoretical and empirical research on OI, there seems to exist, in the prevailing discourse of scholars and practitioners, the tendency to exclude the less successful experiences that occur during the innovation process. But such (in) visible side of OI must also be researched, as it is crucial to integrate into the interpretation of OI, not only the advances, successes, and advantages but also the setbacks, failures, and constraints. Such setbacks can be seen as the unintended consequences of the innovation process [3]. But OI requires learning both from successes as well as from failures [3, 4].

© IFIP International Federation for Information Processing 2019
Published by Springer Nature Switzerland AG 2019
L. M. Camarinha-Matos et al. (Eds.): PRO-VE 2019, IFIP AICT 568, pp. 103–114, 2019.
https://doi.org/10.1007/978-3-030-28464-0_10

From an epistemological perspective, more than a final result, it is the trajectory that must be understood to accurately know the OI concept and the elements that systemically combine to reach it. There are certainly contingency factors in the process, but there are also structural factors that underlie the social construction of OI. What paths have been taken? What mishaps have been overcome? What choices have been made? Therefore, much more research analysis on this topic is needed at the level of academia. The main goal in this paper is to analyse the mindset of OI practitioners regarding risk and other factors, e.g. trust, incorporating both positive and negative elements of OI in our research. For this, we aim at understanding the narratives and practices of OI actors regarding these elements. Despite recent research efforts, risk in OI lacks a deeper and more systematic analysis [5, 6].

We hypothesize that the apparent lack of risk assessment research in literature might be associated with the way the OI concept is usually portrayed, with more favourable narratives in which failures and setbacks are less likely to arise. For this purpose, we proceed to an exploratory analysis of the elements underlying the mindset of OI practitioners, starting with literature analysis. For this, Text Mining and Sentiment Analysis were applied to web documents containing interviews addressing risk in OI, which were available online during the year 2018. Afterwards, semi-directive interviews were conducted with OI practitioners (at the level of company managers) and we finish with results analysis and synthesis.

2 Background

Considering the scope and depth of the topics involved in open innovation, in this work we concentrate efforts focusing on the aspects that are mostly relevant to the defined research goals. In this way, we start by revisiting the concept of OI, then moving on to a perspective around the mindset that characterize the practitioners. We conclude this section with a synthesis concerning risk in OI.

2.1 Revisiting the Concept of Open Innovation

Open innovation is already a recurring strategy used by organizations to help them keep up with market changes and technological development. According to Chesbrough [7], OI is seen as a more profitable form of innovation, because it can reduce costs, accelerate time-to-market, increase product variability on the market "and create new revenue streams for the company"

In addition to the initial concept of OI as proposed by Chesbrough, OI also appears in the discourse of several scientific areas, generally taking an even further positive tone. The term acquired its more positive view due to its instrumentality from the social, political and material perspectives [3]. This is what we can commonly refer to as the bright side of OI. Although tendentially less visible, while not less relevant, it starts becoming increasingly recognized that the less bright side is also a part of the innovation dynamics, i.e., the other side of the same coin [8, 9].

In this sense, organizations, in general, tend to highlight their success cases and hide the mishaps, setbacks and failures during their OI projects. Whenever these are reported, they are shown as sporadic episodes, without meaningful relevance in the innovation dynamics. But, to adequately tackle the OI concept, it is crucial to incorporate those less publicizable elements. Such critical aspects are of paramount importance to innovation in general, and to OI in particular, as difficulties, and often the failures, frequently allow reaching increased achievements in knowledge and results. Then, we need to focus also at the Innovation practitioners. To walk the path of OI, practitioners need to aggregate several OI compatible attitudes, allowing them to be able to benefit from successes and learn from failures.

2.2   The Open Innovation Mindset

When Chesbrough colloquially placed the question "What is open innovation?", he answered that it mainly means having a much more open mindset and much more engaged with both the inside and outside world [10].

Furthermore, as mentioned by Björling in [11], participating in OI requires having some important attitudes, namely, that we must be "open to change", because the world is constantly changing. We need to "embrace creativity", recognizing that instead of "management processes" and "organizational structures," the starting point of OI is creativity, which requires a certain type of culture and organizations to make it possible. Another important facet is to have the ability and courage to "think big" and proceed beyond current norms and truths in the marketplace. This implies extending beyond normal/ordinary thinking and analysis. The author also states that OI implies to "show courage" to constantly rethink how things can be done. Finally, he argues that in OI, we must "think and act quickly" since innovations typically comprise agile processes.

In this regard, mindset can be understood as having a way of thinking or having psychological predispositions, which are tied to corresponding attitudes, ideas, beliefs and patterns of behavior. As such, it is scientifically important and strategically interesting to determine and accurately characterize the OI practitioners' mindset.

2.3   A Risk Perspective in Open Innovation

To properly establish an OI risk perspective, it is important to start by contrasting the two innovation models, internal and open.

Within company boundaries, innovation projects include practitioners who are subjected to management and supervision processes, in which risk control mechanisms can be used, allowing to deterministically anticipate and circumscribe contingencies and failures. Therefore, the "internal" innovation, typically supported by Research and Development Innovation (RDI) management systems and projects, has been already consolidated [12, 13] as well as the internationally consolidated risk assessment methods and tools for risk evaluation [14] within a company. In short, despite its intrinsic uncertainty and significant rate of products failures, internal innovation can be handled within management practices.

On the other hand, OI is characterized by its practitioners' autonomy in an environment which favors creativity, knowledge sharing, collaboration, and trustworthiness. As such innovation process are much more complex and much more unpredictable. Furthermore, due to partners' self-interests, relatively frequent conflicting goals and lack of preparedness, there is a growing risk of failures. On each failure, both resources and time are lost. For instance, intellectual property can be taken away and used by other actors for their benefit. In this sense, risk assessment is considered far more challenging in OI contexts. Furthermore, as mentioned in [15], the failure rate of a new product's development is around 35%, and this just considering the products that could reach the market phase. Other sources [16–18] report that failure rate can go up to 80% if the failures in the preliminary stages are also considered. Therefore, although risk models are difficult to apply in OI, their effective use could have significant impacts on OI outcomes.

3   Exploratory Study

In this chapter, we describe the methodological approach applied to characterize the mindset of practitioners in OI. The approach includes two distinct methods.

As illustrated in Fig. 1, the first method involves Text Mining and Sentiment Analysis performed on interviews recorded in on-line documents provided throughout the year 2018. The second method consisted on semi-directive interviews conducted CEOs and CTOs, who are OI practitioners.

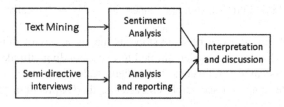

Fig. 1.   Phases in our research method.

Sentiment Analysis is a widely used method particularly in the Social and Behavioral Sciences, as well as in Web-based services for characterization of online information and users from Online Social Networks [19–21]. The semi-directive interview can be seen as a methodologically adequate technique to more deeply enquired entrepreneurs and managers regarding OI, as it allows collecting information of qualitative nature, through interaction with interviewees, in which the discourses, feelings, emotions, and contexts intersect together. Therefore, sentiment analysis of online interview documents (extensive analysis) combined with face-to-face interviews results in a methodological approach that enhances the interpretation framework.

3.1   Exploratory Analysis of Online Documents

3.1.1   Research Method Description

The research method followed in this phase involved several steps which are represented in Fig. 2. Firstly, we searched documents containing interviews regarding OI. Then these documents were downloaded to a local repository to be further checked and analyzed, and in the final steps subject to Text Mining and Sentiment Analysis.

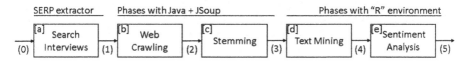

Fig. 2. Steps comprising the text mining and sentiment analysis of interviews.

The interviews were collected from online documents made available during the year 2018, with the search engine, "Google Search". We searched for documents of that year that contained the terms "open innovation" and "interview." This search performed in step (a) resulted in 18,093 URL links of potential interview documents.

In the next step (b), each site was visited, and its content downloaded and recorded in a local file. For this part, we developed a small Java application integrating the JSoup library [22] for extracting the documents' contents. However, after inspecting the content of some documents, we found that many of them did not correspond to interviews. Thus, it was also developed a filter for identifying only valid interview documents. This filter is composed of a regular expression which tracks sentences ending with a question mark. The rationale is that if each document arose as a result of a search with the keyword "interview," the odds of being a document with an interview is higher. If the document contains questions, then it must be an interview. After inspecting a sample of the downloaded documents, we verified that documents with at least five questions were interviews. To reduce false positive documents, we collected documents with at least ten questions inside. The next step included the elimination of "stop words" and the stemming of the documents' terms (step (c)) [23]. During the stemming transformation, if each yielded word did not belong to the dictionary, then we considered the original word, as we needed valid words for the sentiment analysis part. The remaining steps are synthesized in Table 1.

In steps (d) and (e), we relied on the "R" environment [24], for its good features on Text mining, including Sentiment Analysis. With R, we proceed to the determination of the document-term matrix, but its transformed form, using the "inverse document frequency" formula (Tf-idf), which reduces the importance of terms that are too common across the documents. Phase (e), corresponding to the sentiment analysis, was also performed within the R environment, using the scripts illustrated and described in [25].

Table 1. Description of steps involved in text mining and sentiment analysis

Inputs	Steps	Description
(0)		Keyword search: "open innovation" AND interview, for the year 2018
	(a)	Find documents with Google Search engine. Considering documents with at least ten questions
(1)		Set of URLs obtained with a SERP extractor
	(b)	Small Java App with JSoup that visits each URL and saves its content in a local filesystem. Non-English documents are eliminated
(2)		Collection of documents in a folder named "Corpus"
	(c)	Elimination of Stop words and stemming. Stemming of each word is considered only if the transformed term is still a word in the dictionary
(3)		Collection of documents in a folder named "Corpus"
	(d)	Download corpus; DTM determination "tidytext" and "tm" libraries inside R environment
(4)		Matrix dtm_tfidf
	(e)	Application of sentiment analysis
(5)		Plot sentiment analysis chart

3.1.2 Obtained Results

Figure 3 presents the chart obtained during sentiment analysis. An initial general interpretation suggests that there is a generally positive attitude towards OI.

On the positive side, such words as "capability", "patient", "award", "sustainability", "flexibility", "talent", "master" and "skill" match with the more frequent sentiments detected, followed by the term "trust", which corresponds to an important sentiment in collaboration. The other terms appearing on the positive side, namely "skills", "agility", "competitive", "intelligence" and "creativity" allow us to, in principle, confirm the kinds of attitudes, or mindset, related to open innovation, as portrayed in Sect. 2.2.

On the negative side, the sentiment analysis highlighted several terms that also meet the topics addressed in this work. The term "risk" is the most important element appearing on the negative sentiment analysis, which raises a question by itself. Why is risk the most cited element from the interviews? Considering that Sentiment Analysis of these interviews yields a more positive than negative tone, perhaps OI participants feel that in spite of the dangers, OI is a strategy that is worth to take. This result supports the argument that risk is an intrinsically major concern of OI. It also might mean that risk in OI deserves much more attention by researchers. Other terms that may also be tied to risk are "disruption" and "conflict", which are concerns that are known to increase the risk of Open Innovation partnerships failure.

The term disruption is interesting in this regard. Costumers benefit from "disruptive technology", which drive the creation of innovative products, so disruptiveness is seen a positive element. Researchers of innovation, and similarly in other areas, like to conceive innovation as a "disruptive phenomenon", so disruptiveness is seen in a more positive mood. However, companies may perceive "disruptive" events with more cautious eyes. We would say that "disruptive technologies" or similar situations may

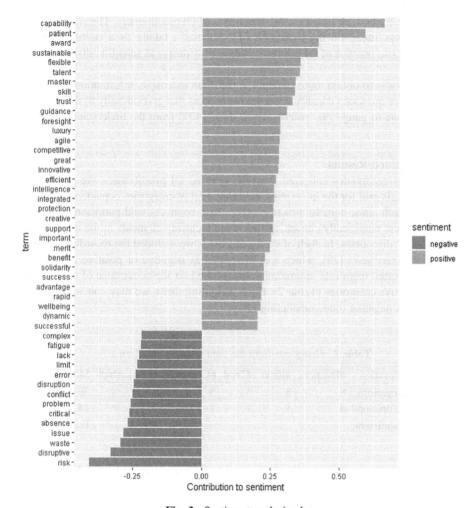

Fig. 3. Sentiment analysis plot

frequently cause both industrial and market shifts that companies may find threatening and detrimental for their business models. Therefore, from the companies point of view "disruptive" cases might be seen as negative.

3.2 Interviews with OI Practitioners

3.2.1 Methodological Steps

In the scope of empirical research, we complementarily conducted semi-directive interviews with three CEOs and two managers from four information technology (IT) companies. The interviews were carried out during March and April 2019. We defined several questions oriented to OI practices in companies' contexts (interview script). The collection of qualitative information from the interviewees' discourses allowed to complement the sentimental analysis and the construction of an interpretative framework based on the experience of OI practitioners. The way to reach companies was based on the technique of "snowball", taking as a starting point a company, whose practice of OI is already a case of widespread scientific dissemination [26].

Our goal was to obtain more in depth, rather than extensive, information regarding OI. Qualitative questions constitute a reflexive process that gives density to the analysis and allows one to gauge the "microscopic" details [27] from the understanding of OI practitioners.

3.2.2   Obtained Results

Based on the testimonies collected from the selected OI practitioners, we prepared a content analysis grid for the interviews, covering a set of categories considered relevant for our research aims, namely, practices, risk, trust, contracts, and partnerships. These categories were empirically chosen, as they were recurring elements in the interviewed practitioners' discourses. In each of these categories, we included the recording units of the various interviews [28], which we interpreted as negative or positive discourses, and we converted them into enumeration units based on the occurrence of the records in the respective categories (Table 2). From weighting them, we may conclude a more positive than negative tone considering OI.

Table 2. Categories from the semi-directive interviews

Open innovation	#Practices	#Risks	#Trust	#Contracts	#Partnerships	SCORE
Positive opinions	8	8	4	5	5	30
Negative opinions	4	5	2	1	2	14
Overall sentiment						Positive

In the remaining of this section, we present the more in-depth and richer insights provided by the interviewed OI practitioners.

Practices and Partnerships

From the analysis of the interviews, we obtained relevant information that allows deepening the aspect regarding the mindset of the participants in open innovation. One of the interviewees mentions that *"OI is a virtuous concept, enabler of various businesses, but that from concept to practice goes a great distance."* He added that *"we need to have a mindset for open innovation"*. There is a clear idea that practicing OI requires a specific form of thinking and a particular attitude. It means accepting the risk, vulnerability, and uncertainty.

OI is, in general, seen from a positive perspective, *"several initiatives fit into open innovation. We have an area dedicated to identifying possible partners, whether national or international. The fact that we open and share with other companies we all win. We are not going from scratch; we start from a more advanced level"*. But it is also said that *"they share little of the failures, which is inevitable and integral and essential for us to reach the part of success. It is a very great wealth. There are situations of contingency success"*.

Nevertheless, the experiences are successful; there are paths with advances and retreats until the final result. As the interviewee stresses, both negative and positive experiences are important and should be shared as they allow for joint learning to deal with the complexity of problems and solutions.

Risk, Trust, and Contracts

The OI practitioners' discourse points to different practices taking into account the structure of the company and the type of business. There is, however, a coincident narrative in the risk perspective. More risk requires more trust. And the idea that OI is risky is consensual. As the interviewee adds "*there is no innovation without risk*".

The words of the CEOs make us confirm that the relationship with the partners is essential to the existence of trust, as a way to minimize the risk. It is crucial that the development of the business takes place within a calculated risk framework, as one of the interviewees indicates, which allows for the establishment of commitments and guaranteeing the delivery of products/services by the expectations of the clients. "*When we go with other companies, we have more risk, in principle. We have a very close relationship, but we have no control. It is important to look at the risk to do the math and say is between 40 and 50.*"

Risk arises with a double face, the challenge of the business itself, and the business in the framework of an OI paradigm, and the risk that must be safeguarded in the relationship with partners. One of the aspects that are repeatedly underlined is precisely risk acceptance. Nevertheless, there are nuances in terms of risk in the interviewees' discourse. Important in the study of trust is the issue of risk. The border of trust can be defined by mistrust. It is the development of trust that lays the foundation for trusting one partner more than another and deciding the level of risk to which it is prudent to incur.

There are referred forms of contracting that define rules of understanding between the partners and with the customers regarding the sharing of intellectual property. As one of the interviewees says "*we sign agreements with all companies*".

There is, however, the feeling that more important than these contracts are the behavior of partners and the building of relationships of trust. "*We have a lot of memorandums of understanding (MoU) that are practically replicated from each other, but it's worth it.*" Another interviewee adds: "*It is important to have trusted partners to embrace the projects.*" In this way, risk containment through formal means (contracts) can be used as a device not to eliminate its exposure to risk, but to reduce exposure. As mentioned before, there is no OI without risk. In conclusion, creativity and pro-activity are characteristics that, in one way or another, refer to: we must go further, search for new paths, new methodologies, new approaches, and not be afraid to embrace new projects, ideally with partners in which we have trust, but when it does not happen, the stance is to go to the market to look for new partners to respond to new business.

4 Discussion and Conclusions

4.1 Summary of the Developed Work

In this paper, we present a research approach for exploring the mindset for risk in OI The approach involved the application of two specific methods: the first one was based on the application of "text mining" and sentiment analysis performed on documents containing interviews, which were provided online during the year 2018. The second method consisted of semi-directive interviews addressed to OI practitioners.

4.2 Critical Analysis of the Application of the Two Methods

Based on the results of both research methods, it was emphasized that participants take a more positive than a negative stance towards OI, which is consistent with the theoretical and empirical manifestations mentioned in the literature.

From the analysis of interview documents available online, the positive side of sentiment analysis includes the trust term, which represents a crucial attitude in collaboration and OI. The risk appeared as the term that most contributes to the negative side of the sentiment chart.

From the CEOs interviews, the main idea that stands out is a relatively strong will to engage in innovation, although with safeguards that each practitioner applies as a way to mitigate risk. But they embrace it, as one stated, "There is no innovation without risk".

These results give a better understanding of the main mindset, positive and negative perspectives, regarding OI, from which it was possible to determine that risk plays an important role. There is also an apparent dissonance between the importance of risk in OI and the emergence in their research by academics.

Therefore, the combination of both research approaches and the literature confirm the idea that entrepreneurs should display OI enhancer mindsets, which maximize the success, like being open, trust partners, taking risks, adapt to changes, challenge tradition, and collaborate.

As a final remark, despite the theoretical character associated with the OI, it is through the interpretation of social practices, incorporating positive and negative occurrences, that the very concept of open-innovation achieves greater conceptual maturity.

We identified potential lines of research for future work. One such line consists of exploring the trust versus risk dichotomy that was recurrent in the results provided from both research methods. Although a more challenging goal, we also aim to develop work to integrate the OI mindset concept in risk assessment and into management processes.

Acknowledgments. A special thanks to A-to-Be, Do iT Lean, Fordesi and MakeWise companies for the valuable contributions for the performed research.

This work has been partially supported by Interuniversity Center for the History of Science and Technology (CIUHCT) (Portuguese FCT-PEST program UID/HIS/00286/2019) Center of Technology and Systems (CTS) – Uninova, (Portuguese FCT-PEST program UID/EEA/00066/2019), and UNIDEMI - Research and Development Unit for Mechanical and Industrial Engineering (Portuguese FCT-PEST program UID/EMS/00667/2019).

References

1. Chesbrough, H.: Managing open innovation. Res.-Technol. Manag. **47**(1), 23–26 (2004). https://doi.org/10.1080/08956308.2004.11671604
2. Felin, T., Zenger, T.R.: Closed or open innovation? Problem solving and the governance choice. Res. Policy **43**(5), 914–925 (2014)
3. Godin, B., Vinck, D.: Introduction: innovation – from the forbidden to a cliché. In: Godin, B., Vinck, D. (eds.) Critical Studies of Innovation: Alternative Approaches to the Pro-Innovation Bias. Edward Elgar Publishing (2017)
4. Sveiby, K.: Unattended consequences of innovation. In: Godin, B., Vinck, D. (eds.) Critical Studies of Innovation: Alternative Approaches to the Pro-innovation Bias. Edward Elgar Publishing (2017)
5. Rosas, J., Macedo, P., Tenera, A., Abreu, A., Urze, P.: Risk assessment in open innovation networks. In: Camarinha-Matos, Luis M., Bénaben, F., Picard, W. (eds.) PRO-VE 2015. IAICT, vol. 463, pp. 27–38. Springer, Cham (2015). https://doi.org/10.1007/978-3-319-24141-8_3
6. Rosas, J., Urze, P., Tenera, A., Abreu, A., Camarinha-Matos, L.M.: Exploratory study on risk management in open innovation. In: Camarinha-Matos, L.M., Afsarmanesh, H., Fornasiero, R. (eds.) PRO-VE 2017. IAICT, vol. 506, pp. 527–540. Springer, Cham (2017). https://doi.org/10.1007/978-3-319-65151-4_47
7. Chesbrough, H.: Everything You Need to Know About Open Innovation (2011). https://www.forbes.com/sites/henrychesbrough/2011/03/21/everything-you-need-to-know-about-open-innovation/#741310f175f4. Accessed 20 Apr 2019
8. Vinck, D.: Learning thanks to innovation failure. In: Godin, B., Vinck, D. (eds.) Critical Studies of Innovation: Alternative Approaches to the Pro-innovation Bias. Edward Elgar Publishing (2017)
9. Martin, B.R.: Innovation studies: an emerging agenda. In: Fagerberg, J., Martin, B.R., Andersen, E.S. (eds.) Innovation Studies: Evolution and Future Challenges, Oxford (2013)
10. A growth strategy for the digital age: the key is Open Innovation, Fujistu (2018). https://www.fujitsu.com/pt/vision/insights/201805event/. Accessed 20 Apr 2018
11. Björling, M.E.: 5 key steps to creating an innovation mindset. https://www.ericsson.com/en/blog/2018/5/5-key-steps-to-creating-an-innovation-mindset. Accessed 10 Apr 2018
12. NP 4457: Gestão da Inovação, Desenvolvimento e Inovação (IDI)/Management of Research, Development and Innovation (RDI): Requisitos do sistema de gestão IDI/Management system requirements of RDI activities, IPQ Technical Committee CT169, Instituto Português da Qualidade (IPQ) (2007)
13. NP 4458: Gestão da Inovação, Desenvolvimento e Inovação (IDI)/ Management of Research, Development and Innovation (RDI): Requisitos de um projeto de gestão IDI/ Requirements for RDI project, IPQ Technical Committee CT169, Instituto Português da Qualidade (IPQ) (2007)
14. IEC 31010: Risk management – Risk assessment techniques, Technical Committee, ISO/TC 262, ISO/IC (2009)
15. Castellion, G., Markham, S.K.: Perspective: new product failure rates: influence of argumentum ad populum and self-interest. J. Prod. Innov. Manag. **30**(5), 976–979 (2013)
16. Simoons, P.: The 80% rule of business partnerships (2013). https://www.petersimoons.com/2013/07/the-80-percent-rule/. Accessed 25 Mar 2017
17. Fisher, A.: Why most innovations are great big failures (2014). http://fortune.com/2014/10/07/innovation-failure/. Accessed 20 Feb 2017

18. Martinez, M.G. (ed.): Open Innovation in the Food and Beverage Industry. Elsevier, Amsterdam (2013). Hewitt-Dundas, N., Roper, S.: Exploring market failures in open innovation. Int. Small Bus. J. (2017). https://doi.org/10.1177/2f0266242617696347
19. Liu, B.: Sentiment analysis and subjectivity. Handb. Nat. Lang. Process. 2(2010), 627–666 (2010)
20. Farhadloo, M., Rolland, E.: Fundamentals of sentiment analysis and its applications. In: Pedrycz, W., Chen, S.-M. (eds.) Sentiment Analysis and Ontology Engineering. SCI, vol. 639, pp. 1–24. Springer, Cham (2016). https://doi.org/10.1007/978-3-319-30319-2_1
21. Kaushik, A., Naithani, S.: A study on sentiment analysis: methods and tools. Int. J. Sci. Res. (IJSR) 4, 287–291 (2014)
22. jsoup: Java HTML Parser (2018). https://jsoup.org/. Accessed 20 Mar 2019
23. Aggarwal, C.C., Zhai, C.: A survey of text clustering algorithms. In: Aggarwal, C., Zhai, C. (eds.) Mining Text Data, pp. 77–128. Springer, Heidelberg (2012)
24. R: A Language and Environment for Statistical Computing (2019). https://www.r-project.org/
25. Silge, J., Robinson, D.: Text Mining with R: A Tidy Approach. O'Reilly Media, Inc. (2017) https://www.tidytextmining.com/dtm.html. Accessed 01 Apr 2019
26. Urze, P., Abreu, A.: Knowledge transfer assessment in a co-innovation network. In: Camarinha-Matos, L.M., Xu, L., Afsarmanesh, H. (eds.) PRO-VE 2012. IAICT, vol. 380, pp. 605–615. Springer, Heidelberg (2012). https://doi.org/10.1007/978-3-642-32775-9_60
27. Geertz, C.: The Interpretation of Cultures: Selected Essays. Basic Books, New York (1973)
28. Bardin, L.: Análise de conteúdo. Edições, Lisboa (2008)

Developing a Green Product-Based in an Open Innovation Environment. Case Study: Electrical Vehicle

Ricardo Santos[1,3]([✉]) [iD], Antonio Abreu[2,3] [iD], and Vitor Anes[3] [iD]

[1] GOVCOPP - University of Aveiro, Aveiro, Portugal
ricardosimoessantos84@ua.pt
[2] CTS Uninova, Faculdade de Ciências E Tecnologia,
Universidade Nova de Lisboa, Lisbon, Portugal
[3] ISEL- Instituto Superior de Engenharia de Lisboa,
Instituto Politécnico de Lisboa, Lisbon, Portugal

Abstract. In order to respond to new market challenges, companies have attempted to develop open innovation processes with other organizations such as research centers and higher-education institutions. However, it is also frequently mentioned by several companies that the lack of models that support open innovation in a sustainable way, involving higher-education institutions or research centers and companies in the context of a collaborative environment, is an obstacle for a wider acceptance of this way of promoting innovation processes. Starting with some discussion about innovation models in a collaborative context, this paper discusses the developed of an electric vehicle based on an open-innovation approach among several companies and a Portuguese university.

Keywords: Business sustainability · Open innovation ·
New product development · Collaborative networks

1 Introduction

Currently, there are even more electric vehicles in the market, mainly due to the competitiveness levels achieved, as well as the increasingly affordable acquisition costs, coupled in turn, with a greater autonomy and energy efficiency, placing therefore this vehicle, in a position, even more closed by the internal combustion vehicles.

The increasingly need of competitiveness by the companies, as well as the need to expand their competences, know-how and create substantial competitive advantage, lead them, to form alliances, partnerships and collaborative networks with outsiders in order to overcome potential capacity limitations, knowledge gaps, promoting therefore, innovative and dynamic relationships, useful for future projects for instance [1–3].

Open Innovation (OI), allows to distribute innovation across organizational boundaries, by using collaborative networks and a wide range of external actors and sources to help them to achieve and sustain innovation and competitiveness as well [4, 5].

© IFIP International Federation for Information Processing 2019
Published by Springer Nature Switzerland AG 2019
L. M. Camarinha-Matos et al. (Eds.): PRO-VE 2019, IFIP AICT 568, pp. 115–127, 2019.
https://doi.org/10.1007/978-3-030-28464-0_11

However, there seems to be a lack of evidence of successfully applied models, to support the way that the organizations, uses OI, to develop new products or services in the collaborative network's context, especially regarding the electrical vehicle's development.

In this work it's presented an Open Innovation model to support the decision makers of the collaborative network, by planning the development of a green product such an electric vehicle in an open innovation context.

The proposed approach combines collaborative networks, regarding different partnerships (suppliers, government, university, etc.) with a model of innovation management, regarding New Products Development (NPD) concept, in order to accelerate the development of an electrical vehicle, used as a case study here.

Evidences of perceived benefits in this case study, and regarding OI context, will also be presented in this work.

Therefore, and based on what was referred before, the research question is:

How to support the green product development in an open innovation context?

2 Literature Review

Various literature streams are synthetized here, in order to highlight the multidisciplinary approaches regarding open innovation (OI), including OI models.

The OI, can be defined as "the use of purposive inflows and outflows of knowledge to accelerate internal innovation, and expand the markets for external use of innovation, respectively" [7].

On the center of this definition is the triangular relationship among outflow (inside-out), inflow (outside-in) and coupled (both directions) open innovation process [8]. This concept has received wide acceptance on literature [9], as well as some criticism, by some authors like [10].

Authors, like [12], defines OI as "a model using a wide range of external actors and sources to help them to achieve and sustain innovation".

OI is also based on collaborative relationships-organizational alliances and partnerships [13] who are willing to work together by sharing ideas, know-how, experiences and knowledge to generate value, by achieving innovative outcomes [14].

In line with this concept, authors such as [15] perceive three levels of collaborative innovation, namely: management of interorganizational collaboration process, management of the overall innovation process and creation of a new collaborative knowledge.

To expand their competences, their know-how and achieve substantial competitive advantage, organizations share the need to form alliances, partnerships and collaborative networks with outsiders to overcome potential capacity limitations, knowledge gaps, develop the ability to jointly work into new projects and promote [1].

There are several open innovation models that can be found on literature [16, 17].

One of the OI models most used, is the InnoCentive Model [10]. Created in 2001, InnoCentive is a model of OI, supported in a web platform that bears the same name [18]. This model consists of six steps that begins with the identification of problems and ideas, the formulation of a challenge, the specification of intellectual property agreements, the publication of the challenge, the evaluation of solutions and an award to finalize with the transfer of intellectual property [18, 19].

Other model found on literature, more recent and widely used, is created by Procter & Gamble P & G, which is defined as "Connect+Develop" [17].

This model works in both directions inwards and outward, and ranges from registered trademarks to packaging, from marketing models to engineering, and from commercial services to design [20].

The chain-linked model (CLM), developed by Kline and Rosenberg in 1985 [19] is an attempt to describe complexities in the innovation process.

This model is based on a concept called "*systemism*" [20], which considers innovation as a system. *Systemism,* allows the possibility to imagine different scenarios; high *versus* low research intensity innovation, routine *versus* breakthrough innovation, methodic *versus* empirical innovation, local *versus* global multinational level innovation, making CLM an important innovation model widely used today [17].

Although, the existence of an academic consensus, regarding the value of this model [17, 21], some authors propose that such model, can be improved to be more contextualized with other contexts, such as open innovation [21].

3   Proposed Open Innovation Model

The present open innovation model, proposed here, was designed with the aim to serve companies of any size and business, in the transition to an Open Innovation (OI) context.

The purpose of this approach is to contribute with a tool, to support the innovation management and the information associated.

The proposed model, was based on four assumptions, as follows:

- Generalize the classical and very influential model of chain linking from Kline and Rosenberg model [19];
- Accommodate the concepts of the 4th Edition of the Oslo Manual [22];
- Consider innovation in both industry assets (tangible and intangible) and regarding low-tech companies as well as high-tech ones;
- Innovation results from a chain of interactions between the knowledge from OI's network and the organizations, regarding its external environment;

The proposed model, besides incorporating the assumptions referred above, also intends to structure the process of developing a product/service in a collaborative context, which is supported by a set of knowledge, necessary for its development.

This type of knowledge, needed to reach product/service innovation, is shared with a set of Open Innovation Network (OIN) partners (Pn), which makes the collaboration network, necessary for the development of the product/service in question.

In general, the model can be divided into four different groups of components; Stages of product development (Sn), Interfaces (In), Knowledge Interface groups (KIn) and Process groups (Pr).

These components, can be briefly described, as follows:

- **Stages of product development (Sn)** – Consists in a set of monitor indicators, regarding the product/service development, to support the project management;
- **Interfaces (In)** – Divided into 3 groups, works as channels in which the transfer of knowledge, takes place between the OI's network and the external environment (EE) of the open innovation network, through the interaction between the different partners (Pn) and the corresponding External Collaborators (ECn).
  For each interface, are assigned a set of Partners (Pn), which are responsible to establish and control the interactions between Pn and ECn;
- **Knowledge interface groups (KIn)** – The knowledge changed between Pn and ECn, are organized into 3 types of knowledge (Kin), regarding the correspondent interface (In) (see Table 1). The mechanism of such transfer, is exemplified on Fig. 1;
- **Process groups (Pr)** - Is where the innovations will be applied to develop the product and it results from the transfer and development of different knowledge types (Kn), occurred between the collaborative network partners (Pn), and also between Pn and the External Collaborators (ECn), i.e. from the outside of OI's network (Fig. 1).

On Fig. 1, are presented the four components referred before.

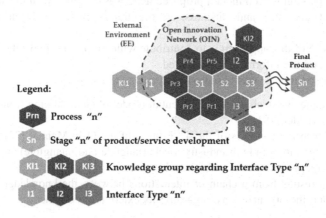

Fig. 1. Model components

Based on what was referred before, and through Fig. 1, the model's components, can better described, as it follows:

- KI1 - Existing market knowledge (needs preferences values)
- KI2 - Existing Organizational Knowledge
- KI3 - Existing scientific and technological knowledge
- Pr1 - Potential Market Assessment, Economic Viability Assessment, Selection of ideas Projects

- Pr2 - Invention, Basic Sketches, Service Design
- Pr3 - Detailed Drawing
- Pr4 - Redesign Demonstration or Test and Production
- Pr5 - Commercialization or Implementation
- I1- Technology watch/Technology forecast
- I2- Market research
- I3- Knowledge research

In general terms, the innovation process usually starts from a potential market perspective. The activities, regarding interfaces I1, I2 and I3, allows the emergence of ideas to satisfy new market needs, not only by improving products or processes, but also by improving the open innovations' organization to better market the products and reach consumers (Pr1).

The ideas, with technological and economic viability, are then selected and give rise to innovation. The invention, product design or service design, are the first step of the project (Pr2), followed by the detailed design (Pr3), in order to better specify the product/service.

After the Redesign Demonstration or Test and Production process group (Pr4), the process of innovation continues, until the commercialization or implementation of its final result is achieved, which can be related to a product, process, marketing or even organizational (Pr4).

Interactions may occur between the different processes of the chain, since that the innovation does not follow a linear path.

The knowledge regarding each process (KnPrn), needed to develop innovation projects, may be internally available through the different partners (Pn) of the open innovation network, or be obtained abroad through the External Environment (EE) between Pn and the EE's External Collaborators (ECn).

Regarding the knowledge transfer mechanisms, there are 2 types used in this model.

In Fig. 2, are presented two examples of how these two types of mechanisms occur.

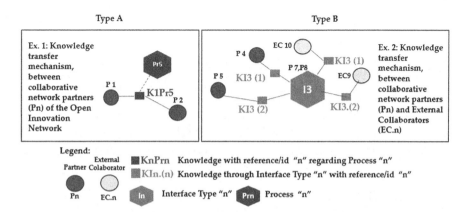

Fig. 2. The two types of knowledge's transferred mechanisms used (Examples): A–Between Partners, B– Between Partners (Pn) and External Collaborators (EC.n)

Through Fig. 2, and more specifically, through Example 1 (Ex.1), it can be seen an interaction between 2 open innovation's partners, where the knowledge (K1Pr5), related to Process 5 (Pr5), is transferred between P1 and P2.

In the same figure, and regarding Example 2 (Ex.2), there are some differences, since between each knowledge transfer, there is an interface (In), which controls and monitories, each knowledge transfer, regarding to group Kn, which is related to In. This control occurs in order to manage the knowledge transfer, according to the project needs, promoting therefore efficiency.

On Ex.2, there are two interactions, that can be observed; one, between P5 and EC.9 (KI3(2)) and the other one, between P4 and EC.10 (KI3(1)).

In more detail, and based on Fig. 1, the model assumes the following components, listed on Table 1:

Table 1. Components, regarding the proposed model

Knowledge interface (KIn)	KIn(n)	Actors involved
KI1 - Existing market knowledge (needs preferences values)	KI1(1)..KI1(n)	P1..Pn| EC1..ECn
KI2 - Existing Organizational Knowledge	KI2(1)..KI2(n)	P1..Pn| EC1..ECn
KI3 - Existing scientific and technological knowledge	KI3(1)..KI3(n)	P1..Pn| EC1..ECn
Process (Prn)	KnPrn	Actors involved
Pr1 - Potential Market Assessment, Economic Viability Assessment, Selection of ideas Projects	K1Pr1..KnPr1	P1,..,Pn
Pr2 - Invention, Basic Sketches, Service Design	K1Pr2..KnPr2	P1,..,Pn
Pr3 - Detailed Drawing	K1Pr3..KnPr3	P1,..,Pn
Pr4 - Redesign Demonstration or Test and Production	K1Pr4..KnPr4	P1,..,Pn
Pr5 - Commercialization or Implementation	K1Pr5..KnPr5	P1,..,Pn

Table 1 allows to assign, each knowledge to be transferred, to a set of actors, involved in the correspondent process. The same, can be preform through Table 2, and regarding each models' interface (I1, I2, I3), where a set of partners, can assign the task (isolated or in group) of managing each interface, as innovation managers.

Table 2. Assignment of innovation managers

Interfaces (In)	Assignment of innovation managers
I1- Technology watch/technology forecast	P1, .., Pn
I2- Market research	P1, .., Pn
I3- Knowledge research	P1, .., Pn

Both tables allows to gain control over the process of product/service development, not only between the Partners (Pn) of Open Innovation Network (OIN), but also between Partners (Pn) from OIN and the External Collaborators (ECn), from the External Environment (EE), by identifying the actors/organizations, involved on each knowledge transfer.

Based on what was referred before, the model can be therefore integrated in an open innovation context (Fig. 3).

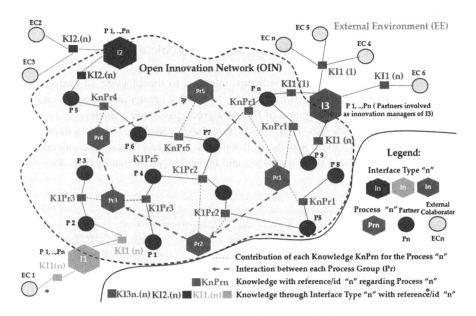

Fig. 3. Proposed model, integrated in open innovation context

Based on what was referred before, The knowledge required and not obtainable by the external collaborators (ECn), will have to be developed and/or transferred, between the Partners (Pn), of the open innovation network.

According to Fig. 3, each knowledge transferred (KnPrn) between the Partners (Pn), is a contribution to the Process Group (Prn), which is one of the 5 Process Groups, that composes the linked chain, necessary to develop the product or service, which follows a sequence order. This last concept is based on the work of Kline and Rosenberg [18].

The whole development product/service's process is composed by a set of Process Groups, that composes the chain, namely: Pr1, Pr2, Pr3, Pr4 and ending in Pr5.

For product/service's continues improving, this chain can continue to Process Group 1 (Pr1), from Pr5 directly, until the product/service objectives are accomplished.

The knowledge required and obtainable by the external collaborators (ECn), will have to be transferred between the Partners (Pn) and the correspondent External Collaborators (EC.n) involved in the process.

The knowledge to be transferred on this context (Kin.(n)), will be transferred from the respective Interface (In), which will be managed by the Partners (Pn) of the network (isolated or in group) assigned for his function.

Regarding the three interfaces referred above, they don't have to exist simultaneously, and they don't have to constitute disjoint entities as well.

In this sense, the product development process, occurs in a collaboration context, by incorporating the different innovations, resulted from the knowledge transferred, associated within the various network partners and external collaborators as well, resulting thus, into a final product/service.

4   Application to a Case Study: Electric Vehicle

A Portuguese company of electric vehicles, intended to manufacture an electric passenger vehicle (2 seats), energy efficient, safer, and with a greater autonomy, in order to be available in the market segment of two-seat green passenger vehicles.

The insufficient know-how for its production, have leaded the company to produce the vehicle in collaboration with several entities, including industries, universities, Research & Development (R&D) centers, and consultancy companies (Fig. 4).

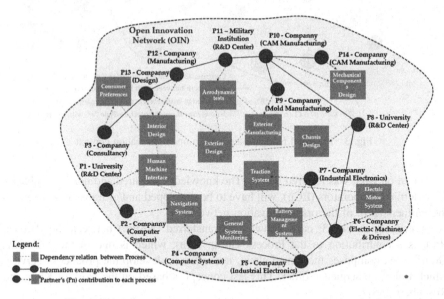

Fig. 4. Diversity of partners and respective competencies involved

It was created 14 partnerships, involved industries from different areas, as well as two R & D centers (from two Portuguese universities) and a Portuguese military institution) with the aim to develop and test the new components of the car. It was also intended to manufacture a vehicle that would exploit the concept of reverse trike, i.e. a vehicle having 3 wheels on its constitution-base.

The partnerships, established with the two R & D centers, have consisted on a interdisciplinary involvement of fellow students and other researchers from several areas of engineering (Electrical, Mechanics, Computers and Electronics), where there was an intervention in several disciplinary areas, regarding the vehicle's development (Fig. 4).

The existing competences, together with those resulting from the interaction with the different partners, have allowed the development of a set of other competences necessary for the development of the vehicle.

Still in the scope of the development of the vehicle, there were concerns with the communication abroad, namely with the marketing and sales areas, with all support being assumed by two consulting companies in Marketing and Advertising (Fig. 4).

The model application is presented on Table 3.

Table 3. Model application (through Table 1)

Knowledge (K)	KIn(n)	Actors involved
K1	KI1(1) - Market trends	P5, EC7
	KI1(6) - Consumer preferences	P5, EC7
K2	KI2(1) - Assembly method	P11, EC2
	KI2(9) - Innovation management method	P4, EC7
K3	KI3(1)- New Software to develop HMI system	P2, EC10
	.... -	....
	KI3(72) - New Protocol Communication (car lights, error code diagnosis)	P1, EC12
Process (Pr)	*KIn(n)*	*Actors involved*
Pr1	K01Pr1 – Market Annalys (from: K1C1 & K1C2)	P1, P2, P3
	K02Pr1 – Innovation Management (from: K2C2)	P11, P13
	K03Pr1 – Systems Engineering (from: K2C2)	P2, P12
Pr2	K01Pr2 – Traction development system	P8, P7
	K02Pr2 – HMI development (from: K3C1)	P2, P11
	..... -	....
	K87Pr2 – GPS Navigation System	P4
Pr3	K01Pr3 – System components design	P5, P8
	K02Pr3 – Chassis' design	P2, P5, P9
	..... -	....
	K23Pr3 – Interior design	P1, P7
Pr4	K01Pr4 - Assembling methods	P5, P7
	K02Pr4 – Aerodynamics tests	P2, P3
	... -	....
	K34Pr4 – Vehicle performance tests	P9, P13
Pr5	K01Pr5 – Marketing &Sales	P5, P6
	K02Pr5 -	....
	K12Pr5 - Logistics	P10, P14
Interfaces (I)	*Assignment of innovation managers*	
I1	P5, P8	
I2	P3, P10	
I3	P7, P11	

Through Table 3, it can be seen, the relationship between the knowledge transferred and each process group (Prn).

Based on the model proposed before, the partners involved in the project, are presented in Fig. 5, as well as the knowledge transfers preformed.

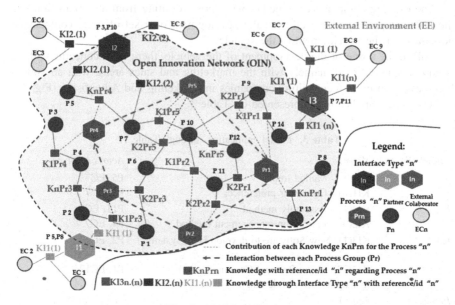

Fig. 5. Model application

The partners (Pn) were also mapped in this methodology, which has helped the innovation managers, regarding I1, I2 and I3, to identify the necessities of in terms of knowledge, associated to each process group (Prn).

The performed tests, regarding the development of the vehicle, have allowed feedback, regarding the components developed by the partner companies, in order to improve them later. One of these tests have involved the aerodynamics of the vehicle, carried out in partnership with a military institution, to optimize the aerodynamic coefficient of the vehicle.

Other tests carried out, was related to the vehicle's battery system, whose performance allowed adjustments in the thermal behavior of the batteries with the load management system developed between the partner companies of the area and the partner universities. These partnerships, have proved to be crucial to the good performance of the vehicle, allowing both companies to gain insight into the development of LiFePO4 (lithium phosphate) batteries for other applications.

Benefits from Collaboration

The benefits of collaboration can be better understood, by presenting 2 scenarios, regarding the development of the electrical vehicle, through the company which have promoted the project, namely; 1, Isolated context and 2, Collaborative context.

On first scenario (isolated context), there is a lack of knowledge, needed by the company as well as other assets, to develop the product, resulting therefore in additional costs, including time. This scenario would delay the development of some specific systems, such as the car battery system for example, which was design specifically for that vehicle, given its specificities.

Regarding the second scenario (collaborative context), the company had for example, the possibility to learn from the development of the chassis of the car, as well as the other company and the R&D center involved, which have allowed, to produce new knowledge for both partners, and at the same time, accelerate the chassis process design, given the proximity between both partners, to better discuss the project.

In this sense, and given the knowledge transferred between the different partners of the network, as well as the knowledge transferred from the outside to inside of the network, there was additional competences achieved by all the partners involved, which would be harder, or even impossible in the "isolated context" scenario.

Additionally, and given the proximity between the collaboration partners, the product's time-to-market, was also reduced, regarding the collaboration context, which has allowed the developed product to be more competitive into the segment market of two-seat green passenger vehicles, given the pioneer's strategic advantage.

5   Conclusions and Further Work

In this work, it was presented an approach to manage innovation in collaborative context (Open Innovation). A case study was used for its application, by presenting a collaboration network, originally created by a company to produce a green product: an electrical vehicle. The advantages in recurring to Open Innovation, are showed in this work. One of them was cost reduction, regarding the competences, needed to the product developed. Given the collaboration context, the product time-to-market, was also reduced, allowing the company (promoter) to be more competitive in this market segment. The proposal model, proposed and applied in this work, was based on a model existed in literature, although adapted to the collaborative context.

The approach presented here, has allowed to map the partners, involved in this project, as well as the competences needed to develop the final product, by distinguish the competences associated to the internal partners, from the competences associated to the external ones. Based on these last ones, and regarding the collaborative context, it was possible to developed additional competences for every partner of the network.

Given the benefits showed in this work, the approach proposed here, could be applied into other industries, although, and besides the adjustments to be made, there is a need of systematize the external knowledge, i.e., the knowledge group, from the outside of the network, that will be created by the external research, to be applied on network.

Acknowledgments. This work was partially supported by FCT, through CTS, project UID/EEA/00066/2019.

References

1. Pisano, G.P., Verganti, R.: Which kind of collaboration is right for you? Harvard Bus. Rev. **86**, 78–86 (2008)
2. Camarinha-Matos, L.M., Afsarmanesh, H., Abreu, A.: Targeting major new trends. In: Camarinha-Matos, L.M., Afsarmanesh, H. (eds.) Collaborative Networked Organizations. Springer, Boston (2004). https://doi.org/10.1007/1-4020-7833-1_8
3. Urze, P., Abreu, A.: System thinking to understand networked innovation. In: Camarinha-Matos, Luis M., Afsarmanesh, H. (eds.) PRO-VE 2014. IAICT, vol. 434, pp. 327–335. Springer, Heidelberg (2014). https://doi.org/10.1007/978-3-662-44745-1_32
4. Urze, P., Abreu, A.: Circulation of knowledge in a co-innovation network: an assessment approach. In: Camarinha-Matos, Luis M., Scherer, Raimar J. (eds.) PRO-VE 2013. IAICT, vol. 408, pp. 103–110. Springer, Heidelberg (2013). https://doi.org/10.1007/978-3-642-40543-3_11
5. Abreu, A., Camarinha-Matos, Luis M.: An approach to measure social capital in collaborative networks. In: Camarinha-Matos, Luis M., Pereira-Klen, A., Afsarmanesh, H. (eds.) PRO-VE 2011. IAICT, vol. 362, pp. 29–40. Springer, Heidelberg (2011). https://doi.org/10.1007/978-3-642-23330-2_4
6. Enkel, E., Gassmann, O., Chesbrough, H.: Open R&D and open innovation: exploring the phenomenon. R&D Manag. **39**, 311–316 (2009)
7. Huizingh, E.: Open innovation: state of the art and future perspectives. Technovation. **31**, 2–9 (2011)
8. Linstone, H.A.: Comment on "is open innovation a field of study or a communication barrier to theory development"? Technovation **30**, 556 (2010)
9. Trott, P., Hartmann, D.A.P.: Why open innovation is old wine in new bottles international. J. Innov. Manag. **13**, 715–736 (2009)
10. Slowinski, G., Sagal, W.: Good practices in open innovation. Technol. Manag. **53**, 38–45 (2010)
11. Chatenier, E., Verstegen, M.A.A.J., Biemans, A.J.H., Mulder, M., Omta, F.W.S.O.: Identification of competencies for professionals in open innovation teams. R&D Manag. **40**, 271 (2010)
12. Adler, K.: Social capital: prospect for a new concept. Acad. Manag. Rev. **27**(1), 17–40 (2002)
13. Urze, P., Abreu, A.: Knowledge transfer assessment in a co-innovation network. In: Camarinha-Matos, Luis M., Xu, L., Afsarmanesh, H. (eds.) PRO-VE 2012. IAICT, vol. 380, pp. 605–615. Springer, Heidelberg (2012). https://doi.org/10.1007/978-3-642-32775-9_60
14. Urze, P., Abreu, A.: Mapping patterns of co-innovation networks. In: Afsarmanesh, H., Camarinha-Matos, Luis M., Lucas Soares, A. (eds.) PRO-VE 2016. IAICT, vol. 480, pp. 241–252. Springer, Cham (2016). https://doi.org/10.1007/978-3-319-45390-3_21
15. Abreu, A., Urze, P.: System thinking shaping innovation ecosystems. Open Eng. **6**, 418–425 (2016)
16. Innocentive. https://www.innocentive.com/
17. Galeano, C.P., Gaviria, P.A.: Open innovation models, a literature review with a focus on SMEs. In: 2016 11th Iberian Conference on Information Systems and Technologies, pp. 1–13. Las Palmas (2016)
18. Proctor & Gamble: Connect and Development. https://www.pgconnectdevelop.com/pg-connection-portal/ctx/noauth/PortalHome.do

19. Kline, S.J., Rosenberg, N.: An overview of innovation. In: Landau, R., Rosenberg, N. (eds.) The Positive Sum Strategy: Harnessing Technology for Economic Growth, pp. 275–305. National Academy Press, Washington (1986)
20. Micaëlli, J.-P., Forest, J., Coatanéa, E..: How to improve Kline and Rosenberg's chain-linked model of innovation: building blocks and diagram-based languages. J. Innov. Econ. Manag. **3**, 59–77 (2014)
21. Forrester, J.: Principles of Systems. Wright Allen, Cambridge (1967)
22. OECD/Eurostat: Oslo Manual 2018: Guidelines for Collecting, Reporting and Using Data on Innovation, 4th edn. The Measurement of Scientific, Technological and Innovation Activities. OECD Publishing. Paris/Eurostat, Luxembourg (2018)

Commute Green! The Potential of Enterprise Social Networks for Ecological Mobility Concepts

Christian Zinke-Wehlmann[✉] and Julia Friedrich[✉]

Institute for Applied Informatics (InfAI), Gordelerring 9,
04109 Leipzig, Germany
{zinke, friedrich}@infai.org

Abstract. The paper discusses the potential of collaborative networks (CN) to support eco-friendly commuting and create ecological benefits. It therefore develops framework conditions within the concept of social business. The objective is to show up solutions to reduce air pollution, frustration, stress caused by rush hour traffic related to the inflexible working hours. Therefore, relevant social business framework conditions to support eco-friendly behavior have been identified. As a result, the paper shows how social business can combine digitally driven empowerment of workers and corporate responsibility for human and environment. It points out the potential for ecological as well as for social benefits.

Keywords: Social business · Enterprise social network ·
Ecological mobility concepts · Sustainable commute · Gamification

1   Introduction

The success of social network technology and digital collaboration leads to a transformation of work [1–3]. This transformation concerns internal communication and collaboration processes [4, 5] like knowledge exchange [6] as well as external marketing activities [7] and business innovation processes [8, 9]. Moreover, the popularity of social media and social software that allow every participant to be heard and every voice to matter lead to a transformation of workers' self-conception [10, 11]. Concurrently to this, in the times of raising awareness for climate change [12, 13] people start or intensify the reconsideration of their own lifestyle[1] which is particularly apparent in the popularity of the Fridays for future (FFF) movement [14, 15]. Increasing pollution and politically driven debates like the regulation or restriction of diesel vehicles in European countries [16] bring the idea of a (personal) ecological footprint [17, 18] into focus.

In the sense of corporate responsibility for human and environment, a modern employer is expected to take these idealistic values of his employees into account. Moreover, the so-called "war for talents" [19] puts high pressure on companies to

---

[1] Green consumption [16, 17], veganism [18, 19] or sustainable living [20] represent the growing environmental awareness and can be understood as a modern lifestyle forms.

© IFIP International Federation for Information Processing 2019
Published by Springer Nature Switzerland AG 2019
L. M. Camarinha-Matos et al. (Eds.): PRO-VE 2019, IFIP AICT 568, pp. 128–139, 2019.
https://doi.org/10.1007/978-3-030-28464-0_12

create attractive work environments and to respond to the needs of their employees in the spirit of the new work concept [20]. The combination of a digitally driven empowerment of workers and the sense for ecological issues gives rise to new demands on companies. Moreover, in accordance to the new work concept [20], these individual and internal attitudes towards sustainability and environmental awareness need to be consistent.

The idea of the research project SB: digital, where this work is conducted, is to meet these modern work requirements by creating an added value for workers and companies through the concept of social business [21]. Within the context of the project, social business is understood as a strategy and framework whose application is linked to the generation of a social, ecological and economic benefit as a primary goal from the use of social or collaborative networks (CNs), e.g. enterprise social networks, virtual organizations or virtual enterprises [1]. Thereof, the main research question of our work is: How can Social Business create framework conditions for a sustainable support of ecological commute behavior?

2   Methodology

In order to address the research question on how social business can support environmental-friendly commute behavior, we have chosen a design-oriented approach [22]. The presented results need to be understood as conceptual work and have not yet been tested due to the not yet completed implementation phase. According to Peffers [22], who developed a generative procedure for computer science, there are six essential steps in design science: (I) problem explanation, (II) development of solution approach, (III) artifact design and implementation, (IV) demonstration, (V) evaluation (and initiation of another design cycle, if necessary) and (VI) result communication. While we have already described the problem (I), the objective of this work is to conceptualize (II) and design (III) a solution approach in order to analyze the potential of CN and to identify relevant social business framework conditions to support eco-friendly behavior. These framework conditions are inspired by the Human-Technology-Organization analyze framework [23, 24] and the analysis of socio-technical systems [25]. The main idea is to analyze the influencing and conductive factors and conditions for eco-friendly behavior within organizations/CNs from three main perspectives: the organizational, the human and the technological. The exemplarily presented "every-day case" is based on an empirical business case from the project SB: Digital. Thus, here it represents an adapted case-study, in the way Yin understand it: "The all-encompassing feature of a case study is its intense focus on a single phenomenon within its real-life context...[Case studies are] research situations where the number of variables of interest far outstrips the number of data points" [25]. The following chapter will introduce the case.

The Case: Commuting - An Everyday Life Scenario: In Germany, more than 50% of all employees have strict working time conditions (rigid working hours, less influence on pause times and limited selectable vacation within determined time slots) and only 9% of dependent workers have agreements regarding home office with their employer [26]. In other words, this means that the majority of employees must be at work at fixed times. The resulting commute overload causes rush hours on the streets, especially in business districts. "A commuter is defined as every employee whose workplace is outside its local community" [27]. In 2016 for almost 70 % of employees, the daily commute distance between home and work was at least 5 km, of which 20 % had to cover a distance between 5 to 10 km [28]. Furthermore, 67,7 % of all commuters, used a car for commuting [28]. The standard vehicle occupancy in Germany during commute is 1,2 persons per car [29]. Furthermore, even new cars have an average CO_2 emission of 118.5 g/km [30] - no congestion factored. This shows, that car sharing or an occasional change from motorized private transport to active commute (bike, walking) or public transport would have a significant impact on emissions [31, 32]. By understanding commuting as a social phenomenon, which affects everyone and that requires for a joint solution, every passive commuter (car, public transport) could reduce its own environmental footprint significantly.

3   Background and Related Work

3.1   Collaborative Networks and Enterprise Social Networks

Enterprise Social Networks (ESN) are well known web-based platforms for digital communication and exchange of digital artifacts [33]. Via individual profiles, employees can present themselves and their work but also connect and communicate with other employees [34]. Examples are platforms like wikis, microblogs and social networking platforms [35]. CNs are cross-organizational network, where social interaction via ESN is time- and location-independent [36]. This allows employees to stay connected across national borders and time zones. Companies often implement ESN with the goal of increasing productivity or innovation [33]. However, although the potential of ESN as a platform for internal as well as inter-company knowledge exchange between actors has been recognized [37], there is no research on the possible use of ESN to promote environmentally friendly behavior. Thus, this paper does not address the major topics of ecological product or process innovation but puts the focus on framework conditions to support individual eco-friendly behavior change in the context of cross-organizational collaboration.

3.2   Motivation for Behavioral Change

The main objective of a business commute project as we describe it, is to motivate employees for a change of behavior. A growing number of communities all over the world is already trying to establish sustainable mobility concepts [38, 39]. Even though the primary motives of the stakeholders may differ, the commute project needs to take all perspective into consideration to assure a long-lasting success by addressing intrinsic motives. A purely incentive based extrinsic motivation causes only a short change of behavior but not a sustainable change of attitude [40]. The motive of the company, for example, might be a mitigation of the parking space shortage or the whish for stress reduction to prevent sick leaves. The employees, on the other hand, might also wish to avoid stressful commuting with traffic and long-lasting searches for parking spaces [41] or strive for a more sustainable living and environmental awareness. In a first step, all the different objectives towards commute as well as barriers and factors for individual resistance should be identified.

Change of behavior patterns towards pro-environmental behavior requires for pressure or strong individual motivation. But as Ölander and Thøgersen [42] note, the free choice of the individuum is the decisive point to ensure "consistency between attitudes and behaviour" and, thus, a sustainable change of behavior. Motivation can be addressed by incentives. Incentives address individual motives and can thus be enhancer but cannot create motivation which is not at least subliminally present which means that they cannot be able to cause behavioral change if they are not compatible with the individual value system [43, 44]. Moreover, incentives need to be desirable for the addressee [45]. Both motivation and ability are key determinants for human behavior. While a lot of psychological works "studying behavior as a function of processes internal to the individual" [46], we agree with the idea that behavior change need the integration of external and internal functions as independent variables - e.g. resources and social embedment (e.g. in terms of relatedness). The most powerful advantage of CNs is the community aspect. Online communities strengthen feelings of relatedness [47]. In the context of badge systems, Kwon et al. [48] describe the effect of social incentives that work through comparison and social benchmarking. But online communities are not only useful in the context of incentive creation but can furthermore be used to promote a value system and create awareness for community relevant aspects such as ecology. Thus, social comparison and the growing awareness for ecological sustainability can both be exploited in order to establish a shared value system within CNs.

4 Social Business Framework Conditions for Eco-friendly Behavior

Within this chapter, we are going to identify and initiate the design of artefacts within the developed framework conditions on the presented case. These artefacts need to be elaborated in on-going work. A general overview which shows the relations between the three different analysis layers of human, CN and technology and interdependencies in terms of behavior change can be found in Fig. 1.

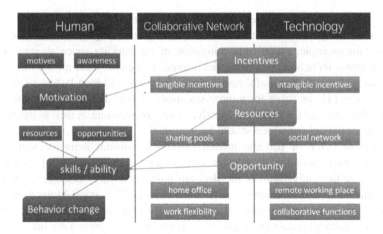

Fig. 1. Social business framework conditions

4.1 The Human Factor

To initiate a change of behavior, humans need to be motivated, which works both positively by addressing motives and the individual value system[2] as well as negatively by addressing environmental concerns and clarifying the negative consequences of a non-changing of e.g. commute behavior [50]. Furthermore, they require for the ability in terms of resources and opportunities to behave different. Intrinsic motivation is one of the key factors for a sustainable change of behavior and an ultimately as a result of personal experience and internalization change of attitude [40], but the problem is that there is no single way to motivate, every individual have to be motivated in different ways. Communities and companies can, therefore, act as "motivators" and create both awareness and incentives to support motivational growth and to initiate behavioral change. Next to the **individual motivation**, employees need the ability to change. This means, that they require for adequate **resources** (Do I have the capabilities?) as well as for the **opportunity** (Is it doable for me?) to change their commute routine. As it has been shown in Fig. 1, all three components, namely motivation, resources and opportunity, are key factors for the human behavior. Within this work, we do not go into deep psychological discourses like, e.g., Ohtomo and Hirose [51] did. Instead, we focus on the overall framework conditions (human, organization, technology) and its relations. More precisely, we ask, which framework conditions are supporting the motivation, the resources and the opportunities of employee to behave in an eco-friendlier way?

---

[2] EU study show: "the more the individuals think that they are playing an important role in protecting the environment, the higher the probability of behaving ecologically" [49].

4.2   The Collaborative Network

To have the greatest possible impact, we believe that collaborative networks in forms of regional limited ESN, established for industry parks and conurbation, supports business independent, cross-organizational cooperation. In addition, a regional reference enables a stronger identification with the commute project as well as a social embedding in a shared value system. All organizations as well as the local administration do need to develop a framework specifically and individually for the target conurbation (based on infrastructure (traffic, schools, public transport etc.), types of enterprises and employee, landscape etc.). Even local administrations can have the role of mediator for the eco-driven collaboration network and give general advices and help lines like [52] suggest for SME. Enterprises do have the possibilities to share cost, attract working place and motivate employee. Within the network, important resources can be set. Likewise, tangible incentives can be created in order to strengthen awareness and collective rethinking of commute behavior and using network effects. A collection of examples is given in Fig. 2.

Beside the resources and opportunities, collaborative networks also can set different incentives. Based on the different point systems, individual points can be transferred into vouchers, convertible, e.g., for bicycle equipment or free public transport rides. On a group level, points can be transformed into team events or included, e.g., into donation campaigns for regional ecological project. As it has been shown be Ettema et al. [53], monetary incentives with no further contextualization towards mode switching have no lasting effect on behavior once they are withdrawn.

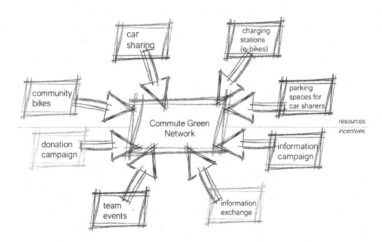

Fig. 2 Network design approaches to support ecological commute behavior

Table 1. Incentive potential for pro-ecological behavior change

	Motivation	Eco-friendly embedment	Social embedment
Voucher	(+) tangible incentive like e-bike voucher have ecological impact and support attitude change through experience	(+) corresponding to the intended action (bike repairing), regional- and ecological adaptable	(+/−) vouchers for group activities foster joint objectives, but may cause rivalry between individuals / teams
Financial incentives	(+/−) strong extrinsic incentive for short-term behavioral adjustment	(−) no relevance for eco-friendly attitude	(−) high chance of rivalry
Free working time	(+/−) highly motivating, less connection to eco-friendly attitude	(−) no relevance for eco-friendly attitude	(−) high chance of rivalry
Funding campaigns	(+) addresses intrinsic motivation / altruism	(+) regional- and ecological adaptable	(+) joint design of the (working) environment foster teamwork
Equipment	(+/-) extrinsic incentive for short-term behavioral adjustment	(+) regional- and ecological adaptable	(+/-) foster teamwork, may strengthen silo-mentality (team vs. team)
Team events	(+/−) foster affiliation, potential negative impact on voicing concerns	(+) regional- and ecological adaptable	(+) foster teamwork to achieve joint objective

From our point of view, it is important not only to set any tangible incentives, but also to adapt these incentives for the context (to foster eco-friendly behavior and acting). Moreover, the social embedment is one of the key concepts to foster motivation. Thus, it seems useful to analyze potential incentives regarding their motivation opportunity, their adaptability (and embedment) to eco-friendly concepts and their social embedment as it is done in Table 1.

4.3 Technology to Set Incentives in CNs Promoting Ecological Behavior

The technological basis for a collaborative network built the digital social network (e.g. Humhub) that allows for a barrier free digital communication between multiple stakeholders (e.g. companies in an industrial estate). It is an important resource[3] for all actors. The network as itself supports a seamless and open information exchange between all stakeholders. This way, users are supported in building car sharing communities to enhance the car occupancy or share their favorite (bike) routes or running tracks.

Within the application, it is furthermore possible to provide useful information to employees which may have an impact on their mobility behavior. Such information

---

[3] The term resource is ambiguous. Here it refers also to the capabilities.

might be the daily weather prognosis, current fine dust load of the region or traffic jams on the commute route.

Based on this technical system, it is possible to use gamification in order to create **incentives** for users. Due to its positive impact on motivation [54] and behavior change, we chose a gamification approach for the incentive design process. In general, in the consideration of incentives, a distinction between internal and external incentives is made [55]. While internal incentive are an integral part of an activity [56] and trigger emotions like fun or ambition, external incentives like bonus payments or reputation are tied to preconditions [57] and can thus be understood as tangible compensation that require for a certain effort. The following Table 2 shows exemplary incentives that are the result of the artifact design.

Table 2. Incentives to promote ecological commute behavior

Gamification element	Addressed motivation	Implementation
Points	Ambition	(1) specific mobility behavior according to the environmental footprint (2) saved fuel costs with car sharing
Meaningful story (virtual parc)	Relatedness	(3) individual growing trees (including employees/alias name plate) (4) leaves can be "earned" by passing challenges/ redeeming of points
Time comparison	Self-efficiency, comparison, fun	(5) visualization of commute distance/route & time (individual time tracking from the apartment door to the workplace) (6) showing differences for different variants (bicycle vs. car, etc.) (7) Visualization of times spent in traffic jams and avoided congestion times when using bicycles/public transport
Feedback (eco statistics)	Relatedness, progression, altruism	(8) visualization of personal/group CO^2 commute footprint (9) (real-time) ecological company footprint
Feedback (health statistics)	Ambition, fun	(10) burned bike calories / walked steps (11) conversion of calories into favorite food to choose (you burned x calories, that corresponds to 2 pieces of cake/1 burger in the cafeteria/…) (12) active commute time
Simulation	Ambition, altruism	(13) effects of (partial) changeover from car to car sharing/ cycling/public transport on pollution/ CO^2 footprint
Challenge & rewards	Ambition, fun	(14) badges for achievement of target time/calories/emission (15) achievement of target, based on individual and group points

What have to be taken into account in the design and implementation of incentives is, that they need to be adjusted to the corporate culture [54]. Moreover, in order to support the consciousness building for pro-environmental behavior, the design of incentives should be adapted to the context (e.g., leaves for the virtual tree instead of simple points). Furthermore, it has to be kept in mind, that incentives do not unfold their potential automatically, but need to be designed to meet the needs of their recipients [58]. Additionally, it is important to consider, that incentives that put a hugh pressure on its recipients by primarily focusing on competition and rivalry, such as rankings and associated tangible rewards, bear the risk of cheating [59] and a displacement of positive motives (pro-ecological behavior) by negative motivation (egoism, status) [60].

Enabling social collaboration through digital resources and intangible incentives, created through gamification, is a promising approach to foster eco-friendly commute behavior. Moreover, the work conditions of the employee do also affect it. In order to achieve more flexibility in commuting, employers must be open to change, particularly with regard to time constraints. On technical side, that includes a **remote working** place with collaborative functions to enable social collaboration (e.g. to have the flexibility to negotiate travel times).

5   Discussion and Future Directions

We have discussed social business framework conditions to enable eco-friendly behavior within collaborative networks. Therefore, we developed and discussed different conditions of the human, technology and organizations dimensions. Our main requirement or condition is to set up a digital environment, where employees get the possibility to interact and collaborate. Within the project SB: Digital, we discuss the different technical and organizational conditions in various environments and first deployments of technical features (point system, alternate vehicle suggestion) have been started. In further steps we plan to implement the presented approach (in parts) and evaluate the mode of action, benefits and risks as well as the barriers and contexts. While some validation aspects can be part of the technical solution (e.g. bike and share usages), other aspects, like stress level, will be harder discoverable. Therefor specific methods have to be developed.

Acknowledgments. The German Federal Ministry of Education and Research have funded the work leading to this publication under grant number 02L15A070 (Project: SB:Digital). The authors thank for the funding.

References

1. Camarinha-Matos, L.M., Afsarmanesh, H.: Collaborative networks. In: Wang, K., Kovacs, G.L., Wozny, M., Fang, M. (eds.) PROLAMAT 2006. IIFIP, vol. 207, pp. 26–40. Springer, Boston, MA (2006). https://doi.org/10.1007/0-387-34403-9_4
2. Patroni, J., von Briel, F., Recker, J.: How enterprise social media can facilitate innovation. IT Prof. **18**, 34–41 (2016)

3. Westerman, G., Bonnet, D., McAfee, A.: Leading digital turning technology into business transformation. Harvard Business Review Press, Boston (2014)
4. Reychav, I., Ndicu, M., Wu, D.: Leveraging social networks in the adoption of mobile technologies for collaboration. Comput. Hum. Behav. **58**, 443–453 (2016)
5. Cook, N.: Enterprise 2.0. Routledge (2017)
6. Majchrzak, A., Faraj, S., Kane, G.C., Azad, B.: The contradictory influence of social media affordances on online communal knowledge sharing. J. Comput.-Mediat. Commun. **19**, 38–55 (2013)
7. Alalwan, A.A., Rana, N.P., Dwivedi, Y.K., Algharabat, R.: Social media in marketing: a review and analysis of the existing literature. Telematics Inform. **34**, 1177–1190 (2017)
8. Lehmkuhl, T., Baumol, U., Jung, R.: Towards a maturity model for the adoption of social media as a means of organizational innovation. In: 2013 46th Hawaii International Conference on System Sciences, pp. 3067–3076. IEEE (2013)
9. Kuegler, M., Smolnik, S., Kane, G.: What's in IT for employees? understanding the relationship between use and performance in enterprise social software. J. Strateg. Inf. Syst. **24**, 90–112 (2015)
10. Weinberg, B.D., de Ruyter, K., Dellarocas, C., Buck, M., Keeling, D.I.: Destination social business: exploring an organization's journey with social media, collaborative community and expressive individuality. J. Interact. Mark. **27**, 299–310 (2013)
11. Schneckenberg, D.: Web 2.0 and the empowerment of the knowledge worker. J. Knowl. Manag. **13**, 509–520 (2009)
12. Biesbroek, G.R., et al.: Europe adapts to climate change: comparing national adaptation strategies. Glob. Environ. Change **20**, 440–450 (2010)
13. Sarkodie, S.A., Strezov, V.: Economic, social and governance adaptation readiness for mitigation of climate change vulnerability: evidence from 192 countries. Sci Total Environ. **656**, 150–164 (2019)
14. Fridays for Future. https://fridaysforfuture.org/
15. Taylor, M., Neslen, A., Brooks, L.: Youth climate strikes to take place in more than 100 countries. http://www.theguardian.com/education/2019/mar/14/youth-climate-strikes-to-take-place-in-almost-100-countries-greta-thunberg
16. Diesel Information Hub: Where in Europe can I drive my diesel car?. https://dieselinformation.aecc.eu/where-in-europe-can-i-drive-my-diesel-car/
17. Global Footprint Network. https://www.footprintnetwork.org/
18. Wackernagel, M., Rees, W.E.: Our ecological footprint. Reducing human impact on the earth. New Society Publishers, Gabriola Island (1998)
19. Beechler, S., Woodward, I.C.: The global "war for talent". J. Int. Manag. **15**, 273–285 (2009)
20. Hackl, B., Wagner, M., Attmer, L., Baumann, D.: New Work: Auf dem Weg zur neuen Arbeitswelt. Springer Fachmedien Wiesbaden, Wiesbaden (2017)
21. Digitale Soziale Netzwerke als Mittel zur Gestaltung attraktiver Arbeit. https://sbdigitial.infai.org
22. Peffers, K., et al.: The design science research process: a model for producing and presenting information systems research. In: Proceedings of First International Conference on Design Science Research in Information Systems and Technology DESRIST, pp. 83–106 (2006)
23. Strohm, O., Escher, O.P. (eds.): Unternehmen arbeitspsychologisch bewerten. Ein Mehr-Ebenen-Ansatz unter besonderer Berücksichtigung von Mensch, Technik und Organisation. vdf Hochschulverl. an der ETH Zürich, Zürich (1997)
24. Ulich, E.: Arbeitssysteme als Soziotechnische Systeme – eine Erinnerung. Psychol. Everyday Act. **6**(1), 4–12 (2013). ISSN 1998-9970
25. Yin, R.K.: Case study research. Design and methods. Sage, Los Angeles (2009)

26. Wöhrmann, A.M., et al.: Arbeitszeitreport Deutschland 2016. Verlag Kettler GmbH, Bönen (2016)
27. Peine, K., Helferich, A.: MyQommute—an app as sustainable mobility concept. In: 2018 IEEE International Conference on Engineering, Technology and Innovation (ICE/ITMC), ICE/IEEE ITMC, Stuttgart, 17 June–20 June 2018, pp. 1–9. IEEE, Piscataway (2018)
28. Statistisches Bundesamt: Erwerbstätige nach Stellung im Beruf, Entfernung, Zeitaufwand und benutztem Verkehrsmittel für den Hinweg zur Arbeitsstätte 2016 in % (2016). https://www.destatis.de/DE/Themen/Arbeit/Arbeitsmarkt/Erwerbstaetigkeit/Tabellen/pendler1.html
29. Lenz, B., et al.: Mobilität in Deutschland 2008. Bonn, Berlin (2010)
30. No improvements on average CO2 emissions from new cars (2017)
31. Bearman, N., Singleton, A.D.: Modelling the potential impact on CO2 emissions of an increased uptake of active travel for the home to school commute using individual level data. J. Transp. Health **1**, 295–304 (2014)
32. Farrell, S., McNamara, D., Caulfield, B.: Estimating the potential success of sustainable transport measures for a small town. Transp. Res. Rec.: J. Transp. Res. Board **2163**(1), 97–102 (2010)
33. McAfee, A.: Enterprise 2.0: the dawn of emergent collaboration. IEEE Eng. Manag. Rev. **34**, 38 (2006)
34. Subramaniam, N., Nandhakumar, J., Baptista John, J.: Exploring social network interactions in enterprise systems: the role of virtual co-presence. Inf. Syst. J. **23**, 475–499 (2013)
35. Behrendt, S., Richter, A., Trier, M.: Mixed methods analysis of enterprise social networks. Comput. Netw. **75**, 560–577 (2014)
36. Qureshi, S.: Adaptation in distributed projects: collaborative processes in digital natives and digital immigrants. In: Proceedings of the 39th Annual Hawaii International Conference on System Sciences (HICSS 2006), p. 202c. IEEE (2006)
37. Mack, D., Vilberger, D.: Leitfäden: Wie geht man systematisch vor für den Social-Media-Einsatz? (Social-Media-Navigator). Social Media für KMU, pp. 63–99. Springer, Wiesbaden (2016). https://doi.org/10.1007/978-3-658-07739-6_5
38. SHARE-North: Shares Mobility Solutions for a Liveable and Low-Carbon North Sea Region. https://share-north.eu/partners/
39. Gudmundsson, H.: Making concepts matter: sustainable mobility and indicator systems in transport policy. Int. Soc. Sci. J. **55**, 199–217 (2003)
40. Finke, I., Will, M.: Motivation for knowledge management. In: Mertins, K., Heisig, P., Vorbeck, J. (eds.) Knowledge Management, pp. 66–91. Springer, Heidelberg (2003). https://doi.org/10.1007/978-3-540-24778-4_4
41. Gatersleben, B., Uzzell, D.: Affective appraisals of the daily commute. Environ. Behav. **39**, 416–431 (2007)
42. ölander, F., ThØgersen, J.: Understanding of consumer behaviour as a prerequisite for environmental protection. J Consum. Policy **18**, 345–385 (1995)
43. Gneezy, U., Meier, S., Rey-Biel, P.: When and why incentives (don't) work to modify behavior. J. Econ. Perspect. **25**, 191–210 (2011)
44. Kohn, A.: Why incentive plans cannot work. Harvard Bus. Rev. 54–63 (1993)
45. Brandenberg, A.: Anreizsysteme zur Unternehmenssteuerung. Deutscher Universitätsverlag, Wiesbaden (2001). https://doi.org/10.1007/978-3-663-08251-4
46. Guagnano, G.A., Stern, P.C., Dietz, T.: Influences on attitude-behavior relationships. Environ. Behav. **27**, 699–718 (1995)
47. Moisander, J.: Group identity, personal ethics and sustainable development suggesting new directions for social marketing research. In: Jochem, E., Sathaye, J., Bouille, D. (eds.) Society, Behaviour, and Climate Change Mitigation, vol. 8, pp. 127–156. Kluwer Academic Publishers, Dordrecht (2003). https://doi.org/10.1007/0-306-48160-X_5

48. Kwon, K.H., Halavais, A., Havener, S.: Tweeting badges: user motivations for displaying achievement in publicly networked environments. Cyberpsychol. Behav. Soc. Netw. **18**, 93–100 (2015)

49. Lajunen, T., Parker, D., Summala, H.: Does traffic congestion increase driver aggression? Transp. Res. Part F: Traffic Psychol. Behav. **2**, 225–236 (1999)

50. Kollmuss, A., Agyeman, J.: Mind the gap: why do people act environmentally and what are the barriers to pro-environmental behavior? Environ. Educ. Res. **8**, 239–260 (2002)

51. Ohtomo, S., Hirose, Y.: The dual-process of reactive and intentional decision-making involved in eco-friendly behavior. J. Environ. Psychol. **27**, 117–125 (2007)

52. Klewitz, J., Hansen, E.G.: Sustainability-oriented innovation of SMEs: a systematic review. J. Cleaner Prod. **65**, 57–75 (2014)

53. Ettema, D., Knockaert, J., Verhoef, E.: Using incentives as traffic management tool: empirical results of the "peak avoidance" experiment. Transp. Lett. **2**, 39–51 (2010)

54. Hamari, J., Koivisto, J., Sarsa, H.: Does gamification work? a literature review of empirical studies on gamification. In: 47th Hawaii International Conference on System Sciences (HICSS), pp. 3025–3034 (2014)

55. Friedrich, J., Becker, M., Kramer, F., Wirth, M., Schneider, M.: Incentive design and gamification for knowledge management. J. Bus. Res. (2019)

56. Zaunmüller, H.: Anreizsysteme für das Wissensmanagement in KMU. Deutscher Universitätsverlag, Wiesbaden (2005)

57. Fishbach, A., Choi, J.: When thinking about goals undermines goal pursuit. Organ. Behav. Hum. Decis. Processes **118**, 99–107 (2012)

58. Suh, A., Wagner, C.: How gamification of an enterprise collaboration system increases knowledge contribution: an affordance approach. J. Knowl. Manag. **21**, 416–431 (2017)

59. Pascual-Ezama, D., Dunfield, D., Gil-Gomez de Liano, B., Prelec, D.: Peer effects in unethical behavior: standing or reputation? PloS one **10**, e0122305 (2015)

60. Hanus, M.D., Fox, J.: Assessing the effects of gamification in the classroom: a longitudinal study on intrinsic motivation, social comparison, satisfaction, effort, and academic performance. Comput. Educ. **80**, 152–161 (2015)

Managing Disruption in Collaboration

Development of a Methodology for the Analysis and Evaluation of Alternative Actions in Disruption Management in Production

Ben Luetkehoff[(✉)], Volker Stich, Moritz Schroeter,
and Felix Steinlein

FIR e.V., Campus-Boulevard 55, 52074 Aachen, Germany
ben.luetkehoff@fir.rwth-aachen.de

Abstract. Due to Digital Transformation, also called Industry 4.0 or the Industrial Internet of Things, the barrier for implementing data collecting technology on the shop floor has decreased dramatically in the past years – leading to an increasingly growing amount of data from a multitude of IT systems in production companies worldwide. Despite that, the production controller still relies heavily on intrinsic knowledge and intuition for the management of disruptions in production. Thanks to advances in the fields of production control and artificial intelligence, potentials for the collected data for disruption management arise. However, in order to transform data into usable information and allow drawing conclusions for disruption management in production, the relevant data-objects, disturbances and alternative actions must be known. Thus, the decision-making can be supported, reducing the decision latency and increasing benefit of alternative actions. Therefore, the goal of this paper is to discuss the prerequisites necessary to perform a data based disruption management and the methodology itself, serving as an approach to allow companies to build a data basis, classify disruptions and alternative actions in order to improve decision making in the future.

Keywords: Decision making · Decision support · Disruption management · Reaction strategy

1 Introduction

Offering customer specific products defines small and medium enterprises (SMEs), especially mechanical and plant engineering companies. This, combined with increasing product varieties and deceasing product lifecycles, leads to highly complex production processes, which in turn lead to an increasing amount of potential disturbances [1, 2]. These company-internal or -external disturbances are to blame for disruptions and their effect on, for example, delivery dates. Efficient Production Planning and Control systems are the most important means to react to this changing environment [3]. However, while solutions – even automated ones – exist in the field of detailed planning, the production controller is usually left unsupported in many areas when it comes to disruption management [4]. This makes the job of a production controller increasingly difficult. They need to comprehend the effect of the disturbances

© IFIP International Federation for Information Processing 2019
Published by Springer Nature Switzerland AG 2019
L. M. Camarinha-Matos et al. (Eds.): PRO-VE 2019, IFIP AICT 568, pp. 143–150, 2019.
https://doi.org/10.1007/978-3-030-28464-0_13

on production as well as the outcomes of the possible alternatives with regard to the production system and the logistical target system of the company. Therefore, the goal of this paper is to introduce a methodology that supports the production controller by providing possible alternative actions in disruption management for production. The methodology is part of the research project "iProd" with the goal of developing a collaborative platform [5, 6].

This paper starts by discussing the motivation of the subject in a more detailed manner. Afterwards, the state of the art discusses the current solutions found in practice and in research. As a basis for the methodology to be developed, requirements are collected and discussed. Section 5 will introduce the methodology itself, covering the aspects of the data model, setting up rules as well as the analysis and derivation of alternative actions. The findings will be concluded and a short outlook on upcoming research will be given.

2 Motivation

Production Planning and Control plans the current production program at regular intervals in advance according to type and quantity over several planning periods. Its goal is to implement the program with given or planned capacities as economically as possible while taking unavoidable disruptions such as personnel losses, delivery delays or rejects into account [7].

Disruption management therefore is part of the short-term production management and closes the gap between regular production control and closed-loop production control [6]. The goal is a short, medium and long-term reduction of disruptions. Generally, preventive disruption management takes place to avoid disruptions before they arise, whereas reactive disruption management starts only after the occurrence of a malfunction in order to reduce its effect [8]. For this, appropriate reaction strategies (i.e. prefabricated decisions that intervene through the system and define measures to eliminate the disruption) are required. These are control processes that eliminate operational interruptions or occur as preventive measures to prevent malfunctions [9]. Dealing with disruptions in an organized way has several advantages, since the time it takes to react to a disturbance can be shortened noticeably. This leads – aside from the time-benefit – to a higher benefit of the adaption itself [10].

Within the research project "iProd", a collaborative platform is developed, that allows the analysis of production data using Artificial Intelligence (AI). The presented method is part of the project and deals with the disruption management as part of the platform. Due to the connectivity to the shop floor and IT-systems within the company, the platform notices the disruption, analyzes it and feeds it back to the system. Thus, the presented methodology is the backbone of the collaborative platform which in turn allows a closed-loop production control [6] (Fig. 1).

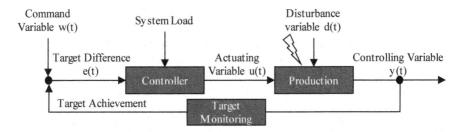

Fig. 1. Closed-loop production control [according to 11]

3 State of the Art

The state of the art shows an analysis of the research already available in the areas of disruption management, reaction strategies and simulation. Moreover, the industry also provides solutions in the field of disruption management, which this chapter will also discuss.

3.1 Literature in the Field of Disruption Management, Reaction Strategies and in the Field of Simulation

The literature review showed research focusing on the classification of disruptions in production processes as well as preventive and reactive disruption management, e.g. for customer specific production [8, 12]. Other researchers focus on the evaluation of countermeasures. The focus here lies on mathematical models [13] or very specific areas in production, such as the assembly [14]. Moreover, there are different approaches in the field of simulation (discrete event as well as agent based) in the context of production [15–19]. Comparing the relevant literature references shows that research-based approaches to simulation-based decision support are often limited to certain use cases or cannot be transferred to other industries.

3.2 State of the Art in the Industry

In practice, approaches for decision support can already be found in the area of ERP (Enterprise Resource Planning), APS (Advanced Planning and Scheduling) as well as MES (Manufacturing Execution System) systems.

ME systems integrate information relevant to production (personnel, material resources, production equipment including tools and fixtures) and link them to the planning framework conditions from the higher-level systems [20]. This way, MES generate more realistic plans than ERP systems and can react promptly to changes (e.g. due to disruptions in the production area) and calculate and initiate plan changes. ERP and MES cannot replace the production planner during planning and should rather support him interactively. However, the support of the production planner is prevented by the lack of transparency of the algorithms and the IT system structures, since the comprehensibility of the calculation by the production planner is a prerequisite for checking and supplementing the calculated proposal [21].

APS systems also obtain their data from ongoing value-added processes from transaction-based ERP and ME systems but deliver more exact planning results. APS systems generate plans based on advanced mathematical models. On the operational level, the detailed planning takes place throughout the entire supply chain. Here, most of the parameters and dependencies are already known; it is simply a matter of getting the optimum planning results out of the input. Thus, Companies can plan their requirements, quantities, due-dates, capacities to the point of distribution and logistics across the entire supply chain. Unfortunately, the planning horizon of APS systems ranges from days to weeks and is therefore not fast enough for short-term disruption management. The exact scope of APS systems remain to be defined.

In summary, it can be stated that there is no holistic recording and evaluation model of alternative actions for short-term disruption management. In the literature, there are various papers on aspects such as disruption management, reaction strategies, simulation and quantitative evaluation alternative actions. The research deficit is therefore a decision support system for short-term production control in the field of disruption management.

4   Requirements

The proposed concept must meet specific requirements to fulfill the need of the methodology. First, the data basis must be up to date and at the same time have access to historical values and planning data. Since the response time in short term production management is highly important, the evaluation of alternative actions must happen in or close to real-time. The goal of this methodology is that it either serves as an extension of existing IT systems or the production controllers themselves can work with the solution (e.g. for mobile use). Therefore, the interface must be open and allow displaying the results in a self-explanatory and user-centric manner [22].

Aside from the above-mentioned requirements, the following questions arise and need to be addressed when implementing the model: (1) Which decision cases occur in production? Which data is therefore required as input for a decision tool? (2) What effects do the potential measures have and how can these effects be quantified? (3) Which information must be prepared for the decision maker and how?

5   Methodology

The methodology consists of several steps that allow an evaluation of the reaction strategy and the selection of the most promising one. The first step consists of setting up the relevant data model (i.e. which data can be found where). The second step is to collect the existing and potential disruptions as well as counter measures manually (e.g. by interviewing the production controller) and automatically (e.g. by analyzing the historical data). Based on this, rules for the identification of future disruptions and the derivation of alternative actions. The basic framework for the methodology is illustrated in Fig. 2.

5.1   Identification of Relevant Data

In many companies, the worker or production controller notices disruptions, however, the goal is that the system can detect them automatically. The latter is done via an automatic transfer of order data from the ERP and ME system as well as from production or machine data acquisition (PDA/MDA). Manual input from the worker is required if the data cannot be transferred from the IT systems automatically. This input may contain additional parameters for the in-house production such as shift plans (e.g. from a human resource system), amount and qualification of workers, disruptions or maintenance at resources, blocked parts as well as the availability of resources from Production Data Acquisition (PDA).

In this first step, it is necessary to define the scope of disruption management within the company in order to identify the relevant data objects. The typology of the company in focus will heavily determine the needed data. For example, while for one company the batch-number and size may be relevant, others simply do not produce batches. This data then needs to be allocated (i.e. which databank stores this data, e.g. ERP system) and its meaning defined. This means that, even within the same company, the understanding of the used vocabulary may differ.

5.2   Collecting Disruptions, Alternative Actions and Rules

The goal of the digital transformation in production is to support the worker and to turn their implicit knowledge into usable data for IT systems. Thus, when setting up this methodology for disruption management, the worker needs to be interviewed and the known disruptions as well as their countermeasures need to be collected. If the company already has a reliable database, this can also be used in order to identify disruptions and alternative actions from the past. This step usually results in unveiling missing data which then needs to be added to the data model.

In the presented project, a matrix has been developed, that groups the disruptions in reference objects. Possible causes, their effect and characteristic define the reference object in more detail. The alternative actions are grouped in reaction strategies (i.e. delay, delegation, replanning, relaxation, negotiation and cancellation). Based on the matrix, the reaction strategies can be allocated to the disruptions and thus alternative actions be derived.

5.3   Analyze the Data and Knowledge Base

When a disruption occurs, the first step is to identify the disruption. Depending on the grade of automation within the company, the reaction for disruptions with low impact can be performed automatically, without requiring an intervention of an employee. At the same time, there are disruptions that can solely be solved by manual interventions from an employee. The type of disruption that is the focus of this paper is the type that can be encountered semi-automatically. Here, part of the input can come from the system and the other part still requires some kind of manual input [23].

After the disruption has been identified, it needs to be analyzed in more detail. This is necessary in order to see what the reaction strategy and alternative actions looked like in the past. The AI-tool (Jupyter Notebook) is used to extract the necessary data and analyze them separately regarding the disruption. Afterwards, the analyzed data is fed back via the interface[1]. The result of this analysis depends on the defined scope. An example is a clustering of disruptions according to their conditions (e.g. product variant or past alternative actions) in order to anticipate further disruptions, and therefore enables a short-, medium- and long-term disruption management.

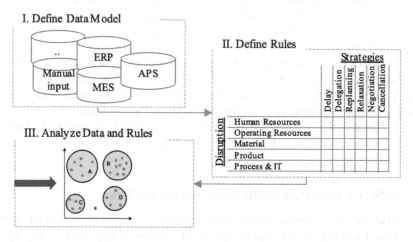

Fig. 2. Methodology to approach disruptions

6   Conclusion and Outlook

Companies try to encounter the turbulent market, customer specific production and thus higher susceptibility to disruptions in production by collecting data and supporting the worker with IT systems. While many aspects of production have already been facilitated by this digital transformation, the disturbance management remains unsupported and mostly based on implicit knowledge and intuition of the worker. In order to improve the decision making process in disruption management, this paper discussed a possible methodology by discussing the data model, rules (disruptions and alternative actions) as well as their analysis briefly. The findings can be used as an extension of existing IT systems or for standalone support systems. However, within the presented project, the methodology still involves many manual steps and is not yet ready for a direct implementation. Future research therefore needs to focus the area of data models for disruption management as well as their ontology. Moreover, the methodology needs validation in practice and standardization of the analysis using AI. For companies it is crucial to collect the implicit knowledge of the worker in order to allow the described methodology in practice.

---

[1] In the presented project, a platform is developed that uses REST API interfaces in order to feed data back to the IT systems or to a web-based dashboard. For more information please see www.projekt-iprod.de and [5, 6].

Acknowledgement. The European Regional Development Fund (ERDF) funded the presented research (grant number EFRE/ERDF-0800924). The authors would like to thank the European Regional Development Fund for the kind support and making this research possible.

References

1. ElMaraghy, H., Schuh, G., ElMaraghy, W., et al.: Product variety management. CIRP Ann. **62**(2), 629–652 (2013)
2. Ferreira, F., Faria, J., Azevedo, A., et al.: Product lifecycle management in knowledge intensive collaborative environments: an application to automotive industry. Int. J. Inf. Manag. **37**(1), 1474–1487 (2017)
3. Böckenkamp, A., Mertens, C., Prasse, C., Stenzel, J., Weichert, F.: A versatile and scalable production planning and control system for small batch series. In: Jeschke, S., Brecher, C., Song, H., Rawat, Danda B. (eds.) Industrial Internet of Things. SSWT, pp. 541–559. Springer, Cham (2017). https://doi.org/10.1007/978-3-319-42559-7_22
4. Schuh, G., Potente, T., Thomas, C., Hauptvogel, A.: Cyber-physical production management. In: Prabhu, V., Taisch, M., Kiritsis, D. (eds.) APMS 2013. IAICT, vol. 415, pp. 477–484. Springer, Heidelberg (2013). https://doi.org/10.1007/978-3-642-41263-9_59
5. Luetkehoff, B., Blum, M., Schroeter, M.: Self-learning production control using algorithms of artificial intelligence. In: Camarinha-Matos, L.M., Afsarmanesh, H., Fornasiero, R. (eds.) Collaboration in a Data-Rich World, vol. 506, pp. 299–306. Springer, Cham (2017)
6. Luetkehoff, B., Blum, M., Schroeter, M.: Development of a collaborative platform for closed loop production control. In: Camarinha-Matos, Luis M., Afsarmanesh, H., Rezgui, Y. (eds.) PRO-VE 2018. IAICT, vol. 534, pp. 278–285. Springer, Cham (2018). https://doi.org/10.1007/978-3-319-99127-6_24
7. Wiendahl, H.-P.: Betriebsorganisation für Ingenieure, 8., überarb. Aufl. Hanser, München (2014)
8. Schwartz, F., Voß, S.: Störungsmanagement in der Produktion—Simulationsstudien für ein hybrides Fließfertigungssystem. Zeitschrift für Planung Unternehmenssteuerung **15**(4), 427–447 (2004)
9. Opfermann, K.: Kostenoptimale Zuverlässigkeit produktiver Systeme. Gabler (1968)
10. Gu, X., Jin, X., Ni, J., et al.: Manufacturing system design for resilience. Proc. CIRP **36**, 135–140 (2015)
11. Wiendahl, H.-P.: Fertigungsregelung: Logistische Beherrschung von Fertigungsabläufen auf Basis des Trichtermodells. Hanser, München (1997)
12. Wünscher, T.: Störungsmanagement im Entwicklungs-und Herstellungsprozess komplexer, kundenindividueller Produkte, Cuvillier (2010)
13. Stich, V., Schröter, M., Jordan, F., Wenger, L., Blum, M.: Assessment of counter-measures for disturbance management in manufacturing environments. In: Lödding, H., Riedel, R., Thoben, K.-D., von Cieminski, G., Kiritsis, D. (eds.) APMS 2017. IAICT, vol. 513, pp. 449–456. Springer, Cham (2017). https://doi.org/10.1007/978-3-319-66923-6_53
14. Burggräf, P., Wagner, J., Lück, K., et al.: Cost-benefit analysis for disruption prevention in low-volume assembly. Prod. Eng. **11**(3), 331–342 (2017)
15. Melouk, S., Fontem, B., Waymire, E., et al.: Stochastic resource allocation using a predictor-based heuristic for optimization via simulation. Comput. Oper. Res. **46**, 38–48 (2014)
16. Krenczyk, D., Olender, M.: Simulation aided production planning and scheduling using game theory approach. AMM **809–810**, 1450–1455 (2015)

17. Burggraef, P., Wagner, J., Dannapfel, M., et al.: Simulating the benefit of disruption prevention in assembly. J. Model. Manag. **14**(1), 214–231 (2018)
18. Greenwood, A., Vanguri, S., Eksioglu, B., et al.: Simulation optimization decision support system for ship panel shop operations. In: Proceedings of the Winter Simulation Conference, 2005, pp. 2078–2086. IEEE (2005)
19. Galaske, N., Anderl, R.: Disruption management for resilient processes in cyber-physical production systems. Proc. CIRP **50**, 442–447 (2016)
20. Kletti, J.: MES - Manufacturing Execution System: Moderne Informationstechnologie Zur Prozessfähigkeit Der Wertschöpfung. Springer, Dordrecht (2006)
21. Gachet, A., Haettenschwiler, P.: A decentralized approach to distributed decision support systems. J. Decis. Syst. **12**(2), 141–158 (2003)
22. Nyhuis, P., Mayer, J., Kuprat, T.: Die Bedeutung von Industrie 4.0 als Enabler für logistische Modelle. Industrie **4**, 79–100 (2014)
23. Meissner, J.: Adaptives Abweichungsmanagement in der Fertigungssteuerung bei Kleinserien. Dissertation, RWTH-Aachen (2018)

Actionable Collaborative Common Operational Picture in Crisis Situation: A Comprehensive Architecture Powered with Social Media Data

Julien Coche[1], Aurélie Montarnal[1(✉)], Andrea Tapia[2],
and Frederick Benaben[1(✉)]

[1] Centre Génie Industriel – Université de Toulouse – IMT Mines Albi,
Albi, France
{julien.coche,aurelia.montarnal,benaben}@mines-albi.fr
[2] College of Information Sciences and Technology,
The Pennsylvania State University, University Park, PA 16801, USA
atapia@ist.psu.edu

Abstract. Previous works in social media processing during crisis management highlight a paradox: citizens are extensively sharing data from the field of the crisis, while decision-makers are looking for information about the emerging risks they need to address. Several tools already exist to help taking advantage of this new important source of data. However, few made their way to decision-makers, mainly because they remain resource-consuming. That is why the question of a tool, able to process social media in near-real time, to deliver actionable information from the field is still pending. Based on a state of the art of the Natural Language Processing tools and systems dedicated to the use of social media data to improve the situational awareness of the decision-makers, this paper aims to describe a way to provide them with a first comprehensive system which asset is to completely address the challenge, from the collection of the data to their interpretation and understanding and finally offer situational models. In this sense, the paper focuses on the thorough detail of the business and consequent technical challenges that are raised, and a work in progress proposal to address them in a comprehensive manner.

Keywords: Social media · Crisis management · Metamodel ·
Natural Language Processing

1 Introduction

Crisis situations are recurrent situations in our societies. Whatever their nature, severity, extent, duration or complexity, these breaks are confusing situations. The need for information then becomes crucial to provide an adequate response to ongoing events. On the one hand, emergency management cells aim at building a common operational picture (COP) from the information sent by the responders on the field. On the other hand, citizens are using more and more social media to share what is

© IFIP International Federation for Information Processing 2019
Published by Springer Nature Switzerland AG 2019
L. M. Camarinha-Matos et al. (Eds.): PRO-VE 2019, IFIP AICT 568, pp. 151–162, 2019.
https://doi.org/10.1007/978-3-030-28464-0_14

happening around them during exceptional events. They tend to react more during crisis situations and share information about it [1]. Social media, such as Twitter, Facebook or Instagram therefore participate in the exchange of information related to the crisis in an unprecedented timely manner. For this reason, it is of utmost importance to be able to integrate citizens' social media data into the COP.

Up to this day, although many tools exist in the literature, such information systems incorporating social media data into the COP are rarely used in the facts. This leads to a paradoxical situation where decision-makers are looking for information to organize their resources during crisis situations and victims and witnesses' willing to share information in real-time is not considered. These social media processing systems and crisis-related resources have already been developed and the most noticeable of them are explored by [2]. Moreover, [3] points out some possible necessary improvements. Among them, *"how the added-value information extracted thanks to such social media-oriented system should be integrated in the decision-making process?"* echoes to this context.

In a collaborative context such as crisis management, where heterogeneous actors are acting conjunctly or simultaneously in a coordinated manner, the ability to design a relevant, trustable and sharable COP is of the highest priority. Dispersed visions and compartmentalized information among responders are totally inappropriate in a context where interdisciplinarity and complementarity of coordinated interoperable responders is, not only the doctrine, but also the best way to have a chance to perform an efficient collaborative response.

Consequently, the point of this article is: **How to fully integrate the information provided by social media data, in times of crisis, into the COP to improve the common understanding and thus the collaborative response of the responders?** The following of this article is structured in three parts. Section 2 presents the most significant social media processing systems, their structure and what needs they aim to address. Based on this, Sect. 3 describes the chosen approach to tackle the broad and comprehensive problematic raised here and illustrates the proposed approach with an example. Finally, Sect. 4 details what are the next steps of this work in progress research.

2 Existing Social Media Processing Systems

Following the fact that people are posting text messages, pictures or videos about their surrounding environment during a crisis, the idea of automatically processing this data emerged. [2] lists several existing systems alongside their literature. Also, these systems address various business concerns.

First, data **collection**. It is achieved by using requests directly executed thanks to the Application Program Interface (API) offered by the social media platforms. As an example, Twitter provides an API that allows to retrieve past messages according to their ID or a username. It also allows to monitor a fraction of the activity through keywords or geoboxes (for location-based collect). This last method is tedious as approximately 1% of the total user has the geolocation turn on their device. Finally, systems such as EMERSE [4] are also using Short Message Service (SMS). But as it is difficult to have such access, this kind of system represent a small fraction of the existing systems. Because of its ease of access, thanks to its freely-available API, Twitter was chosen as the social media platform for this study.

The **processing** of the data is considered as the most difficult task. Some of the main challenges addressed by existing systems are listed below:

- **Event detection** is a task considered by all the existing systems. However, systems such as ESA (Emergency Situation Awareness) [5] aims at detecting bursts on social media, based on trigger put on data volume or specific keywords.
- The most addressed is **filtering**. Most of the systems such as AIDR [6], Tweedr [7], ESA [5], Twitris [8], Twitcident [9] and EMERSE [4] are filtering the tweets according to fact they are related or not to the crisis.
- In order to improve the filtering of the tweets, additional context may be needed. So, **semantic enrichment** aims to add more information to the existing tweets. For example, Twitris [8] proceeds to a sentiment analysis on the tweets in order to add a sentiment feature to the tweets. Also, entities extraction (such as Part of Speech tagging to classify words according to their grammatical role or Named Entities Recognition in NLP) allow to retrieve specific information from the message, such as names (brand, companies, people…), location (place, street name…) or numbers (money, quantities, etc.). Twitcident [9] uses this technique to improve the semantic of the tweets. All these previous elements can then be associated with the metadata of the tweet to infer the context of the monitored event. Systems such as Sense-Place2 [6] can help inferring the location of the user thanks to the locations mentioned in the tweet.
- Filtering is a first good step towards a better use of the social media data. However, in order to improve the usefulness of the tweets, several systems aim to **classify** into different categories or identify **clusters** of tweets. For instance Tweedr [7] classifies the tweets according to their relation to casualties, damage, missing persons, projectile damage and health services. Twitris [8], Twitcident [9], AIDR [6] and EMERSE [4] are also performing a similar classification with different categories. Systems such as CrisisTracker [10] or ESA [5] works at identifying tweets related to the same topic during an event thanks to their metadata, entities, keywords, time period, entities or other relevant features. These features help to filter the data collected and aggregate the associated messages.
- **Veracity** of the data is also a huge concern in crisis management. Social media may convey useful information during an emergency but may also contain rumors or fake news. Identifying rumors is a challenging task, even for humans. To do so, identify and describe what makes a rumor is a key. [11] studies how rumors propagate after March 2012 tsunami on social media. Then, they identify several common features between rumors. Few years later, [12] identify rumor signature during Boston bombing in order to characterize them. Retweets (RT), previous activity, or identifying if the user is present or not at the event site, are all potential features that may be used to assess the veracity of the data on Twitter [13]. This work has made possible to train machine learning models to automatically detect rumors. [14] presents a rumor detector and a classifier. Their model is based on

Twitter NLP tools, a WEKA's[1] framework dedicated to tweets processing. Also, [15] introduces a real-time rumor debunking system, using Support Vector Machine described as effective even with only five tweets.

The systems described previously are summed up in Table 1.

Table 1. Classification of the different systems mentioned in the literature review, according to the business issue they address.

	Filtering	Semantic enrichment	Classification/ clustering	Geotag	Veracity
ESA [5]	x		x	x	
AIDR [6]	x		x		
Tweedr [7]	x		x		
Twitris [8]	x	x	x	x	
Twitcident [9]	x	x	x		
EMERSE [4]	x		x		
Crisistracker [10]			x	x	
SensePlace2 [16]		x		x	
[15]	x				x
[12]	x				x

Collaboration requires adapted medium. So, the way the results of the processing part is **displayed** is crucial. It varies according to the purpose of the system. However, most of them are sharing common elements. A geographical map allows to regroup the information on a single and shared representation. Systems such as Twitris [8] SensePlace2 [16], Twitcident [9], CrisisTracker [10], ESA [5] are plotting the tweets on a map, in order to provide a quick and visual information of the location of the tweets. However, this system requires that the Twitter user enables the geolocation on his/her tweet, which represent only 1% of the total volume. So, systems such as SensePlace2 are going one step further with geolocation inference according to places mentioned in the tweet. Some other common representations such as word clouds or pie charts are used to visually summarize the most frequent words captured by the system. Finally, a timeline of the messages marked as relevant by the system is provided in order to help the user to keep an access to the data.

Also, in order to improve performances, some systems, such as [6, 10], also involve digital citizens during the processing to label some of the data. These new data are then used to train the algorithms online with human annotated data.

Other industrial tools exist in this field. In crisis-related domain, the most famous is Ushahidi, but many commercial/advertising solutions also exist.

---

[1] https://www.cs.waikato.ac.nz/ml/weka/.

To sum up, previous systems aim to filter the flow of information delivered by the social media, classify them according to some, and then display the messages that may be interesting for the decision-makers. But these filtered data ignore the existing environment, the current context of the situation or the organization and the mandatory collaboration. In addition, they do not feed the COP used by the organizations. The processing of these information coming from the social media and the cross-checking with all the other sources of information remain to the user or to the decision-maker. The question of the integration of these data into the organization remains, in particular the automation of the data collection, processing and display to provide actionable information to the responders.

3   Approach: A Step Towards a Better Integration of Social Data

3.1   Research Motivations

Let's consider an example. An emergency agent is using a social media processing system in a crisis cell during a flooding. He/she has a similar system to one of those described in the previous section, i.e., a map, corresponding to the COP used by all the actors of the crisis responder's organization and a timeline of the tweets sent in a specific area. Then, a tweet appears, and it says that *"The dike at Atherton St is about to fail! Help #911"*. Current systems make it possible to display such crisis-related data. But then, the user has to check all the emerging tweets, one-by-one, if there are other data related to this event, maybe send resources to get more information if they are available.

An improved version of the current system would have notified the user that there is a school nearby that can be used as a shelter according to the contingency plan. It would then have triggered an alarm to the crisis cell, offered to send resources to evacuate the place and maybe people to assess whether or not the dike can still hold. In addition, all these elements would have been displayed on the COP. This second version would be a version that integrates the social media data into the actual organization. The following of the paper aims to propose an approach that leads to the second version of the existing systems and which provides (i) an understanding of the situation and (ii) a corresponding decision support.

3.2   Integrating Information into the Collaborative Decision-Making Process

The proposed approach relies on an understanding of the actual rescue organization by the algorithms, to better match it. To do so, such system should be able to match the current logic of the user. In [17] authors highlight that in the American 911 call centers, staff are asking questions in order to answer the "6Ws". During a phone call, questions asked by the call-taker are supposed to answer question **Where** (Where the emergency is occurring), **What** (What is happening? What kind of emergency is it?), **Weapon** (Are they weapons imply in the emergency?), **When** (if the event is not currently eyewitnesses when did the event occur?), **Who** (How many people are concern by the emergency?), and **Why** (Why is the emergency occurring?).

Any answer related to one of these questions is then forwarded to the emergency teams. Moreover, the "6Ws" framework is shared with several call centers in the United States. This behavior highlights that the call-takers follow an underlying mental framework. They are specifically looking for answers to one of these "6Ws".

This observation produces two main results. First, it highlights that in a collaborative environment, it is crucial that the stakeholders share a common vocabulary in order to perform well. Due to the organization of the American 911, where the call centers are in charge of the rescue, and police and firefighters have to work side by side, these implementing a these common concepts and use them in the response phase of a crisis seems an obvious requirement which is yet not always addressed, in particular when it comes to set up an effective collaborative decision in terms of the actions to take.

Secondly, while the "6Ws" were highlighted particularly in a Charleston call center [17], it can be assumed that such framework is or should be used in a generic way, for any crisis related call center or crisis cell, since the intrinsic purpose is precisely to get a good understanding of the situation that would be understood by all crisis stakeholders and responders. In particular, rescue organizations are taking decisions according to a specific set of concepts, such as the environment, the resources that they have, the people involved, the possible additional threats etc.

Such concepts have already been defined in ontologies or metamodels. As a metamodel provides a representation or a framework of an observed situation it enables conceptualizing the elements that make the situation in the form of interdependent concepts. This representation can then be interpreted as a common vocabulary shared between the organizations. Therefore, it becomes possible to describe behavior, processes, and interactions between the different actors according to occurring events.

The current approach of the existing systems is that the decision makers of the organizations are receiving data from the social media, and then have to process them according to their own vocabulary. However, the approach proposed in this paper is to couple this approach with a metamodel that will both (i) provide the common vocabulary to use among all responders and decision makers and (ii) help generating actionable information (i.e. that can be used by a decision support system to provide a collaborative response behavior to better coordinate all stakeholders). These information are organized trough an information model generated according to the metamodel. In this sense, the metamodel is used to provide a situation model which instanciate its concepts and associations between concepts (Fig. 1).

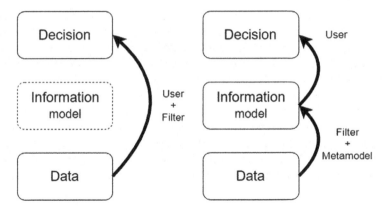

Fig. 1. Differences between the approach proposed in this paper and the one used on existing systems.

Doing so, it would be easier to monitor the operations and collaborate around the COP. So, the system is going to embed a module that is dedicated to the instantiation of the crisis situation models based on the metamodel's classes.

Many people propose metamodels or ontologies that cover concepts involved during an emergency. [18] establishes a metamodel based on the interdependence of networks to study the impact of a crisis. [19] introduces a metamodel focused on crisis entities. It purposes is to describe the activities they carry out with each other in order to respond in the better way to the crisis. [20] defines a metamodel for each of the 4 phases of the crisis (preparedness, mitigation, response and recovery). The application depicted in this paper is only considering the crisis response phase, so the three other phases would not be taken into account during the evaluation. [21] published an ontology to describe data flow, from the event to the decision-maker. Finally, [22] defines an ontology around terrorist risk to help decision-makers prevent terrorist attacks on a territory. All this previous work shows the interest of metamodels and ontology in crisis management.

Previous work linked to these points has been done in order to correlate sensors data to several metamodels' entities. [23] develops how they correlate sensor data with different entities from a metamodel in the use case of the Loire floods. In this case, the data coming from the sensors are automatically processed using [19]. This way, the system maintains a COP where water level data are considered in order to indicate the consequences of a water rise.

4   Current Implementation

Following the previous assumption, the evolution proposed in this paper is to enhanced existing systems thanks to a metamodel, alongside the filter. The proposed architecture is represented in Fig. 2. It is composed of different modules, each achieving a different operation of the global processing. The first module is the data collection module

(*Tweet collection* in the figure). Then, the *Information extraction* module is composed of a first classifier able to identify if the data is related to a crisis or not and proceed to semantic enrichment or data normalization in order to contextualize the collected and relevant data. Next comes the *Reconciliation modules*. Paired with the *Metamodel*, it classifies the information contained in the tweets with the concepts that fit best. This outputs a situation model, which then feeds the COP. However, this solution raises several challenges. First, the classifier contained in the *Reconciliation module* needs to "reconcile" the data it receives, with the metamodel classes, in order to instantiate them. Secondly, the modules need to handle the relations between the different classes instantiated previously in order to extract the underlying links between the different data (i.e. correlate data together and relevantly generate consistent parts of situational models).

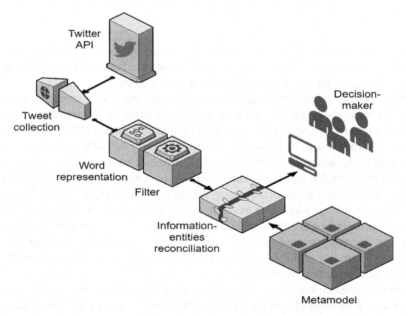

Fig. 2. Architecture of the proposed solution with the different elements that may composed the final system.

4.1 Metamodel Chosen in This Approach

Crisis situation modelling brings constraints in the choice of a metamodel. First, it must be instantiable and provide a model of the crisis situation, either manually or automatically. Crisis situations also require an evolution of these models to keep them up to date based on information acquired throughout the rescue operations. Finally, the models generated must be usable by its users and, here, specifically by most of the users. So, these criterions can be summarized in the following requirements: (i) instantiate it manually and/or automatically, (ii) continuously update the built model

(iii) exploit it. The system developed in this paper proposes to use the metamodel described in [19], which allows to describe the management of the concepts underlying in crisis resolution. In addition, it also fits to the previous criterions mentioned. First, it is instantiable as shown by [24], but also because it fits with concepts already handled by first responders, the "6Ws", which can be easily link to the metamodel classes (Who-Actors, Where-Environment, What-Threat etc.). Secondly, the situation model can be changed according to occurring events and the different data it receives. Finally, it responds to the goal set previously: enable a better collaboration through common concepts shared between the stakeholders, and it is usable to display a COP. Consequently, this metamodel is the framework used to design the information in the proposed approach.

4.2   Filtering the Data Flow

The filtering task is crucial, as it reduces the processing load on humans and allow to process only crisis-related data. Data filtering is already achieving acceptable performances according to the literature. Consequently, the system presented in this paper do not intend to improve this component. Filtering the data will reimplement existing solutions used and tested through systems such as those presented in the literature review (see Sect. 2). This will be implemented in the *Tweet collection* module. Once the data is filtered, it is then possible to organize them and extract meaningful information which will then ultimately lead to the instantiation of the different classes of the metamodel.

4.3   Information Representation and Word Embeddings

However, being able to extract information from tweets requires that the algorithms can catch the meaning behind the words used in the tweets. To get such representation of words, the proposed solution uses a word embedding. A word embedding contains all the words found in the corpus and represent them through a vector according to the context in which they are found. The context is represented by the words surrounding the targeted word. The result is a n dimensional space (where n is set during the training time) containing m vectors (where m is the number of different words in the dataset). Figure 3(a) represents a 2D representation of a word embedding, after a reduction of the n dimensions using the t-SNE algorithm [26]. The interesting feature of word embeddings is that while each word keeps its semantic sense, it is expressed according to all other words' semantic.

Here, the proposed solution relies on a crisis-related dataset, in order to better capture the vocabulary related to crisis. However, tweets sometime contain words that are missing in the word embedding. This issue is common for domain-specific word embeddings. The obvious way to overcome this issue is to get more data, which allows to get the missing words. But [27] proposes another solution which consists in starting from general word embeddings (with an important vocabulary therefore) and make them domain-specific. To do this, they modify it by emphasizing the areas of the vocabulary that are related to the domain targeted. Also, this proposition suits well the following of the proposed approach.

Thus, the resulting *Information Extraction* module ensures a filtering step to only keep crisis-related tweets and then an information representation step were all words used in the remaining dataset are confronted to one another, in order to provide a crisis-specific semantic context.

4.4 Information/Classes Reconciliation Through Clustering

Using this representation of words and their semantic, the system is going to fit the information contained in the tweets with the classes of the metamodel. To do this, the approach adopted is to identify the semantic clusters present in the word embedding. This will be accomplished using clustering algorithms. Figure 3(b) represents a possible cluster in a word embedding. Word clusters that are semantically close to a metamodel class are then highlighted, as performed in [27].

All this work will be incorporated into the *Information/Classes Reconciliation* module. The output of this module is mapped on the COP with the different instances identified on social networks, linked to the other instances that may interconnect each other's. Developing this part should be iterative, as it will require to tune the word representation and the clustering in order to get sufficient results.

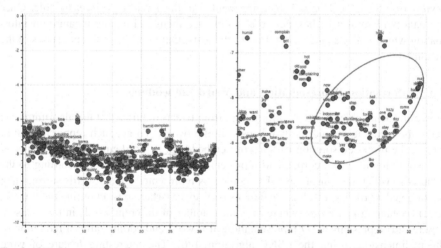

Fig. 3. 2D representation of a word embedding created using the Singapore_Haze_2013 dataset from the CrisisLex archive [28]. Figure (a) gives an overview of the word embedding. Figure (b) gives an overview of a cluster of terms related to "haze".

5   Conclusion

This paper presented a novel social media analysis system which aimed to improve the COPs used in crisis cells with a better integration of social media data and a better sharing of this information.

The contributions are: (i) a system which takes away social media processing from humans, to let them focus on decision making (ii) instantiate an information model thanks to semantic clusters found in a word embedding. This information model is generated according to the classes provided by a metamodel.

Future work will consist in further experimentation of the modules in order to provide consistent outputs for crisis responders. Reconciliation between the entities extracted from the classifier and the model is going to require time to find the appropriate parameters for the word embedding and the clustering algorithm.

Moreover, in order to improve accuracy and/or veracity of the data, it may be interesting to merge the data coming from social media data and data coming from sensors placed on the ground (water level, CCTV…). Also, this work is not dedicated only to crisis management and results may be reused in supply chain management, by replacing the data coming from the social media with data from the Internet of Things.

References

1. Blanford, J.I., et al.: Tweeting and tornadoes. In: ISCRAM 2014 Conference Proceedings – 11th International Conference on Information Systems for Crisis Response and Management, University Park, PA, pp. 319–323 (2014)
2. Imran, M., Castillo, C., Diaz, F., Vieweg, S.: Processing social media messages in mass emergency: a survey, arXiv:1407.7071 Cs, July 2014
3. Imran, M., Castillo, C., Diaz, F., Vieweg, S.: Processing social media messages in mass emergency: survey summary. In: Companion of The Web Conference 2018 - WWW 2018, Lyon, France, pp. 507–511 (2018)
4. Caragea, C., et al.: Classifying text messages for the haiti earthquake, p. 10 (2011)
5. Cameron, M.A., Power, R., Robinson, B., Yin, J.: Emergency situation awareness from twitter for crisis management, In: Proceedings of the 21st International Conference on World Wide Web, New York, NY, USA, pp. 695–698 (2012)
6. Imran, M., Castillo, C., Lucas, J., Meier, P., Vieweg, S.: AIDR: artificial intelligence for disaster response. In: Proceedings of the Companion Publication of the 23rd International Conference on World Wide Web Companion, October, pp. 159–162 (2014)
7. Ashktorab, Z., Brown, C., Nandi, M., Culotta, A.: Tweedr: mining twitter to inform, p. 5 (2014)
8. Purohit, H., Sheth, A.: Twitris v3: from citizen sensing to analysis, coordination and action, p. 2
9. Abel, F., Hauff, C., Houben, G.-J., Stronkman, R., Tao, K.: Semantics + Filtering + Search = Twitcident. exploring information in social web streams. In: Proceedings of the 23rd ACM Conference on Hypertext and Social Media, New York, NY, USA, pp. 285–294 (2012)
10. Rogstadius, J., Vukovic, M., Teixeira, C.A., Kostakos, V., Karapanos, E., Laredo, J.A.: CrisisTracker: crowdsourced social media curation for disaster awareness. IBM J. Res. Dev., 57(5), 4:1–4:13 (2013)
11. Takahashi, T., Igata, N.: Rumor detection on Twitter. In: The 6th International Conference on Soft Computing and Intelligent Systems, and The 13th International Symposium on Advanced Intelligence Systems, Kobe, Japan, pp. 452–457 (2012)
12. Maddock, J., Starbird, K., Al-Hassani, H.K., Sandoval, D.E., Orand, M., Mason, R.M.: Characterizing online rumoring behavior using multi-dimensional signatures. In: Proceedings of the 18th ACM Conference on Computer Supported Cooperative Work & Social Computing, New York, NY, USA, pp. 228–241 (2015)

13. Starbird, K., Muzny, G., Palen, L.: Learning from the crowd: collaborative filtering techniques for identifying on-the-ground Twitterers during mass disruptions, p. 10 (2012)
14. Hamidian, S., Diab, M.: Rumor detection and Classification for Twitter data, p. 7 (2015)
15. Liu, X., Nourbakhsh, A., Li, Q., Fang, R., Shah, S.: Real-time rumor debunking on Twitter, In: Proceedings of the 24th ACM International on Conference on Information and Knowledge Management - CIKM 2015, Melbourne, Australia, pp. 1867–1870 (2015)
16. MacEachren, A.M., et al.: SensePlace2: GeoTwitter analytics support for situational awareness. In: 2011 IEEE Conference on Visual Analytics Science and Technology (VAST), pp. 181–190 (2011)
17. Kropczynski, J., et al.: Identifying actionable information on social media for emergency dispatch, p. 11 (2018)
18. Kruchten, P., Woo, C., Monu, K., Sotoodeh, M.: A conceptual model of disasters encompassing multiple stakeholder domains. Int. J. Emerg. Manag. 5(1/2), 25 (2008)
19. Bénaben, F., Lauras, M., Truptil, S., Salatgé, N.: A metamodel for knowledge management in crisis management. In: 2016 49th Hawaii International Conference on System Sciences (HICSS), pp. 126–135 (2016)
20. Othman, S.H., Beydoun, G., Sugumaran, V.: Development and validation of a disaster management metamodel (DMM), Inf. Process. Manag. 50(2), 235 271 (2014)
21. Han, Y., Xu, W.: An ontology-oriented decision support system for emergency management based on information fusion. In: Proceedings of the 1st ACM SIGSPATIAL International Workshop on the Use of GIS in Emergency Management, New York, NY, USA, pp. 15:1–15:8 (2015)
22. Bennani, S., Maalel, A., Ghezala, H.B., Abed, M.: Towards a decision support model for the resolution of episodic problems based on ontology and case bases reasoning: application to terrorism attacks. In: 2017 IEEE/ACS 14th International Conference on Computer Systems and Applications (AICCSA), Hammamet, pp. 1502–1509 (2017)
23. Fertier, A.: Interprétation automatique de données hétérogènes pour la modélisation de situations collaboratives: Application à la gestion de crise (2018)
24. Fertier, A., Montarnal, A., Truptil, S., Barthe-Delanoë, A.-M., Bénaben, F.L: A situation model to support collaboration and decision-making inside crisis cells, in real time, p. 9 (2017)
25. Mikolov, T., Sutskever, I., Chen, K., Corrado, G.S., Dean, J.: Distributed representations of words and phrases and their compositionality, p. 9
26. van der Maaten, L., Hinton, G.: Visualizing data using t-SNE. J. Mach. Learn. Res. 9, 2579–2605 (2008)
27. Karisani, P., Agichtein, E.: Did you really just have a heart attack?: Towards robust detection of personal health mentions in social media. In: Proceedings of the 2018 World Wide Web Conference, Republic and Canton of Geneva, Switzerland, pp. 137–146 (2018)
28. Olteanu, A., Vieweg, S., Castillo, C.: What to expect when the unexpected happens: social media communications across crises. In: Proceedings of the 18th ACM Conference on Computer Supported Cooperative Work & Social Computing - CSCW 2015, Vancouver, BC, Canada, pp. 994–1009 (2015)

A Knowledge-Based System for Collecting and Integrating Production Information

Giulia Bruno[(⊠)], Emiliano Traini, and Franco Lombardi

Department of Management and Production Engineering, Politecnico di Torino,
Corso Duca degli Abruzzi 24, 10129 Turin, Italy
{giulia.bruno,emiliano.traini,
franco.lombardi}@polito.it

Abstract. Design and production departments are scarcely integrated in manufacturing companies. This fact, especially for companies with a highly customized production, is very critical, since the collaboration between the two
departments is essential to reduce the trial-and-errors cycles to design new
products and process. It is therefore necessary to collect data from the shop
floor, especially the ones related to anomalies or critical situations, and make
them at disposal to be used to improve the design of the next products and
processes. The aim of this paper is to develop a knowledge-based system to
digitalize and collect data regarding anomalies at the shop floor, and to integrate
them with data coming from the design phase, in order to reduce the time for
finalizing a new product. A case study has been developed for a car prototyping
company to illustrate the potentiality of the proposed solution.

Keywords: Industry 4.0 · PLM · MES · Knowledge management

1 Introduction

Today market is characterized by a by high volatility and quick dynamics. To compete
in such market, small and medium sized manufacturing companies focus on product
innovation and customization [1–3]. Effective collaboration and knowledge sharing
among experts and technicians is the winning strategy for such manufacturing systems.
In fact, decision making mainly relies on the human learning process based on product
case-histories, which enables operators to react autonomously to improve the manu-
facturability. In addition, companies are addressing a digital transformation, by using
data to improve their production processes and achieve greater consistency.

Several commercial software applications are already available for product lifecycle
management (PLM) and manufacturing execution control (MES). PLM systems make
at disposal of designers shared product databases. The fact that PLM systems are
accessible by different people and departments allows the collaborative development of
products, enabling sharing and reuse of information. However, PLM systems are not
integrated with the manufacturing execution systems (MES), which took control of the
factory operations, from production order release testing of the finished product. MES
systems are used to control in real time the progress of orders and to associate to each
production order the information about the parameters and results of the operations.

© IFIP International Federation for Information Processing 2019
Published by Springer Nature Switzerland AG 2019
L. M. Camarinha-Matos et al. (Eds.): PRO-VE 2019, IFIP AICT 568, pp. 163–170, 2019.
https://doi.org/10.1007/978-3-030-28464-0_15

Through the real-time monitoring, it is therefore possible to control the progression of tasks and compare it with the production planning. In case of delays, the planning can be readjusted accordingly.

However, without a connection between PLM and MES, it is difficult for a designer to find data related to the anomalies occurred during the manufacturing process in the shop floor. This data could be of great importance at the design stage of a new product, especially for companies that realize prototypes, since, to design a new process, they usually need several trial-and-errors cycles before find the final one. For such companies, the knowledge of the trial-and-errors cycles that contribute to develop past products and processes, without the presence of a formalized and structured system, remains in the minds of the people, or, at best, transferred verbally, and then, over time, inevitably lost [4, 5]. Similarly, it is also difficult for a production manager to find information related to the checks to perform before and after the execution of an operation on a machine, and for an operator to report in a structured way the occurrence of problems and anomalies during the production.

Based on such needs, the aim of the paper is to develop a framework able to: (i) collect data regarding anomalies at the shop floor, in addition to the other data regarding the production monitoring typical of MES systems, (ii) integrate data coming from PLM and MES to reduce the number of trial-and-errors cycles to find the final production process of a new product.

The rest of the paper is organized as follows. Section 2 summarizes the relevant literature available on the topic. Section 3 describes the proposed method and the definition of the data model to structure the knowledge-based system. Section 4 presents the application of the framework in the use case of an Italian company producing car prototypes. Finally, Sect. 5 draws conclusions and states future work perspectives.

2 Related Works

Previous works addressed the issue of structuring and formalising product-related knowledge [6–9], while several international research projects addressed the development of industrial knowledge sharing systems (e.g., amePLM [10], ICP4Life [11], Know4car [12], Manutelligence [13]). The importance of collaboration between design and manufacturing is highlighted in several papers [14, 15]. However, the practical use of tools for supporting knowledge management is still very low. The GeCo Observatory (http://www.homeappliancesworld.com/2015/06/01/italian-manufacturing-innovation-is-possible) found, on a sample of more than 100 Italian manufacturing companies, that the most used methods to explicit knowledge remain the traditional verbal or written communication, while the use of more structured software systems is severely limited.

Two lacks can be identified in both current scientific literature and research projects. The first one is that they did not address specifically the highly customized/prototypal production, where the presence of many alternative routings and operations makes very difficult to manage all the manufacturing variables together, in an efficient way, without increasing wastes of time and costs. The second one is that they did not address the problem of collecting data related to failures and anomalies occurring at the shop floor, and make them available for the designers, to allow them learning from past problems when designing new products and processes.

The main technical innovations proposed by our work are the following: (i) open source architecture for PLM, KBS and MES, (ii) advanced data model to relate data from PLM and MES, and (iii) possibility of storing data related to anomalies occurred during the production.

3 Method

Three systems are used to manage manufacturing information: PLM, MES and Enterprise Resource Planning (ERP). The integration of ERP and MES allows the organization an efficient management of the inventory. In fact, an ERP systems can more efficiently manage the purchase functions if it knows the consumption of raw materials in real time. The integration between ERP and MES is based on the IEC 62264 standard, a model that standardizes the exchange of information between business systems and production control systems. In order to guarantee a consistent flow of information in the company, the integration between PLM-ERP has also to be implemented. The most significant improvement is the integration of the organizational data, ensuring that all areas can access the updated product data.

These two integrations are not capable of guaranteeing the right flow of information between PLM and MES, because the ERP does not have an adequate structure to accept and store detailed data of the product. Therefore, the PLM-MES integration is necessary.

3.1 Knowledge-Based System

The method we propose is to develop a central Knowledge based System (KBS), acting as integrator of the ERP, PLM and MES. The proposed system will allow (i) to collect all the information regarding the critical realizations of new components in a structured way, so that the added values of the experience breakthrough, as well as other useful tips, could be provided to the users, and (ii) to reuse the knowledge, i.e. help designers to define more reliable processes for new products, reducing the "trial-and-error" cycles in the development of forming processes.

In fact, when a customer makes an order, it means that the company must define the sequence of activities to obtain the required product. If the historical data regarding previous products are stored in the KBS, it can be used to find the closest product already produced in the past that needs less changes to be adapted to the new shop order. The chosen product is then found in the PLM platform where the needed changes can be done. The information associated to the new product is sent to the KBS and made accessible to the MES. The MES uses the product information to manage the production and, when the production is finished, it reports in the KBS the information related to the execution of each activity and the success or failure of the product. In case of failure, the company can check the intermediate results reported for each activity and decide how to proceed to obtain a better solution.

3.2 KBS Data Model

The KBS contains the subset of data relevant for all the three systems and acting as a bridge among them. In the following, we focus in particular on the integration between PLM and MES. Figure 1 shows the structure of the KBS through an entity-relationship model.

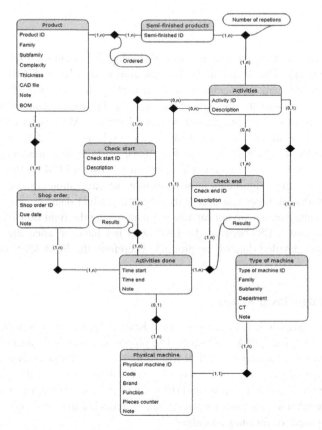

Fig. 1. UML class diagram of the data model of the KBS.

The product entity contains information about the classification, the CAD file, the BOM and other general characteristics of the products. The amount of the semi-finished product is connected to it, which identifies the status of the semi-finished products specifying the next activity to be carried out. This is the reason why there is also the activity entity that characterizes the particular activity, explaining the check start, the check-ends and the machines necessary to carry it out. To each type of machine are then associated the physical machines available in the company. These entities are provided by the PLM and are subsequently used by the MES.

To the entities associated with the PLM activity are added entities that model the data provided by the MES, i.e. the data coming from the production. The fundamental entity is the one related to the shop order. In the KBS all the shop orders taken in charge and on which the company has worked are stored. This entity is connected to the product, as each shop order concerns a single and specific product, so a single and specific product lifecycle. The shop order is also connected to the activity carried out, connected itself to the verification checks. It models the data structure from which we can extract the history of all the activities divided by shop order and consequently by product and results obtained.

3.3 KBS Implementation

The KBS was implemented as a PostgreSQL database (www.postgresql.org), with the set of tables needed to represent the UML diagram of Fig. 1. The open source PLM software ARAS (www.aras.com) was exploited to digitalise and store the information related to the resources of the company and the production process of each product. Through an automatic procedure, the information related to the entities of Product, Semi-finished products, Activity, Check start, Check end, and Type of machine, together with their relationships, are periodically extracted from the PLM system and inserted in the KBS, to make them available to the MES and ERP systems.

The MES platform JPiano (https://www.aecsoluzioni.it/wp/en/jpiano-panoramica/jpiano-prodotti) was used to implement the MES system. As for PLM, also from the MES the information related to the entities of Activities done and Physical machine, and their relationships and the ones with the Check start and Check end are periodically extracted and inserted in the KBS.

Further details on the implementation in a use case are reported in the following section.

4   Use Case

The framework was applied in an Italian company that operates in the automotive sector, producing prototype bodywork components for passenger cars and other kinds of vehicles. Currently, all the information generated during the production process is only written on paper.

The process for the realization of a prototype bodywork component starts with the delivery, by the costumer, of the CAD model of the requested piece. The CAD model is received by the technical office that defines the production process, the design of the dies and the material to be used. Once the dies have been constructed, the metal sheets used to make the body part are sent to the Laser office where the metal sheet is trimmed using a two-dimensional laser to obtain the appropriate shape outline. After the sheets have been cut, they are transported to the presses area where they undergo the first press operation. The semi-finished items are then returned to the laser section where 3D lasers cut the metal sheet according to specific laser paths obtaining the final measures of the piece and creating slots and holes.

We started the development of our framework with the implementation in ARAS of several graphic user interfaces in order to allow the users to store the data corresponding to the structure represented in Fig. 1. As an example, Fig. 2 presents the user interface to insert the information related the Type of machine entity. Similar interfaces were created for Activities, Product, Check start and Check end. For each activity, the corresponding machine, check starts and check ends can be added by selecting them from the drop down menus created.

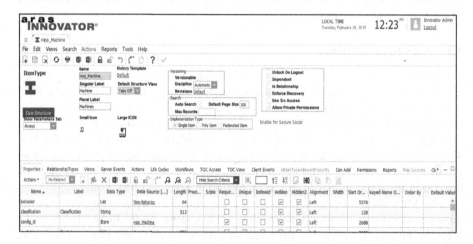

Fig. 2. Screenshot of Aras PLM implementation: Machine.

One of the main potentialities of our framework is the capability of inserting Check start and Check ends related to an activity. Examples of Check starts created for the use case are reported in Table 1. The Check starts represent the controls that the operators have to do before starting the execution of an activity on a machine. The list of Check starts for each Activity are set in the PLM and then transmitted to the KBS, so that they are accessible by the MES. In this way, the MES can show to the operators the Check starts when they start the execution of an activity. The results of the Check starts are inserted by the operators in the MES, which transmit them to the KBS, so they are accessible from the PLM.

Table 1. Examples of Check starts related to the Activities of the use case.

Activity	Check start
3D laser welding	Presence of a dedicated head
	Presence of pincers for fixing the piece on the stand
	Set of self-learning programming mode of welding path
Press punching	Presence of the mold
	Presence of mold mounting brackets
	Presence of supports for handling sheet metal

(*continued*)

Table 1. (*continued*)

Activity	Check start
Deep drawing	Presence of the mold
	Presence of mold mounting brackets
	Presence of supports for handling sheet metal
	Presence of nylon sheets
	Presence of oil
3D Laser finishing	Routes loaded with USB device
	Presence of U-bolts for positioning the sheet
	Presence of pincers for fixing the piece on the U-bolt
	Presence of reference holes
Manual molding	Presence of molds from the press department
	Presence of gauges and hammers

Similarly, also for the Check ends, for each activity it is possible to specify which are the controls to do at the end of the operation. In the current version of the framework, the Check end is a free text where the operator can write if something went wrong during the operation. A more complex data collection, including the possibility of uploading a photo or a video of the anomalous results, is under development.

In ARAS, it is also possible to define a production process (i.e., the relationship between Activities and Product) by using the Process Plan module. In order to populate a process plan, a designer/planner can easily add the activities by selecting the activities from 'list of Activities' created before. The execution of each activity is then recorded by the MES, which insert the actual start and end date for each activity, so that a comparison between the planned dates and the actual ones can be performed.

To replicate data from ARAS to the KBS, a merge replication [16] was implemented. Merge replication starts with a snapshot of the source database objects and data. Subsequent data changes and schema modifications made at the source database and at the destination database are tracked with triggers. The source synchronizes with the destination when connected to the network and exchanges all rows that have changed since the last time synchronization occurred. In this way, the content of the PLM and the KBS are continuously updated and synchronized.

5 Conclusions

The objective of this paper is to propose a framework to integrate design and production data, since, especially in small manufacturing companies, they often remain separated and stored in two different systems: PLM and MES. The framework is based on a knowledge based system, which collects and integrates two subsets of data, one from PLM and one from MES, making such data accessible by both the systems. In this way, anomalies that occur at the shop floor during the production can be easily found by designers, who can use them to improve the process in order to improve the design of the following products. Furthermore, the proposed framework allows the data retrieval of previous products and its re-usage to define variants and changes to them.

Future works will consider on the one hand data analysis techniques for using the stored data in the KBS, and on the other hand a more comprehensive integration considering also the ERP system. Furthermore, a set of key performance indicators to evaluate the efficacy of the proposed framework in terms of reduction of time to finalize the process development will be studied.

References

1. Wortmann, J.C., Muntslag, D.R., Timmermans, P.J.M.: Customer-Driven Manufacturing. Chapman & Hall, London (1997)
2. Tu, Y.: Production planning and control in a virtual one-of-a-kind production company. Comput. Ind. **34**(3), 271–283 (1997)
3. Dean, P.R., Tu, Y.L., Xue, D.: An information system for one-of-a-kind production. Int. J. Prod. Res. **47**(4), 1071–1087 (2009)
4. Bruno, G., Antonelli, D., Korf, R., Zimmermann, N.: Exploitation of a semantic platform to store and reuse PLM knowledge. IFIP Adv. Inf. Commun. Technol. **438**, 59–66 (2014)
5. Bruno, G., Taurino, T., Villa, A.: An approach to support SMEs in manufacturing knowledge organization. J. Intell. Manuf. **29**(6), 1379–1392 (2018)
6. Chungoora, N., et al.: A model-driven ontology approach for manufacturing interoperability and knowledge sharing. Comput. Ind. **64**(4), 392–401 (2013)
7. David, M., Rowe, F.: What does PLMS (product lifecycle management systems) manage: data or documents? Complement. Cont. SMEs Comput. Ind. **75**, 140–150 (2015)
8. Efthymiou, K., Sipsas, K., Mourtzis, D., Chryssolouris, G.: On knowledge reuse for manufacturing systems design and planning: a semantic technology approach. CIRP J. Manuf. Sci. Technol. **8**, 1–11 (2015)
9. Igba, J., Alemzadeh, K., Gibbons, P.M., Henningsen, K.: A framework for optimizing product performance through feedback and reuse of in-service experience. Robot. Comput.-Integr. Manuf. **36**, 2–12 (2015)
10. Bruno, G., Korf, R., Lentes, J., Zimmermann, N.: Efficient management of product lifecycle information through a semantic platform. Int. J. Prod. Lifecycle Manag. **9**(1), 45–64 (2016)
11. Elgamma, A., Papazoglou, M., Krämer, B., Constantinescu, C.: Design for customization: a new paradigm for product-service system development. Proc. CIRP **64**, 345–350 (2017)
12. Ebrahimi, A.H., Johansson, P.E.C., Bengtsson, K., Åkesson, K.: Managing product and production variety – a language workbench approach. Proc. CIRP **17**, 338–344 (2014)
13. Petrucciani, M., Marangi, L., Agosta, M., Stevanella, M.: A platform for product-service design and manufacturing intelligence. In: Cattaneo, L., Terzi, S. (eds.) Models, Methods and Tools for Product Service Design. SAST, pp. 45–61. Springer, Cham (2019). https://doi.org/10.1007/978-3-319-95849-1_4
14. Ming, X.G., Yan, J.Q., Lu, W.F., et al.: Mass production of tooling product families via modular feature-based design to manufacturing collaboration in PLM. J. Intell. Manuf. **18**, 185 (2007)
15. Pouchard, L., Ivezic, N., Schlenoff, C.: Ontology engineering for distributed collaboration in manufacturing. In: Proceedings of the AIS2000 Conference (2000)
16. Hammond, B. Merge replication in Microsoft's SQL server 7.0. In: Proceedings of the 1999 ACM SIGMOD International Conference on Management of Data, vol. 527 (1999)

Big Data and Learning

Interactive Machine Learning: Managing Information Richness in Highly Anonymized Conversation Data

Ari Alamäki[1(✉)], Lili Aunimo[1], Harri Ketamo[2], and Lasse Parvinen[3]

[1] Haaga-Helia University of Applied Sciences, Helsinki, Finland
{ari.alamaki,lili.aunimo}@haaga-helia.fi
[2] HeadAI Oy, Pori, Finland
harri.ketamo@headai.com
[3] Terveystalo Oy, Helsinki, Finland
lasse.parvinen@terveystalo.com

Abstract. This case study focuses on an experiment analysing textual conversation data using machine learning algorithms and shows that sharing data across organisational boundaries requires anonymisation that decreases that data's information richness. Additionally, sharing data between organisations, conducting data analytics and collaborating to create new business insight requires inter-organisational collaboration. This study shows that analysing highly anonymised and professional conversation data challenges the capabilities of artificial intelligence. Machine learning algorithms alone cannot learn the internal connections and meanings of information cues. This experiment is therefore in line with prior research in interactive machine learning where data scientists, specialists and computational agents interact. This study reveals that, alongside humans, computational agents will be important actors in collaborative networks. Thus, humans are needed in several phases of the machine learning process for facilitating and training. This calls for collaborative working in multi-disciplinary teams of data scientists and substance experts interacting with computational agents.

Keywords: Interactive machine learning · Unstructured text · Big data · Anonymisation · Information richness · Collaboration · Privacy

1 Introduction

Sharing data between organisations is becoming an important process for the co-creation of value in collaborative networks [1, 2]. But in most business or scientific research cases, sharing data over organisational boundaries requires anonymisation. For example, the European General Data Protection Regulation (GDPR) allows the secondary use of data, but pseudonymisation or anonymisation is required depending on the intended use for that information (EU GDPR, Article 89). There is, however, little research on how anonymisation affects the way in which data are used or how machine learning algorithms are able to process highly anonymised, unstructured textual data.

© IFIP International Federation for Information Processing 2019
Published by Springer Nature Switzerland AG 2019
L. M. Camarinha-Matos et al. (Eds.): PRO-VE 2019, IFIP AICT 568, pp. 173–184, 2019.
https://doi.org/10.1007/978-3-030-28464-0_16

Sharing data between multiple organisations is becoming more and more common, with organisations looking to enrich their own data analysis by combining it with third party data. Gaining deeper business insight and ensuring the reliability of results both require the processing of several data sets and a collaborative network of organisations. Many organisations are also seeking new value by combining inter-organisational data and advanced data analytics methods such as machine learning [1]. Sharing data will become a crucial process in the digital transformation of business processes in the value chains of ecosystems. Additionally, machine learning is becoming a vital part of the process of digitising data that has been analysed.

There are numerous benefits to sharing data sets for collaborative networks of organisations. But there are also challenges. One is data privacy, anonymisation and the loss of information richness. Preserving data privacy is very important from the points of view of both lawful use and trust. Very often, data that have monetary value include confidential information. Organisations protect their customers' privacy by anonymising data before they use them in their own business processes, but they also anonymise data that are shared with their partner companies. However, anonymisation typically reduces the information richness of the data and thus also the value that can be created from the data.

Prior research on the relationship between anonymisation and information richness in sharing data between organisations is scant. This is even more true in the realm of natural language data. Organisations are increasingly sharing natural language text data, for example, data from voice messages, chat conversations and customer communications. The techniques for anonymising natural language data differ significantly from the many techniques used for anonymising sensitive structured data, such as k-anonymity [3], a traditional anonymisation model that has been used when sharing aggregated health records. In the field of electronic health record anonymisation, the trade-off between privacy and loss of accuracy is a well-studied problem [4, 5].

As with structured data, anonymisation the identity of any text data user may significantly decrease those data's information richness. However, the problem of how to preserve information richness while conserving data privacy has not been widely studied in relation to textual natural language data. This has resulted in two practical consequences: (1) Sensitive textual data are not shared outside the organisation at all, in the fear of breaking privacy regulations; or (2) if the data are shared, they are anonymised using unnecessary obfuscating anonymisation methods, resulting in a dramatic loss in data richness.

The goal of this experiment was to study machine learning and highly anonymized conversation data in the inter-organizational setting. This study also seeks to define information richness in textual conversation data, study the relationship between data anonymisation and information richness, and, lastly, describe the machine learning experiments related to using highly anonymised conversation data. Additionally, it suggests a model for how machine learning algorithms could create useful insight from highly anonymised textual conversation data.

The study contributes to discussions related to using big data, information management and artificial intelligence to automate business processes. The paper is organised as follows. After this introduction, Sect. 2 reviews the essence of anonymisation and information richness in conversation data. Section 3 describes the research method and data used in the case study. In Sect. 4, we then present our findings. In conclusion, Sects. 5 and 6 discuss the contributions this study makes to the field.

2   Anonymisation and Information Richness

Information Richness and Conversation Data
In-person conversations between customers and service providers use a wide range of symbolic systems and therefore contain semantically rich information. Conveying verbal and non-verbal messages in these conversations facilitates mutual understanding. When conversation takes place via the online chat, information is not semantically as rich as in face-to-face situations. However, using video as a part of a chat conversation does enable non-verbal cues to be transmitted and interpreted, allowing for a less ambiguous understanding than with simple textual information. Textual interaction does not create logical connections between various symbolic systems and cannot convey the meanings of conditional events or causes as well as multimedia or face-to-face interaction [6, 7]. This means that analysing chat conversations that include only textual information results in a decrease in information richness as compared to analysing multimedia or physical conversations. In addition, the anonymisation of textual conversation data decreases semantic information.

The concept of information richness [8, 9] provides a theoretical framework for discussing the richness of conversational data before and after anonymisation. Information richness refers to the data mediums, such as text, audio or voice, that deliver informational or emotional cues. The structure of text includes the logical connections and cues that form stories and meanings. Information richness, also referred to as media richness, is an objective property of media that indicates the extent to which a medium can facilitate understanding or interpretation within a specific amount of time [10, 11]. Information richness does not have a causal connection to the actual performance of communication [12]. Thus, richness of information does not directly correlate to the richness of data being used in data analytics. One level of information richness may also result in different levels of understanding for a particular piece of communication [13, 14]. Similarly, results may change over time [15], as information is also context-dependent.

Anonymisation and Data Analytics
The European Union (EU) [16] defines personal data as information concerning an identified or identifiable natural person. A person can be identified directly or indirectly by these data, which could include an *"identification number, location data, an online identifier or [...] one or more factors specific to the physical, physiological, genetic, mental, economic, cultural or social identity of that natural person"* [16].

Data anonymisation refers to the process of obfuscating data so that they cannot be used to identify any individual. Personal identifiers can be categorised into two classes: (1) identifying attributes, such as social security numbers, names, driver license IDs, etc.; and (2) quasi-identifiers, which are a combination of key attributes that can be used to narrow down identity to a certain individual. The terms de-identification and pseydonymisation are also used in this area. De-identification is sometimes used interchangeably with anonymisation [5], while anonymisation is sometimes used in a stronger sense, denoting an irreversible form of de-identification [17]. In this article, we use the latter interpretation of anonymisation. Pseudonymisation refers to the process of personal identifiers being replaced with artificial identifiers. Pseudonymised data can be re-identified if additional information is available. Encrypting is a commonly used pseudonymisation technique. An important difference between anonymisation and pseudonymisation is that pseudonymised data still fall under the scope of privacy legislation, while anonymised data do not [18].

In medical fields, structured data are typically shared between organisations in integrated health care and public health studies. Based on consent and ethical approval, patient records can be used for secondary purposes that include clinical trials and studies, even if the data in those records are not anonymised. However, as clinical data are increasingly shared between organisations, the techniques used to anonymise those data need more attention. When different datasets are linked with each other and when intelligent algorithms are used to mine the data, even anonymised data records can contain attributes that allow for an individual's identity to be narrowed down.

There are several methods for anonymising structured data. These include directory replacement, masking, scrambling and blurring. There are also several measures designed to tackle the problem of indirect identifiers, a problem which arises when datasets are joined (in the medical field, this is called record linkage) so that a new dataset includes records that identify an individual even if all direct identifiers have been removed. For example, if information about patients' native languages is added to a set of records that have been linked, a single patient with a unique combination of nationality and native language may be identifiable in that combined dataset. The problem with establishing sound methods for removing all indirect identifiers from a single dataset is that it is not always possible to predict which sensitive datasets might be combined in the future. Changes to datasets over time also affect the indirect identifiers. Methods based on k-anonymity are a well-known solution for de-identification of combined datasets [3]. K-anonymity requires that every individual must be indistinguishable from at least k other individuals within that dataset, where a greater k value correlates with stronger de-identification levels in the data.

Joining two datasets, i.e. record linkage, often occurs when data originating from different organisations is combined for research purposes [19]. The main principle behind secure record linkage is that information identifying a patient is separated from actual health-related information. This has resulted in the creation of independent linkage centres that ensure this principle is adhered to [19].

As stated before, research on the effects of data anonymisation on the information richness of textual data is scarce. As several authors have stated, de-identifying free text is more complex that de-identifying structured data [see, for example, 20]. Cardinal [21] presents a method for anonymising psychiatric patients' textual records which is based on fuzzy matching of recognizable phrases. This method uses cryptography to map patient identifiers to research identifiers (also called pseudonyms).

3 Methods

The Case Experiment
In this study, we analyse a case in which anonymised natural language chat data were shared between two organisations. These data were analysed using machine learning and neural network methodologies. The organisations represent different roles in the value chain of an ecosystem, making this case particularly relevant when considering the challenges of anonymisation and information richness. The study also provides a case experiment for using machine learning to analyse highly anonymised conversation data.

We used the Headai-artificial intelligence platform (https://www.headai.com/), which utilises machine learning methods. The platform combines semantic neuro-computing and learning algorithms to create semantic neural networks and deep insight based on unstructured or structured data. The data used in the study consist of medical information, an example of sensitive information with a high requirement for anonymisation. The data included 57,000 dialogue-loops and more than 800,000 trigger-response pairs. The data were anonymised using strict standards, removing all indications of personal information. After that, machine learning methods were applied to the data.

The Case Study Method
Since the aim of this research is to develop a new understanding of the relationship between anonymisation and information richness, the method we adopted is the case study approach [22]. We extended our research approach to include abductive quali-tative research methods, [23] since our goal is to build a new model that assists companies in managing anonymisation without losing information richness. The abductive research method enabled the researchers to build explanations from the findings and elaborate on a conceptual model that combines a literature review and the study's empirical findings. This method also enabled researchers to simultaneously process prior literature on anonymisation and information richness and the analysis of the data gathered in the experiment [22]. Using an iterative research process allowed for a deeper understanding of the experiment results while also contributing to the model of anonymisation.

The Machine Learning Experiment Procedure
This scientific research experiment grew out of the needs of a specific healthcare service provider. This organisation wanted to learn about patterns in chat conversations between patients and healthcare professionals. These chat conversations followed similar question-and-answer formats. The goal was to find patterns that could later be used to automate or improve customer experience, or to streamline business processes by improving information management practices related to the chat conversations. The conversation data were highly anonymised before being provided to data scientists (Fig. 1).

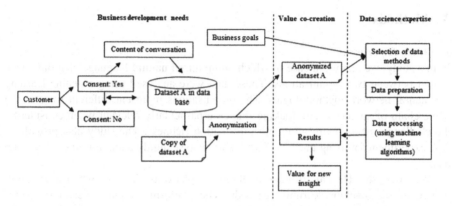

Fig. 1. Experiment procedure

The anonymised data were tested using analytic methods including Bayesian machine learning, support vector machines and feedforward networks. They were then prepared for deeper analyses that would increase the understanding of conversation dialogues. Data were used to train machine learning algorithms, but due to the high levels of anonymisation, special vocabulary and open conversation flows, several human-machine loops were needed to identify the dialogue used to create patterns.

4   Results

Our experiment showed that highly anonymised sensitive data included significantly less information than original datasets. In fact, the anonymised dataset was another dataset compared to the original dataset, in practice. The anonymised dataset excluded the job titles or roles of patients and healthcare experts, since this might have included personal information such as names, titles or organisations. Although machine learning did recognise question-answer pairs, it did not recognise which conversation partner was asking a question and which was answering and artificial intelligence could not conclude who was a patient and who a healthcare (although a human could easily make this determination based on the conversation content). The following question-answer pair illustrates the challenge that machines without the necessary algorithms have in concluding which conversation partner represents which role, as compared to human listeners: *"My children had fevers and coughs yesterday"/"Would you like to make an appointment with a paediatrician?"*

The experiment showed that, although this conversation was a professional discussion between a patient and healthcare expert, it nevertheless included lots of conversation with "blank substance," which we also call noise. This type of content includes words such as *"hello"*, *"hi"*, *"how can I help you?"*, *"what is your address?"* and *"video does work"*. This meant that data modelling using existing machine learning methods, such as Bayesian machine learning, support vector machines and feedforward networks, did not immediately detect meaningful patterns of conversation. These machine learning methods work well in analyses of question-answer data or news data, which include sentences with straightforward meanings and textual data with a lot of different kinds of content. The preliminary analyses revealed that the kind of professional conversation in this case study includes a lot of noise. This needed to be taken into account in order for the machine learning algorithms to be able to successfully detect which repeated question-answer pairs were useful for creating new business insight as opposed to being only noise.

Unlike conversations in public discussion forums, the data in this study followed a linear path. Noise was removed from the analyses, which helped create larger entities and more meaningful question-answer pairs. In this phase, human analysis was needed to differentiate noise from substantive conversation. After this, the basic Bayesian machine learning algorithms began to work properly and were improved by the use of reinforcement learning principles. Additionally, an analysis that recognised the meanings of words also helped to find the essential topics across all conversations. These findings could help service providers incorporate additional useful information into chat conversations, for example, related articles or instructions.

5 Discussion

Our experiment showed that applying machine learning to highly anonymised data requires several human-machine loops to aid in training the artificial intelligence software that is being used. This finding supports Holzinger's [24] research, which showed that using machine learning to generate meaningful results from sensitive and complex medical information requires several rounds of expert training. In interactive machine learning, human agents (experts) interact with computational agents in order to train those computational agents to create meaningful and correct analyses. The human agent or expert also needs to perform a final check to ensure the meaningfulness of analytic results. This kind of machine learning is especially relevant in new scenarios where neither data scientists nor experts have prior experience. A new approach is needed for developing and training machine learning algorithms so that they compute in a meaningful way. For example, analysing of professional conversation data or abstract and domain-specific data require typically several human-machine interactions.

There is little existing literature on the role of anonymisation and machine learning. This study has filled that gap by showing that anonymisation causes problems for machine learning. Unlike prior research, the present study examined highly anonymised data and its information richness using real-life data. Service providers need to anonymise highly sensitive conversation data—typically natural language data (text, voice, audio, image) that includes personal information or other identifying information not located in separated columns in the database. These data differ from structured textual data that locates in database cells according to the data model of software system. Locating direct identifiers that need to be anonymised is significantly easier in structured data sets, because the identifying data are located in specific columns and cells. For example, in unstructured conversation data, it is difficult to locate all personally identifying information because names, addresses or other physical, physiological, genetic, mental, economic, cultural, social or ethnic data are a part of the conversation. In addition to recognizing direct identifiers such as proper names, the data should also preserve at least some of the content of the information, such as different actor types (patient, physician, possibly a patient's relatives, etc.). If these were recognized in the data, the anonymisation method could consist of replacing personal identifiers with general terms, for example, all patient names may read "patient", all home addresses "home address" and so on. However, if simplistic anonymisation methods are used, this creates an unintended loss of information cues and their logical connections, which are needed for a full understanding of the meanings of sentences. One advantage of unstructured conversation data is that they provide richer conversation samples, unlike data that is entered into pre-defined information categories.

The findings of this study pointed out that anonymisation resulted in some loss of significant informational cues and that this, in turn, destroyed sentence logic and decreased information richness. This is not necessarily a problem for humans, who can easily determine which question-answer pairs belong together, however, machine learning interprets words mechanically and needs informational cues in order to create patterns. For example, machine learning needs to conclude who is a patient in a conversation. If informational cues do not have a clear logical connection to meaning, then machine learning algorithms cannot determine their internal connections. An issue may be, for example, stated as suggestion, example, conclusion, diagnostic or warning in the conversation. Thus, human agents or experts are needed in several phases of the machine learning process in order to facilitate and train machine learning. This consists of an iterative process of selecting the proper methods by running several trial-and-error loops that can map concepts logically and locate meaningful patterns. This calls for collaborative and multi-disciplinary teams of data scientists and substance experts interacting with computational agents. For example, substance experts can explain to data scientists why conversation goes forward with certain logic or why some experts ask questions before they present their recommendations.

Collaborative networks are data-rich environments that have started to adopt new technologies such as artificial intelligence and data management [25–27]. These findings contribute to discussions around the ways in which data are often used across collaborative networks. Healthcare sector is one of industries that are adopting data management and machine learning within collaborative networks [28]. Healthcare and social welfare data, for example, can be shared and used in these networks, but it must be anonymised. This study demonstrates that the anonymisation of unstructured clinical or patient textual data often results in a significant loss of information richness. Thus, the secondary use of highly anonymised data creates potential reliability and validity problems for the interpretation of results, if these issues are not taken into account when conducting machine learning analytics, especially given that artificial intelligence software cannot automatically manage these challenges. Healthcare companies can, in addition, request their customers' consent to use their data for the company's own purposes, which allows for the use of richer information. The kind of anonymisation required when sharing personal data across organisational boundaries should pay particular attention to linguistic challenges and differences. For example, some languages have several word endings that pose a challenge when trying to locate all personal identifiers in a set of unstructured textual data. Data are anonymised, and their processing falls outside the scope of GDPR when it no longer includes any identifiable personal data [18].

The proposed method for anonymising unstructured textual data uses natural language processing techniques to identify all personal identifiers and to classify them according to a domain-specific ontology. Once this has been done, all personal identifiers are replaced with terms from that ontology. The first phase of the identification of personal identifiers is achieved using an off-the-shelf named entity recognition software. Named entity recognition software uses lemmatization or the stemming of words, as well as syntactic sentence analysis, to classify entities into categories such as: names of persons, organisations, locations, expressions of time, currency and other numerical expressions (see, for example, the GATE software created by the University of Sheffield). When these named entities have been identified, a human specialist is brought in to produce training data for the domain-specific personal identifier recognizer. This involves marking in the processed text all entities listed in the domain-specific ontology, which contains a hierarchy of terms. Based on this training corpus, patterns for identifying ontology-specific personal identifiers are created. Anonymisation is achieved by replacing the specific entities recognised in the text with the corresponding term from the ontology.

In many practical cases, researchers end up facing an overly anonymised dataset. This is typically because organisations wish to stay on the safe side of privacy regulations. While this is understandable from the organisation's point of view, for a researcher, this often strips the data of most of its utility. To tackle this challenge, we propose using an interactive machine learning method with a human specialist in the loop to assist the algorithm. This method uses machine learning in an iterative manner. After the first iteration with initial training data, a human specialist inspects the results and makes one systematic improvement to the training data. The goal of this improvement is to add to the data's information richness. For example, in our case study, the first iteration consisted of a human agent classifying the parts of the conversation as either belonging to the physician or the patient. After this, the algorithm is run again and the iteration starts from the beginning. This iterative process ends either when the results of the machine learning algorithm are satisfactory with regard to the task at hand or when the human expert cannot do any systematic improvements to the training data.

6   Conclusion

This study's results contribute to debates related to information processing and management and artificial intelligence in several ways. First, by reviewing the relationship between anonymisation and information richness in unstructured conversation data and secondly, by demonstrating that an interactive machine learning method in which humans and computational agents collaborate is the best mode of analysing highly anonymised conversation data.

These findings highlight that the digital transformation of business intelligence processes is not linear, but that it instead requires multi-disciplinary teamwork in inter-organisational settings. Incorporating artificial intelligence into business processes requires an understanding the role anonymisation plays in information richness and machine learning methods. The insight generated by artificial intelligence is directly dependent on the ways in which data and human-machine interaction takes place.

This study's most basic limitation is that its reliance on a specific case study limits the results' transferability. Nonetheless, the findings provide a basic understanding of anonymisation, information richness and interactive machine learning. The present research raised questions concerning interactive machine learning which merit further examination. This study's results should also encourage researchers to conduct empirical research into how best to involve topic experts in the process of interactive machine learning, in particular when data scientists are not able to solve all domain-related conceptual and procedural problems.

In future research, the method proposed for anonymising unstructured textual data should be augmented with the capability to measure the level of anonymisation achieved with the data at hand. It should also be possible to define the desired level of anonymity beforehand. These two steps could be achieved by forming a structured database record based on each dialogue loop. The columns would consist of named entity classes and the rows would consist of the corresponding ontology-specific named entities extracted from a dialogue loop. The k-anonymity level of the anonymised data set could then be measured. If that level is lower than desired, the anonymisation method could replace the currently used ontology terms in the data with the original term. For example, the expression of location "City name: Kauniainen: role: home address" would be replaced by the "District name: Uusimaa, role: home address". In the original data, the location was the exact home address.

Acknowledgments. The authors would like to thank the Big data big business-project, all the parties behind the project, and Business Finland – for its support for this study.

References

1. Alamäki, A., Rantala, T., Valkokari, K., Palomäki, K.: Business roles in creating value from data in collaborative networks. In: Camarinha-Matos, L.M., Afsarmanesh, H., Rezgui, Y. (eds.) PRO-VE 2018. IAICT, vol. 534, pp. 612–622. Springer, Cham (2018). https://doi.org/10.1007/978-3-319-99127-6_53
2. Lindquist, J.: Data science under GDPR with pseudonymisation in the data pipeline. Dativa (2018). https://www.dativa.com/data-science-gdpr-pseudonymisation-data-pipeline
3. Sweeney, L.: k-anonymity: A model for protecting privacy. Int. J. Uncertainty Fuzziness Knowl. Based Syst. **10**(05), 557–570 (2002)
4. Lu, Y., Sinnott, R.O., Verspoor, K., Parampalli, U.: Privacy-preserving access control in electronic health record linkage. In: 17th IEEE International Conference on Trust, Security and Privacy in Computing and Communications (TrustCom)/12th IEEE International Conference on Big Data Science And Engineering (BigDataSE), pp. 1079–1090 (2018)
5. Board on Health Sciences Policy, Institute of Medicine (2015). https://www.ncbi.nlm.nih.gov/books/NBK285994/
6. Lim, K.H., Benbasat, I.: The effect of multimedia on perceived equivocality and perceived usefulness of information systems. MIS Q. **24**, 449–471 (2000)

7. Salomon, G.: Interaction of Media, Cognition, and Learning: An Exploration of How Symbolic Forms Cultivate Mental Skills and Affect Knowledge Acquisition. Jossey-Bass, San Francisco (1979)

8. Daft, R.L., Lengel, R.H.: Information Richness: A New Approach to Managerial Behavior and Organisation Design (No. TR-ONR-DG-02). College of Business Administration, Texas A&M University, College Station (1983)

9. Daft, R.L., Lengel, R.H.: Organisational information requirements, media richness and structural design. Manag. Sci. **32**(5), 554–571 (1986)

10. Sun, P.C., Cheng, H.K.: The design of instructional multimedia in e-learning: a media richness theory-based approach. Comput. Educ. **49**(3), 662–676 (2007)

11. Alamäki, A., Pesonen, J., Dirin, A.: Triggering effects of mobile video marketing in nature tourism: media richness perspective. Inf. Process. Manag. **56**(3), 756–770 (2019)

12. Dennis, A.R., Kinney, S.T.: Testing media richness theory in the new media: the effects of cues, feedback, and task equivocality. Inf. Syst. Res. **9**(3), 256–274 (1998)

13. Mayer, R.E.: Multimedia Learning, 2nd edn. Cambridge University Press, New York (2009)

14. Fiorella, L., Mayer, R.E.: Effects of observing the instructor draw diagrams on learning from multimedia messages. J. Educ. Psychol. **108**(4), 528 (2016)

15. Tan, W.K., Tan, C.H., Teo, H.H.: Conveying information effectively in a virtual world: insights from synthesized task closure and media richness. J. Am. Soc. Inform. Sci. Technol. **63**(6), 1198–1212 (2012)

16. GDPR Regulation (EU) 2016/679 of the European Parliament and of the Council of 27 April 2016. Official J. Eur Union (2016). https://eur-lex.europa.eu/legal-content/EN/TXT/HTML/?uri=CELEX:32016R0679&from=EN

17. Garfinkel, S.: De-identification of Personal Information (NISTIR 8053). U.S. National Institute of Standards and Technology (2015). http://nvlpubs.nist.gov/nistpubs/ir/2015/NIST.IR.8053.pdf

18. European Medicines Agency Data Anonymisation: A key enabler for clinical data sharing. In: Workshop Report, 30 November–1 December 2017, EMA/796532/2018 (2018)

19. Winkler, W.E.: Overview of record linkage and current research directions. Technical report Statistical Research Report Series RRS2006/02, US Bureau of the Census, Washington, D.C. (2006)

20. Uzuner, O., Luo, Y., Szolovits, P.: Evaluating the state-of-the-art in automatic deidentification. J. Am. Med. Inform. Assoc. (JAMIA) **14**, 550–563 (2007)

21. Cardinal, R.N.: Clinical records anonymisation and text extraction (CRATE): an open-source software system. BMC Med. Inform. Decis. Mak. **17**(1), 50 (2017)

22. Eisenhardt, K.M., Graebner, M.: Theory building from cases: opportunities and challenges. Acad. Manag. J. **50**(1), 25–32 (2007)

23. Dubois, A., Gadde, L.E.: Systematic combining: an abductive approach to case research. J. Bus. Res. **55**(7), 553–560 (2002)

24. Holzinger, A.: Interactive machine learning for health informatics: when do we need the human-in-the-loop? Brain Inform. **3**(2), 119–131 (2016)

25. Camarinha-Matos, L.M., Fornasiero, R., Afsarmanesh, H.: Collaborative networks as a core enabler of industry 4.0. In: Camarinha-Matos, L.M., Afsarmanesh, H., Fornasiero, R. (eds.) PRO-VE 2017. IAICT, vol. 506, pp. 3–17. Springer, Cham (2017). https://doi.org/10.1007/978-3-319-65151-4_1

26. Serrano, D.C., et al.: A framework to support industry 40: chemical company case study. In: Camarinha-Matos, L., Afsarmanesh, H., Rezgui, Y. (eds.) PRO-VE 2018. IAICT, vol. 534, pp. 387–395. Springer, Cham (2018). https://doi.org/10.1007/978-3-319-99127-6_33

27. Valkokari, K., Rantala, T., Alamäki, A., Palomäki, K.: Business impacts of technology disruption - a design science approach to cognitive systems' adoption within collaborative networks. In: Camarinha-Matos, L.M., Afsarmanesh, H., Rezgui, Y. (eds.) PRO-VE 2018. IAICT, vol. 534, pp. 337–348. Springer, Cham (2018). https://doi.org/10.1007/978-3-319-99127-6_29
28. Macedo, P., Madeira, R.N., Camarinha-Matos, L.M.: Cognitive services for collaborative mHealth: the OnParkinson case study. In: Camarinha-Matos, L.M., Afsarmanesh, H., Rezgui, Y. (eds.) PRO-VE 2018. IAICT, vol. 534, pp. 442–453. Springer, Cham (2018). https://doi.org/10.1007/978-3-319-99127-6_38

Methods of Data Mining for Quality Assurance in Glassworks

Łukasz Paśko[(✉)] and Paweł Litwin

Faculty of Mechanical Engineering and Aeronautics,
Rzeszow University of Technology, Al. Powstancow Warszawy 12,
35-959 Rzeszow, Poland
{lpasko, plitwin}@prz.edu.pl

Abstract. In manufacturing enterprises implementing the idea of Industry 4.0, devices that generate data are increasingly used. Over time, huge data sets are created. These collections, known as Big Data, are very important to the company because they can contain valuable information. One of the goals of today's enterprises is to discover this information and transform it into knowledge. The aim of the article is to present the methodology of exploration of large data sets from the manufacturing process in glassworks. The result of the research is knowledge about the parameters of the manufacturing process causing defects in the products.

Keywords: Big Data · Data mining · Quality assurance · Glass industry

1 Introduction

Today's manufacturing companies increasingly use different types of devices that generate data. This data may contain crucial information. An important area of modern enterprises' activities is discovering this information. Such task requires processing a large amount of data. Then the identified information is transformed into knowledge understood as information that has been confirmed and can be used to support decision-making [1].

The crucial stage of knowledge discovery process is data mining (DM). DM is defined as the automatic search for unknown dependencies and patterns hidden in the data. The detected information should then be presented to the user in an intelligible form, e.g. in the form of logical rules or visualizations [1].

In the research literature on production engineering, an increasing number of DM applications has been observed for several years. Examples include: scheduling and production planning [2], customer needs research [3], machine failure prediction [4], improvement of the assembly process [5], supply chain management [6] or product design [7].

Also in collaborative networks are places where DM methods can be used. A collaborative network has the potential to collect huge amount of data about its collaborative activities. For this reason, there is a need to extract significant patterns out from data and utilize them in a collaborative network. The authors of the paper [8] propose a framework for DM in the design of collaborative virtual environments. Modeling of collaboration

L. M. Camarinha-Matos et al. (Eds.): PRO-VE 2019, IFIP AICT 568, pp. 185–192, 2019.
https://doi.org/10.1007/978-3-030-28464-0_17

networks is also the topic of the work [9]. The aim of the paper is exploration of the structural and the dynamic features of collaboration to demonstrate that there is a unified modeling approach for reproduce these features in different domains. Proposed model allows understand collaboration patterns in two different domains: research and development alliances between firms, and co-authorship relations between scientists. In the work [10], the authors draw attention to prediction of collaborative relationships in the form of collaboration platform where firms can address works to solve problems together. A similar topic is discussed in the paper [11], which presents an analytic framework for managing extended networks in supply chains.

The authors of the work attempt to demonstrate the suitability of using DM methods to ensure the quality of products and propose the methodology for analyzing industrial data in glassworks.

2 Data Analysis Methods Applications to Quality Assurance

Many applications of data analysis in manufacturing enterprises are related to the product quality. A large part of the research concerns the influence of input parameters of the manufacturing system on the quality of products. Usually the data analyzed includes parameters of the manufacturing process (MP), properties of materials used, employees (e.g. seniority, age), equipment and tools status (e.g. number of days since the last failure, number of hours worked), and the environment of the production system (e.g. atmospheric conditions, day of week).

Many publications using DM in the field of quality assurance come from the metallurgical industry. The aim of the research [12] was to use neural networks and multiple regressions to predict the quality of galvanized steel. Paper [13] presents models of neural networks that predict the influence of process parameters on the properties of products manufactured in a pressure die-casting process. The article [14] presents the use of Kohonen's neural networks to identify key factors affecting the quality of steel after the rolling process. Work [15] shows that data recorded with automatic sensors in the cutting process can be used to monitor the quality of products. In [16], Bayesian neural networks were used to determine the appropriate parameters of the sintering process. In [17], grouping algorithms, similarity measures, and distance measures were used to improve production schedules. In work [18], a method for determining the correlation between a sequence of machines and the quality of products is proposed, based on association rules.

All the above-mentioned works focus on a strictly defined field of industry and describe only selected cases of the use of DM in the context of product quality assurance. There are no solutions in the literature describing the use of DM techniques that comprehensively cover all stages of manufacturing.

In addition, it should be noted that the applications of DM in the area of quality assurance are mainly focused on the processing of metals, and the glass industry is an area in which there is a small number of studies [19].

The aim of this article is to present the concept of methodology for the analysis of large data sets from a production system in glassworks. The result of the research is expected to be the knowledge about the impact of MP parameters on the occurrence of defects in the products.

3 Problem Statement and Data Source Description

Analysis of industry data is a non-trivial task, because of the attributes that can be assigned to this data. The Big Data concept defines them as 3V: volume, velocity, variety. Volume refers to a large amount of data, velocity concerns the speed of data inflow and analysis, and variety indicates the heterogeneity of data. An additional difficulty is to determine the technique of extracting knowledge that will best suit to a given problem. These difficulties indicate the need to develop some general methods and guidelines that will be useful for researchers. A glassworks factory is an example of a company where large amounts of data are generated. There are 4 glass furnaces and 14 production lines in the analyzed glassworks. The daily production volume is over 5 million. The manufacturing is continuous, and as a result, data regarding process parameters are recorded 24 h a day, 7 days a week. Data sets created in this way may be used when there are problems with ensuring high quality of products.

In the glassworks, at automatic quality control stations, an anomaly was recorded. The anomaly involves the occurrence of periods in which an increased number of defective products is observed. Periods of the increased number of defective products last from a few to over a dozen days. During this time, the number of defective products is about three times higher than the average. The abovementioned anomaly is that air bubbles occur in the product's head. The bubbles appearing on the surface of the seal are particularly dangerous; product with the defect becomes useless. It should be noted that with the use of the statistical data analysis methods, glassworks' employees were not able to determine the reason for the periods of increased defectiveness of the products. The aim of the research is to identify the parameters that are responsible for periods of increased number of products with the defect. Because the glassworks collects extensive datasets containing the values of hundreds of MP parameters, there was decided to find the reason of increased number of defective products using DM methods.

The quantity and dynamics of the collected data (values of most parameters are registered every second) justifies the use of artificial intelligence and machine learning methods. In addition, the research issue also includes the appropriate presentation of knowledge, so that it is understandable for decision-makers. The knowledge base, which is an integral part of the decision support system (DSS), should contain decision rules acquired by appropriate methods of induction.

Data from the production process monitoring system were recorded within a period of 27 days and can be divided into three groups:

1. The number of products with the defect recorded on three manufacturing lines.
2. Parameters characterizing the MP, concerning: operation of the glass furnace (glass level and temperature, electric and gas heating power); work of three forehearths (glass temperature and heating); cooling of moulds.
3. Meteorological data describing weather conditions outside the production hall, such as air temperature, atmospheric pressure and humidity.

Data regarding the number of defective products are recorded at quality control stations located at the so-called cold end of the production line. Based on them, three variables were defined, which will be explained (output) variables during the test.

Parameters of the MP, together with meteorological data, will be used as explanatory (input) variables. The first device from the hot end is a glass furnace. Based on data obtained from sensors located in the furnace, 11 variables were defined, that describe the operation of the furnace and ventilation, as well as the level and temperature of the liquid glass. The next device in the MP is a forehearth, which receives liquid glass from the glass furnace. Glass moving through forehearth gets the right consistency and temperature. The acquired forehearth parameters refer to the air pressure, the position of the air supply valves and the temperature of the glass. At the end of forehearth, liquid glass is divided into portions (so-called gobs). A total of 139 parameters were registered in the forehearths. Gobs are moving to moulds that give them the shape of the product. Another group of acquired parameters describes the cooling of moulds, where nine parameters were registered. The number of registered parameters is shown in Table 1.

Table 1. The set of explanatory variables

The number of parameters used as explanatory variables				
Glass furnace	Forehearths	Moulds cooling	Meteorological data	Total
11	139	9	3	162

4 Research Methodology and Preliminary Results

In the paper [20], it was shown that DM methods can be used to generate one of four types of information:

- logical rules based on IF (conditions) THEN (conclusion) construction;
- relative significance of explanatory variables expressing their impact on the explained variable;
- predicted values of explained variables;
- results of grouping explanatory variables.

The analysis focuses on obtaining the four types of information, enabling the understanding of the relationship between the parameters of the production process and the number of defective products. Figure 1 presents the assumed research plan, leading to the automatic acquisition of knowledge from production data, and then to develop a decision support system in the quality assurance process. Data selection is aimed at choosing the right data that may potentially contain knowledge about the problem being studied. Preparation for analysis includes handling of missing data and outliers as well as generation of basic statistics describing the data. The principal component analysis (PCA) in the literature is most often used as a method of reducing dimensionality, i.e. reducing the number of explanatory variables.

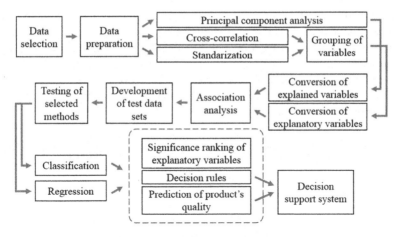

Fig. 1. Proposed research plan

In the proposed approach, PCA plays a slightly different role - it is used for grouping observations. The expected results of PCA are the principal components, which are a linear combination of explanatory variables, and graphs presenting the view of observations (cases) on the plane of the principal components. The graphs will allow to identify groups (clusters) of observations. The clusters will help in the implementation of the next stage - the conversion of explained variables. An example of the application of this approach is the analysis of parameters obtained from one of the manufacturing lines. The eigenvalues of the 20 principal components are presented in the scree plot shown in Fig. 2.

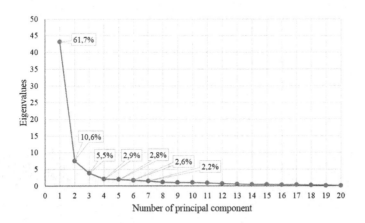

Fig. 2. A scree plot for 20 principal components

The selection of the principal components for further analysis assumes determining the division point at the place where the eigenvalues of subsequent components cease to decrease significantly. For the further analyzes the principal components number 1 to

4 are selected. It is worth noting that the percentage values of the four main components cover in total over 80% of the variability of the explained variables. This example
shows the high usefulness of PCA in application to the reduction of the dimensionality
of the analyzed dataset.

For each pair of four principal components, observations were projected onto the
plane. The points shown in the charts are individual cases from the data set. Charts in
which component No. 1 is present contain clear clusters of observations (Fig. 3).

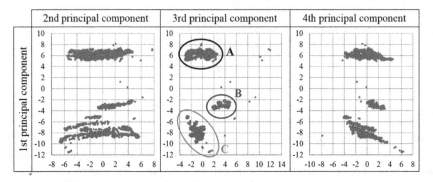

Fig. 3. Observations for selected pairs of four principal components

Particularly compact clusters of observations appear in the graphs of components
No. 1 and 3, where they are marked with letters A, B and C.

The next stage of the analysis is the conversion of explained variables. At this stage
of the research, data cases belonging to clusters A, B and C were projected onto a
chronological graph showing the number of products with the defect (Fig. 4).

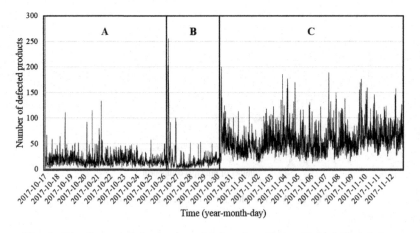

Fig. 4. The diagram of the number of defected products with identified classes

It turns out that data cases belonging to cluster A are at the beginning of the graph, cases from cluster B are in the middle, and the final part of the chart is occupied by cases from cluster C. Therefore, the clusters found can be used to separate observation classes on the graph of the number of defective products, i.e. to convert a quantitative variable into a qualitative one. In addition to the "increased number of defective products" and "acceptable number of defective products" corresponding to clusters C and A, the PCA suggests also taking into account the third "predicting" class, covering a period of a few days before the sudden increase in the number of defective products.

The research carried out so far allows the first conclusions. The PCA showed the variables, which have the highest impact on the data set's variability. These are temperatures of liquid glass, whose values were measured in three zones of the forehearth. The variables are the main candidates for recognition as a cause of products' defects, because the clusters obtained from PCA are compatible with the variability of the number of defected products, what is depicted in the Fig. 4.

5 Summary

The paper presents a DM application for acquiring knowledge from large data sets in the glassworks. The article proposes a proprietary research plan aiming to develop a decision support system in the quality assurance. Part of the plan, which was implemented, allowed for identification of the parameters of the production process responsible for the increased defectiveness of the products. Preliminary results have been positively verified in the glassworks. The implementation of the full range of research (Fig. 1) will allow to build and test a DSS for quality assurance. Both the research problem and the proposed solution method can be successfully used in education in the field of Industry 4.0 and Big Data concepts. The plan of further work envisages extending the data analysis to a collaboration network including glassworks' suppliers (materials, industrial automation systems, energy) in order to obtain a more complete picture of the parameters affecting the glass MP.

References

1. Larose, D.T.: Odkrywanie wiedzy z danych: wprowadzenie do eksploracji danych. Wydawnictwo Naukowe PWN, Warsaw (2006)
2. Wang, Y., Zhang, Y., Yu, Y., Zhang, C.: Data mining based approach for jobshop scheduling. In: Qi, E., Shen, J., Dou, R. (eds.) Proceedings of 2013 4th International Asia Conference on Industrial Engineering and Management Innovation (IEMI2013), pp. 761–771. Springer, Heidelberg (2014). https://doi.org/10.1007/978-3-642-40060-5_73
3. Kittidecha, C., Yamada, K.: Application of Kansei engineering and data mining in the thai ceramic manufacturing. J. Ind. Eng. Int. **14**(4), 757–766 (2018)
4. Ruschel, E., Santos, E.A.P., Loures, E.F.R.: Establishment of maintenance inspection intervals: an application of process mining techniques in manufacturing. J. Intell. Manuf. 1–20 (2018). Springer, Heidelberg. https://doi.org/10.1007/s10845-018-1434-7
5. Knosala, R.: Zastosowania metod sztucznej inteligencji w inzynierii produkcji. WNT, Warsaw (2002)

6. Akhtar, M.D., Manupati, V.K., Varela, M.L.R., Putnik, G.D., Madureira, A.M., Abraham, A.: Manufacturing services classification in a decentralized supply chain using text mining. In: Abraham, A., Muhuri, P.Kr., Muda, A.K., Gandhi, N. (eds.) HIS 2017. AISC, vol. 734, pp. 186–193. Springer, Cham (2018). https://doi.org/10.1007/978-3-319-76351-4_19

7. Giess, M.D., Culley, S.J.: Investigating manufacturing data for use within design. In: DS 31: Proceedings of ICED 03, the 14th International Conference on Engineering Design, Stockholm (2003)

8. Biuk-Aghai, R.P., Simoff, S.J.: An integrative framework for knowledge extraction in collaborative virtual environments. In: Proceedings of the 2001 International ACM SIGGROUP Conference on Supporting Group Work, New York, pp. 61–70 (2001)

9. Tomasello, M.V., Vaccario, G., Schweitzer, F.: Data-driven modeling of collaboration networks: a cross-domain analysis. EPJ Data Sci. **6** (2017). https://doi.org/10.1140/epjds/s13688-017-0117-5

10. Zuo, Y., Kajikawa, Y.: Prediction of collaborative relationships by using network representation learning. In: 2017 IEEE International Conference on Systems, Man, and Cybernetics, pp. 69–74 (2017)

11. Cox, A., Sanderson, J., Watson, G.: Supply chains and power regimes: toward an analytic framework for managing extended networks of buyer and supplier relationships. J. Supply Chain Manag. **37**, 28–35 (2001)

12. Mere, J.B.O., Marcos, A.G., Gonzalez, J.A., Rubio, V.L.: Estimation of mechanical properties of steel strip in hot dip galvanising lines. Ironmaking Steelmaking **31**(1), 43–50 (2004)

13. Krimpenis, A., Benardos, P.G., Vosniakos, G.-C., Koukouvitaki, A.: Simulation-based selection of optimum pressure die-casting process parameters using neural nets and genetic algorithms. Int. J. Adv. Manuf. Technol. **27**(5), 509–517 (2006)

14. Cser, L., Gulyás, J., Szücs, L., Horváth, A., Árvai, L., Baross, B.: Different kinds of neural networks in control and monitoring of hot rolling mill. In: Monostori, L., Váncza, J., Ali, M. (eds.) IEA/AIE 2001. LNCS (LNAI), vol. 2070, pp. 791–796. Springer, Heidelberg (2001). https://doi.org/10.1007/3-540-45517-5_86

15. Chang, D.S., Jiang, S.-T.: Assessing quality performance based on the on-line sensor measurements using neural networks. Comput. Ind. Eng. **42**(2), 417–424 (2002)

16. Cherian, R.P., Midha, P.S., Pipe, A.G.: Modelling the relationship between process parameters and mechanical properties using Bayesian neural networks for powder metal parts. Int. J. Prod. Res. **38**(10), 2201–2214 (2000)

17. Hu, C.-H., Su, S.-F.: Hierarchical clustering methods for semiconductor manufacturing data. In: IEEE International Conference on Networking, Sensing and Control, vol. 2, pp. 1063–1068 (2004)

18. Chen, W.-C., Tseng, S.-S., Wang, C.-Y.: A novel manufacturing defect detection method using association rule mining techniques. Expert Syst. Appl. **29**(4), 807–815 (2005)

19. Koksal, G., Batmaz, I., Testik, M.C.: A review of data mining applications for quality improvement in manufacturing industry. Expert Syst. Appl. **38**(10), 13448–13467 (2011)

20. Perzyk, M., Soroczynski, A.: Comparative study of decision trees and rough sets theory as knowledge extraction tools for design and control of industrial processes. Int. J. Ind. Manuf. Eng., **4**(1), 234–239 (2010)

A Digital-Enabled Framework for Intelligent Collaboration in Small Teams

Juanqiong Gou[1], Qinghua Liu[1(✉)], Wenxin Mu[1], Wenchi Ying[1],
Hamideh Afsarmanesh[2], and Frederick Benaben[3]

[1] School of Economic and Management,
Beijing Jiaotong University, Beijing, China
{jqgou,18120615,wxmu,wcying}@bjtu.edu.cn
[2] Institute of Informatics, University of Amsterdam,
Amsterdam, The Netherlands
h.afsarmanesh@uva.nl
[3] École des Mines d'Albi-Carmaux, Albi, France
frederick.benaben@mines-albi.fr

Abstract. Socialized value creation in networked organizations is the new paradigm of digital organizations. In dynamic and uncertain environment, small teams and big organizations can benefit from interaction with intelligent assistance. For that purpose, various behavior and relationships in situations should be effectively collected and fused. This paper proposes very early steps toward developing theoretical method for the intelligent collaboration of small teams and their big organization environment. Three main subjects are addressed in this paper: (i) Behavior intelligence support for virtual organizations; (ii) Situations behavior digitization, focusing on scenario recognition and modeling; (iii) Data fusion and behavior pattern mining, based on situation-based behavior modeling and heterogeneous behavior model fusion.

Keywords: Intelligent collaboration · Collaborative Networks ·
Digital platform · Situations

1 Introduction

In big data environment, value creation in a social and networked way driven by real-time market insight [1] is a new trend. It also provides a new paradigm, which information system field strives to establish and analyze. For this, establishment of organizational network ecosystems and its collaboration mechanism provide the core foundation.

There are two trends defined in organizational ecological evolution [1]. One is driven by business model innovation, in which more external organizations and users are included in the value creation system. The other trend, which we will concentrate more in this paper, is to let employees participate in value creation and value

J. Gou—The presented research works have been supported by "Science and Technology Development Center, Ministry of Education" (2018A02008).

L. M. Camarinha-Matos et al. (Eds.): PRO-VE 2019, IFIP AICT 568, pp. 193–202, 2019.
https://doi.org/10.1007/978-3-030-28464-0_18

distribution. In this way, internal boundaries of organizations are being weakened, and new organizational structures are emerging to replace the traditional "company + employees" structure which driven by its leaders. Among them, "big organization + small teams" is a well-recognized organizational structure [2]. Here, "big organization" doesn't mean organizations which is pretty huge, but a concept corresponding with "small teams", acting as a platform to support mall teams with internal and external resources. In this structure, small teams can be established rapidly to make agile response to emerged opportunity, and the big organization can support small teams with internal and external resources. However, in existing organization management, small teams cannot make effective interactions with the big organization during their life cycles, which makes it hard to fully exploit the advantages in this organizational structure [3]. Therefore, between the collaboration in small teams and the overall resources organizing in the big organization, a systemic contradiction appears. This makes it challenging to perform unified modeling and operation management in a single environment.

Referred to the theory of Collaborative Networks [4], this study aims to provide theoretical methods for intelligent collaboration of small teams in big organization environment with high-level design to realize the new vision.

The paper is structured as follows. Section 2 gives an overview of existing contributions that help to solve the mentioned tasks. Section 3 presents a framework aimed at providing a theoretical method for intelligent collaboration in small teams in a big organization environment. Section 4 details the early steps on three main subjects to achieve a theoretical vision for this research in the previous section by digital platforms. Finally, Sect. 5 presents the conclusion.

2 Related Works

2.1 Collaborative Networks

New organization forms need theoretical models to formalize them. The paradigm of Collaborative Networks (CN) provides a new perspective for solving the challenge of small teams' collaboration in big organizations [4]. Collaborative Networks address reconstructing organizations into two high levels of Collaborative Networked Organizations (CNO) namely: the goal-oriented networks and longer-term strategic alliances [5].

Virtual organization is a typical form of goal-oriented networks. Compared with the general understanding of the concept of virtual organization in the field of organizational management, the theory of Collaborative Networks emphasizes the dynamism of VO, which requires VOs themselves to be either driven by continuous production/service provision activities, or driven by the goal of grasping a single collaboration opportunity [5].

Longer-term strategic alliance, mostly represented as a VO Breeding Environment (VBE), is an association or pool of organizations and their related supporting institutions [6]. Members in a VBE have both the potential and the will to share resources and cooperate with each other through the establishment of a "base" long-term cooperation agreement. When a business opportunity is identified by one member of VBE that acts as a broker, a subset of these organizations will be selected to form a VO, in order to fulfill the opportunity. A breeding environment, as a long-term networked structure, provides in advance the adequate base environment for the establishment of the cooperation agreements, the provision of common co-working and co-development infrastructures, generating the common ontologies, and establishing mutual trust as the main aspects, which are necessary to facilitate building a new VO [7]. For small teams in a big organization environment, the theory of CN addresses the needed digital models, prototype systems and key technical methods.

With the continuous growth and dynamic evolvement of CNOs, it is necessary for VOs to preserve and enhance its digital integration with VBE. In other words, it is necessary to establish the collaborative mechanism for VO-VBE at two levels: (i) to drive VBEs gathering information dynamically, realizing the intelligent service to support VOs, and (ii) to help digital management of VOs and their information feedback to VBEs.

2.2   Situations and Artificial Intelligence

Artificial intelligence (AI) is "designed to realize human intelligence by machine means" [8]. Since the late 1970s, AI has shown great promise in improving human decision-making processes in various business endeavors due to its ability to recognize business patterns, learn business phenomena, seek information, and analyses data intelligently [9]. In our research, we aim to provide small teams varies kinds of service based on data assets of their big organization environment. These services will help small teams just like extra partners, giving them proper information at proper time, so that small teams can collaborate "intelligently".

A situation can be defined as "a snapshot of a complete world state at a particular time" [10]. It is "the missing link" to organize and fuse diverse data resources for computational intelligence in software development [11]. Big data brings artificial intelligence into situation applications [12] and brings fundamental changes to the computing architecture and application models [3]. In information systems, collaboration in small teams mainly relies on situation applications, and its behavior data is integrated with the enterprise legacy system to form enterprise data assets. However, how to build a digital collaborative platform based on data assets and make full use of artificial intelligence is still a problem remained to be studied. Since it can help to better solve the organizational collaboration challenges between the small teams their big organization environment, solving this problem constitutes the core entry point of our research.

3   Overview of Objectives

In traditional management models, an enterprise has vertical boundaries (departments) and horizontal boundaries (levels) dividing its members and resources into small "cells". While in theory of Collaborative Networks, VOs can be created from a VBE triggered by a specific business/collaboration opportunity. One of the main ideas of our research is to apply VO-VBE model into a single enterprise environment. In this way, a VBE doesn't act as a long-term association of autonomous organizations, but a collection of members and resources within a single enterprise. This shows the following advantage: the potential of creating goal-oriented, dynamic organization models replaces the traditional static model, which in turn makes it possible for enterprises to make quick reactions toward emerging opportunities and act as a "big organization" from which "small teams" can be produced continuously.

Actually, the VO-VBE model not only provides a new view for organization itself, but also creates new views for businesses, resources and data assets. Based on this, our research fuses these views into the VO-VBE model and proposes a comprehensive mechanism for small teams/big organizations, while supporting high-frequency interactions to fully exploit their advantages.

As is shown in Fig. 1, a VBE can be assumed as a pool of a wide variety of resources within a big organization. Each small circle in the VBE pool in Fig. 1 is a unit containing some kinds of resources, such as a machine, space or other infrastructure. A human, such as an expert with specific skills, or a partnership with external organizations can also be resources needed to support VOs.

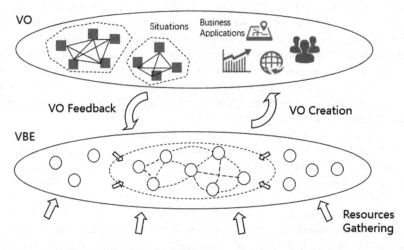

Fig. 1. Digital-enabled VO-VBE collaboration framework

There are two kinds of arrows around and inside the VBE resources pool. One represents all kinds of resources being gathered from the "open universe" of external resources. In this process, administrators or other agents of the VBE bring these nodes and resources into the boundary of the VBE. In other words, VBE makes all resources ready and prepared for potential participation [13], while this will include making some agreements or preparing complete profiles of resources, etc. With this process, which will be further explained below, the VBE provides a sound base for VO creation, no matter which building situations or business applications emerge.

The other arrows inside the VBE pool, however, represent the process of building strong connections between members of resources. The VO-VBE model describes a dynamic collaboration mechanism, and that means assignment of resources to collaboration is also dynamic. For example, after a period of collaboration in a VO, members in the VO gain more experience and knowledge, and will have a better understanding of their partners, skills and infrastructures. These new experiences, knowledge and understanding, can be conveyed back to VBE as new connections, and make relevant members and resources "more prepared" to collaborate for the next times. This process is shown in Fig. 1 as "VO Feedback" and arrows inside the VBE pool pointing from single circles to connected circles.

While the VBE in this model concentrates mainly on resources, the VO layer focuses more on business. As VOs in theory of Collaborative Networks are highly goal-oriented and dynamic, their goals and business can be modeled as several situations, or a chain of situations. Situation models contain possible elements required to describe certain business [14]. They can be built to fit newly emerged opportunities and can also come from predesigned situations from the VBE resources pool. Based on situations which carry all the business information, a final model for business applications becomes clear. In other words, which members and resources are relevant, what kinds of information need to communicate and how to communicate, what processes are needed and what is the purpose of each process etc. The situation-based business applications also make it possible to provide VO members with various kinds of AI service. As we will explain in the next section, during the whole lifecycle of VOs, the situations, business applications, behavior data and all other kinds of connections are feeding back to the VBE. This will make the big organization better prepared for the subsequent planned small teams' collaborations.

4 High-Level Design of Proposed Framework

In order to realize the required theoretical framework described above, in our proposed model, three components must be developed. The following main aspects are shown in Fig. 2: (i) Behavior intelligence support for VOs, addressing the VO situation applications and their intelligent processing; (ii) situations digitization, addressing steps involved in situation modeling and VO creation; (iii) data fusion and behavior pattern mining, addressing steps to realize a VBE resources pool. In the next three subsections, we describe each of these components with more details. So far, the proof-of-concept about framework in 3 is in progress. We are proceeding our work cooperating with two Chinese software companies on these three components.

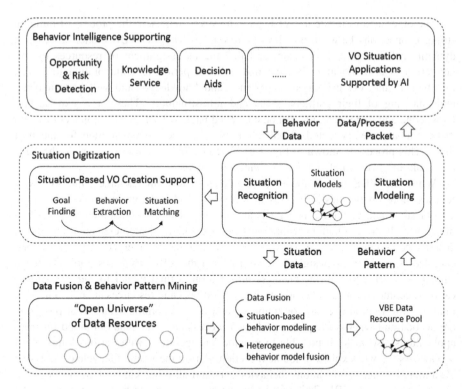

Fig. 2. High-level design of proposed framework

To make this high-level design more concrete, we suppose that there is a regional manufacturing network, acting as a "big organization" or VBE. Mike is a broker of this network mainly in charge of marketing affairs. One day, Mike got a requirement to do a market research for a new product. On the digital platform, this task was recomposed into several situations automatically: team creation, research planning, research data collection, data analysis, etc.

4.1 Behavior Intelligence Supporting for VOs

This component focuses on various kinds of VO situation applications, such as opportunity/risk detection, knowledge service, decision aids etc. Realization of these behavior intelligence applications will be considered as the means to provide an ideal vision for small teams' collaboration in the future. This vision needs to be based on a well-implemented VBE digital platform, and just as it was described above, behavior data from all running applications will be fed back to situation digitization and finally make a close loop with the whole VBE digital platform.

In the example of Mike and his market research, the situation applications in team creation phase may include team composition and partner recommendation. The VBE digital platform can help Mike find appropriate partners based on their past behaviors in the same or other situations. The behavior data may imply that a potential partner has related experience before so that AI can recommend him or her to Mike. At the same time, behaviors in this situation will also be recorded, such as what kind of partners does Mike prefer or what ability is needed in this kind of task, to help collaboration in other small teams in the future.

In the information system for the small team and its big organization, the situation application will receive the data packets and process packets, and the following is planned: firstly, the data packet will be parsed to form a visual interface guided by the situation behavior, which is the visualization of the situation participants' behavior mode; secondly, the process packet is parsed to form the situation application with behavior mode's visual interface.

Incorporating AI in its development, this structure assists VO decision-making and behavior guidance by identifying dynamic opportunities and risks in situations, thus enhancing intelligent operation for small teams.

4.2   Situation Digitization

To realize the VO situation applications that we mentioned in Sect. 4.1, situations need to be recognized and represented from reality to information systems, and we call this part of works situation digitization. This component focuses on the collection of information from processes of situations, design of the required situation models, definition and representation of related behaviors, and implementation of the collection and storage of data for these aspects. Actually, this part of the research can be regarded the connection between VO and VBE.

Situation Recognition. There are two sources to get information for situation recognition, thus laying the foundation for the construction of the specific situation model. The first source is the demands, which mainly include the observation method or the interview method. Getting situation recognition information from demands requires observation and investigation of the key participants in the situations, so that the activities of the participants in a certain period can be sorted out and concisely defined, and then the specific situations will be summarized. The second source is the collected data. Gathering situation information from data mainly requires analyzing the data generated during the interaction of the participants. The data can be either structured data or unstructured data. Then for different characteristics of the data, proper analysis and mining methods will be applied to summarize important information related to the situation (such as the situation mode, key processes involved in the situation, etc.) as they are needed to provide a basis for the classification of situations. In our market research example, most situations have already been recognized or defined from demand by knowledge and experience from experts. But if data showing that Mike and his team did much behaviors not suit for existing situation mode, the AI of the digital platform will decide whether to model a new situation.

Situation Modeling. Situation model in our research bases on the design of meta-model for collaborative situations in [15], which mainly include context, partners, objectives and behavior. Elements and relationships between elements will be described, and we will use ontology or UML to represent them. The collaborative situations will be manually classified according to the collected situation information. Here, the situations are mainly classified into two types: process-based situations and interactive situations. Process-based situations are service-oriented, and their aim is to transfer information or resources from one entity to another, such as data collection or data analysis of Mike's market research. This kind of situations is built around the process and includes multiple sets of processes and collaboration between processes. Interactive situations are based on frequent interactions, such as instant messaging, face-to-face brainstorming etc. Thus, the information generated in this kind of situations is potentially dynamic and unstructured. Appropriate modeling methods will be selected according to different situation types, but both types are based on the basic structure of the metamodel.

Situation-Based VO Creation. When the required situation models are established, the subsequent tasks include identifying, defining, and describing the behaviors for the VO, and determining the virtual organization network that can achieve the collaborative goals. Here, we first find and refine the collaborative goals, such as finding proper partners, collecting available research data. Second, extract behavior or the events and activities related to the behavior in the situation model, and then determine the key behavior or activities, which should be the activities that can be further subdivided into participant behavior according to the requirements of the behavior collection. Finally, the collaborative goals will be matched with the situation behavior, and the participants and resources will be selected from the VBE resource pool to complete the creation of the VO. In other words, this step is to match each situation with relevant participants and to find out what kind of behaviors they will do and what processes and resources are needed to complete the goals.

4.3 Data Fusion and Behavior Pattern Mining

This component mainly focuses on realizing ideas about VBE resource pool which were mentioned in Sect. 3. Its main functionality includes situation-based behavior modeling and data fusion. The component will involve developing effective data sharing mechanisms in VBE. Further, data collection, data cleaning, and data fusion technologies will be developed to implement data management for related behavior pattern discovery and mining. Following are the four main aspects to be supported by this component.

Data Fusion. Since the interactive behavior data in situations or other kinds of data describing resources is mostly unstructured text, such as online message between members in market research team. Here the data must be pre-processed and then fused. The unstructured or semi-structured data should be dimension-reduced, and then the heterogeneous data is realized through pattern alignment and instance alignment. The application of an appropriate data sharing mechanism and an enhanced VBE resources pool for data will be established. This is also a prerequisite for the following aspects.

Situation-Based Behavior Modeling. We use appropriate modeling methods such as the OWL primitives to construct multi-dimensional situation ontology, in order to complete the description of basic behavior. Second, in each situation, we select the appropriate machine learning algorithm to effectively analyze behavior of data and realize data-driven behavior model. Finally, in each situation, the behavior models obtained by knowledge-driven and data-driven methods are encoded and stored.

Heterogeneous Behavior Model Fusion. Data fusion methods are divided into incremental fusion and full-scale fusion. Since in practice it is not possible to obtain all data models once, our research proposes an incremental heterogeneous data model fusion method, which is mainly divided into three steps: (i) data parsing, (ii) pattern alignment, and (iii) instance alignment.

5 Conclusion

The main topic addressed in this paper is how to enhance collaborative evolvement for small teams and their big organization environment on digital platforms, giving small teams more intelligent assistance and promoting frequent interactions to fulfill their goals in a dynamic environment.

Virtual organization – VO, and virtual organizations breeding environment – VBE, are two typical organizational models introduced for Collaborative Networks. We propose a VO-VBE two-layer model to provide a possible perspective to solve systemic differences and sometimes even contradictions between the business goals and the operation mechanism applied to small teams and their big organizations. As big data brings artificial intelligence into the situation application, situations show a perspective that can help organizations to fulfill digital collaboration with artificial intelligence.

Based on existing research, this paper proposes the high-level framework for intelligent collaboration in small teams in their big organization environment. This framework fuses several state-of-the-art views, through which the VBE layer concentrates mainly on resources and the VO layer focuses on business. VBE will then give strong support for VO creation by resources and situations, while during the whole lifecycle of VOs all kinds of connections and situation behavior information will be fed back to the VBE to enhance next collaboration.

The final realization of the framework needs to be based on developing effective information systems and tools. This paper addresses three main components of works to achieve the goals for this framework: (i) behavior intelligence support provides the base to achieve intelligent VO operation; (ii) situations digitization can be regarded as a connection between VO and VBE to complete a dynamic link of resources and situations; finally, (iii) data fusion and behavior pattern mining focuses on realizing VBE resources pool, including an effective data sharing mechanism and the implementation of data collection for related behavior pattern discovery and mining.

To sum up, several key issues for the social value creation and network of small teams are addressed at the high level in this paper. Next steps of our work address the development and final establishment of organizational network ecosystem and collaboration mechanisms supporting small teams.

References

1. Feng, Z., Guo, X., Zeng, D., Chen, Y., Chen, G.: On the research frontiers of business management in the context of big data. J. Manag. Sci. China **16**, 1–9 (2013)
2. Xiao, J., Mao, Y., Xie, K.: Transformation of Chinese manufacturing industry: insight from intelligent manufacturing system based on internet and big data. Mod. Ind. Econ. **2**, 5–16 (2016)
3. Gou, J., Li, N., Mu, W., Liu, Q., Lv, X.: Chinese collaborative software in digital transformation era. In: Camarinha-Matos, L.M., Afsarmanesh, H., Rezgui, Y. (eds.) PRO-VE 2018. IAICT, vol. 534, pp. 601–611. Springer, Cham (2018). https://doi.org/10.1007/978-3-319-99127-6_52
4. Camarinha-Matos, L., Afsarmanesh, H.: Collaborative networks: a new scientific discipline. J. Intell. Manuf. **16**, 439–452 (2005)
5. Camarinha-Matos, L.M., Afsarmanesh, H.: Classes of collaborative networks. In: Networked & Virtual Organizations, pp. 193–198. Idea Group (2008)
6. Afsarmanesh, H., Camarinha-Matos, L.M., Msanjila, S.S.: Models, methodologies, and tools supporting establishment and management of second-generation VBEs. IEEE Trans. Syst. Man Cybern. C **41**(5), 692–710 (2011)
7. Afsarmanesh, H., Camarinha-Matos, L.M.: A framework for management of virtual organization breeding environments. In: Camarinha-Matos, L.M., Afsarmanesh, H., Ortiz, A. (eds.) PRO-VE 2005. ITIFIP, vol. 186, pp. 35–48. Springer, Boston, MA (2005). https://doi.org/10.1007/0-387-29360-4_4
8. Cai, S., Xue, X., Wu, L.: Artificial intelligence and human intelligence: a view on human-computer competition from the five-level theory of cognitive science. J. Peking Uni. (Philos. Soc. Sci.) **53**, 140–155 (2016)
9. Min, H.: Artificial intelligence in supply chain management: theory and applications. Int. J. Logistics Res. Appl. **13**, 13–39 (2010)
10. Magoutas, B., Mentzas, G., Apostolou, D.: Proactive situation management in the future internet: the case of the smart power grid. In: International Workshop on Database & Expert Systems Applications (2012)
11. Chang, C.K.: Situation analytics—at the dawn of a new software engineering paradigm. Sci. China Inf. Sci. **61**, 050101 (2018)
12. Banuls, V.A., Turoff, M., Hiltz, S.R.: Collaborative scenario modeling in emergency management through cross-impact. Technol. Forecast. Soc. Change **80**, 1756–1774 (2013)
13. Afsarmanesh, H., Camarinha-Matos, L.M., Ermilova, E.: VBE Reference Framework. In: Camarinha-Matos, L.M., Afsarmanesh, H., Ollus, M. (eds.) Methods and Tools for Collaborative Networked Organizations, 35–68. Springer, Boston (2008). https://doi.org/10.1007/978-0-387-79424-2_2
14. Bidoux, L., Bénaben, F., Pignon, J.-P.: A metamodel for collaboration formalization. In: Camarinha-Matos, L.M., Afsarmanesh, H. (eds.) PRO-VE 2014. IAICT, vol. 434, pp. 375–383. Springer, Heidelberg (2014). https://doi.org/10.1007/978-3-662-44745-1_37
15. Benaben, F., Li, J., Gou, J.: A tentative framework for risk and opportunity detection in a collaborative environment based on data interpretation. In: HICSS 2019 (2019). https://doi.org/10.24251/hicss.2019.369

Collaborative Knowledge Management

Supporting Transparent Information/Knowledge Federation in Collaborative Administrative Environments

Beibei Pang[1(✉)], Hamideh Afsarmanesh[2], Juanqiong Gou[1], and Wenxin Mu[1]

[1] School of Economics and Management, Beijing Jiaotong University, Beijing, China
{16113125,jqgou,wxmu}@bjtu.edu.cn
[2] University of Amsterdam, Amsterdam, The Netherlands
h.afsarmanesh@uva.nl

Abstract. Leading edge ICT facilitates obtaining and interoperating information within collaborative networks (CNs), providing the base to tackle more advanced challenges. The paper addresses provision of transparent federated information/knowledge within administrative CNs. We introduce a methodology and mechanisms for incremental ontology development. The paper first identifies four typical sources of information/knowledge at the organizations involved in targeted emerging CNs, including: (i) database schemas, (ii) mission statements and main application scenarios, (iii) textual communications, and (iv) governance policies. It then introduces a systematic methodology to develop their meta-data and unify them into an ontology. This methodology consists of four semi-automated steps to gradually develop and enhance an ontology for the environment. The paper describes and exemplifies these steps and their mechanisms. An example real emerging case in the field of higher education administration in China is presented to serve as the proof of concept and verification of our proposed solution approach.

Keywords: Collaborative network · Knowledge federation · Unified ontology

1 Introduction

"A collaborative network (CN) is an alliance constituted by a variety of entities (e.g. organizations and people) that are largely autonomous, geographically distributed, and heterogeneous in terms of their operating environments, culture, values, and goals, but that collaborate to better achieve common or compatible goals, and whose interactions are achieved through computer networks [1]." Advanced ICT and emerging technologies provide the base to facilitate obtaining, sharing and exchange of various types of information/knowledge in collaborative networks [2]. Focusing on administrative CNs, we consider the application case of federating varied information/ knowledge sources as for instance illustrated in Fig. 1. Suppose that there are several organizations including some universities and enterprises that collaborate to achieve the following common goals: (i) obtaining the progress track of students throughout their life cycle;

© IFIP International Federation for Information Processing 2019
Published by Springer Nature Switzerland AG 2019
L. M. Camarinha-Matos et al. (Eds.): PRO-VE 2019, IFIP AICT 568, pp. 205–219, 2019.
https://doi.org/10.1007/978-3-030-28464-0_19

(ii) generating training advices to universities on how to supervise and promote good students, and (iii) producing advices to employers for their recruitment plans, according to students' background experience and school performance. To achieve these common goals, it is necessary to first identify the information/ knowledge to be shared among these organizations, such as the undergraduate, masters, PhD records of students in different universities, their working experience records at various enterprises, as well as the missions and governing policies at these universities related to supervising/ promoting students. Furthermore, it is necessary to then integrate and federate these information/knowledge, generating both a unified and transparent pool that can be accessed by all actors in this environment, e.g. from the students and staff at universities to analysts and decision makers at enterprises, while supporting fair analysis of all students in this environment.

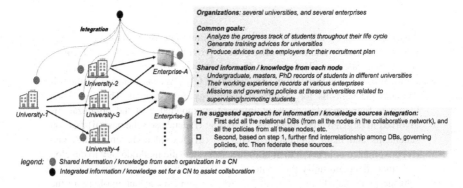

Fig. 1. An example application case of CN in higher education environment

In this process, we first identify four main kinds of information/knowledge sources, including: (i) relational databases, (ii) existing mission statements and example application scenarios, usually characterized by their fragmented, lightweight and behavior-intensive features, (iii) textual communications among its stakeholders, mostly gathered through fragmented application cases and (iv) governance policies. Each of the above organizations, being a university or an enterprise, in this CN has one or more kinds of these four information/knowledge sources. In order to realize the federation of all these heterogeneous knowledge sources, we first analyze each data source, identify some inherent challenges, and define its related meta-data applying object-oriented principles, and second extract semantic relations among all these different pieces of information/knowledge. We then create a unified ontology for this collaborative environment, and formalize it using the OWL [3]. In our approach, we consider and apply current state of the art approaches for integrating databases, and for gathering governing policies [2] [8]. Thus, the paper does not address these aspects in details, and rather focuses on challenges that are not yet addressed. We specifically describe and tackle the following obstacles in this paper, since they are faced in achieving the information/knowledge federation goal in administrative CNs:

- For relational database schemas, knowledge is typically represented as tables, and attributes are classified as primary key, foreign key, etc. These are typically captured using the data definition language (DDL). The challenge faced here is to automate transforming relational schemas represented as DDL information, into the OWL elements for the unified ontology.
- For extracting meta-data from application scenarios, typically their knowledge from every source has completely different organizational structure, and the relationship between different knowledge pieces is not well expressed. There are also usually some knowledge overlaps with the knowledge presented through the relational schema. The challenge faced here is how to semi-automatically deal with resolving these problems.
- For textual data gathered from different communications in the environment, data is usually recorded together with some timestamps. The challenge faced here is first to convert these into structured formats, and then to automatically extract semantic information from text corpora, and generate their meta-data.
- For generating meta-data related to the governing policies of the environment, since their expression formats are quite flexible, only few studies have so far treated them. But in fact these represent an important knowledge source in administrative environments. This is especially the case for capturing the temporal data behavior that is usually hidden elsewhere, and only present in governing policies. Therefore, the challenges faced here are complex and at present we can only manually identify and formalize these temporal data behaviors in order to represent them in OWL format for the ontology.

Aiming to address the above-mentioned obstacles, we introduce our systematic methodology to knowledge source's meta-data unification that consists of four semi-automated steps, that gradually develop a unified ontology for the environment, formalized in OWL. This article is structured according to the following sections. Section 2 represents the related work. Sections 3 and 4 describe a methodology to facilitate identification and resolution of the main encountered typical inconsistencies among heterogeneous knowledge sources within collaborative environments. Section 5 concludes this research work and provides some perspectives for future plans.

2 Related Work

Influenced by [3], we define knowledge as the set of collected information together with their context, which could be understood, formatted, and shared without ambiguity by the environment stakeholders. In this paper, we aim at developing an ontology to support collaboration within administrative CNs. We address different kinds of information and/or knowledge that can be shared by the involved organizations. Please note that for simplicity reasons, in the remaining of this paper we mostly refer to the information/knowledge as "knowledge", and to the sources of information and/or knowledge as "knowledge sources". We then focus on generating the common/unified meta-data from all addressed sources. Our related research review focuses on three main challenging aspects: (i) unification of heterogeneous knowledge sources, (ii) specification and management of governing policies, and (iii) topic modeling for the content of textual communications.

2.1   Unification of Heterogeneous Knowledge Sources

Research areas related to unification of heterogeneous knowledge sources in collaborative networks either address the ontology based knowledge integration [4], or the ontology based data base integration [2, 5]. The unified ontology represents all types of data in uniform format and realizes intelligent analysis on integrated data sets [4]. It can also guide the integration of heterogeneous data bases [5]. State of the art in ontology based unification methods can be summarized as: first identifying different knowledge sources [2, 6], second formalizing and generating ontology for each source, and third integrating ontologies by using semantic similarity (i.e. graph based or content based) research methods [2, 7]. However, the state of the art research primarily focuses on addressing similar types of knowledge sources, such as research on integrating a number of databases [5], or research on integrating several XML documents [6]. In our research however, we design a methodology that handles four representative knowledge sources that are typically heterogeneous, and we aim to unify all these varied meta-data into one ontology. To the best of our knowledge, the current existing approaches have not yet addressed this problem area. We therefore propose a systematic approach to knowledge source unification for administrative CNs, through a methodology consisting of four semi-automated unification steps, gradually developing and enhancing the unified ontology for this environment.

2.2   Specification and Management of Governing Policies

A few studies capture and model the governance policies in the environment. one closely related research addresses enterprise modeling field [8], in which three relations are identified for business rules, namely the is-a relation, support relation, and hinder relation. For example, a governing rule states that: *"if the training plan of students that can be updated systematically every four years support our planned goal, then you must organize relevant revision work every four year"*. Since policies are typically defined flexibly at every node in the network, they do not typically have a uniform format. In our research, we focus on extracting relevant semantics from governing policies in the environment, in order to integrate these with their related concepts in relational schemas or other meta-data. This in turn helps knowledge transfer between policy makers and executors, as well as benefiting the intelligent check whether these policies are being executed as expected. Semantics like temporal data behavior, complex causal relationship are identified by our methodology. In this paper however, we only address the temporal data behavior, and our approach is rooted in temporal data bases [9]. We will describe and formalize temporal data behavior patterns, reflected from governing policies in the environment.

2.3   Topic Modelling for the Content of Textual Communications

Topic models are commonly used to extract topics from texts, by simulating the human thinking process. Related topic models include Latent Semantic Analysis (LSA) [10], Probability Latent Semantic Analysis (PLSA) [11], and Latent Dirichlet Distribution (LDA) [12]. LSA breaks the previous thinking of text representation based on "dictionary space", and introduces a semantic dimension. However, the basis of the LSA methodology is derived from linear algebra, and the results of the operation are negative in many dimensions. Hofmann proposes a new method PLSA based on reliable probability statistics for the defects of LSA. But PLSA does not provide a probabilistic model at the document level, which leads to a linear increase in the number of parameters to be estimated in the model, depending on the size of the corpus. LDA has further extended the PLSA model by introducing a Dirichlet prior distribution. This approach overcomes the shortage of PLSA parameters as the document set grows linearly, thus forming a widely used probability topic model [13]. In our previous work, LDA model has been used in the first step of extracting domain knowledge in education field [14]. In this paper, LDA model will be used to enhance the ontology's data properties through parsing the content of textual communications.

3 Research Approach

We use the application case mentioned in Sect. 1 as the input and proof of concept for our approach. The considered four knowledge sources include: source #1: integrated relational schemas of databases from universities and enterprises; source #2: gathered meta-data from application scenarios, such as students take part in lectures information; source #3: gathered textual communications between students and education staff; source #4: gathered governing policies from universities.

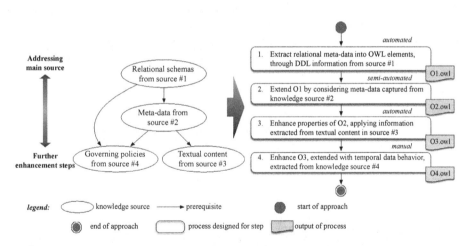

Fig. 2. Unification methodology flowchart

We introduce our step-wise knowledge federation methodology as depicted in Fig. 2. The methodology starts by first tackling the main source #1. This source contains the basic structure and conceptual model of the main entities in the environment, thus providing the tarp for our unification process. Second, the meta-data from source #2 will be generated from application scenarios, in order to extend the basic structure from source #1. Third, from source #3, some semantic information can be extracted to further extend the generated unified model. Furthermore, another important source is the governing policies. In our approach, temporal data behaviors are extracted from these policies. Since description objects related to governing policies are mainly defined on top of the knowledge sources mentioned above, it is necessary to first formalize the above knowledge and then integrate the governing policies. As shown on the right half of Fig. 2, in our proposed methodology, steps 1 and 3 are fully automated, while step 2 is semi-automated, and step 4 is manual. Every step enhances/extends the ontology generated in previous step, as shown by O1 to O4.

4   Detailed Meta-data Unification Methodology

In order to better explain the addressed knowledge types and their meta-data, from each of the four knowledge sources, we provide some simple and easy to understand examples for each discussed aspects. Please note that to help with better understanding of the examples in this section, a partial information/knowledge from each of the four sources are provided as annex at the end of this paper.

4.1   Step 1: Extract Relational Meta-data to OWL Through DDL Information

This step turns relational schemas into OWL. Some relevant examples are shown in Table 1. The Algorithm 1 in Fig. 3 represents this process and its three functions. Function F1.1 converts each table to a class. Function F1.2 converts attributes (if not foreign keys) to data properties, and adds the related class generated by function F1.1 as the domain class for each data property. Function F1.3 converts the relational foreign keys to object properties one by one, and specifies their respective domain and range classes according to the reference relation specified in the schema.

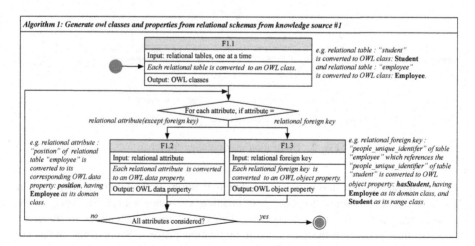

Fig. 3. Algorithm 1: Generates OWL classes and properties from relational schemas

4.2   Step 2: Extend O1 Through Meta-data from Knowledge Source #2

Unlike the concise definition provided by relational schemas, typically there is no uniform specification for meta-data from knowledge source #2. Here, usually the meta-data only contains some tables and some definition of their related fields. So in this step, it is necessary to first manually analyze and organize these meta-data as explained below, and then to formalize them further in OWL. Some relevant examples are shown in Table 2. In our proposed method, fields of tables from the source #2 are specifically classified into the following four categories:

(a) *sameAs* relation

The *sameAs* relation means that the field is already addressed and exists either in O1 or in another already categorized extracted table from the source #2, e.g. *user_name* of table *take_extracurricular_lecture* is *sameAs student_name* of class *Student* in O1.

(b) user defined relation

This is defined in special situations of a field in a table when the domain class is not the class that corresponds to its own table in the meta-data. e.g. *mobile* field in table *take_extracurricular_lecture* is intended to describe the students' mobile contact information. Therefore, this field is not semantically related to taking extracurricular lectures. Rather, it will be converted to a data property of the class *Student* in OWL.

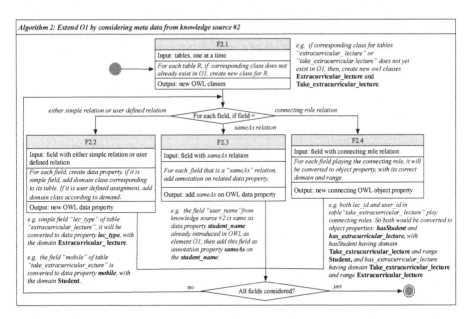

Fig. 4. Algorithm 2: Extends O1 by considering meta-data from knowledge source #2

(c) connecting role relation

Some fields play the role of connecting two tables, or connecting a table with a class. e.g. consider if table *take_extracurricular_lecture* and table *extracurricular_lecture* both have the field *lec_id*, and the *lec_id* in table *take_extracurricular_lecture* is used to describe which lectures are considered as extra-curricular. So in OWL the *lec_id* in table *take_extracurricular_lecture* will be converted to an object property, in order to link the class *take_extracurricular_lecture* and the class *extracurricular_lecture* with each other, as created by function F2.1 in Fig. 4.

(d) simple relation

We call all other fields that do not satisfy the above three classifications simple fields, e.g. the *lec_type* of table *extracurricular_lecture*.

After manually sorting out the above four kinds of fields, our algorithm 2 will be executed to extend the output of step 1 of the methodology, as also shown in Fig. 4. There are four functions defined in algorithm 2. Function F2.1 converts tables one by one to classes, if their corresponding classes are not yet present in O1. Based on result of function F2.1, Function F2.2 handles the simple and user defined relations, and accordingly adds their suitable domain classes. In function F2.3, fields with *sameAs* relation will appear as annotations on their related data properties. In function F2.4, each field that plays a connecting role will be converted to an object property, and its domain and range classes will be defined according to its role.

4.3   Step 3: Extend Data Properties of O2 with Knowledge Source #3

Rooted in our earlier study [14], we introduce our approach in step 3. There are three main sub steps that generate new meta-data from the recorded text provided through this knowledge source, and further extend the O2 as sub data properties. We first briefly address how the gathered texts are preprocessed and then describe how semantics are extracted from them, in order to create new meta-data elements in OWL. Some relevant examples are shown in Table 3. More information about our approach to automate step 3, related to functions F3.1 and F3.2 are described below (Fig. 5).

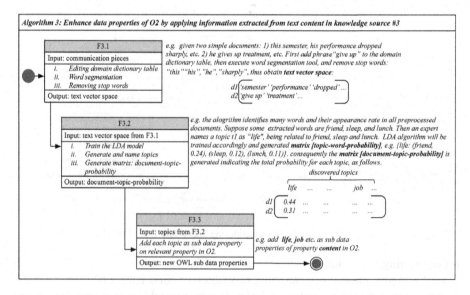

Fig. 5. Algorithm 3: Enhances data properties of O2, by applying information extracted from text content in knowledge source #3 (for more description of these examples, see [14])

4.3.1   Data Pre-processing by Function F3.1

Preprocessing of the acquired text data involves the following tasks. Each piece of recorded communication represents a "document" in this process. Pre-processing program first removes all carriage return characters in each document, then assembles all documents into one "integrated document", while separating the original documents by adding carriage return characters. In the next step, the document set is word segmented. In order to improve the accuracy of word segmentation, a domain dictionary table and a stop-use dictionary table are manually constructed, as described below under (1) and (2). Clearly, the language for the content presented in the two tables must be with the same as the language for the text being processed.

(1) The domain dictionary table avoids incorrect segmentation of domain-specific words (e.g. in English, "give up" into "give" and "up") by word segmentation tools.
(2) The stop-use dictionary keeps track of meaningless words such as "the" and "in" that appear in the document of word segmentation.

4.3.2   Topic Based Semantic Extraction by Function F3.2

We apply the LDA model [12], mentioned in Sect. 2.3, as follows:

(1) *LDA topic modeling* – "Topic" represents a concept and the conditional probability of a series of words. Each word in a document is characterized by the process of "selecting a topic t with a certain probability, and selecting a certain word w from the topic t with a certain probability." So for a document d, the probability of each word appearing in it can be calculated by: $p(w|d = \sum_t p(w|t) \times p(t|d))$ In this formula, w is word, d is document, t is topic, and p is probability. For one document, this can be represented by $C = \Phi \times \Theta$, as in the following matrix (Fig. 6):

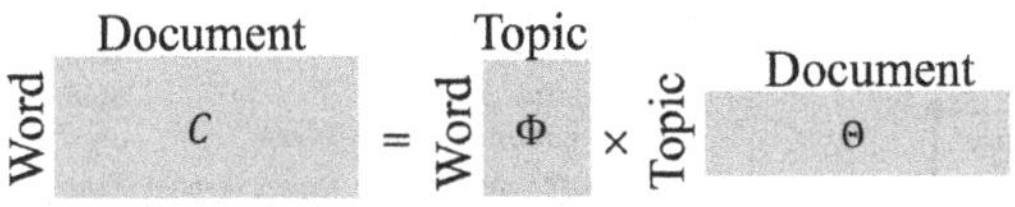

Fig. 6. Topic modeling theory

The "document-word" matrix represents the word appearance's frequency in each document. The "topic-word" matrix represents the probability of occurrence of each word in each topic. The "document-topic" matrix represents the frequency of each topic appearing in each document. Given the pre-processed document set, the "document-word" matrix on the left can be obtained by segmenting different documents, and calculating the frequency of each word in each document.

Our topic model is then trained by learning from the matrix on the left, to derive the two matrices on the right. For this training, we apply the Dirichlet distribution [12], which identifies appropriate number of topics in document set. The basic idea there is to identify all topics when similarity between the topics is the smallest. Therefore, appropriate numbers of topics will be identified by the LDA method.

(2) *Naming each topic* – Here, we apply the LDA model and generate the set of (*topicID, word, probability*), that describe the distribution of words that are related to each topic. Combined with the domain knowledge, the topic names are defined.

(3) *Generating topics distribution of each document* – We apply the LDA topic model to generate the set of (*documentID, topicID, probability*), which represent the probability distribution of each document under each topic. Combined with the set generated in (2), we therefore produce: (*documentID, topicName, probability*).

4.4 Step 4: Extend O3 by Governing Policies from Knowledge Source #4

This step focuses on extraction of "temporal data behavior" concepts, e.g. related to environment policies (relevant examples see Table 4), as necessary regulation constraints can enhance the conceptual model of the collaborative environment. For the interest of this paper, three kinds of behavior for temporal entities are considered and classified, as described below:

(i) *Discrete temporal behavior* – Discrete temporal data properties represent events that can be recorded only at specific points in time, such as check in time of every student for a lecture or the lecture's start time, then for example, a discrete temporal behavior rule related to such a lecture will state that the value of check in time for a student should be minimum 15 min earlier than the value of start time. This time behavior can be modeled as a time constraint on data property on the defined values (Fig. 7).

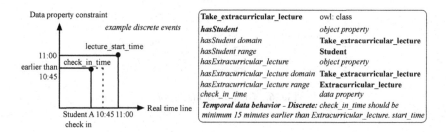

Fig. 7. Example of temporal rule on discrete behavior

(ii) *Stepwise & constant temporal behavior* – Here we mainly consider two specific cases of stepwise & constant temporal behavior, as addressed below.

(a) Situation1: constant step duration – As an example of a time constraint on class instances, suppose that since a decade ago the definition of the students' training plan changes once every 4 years. Given this policy, the behavior of every instance

in class "Training plan" while being constant, changes with steps of exactly 4 years (Fig. 8).

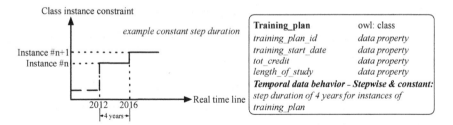

Fig. 8. Example of temporal rule on constant step duration behavior

(b) Situation2: variable step duration – As an example of a time constraint on data properties, consider different governing policies related to the minimum required outcomes to pass a postgraduate innovation project at a school. Suppose that between Sept.2013 and Sept.2017, the minimum required outcomes were two papers, but that after Sept.2018, the required outcomes are either 1 high impact publication or 3 papers. Valid time for the requirements can be represented by the interval: (t1, t2), where t1 and t2 correspond to the start and end date of the period respectively. In order to also support the case when the end time is not known, we introduce ** symbol that indicates the expiration date would be the date of next potential start time (Fig. 9).

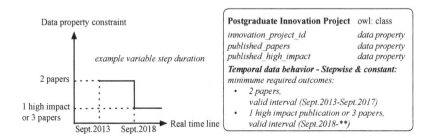

Fig. 9. Example of temporal rule on variable step duration behavior

(iii) Period based temporal behavior – As another example of time constraint on class instances, consider a period-based governing policy to capture the behavior of events that may occur on each entity (e.g. a student) in an environment, over a period of time (e.g. study in a program). For example, a policy can state that for each student, the total number of months of leave from school cannot go over 24 months (Fig. 10).

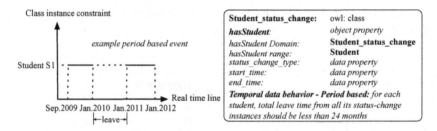

Fig. 10. Example of temporal rule on period based behavior

The Algorithm 4 and its three functions in Fig. 11 represents the process we introduce for step 4 of our approach. In function F4.1, temporal behavior concepts mentioned above are added into O3 as annotation properties. Function F4.2 extracts discrete or period based temporal behavior from governing policies. In function F4.3, two situations of stepwise & constant temporal behavior are considered, compared with function F4.2, an important process here is adding of step duration or valid time constraints on each related rule. Therefore, O4 is generated as the output of this step, as well as the final output of our knowledge federation approach.

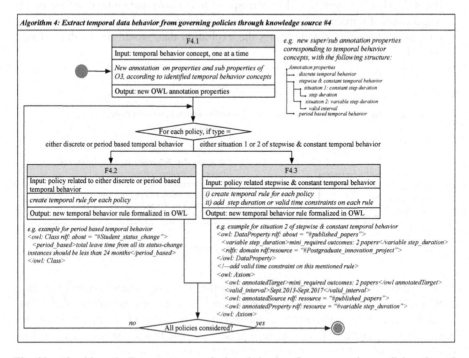

Fig. 11. Algorithm 4: Extracts temporal data behavior from governing policies through knowledge source #4

4.5   Discussion

This section provides details of our proposed methodology. We extract/federate meta-data from four kinds of knowledge sources, as mentioned in Sect. 1. The meta-data extracted from integrated relational schemas provide the tarp for our unification approach, while information from other sources are used to extract semantics to further enhance the unified ontology. The other considered sources include: (i) meta-data generated from mission statements and application scenarios, (ii) meta-data extracted from textual communications, through LDA model that are converted to sub data properties used to enhance already generated data property, and (iii) meta-data generated from governing policies used to enhance conceptual models by adding time constraints on class instances or on data property values. Through our approach, these four kinds of heterogeneous knowledge sources are unified, and in turn effectively supporting knowledge interoperability in administrative CNs. Nevertheless, our proposed methodology is relatively general and applicable to other relevant administrative CN cases. A point of caution for the current approach is related to data privacy. In other words, the approach to providing information/knowledge transparency needs to be carefully adjusted to the type of environment stakeholders. This means that not all users, e.g. student, administrative staff, etc., can see everything transparently, rather the interface accessible to every kind of user, must concisely correspond to the user's level of information/ knowledge visibility.

5   Conclusion and Future Works

To realize federation of varied knowledge sources in administrative CNs, we propose a systematic methodology and a set of mechanisms for federation of four typical types of knowledge sources shared within collaborative environments. Our introduced mechanisms support semi-automation of the methodology steps and incremental generation of a unified ontology capturing all shared knowledge from heterogeneous sources. As a proof of concept, our approach is exemplified for a real emerging case in higher education administration environment. As the next steps of our research, we intend to address knowledge unification for several other types of sources that we identify in collaborative administration networks. These include: entity relationship diagrams (ERD), data dictionaries accessible from relational data bases, standard regulation documents, and data captured through cyber physical devices. We also intend to further tackle other kinds of temporal data behaviors, including those with complex causal relations, as well as addressing interactive application scenarios and information communicated among the environment stakeholders.

We are currently in the process of developing mostly automated mechanisms to handle knowledge unification, which will be addressed in forthcoming publications.

Acknowledgments. The present research has been partially supported by the Fundamental Research Funds for the Central Universities of China (2017YJS081) and Research on Behavioral Intelligence Based on Collaborative Scenarios in High Education Environment (2018A02008). This research is also partially supported by the ARCON-ACM project at the University of Amsterdam.

Annexed Tables

Table 1. Example of integrated relational schemas related to knowledge source #1

student (people_unique_identifier (PK), name, birth_date)
student_degree (student_id(PK), people_unique_identifier (FK), discipline_id(FK),
entry_year, university_name, degree_type)
discipline(discipline_id(PK), title, start_time, end_time, teaching_language)
graduate_innovation_project (innovation_project_id (PK), project_manager_id(FK),
published_papers, published_high_impact)
training plan (training_plan_id(PK), discipline_id(FK), training_start_date, tot_credit,
length_of_study)
student_status_change (student_status_change_id(PK), student_id(FK), status_change_type,
start_time, end_time)
employee (employee_id (PK), people_unique_identifier (FK), position, enterprise_name,
salary_level, entry_date)

Table 2. Example of gathered meta-data related to knowledge source #2

extracurricular_lecture		take_extracurricular_lecture		communication_information	
lec_id	end_time	lec_id	check_in_time	staff_id	end_time
lec_title	total_nmu	user_id	mobile	stu_id	content
start_time	lec_type	user_name		start_time	

Table 3. Example of communication's content related to knowledge source #3

Example of one document:
Yesterday, I had a conversation with Student A. He just received an intern offer from a company ranked in Fortune 500. This is an opportunity that many students dream of. However, since he is going to take an important National Civil Servant Examination, it seems hard for him to balance both, and he looked really anxious.

Table 4. Example of gathered governing policies related to knowledge source #4

a. Between Sept.2013 and Sept.2017, the minimum required outcomes to pass a postgraduate innovation project were two papers, but that after Sept.2018, the required outcomes are either 1 high impact publication or 3 papers. (*from university-1*)
b. The value of check in time for a student should be minimum 15 minutes earlier than the value of extracurricular lecture's start time. (*from university-2*)
c. The definition of the students' training plan systematically changes once every 4 years. (*from university-3*)
d. For each student, total leave time from all its status-change instances should be less than 24 months. (*from university-1, university-2 and university-3*)

References

1. Camarinha-Matos, L.M., Afsarmanesh, H.: On reference models for collaborative networked organizations. Int. J. Prod. Res. **46**(9), 2453–2469 (2008)
2. Unal, O., Afsarmanesh, H.: Semi-automated schema integration with SASMINT. Knowl. Inf. Syst. **23**(1), 99–128 (2010)
3. Ekaterina, E.: Management of information in virtual organizations breeding environments. Ph.D. dissertation, University of Amsterdam, Netherlands (2014)
4. García, M.D.M.R., García-Nieto, J., Aldana-Montes, J.F.: An ontology-based data integration approach for web analytics in e-commerce. Expert Syst. **63**, 20–34 (2016)
5. Li, L., Wei, Y., Tian, F.: A Framework for ontology-based top-K global schema generation. J. Data Semant. **6**(1), 31–53 (2017)
6. Tekli, J., Charbel, N., Chbeir, R.: Building semantic trees from XML documents. Web Semant. **37**, 1–24 (2016)
7. Zhu, G., Iglesias, C.A.: Computing semantic similarity of concepts in knowledge graphs. IEEE Trans. Knowl. Data Eng. **29**(1), 72–85 (2017)
8. Sandkuhl, K., Stirna, J., Persson, A., Wißotzki, M.: Enterprise Modeling: Tackling Business Challenges with the 4EM Method. Springer, Heidelberg (2014). https://doi.org/10.1007/978-3-662-43725-4
9. Date, C.J., Darwen, H., Lorentzos, N.: Temporal Data & the Relational Model. Morgan Kaufmann, San Francisco (2002)
10. Landauer, T.K., Foltz, P.W., Laham, D.: An introduction to latent semantic analysis. Discourse Process. **25**(2–3), 259–284 (1998)
11. Hofmann, T.: Probabilistic latent semantic analysis. In: Proceedings of the Fifteenth Conference on Uncertainty in Artificial Intelligence, pp. 289–296. Morgan Kaufmann, San Francisco (1999)
12. Blei, D.M., Ng, A.Y., Jordan, M.I.: Latent Dirichlet allocation. J. Mach. Learn. Res. **3**, 993–1022 (2003)
13. Della Rocca, P., Senatore, S., Loia, V.: A semantic-grained perspective of latent knowledge modeling. Inf. Fusion. **36**, 52–67 (2017)
14. Pang, B., Gou, J., Mu, W.: Extracting topics and their relationship from college student mentoring. Data Anal. Knowl. Discov. **2**(6), 92–101 (2018). (in Chinese)

A Method of Ontology Evolution and Concept Evaluation Based on Knowledge Discovery in the Heavy Haul Railway Risk System

Tiancheng Cao[1(✉)], Wenxin Mu[1], Aurélie Montarnal[2],
and Anne-Marie Barthe-Delanoë[3]

[1] School of Economics and Management,
Beijing Jiaotong University, Beijing, China
{18120606,wxmu}@bjtu.edu.cn
[2] École des mines d'Albi-Carmaux, Albi, France
aurelie.montarnal@mines-albi.fr
[3] Ecole Nationale Supérieure des Ingénieurs en Arts Chimiques
et Technologiques, Toulouse, France
annemarie.barthe@ensiacet.fr

Abstract. The risk pre-control of heavy haul railways is a collaborative scenario with multi-department linkage and the risk analysis model relies on multiple data sources. As a tool for knowledge formal modeling, Ontology and knowledge graph can achieve knowledge discovery, reasoning and decision support based on multi-dimensional heterogeneous data. This paper restores unusual context with participant behavior data as the core, establishes a basic Scenario-Risk-Accident Chain (SRAC) ontology framework. Under collaborative relationships formed by reasoning rules between context and risk, this paper establishes evolution mechanism of SRAC to introduce new knowledge, such as knowledge extracted from device detection data. New entities are added to the risk concept tree through semantic similarity algorithms. In addition, researchers added weight attribute to the risk ontology. With quantitative representation of risk concepts, this paper uses risk relevance mining to establish associated-subgraphs, establishes a new method for potential accident level assessment through maximum flow search mechanism.

Keywords: Ontology evolution · Risk knowledge reasoning · Semantic similarity · Maximum flow · Collaboration

1 Introduction

The train operation safety of heavy haul railways, as a systematic project, comprehensively consider the transportation organization, vehicle operating characteristics, signal system, personnel behavior and other factors to analyze the cause mechanism of the accident. Under the collaboration system of railway safety impact factors, both Analysis of Heterogeneous Knowledge and Knowledge Reasoning Ability should be involved in the risk analysis model. For the analysis of heterogeneous knowledge, for instance, some major accidents are caused by human factors, e.g. personal skills. If the

© IFIP International Federation for Information Processing 2019
Published by Springer Nature Switzerland AG 2019
L. M. Camarinha-Matos et al. (Eds.): PRO-VE 2019, IFIP AICT 568, pp. 220–233, 2019.
https://doi.org/10.1007/978-3-030-28464-0_20

risk analysis model comprehensively analyzes the personnel behavior data and equipment operation data such as line orbit, the analysis conclusions about the accident cause mechanism are possible to mine implicit information: the combined effect of personal skill negligence and line aging makes the accident escalate, resulting in more serious consequences. The multi-dimensional analysis helps to advise on the later risk control and prevention in different aspects such as personnel management and equipment maintenance. That is, the decision support under multiple data sources can extract more implicit information than the model with single data source output. For knowledge reasoning, the risk analysis model should establish conceptual mapping and knowledge graphs within heterogeneous knowledge. For example, the aging of line on equipment layer can often infer that the security supervision mechanism on the management layer is not perfect, so the knowledge in management domain can be mapped with the knowledge in equipment domain. Based on concept mapping, this knowledge network structure makes the multi-data source not only a simple combination, but also it makes that the internal logic inside the knowledge is found by reasoning rules. The analysis results will be more intelligent, more accurately restore real situations of railway production environment (Fig. 1).

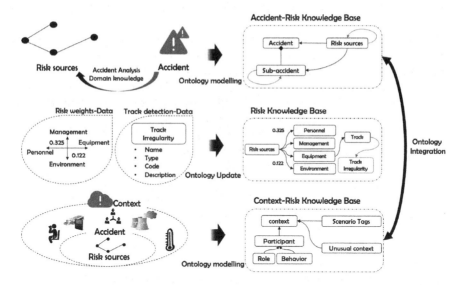

Fig. 1. Research framework

In order to make the risk analysis model constructed in this paper have the above two capabilities, it is necessary to conceptualize knowledge, establish inter-concept relationship and reasoning rules. In this paper, Sect. 3 introduces the SRAC model (Scenario-Risk-Accident Chain). This model uses the association rule mining and expert rules reasoning to construct a knowledge reasoning framework from the unusual context knowledge to the risk source knowledge, so that the ontology has an initiatory reasoning ability. It is the basis for the implementation of ontology evolution. Section 4 defines concept mapping rules and concept updating mechanism of risk ontology. This section introduces the weight attribute of safety indicators and other knowledge such as "track irregularity" into the original ontology. In the environment supporting ontology evolution and heterogeneous knowledge integration, this paper constructs a new risk evaluation method in Sect. 5. The implementation methods are based on knowledge graph and semantic similarity. Based on the SRAC reasoning framework and the ontology evolution algorithms, this paper tend to construct a knowledge reasoning evolution platform (KREP) in risk reasoning domain.

2 Related Works

This paper mainly studies the risk knowledge discovery and heterogeneous knowledge integration and interoperability under the multi-sector collaboration scenario in the heavy haul railway domain. With the knowledge discovery and ontology as keywords, 22 strong related articles are searched and screened in the web of science. The research of knowledge discovery is mainly divided into three categories: (1) Related techniques and algorithms for knowledge extraction from data. (2) Research on the construction of knowledge management and reasoning models. (3) Research on the data and knowledge interoperability in collaborative scenarios.

At the algorithm level of extracting knowledge from data, data features and semantic relationships are the focus of the research. In the scenario of big data, in multi-database integration environment, [1] give general algorithms and basic algorithms for different aspects of network paradox knowledge discovery. Based on rough set theory, [2] use parallel-reduction algorithm for knowledge extraction and it is suitable for large data sets with different roughness. In the process of constructing enterprise knowledge graphs, the inconsistency and knowledge conflicts are solved by [3] using the associated data paradigm algorithm. In the research of knowledge reasoning models, Ontology and Semantic Web [4] are widely used for organization the scattered knowledge extracted by factor analysis, cluster analysis methods and difference matrix [5], such as hotspot information. In addition to traditional classification, [6] also explored the fuzzy representation of knowledge and rules.

For the construction of knowledge management models and reasoning models, it involves generalized representation of knowledge and meta-model abstraction based on business activities. Based on ontology, Petri net [7], BPMN model [8], etc., the main research object is the definition of the rules and concept attributes in the model layer and the relationship between the established features in the business. The knowledge base and the feature library are continuously enriched based on existing models in the running environment. [9] recommended investment types for investors by mining the frequent characteristics of stock price changes, and the concept extraction is also transferred from indicators to contextual information such as the subject of sale and the scope of amount. The impact of context on decision-making is increasingly valued by researchers and the real-time access to information [10]. For the information overload problem of browsing rather than search process, [11] used social network analysis method to analyze the edge of important knowledge map, so as to guide the important knowledge of different user types in learning field to achieve good results. The knowledge management model begins to provide contextual interfaces, and the flexibility of the interface is also a problem that needs to be solved. [12] in the study of process behavior prediction problems, established a decomposition machine model and active k-tuples, it is easy to add known features of the process model, rather than predefined hard rules. [13] also expressed the necessity to mine the generalized connection of multi-dimensional knowledge from the unified process of preprocessing, mining and post-processing of knowledge discovery.

For research on data and knowledge interoperability, focusing on applied research and architectural design, [14] construct a knowledge management framework for distributed health care systems consisting of data- and knowledge-bases, it combines patient data and the mined knowledge to enable decision making in a higher level. [15] have emphasized the importance of interaction and iteration of the knowledge discovery process through case studies. The complex synergy between the dynamics of business scenarios and business objects constitutes the heterogeneity and time-varying of perceived data. In an open collaborative scenario [16], data changes will influence the decision model [17], Research on the update mechanism of the knowledge reasoning model is particularly important, when dealing with complex contexts, relative to the above state for enriching knowledge base and feature databases. Some attempt to model evolution are researched. [18] used a comprehensive flood ontology with a scalable structure to develop a network-based emergency preparedness and response knowledge system that embodies concepts/rules to update by establishing a number of extensible interfaces. [19] designed a framework for the simultaneous involvement of users and experts in the design process of geospatial data risk identification to avoid risk about improper use of spatial data. [20] used ontology-based weighted data normalized transduction neural fuzzy reasoning to combine personal portraits with existing ontology to establish a personal diabetes risk model, and vice versa [21]. The individualized modeling data of individuals on the impact of chronic disease ontology structure will be the research focus. [22] construct an ontology that represents the temporal relationship between semantic details and text elements in the knowledge domain, combining with SVD technology, the strength of association rules could change with time. And [23] also provides a good case for evolution of rules for the model.

To summarize, there are two problems remain:

- The lack of multi-heterogeneous data management makes it difficult to form knowledge for decision support. It's necessary to apply mathematical models to conceptualize heterogeneous data, especially for complex railway management scenario.
- The new concepts/rules are separated from the original knowledge structure model. But knowledge modeling and automatically updating are necessary, especially for the potential risk mining in continuous railway operation. New knowledge should be integrated into the previous reasoning model to support automatic evolution.

3   Ontology Reasoning Framework

This chapter introduces the scenario-risk-accident chain (SRAC) ontology model that was constructed in the previous period. The research domain of this paper is specified by this ontology reasoning framework. In heavy haul railway domain, the occurrence of major accidents is often in the form of accident chains. Different accidents in the chain can be traced back to different risk sources. There are often multiple risk sources with interaction in accident chains. Figure 2 is the classification of risk factors.

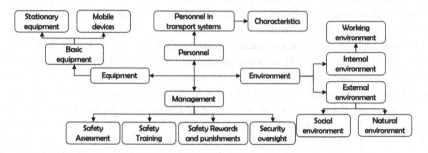

Fig. 2. Concept classification in the risk ontology

Among the risk sources, their accumulation is important implicit knowledge, e.g. "Personnel-personal skills" and "Management-safety training" are relevant, "equipment-aging" and "Environment - extreme environment" also. Define a model to describe the accumulation relationship is important. For the purpose of mining potential risk sources and evaluating risk levels through context knowledge in collaborative railway accident scenarios, we construct a SRAC model in Fig. 3. The model is obtained by the integration of risk ontology and context ontology. The risk ontology is built following Fig. 2. In this model, we use reasoning rules to describe the "produce", "accumulate" among context, risk sources, and accidents.

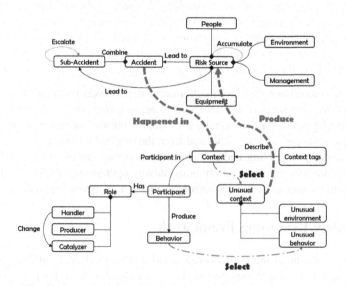

Fig. 3. Scenario-risk-accident chain model (top level structure)

For the relationships in the model, since the model mines potential risk sources based on context knowledge, the "produce" relationship must be automatically derived. And the "accumulate" shows collaborative relations among risk sources. It is constructed by expert rules, e.g. correlating risk sources occurring at the same place or at the same time; correlating ones in frequent item sets using Apriori algorithm. The rules and relations are important foundations for knowledge graph implementation in Sect. 5.

In summarize, the SRAC model constructs a reasoning chain between participants' unusual behavior/context and accident knowledge, intermediating for risk sources which includes self-association.

4 Ontology Evolution

Within the scope of the SRAC model, research is conducted on both the risk ontology extension and the potential accident level assessment. To archive a quantitative risk assessment model, it is necessary to give weight for different risk factors. In this section, this paper draws on the railway safety indicators architecture constructed by other scholars, and analyzes its similarity and knowledge heterogeneity with the risk ontology in this paper. Then this section defines concept mapping rules and concept updating mechanism. This mechanism helps to add weight attribute and other knowledge to achieve ontology evolution.

4.1 Heterogeneous Knowledge Analysis

In order to introduce weight attribute for risk evaluation, we can refer to some existing index system and weight analysis research work. But different risk indicator system has knowledge heterogeneity problems.

In view of the construction of a safety impact factor indicators system [24] in Fig. 4, the relevant scholars build a three-level indicator system from the perspective of people, equipment, environment and management. This indicator architecture is mainly based on the universal safety theory of high-speed railway, it collects risk, fault and accident data in railway-related operations. It builds a safety knowledge analysis table based on some calculation such as factor reduction, conditional attribute ratio, etc. Some key factors are calculated to compare their weights.

This paper introduces those weight attributes into SRAC from the perspective of ontology evolution and concept updating, thus form a new method of risk assessment in a more quantitative level.

The concept in the safety impact indicator system (Fig. 4) and the risk sources in the accident-risk ontology (Fig. 2) are obviously heterogeneous. If the weight of the safety impact factors is introduced into the ontology as the attribute of risk concepts, it

Attribute		2-level Attribute		3-level Attribute	
Indicator	Weight	Indicator	Weight	Indicator	Weight
People	0.352	Physiological quality	0.103	visual & acoustic	0.065
				......	......
		Psychological quality	0.089	Rapid response	......
		Personal skills	0.077	......	......
		......	......	......	......
Equipment	0.212	Line and tracks	0.067	carrying capacity	0.011
				bridge intensity	......
		Power supply	0.042	......	......
		......	......	......	......
Environment	0.122	......	......	Man-made destruction	......
Management	0.314	......	......	......	......

Indicator Classification

Rough Set Calculation   Rough Set Calculation   Rough Set Calculation

Fig. 4. Safety impact factor indicators architecture - a 3 level example

can indicate the impact degree on the potential accident in the knowledge reasoning process. The prerequisite is to achieve interoperability between safety indicator knowledge and risk source knowledge through inter-concept mapping. A necessary process is to analyze the concept similarity of different systems. The mapping rules between the management and personnel elements is shown in Fig. 5. By similar concept recognition, this paper can introduce those weight attributes into SRAC from the perspective of concept updating.

Rule 1-1. People: Sum (Railway Safety. Influence Factors. People) → Accident Risk Ontology. People. Characteristics.

Rule 2-1. Safety Assessment: Railway Safety. Influence Factors. Management. Safety Assessment → Accident Risk Ontology. Management. Safety Assessment.

Rule 2-2. Safety Training: Railway Safety. Influence Factors. Management. Safety Training → Accident Risk Ontology. Management. Safety Training.

Rule 2-3. Safety Rewards and Punishment: Railway Safety. Influence Factors. Management. Rewards and Punishment → Accident Risk Ontology. Management. Rewards and Punishment.

Rule 2-4. Safety Supervision: Railway Safety. Influence Factors. Management. Safety Supervision → Accident Risk Ontology. Management. Safety Supervision.

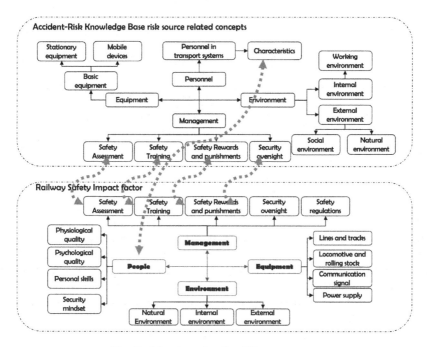

Fig. 5. Mapping rules for different systems

4.2   Knowledge Integration

In Sect. 4.1, this paper updates the attributes of some concepts in SRAC through the similar concept mapping. This update process does not introduce new business knowledge. But with the progress of the railway operation business and risk control tasks, new business knowledge is produced continuously. Based on the detection data of the irregularity of railway tracks, this section analyzes how to integrate "track irregularity" concepts into existing risk ontology and complete concept updating. The track irregularity in geometry can cause the vibration of the rolling stock and the force of the wheel-rail action, which is the source of the disturbance of the wheel-rail system. Through analysis and prediction of the track irregularity in Fig. 6, it can effectively grasp the trend of its state change and provide a scientific basis for the track maintenance and repair work.

Combined with the nonlinear mapping ability of the neural network, the BP neural network can be used to predict the state of the track irregularity. The input of neural network is a large amount of dynamic track inspection data generated by the track detection vehicle during the inspection process, the output is some prediction values of track parameters in next month. Through expert rules of the "track irregularity classification standard" and "over-limit condition coding rule", the knowledge of line condition can be reasoned from the prediction values of track parameters.

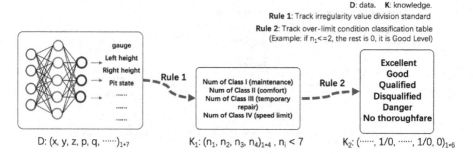

Fig. 6. Early warning mechanism of track irregularity

In view of the new knowledge structure of "track irregularity", this paper considers adding it to the risk ontology, realizes a method for the automatic updating of concepts to reduce excessive reliance on domain experts. After the risk ontology is updated, the track irregularity concept, as a new risk source concept, join the self-learning of the risk-related knowledge base. The other personnel, management, and environmental risk factors associated with "track irregularity" can be mined and related, which are all implicit knowledge.

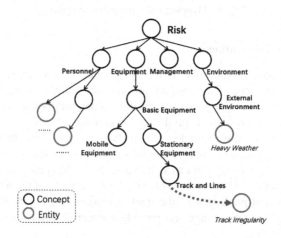

Fig. 7. Add track irregularity to risk concepts tree

Integrating new concepts into the concept tree (risk ontology) requires calculating the similarity between the new concept and the existing ones, and selecting the most appropriate parent concept as an insertion position. In Fig. 7, "track irregularity" is inserted behind the concept "track and lines", using the semantic similarity algorithm based on word2vec model, which has detailed introduction in Sect. 5. This method has achieved good results on more concrete concepts and instance layers, and the addition operation can be performed. However, this algorithm does not accurately mine specific semantic features of abstract concepts such as "Management" because words contained in abstract ones have strong universality. Therefore, the dynamic change of the ontology structure still requires further model and algorithm design.

5 Implementations

The scenario-risk-accident chain ontology includes custom knowledge reasoning rules. In order to ensure the stability and adapt to ontology reasoning ability with big data magnitude, this paper use Neo4j graph database to support ontology construction and knowledge reasoning process. This chapter migrates the risk knowledge base originally represented by OWL to graph database to support efficient reasoning and custom search. This paper tends to build a knowledge reasoning evolution platform (KREP) based on the Django framework and Python. A brief architecture is shown in Fig. 8. Encapsulating the risk knowledge reasoning services is for decision support. The new knowledge interface is for knowledge base updating.

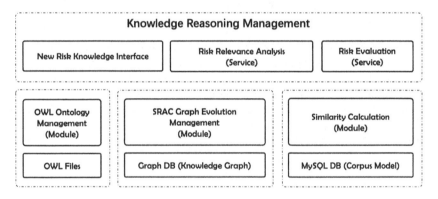

Fig. 8. A brief architecture of the core of risk knowledge reasoning evolution platform

As shown in Fig. 9, after risk source entities are divided into four categories according to personnel, equipment, management, and environment, the risk entities are introduced into the risk knowledge base, and the n-level cascade effect relationship is established, the cascade number is about 1 to 4 times. The Cypher query in Neo4j can search the knowledge graph and complete some simple reasoning tasks about risk escalation or association.

The part of knowledge graph shows the upgrade relation among risk sources. The upgrade relation is one of the forms of "accumulate". From this result of cypher query, we could find many sub-graphs that describe the potential relationships among the risk sources. On this basis, each risk entity needs to complete the updating of the weight attributes according to the mapping rules established in Sect. 4.1, which is implemented by Python programming. After adding weights to risk factors in the risk knowledge graph, the risk level of potential accidents can be quantified.

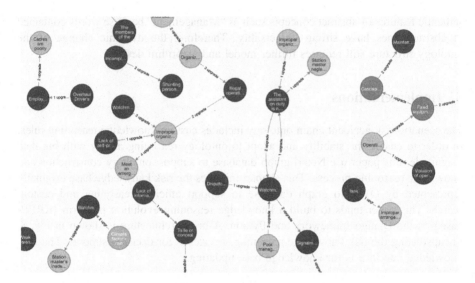

Fig. 9. Part of knowledge graph about risk entities

When one risk occurs, the other risks associated with it can be extracted according to the association mining algorithm, which is equivalent to extracting a directed subgraph from the knowledge graph shown in Fig. 9. The risk source contained in the subgraph could infer a potential accident based on the SRAC model. The problem level prediction for the potential accident is transformed into the problem of maximum flow for graph with multiple source/multiple sinks. The value of the maximum flow is the predicted value of the level of the potential accident.

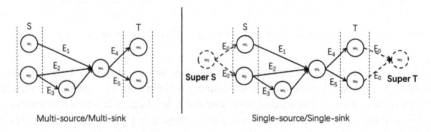

Multi-source/Multi-sink   Single-source/Single-sink

Fig. 10. Equivalent flow problem of potential accident level prediction

The left side of Fig. 10 represents the risk subgraph consisting of risk (node) and risk associations (edge). To measure the maximum level of potential accidents in this subgraph, that is, to find the maximum flow in the graph. This paper defines the weights as W_i, which are calculated using the rough set from Fig. 4. The similarity between the risk nodes is defined as E_i. The purpose is to find the link in the graph that can make $\sum |S_i + E_i|$ the largest. Since the subgraph extracted from the risk knowledge map may have multiple source points S and multiple sink points T, the problem can be transformed into a single source/single sink problem on the right side of Fig. 10, thereby turning the problem into a classic maximum flow problem in Graph theory. Let the W vector in the graph be (0.3, 0.2, 0.05, 0.1, 0.3, 0.2), and the E vector be (0.2, 0.05, 0.1, 0.2, 0.2), then the link corresponding to the largest stream in the risk graph is (w1, w4, w5), the reference value of the potential accident level is 1.1. To evaluate the risk level and integrate new knowledge to the original ontology both needs the value of concept similarity and entity similarity. For an appropriate model, we use word2vec model to evaluate similarity values in Table 1.

Table 1. Examples of similarity with "track irregularity"

ID	Entity/concept name	Similarity ("track irregularity")
1	Track and lines	0.61
2	Interruption on lines	0.43
3	Wrong operation by workers	0.18
4	People's weak business ability	0.02
5	......	......

We select the 10-year heavy haul railway accident analysis reports in 2006–2016 for training. These reports are prepared for the corpus. The training results of word2vec (word embedding) - word vectors, is a good way to measure the similarity between the words. But the form of risk source is usually phrases or sentences. In this paper, we use the word segmentation tools to transform the sentences into word sequence vectors. After that, this paper calculates the similarity between the word sequence of the target concept and the sequence of the original concepts. Then the result is the concept similarity. The process of integrating new risk knowledge with original risk concept tree is equivalent to find an appropriate subclass for a new risk entity. we consider the conceptual similarity and attribute similarity to evaluate the similarity of two knowledge nodes in graph database. For it involves the similarity comparison of texts. Therefore, this task requires corpus training in special scenarios, the quality of corpus and word segmentation has a great influence on the results.

6 Conclusion

In the Scenario-Risk-Accident chain framework, this paper uses ontology and knowledge graph to formalize accident cause mechanisms in collaboration scenarios. This paper discusses attribute and concept updating with multi-dimensional heterogeneous risk knowledge in heavy haul railway accident-handling collaboration processes. We establish a risk ontology evolution mechanism using conceptual semantics. By introducing weight attribute of risks, a maximum link search of knowledge graph is completed on risk relevance basis. A new quantitative evaluation method of potential accident level is proposed. There are two parts of future work:

- Ontology updating method based on semantic similarity has achieved good results on entity sets. However, due to the abstraction of ontology concepts, similar features between concepts are difficult to extract through semantics, which still needs artificial participation. Therefore, the model for extracting more detailed features to support automatic updates of ontology concepts will be the focus of future research.
- The ontology evolution mechanism is for adding elements, but does not involve reconstruction of the ontology structure. In order to enhance the flexibility of the ontology, it is necessary to do fuzzification on the ontology concept definition and set fuzzy reasoning rules. Thereby the adaptability to complex collaborative scenarios could be enhanced.

Acknowledgments. The presented research works have been supported by "the National Science Foundation for Young Scientists of China" (61703032, Context based Multi-dimension ontology modeling and alignment). The authors would like to thank the project partners for their advice and comments.

References

1. Zhang, C., He, L., Mao, Y., Xiao, B.: Knowledge discovery of network public opinion in the concept of smart city. In: Industrial Electronics and Applications, pp. 1197–1202 (2015)
2. Chowdhury, T., Chakraborty, S., Setua, S.K.: Knowledge extraction from big data using MapReduce-based parallel-reduct algorithm. In: International Conference on Computer Science and Network Technology, pp. 240–246 (2017)
3. Miao, Q., Meng, Y., Zhang, B.: Chinese enterprise knowledge graph construction based on linked data. In: IEEE International Conference on Semantic Computing, pp. 153–154 (2015)
4. Li, Y., Thomas, M.A., Osei-Bryson, K.-M.: Ontology-based data mining model management for self-service knowledge discovery. Inf. Syst. Front. **19**, 925–943 (2017)
5. Wang, X., Liu, J., Sheng, F.: Analysis of hotspots in the field of domestic knowledge discovery based on co-word analysis method. Cybern. Inf. Technol. **14**, 145–158 (2014)
6. Soundappan, S.J., Sugumar, R.: Optimal knowledge extraction technique based on hybridisation of improved artificial bee colony algorithm and cuckoo search algorithm. Int. J. Bus. Intell. Data Min. **11**, 338 (2016)
7. Liu, H.C., You, J.X., Li, Z.W., Tian, G.: Fuzzy Petri nets for knowledge representation and reasoning. Eng. Appl. Artif. Intell. **60**, 45–56 (2017)
8. Ligęza, A., Potempa, T.: Artificial intelligence for knowledge management with BPMN and rules. In: Mercier-Laurent, E., Boulanger, D. (eds.) AI4KM 2012. IAICT, vol. 422, pp. 19–37. Springer, Heidelberg (2014). https://doi.org/10.1007/978-3-642-54897-0_2
9. Ha, Y.M., Park, S., Kim, S.W., Won, J.I., Yoon, J.H.: A stock recommendation system exploiting rule discovery in stock databases. Inf. Softw. Technol. **51**, 1140–1149 (2009)
10. Abu Muntalib, S., Sidi, F., Jabar, M.A., Ishak, I.: Big data trend: knowledge discovery on the unstructured data (2014)
11. Hao, J., Yan, Y., Gong, L., Wang, G., Lin, J.: Knowledge map-based method for domain knowledge browsing. Decis. Support Syst. **61**, 106–114 (2014)
12. Lee, W.L.J., Parra, D., Munoz-Gama, J., Sepúlveda, M.: Predicting process behavior meets factorization machines. Expert Syst. Appl. **112**, 87–98 (2018)
13. Huanyu, Z., Xin, L.: Research on the application of knowledge discovery in digital library service (2017)

14. Kazemzadeh, R.S., Sartipi, K.: Interoperability of data and knowledge in distributed health care systems. In: IEEE International Workshop on Software Technology & Engineering Practice (2005)
15. Schmidt, C., Sun, W.N.: Synthesizing agile and knowledge discovery: case study results. J. Comput. Inf. Syst. **58**(2), 142–150 (2016)
16. Allarakhia, M.: Evolving models of collaborative drug discovery: managing intellectual capital assets. Expert Opin. Drug Discov. **13**(6), 473–476 (2018)
17. Usai, A., Pironti, M., Mital, M., Mejri, C.A.: Knowledge discovery out of text data: a systematic review via text mining. J. Knowl. Manag. **22**, 1471–1488 (2018)
18. Sermet, Y., Demir, I.: An intelligent system on knowledge generation and communication about flooding. Environ. Model Softw. **108**, 51–60 (2018)
19. Grira, J., Bédard, Y., Roche, S., Devillers, R.: Towards a collaborative knowledge discovery system for enriching semantic information about risks of geospatial data, vol. 40, pp. 53–58 (2013)
20. Verma, A., Fiasché, M., Cuzzola, M., Morabito, F.C., Irrera, G.: Knowledge discovery and risk prediction for chronic diseases: an integrated approach. In: Engineering Applications of Neural Networks - INNS EANN-SIG International Conference, EANN 2011 and IFIP WG 12.5 International Conference, AIAI 2011, Corfu, Greece, 15–18 September 2011, Proceedings, pp. 270–279 (2011)
21. Qu, M., Chang, Y., Reddy, Y.V., Reddy, S.: A behavior centric service discovery model for building knowledge advantage machine. In: Advanced Information Technology, Electronic and Automation Control Conference, pp. 630–634 (2017)
22. Woszezenki, C.R., Goncalves, A.L., de Souza, J.A.: A knowledge discovery model based on semantic and temporal associations between textual elements. IEEE Lat. Am. Trans. **16**, 1243–1249 (2018)
23. Chen, Q., Fan, Z., Kaleshi, D., Armour, S.: Rule induction-based knowledge discovery for energy efficiency. IEEE Access **3**, 1423–1436 (2015)
24. Peng, L.Y., Feng, Y.Q., Gou, J.Q., Li, X.W.: Heavy haul railway safety factors selection and weight analysis. China Saf. Sci. J. **28**(2), 116–121 (2018)

Designing a Trusted Data Brokerage Framework in the Aviation Domain

Evmorfia Biliri[1(✉)], Minas Pertselakis[1], Marios Phinikettos[1],
Marios Zacharias[2], Fenareti Lampathaki[1], and Dimitrios Alexandrou[3]

[1] Suite5 Data Intelligence Solutions Limited,
95B Arch. Makariou III, 3020 Limassol, Cyprus
{evmorfia,minas,marios,fenareti}@suite5.eu
[2] Singularlogic Anonymi Etaireia Pliroforiakon Systimaton Kai
Efarmogon Pliroforikis, 3 Achaias, 145 64 Kifisia, Greece
mzacharias@singularlogic.eu
[3] UBITECH, 8 Thessalias, 152 31 Chalandri, Greece
dalexandrou@ubitech.eu

Abstract. In recent years, there is growing interest in the ways the European aviation industry can leverage the multi-source data fusion towards augmented domain intelligence. However, privacy, legal and organisational policies together with technical limitations, hinder data sharing and, thus, its benefits. The current paper presents the ICARUS data policy and assets brokerage framework, which aims to (a) formalise the data attributes and qualities that affect how aviation data assets can be shared and handled subsequently to their acquisition, including licenses, IPR, characterisation of sensitivity and privacy risks, and (b) enable the creation of machine-processable data contracts for the aviation industry. This involves expressing contractual terms pertaining to data trading agreements into a machine-processable language and supporting the diverse interactions among stakeholders in aviation data sharing scenarios through a trusted and robust system based on the Ethereum platform.

Keywords: Data brokerage · Collaboration platform · Aviation

1 Introduction

The aviation industry encompasses all the activities that are directly dependent on transporting people and goods by air. This covers airport and airlines operations, aircraft construction and maintenance, air traffic control and regulation, passenger and freight services, among others. Aviation stakeholders produce and consume, nowadays, vast amounts of data and the industry is already investing on them, aiming to utilise their full potential in order to improve passenger experience and flight efficiency, expand sales and reduce costs.

In this direction, the emergence of big-data technologies has pushed the aviation domain many steps forward: the collection and storage of massive data sets has become easier, the parallel processing provides the necessary computation infrastructure, and data science has developed the prerequisite tools that can provide insights and

L. M. Camarinha-Matos et al. (Eds.): PRO-VE 2019, IFIP AICT 568, pp. 234–241, 2019.
https://doi.org/10.1007/978-3-030-28464-0_21

predictions directly from high volumes of data. Recent academic works on machine learning techniques for aviation applications provide strong proof regarding the ways in which data analytics can contribute to significant domain issues, indicatively including air travel demand modelling and operational safety and quality [1–3]. However, they also hint to the lack of cross-section data availability in real-world cases, i.e. at scale, which hinders the development of more powerful multi-source data analytics solutions. One of the main reasons for this is that the highly competitive business players of the aviation sector remain sceptical when data diffusion and sharing comes into the discussion. Beyond technical limitations that need to be overcome, establishing trust and fairness in the scope of data sharing is also an important, yet highly challenging first step towards a sustainable collaborative network spanning across the broader aviation ecosystem.

Several EU projects and works in literature have tackled in the past the challenges of collaborative networks and platforms for enterprises [4, 5] even for data sharing [6]. Most of these solutions however prefer to follow a more generic approach, ignoring the special characteristics and peculiarities of serving a particular domain. The few exceptions to this rule, like [7], which explores business scenarios in the solar energy domain, do not involve the data analytics target of collaboration, nor the data sharing and asset exchange using a clear and secure framework for intellectual property rights (IPR).

The ICARUS project aims to fill this gap by bringing together all aviation related stakeholders and accelerate their collaboration on data exploration and analysis through an innovative big data enabled sharing and collaboration platform, removing current barriers in data aggregation, sharing and IPR protection. These features, combined with a targeted aviation oriented data model and metadata model, constitute the novelty of the proposed framework.

2 Background

2.1 Data Sharing Motivation and Initiatives in Aviation

Data sharing is not a new concept for the aviation industry. GAIN, the Global Aviation Information Network, was proposed by the Federal Aviation Administration (FAA) in 1996. Since then, numerous multi-airline and multi-national data sharing programs and initiatives which involve centralising airline flight data storage have been established: Flight Data eXchange (FDX) is an aggregated de-identified database of FDA/FOQA type events that allows to identify commercial flight safety issues for a wide variety of safety topics. The ASIAS program, developed by FAA and the aviation industry aims to promote an open exchange of safety information. Over 90% of IATA member carriers have agreed to participate in GADM, the IATA Global Aviation Data Management programme and platform. STEADESTM, the IATA's aviation safety incident data management and analysis program that constitutes one of the GADM data sources, has over 200 members. SKYbrary is an electronic repository of safety knowledge related to flight operations, air traffic management (ATM) and aviation safety. Partners of the European Airport Collaborative Decision Making (A-CDM) share timely information through adapted procedures and tools enabling real-time collaborative decision-making.

The information being shared is broad and includes, among others, aeronautical data, flight trajectories, aerodrome operations, historical and current meteorological data, surveillance data (e.g. from radars). The primary goal of such initiatives is to ensure safety in the air travel, which in turn requires the optimisation of a wide range of operations, e.g. the way Airline Operations Centres plan flight routings. Nevertheless, the launch of such Aviation Data Exchange programmes has opened the door to data sharing with trusted third parties [8].

Advantages of data sharing in the aviation industry are numerous and multi-facetted and bolster the development of further larger-scale collaborations. IATA, Eurocontrol and other core stakeholders of the aviation industry but also stakeholders of the broader spectrum, all report on the expected advantages of collaborations built on shared data and insights [9]. Ad-hoc collaborations, such as EasyJet's partnership with Gatwick Airport [10] and Aer Lingus' partnership with the Dublin airport [11], are emerging, while Airbus has launched the Skywise platform that aspires to become the reference platform for core aviation stakeholders. However, an inclusive solution for the aviation industry has not been established yet.

2.2 Data IPR and Marketplaces

Even when incentives for data sharing are strong and the expected benefits are well comprehended, privacy, legal and organisational policies and even infrastructure limitations may hinder data sharing and, thus, the benefits that stem from it. An important milestone towards addressing such limitations is the definition of a clear and robust IPR framework. [12] analysed data sharing agreements from industry, academia and government and identified six high-level aspects of data licenses that affect data sharing: (i) attributes regarding the project and the agreement itself, e.g. description of data, (ii) privacy & protection of sensitive information, (iii) access policies, (iv) legal and financial responsibility, data ownership and rights, (v) compliance, (vi) permissible interactions during data handling. Each of the aforementioned aspects encapsulates numerous more specific attributes and properties of the sharing agreement and the underlying data assets. Depending on the context where they are used, specific practices and derived terms are found, e.g. the work presented in [13] regarding only the pricing aspects. The definition of a concrete data IPR handling process to cover broader and more generic data sharing needs, like the ones manifesting in the emerging data marketplaces, is a challenging task, especially when many-to-many data marketplaces are examined, which is the case in ICARUS. As explained in [14], these marketplaces often emphasise on data discoverability and other facilitation activities, including online payment. In their most common form, the platforms do not have ownership of the data, but only act as intermediaries that facilitate transactions, therefore it is extremely important for the interacting parties to be presented with an intuitive yet trustful way of engaging into such transactions which are gradually starting to pertain to machine processable data contracts. In this context, there is an emerging need to develop contract engines that provide querying and validation mechanisms for access to and usage rights of data assets, as well as the status of the agreements being performed. However, the majority of existing marketplaces are far from this level of automation and lack an adequately expressive, but not prohibitively-for implementation - complex, information model [15]. Establishing rigorous provenance through verifiable information for the data being shared/sold is under this prism of paramount importance to increase trust between interacting stakeholders. Towards this goal, distributed ledger technologies (DLTs) are now being leveraged in the design of the decentralised multilateral platforms (e.g. [16, 17]). The advantages of DLTs in this context are numerous and widely accepted and include transparency and data democratisation [18].

3   ICARUS Data Policy and Assets Brokerage Framework

The landscape review presented in Sect. 2 reveals that although both research- and industry-oriented approaches are emerging for facilitated data sharing in various domains and stakeholders in the aviation industry have begun to grasp the underlying potential of collaborative data analysis, no concrete solution has been proposed and implemented for the aviation industry. One of the key identified reasons is that data trading is not a primary activity for most ATM stakeholders, hence their incentivisation to participate in this activity is largely affected not only by the envisioned benefits, but also by the effort that will need to be devoted into understanding, learning how to use and ultimately engaging a data sharing and collaboration platform. Furthermore, strong KYC (Know-Your-Customer) requirements in the aviation industry, make it hard for stakeholders to trust a broader data marketplace initiative. Finally, apart from the technical difficulties, data privacy and sensitivity aspects especially in the GDPR context are troublesome for many aviation stakeholders.

In this perspective, the proposed ICARUS Data Policy and Assets Brokerage Framework has a dual role:

1. To formalise all data attributes and qualities that affect, or are in any way relevant to, the ways in which data assets can be shared/traded and handled subsequently to their acquisition. This involves licenses, IPR, characterisation of sensitivity and privacy risk levels, but also more generic metadata regarding data content and structure, as well as properties derived from the underlying data model. It should be noted that at least in its initial version, the ICARUS platform will not handle any type of personal data, hence GDPR compliance is not discussed in the current work.
2. To enable the creation of structured, machine-processable data contracts for the aviation industry. This entails the expression of contractual terms pertaining to data trading agreements into an appropriate machine-processable language. The framework foresees the interactions of stakeholders in aviation data sharing scenarios and defines the system's functionalities in this context.

3.1   Data Sharing and IPR Model

ICARUS adopts a DLT-based solution for data brokerage to ensure the robustness of the framework and increase transparency and trust. The first step towards delivering the ICARUS data sharing system was to select a set of clearly defined properties that can be used to compose a virtual representation of a data sharing contract, i.e. to identify the data license and IPR attributes and policies. For this process, the insights gained through the literature review were combined with findings from the traditional data sharing agreement documents used by the ICARUS industry partners. The ICARUS data sharing framework is built on top of three core entities, namely the Data Asset, the Policy and the Contract and two supporting entities, namely Attributes and Terms, with the latter being specified as one of Prohibition, Permission and Obligation, as shown in Fig. 1.

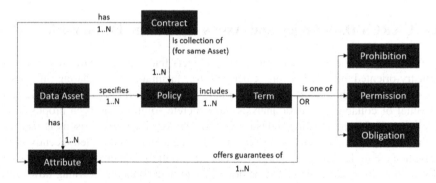

Fig. 1. High-level view of ICARUS data sharing model

For each of the presented entities, concrete instantiations are defined, like the ones presented in Table 1 for policies. Balancing expressivity with applicability was necessary, therefore the adopted model is simplified when compared to the complete set of considerations and options of data trading in aviation. Yet the performed assumptions were deemed reasonable for the initial piloting applications of the system and in any case do not harm the future extension and refinement of the framework.

Table 1. Indicative terms definition for the ICARUS data brokerage framework

Policy category	Indicative terms
Data asset	description; encrypted & unencrypted columns; included data model entities from the ICARUS aviation data model; provider; creator; contributor; version; created date; modified date; published date
Contract	temporal validity; spatial validity & coverage; validation date; liability; involved provider; involved consumer; termination clause
Responsibility	ownership; addressed to; liability & indemnification
Rights and usage	license & copyright notice; derivation; attribution; reproduction; distribution; target purpose; target industry; re-context allowed
Quality	accuracy; completeness; consistency; credibility; accessibility & online availability
Privacy and protection	privacy & sensitivity compliance (levels, disclaimers, guarantees); liability; applicable law

3.2   Data License and Agreement Manager

The ICARUS data brokerage framework includes the conceptual work on the IPR and license terms, the design of the envisioned and allowed data sharing workflows and, finally, the instantiation of the above in a prototype entitled *data license and agreement manager* that implements the designed functionalities. This component as part of the complete ICARUS platform, is responsible for handling all processes related to the data licenses and IPR attributes, as well as the drafting, signing, and enforcing the smart data contracts that correspond to data sharing agreements between platform users. Its smart contract functionalities are developed on Ethereum, a popular decentralised platform for smart contracts, using the Truffle Framework. The component has three interconnected roles:

1. It allows the users to define, review and update the data license and IPR attributes discussed in the previous section.
2. It allows users to draft, review, negotiate on, and sign a smart data contract that concretely defines the terms under which a dataset will be shared.
3. It handles all processes required to prepare a smart contract for each (paid) asset transaction and, finally, upload it to the blockchain. Depending on the exact terms and attributes included in a contract, the corresponding key-value pairs are stored either as-is or hashed in the blockchain. The component enables the activation (i.e. status change) of a smart contract when both parties - data owner (seller), data consumer (buyer) - approve it and the payment is completed and can also report on the validity of a given smart contract.

Assuming the first step (step 0) of defining the data license, IPR and access policies foreseen by the framework has been completed for a given data asset by its owner (provider), the data brokerage process has the following three high-level phases:

Phase I - Data Assets Exploration: The workflow is initiated by an ICARUS user performing a query to search for data. The search functionality is facilitated by the fact that all data assets conform to the same data model and there is rich additional information defined by the designed metadata and sharing model, which ensures that the results presented to the user adhere to the limitations imposed by the defined terms and policies.

Phase II - Smart Contract Drafting: The step includes the definition of and negotiation upon the terms of the data sharing contract to be signed (Fig. 2). Different statuses are foreseen for the smart contract in order to denote whether it is in draft, negotiating, accepted or rejected state.

Phase III - Smart Contract Validation: If the contract reaches the "Accepted" status and the payment obligations are satisfied, the ICARUS platform will allow the consumer to obtain the dataset to use either externally to the platform or to explore and perform analytics on it leveraging the ICARUS functionalities. To avoid issues caused by potentially malicious data providers, a security mechanism to bypass the data provider's validation process is foreseen to address cases where the consumer has proof of a completed payment, but the provider does not honour the agreement.

The proposed framework has been presented to 15 different aviation stakeholders (representing airlines, airports, ground handlers, and generally aviation data providers) during the external validation activities performed in the ICARUS project so far, and has gathered unanimously positive and enthusiastic feedback.

Fig. 2. Contract drafting page

4   Conclusions and Next Steps

The ICARUS policy and brokerage framework sets the foundations of the ICARUS platform that will link data providers and data consumers at all levels of the data value chain in the aviation industry, through a combination of state-of-the-art approaches in academia and industry regarding data brokerage and IPR.

It needs to be noted that the enforceability aspects of smart contracts constitute one of the major challenges, both from a technical and legal perspective. In this context, the future work along the proposed framework will focus on two parallel streams: (a) to investigate how the complexities of multi-sharing, i.e. sharing multiple datasets among multiple stakeholders, can be addressed based on license compatibility analysis, and (b) to conclude the framework's evaluation and validation process by a broader group of aviation stakeholders, which is currently ongoing in the context of the ICARUS project, and leverage the respective feedback to further improve the presented approach.

Acknowledgments. This work has been created in the context of the ICARUS project, that has received funding from the European Union's Horizon 2020 research and innovation programme under grant agreement No. 780792.

References

1. Maheshwari, A., Davendralingam, N., DeLaurentis, D.A.: A comparative study of machine learning techniques for aviation applications. In: Aviation Technology, Integration, and Operations Conference, p. 3980 (2018)
2. Ariyawansa, C.M., Aponso, A.C.: Review on state of art data mining and machine learning techniques for intelligent airport systems. In: 2016 2nd International Conference Information Management (ICIM), pp. 134–138. IEEE (2016)
3. Gavrilovski, A., et al.: Challenges and opportunities in flight data mining: a review of the state of the art. In: AIAA Infotech@ Aerospace, p. 0923 (2016)
4. Camarinha-Matos, L.M., Afsarmanesh, H., Ollus, M.: ECOLEAD and CNO base concepts. In: Camarinha-Matos, L.M., Afsarmanesh, H., Ollus, M. (eds.) Methods and Tools for Collaborative Networked Organizations, pp. 3–32. Springer, Boston (2008). https://doi.org/10.1007/978-0-387-79424-2_1
5. Facca, F.M., Komazec, S., Guglielmina, C., Gusmeroli, S.: COIN: platform and services for SaaS in enterprise interoperability and enterprise collaboration. In: 2009 IEEE International Conference on Semantic Computing, pp. 543–550. IEEE (2009)
6. Biliri, E., et al.: Big data analytics in public safety and personal security: challenges and potential. In: 2017 International Conference on Engineering, Technology and Innovation (ICE/ITMC), pp. 1382–1386. IEEE (2017)
7. Camarinha-Matos, L.M., Macedo, P., Ferrada, F., Oliveira, A.I.: Collaborative business scenarios in a service-enhanced products ecosystem. In: Camarinha-Matos, L.M., Xu, L., Afsarmanesh, H. (eds.) PRO-VE 2012. IAICT, vol. 380, pp. 13–25. Springer, Heidelberg (2012). https://doi.org/10.1007/978-3-642-32775-9_2
8. Aviation Data Exchange Programmes Worldwide. https://datascience.aero/aviation-data-exchange-programmes-worldwide/
9. Performance Success Stories - Data Sharing Helps Airlines Reduce Delays. https://www.faa.gov/nextgen/snapshots/stories/?slide=9
10. EasyJet and Gatwick Launch Mobile Host to Simplify Airport Experience. https://www.futuretravelexperience.com/2015/04/easyjet-and-gatwick-launch-mobile-host-for-iphone/
11. Data Sharing Transformation Driving Kerb to Gate Improvements at Dublin Airport. https://www.futuretravelexperience.com/2015/04/data-sharing-transformation-driving-kerb-gate-improvements-dublin-airport
12. Grabus, S., Greenberg, J.: Toward a metadata framework for sharing sensitive and closed data: an analysis of data sharing agreement attributes. In: Garoufallou, E., Virkus, S., Siatri, R., Koutsomiha, D. (eds.) MTSR 2017. CCIS, vol. 755, pp. 300–311. Springer, Cham (2017). https://doi.org/10.1007/978-3-319-70863-8_29
13. Cao, T.D., Pham, T.V., Vu, Q.H., Truong, H.L., Le, D.H., Dustdar, S.: MARSA: a marketplace for realtime human sensing data. ACM Trans. Internet Technol. (TOIT) **16**(3), 16 (2016)
14. Koutroumpis, P., Leiponen, A., Thomas, L.: The (unfulfilled) potential of data marketplaces, vol 53. The Research Institute of the Finnish Economy (2017)
15. Vu, Q.H., Pham, T.V., Truong, H.L., Dustdar, S., Asal, R.: DEMODS: a description model for data-as-a-service. In: 2012 IEEE 26th International Conference on Advanced Information Networking and Applications, pp. 605–612. IEEE (2012)
16. IOTA. https://www.iota.org/
17. Wibson. https://wibson.org/
18. Özyilmaz, K.R., Doğan, M., Yurdakul, A.: IDMoB: IoT data marketplace on blockchain. In: 2018 Crypto Valley Conference on Blockchain Technology (CVCBT), pp. 11–19. IEEE, June 2018

Collaborative Business Ecosystems and Processes

A Model of Evolution of a Collaborative Business Ecosystem Influenced by Performance Indicators

Paula Graça[1,2(✉)] and Luis M. Camarinha-Matos[1(✉)]

[1] Faculty of Sciences and Technology and Uninova CTS,
NOVA University of Lisbon, Campus de Caparica, 2829-516 Caparica, Portugal
cam@uninova.pt
[2] Instituto Superior de Engenharia de Lisboa, Instituto Politécnico de Lisboa,
Rua Conselheiro Emídio Navarro 1, 1959-007 Lisbon, Portugal
mgraca@deetc.isel.pt

Abstract. The materialization of the 4th Industrial Revolution needs to emphasize the role of collaboration. Traditional business ecosystems have evolved to hyper-connected organizations facing more advanced collaboration models, dynamic networks, and more complex smart systems. Emerging collaborative aspects in this context need to be identified, and tools developed to help organizations coping with changing environment, market, and societal needs. As such, an assessment model is proposed to measure the expected self-adjustment of organizations in a collaborative business ecosystem, induced by performance indicators, in order to improve the organizations themselves and the ecosystem as a whole. Organizations with distinct profiles, categorized by classes of responsiveness, respond differently to the collaboration opportunities they may receive, or are more likely to invite others to collaborate. This behaviour is expected to be influenced by the variation in importance (weight) of each specific performance indicator adopted in a given business ecosystem, as the organizations, like individuals, tend to evolve according to how they are evaluated. To assess the proposed approach, an experiment has been set up using a simulation model based on system dynamics and agents. Preliminary results, based on a number of relevant scenarios, are presented and discussed.

Keywords: Collaborative Networks · Business ecosystem ·
Performance indicators · System dynamics · Agent based modelling

1 Introduction

Business ecosystems are continuously evolving, accompanying the growing use of digital and collaborative platforms. Nowadays, they are shifting towards the age of Industry 4.0, more specifically to the notion of Collaborative Industry 4.0 [1]. The expression Business Ecosystem was first introduced by Moore and inspired by ecological ecosystems [2]. On the other hand, a business ecosystem it is also considered in the research area of Collaborative Networks (CN) [3], which has a wider scope.

© IFIP International Federation for Information Processing 2019
Published by Springer Nature Switzerland AG 2019
L. M. Camarinha-Matos et al. (Eds.): PRO-VE 2019, IFIP AICT 568, pp. 245–258, 2019.
https://doi.org/10.1007/978-3-030-28464-0_22

As such and aiming to emphasize the collaboration dimension, the term Collaborative Business Ecosystem (CBE) has been introduced in [4] and a model proposed [5].

The aim of the present work is to assess the influence of performance indicators in a CBE, expecting to improve its behaviour and that of its individual organizations. There are several mechanisms to evaluate organizations individually, of which the balanced score cards (BSCs) [6] are the best-known. However, to evaluate collaboration benefits, only limited contributions can be found in the literature. As an example, [7] proposes a conceptual model for value systems in CNs, and suggests a method for assessing the alignment of the value systems of their members [8]. Other examples in the field of supply chain collaboration (SCC), a relatively new research area that is growing fast [9], identify collaboration to improve performance in traditional SCs and propose a wide variety of methods and metrics in [10–12]. Finally, the social network analysis (SNA) proposes a set of metrics related to the structure of the network, namely in [13] and [14], consisting of the most adequate approach as a contribution to the establishment of the performance indicators of the CBE.

For the evaluation of the CBE in this work, two of the performance indicators proposed in [5] and [15] (CI – Contribution Indicator and PI – Prestige Indicator) are detailed, as well as a proposal for an influence mechanism. For experimental assessment, the CBE is simulated by a Performance Assessment and Adjustment Model (PAAM) as proposed in [5], using agent based modelling (ABM) and system dynamics (SD) [16].

The remaining sections of this paper are organized as follows: section two describes the proposed simulation model, presenting its collaborative and assessment environment; section three shows how to calculate two of the performance indicators used to illustrate the assessment; section four presents the experimental evaluation of the model using a parametrized scenario to assess and verify the influence of indicators in its evolution, including a discussion of results. The last section summarizes the results and identifies the ongoing research and future work.

2   A Simulation Model of a CBE

The PAAM model illustrated in Fig. 1, simulates a CBE environment populated by organizations (the agents) of different profiles, classified according to classes of responsiveness described in Table 1, thus allowing the establishment of diversified behaviors. To better respond to market opportunities, it is assumed that organizations collaborate by creating collaboration opportunities (*CoOps*) that they send and receive from each other. These collaborations generate "links" between organizations, weighted by the number of times they collaborate (*#CoOps*). The higher values of *#CoOps* mean stronger collaboration.

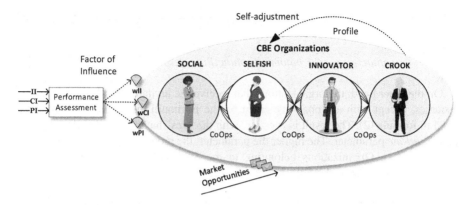

Fig. 1. PAAM (Performance Assessment and Adjustment Model) for a CBE.

For a certain CBE, a variable number of organizations of each class of responsiveness can be used among those considered in Table 1: Social, Selfish, Innovator, and Crook, to better reproduce diversity in a true CBE. Each class is composed of three parameters to characterize the agents, whose values presented in Table 1 are merely illustrative and can be adjusted for each simulation scenario. These parameters (decimal values ranging from 0 to 1), are used as the probability of successful attempts in the distribution functions adopted by the model to simulate the random behaviour of the agents.

Table 1. Description of the classes of responsiveness of organizations.

Classes of responsiveness of organizations					
	Parameters [0..1]	Social	Selfish	Innovator	Crook
Contact rate	Willingness to invite others to collaborate	0,8	0,1	0,4	0,3
Accept rate	Readiness to accept invitations	0,7	0,2	0,5	0,3
New products rate	Tendency to accept opportunities related to innovation	0,2	0,2	0,9	0,3

2.1 Collaborative Environment

When an organization wants to collaborate with other organizations in the CBE, it requests so by sending a *CoOp (taskDescription, resourcesToAssign)*, describing the task and specifying the amount of resources assigned. This amount is given by a binomial distribution as illustrated in formula (1), to get a value bounded between [0, *resourcesToAssign*] with a probability equal to the *contactRate* parameter. The higher the parameter, the more likely it is to get more resources to distribute. Organizations belonging to the Social class have the highest *contactRate* and those of the Selfish class the lowest.

$$contact_{to_{collaborate}} = binomial(contactRate, resourcesToAssign) \tag{1}$$

On the other hand, the organizations that receive the invitations, if having available resources, accept with a probability given by the Bernoulli distribution [17] as illustrated in formula (2). The result is "yes/no" with the "yes" having a probability equal to the *acceptRate* parameter. The higher the parameter, the more likely the collaboration is to be accepted. Organizations belonging to the Social class also have the highest *acceptRate* and those of the Selfish class the lowest.

$$accept_{collaboration} = bernoulli(acceptRate) \&\& resourcesAvailable \tag{2}$$

Finally, if the *CoOp* refers to a task related to innovation, which may result in the development of new products or patents, then the organizations also accept the collaboration according to the Bernoulli distribution as illustrated in formula (3), but with a probability equal to the *newProductsRate* parameter. The higher the parameter, the more likely the collaboration is to be accepted. Organizations belonging to the Innovators class have the highest *newProductRate* and those of the Social and the Selfish class the lowest.

$$accept_{collaboration} = bernoulli(newProductsRate) \&\& resourcesAvailable \tag{3}$$

2.2   Assessment Environment

A performance assessment mechanism can be used to assess the CBE and its individual organizations, based on the indicators proposed in [5] and [15]: the Innovation Indicator (II), to evaluate the proficiency of the organizations to create new products or patents; the Contribution Indicator (CI), to evaluate the value generated by the collaboration; and the Prestige Indicator (PI), to evaluate the prominence of a particular organization over others, to participate in collaboration.

The weight (significance) given to each performance indicator by the CBE manager, is expected to act as a factor of influence, resulting in a certain achievement of organizations, which as individuals, tend to adjust according to the way they are evaluated. For demonstrative purposes, a scenario of simulation was created with three main components of common business activity: research and development (R&D), Consulting, and Inner tasks. For the realization of each component, the organizations allocate a given percentage of resources according to their class of responsiveness. Table 2 illustrates a sample of a possible allocation used in the current experiment (the Crook class was not considered).

Table 2. Sample of resources allocation by business activity and class of responsiveness.

Resources allocation				
Activity	Social	Selfish	Innovator	Crook
R&D	10%	10%	30%	N/A
Consulting	70%	60%	60%	N/A
Inner tasks	20%	30%	10%	N/A

It is assumed that the variation in the weights of the performance indicators by the CBE manager, will act as a factor of influence over the organizations, causing their self-adjustment trying to improve their profile, resulting in an improvement of the CBE as a whole. Therefore, as illustrated in Fig. 2, it is considered that an influence mechanism acts on the percentage of resources allocated to each business activity, called respectively *slice for R&D*, *slice for Consulting* and *slice for InnerTasks*. The factor of influence (FI) of the mechanism, is expressed as a percentage (for instance 10%) of improvement to be distributed among the slices according to the weights of the performance indicators (*wII*, *wCI* and *wPI*), causing a reallocation of resources and a consequent self-adjustment of the organizations' behaviour. It is also assumed that the resources for R&D are influenced by the weight *wII*, and the resources for consulting, are influenced by the weights *wCI* and *wPI*.

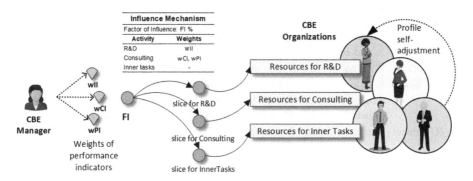

Fig. 2. Detail of the influence mechanism used for the presented simulation model.

Considering the resources allocation of Table 2 as a base distribution, the influence mechanism can be expressed by formulas (4), (5) and (6).

$$slice_{forR\&D} = slice_{forR\&D_{base}} - \frac{FI}{3} + \frac{wII * FI}{wII + wCI + wPI} \tag{4}$$

$$slice_{forConsulting} = slice_{forConsulting_{base}} - \frac{FI}{3} + \frac{(wCI + wPI) * FI}{wII + wCI + wPI} \tag{5}$$

$$slice_{forInnerTasks} = slice_{forInnerTask_{base}} - \frac{FI}{3} \qquad (6)$$

According to these formulas, the influence mechanism subtracts the FI equally from the three slices of resources, so that it can be redistributed by considering the weights of the indicators.

3 Performance Indicators to Assess the Influence on the CBE

Two of the performance indicators proposed in [5], are used in this work to assess the CBE and the influence on the behaviour of its organizations in terms of collaboration. The Contribution Indicator (CI),to measure the total value created by collaboration in the CBE as a whole and that of its individual organizations, and the Prestige Indicator (PI), to measure the influence/prominence of the organizations in the CBE.

Tables 3 and 4 describe the metrics used to calculate the performance indicators CI and PI, of the organizations' collaboration and that of the CBE as a whole.

Table 3. Metrics of the Contribution Indicator.

Metrics of the Contribution Indicator (CI)	
Metric	Description
$O_1,...,O_n$	Organizations in the CBE
#O	Number of organizations in the CBE
#CoO$_{pi}$ in	No. of collaboration opportunities the organization O; gamed from the CBE
#CoO$_{pi}$ out	No. of collaboration opportunities the organization O; brought in the CBE
$\sum_i$ #CoO$_{pi}$	Total no. of collaboration opportunities created in the CBE
$C_D(O_i)$ in/out	Weighted indegree/outdegree centrality (C_D) of the organization O_i in the CBE, which stands for the sum of direct connections in/out of O_i to the n organizations O_j, with weight #CoO$_{pij}$
$C_D(O^*)$ in/out	Maximum indegree/outdegree centrality of O_i

The CI_i in of an organization, assesses the contribution of the organization O_i in terms of accepted collaboration opportunities. The value CI_i in is thus obtained by the weighted degree centrality of O_i calculated by formula (7), which is more related to the popularity of organizations [18].

$$CI_i in = \frac{C_D(O_i)in}{C_D(O^*)in} = \frac{\sum_j O_{ij} \#CoOp_{ij} in}{\max \sum_j O_{ij} \#CoOp_{ij} in} \qquad (7)$$

The CI_i out of an organization, assesses the contribution of the organization O_i in terms of created collaboration opportunities. The value CI_i out is thus obtained by the weighted outdegree centrality of O_i calculated by formula (8), which is more related to the activity of organizations [18]. These values are normalized between 0 and 1 in relation to the maximum degree centrality for the current network.

$$CI_i out = \frac{C_D(O_i)out}{C_D(O^*)out} = \frac{\sum_j O_{ij} \#CoOp_{ij}out}{max \sum_j O_{ij} \#CoOp_{ij}out} \qquad (8)$$

The CI_{CBE} in and the CI_{CBE} out of the CBE, assess respectively the degree to which the most popular organization in terms of accepted collaboration opportunities and the most active organization in terms of created collaboration opportunities, exceeds the contribution of the others. The values CI_{CBE} in and CI_{CBE} out are thus obtained by the weighted degree centrality of the CBE as a whole calculated by formulas (9) and (10), i.e. the sum of differences between the contribution of the most popular/active organization (O^*) and that of all organizations in the CBE. These values are normalized between 0 and 1 in relation to the maximum possible sum of differences of degree centralities for the current network.

$$CI_{CBE}in = \frac{C_D(CBE)in}{maxC_D(CBE)in} = \frac{\sum_i [C_D(O^*)in - C_D(O_i)in]}{C_D(O^*)in * (\#O - 1)} \qquad (9)$$

$$CI_{CBE}out = \frac{C_D(CBE)out}{maxC_D(CBE)out} = \frac{\sum_i [C_D(O^*)out - C_D(O_i)out]}{C_D(O^*)out * (\#O - 1)} \qquad (10)$$

The $CI_{CBE}t$, calculated by formula (11), is a ratio of the total number of collaboration opportunities created in the CBE by the total number of organizations.

$$CI_{CBE}t = \frac{\sum_i \#CoOpi}{\#O} \qquad (11)$$

Table 4. Metrics of the Prestige Indicator.

Metrics of the Prestige Indicator (PI)	
Metric	Description
$O_1,...,O_n$	Organizations in the CBE
#O	Number of organizations in the CBE
$\#CoO_{pi}$ in	No. of income collaboration opportunities the organization O_i participated in the CBE
$\#CoO_{pi}$ out	No. of outcome collaboration opportunities the organization O_i participated in the CBE
$\#CoO_{pkj}$ in/out	No. of income/outcome collaboration opportunities between the organization O_k and O_j in the CBE
$C_B(O_i)$ in/out	Weighted income/outcome betweenness centrality (C_B) of the organization O_i in the CBE, which stands for the sum of overall partial betweenness of O_i relative to all pairs O_{kj}, assuming that connections between O_k and O_j have weight of $\#CoO_{pki}$
$C_B(O^*)$ in/out	Maximum income/outcome betweenness centrality of O_i

The PI_i *in* of an organization, assesses the prominence of the organization O_i in terms of accepted collaboration opportunities. It means the extent to which a node (organization) is part of transactions (collaboration) among other nodes [18]. Using Freeman's betweenness measure [13], this means the number of times that an organization is on the shortest paths among all pairs of the other organizations. In a binary network, the shortest path means the smallest number of intermediate nodes between two organizations. However, in weighted networks, the transactions (collaboration) between two nodes (organizations) might be faster (more expressive) with more intermediate nodes that are strongly connected [18]. This is due to the fact that stronger intermediate nodes mean more collaboration between organizations. The value PI_i *in* is thus obtained by the weighted betweenness centrality calculated by formula (12), which stands for the sum of overall partial betweenness of O_i relative to all pairs O_{kj} assuming that connections between any O_k organization and any other O_j have weight of $\#CoOp_{kj}$ *in*.

$$PI_i in = \frac{C_B(O_i)in}{C_B(O^*)in} = \frac{\sum_k \sum_j O_{kj}(O_i)in}{\max \sum_k \sum_j O_{kj}(O_i)in} \tag{12}$$

The PI_i *out* of an organization, assesses the prominence of the organization O_i in terms of created collaboration opportunities. Similarly to PI_i *in*, PI_i *out* is calculated by formula (13). These values are normalized between 0 and 1 in relation to the maximum betweenness centrality for the current network.

$$PI_i out = \frac{C_B(O_i)out}{C_B(O^*)out} = \frac{\sum_k \sum_j O_{kj}(O_i)out}{\max \sum_k \sum_j O_{kj}(O_i)out} \tag{13}$$

The PI_{CBE} *in* and PI_{CBE} *out* of the CBE, assess respectively the degree to which the most prominent organization in terms of accepted collaboration opportunities and the most prominent organization in terms of created collaboration opportunities, exceeds the contribution of the others. The values PI_{CBE} *in* and PI_{CBE} *out* are thus obtained by the weighted betweenness centrality of the CBE as a whole calculated by formulas (14) and (15), i.e. the average of the differences between the preponderance of the most influent organization (O^*) and that of all organizations in the CBE. These values are normalized between 0 and 1 in relation to the maximum possible sum of differences of betweenness centralities for the current network.

$$PI_{CBE} in = \frac{C_B(CBE)in}{maxC_B(CBE)in} = \frac{\sum_i [C_B(O^*)in - C_B(O_i)in]}{C_B(O^*)in * (\#O - 1)} \tag{14}$$

$$PI_{CBE} out = \frac{C_B(CBE)out}{maxC_B(CBE)out} = \frac{\sum_i [C_B(O^*)out - C_B(O_i)out]}{C_B(O^*)out * (\#O - 1)} \tag{15}$$

The PI indicator, as shown in formulas (12), (13), (14) and (15), uses the betweenness centrality to evaluate the preponderance of organizations' collaboration in the CBE. For this, the Floyd-Warshall algorithm [19] was applied to find the shortest paths in the weighted graph represented by the CBE and its organizations connected by collaboration opportunities. The algorithm starts with a distance matrix D with n lines and n columns, where n is the number of nodes ($\#O$) and each position of the matrix $D[i, j]$ contains the weight ($\#CoOp_{ij}$) between the node i (O_i) and node j (O_j). Because the shortest paths in the CBE mean stronger connections between the organizations, i.e. more collaboration, the inverse of the $\#CoOp_{ij}$ is used, resulting in the matrix (16).

$$D^n = \left\{ \begin{array}{ccccc} \infty & \frac{1}{\#CoOp_{0,1}} & \cdots & \frac{1}{\#CoOp_{0,n-1}} \\ \frac{1}{\#CoOp_{1,0}} & \infty & \cdots & \frac{1}{\#CoOp_{1,n-1}} \\ \frac{1}{\#CoOp_{2,0}} & \frac{1}{\#CoOp_{2,1}} & \cdots & \frac{1}{\#CoOp_{2,n-1}} \\ \cdots & \cdots & \cdots & \cdots \\ \cdots & \cdots & \cdots & \cdots \\ \frac{1}{\#CoOp_{n-1,0}} & \frac{1}{\#CoOp_{n-1,1}} & \cdots & \infty \end{array} \right\} \tag{16}$$

The shortest paths matrix is then obtained after $k = 0..n-1$ iterations over the D^n distance matrix, where in each k iteration, the D^k matrix is calculated according to formula (17).

$$D_{ij}^n = \min\left(D_{ij}^{n-1}, D_{ik}^{n-1} + D_{kj}^{n-1}\right) \tag{17}$$

Finally, to compute the betweenness centrality of each node, i.e. the number of times that an organization O_i is on the shortest paths among all pairs of the other organizations O_{kj}, the Floyd-Warshall algorithm [19] had to be improved. A path matrix P was used to register the shortest paths between all pairs, starting with the matrix P^0 calculated according to (18).

$$P_{il}^0 = \left\{ \begin{array}{l} null \ if \ i = j \ or \ D_{ij} = \infty \\ i \ in \ all \ other \ cases \end{array} \right. \tag{18}$$

The final P^n matrix is reached after $k = 0..n-1$ iterations, where in each k iteration, the P^k matrix is calculated according to formula (19).

$$P_{ij}^n = \left\{ \begin{array}{l} P_{ij}^{n-1} \ if \ D_{ij}^{n-1} < D_{ik}^{n-1} + D_{kj}^{n-1} \\ P_{ij}^{n-1} \cup P_{kj}^{n-1} \ if \ D_{ij}^{n-1} = D_{ik}^{n-1} + D_{kj}^{n-1} \\ P_{kj}^{n-1} \ if \ D_{ij}^{n-1} D_{ik}^{n-1} + D_{kj}^{n-1} \end{array} \right. \tag{19}$$

All the metrics and formulas described in this chapter, were used to calculate the performance indicators in the experimental evaluation of the CBE.

4   Experimental Evaluation of the CBE

To build the proposed PAAM described in Sect. 2, for the experimental evaluation of the CBE, and to implement the performance indicators described in Sect. 3, the AnyLogic Multimethod Simulation Software [16] was used. The model depicted in

Fig. 3, simulates an environment (the CBE), populated by agents (the organizations), whose behaviour is represented by state-charts and system dynamics, to represent stocks and flows of resources.

The income market opportunities (*incomingMarketOps*) are also modelled by agents arriving at a rate of 1.000/year plus a 25% of opportunities for new products or patents, following the Poisson distribution (adequate for modelling the number of times an event occurs in an interval of time) [20]. Each *incomingMarketOps* is composed of a task description (research or consulting) and a number of resources (days-man) estimated to perform the task (generated by a uniform distribution bounded by [1..50 days-man]).

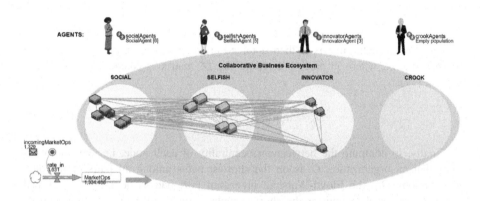

Fig. 3. PAAM model after an iteration of one year.

The organizations, whose profile is differentiated by classes of responsiveness, respond to *incomeMarketOps* interacting by sending and receiving collaboration opportunities (*CoOps*). To fulfil the tasks, the available resources are consumed according to the type of business activity (*R&D*, *Consulting* or *Inner tasks*) and the amount of estimated resources. The influence mechanism of the Fig. 2 induces a reallocation of resources causing a self-adjustment in the profile of the organizations.

For the present experimental evaluation, the PAAM simulation model was parametrized to represent a CBE composed of 6 Social organizations, 5 Selfish and 3 Innovative. The organizations were configured with the values described in Tables 1 and 2, having an initial amount of resources of 1.500/year (day-man).

Running the model considering the interval of one year, the performance indicators CI and PI were calculated, resulting in the values displayed in Table 5. Columns CI_i *in* and CI_i *out* show respectively the contribution of the organization O_i in terms of accepted *CoOps*, and the contribution in terms of created *CoOps* by inviting other organizations to collaborate. On the other hand, columns PI_i *in* and PI_i *out* show respectively the prominence of the organization O_i, i.e. the extent to which O_i is part of the collaboration among the other organizations in terms of accepted or invited *CoOps*. Finally, the performance indicators related to the whole CBE, have the following results: $CI_{CBE}t = 26,4$ is the ratio of the total number of *CoOps* generated in the CBE by the total number of organizations; CI_{CBE} *in* = 0,444 and CI_{CBE} *out* = 0,214, are respectively the degree to which the most popular organization (*#CoOps* received) and the most active (*#CoOps* created), exceeds the contribution of the others; PI_{CBE} *in* = 0,776 and PI_{CBE} *out* = 0,686, are respectively the degree to which the most prominent organization (being part of the *CoOps* received or created) exceeds the contribution of the others.

Table 5. Values of the CI and PI for each individual organization and for the CBE.

Contribution and Prestige Indicators (CI and PI)				
Class of Resp.	CI_i in	CI_i out	PI_i in	PI_i out
Social	0,89	0,97	1,00	0,83
	0,58	1,00	0,44	0,63
	0,64	0,76	0,17	0,12
	0,76	0,64	0,17	0,33
	0,82	0,82	0,68	0,97
	0,71	0,70	0,16	0,21
Selfish	0,20	0,58	0,00	0,00
	0,27	0,85	0,00	0,00
	0,20	0,94	0,33	0,33
	0,20	0,73	0,00	0,00
	0,22	0,79	0,00	0,00
Innovator	0,76	0,85	0,71	1,00
	1,00	0,94	0,54	0,96
	0,98	0,67	0,01	0,01
	CI_{CBE} t	26,4		
	CI_{CBE} in	0,444	PI_{CBE} in	0,776
	CI_{CBE} out	0,214	PI_{CBE} out	0,686

The indicators CI_{CBE} *in/out* reveal a better distribution of the collaboration than the PI_{CBE} *in/out*, since these values are normalized between 0 and 1, with zero indicating an equal distribution of collaboration among all organizations.

Running the model again for a period of one year and parameterizing the influence mechanism as shown in Table 6, the results of Table 7 were achieved.

Table 6. Parametrization of the influence mechanism.

Influence mechanism			
Factor of influence	Weights		
FI	wII	wCI	wPI
10%	1	4	2

Comparing the results of Tables 5 and 7, it can be observed that the more significant difference in the CBE after applying the influence mechanism, is that all the organizations tried to be more active creating more *CoOps*. The indicator $CI_{CBE}t$ increased from 26,4 to 26,7 (showing a higher average of collaboration opportunities by organization, although not very significant), and the CI_i *out*(invites to collaborate sent by organization) also increased for almost all the organizations, flattening CI_{CBE} *out* from 0,214 to 0,178 (showing a more uniform collaboration among organizations) at the same time. On the other hand, the PI_i *in* also had an increase (more prestige concerning invitations received) but only in the Social and Innovator classes, resulting in a better PI_{CBE} *in* from 0,776 to 0,742 (showing a more uniformization of the prestige among organization), but still showing a high polarized distribution. Finally, no further significant differences were registered.

Table 7. Values of the CI and PI for each individual organization and for the CBE, after the influence mechanism.

Contribution and Prestige Indicators (CI and PI)			
Class of Resp.	CI_i in	CI_i out	PI_i in	PI_i out
Social	0,85	1,00	1,00	0,77
	0,55	1,00	0,45	0,57
	0,62	0,81	0,22	0,15
	0,72	0,66	0,22	0,36
	0,79	0,88	0,76	0,99
	0,66	0,78	0,18	0,21
Selfish	0,21	0,56	0,00	0,00
	0,26	0,91	0,00	0,00
	0,21	0,97	0,33	0,33
	0,17	0,78	0,00	0,00
	0,23	0,81	0,00	0,00
Innovator	0,72	0,88	0,79	1,00
	1,00	0,97	0,71	0,98
	0,96	0,69	0,15	0,02
	CI_{CBE} t	26,7		
	CI_{CBE} in	0,465	PI_{CBE} in	0,742
	CI_{CBE} out	0,178	PI_{CBE} out	0,687

Although the previous observed responses of a CBE and its individual organizations, to the proposed influence mechanism are not very significant so far, these are preliminary results using arbitrary parameters so that the modelling and simulation concept can be illustrated. Other improvements to the influence mechanism should be made as well as the adjustment of the parameters used in order to obtain more meaningful conclusions.

5   Conclusions and Further Work

The PAAM model and the experimental evaluation in the previous section showed that a CBE can be evaluated through performance indicators, more specifically, the proposed CI and PI. It also showed that a CBE can evolve by self-adjusting of the behaviour of its organizations, when influenced by the variation of the weights (significance) of the adopted performance indicators.

The ongoing work is related to the improvement of the influence mechanism, enhancing the calculation formulas by introducing more variables in addition to the allocated resources.

Future work includes the calculation of the Innovation Indicator (II), correlating it with collaboration. On the other hand, the PAAM model should be more dynamic, basing the decision to collaborate not on distribution functions, but depending on the performance of organizations. Finally, more refined and tested simulation scenarios should be carried out using all classes of responsiveness with different and dynamic parametrizations.

Acknowledgments. This work benefited from the ongoing research within the CoDIS (Collaborative Networks and Distributed Industrial Systems Group) which is part of both the New University of Lisbon (UNL) - Faculty of Sciences and Technology, and the UNINOVA - CTS (Center of Technology and Systems). Partial support also comes from Fundação para a Ciência e Tecnologia through the PEST program UID/EEA/00066/2019.

References

1. Camarinha-Matos, L.M., Fornasiero, R., Afsarmanesh, H.: Collaborative networks as a core enabler of Industry 4.0. In: Camarinha-Matos, L.M., Afsarmanesh, H., Fornasiero, R. (eds.) PRO-VE 2017. IAICT, vol. 506, pp. 3–17. Springer, Cham (2017). https://doi.org/10.1007/978-3-319-65151-4_1
2. Moore, J.F.: Predators and prey: a new ecology of competition. Harvard Bus. Rev. **71**(3), 75–86 (1993)
3. Camarinha-Matos, L.M., Afsarmanesh, H.: Collaborative networks: a new scientific discipline. J. Intell. Manuf. **16**(4–5), 439–452 (2005)
4. Graça, P., Camarinha-Matos, L.M.: The need of performance indicators for collaborative business ecosystems. In: Camarinha-Matos, L.M., Baldissera, T.A., Di Orio, G., Marques, F. (eds.) DoCEIS 2015. IAICT, vol. 450, pp. 22–30. Springer, Cham (2015). https://doi.org/10.1007/978-3-319-16766-4_3
5. Graça, P., Camarinha-Matos, L.M.: Evolution of a collaborative business ecosystem in response to performance indicators. In: Camarinha-Matos, L.M., Afsarmanesh, H., Fornasiero, R. (eds.) PRO-VE 2017. IAICT, vol. 506, pp. 629–640. Springer, Cham (2017). https://doi.org/10.1007/978-3-319-65151-4_55
6. Kaplan, R.S., Norton, D.P.: The Balanced Scorecard: Translating Strategy into Action. Harvard Business Press, Brighton (1996)
7. Camarinha-Matos, L.M., Macedo, P.: A conceptual model of value systems in collaborative networks. J. Intell. Manuf. **21**(3), 287–299 (2010)
8. Macedo, P., Camarinha-Matos, L.M.: A qualitative approach to assess the alignment of value systems in collaborative enterprises networks. Comput. Ind. Eng. **64**(1), 412–424 (2013)

9. Ramanathan, U.: Performance of supply chain collaboration – a simulation study. Expert Syst. Appl. **41**(1), 210–220 (2014)
10. Vereecke, A., Muylle, S.: Performance improvement through supply chain collaboration in Europe. Int. J. Oper. Prod. Manag. **26**(11), 1176–1198 (2006)
11. Lorentz, H., et al.: Supply chain collaboration performance metrics: a conceptual framework. Benchmarking Int. J. **18**(6), 856–872 (2011)
12. Ramanathan, U., Gunasekaran, A.: Supply chain collaboration: impact of success in long-term partnerships. Int. J. Prod. Econ. **147**, 252–259 (2014)
13. Freeman, L.C.: Centrality in social networks conceptual clarification. Soc. Netw. **1**(3), 215–239 (1978)
14. Jackson, M.O.: Social and Economic Networks, vol. 3. Princeton University Press, Princeton (2008)
15. Graça, P., Camarinha-Matos, L.M.: A proposal of performance indicators for collaborative business ecosystems. In: Afsarmanesh, H., Camarinha-Matos, L.M., Lucas Soares, A. (eds.) PRO-VE 2016. IAICT, vol. 480, pp. 253–264. Springer, Cham (2016). https://doi.org/10.1007/978-3-319-45390-3_22
16. Borshchev, A.: The Big Book of Simulation Modeling: Multimethod Modeling with AnyLogic 6. AnyLogic North America, Chicago (2013)
17. JHCW: Introduction to mathematical probability. Sci. Prog. **33**(130), 350–350 (1938). (1933)
18. Opsahl, T., Agneessens, F., Skvoretz, J.: Node centrality in weighted networks: generalizing degree and shortest paths. Soc. Netw. **32**(3), 245–251 (2010)
19. Floyd, R.W.: Algorithm 97: shortest path. Commun. ACM **5**(6), 345 (1962)
20. Haight, F.A.: Handbook of the Poisson Distribution. Wiley, New York (1967)

Verifying for Compliance to Data Constraints in Collaborative Business Processes

John Paul Kasse[1], Lai Xu[1(✉)], Paul de Vrieze[1], and Yuewei Bai[2]

[1] Department of Computing and Informatics,
Faculty of Science and Technology, Bournemouth University,
Poole BH12 5BB, UK
{jkasse, lxu, pdvrieze}@bournemouth.ac.uk
[2] Industry Engineering of Engineering College,
Shanghai Polytechnic University, Shanghai, China
ywbai@sspu.edu.cn

Abstract. Production processes are nowadays fragmented across different companies and organized in global collaborative networks. This is the result of the first wave of globalization that, among the various factors, was enabled by the diffusion of Internet-based Information and Communication Technologies (ICTs) at the beginning of the years 2000. The recent wave of new technologies possibly leading to the fourth industrial revolution – the so-called Industry 4.0 – is further multiplying opportunities. Accessing global customers opens great opportunities for organizations, including small and medium enterprises (SMEs), but it requires the ability to adapt to different requirements and conditions, volatile demand patterns and fast-changing technologies. Regardless of the industrial sector, the processes used in an organization must be compliant to rules, standards, laws and regulations. Non-compliance subjects enterprises to litigation and financial fines. Thus, compliance verification is a major concern, not only to keep pace with changing regulations but also to address the rising concerns of security, product and service quality and data privacy. The software, in particular process automation, used must be designed accordingly. In relation to process management, we propose a new way to pro-actively check the compliance of current running business processes using Descriptive Logic and Linear Temporal Logic to describe the constraints related to data. Related algorithms are presented to detect the potential violations.

Keywords: Compliance · Collaborative business processes · Virtual factory · Business Process Verification · Algorithm

1 Introduction

Compliance is about adherence to regulations, guidelines or predefined legal requirements like norms, laws and standards. Compliance verification in business process management is addressed at different levels of the life cycle i.e. deign time, runtime, post runtime. A hybrid approach addresses compliance verification for all levels [1]. Moreover, existing research has made significant contribution to addressing verification of models for compliance with a range of requirements such as, activity ordering

L. M. Camarinha-Matos et al. (Eds.): PRO-VE 2019, IFIP AICT 568, pp. 259–270, 2019.
https://doi.org/10.1007/978-3-030-28464-0_23

requirements [2–9], resource assignment constraints [10–13], data requirements [14, 15], security requirements [16–20] and privacy [21–27], compliance between process variants [28–31]. These works show the state of the art in business processes compliance management and verification. They have also resulted into various compliance approaches, frameworks, methods, languages and tools. However, more compliance challenges need to be addressed to fully support collaborative processes in the context of a virtual factory.

In this paper, we look at the compliance of running collaborative business processes with data constraints. The paper proposes a new way to describe data constraints using descriptive logic (DL) and Linear Temporal Logic (LTL). The traces of the running processes are used to check whether the current collaborative business processes are compliant with the data constraints described in DL and LTL.

The structure of the paper is as follows: related work is presented in Sect. 2. Section 3 introduces an exemplary business process and related traces. DL and LTL are used to express the data constraints in Sect. 4. Section 5 shows how to present compliance properties as well as related verification algorithms. Future work and conclusion are presented in Sect. 6.

2 Related Work

Pesic et al. propose DECLARE, a declarative constraint based specification language and model compliance checking in relation to ordering requirements [2, 3]. The language is limited to control flow checking. Similar work is presented by Awad et al. and Wynn et al. Awad et al., propose a BPMN-Q language which extends BPMN to search for segments of a process model affected by changes and verify their compliancy in terms of control flow.

Whereas Wynn extends YAWL language with reset nets to determine correctness of business processes with cancellation and OR joins, other work by Elgammal et al. and Taghiabadi present compliance frameworks for managing the compliance of a business process during its life cycle. The constraints are organised according to patterns like control flow, resources, temporal and data [7, 9]. Despite the fact that the frameworks comprehensively cover all perspectives of the business process, the proposed languages employ complex mathematics and logics that are not intuitive for ordinary end users.

Data specific constraint checking approaches check compliance between the model and data requirements. Knuplesch et al. propose a graph method for modelling compliance rules and address verification through structured compliance checking based on compliance rules and data checking based on abstracted data [14]. The resultant graph based approach is data constraint based. Borrego and Barbara enhance earlier work of Declare to include data requirements compliance checking [15]. In this paper we extend our earlier work for supporting compliance verification in collaborative business processes [32–34]. Related work remains limited in various ways; the compliance management framework by Elgammal et al. results into a compliance request language in which constraints can be specified by ignores their verification. Taghiabadi' s compliance approach caters for verification for control flow and data constraints. However, its application to collaborative environments is not demonstrated, it is also a domain specific approach and so is Declare language. Wynn et al.'s work based on YAWL is geared towards control flow verification to achieve model soundness. Data constraints are not considered by the authors. Moreover, non of these works presents mechanism easily comprehensible for non-expert end users. This limits their application. Our work leverages previous work by supporting specification of data constraints and verifying for their compliancy with collaborative business processes using an approach that empolys syntactic and semantic mechanism close to natural language. Besides, we provide a coarse grained approach in which we cater for data constraints in terms of accessibility, authentication and privacy by means of access control and authorisation. This is a valuable contribution in the wake of revised compliance requirements of the 2008 general data protection regulation.

3   An Exemplary Business Process and Related Traces

We adopt an abstracted industry based use case, the Pick and Pack business process proposed in [33]. In this case, customers submit orders online after registering on the system. Stores' staffs check order details, and proceed to process the order as Fig. 1 illustrates.

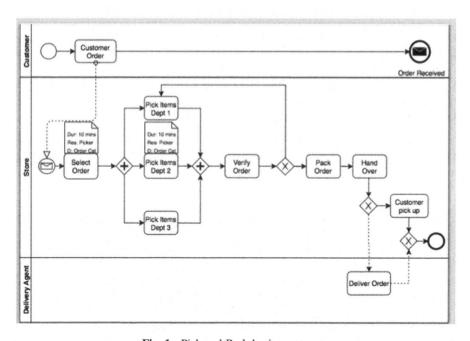

Fig. 1. Pick and Pack business process

Order processing involves activities summarised in Table 1 and assigned roles: Based on the role assignments, the following resource assignment conditions apply;

1. Pickers cannot participate in the verification of orders.
2. Packers can also do the verify order task.
3. Pickers can participate in hand over task at peak times
4. Supervisors oversee other employees and can execute any task.

Supervisors delegate or share rights of task execution to other staff, e.g. supervisors can delegate pickers to pack items.

Table 1. Process activities and role assignments

Activity	Description	Role
Select order	Order is chosen from a pool of pending orders	Picker
Pick items	Order items are picked	Picker
Verify order	Right order in terms of items and quantities	Verifiers
Pack order	Order is packed	Packers
Hand over/Deliver order	Orders ready for picked up or delivery by agent	Customer service

Relatedly, the constraints governing data access are summarized;

1. Supervisors have full data access and can grant access to other staff.
2. Basic data must be accessible and available for staff to execute tasks that do not need much restriction and control. E.g. order list data.
3. Access control and authorization is observed for restricted data. For example, customer personal data, financial data among others.
4. For security of data and system, users must be authenticated by the system.

For illustration purposes, the business process is considered in terms of activities while traces are used as a mechanism to derive process execution to facilitate checking compliance to constraints. Table 2 lists sample traces based on the use case.

Table 2. Exemplified log showing events, activities, constraints and process instances

Event	Activity	Constraints		Process instance
		Accessible Data	Time (units)	
e_1	Select order	OrderList	Duration [6]	P_1
e_2	Hand over order	Customer orderlist	Delay [10]	P_1
e_3	Select order	Orderlist	Between [10]	P_1
e_4	Pick items	ProductList	Duration [15]	P_1
e_5	Pickup or delivery	Contactlist	Duration [20]	P_1
e_6	Select order	Customer address	Duration [10]	P_1

4 Constraint Expression in Description Logic and LTL

To achieve constraint expression, descriptive logic (DL) [35] and LTL are adopted. While using DL, the business process is the domain of discourse with activities and constraints as concepts. The intention is to support expression of constraint require- ments in a way close to natural language for easy intuition by non-experts yet expressive enough to support reasoning. DL is known for knowledge base represen- tation and building in knowledge management systems [35]. Its application in business process design however has not received much attention with fewer applications in [10, 11]. The limitation is due to lack of known syntax to express unique business process requirements.

To enhance its expressiveness, we adopt logical operators and quantifier operators from temporal logic. Temporal logic is a formal method founded on mathematics. Models are specified and checked for correctness against a set of properties expressed as event orderings in time [36]. Role representation establishes a link between the constraints and the activities while the role restrictions impose specific existential and value restrictions of a constraint over the activity. We use unary predicates to represent sets of individual constraints while binary predicates denote relationships between individual constraints. We further use composite predicates to denote relationships between different constraints.

4.1 Expressions of Data Requirements as Constraints in DL and LTL

Data constraints are based on data patterns [37] and represented as unary predicate expressions using DL and logical operators and quantifiers from LTL. Task execution requires access to data. E.g., 'delivery' task needs access to customer address and contact to be accessible. Further still, actions that a user can do must be pre-authorized i.e. action to read, write, modify. Thus, task data assignment TD is composed of a task, data object (o), value (v) and action (∂). TD assignment is achieved by a function $f : a \rightarrow o, v, \partial$ which maps data item attributes like value and action to a task. Figure 2 exemplifies task data assignment and the required attributes.

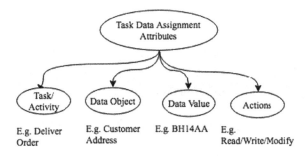

Fig. 2. Task and data assignment attributes

Using DL constructs, the expression for *TD* is derived as; $TD = a \to (o \sqcap v \sqcap \partial)$ and formalized as; $a \to (o \wedge v \wedge \partial)$ in LTL. Based on Fig. 2, the use case, it follows that;

$$TD = [Deliver_{Order} \to (customer\_address \sqcap BH14AA \sqcap Read)]$$

Table 3 presents some examples of expressions as derived for data constraints in;

Table 3. Data constant expression in DL

DL data unary expressions	Description
$\forall$data $\to$ visible/$\exists$data $\to$ visible	All/some data is visible
$\forall$data $\to$ valid/$\exists$data $\to$ valid	All/some is valid data
$\forall$data $\to$ ¬available/$\exists$data $\to$ ¬available	All/some data not available
$\forall$data $\to$ accessible/$\exists$data $\to$ accessible	All/some data is accessible
$\forall$data $\to$ privacy/$\exists$data $\to$ privacy	All/some data classified as private
$\forall$data $\to$ authentic/$\exists$data $\to$ authentic	All/some data classified as private
DL data binary expressions	*Description*
$\forall$data $\to$ (visible $\sqcap$ accessible)/ $\exists$data $\to$ (visible $\sqcap$ accessible)	All/some data has visible and accessible constraints
$\forall$data $\to$ (authentic $\sqcap$ privacy)/ $\exists$data $\to$ (authentic $\sqcap$ privacy)	All/some has authenticity and privacy constraints

5 Verification Algorithms for Compliance to Data Constraints

Data constraints are based on Boolean conditional evaluations where the condition is either true or false. Depending on the outcome of the conditional evaluation assessed against predefined access policies, access is granted or denied. To check for compliance, a constraint is satisfied if a trace is true for the given conditions, and the constraint is violated if trace is otherwise. To that effect, the following specifications and definitions are useful for the data constraints compliance checking algorithm.

Given a set of activities a_1, a_2 and a_3 whose execution by role actor (r_1) requires product catalogue data (Pcd). Access to this data is constrained by access and availability. If the assignment is true per the executed behavior, then the trace (σ) satisfies ($\models$) the constraint.

Definition 1: Accessibility and Availability (AA)

$$\sigma \in (((a_1, a_2, a_3), r_1) : (Pcd.[Read]) : AA \tag{1}$$

If $\sigma = True$ then $\sigma \models AA$
The definition specifies accessibility and availability constraints for Pcd data object with action read granted to r_1 for execution of activities a_1, a_2 and a_3. During verification, the data compliance verification algorithm checks for compliance to the

constraint for the data object, action by the user and tasks. If the outcome shows that the trace is true, then the availability and accessibility constraints satisfied. Otherwise, it is a violation detected for the AA constraint.

Definition 2: Authentication

$$\sigma \in (((a_1, a_2, a_3), r_1) : (Pcd.[True/False]) : Authentication \tag{2}$$

If $\sigma = True$) **then** $\sigma \vDash Authentication$
The definition specifies access control by authentication granted for Pcd data with actions to read and write for role actor (r_1) who executes activities a_1, a_2 and a_3. Satisfaction of the authentication constraint is achieved if the trace of the executed events exhibits the specified behavior. Otherwise, a violation is detected for the constraint.

Definition 3: Privacy (Prv)

$$\sigma \in (((a_1, a_2, a_3), r_1) : (Pcd.[Read]) : Prv \tag{3}$$

If $\sigma = True$ **then** $\sigma \vDash Prv$
The definition specifies Privacy constraint for accessing Pcd data where action to read private data is to be granted for the resource actor r_1 who executes activities a_1, a_2 and a_3. During verification using the privacy compliance verification algorithm, the constraint is checked if it is satisfied before access is granted to private data. If trace is true to the specification, then the constraint is satisfied and thus compliance achieved. Otherwise, it is a violation detected for the privacy constraint.

5.1 Data Constraints Verification Algorithms

In this section, four algorithms are introduced, namely access and availability, authentication and privacy data constraints compliancy verification algorithms. At the end, an overall data constraint compliancy verification algorithm is presented.

Access and Availability Constraint Verification
Verifying Access and Availability data constraint ensures that basic non-exclusive data is accessible and available with less restriction to enable accomplishment of basic tasks. Algorithm 1 is composed to the effect. Violation occurs if role actors or tasks are denied access to data or where the permitted action type differs from the initial assignment, e.g. modify action type instead of read action type.

Algorithm 1 Access and Availability Compliance Verification

1: $InPut$:

   a. All Process Instances, Traces and Activities events

   b. Constraints (AA)

2: **for** all data with constraint $C = (AA : [Read/Write/Modify])$ for actors (r) **do**

   Assign = r,e.ac: $\rightarrow$ AA= Data Item.[Read/Write/Modify]

3:    **if** $(Assign \neq\in seen, finished \neq AA)$ **then**

   Violation: "Deadlock due to denied access to data. AA constraint violated"

   Return No violation of AA constraint for the provided processes if $AA \in$ seen

   and $AA \in$ finished

Violation of AA constraint as per Algorithm 1 exists when tasks or their actors(r, e. ac) are denied access. The violation results into to a deadlock or livelock. Deadlock occurs if running activities are denied access to data necessary for the process to progress, while livelock occurs when a task denied data access stays in waiting mode stagnating process execution. Another form of violation occurs when a task executes without necessary data resulting into wrong outcomes which compromise data integrity.

Verifying Compliancy with Authentication Data Constraint

Authentication Algorithm 2 verifies for compliance by checking that role actor credentials match the credentials stored in a database of authorized actors and their access privileges over tasks. Two forms of authentication errors lead to violations, i.e.;

- Access leakage which occurs when non-authenticated users gain access to data. This is traced from running or finished events
- Deadlocks which occur when users are authorised to execute activities but access to data is denied for technical or logical reasons e.g. improper configurations.

Algorithm 2 Authenticity Data Constraint Checking

1: $InPut$:

   a. All Process Instances in the business process

   b. Constraints (Authenticity)

2: **for** all data with constraint C.Auth = Data item.$[True/False]$) **do**

   $assign \equiv r, e.ac :\rightarrow Auth = DataItem.[True/False]$

3:    **if** $(Assign \neq\in seen, finished)$ **then**

   Violation: "authenticated are denied access to restricted data."

4:       **if** $\exists$ actor $r_n \in Assign$ **then**

   Violation: "Access leakage, non-authenticated actor accessed data. "

   Return No violation of Authenticity constraint for the provided business process.

When data constrained by authenticity constraint exists outside the constraint it leads to access leakage since it will be accessible by users without authentication or if it is accessed by non-authenticated role actors. Similarly, where data is not accessible to authenticated actors leads to a deadlock since they cannot progress with the current work being executed.

Verifying Compliancy with Privacy Data Constraints

Privacy constraint is enforced by means of access control and authorization. Authorization involves the process of validating that the authenticated user is granted permission to access the requested resources. Privacy as a data constraint restricts access to data regarded private as defined by GDPR. Data restricted from public access is enforced by authorization. Algorithm 3 checks whether the process is complying with the privacy data constraint. Violation to privacy constraint is checked targeting two forms of errors; deadlocks and privacy breach.

- Deadlocks occur when the executing events authorised to access data are denied access for technical or logical reasons e.g. improper configurations,
- Breach to privacy i.e. non-authorised activities eventually access private data and execute.

Algorithm 3 Privacy Data Constraint Checking

1: $InPut$:

    a. All Pi in the Business process

    b. Constraints (Privacy)

2: **for** all data with constraint (C=Privacy[R/W/M]) for actors (r) **do**

    Assign $\equiv$ r,e.ac: Data Item $\rightarrow$ privacy $\equiv$ Authorise :[Read/Write/Modify]

3:     **if** $(Assign \not\models privacy \in seen, finished)$ **then**

    Violation: "Assigned actors denied access to private data"

4:       **if** $(Assign \neq (Dataclerk, Assessor) \in seen, finished)$ **then**

    Violation: "Access leakage, non authorised actors gain access to private data"

    Return No violation of Privacy constraint for the provided processes if $r, e.ac \in$

    seen and finished

When data constrained by privacy constraint exists outside the constraint, it leads to a leakage since it is accessible by non-authorized actors. Similarly, where authorized data is not visible in 'seen' and 'finished', it implies denied access as a form of violation.

The overall compliance verification Algorithm 4, is a general algorithm that invokes Algorithms 1, 2 and 3 to check whether the entire business process complies with above mentioned data constraints.

Algorithm 4 Overall Compliance Data Constraint Verification Algorithm

1: *InPut*:

      a. All Process Instances in the business process

      b. All Constraints

2: **for** all (Pi) with given constraints C = Control flow, Resource, Data, and Temporal constraints) **do**

      Return violation or compliance of Resource flow constraints /* Check for compliance with Data constraints*/

3:               if e.ac.Exist = True **then**

      Check AA → call algorithm 1

      Check Auth → call algorithm 2

      Check Privacy → call algorithm 3

      Return violation or compliance of Data constraints

      Return overall compliancy or violation of business process with verified constraints.

6 Conclusion and Future Work

Regardless of the industrial sector, compliance is a major concern not only to keep pace with changing regulations but to address the rising concerns of security, product and service quality and data privacy which are fundamental for implementing industry 4.0. With the EU GDPR in force, concerned organizations (European or otherwise) must meet its requirements by reviewing and realigning their business processes. It is necessary for software to be designed accordingly to reduce overheads from organizational measures used in the interim. In this spirit, we propose a new way to check the compliance of current running business processes. DL and LTL are used to describe the constraints related to data. Related algorithms are presented to detect the potential violations, i.e. data access and availability violation, data authentication violation, and data privacy violation. The research of collaborative process model verification covered also control flow and resource constraint verifications. For page limitation, we only present data constraint verification in this paper. Further research related to data constraint verification will carry out the practical implementation and evaluations as the next step.

Acknowledgements. This research is partially funded by the State Key Research and Development Program of China (2017YFE0118700) and it is part of the FIRST project which has received funding from the European Union's Horizon 2020 research and innovation programme under the Marie Skłodowska-Curie grant agreement No. 734599.

References

1. Hashmi, M., Governatori, G., Lam, H.P., Wynn, M.T.: Are we done with business process compliance: state of the art and challenges ahead. Knowl. Inf. Syst. **57**(1), 79–133 (2018)
2. Pesic, M.: Constraint-based workflow management systems: shifting control to users (2008)
3. Pesic, M., Schonenberg, H., Van Der Aalst, W.M.P.: DECLARE: full support for loosely-structured processes. In: Proceedings – IEEE International Enterprise Distributed Object Computing Working, EDOC, pp. 287–298 (2007)
4. Awad, A., Decker, G., Weske, M.: Efficient compliance checking using BPMN-Q and temporal logic. In: Dumas, M., Reichert, M., Shan, M.-C. (eds.) BPM 2008. LNCS, vol. 5240, pp. 326–341. Springer, Heidelberg (2008). https://doi.org/10.1007/978-3-540-85758-7_24
5. van der Aalst, W.M.P., de Beer, H.T., van Dongen, B.F.: Process mining and verification of properties: an approach based on temporal logic. In: Meersman, R., Tari, Z. (eds.) OTM 2005. LNCS, vol. 3760, pp. 130–147. Springer, Heidelberg (2005). https://doi.org/10.1007/11575771_11
6. Speck, A., Witt, S., Feja, S., Lotyzc, A., Pulvermüller, E.: Framework for business process verification. In: Abramowicz, W. (ed.) BIS 2011. LNBIP, vol. 87, pp. 50–61. Springer, Heidelberg (2011). https://doi.org/10.1007/978-3-642-21863-7_5
7. Wynn, M.T., Verbeek, H.M.W., van der Aalst, W.M.P., ter Hofstede, A.H.M., Edmond, D.: Business process verification – finally a reality! Bus. Process Manag. J. **15**(1), 74–92 (2009)
8. Taghiabadi, E.R.: Understanding non-compliance (2017)
9. Elgammal, A., Turetken, O., van den Heuvel, W.J., Papazoglou, M.: Formalizing and appling compliance patterns for business process compliance. Softw. Syst. Model. **15**(1), 119–146 (2016)
10. Cabanillas, C., Resinas, M., Del-Río-Ortega, A., Ruiz-Cortés, A.: Specification and automated design-time analysis of the business process human resource perspective. Inf. Syst. **52**, 55–82 (2015)
11. Del-Río-Ortega, A., Resinas, M., Cabanillas, C., Ruiz-Cortés, A.: Defining and analysing resource-aware process performance indicators. In: CEUR Workshop Proceedings, vol. 998, pp. 57–64 (2013)
12. Huang, Z., Lu, X., Duan, H.: Mining association rules to support resource allocation inbusiness process management. Expert Syst. Appl. **38**, 9483–9490 (2011)
13. Nakatumba, J.: Resource-aware business process management: analysis and support (2013)
14. Knuplesch, D., Ly, L.T., Rinderle-Ma, S., Pfeifer, H., Dadam, P.: On enabling data-aware compliance checking of business process models. In: Parsons, J., Saeki, M., Shoval, P., Woo, C., Wand, Y. (eds.) ER 2010. LNCS, vol. 6412, pp. 332–346. Springer, Heidelberg (2010). https://doi.org/10.1007/978-3-642-16373-9_24
15. Borrego, D., Barba, I.: Conformance checking and diagnosis for declarative business process models in data-aware scenarios. Expert Syst. Appl. **41**(11), 5340–5352 (2014)
16. Salnitri, M., Dalpiaz, F., Giorgini, P.: Modeling and verifying security policies in business processes. In: Bider, I., et al. (eds.) BPMDS/EMMSAD -2014. LNBIP, vol. 175, pp. 200–214. Springer, Heidelberg (2014). https://doi.org/10.1007/978-3-662-43745-2_14
17. Compagna, L., dos Santos, D.R., Ponta, S.E., Ranise, S.: Cerberus: automated synthesis of enforcement mechanisms for security-sensitive business processes. In: Chechik, M., Raskin, J.-F. (eds.) TACAS 2016. LNCS, vol. 9636, pp. 567–572. Springer, Heidelberg (2016). https://doi.org/10.1007/978-3-662-49674-9_36

18. Karjoth, G.: Aligning security and business objectives for process-aware information systems. In: Proceedings of the 5th ACM Conference on Data and Application Security and Privacy - CODASPY 2015, p. 243 (2015)
19. Combi, C., Viganò, L., Zavatteri, M.: Security constraints in temporal role-based. In: Codaspy, pp. 207–218 (2016)
20. Vijay, A.: Security for workflow systems. Inf. Secur. Tech. Rep. **6**(2), 59–68 (2001)
21. Mont, M.C., Thyne, R.: Privacy policy enforcement in enterprises with identity management solutions. J. Comput. Secur. **16**(2), 133–163 (2008)
22. Mont, M.C., Thyne, R.: A systemic approach to automate privacy policy enforcement in enterprises. In: Danezis, G., Golle, P. (eds.) PET 2006. LNCS, vol. 4258, pp. 118–134. Springer, Heidelberg (2006). https://doi.org/10.1007/11957454_7
23. Khan, A.R.: Access control in cloud computing environment. ARPN J. Eng. Appl. Sci. **7**(5), 613–615 (2012)
24. Alshehri, A., Sandhu, R.: Access control models for virtual object communication in cloud-enabled IoT. In: 2017 IEEE International Conference on Information Reuse and Integration (IRI) (2017)
25. Warner, J., Atluri, V.: Inter-instance authorization constraints for secure workflow management, p. 190 (2006)
26. Basin, D.: Optimal workflow-aware authorizations. Proceedings of the 17th ACM Symposium on Access Control Models and Technologies, pp. 93–102. ACM (2012)
27. Tan, K., Crampton, J., Gunter, C.A.: The consistency of task-based authorization constraints in workflow systems. In: Proceedings. 17th IEEE Computer Security Foundations Workshop, pp. 155–169 (2004)
28. Tealeb, A., Awad, A., Galal-Edeen, G.: Context-based variant generation of business process models. In: Bider, I., et al. (eds.) BPMDS/EMMSAD -2014. LNBIP, vol. 175, pp. 363–377. Springer, Heidelberg (2014). https://doi.org/10.1007/978-3-662-43745-2_25
29. Lu, R., Sadiq, S., Governatori, G.: On managing business processes variants. Data Knowl. Eng. **68**(7), 642–664 (2009)
30. Groefsema, H.: Business process variability: a study into process management and verification (2016)
31. Groefsema, H., Bucur, D.: A survey of formal business process verification: from soundness to variability. In: Proceedings of Third International Symposium on Business Modeling and Software Design, pp. 198–203 (2013)
32. Kasse, J.P., Xu, L., de Vrieze, P.T., Yuwei, B.: Process driven access control and authorisation approach (2019)
33. Kasse, J.P., Xu, L., de Vrieze, P., Bai, Y.: The need for compliance verification in collaborative business processes. In: Camarinha-Matos, L.M., Afsarmanesh, H., Rezgui, Y. (eds.) PRO-VE 2018. IAICT, vol. 534, pp. 217–229. Springer, Cham (2018). https://doi.org/10.1007/978-3-319-99127-6_19
34. Kasse, J.P., Xu, L., de Vrieze, P.: A comparative survey of business process verification methods and tools. In: Working Conference on Virtual Enterprises, pp. 355–367 (2017)
35. Baader, F.: Basic description logics. In: Theory Implementations Application, Cambridge (2003)
36. Lowe, G.: Specification of communicating processes: temporal logic versus refusals-based refinement. Formal Aspects Comput. **20**(3), 277–294 (2008)
37. Russell, N., Hofstede, A.H.M., Edmond, D., Van Der Aalst, W.M.P.: Workflow data patterns. Business **66** (2004). No. FIT–TR–2004–01, p. 2004–01

Collaborative Networks Management from a Theory of Constraints Perspective

Alexandra Tenera[1,2(✉)] and João Rosas[1,3]

[1] Faculty of Sciences and Technology, NOVA University of Lisbon,
Caparica, Portugal
abt@fct.unl.pt
[2] Research and Development Unit for Mechanical and Industrial Engineering
(UNIDEMI), Caparica, Portugal
[3] Center of Technology and Systems (CTS), UNINOVA, Caparica, Portugal
jrosas@uninova.pt

Abstract. Collaborative networks are organizational structures that, instead of expressing market behavior, their formation and operation are based on **principles of collaboration**, where trust, reliability, and commitment between partners prevail. These principles allow collaborative networks to share risks and become more competitive. **Collaboration-based strategies** are increasingly important in the face of a growing demand for new and more sophisticated services and products, posing significant challenges for companies that must struggle to fulfill. In this sense, companies need to adapt their business strategies, so they can react and keep up with the pace of change. In this work, we propose a new perspective from the **Theory of Constraints** in Collaborative Networks Management. The adaptation of the **TOC's Five Focusing Steps** and **TOC Thinking Process,** combined with the **Critical Chain Project Management** (CCPM) approach, are proposed to improve Collaborative Networks Management. CCPM is brought into a collaboration context to deal with project network uncertainty. A preliminary motivation example is shown in this position paper, aiming at illustrating this prospective approach in Collaborative Networks Management.

Keywords: Collaborative networks · Theory of Constraints · Critical Chain Project Management

1 Introduction

The increasing level of market globalization is requiring the creation and development of ever more innovative products and services. Competitiveness, innovation, risk, sustainability, resilience, and flexibility are such terms that are increasingly being considered when reflecting on the general state of organizations, countries' economies and even nations, whose results are grounded on the performance of their productive systems. While, in many sectors of activity, increased competitiveness may be related to the modernization of processes associated with technological advances, in others, success may be related, above all, to how companies organize themselves and manage their productive systems.

© IFIP International Federation for Information Processing 2019
Published by Springer Nature Switzerland AG 2019
L. M. Camarinha-Matos et al. (Eds.): PRO-VE 2019, IFIP AICT 568, pp. 271–282, 2019.
https://doi.org/10.1007/978-3-030-28464-0_24

In this context, Project Management and Innovation can contribute to the success of organizations, providing a contribution to increasing performance and improving countries' economies. Innovation projects, if well managed, will allow technological and organizational development and increasingly sustainable solutions which can be obtained through Collaborative Networks (CN) with high added value efficiently using available resources, skills or competencies in ever shorter development cycles.

As a result, the intrinsic characteristics of projects (by definition, unique and temporary), along with the dynamics of organizations and markets, contribute to the fact that change and uncertainty is inevitable. This happens both at project level (e.g. variations in programmed durations, unavailability of resources or materials) and at organizational level (e.g. by limitations of appropriate mechanisms for decision support or sharing information or competences). Considering these aspects, the application of the Theory of Constraints (TOC) in Collaborative Networks Management (CNM) is proposed in this position paper.

Assuming this TOC-based perspective into CNM, we could stipulate that there is always at least one constraint affecting the performance of a CN. Therefore, identifying and exploring this constraint will eventually make possible to subordinate it to the set of CN partners that are most capable of mitigating the mentioned constraint. In this way, the hypothesis that is being explored is that CNM can be improved by applying the principles of TOC into CNs.

In next chapter, a brief introduction to the Theory of Constraints, their corresponding POOGI, and TOC Process Thinking for problem resolution, as well as the Critical Chain Project Management for project and change implementation. In chapter 3, a few directions on how TOC could be used in Collaborative Networks Management are then addressed. Finally, the main conclusions and some points to be addressed in the future work are proposed.

2   Introducing the Theory of Constraints

In this section, we will begin by introducing fundamentals concepts and approaches of the Theory of Constraints, bounding the scopeto the main aspects that can contribute to its application in Collaborative Networks.

2.1   The TOC Core Concepts

The Theory of Constraints, as presented by Goldratt in 1990 [1], has evolved methodologically as well as in its implementation domains [2] since its first publication [3]. Along their evolution, TOC has presented several designations over time. Initially, it was associated to the "Optimized Production Timetable" (OPT) scheduling, but "Timetable" was later replaced by "Technology" [2]. It was also associated with other designations, such as Synchronous Production or Constraints Management (CM), which should be used in their specific domains [4]. TOC is nowadays used as a management paradigm, theory or philosophy, as it includes their own concepts, principles, methods and tools [5–7].

The TOC assumes that in any system, there is always at least one constraint affecting its performance, and that eliminating or attenuating this constraint will increase the system performance. The rationale for this "at least one constraint hypothesis" is that if a system had no constraints, then its performance could increase indefinitely, but this is not possible [1]. The focal point of the TOC thus resembles Liebig's law, when he states that the growth of a system is not controlled by all available resources, but by the less abundant resource, which is intended as a limiting factor [8].

Therefore, in the TOC perspective, contrary to what is commonly assumed, the existence of constraints should not be seen as negative, but rather an opportunity for focusing management actions and decisions on system improvement. As a constraint establishes the maximum performance of a system, its reduction translates directly into improved system performance.

According to the TOC, any organization can be considered a system, i.e. aggregation of interrelated elements, with defined purposes and objectives to support value creation: typically, more profit for stakeholders and more sustainable service level for organizations. A system can also be viewed as a network of interacting processes, not just a set of processes, in which the performance and survival of a system depends mostly on how its processes interact rather than their individual and local capacity or performance. Once the purpose of each system's component has been defined, the TOC concentrates all its efforts on promoting improvements that directly translate into system purposes or objectives and, inevitably, into increasing overall performance. These advantages may even increase, when TOC is combined with other management paradigms [9].

In TOC, several types of constraints can be identified [10–13], typically classified into: (a) physical (resources unavailability, as an example) and (b) strategic, political and organizational constraints (such as rules, regulations, procedures, lack of information, etc.). The physical constraints are the easiest to identify, as their effects can be seen through direct observation. On the other hand, the identification of non-physical constraints can be more difficult to distinguish and manage. In addition, aspects like human skills, behaviors, and attitudes, whether individual or collective, can also be included in this non-physical category.

These constraints may also be considered internal or external to the system. A typical external constraint is the market itself. As such, when a production system has more capacity than the required by market, the constraint becomes external. Whenever corresponding balancing and changes are done, the improvements allow reviewing market share and to look for new opportunities. Organizations should concentrate on capitalizing on these new competitive advantages, instead of focusing on continuous improvement in their internal operations.

Furthermore, it is commonly assumed that in service organizations physical constraints are less relevant than organizational ones [10]. As highlighted in [14], it is usually necessary a full elimination of organizational constraints to boost organization results.

2.2   The TOC Thinking Process Logic

From the TOC perspective, any system performance improvement is based on Five Focusing steps known as the Process Of On Going Improvement (POOGI), which can be synthesized as: (1) identify, (2) explore the constraint, (3) subordinate, (4) elevate the constraint, i.e. improve performance and (5) evaluate the changes made and overcome inertia.

The framework is implemented using TOC specific tools, such as TOC Thinking Processes as designated in [15] (TOC TP), performed in a closed loop of continuous improvement, as shown in Fig. 1.

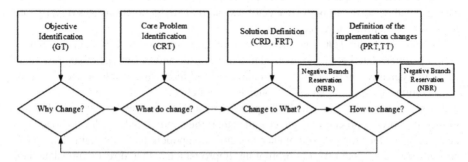

Fig. 1. The TOC Basic Questions and TOC TP tools

As shown in Fig. 1, the TOC TP six logical tools, is used according to a specific set of objectives, namely:

- Goal Tree (GT): clarification and identification of the objective to be achieved under analysis.
- Current Reality Tree (CRT): identification and analysis of system core problems and existing related Undesired Effects (UDE).
- Conflict Resolution Diagram (CRD): identification and resolution of conflicts; also called Evaporating Cloud (EC).
- Future Reality Tree (FRT): search for alternative solutions, characterizing the entities and foreseeable interconnections in the future system, converting the UDEs into desired effects (DE).
- Negative Branch Reservation (NBR): used to identify possible risks of the future solutions and corresponding implementation plan, checking the new system solution against the identified UDEs.
- Prerequisites Tree (PRT): used to ensure the coherence of the solution.
- Transition Tree (TT): to determine the main actions to be taken during the implementation of the solution.

Organizations can be seen as dynamic systems, which undergo changes for their improvement and survival [16]. Although TOC TP is not in the literature traditionally associated with change management, it may support it providing new business perspectives, increasing the managers' sense of control, and allowing more proactive actions [17]. Therefore, the TOC TP presents itself as one of the TOC features with the greatest potential for research exploration [4, 18, 19].

2.3   The TOC in Project Management

TOC principles applied to Project Management practices, the Critical Chain [20] was introduced by Goldratt in 1997, and more conceptuality detailed later on [21–23]. This TOC tool is currently known as Critical Chain Project Management (CCPM).

CCPM can be applied in products or services development projects. Whenever a project is planned, several generic objectives are commonly considered, namely: duration (deadline), cost (budget), resources (materials, equipment, …) and competencies, according to defined specifications or requirements. Among these objectives, time is particularly relevant, as it is a non-cumulative resource, i.e., whether it is used or not, it is spent and cannot be reproduced, resulting in unrecoverable loss of opportunity if not properly exploited.

CCPM applies TOC principles to project scheduling, allowing the best management project duration and resource utilization, while also promoting human resources behavior change. In fact, an effective management of the project execution time, was already highlighted in [24], proposing that in order to maximize the probability of project success, namely the completion of a project within its deadline, a realistic completion date should be established. This should include several types of relationships precedence and resource constraints, in which the only acceptable scheduled durations should be the exact time durations needed to execute the activities, since longer durations would be wasted by the effect of Parkinson's Law [25]. But to ensure that the project is completed on time, the project network must also accommodate uncertainty in the execution of the activities, thus establishing a time buffer at the end of the project and also at the critical chain integration points, known as Feeding buffers. This allows handling sudden changes on the critical activities and preserve management focus.

It is worth to notice that, in addition to the mentioned critical chain scheduling perspective, CCPM must also include specific changes in human behaviors during project activities execution, such as:

- The Relay Runner Behavior or Mentality, e.g., quick activity execution and work deliver as soon as it is completed.
- Full dedicated resources to eliminate or reduce bad multitasking.
- Frequent report of activities expected durations for their completion.
- Prioritize all requests considering the buffer report.
- Use tasks priority lists to dynamically change and assign resources considering buffer penetration reports.

These aspects will have impacts in several other procedural areas of project management, as in costs, quality, communication, risk and procurement in projects [26, 27].

3 Exploring TOC in Collaborative Networks

In this chapter, we will explore the application of TOC in collaborative networks. Although this is a position paper, the authors feel that a motivation example helps to illustrate how the TOC could be applied in the management of a collaborative networks. In the second part of this section, some ideas on how to apply TOC in CNM are provided.

3.1 Motivation Example

This section presents a motivation example illustrating the application of the Theory of Constraints in collaborative networks, focusing in CCPM as starting point.

Typically, a project is specified by a set of activities, with durations and precedencies. For instance, as shown in Table 1, activity a5 can only start after activities a2 and a3 are finished.

Table 1. Project activities precedence table

Activity	Most likely	Pessimist	Optimist	Precedence
a1	3	4	1	–
a2	5	6	2	a1
a3	3	4	2	a1
a4	4	6	3	a1
a5	8	10	5	a2, a3
a6	5	7	3	a3, a4
a7	3	5	1	a5, a6

Each activity requires certain resources, generically represented by r1, r2, ... which might be material, money, equipment, know-how, etc. Assuming it is a collaborative project, these resources are provided by potential partners who will then work together in the execution of the project activities, according to the necessities illustrated in Table 2(a).

Table 2. (a) Required resources in the project, and (b) Availability resources

(a)

Activity	Required resources					
	r1	r2	r3	r4	r5	r6
a1	1			3		2
a2		2			4	
a3	2		5			
a4				4		3
a5		6				
a6	3				2	
a7		2	3	3		

(b)

Partner	Available resources					
	r1	r2	r3	r4	r5	r6
p1	5			5		
p2	2		4		1	
p3		5		5	3	
p4			4		2	1
p5	1	5				
p6						4

Table 2(b) shows a set of partners who, in an earlier collaboration phase, namely partners selection, have already been evaluated in terms of trustworthiness, reliability and past collaborations. In the next phase, the allocation of partners to activities is performed according to the availability of resources for the respective activities.

The TOC's critical chain scheduling allows identification of constraints affecting the project, namely its critical activities. Applying this approach, the project requires 19 days plus 3 for project buffer (PB), which results in 22 estimated days for the project completion, requiring also two Feedings Buffers (FB) as shown in Fig. 2. The project critical activities (which establishes the critical chain) are in red on the project Gantt representation at the right side (a1, a2, a5 and a7).

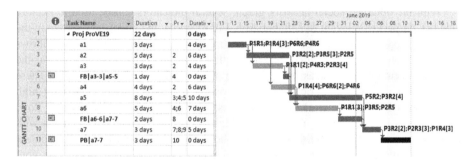

Fig. 2. Project schedule with resource allocation (Color figure online)

While CCPM allows addressing constraints from the project level. We can observe the same information from a collaboration perspective, enabling to focus on other project aspects which might help identify new potential risk factors.

From Fig. 2, we can perceive the interactions that are established between the partners in the project. The assumption here is that partners who work together in the same activity interact more intensively than in different ones. We can represent these interactions in a graph (Fig. 3), which can then be studied with Social Networks Analysis methods. This partners' interaction view can then be used to support collaborative decision making and problem resolutions during project execution.

Each vertex of the graph represents one partner. Each arc and weight represent the number of common project activities between two partners. But in order to represent the proximity concept, the inverse of the number of activities is used. For example, a value of 0.3(333) in the graph indicates that the respective partners work together on three activities (e.g. p1 and p4).

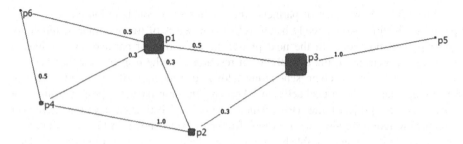

Fig. 3. Social network graph subjacent to the partners participating in the project

With the obtained social network graph, several indicators can be used to explore network properties relevant to collaboration. For example, the node sizes shown in the graph are proportional to the betweenness centrality measure [28]. This measure allows the identification of the network elements with greater authority and control over the flow of information, acting as brokers in the sharing of this information [29]. These authors also indicated empirical research showing that when an element with high betweenness leaves a network, it can cause severe disruptions to information flow. Furthermore, it is suggested in [28] that a high betweenness indicates elements with great influence in the collaboration between the members of a network. In the context of this example, this indicator can then be used in project management, in order to more closely monitor the activities of these partners.

3.2   Potential Research Lines in Collaborative Networks

Collaborative networks are complex and multidimensional structures, requiring the management and supervision of multiple processes that are developing simultaneously. The fundaments of Collaborative Networks, morphology and lifecycle are out of scope of this study, which can be found in [30, 31].

The most important contribution of TOC could be to help handling the complexity of CN management. As stated by Goldratt [1], "Focusing on everything is synonymous with not focusing on anything". TOC could therefore be applied in CN to provide methods to support collaboration contexts, so that a network manager could focus on the most important constraint, or core problem, in a collaborative project. For such, the potential methods from TOC that can be applied in CNM are identified in Table 3, highlighted in bold.

Table 3. Summary of the TOC methods, adapted from [32]

	Prescriptive domain	Reflection and assessment domain
Strategic/Tacit level	Concepts and principles	Problem analysis and resolution
	Main conceptual prescriptions: **The Basic Questions** **The POOGI Five Focusing** Steps **The Six Levels of Resistance**	Logical Tools (**TOC TP**): **Goal Tree (GT)** **Current Reality Tree (CRT)** **Conflict Resolution** **Diagram (CRD) or** **Evaporating Cloud (EC)** **Future Reality Tree (FRT)** **Negative Branch (NBR)** **Prerequisites Tree (PRT)** **Transition Tree (TT)** Validation principles: Categories of Legitimate Reservation (CLR)
Operational level	Specific logical applications	Performance evaluation measures
	Rope-drum-reserve (DBR) **Critical-Chain (CC)** **Buffer Management (BM)** V-A-T Analysis	Throughput, T Inventory/Investment, I Operating Expense, OE

Earlier research works concerning the application of TOC in collaborative networks can be found in [32, 33]. But a more in-depth study must start by attempting to fit the TOC's methods from Table 3 with CNM aspects presented in Table 4. In this table, there are some suggestions of how TOC can be applied in CNM.

Table 4. TOC contributions for collaborative network management

Management aspect	How it can be done (with mappings from Table 3)
Collaborative project definition	Characterization of the project in terms of activity precedencies, required resources, and competencies. TOC methods can use this information to find the critical chain, detect and resolve resource constraints, to manage and adjust the expected project duration (**CCPM**)
Partnership formation	TOC can be applied to help achieve the best possible allocation of partners to project activities, having in mind resources availability and critical chain buffer management (**TOC TP&CCPM**)
Partners selection issues	There are many methods for partners selection. For instance, partners competencies, reliability, trust, collaboration preparedness (and other traits), skills, and resources are some of the ingredients in partners selection approaches. In TOC, these aspects could be explored in terms of availability versus needs in the project activities and evaluate them for eventual conflict issues (**TOC TP**)

(continued)

Table 4. (*continued*)

Management aspect	How it can be done (with mappings from Table 3)
Operation monitoring	TOC can be used to identify deviations from plans, and alert mechanisms can be provided for the VO-planner (**BM**). For instance, eventual disturbances affecting resources availability may pose impacts on the project's critical chain and delay its completion. They can be spotted during project execution (**CCPM**) and resolved by **TOC POOGI/TOC TP**
Performance assessment	Development of new indicators and monitoring rules for the detection of relevant impacts on project planned time objectives (**CCPM**)
Network reconfiguration	TOC can be used to manage change. Whenever there is a shift in goals, activities can be rescheduled, and resources utilization verified for eventual conflicts resolution (**TOC TP & CCPM**)
Risk assessment	As the project progresses, it is possible to observe its status proactively and thus reduce or manage risk of resource or competencies unavailability, spot potential conflicting partners and reduce delays occurrence (**CCPM**)
Trust assessment	There is a significant amount of research works dedicated to trust in collaborative networks, such as [34]. Information provided by trust indicators could be considered in the identification of constraints and risk (**TOC POOGI cycle/TOC TP**)
Collaboration preparedness assessment	The ability to collaborate is a relevant aspect in a collaborative network, as a partner's low score on this trait can be used to foretell relationship issues undermining project execution. Similar to trust, preparedness to collaborate indicators could also be used to assess the need to reconfigure the network (**TOC POOGI/TOC TP**)

4   Main Conclusions and Future Work

This position paper explored the integration of the Theory of Constraints in the context of Collaborative Networks Management. The foundations of this management theory were firstly presented. Then, the methodological integration of TOC into CNM was researched in two parts, starting with a motivation example, and then with an exploratory exercise, to illustrate the correspondence between a few TOC methods and typical phases of CN lifecycle.

The motivation example allowed identify several preliminary results. For instance, from the project definition, the critical chain method allowed identify conflicts in partners' resources utilization. The "betweenness closure" measure, from the realm of Social Networks analysis, was used in the example to identify potential collaboration-related risks. In this regard, disruptions involving partners with high betweenness can pose significant impacts on network performance, including at collaboration level. As such, the example helped highlight potential benefits from the use of TOC in Collaborative Networks Management.

Given the suggested hypotheses, proposed during this position paper, we can expect potential benefits in the use of the Theory of Constraints in collaborative networks. These aspects must be further explored and detailed in future research work. In addition, a CNM/TOC combination should be addressed assuming a multi-disciplinary perspective, involving researchers from distinct areas, namely Industrial Engineering Management, Sociology and Information Technology.

Acknowledgments. This work has been partially supported by UNIDEMI - Research and Development Unit for Mechanical and Industrial Engineering by the Portuguese FCT-PEST program UID/EMS/00667/2019 and by the Center of Technology and Systems (CTS) – Uninova, Portuguese FCT-PEST program UID/EEA/00066/2019.

References

1. Goldratt, E.M.: What is This Thing Called Theory of Constraints and How Should it be Implemented?. North River Press, Great Barrington (1990)
2. Spencer, M.S., Cox, J.: Optimum production technology (OPT) and the theory of constraints (TOC): analysis and genealogy. Int. J. Prod. Res. **33**(6), 1495–1504 (1995)
3. Goldratt, E.M., Cox, J.: The Goal: A Process of Ongoing Improvement, 1st edn. North River Press Publishing Corporation, Great Barrington (1984, 2004)
4. Mabin, V.J., Balderstone, S.J.: The performance of the theory of constraints methodology: analysis and discussion of successful TOC applications. Int. J. Oper. Prod. Manag. **23**(6), 568–595 (2003)
5. Dettmer, H.W.: Goldratt's Theory of Constraints: A Systems Approach to Continuous Improvement. ASQC Quality Press, Milwaukee (1997)
6. Gupta, M., Boyd, L.: Theory of constraints: a theory for operations management. Int. J. Oper. Prod. Manag. **28**(10), 991–1012 (2008)
7. Gupta, A., Bhardwaj, A., Kanda, A.: Fundamental concepts of theory of constraints: an emerging philosophy. Int. J. Econ. Manag. Eng. **4**(10), 2089–2095 (2010)
8. Stamm, M.L., Neitzert, T., Singh, D.P.K.: TQM, TPM, TOC, lean and six sigma-evolution of manufacturing methodologies under the paradigm shift from Taylorism/Fordism to Toyotism (2009)
9. Demchuk, L., Baitsar, R.: Combined usage of theory of constraints, lean and six sigma in quality assurance of manufacturing processes. Key Eng. Mater. **637**, 21–26 (2015). https://doi.org/10.4028/www.scientific.net/KEM.637.21
10. Cox III, J.F., Schleier Jr., J.G. (eds.): Theory of Constraints Handbook. McGraw-Hill, New York (2010)
11. McMullen, T.B.: Introduction to the Theory of Constraints (TOC) Management System. Constraints Management Series. CRC Press, Boca Raton (1998)
12. Sproull, B.: The Ultimate Improvement Cycle: Maximizing Profits Through the Integration of Lean, Six Sigma and the Theory of Constraints, 1st edn. CRC Press, Boca Raton (2009)
13. Watson, K., Blackstone, J., Gardiner, S.: The evolution of a management philosophy: the theory of constraints. J. Oper. Manag. **25**, 387–402 (2007)
14. Rahman, S.: Theory of constraints - a review of the philosophy and its applications. Int. J. Oper. Prod. Manag. **18**, 336–355 (1998)

15. Kim, S., Mabin, V., Davies, J.: The theory of constraints thinking processes: retrospect and prospect. Int. J. Oper. Prod. Manag. **28**(2), 155–184 (2008)
16. Reid, R.A., Cormier, J.R.: Applying the TOC TP: a case study in the service sector. Manag. Serv. Qual.: Int. J. **13**(5), 349–369 (2003)
17. Mabin, V., Forgeson, S., Green, L.: Harnessing resistance: using the theory of constraints to assist change management. J. Eur. Ind. Train. **25**(2/3/4), 168–191 (2001)
18. Kuruvilla, S.J.: Theory of constraints and the thinking process. Int. J. Bus. Insights Transform. **11**(1), 10–14 (2017)
19. Taylor III, L., Rekha, A.: Applying theory of constraints principles and Goldratt's thinking process to the problems associated with inventory control. Franklin Bus. Law J. **2016**(4), 83–104 (2016)
20. Goldratt, E.M.: Critical Chain. North River Press, Great Barrington (1997)
21. Leach, L.: Critical chain project management improves project performance. Project Manag. J. **30**, 39–51 (1999)
22. Leach, L.: Critical Chain Project Management. Artech House, Norwood (2000)
23. Newbold, R.C.: Project Management in the Fast Lane. St. Lucie Press, Boca Raton (1998)
24. Hamburger, D.H.: "On time" project completion-managing the critical path. Project Manag. J. **XVIII**, 79–85 (1987)
25. Parkinson, N.: Parkinson's Law, and Other Studies in Administration. Blurb, Norwood (2018)
26. Leach, L.: Critical Chain Project Management, 2nd edn. Artech House, Boston (2005)
27. Kendall, G., Rollins, S.: Advanced Portfolio Management and the PMO: Multiplying ROI at Warp Speed. IIL- International Institute for Learning, J.Ross Publishing Inc., Fort Lauderdale (2003)
28. Pereira, C.S., Soares, A.L.: Improving the quality of collaboration requirements for information management through social networks analysis. Int. J. Inf. Manag. **27**(2), 86–103 (2007)
29. Sutanto, J., Tan, C.H., Battistini, B., Phang, C.W.: Emergent leadership in virtual collaboration settings: a social network analysis approach. Long Range Plan. **44**(5–6), 421–439 (2011)
30. Camarinha-Matos, L.M., Afsarmanesh, H. (eds.): Collaborative Networks: Reference Modeling. Springer, Heidelberg (2008). https://doi.org/10.1007/978-0-387-79426-6
31. Camarinha-Matos, L.M.: Collaborative networks: a mechanism for enterprise agility and resilience. In: Mertins, K., Bénaben, F., Poler, R., Bourrières, J.-P. (eds.) Enterprise Interoperability VI. PIC, vol. 7, pp. 3–11. Springer, Cham (2014). https://doi.org/10.1007/978-3-319-04948-9_1
32. Tenera, A., Abreu, A.: A TOC perspective to improve the management of collaborative networks. In: Camarinha-Matos, L.M., Picard, W. (eds.) PRO-VE 2008. ITIFIP, vol. 283, pp. 167–176. Springer, Boston, MA (2008). https://doi.org/10.1007/978-0-387-84837-2_17
33. Tenera, A.B., Abreu, A.J.: A critical chain perspective to support management activities in dynamic production networks. In: 2008 IEEE International Engineering Management Conference, pp. 1–5 (2008)
34. Msanjila, S.S., Afsarmanesh, H.: Modelling trust relationships in collaborative networked organisations. Int. J. Technol. Transf. Commercialisation **6**(1), 40–55 (2007)

Collaborative Government and Social Policies

Next Generation Government - Hyperconnected, Smart and Augmented

Adegboyega Ojo[1,2(✉)]

[1] Insight Centre for Data Analytics, Data Science Institute, NUI Galway,
Galway, Republic of Ireland
adegboyega.Ojo@nuigalway.ie
[2] Department of Applied Informatics in Management,
Faculty of Economics and Management,
Gdansk University of Technology, Gdansk, Poland

Abstract. Achieving the Sustainable Development Goals (SDG2030) requires that governments and their various institutions be more agile, collaborate across agency boundaries and national borders, and also develop specific capabilities. Some of the required capabilities are related to developing and sustaining governance networks, digitally transforming public service delivery, building resilience structures within government for crisis and disasters, and harnessing disruptive technologies for new solutions to hitherto unsolved problems. This paper highlights how the integration of *hyper-connectivity*, *"smartness"* and *Artificial Intelligence adoption* within the context of the recent *Post-New Public Management (NPM)* paradigms can generate new capabilities to strengthen government institutions towards achieving their relevant SDG goals.

Keywords: Hyperconnectivity · Smart government · Augmented government ·
Collaborative networks · Post-New Public Management · Artificial intelligence

1 Introduction

Governments are constantly driven to meet citizen demands, operate more efficiently, tackle wicked societal challenges and meet international development and governance commitments such as those related to the Sustainable Development Goals (SDG2030) and the Open Government Partnership (OGP). Through harnessing technological innovations and adopting new public management paradigms, governments are transforming themselves to more effectively achieve their goals [1]. In particular, governments are increasingly collaborating across governance jurisdictions, national and regional borders, and are also developing new partnerships to jointly address common problems.

In the area of technological innovation, government organisations are adopting disruptive technologies such big data and IoT, artificial intelligence, robotics, drones,

---

A. Ojo—Visiting Professor at Department of Applied Informatics in Management, Faculty of Economics and Management, Gdansk University of Technology, Gdansk, Poland.

L. M. Camarinha-Matos et al. (Eds.): PRO-VE 2019, IFIP AICT 568, pp. 285–294, 2019.
https://doi.org/10.1007/978-3-030-28464-0_25

virtual and augmented reality, and digital fabrications [2] to create new services and develop significantly more effective policies. Furthermore, they are also creating resilient data and information infrastructure through the use of blockchains (or distributed ledger) technologies [3].

However, this new wave of disruptive technology adoption in government is enabled by recent public management logics described as post-New Public Management Paradigms (NPM) [4]. These new public management paradigms are characterised by features such as unprecedented transparency, use of shared and integrated services/infrastructures, use of social media, reintegration of fragmented processes, performance governance, cultivation of collaborations networks, participation in public-private partnerships and engagement of citizens [4]. Summarily, these new public administration paradigms agree on the centrality of technological innovation in the improvement of service delivery and policies. These new environments also emphasize obtaining concrete benefits and producing public values from investments in disruptive technologies.

Three major paradigms that are related to recent developments in the government technology arena include Hyperconnectivity, Smartness and AI-Augmentation (the use of AI technologies to augment the capabilities of governments). While these technology paradigms individually deliver significant capabilities, their integration has the potential to radically transform governments with new robust and mutually reinforcing capabilities. This paper highlights how the integration of these three technology paradigms within the context of the post-NPMs can deliver new capabilities that could radically transform and strengthen government institutions towards greater internal efficiency, improved citizen management, more effective policies and better public services.

The objectives of the paper is threefold: (1) highlight the nature of the post-NPM and the supporting government technology paradigms that characterise future government innovation environments; (2) describe some of the new government capabilities that the future government innovation environment potentially enables, and (3) highlight some of the necessary conditions for harnessing these new government capabilities.

2 Creating the Enabling Environment

There is a duality between public management and governance programmes and the supporting technology innovations [5]. Thus, while technological innovations are required to support the implementation of the desired reforms programmes in government environments, the effective adoption of these technologies is also contingent on the adopting environment as shown in Fig. 1.

Following the New Public Management (NPM) agenda which dominated governments thinking between 1985 and 2002, recent public management and governance frameworks explicitly recognise the contributions and influences of technological innovations in government change efforts [6]. Three of these recent public management and governance frameworks include Digital Era Governance (DEG), Public Value Management (PVM) and the New Public Governance (NPG).

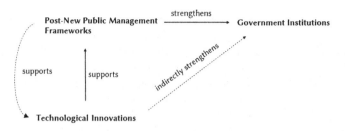

Fig. 1. The duality of Post-NPM & technological innovations

In the first instance, the DEG paradigm focuses on reintegrating functions in the government sphere, adopting needs-based and holistic structures in service delivery, intensifying digitalisation of administrative processes [6]. More recent models of DEG emphasise transparency, the use of social media and the establishment of shared service centres as important tenets of this paradigm [7, 8].

At the centre of the PVM paradigm is the notion of *public value* [9]. The concept of Public value here is more than a summation of individual preferences of citizens. The framework is characterised by: strategy-making for public value creation; performance governance and Innovation.

The NPG paradigm considers both situations where multiple interdependent actors contribute to the delivery of public services as well as the situation in which multiple processes inform policy-making systems. Core elements of the NPG paradigm include the development of networks and collaboration arrangements, forming and leveraging public-private partnerships and engagement of citizens [8]. An important assumption in this paradigm is that *no single government organisation is capable of handling the type of public policy challenges facing governments today, making cooperation, collaboration, and partnering necessary* [8, 10].

Collectively, these paradigms employ technological innovations (or digital technologies) to drive greater openness, enable greater collaborations and new partnerships, engage citizens over new channels, track performance of governments and integrate service delivery [4]. Specific affordances of these three paradigms in contemporary public management and governance environments are given in Table 1.

Table 1. Affordances of Post-NPM paradigms

PM paradigm	What paradigm enables
Digital era governance	• Access to government information • Providing information on a specific policy field of public interest • Publishing open government data • Getting citizens to express their opinions over social media • Crowdsourcing ideas from citizens to tackle societal challenges • Providing shared-service centre for delivery of integrated services

(*continued*)

Table 1. (*continued*)

PM paradigm	What paradigm enables
Public value management	• Public value creation • Understanding public interest and delivering on them collectively • Focus on long-term outcomes and not only short term results • Freedom for managers to be creative (out-of-the-box) and innovate
New public governance	• Development of public-partnerships to share risks and resources • Joined up services and thinking across sectors • Collaboration networks of actors to tackle societal challenges • Co-production with citizens • Dialog with citizens on government performance • Creation of "publics" (different target citizen groups)

3   Technological Support for Post-NPM Paradigms

We consider three government technological (govtech) innovations that support the above post-NPM paradigms – Hyperconnected, Smart and AI-Augmented government. Collectively, these govtech paradigms provide major support for all three post-NPM paradigms. Below we describe these three govtech innovations.

3.1   Hyperconnectivity

Hyperconnectivity is associated with a sharp increase in the interconnectedness of people, organisations and objects [11]. It is enabled by the convergence of the Internet, mobile, social media, Internet-of-things, cloud computing. The concept is also associated with the impact on personal and organisation behaviour is associated with the concept of Hyperconnectivity [12]. Hyperconnectivity focuses on collective behaviour [13] and has the following attributes [12]: perpetual connectivity; ready accessibility; information-rich; interactive; comprises varieties of connections types (machine-to-machine, people-to-machine, etc.); and virtually unlimited in storage allowing for massive data collection.

Hyperconnectivity technology such as social media offers rich information and location independent interaction endowing adopting Governments with a rich information base for policymaking. In addition, hyperconnectivity technologies such as augmented & virtual reality could potentially allow communities to build up a shared understanding of societal and individual needs. They also support bottom-up engagement by citizens to advance their interests [14].

In addition, Hyperconnected Governments have the capability to predict individual needs for public services and the provision of personalised services based on established daily routines or patterns. Furthermore, these governments have the capability to improve communication with their constituents by sharing information more quickly and transparently. It also makes it easier for their citizens to contact them and their agents as well as access public services easily [14].

3.2   Smartness

The notion of *"Smartness"* in digital government literature is associated with attributes including forward-looking, innovativeness, efficiency in resource management and operations, participatory governance and citizen engagement [15]. Smartness in the government sphere has been defined specifically to be related to creative investment in emerging technologies to achieve ability, resilient government structures and infrastructures [1, 16]. According to [1], characteristics of smart government includes: inter-organisational collaboration, information sharing and integration, opening up of government and digital transformation of public services. Similarly, in [15], the notion of smart governance is associated with coordination and integration, service integration, citizen participation and co-production and design of effective regulatory policies.

Smart Governments initiatives utilize hyperconnectivity and AI technologies and a variety of technical artefacts such as interoperability frameworks and standards.

3.3   AI-Augmentation

Artificial Intelligence (AI) refers to systems that exhibit intelligent behaviour by analysing their environment and taking action with some degree of autonomy to achieve specific goals [17]. AI is historically associated with computational solutions which exhibit human-like intelligent behaviour including perceiving, reasoning and acting as humans [18, 19]. Five important classes of problems that could be associated with AI include: search, pattern recognition, learning, planning and induction [20].

AI technologies include [21]: machine learning, computer vision, speech recognition, natural language processing and robotics. There are at least five emerging applications of AI in AI-Augmented Governments in the context of citizen services [22]: (1) answering questions; (2) filling out and searching documents, (3) routing requests, (4) translation and (5) drafting documents. In [21], three core applications of AI in government include: (1) robotic and cognitive automation, enabling the shifting of human labour to high-value work through technologies such as Robotic Process Automation, (2) enabling cognitive insights through better predictive capabilities; and (3) Cognitive engagement through answering citizen queries. Public sector organisations are also increasingly interested in harnessing AI capabilities and data sciences to deliver policy and generate efficiencies particularly in high uncertainty environments [23].

3.4   Integrating Hyperconnectivity, Smartness and AI-Augmentation

We note here that the three Govtech paradigms described above are complementary. A closer look at these paradigms reveals that smart government paradigm is most strategic and relies on the other two paradigms for implementation. The hyperconnectivity generates massive data on relationships and a variety of media for citizen engagement. AI technologies are required to generate insights from hyperconnectivity data and applied to achieve smart government objectives like agility, resilience and service transformation. The interdependencies of the three govtech paradigms are depicted as a virtuous triangle in Fig. 2. The capabilities enabled by three paradigms are also shown in Table 2.

These capabilities also show how the different paradigms may directly support the post-NPM paradigms described earlier in Sect. 2. Specifically, we observe that the Smart Government programmes are well aligned and could support DEG initiatives giving the joint focus on openness, service transformation, co-production and engagement of citizens. Smart Government programmes are also aligned with the PVM initiatives in the area of creativity. Similarly, Hyperconnected Government programmes could provide strong support for NPG initiatives by providing the capability to manage and leverage big data related to collaborations, partnerships and citizen interactions and engagement over social media. AI-Augmented programmes provide concrete services and tools to support all three post-NPM paradigms.

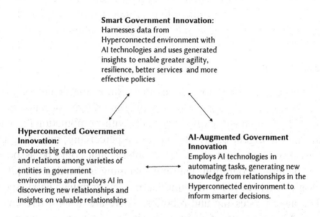

Smart Government Innovation:
Harnesses data from Hyperconnected environment with AI technologies and uses generated insights to enable greater agility, resilience, better services and more effective policies

Hyperconnected Government Innovation:
Produces big data on connections and relations among varieties of entities in government environments and employs AI in discovering new relationships and insights on valuable relationships

AI-Augmented Government Innovation
Employs AI technologies in automating tasks, generating new knowledge from relationships in the Hyperconnected environment to inform smarter decisions.

Fig. 2. Integrating Govtech paradigms

Table 2. Capabilities provided by Govtech paradigms

Govtech paradigm	Capabilities
Hyperconnectivity	• Harness large amount of data and information (big data) about different forms of relationships within the governance system • Leverage rich information base on social media for policymaking • Access to shared understanding of societal and individual needs • Bottom-up engagement by citizens • Predicting individual information and public service needs based on interconnectivity information and delivering services over preferred mobile channels
Smartness	• Inter-organisational collaboration and information sharing • Opening up government • Transformation of public services • Participation, co-production • Regulatory policymaking for the use of smart technologies
AI-Augmented	• Task automation and completion • Predictive & prescriptive analytics • Cognitive engagement & citizen question answering • Knowledge discovery and generation (through induction)

4   New Capabilities Enabled by Convergence

The long-term viability of technological innovation (such as AI) is contingent on effectively embedding it into the delivery of solutions for policy implementation [23]. This embedding is what we denote as convergence here. As shown in Fig. 3, the technological innovation can enable new set of government capabilities when implemented in the context of the post-NPM paradigms described in Sect. 2. Three important capabilities that are enabled by harnessing the technological affordances (right side of Fig. 2) within different post-NPM features are – hyper-openness, self-service (DIY Government) and hyper-collaboration (see arrows).

Hyper-openness capability will allow government to deliver highly-personalised information and knowledge to citizens over old and new channels (e.g. VR) to meet their need proactively. The self-service or "Do-it-Yourself (DIY)" Government capability enables citizens and businesses to initiate the co-production of digital services they require at any time based on the tools and platforms provided by government. This capability also enables notification of citizens and businesses of services they require but unaware of.

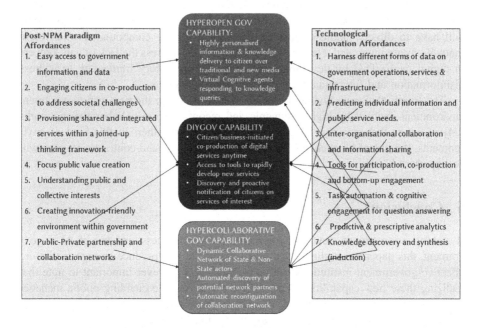

Fig. 3. The Convergence of Post-NPM and Govtech paradigms

The hyper-collaborative Government capability enables the creation of dynamic collaboration networks [24] of state and non-state actors. This form of governance networks will be able to automatically discover and enroll partners and automatically reconfigure the network based on changing circumstances. The resulting governance networks will facilitate flexibility, speed, resource pooling and exchange as well as innovation to tackle complex societal challenges [25, 26].

5 Necessary Conditions for Transitioning to Next-Gen Government

In addition to implementing the post-NPM initiatives to create the enabling environment for implementing the above govtech innovations, there are a number of issues that must be addressed to ensure broadly: safe and ethical use of these technologies, and the availability of the requisite capacity to harness the innovations.

The first challenge is related to a large amount of data generated in hyperconnected environments. Having clear principles to resolve the ownership of individual data is very important [14], considering regulations such as the European Union's General Data Protection Regulation. Another social implication of the unprecedented transparency of public lives associated with hyperconnectivity, in particular, is the need to for stronger privacy protection in future governments [13]. The second issue is related to security. With hyperconnectivity and the use of cyberphysical in smart government environments, security threats are significantly amplified [13]. The third challenge is associated with the ethical use of hyperconnectivity and AI. There is ample evidence that these technologies are already being exploited for terrorist activities, including the active use social media to recruit, radicalize and plan and orchestrate violent activities. AI-powered bots are also being for disinformation purposes. Next-gen governments will have to directly address these threats which will be compounded when these innovations are integrated. Next-gen governments must address the lack of gate keepers in digital media [14] by developing the necessary regulatory framework to address disinformation and future unethical use of these innovations.

The fourth challenge is directly linked to trust issues in the next-gen Government environment enabled by highly dynamic and reconfiguration collaborative networks [24] of actors that may not have history of working together. In this kind of environments, the use of blockchains for ensuring transactions and contracts integrity will be important [2, 3].

6 Conclusions

By taking a convergent view on hyperconnectivity, smartness, and use of AI in government, this paper has outlined how new capabilities that produce stronger and more effective government institutions can be realised. It is however important to note that realizing these new capabilities is contingent on having the enabling public management and administration environment, such as those characterised by the post-NPM initiatives. These new post-NPM environments inter alia enable government institutions to harness the expertise and resources of non-state actors in addressing societal challenges. They also help in overcoming the increasingly limited capacity of governments to effectively leverage new technological innovations like AI or hyperconnectivity [23]. More importantly, addressing the preconditions described in Sect. 5 is a necessary first step into harnessing these new capabilities.

The new capabilities described in Sect. 4 are related to at least two of the four scenarios of the future of government 2030+ described in [14] - DIY democracy and

Super Collaborative Governments. Their "Over-Regulatocracy" scenario is related to the third challenge described in Sect. 5.

Our future work will elaborate on these new government capabilities to better understand possible barriers and preconditions for their development and management in future government environments.

Acknowledgments. This publication has emanated from research supported in part by a research grant from Science Foundation Ireland (SFI) under Grant Number SFI/12/RC/2289, co-funded by the European Regional Development Fund.

References

1. Gil-Garcia, J.R., Helbig, N., Ojo, A.: Being smart: emerging technologies and innovation in the public sector. Gov. Inf. Q. **31**(S1), I1–I8 (2014)
2. Millard, J.: European strategies for e-Governance to 2020 and beyond. In: Ojo, A., Millard, J. (eds.) Government 3.0 – Next Generation Government Technology Infrastructure and Services, vol. 32, pp. 1–25. Springer, Heidelberg (2017). https://doi.org/10.1007/978-3-319-63743-3_1
3. Ojo, A., Adebayo, S.: Blockchain as a next generation government information infrastructure: a review of initiatives in D5 countries. In: Ojo, A., Millard, J. (eds.) Government 3.0 – Next Generation Government Technology Infrastructure and Services, vol. 32, pp. 283–298. Springer, Heidelberg (2017). https://doi.org/10.1007/978-3-319-63743-3_11
4. Ojo, A., Zeleti, F.A., Mellouli, S.: A realist perspective on AI - era public management - an analysis of mechanisms, outcomes and challenges of AI solutions in the public sector. In: Proceedings of dg.o 2019: 20th Annual International Conference on Digital Government Research (dg.o 2019), 18–20 June 2019, pp. 1–12 (2019)
5. Orlikowski, W.J.: The duality of technology: rethinking the concept of technology in organizations. Organ. Sci. **3**(3), 398–427 (1992)
6. Dunleavy, P., Margetts, H., Bastow, S., Tinkler, J.: New public management is dead - Long live digital-era governance. J. Public Adm. Res. Theory **16**(3), 467–494 (2006)
7. Margetts, H., Dunleavy, P.: The second wave of digital-era governance: a quasi-paradigm for government on the web subject areas. Philos. Trans. R. Soc. **371**, 1–17 (2013). No. 20120382
8. Greve, C.: Ideas in public management reform for the 2010s. Digitalization, value creation and involvement. Public Organ. Rev. **15**(1), 49–65 (2015)
9. Stoker, G.: Public value management: a new narrative for networked governance? Am. Rev. Public Adm. **36**(1), 41–57 (2006)
10. Osborne, S.P.: The New Public Governance - Emerging Perspectives on the Theory and Practice of Public Governance. Routledge, Abingdon (2010)
11. Economist: The hyperconnected economy: phase 2 hyperconnected organisations how businesses are adapting (2015)
12. Fredette, J., Marom, R., Steinert, K., Witters, L.: The promise and peril of hyperconnectivity for organizations and societies (2012)
13. Klein, F., Bansal, M., Wohlers, J.: Beyond the noise: the megatrends of tomorrow's world (2017)
14. Joint Research Centre (JRC) of the European Commission: The Future of Government 2030 + - A Citizen Centric Perspective on New Government Models (2019)

15. Ojo, A., Curry, E., Janowski, T.: Designing next generation smart city initiatives - harnessing findings and lessons from a study of ten smart city programs. In: Proceedings of the European Conference on Information Systems (ECIS) 2014, Tel Aviv, Israel, 9–11 June 2014, pp. 0–14 (2014)

16. Mellouli, S., Luna-Reyes, L.F., Zhang, J.: Smart government, citizen participation and open data. Inf. Polity **19**(1–2), 1–4 (2014)

17. Europeam Commission: Communication from the Commission to the European Parliament, the European Council, The Council, The European Economic and Social Committee and the Committee of the Regions - Coordinated Plan on Artificial Intelligence (2018)

18. Feigenbaum, E.A.: Artificial intelligence research. IEEE Trans. Prof. Tech. Group Inf. Theory **IT-9**(4), 248–253 (1962)

19. Simon, H.A.: Artificial intelligence: an empirical science. Artif. Intell. **77**(1), 95–127 (1995)

20. Minsky, M.L.: Steps toward artificial intelligence. In: Proceedings of the IRE, vol. 49, no. 1, pp. 8–30 (1961)

21. Eggers, W.D., Schatsky, D., Viechnicki, P.: AI-augmented government, p. 28 (2017)

22. Mehr, H.: Artificial intelligence for citizen services and government (2017)

23. Mikhaylov, S.J., Esteve, S.J., Campion, S.J.: AI for the public sector: opportunities and challenges of cross-sector collaboration. Philos. Trans. R. Soc. A **376**(2128), 1–26 (2018)

24. Camarinha-Matos, L.M., Afsarmanesh, H.: Collaborative networks. In: Wang, K., Kovacs, G.L., Wozny, M., Fang, M. (eds.) PROLAMAT 2006. IIFIP, vol. 207, pp. 26–40. Springer, Boston, MA (2006). https://doi.org/10.1007/0-387-34403-9_4

25. Estevez, E., Ojo, A., Janowski, T.: Idioms for collaborative government networks – conceptualization and applications to seamless services. In: Camarinha-Matos, L.M., Boucher, X., Afsarmanesh, H. (eds.) PRO-VE 2010. IAICT, vol. 336, pp. 219–226. Springer, Heidelberg (2010). https://doi.org/10.1007/978-3-642-15961-9_26

26. Ojo, A., Mellouli, S.: Deploying governance networks for societal challenges. Gov. Inf. Q. **35**(4), S106–S112 (2018)

Inter-governmental Collaborative Networks for Digital Government Innovation Transfer – Structure, Membership, Operations

Magdalena Ciesielska[1(✉)] and Tomasz Janowski[1,2]

[1] Department of Applied Informatics in Management, Faculty of Management and Economics, Gdańsk University of Technology, Gdańsk, Poland
{magdalena.ciesielska,tomasz.janowski}@pg.edu.pl
[2] Department of E-Governance in Economics and Administration,
Faculty of Business and Globalization, Danube University Krems,
Krems an der Donau, Austria

Abstract. Digital government refers to the transformation of government organizations and their relationships with citizens, business and each other through digital technology. It entails digital innovation in processes, services, organizations, policies, etc. which are increasingly developed and tested in one country and transferred, after adaptation, to other countries. The process of innovation transfer and the underlying information and knowledge sharing increasing take place through networks. The aim of this study is to identify various forms of such networks, their structures, membership criteria and modes of operation. The study relies on the analysis of literature on innovation transfer, collaborative networks and inter-governmental collaboration, and a survey of existing inter-governmental networks for digital government innovation transfer. The key finding is that such networks are a growing form of international collaboration and an instrument in global economy.

Keywords: Digital government · Innovation transfer · Collaborative networks

1 Introduction

Digital government transformation has advanced rapidly over the past 15 years, as shown by increasing number of countries with very high (between 0,75 and 1,00) value of the United Nation's e-Government Development Index (EGDI) [1], from 10 in 2003 to 40 in 2018, and a decrease in the number of countries with "very low" (between 0,00 and 0,25) value of the EGDI, from 38 in 2003 to 16 in 2018. Thus some countries have gained deep knowhow in digital government, making their power, transport, security and other systems ready to interconnect with other systems, while others stand to learn from them, and to connect or even adopt their systems.

However, successful transfer of digital government solutions is difficult due to different conditions – technical, legal, economic, cultural, etc. existing in the donor and recipient countries [2, 3]. This and continuous pressure for improvement in public infrastructure and services, highlight the importance of knowledge sharing and innovation transfer between government organizations [4, 5]. Inter-organizational

L. M. Camarinha-Matos et al. (Eds.): PRO-VE 2019, IFIP AICT 568, pp. 295–307, 2019.
https://doi.org/10.1007/978-3-030-28464-0_26

information sharing delivers higher information quality, improved decision-making, increased productivity, and service integration [6]. Inter-governmental information sharing relies on collaborative actions by diverse agencies from different countries, increasingly coordinated through inter-governmental collaboration networks. Such networks constitute multi-organizational arrangements for solving problems that cannot be achieved, or achieved easily, by a single organization. They rely heavily on informal interaction, persuasion, and information to deal with critical areas [7].

While the existence of networks that specialize in digital government innovation transfer is documented in literature [5, 6, 8], comparative studies are lacking, and questions remain concerning objectives, membership criteria, structure and mode of operation adopted by such networks. This paper aims to fill this gap based on the combination of literature review on technology transfer, collaborative networks and inter-governmental collaboration, four case studies of collaborative networks for inter-governmental technology transfer, and cross-case analysis. The case studies include networks run by countries with advanced digital government capabilities and interest in transferring such capabilities to other countries – Estonia, Korea, Singapore and USA. The main message uncovered by this study is that international digital government collaboration has become an instrument in global economy.

The rest of this paper is structured as follows. Section 2 present a literature review on technology transfer, collaborative networks and inter-governmental collaboration. The main outcome is the framework for inter-governmental networks for digital government technology transfer, which is presented in Sect. 3 along with research questions and how they are addressed. Section 4 presents and analyzes four case studies of such networks using the framework in Sect. 3. Section 5 discusses implications and lessons learns from this work, and Sect. 6 concludes with summary of the findings, limitations of this research, and plans for future work.

2 Background

This section presents the outcomes of a literature review on technology transfer, collaborative networks and inter-governmental collaboration. The review follows the approach described in [9] and the outcomes, described in subsequent sections, lead to the definition of research questions and a framework in Sect. 3.

2.1 Technology Transfer

The introduction of digital technology into government happens in stages of digital government evolution [11], from Electronic Government "when ICT is used to transform the internal organization and working of government", to Electronic Governance "when ICT is used to transform the relationships between government and citizens, businesses, other non-state actors and other arms of government" [10], to Policy-Driven Electronic Governance, which supports "efforts by countries, cities, communities and other territorial and social units to develop themselves" [11].

The process of adapting a digital government application from the donor to the recipient context is referred to as digital government technology transfer [12]. The process is hindered by contextual distances between participant countries which include culture, politics, organizational issues, relations, knowledge, resources, and physical and technical conditions [13].

Digital government is essentially based on imported designs, and digital government applications are isolated technical artefacts [14]. Digital government technology transfer concerns the transformation of government administration, information provision and service delivery by new technologies [15]. In this perspective, digital government initiatives are associated with the deployment of a complex digital infrastructure [16] involving national and local governments, agencies, NGOs, international organization, and citizens [17]. The potential to support sustainable socio-economic development is well supported, e.g. [18].

According to [19], the greater the value of the donor's knowledge stock, the greater its attractiveness to other countries. This is consistent with diffusion of innovation [20], a process by which an innovation is communicated through certain channels among the members of a social system and by which alternation occurs in the structure and function of such system as a kind of social change. While diffusion is crucial to fully benefit from innovation, the diffusion of digital government innovations is uneven [18]. A small number of rich countries are seen as vanguards of digital government, while poor countries experience fragmented digital government implementations. As the deployment of digital government in developing countries should address specific contextual characteristics of such countries and their sectors and organizations [21], international technology transfer should be a learning process based on trust [17], supportive institutional design [22], policy and legal adjustment [17], and the explicit characteristics of the technology being transferred [12].

Technology transfer includes transfer: between individuals, from individuals to groups, between groups, across groups, and from groups to organizations [17, 23]. International technology transfers are guided by profit [24], and include trade flows between parties [17], e.g. a donor country gaining advantage for purchasing raw material from the recipient, and profiting from technology maintenance [25]. However, digital government technology transfer has often bilateral character, e.g. in Mozambique [26], Sri Lanka [16] or Malaysia [27].

2.2   Collaborative Networks

Networks refer to multi-organizational arrangements for solving problems that cannot be achieved, or achieved easily, by a single organization. A collaborative network is a network containing a variety of entities that are mostly independent, geographically dispersed, and varied in terms of operating environment, culture, social capital and goals, but that collaborate to achieve common or compatible goals [28]. Participation in such networks is aligned to increasing competitiveness, reaching new knowledge, sharing risks and resources, and joining complementary skills. A crucial factor for networks and an alternative governance mechanism is trust [29].

According to [30], networks are characterized by: orientation of members and their commitment to goals, organization of the network including the intensity and breadth of its linkages, and the aim including complexity of purpose and the scope of the efforts. The formation and operation of the network reflects the characteristics of its participants and their expectations of the benefits and barriers [31]. Network constitution happens through [32]: activation – prior to successful inter-organizational policy formation; framing – establishing rules, influencing values, and shaping perceptions of the network; and synthesizing – creating the environment and enhancing the conditions for productive interactions among participants.

From the digital government perspective, the concept of public sector knowledge networks is used – inter-organizational relations, policies, structured information, professional knowledge, work processes and technologies brought together to achieve a collective public purpose [31]. They are a type of collaborative networks: led by government entities [32], having some formal elements but not defined by the law [31], enabling members to share knowledge. Network-level knowledge sharing and collaboration assumes that at least three actors pursue a common goal and take collective actions to achieve this goal by producing and sharing skills, expertise, experience, information and data [33].

2.3   Inter-governmental Collaboration for Technology Transfer

Previous concepts should be regarded as the context for inter-governmental collaboration within collaborative networks. In this context, network participants are countries or territorial units, represented by government authorities. Factors that affect multinational digital government collaboration, interoperability and information sharing include: collaboration factors, value network factors, cross-border factors, and integration and interoperability factors [17].

Scarce publications address the structure of inter-governmental collaboration. Thus, a rational formal structure is assumed to be the most effective way to coordinate and control complex relational networks involved in such collaboration [34]. According to [35], three types of inter-organizational collaborations are: public-public, public-nonprofit, and public-private. The first includes horizontal agreements between governments at the same level, and vertical agreements or intergovernmental alliances between levels. The latter need legal authorization, they operate by local agencies. According to [36], inter-organizational trust and collaboration is often not supported by institutional arrangements and organizational structures.

Inter-governmental collaboration takes place in specific contexts. Well connected members introduce trust, norms and social sanctions based on mutual expectations and obligations [37]. Cooperation incentives are greater within networks as "competition is usually minimized" and "organizations generally trust each other to a greater degree" [38]. Within collaborative networks, information is shared easily, and members can build and manage their reputation [39]. Inter-governmental collaboration within networks operates under organizational missions, existing legal and policy frameworks, assigned organizational structures, management practices and each countries' technological infrastructures and capabilities [7].

While research on networks as an element of public policy process is covered in literature, e.g. research on structure, function, management and outcomes of networked forms of organization [17, 32, 40], the topic of organizational networks as an instrument of public management in the international context is relatively recent. This study address this knowledge gap by exploring the structure and operations of inter-governmental collaborative networks for digital government innovation transfer.

3 Research Design and Method

This work studies inter-governmental collaborative networks for digital government innovation transfer. We pursue three research questions:

1. What are the aims, strategies and missions of such networks?
2. What are the membership, structures and operations of such networks?
3. How are the networks facilitating digital government innovation transfer?

These questions were addressed through exploratory and comparative case study research. Such research is focused on understanding the dynamics present within a small number of cases in their real-life context [41]. It is applied when the topic is complex, there is a lot of theory available, and the context is important [42].

The main outcome of the literature review is an integrative framework for inter-governmental collaborative networks for digital government innovation transfer. The framework, depicted in Table 1, is instantiated for particular donor, recipient and the innovation transfer initiative. It consists of general information including objectives, mission, strategy, legal framework and contextual distances [43]; membership criteria including participants [17] and their status [17]; structure including collaboration types [35], structural and individual behavior [17], institutional design [22], managerial tasks and roles [32] and decision-making authority [22]; and operation including incentives and their types [35], transactions [17], trade flows [17], deliverables [17], policy and legal adjustments [17], and information integration [17].

The framework is applied to develop and analyze four case studies of such networks. The enquiry was limited to official websites and legal acts, agreements and statuses available online. Case study selection was based on the donor countries' digital government maturity and active international transfer to third countries.

Table 1. Framework for inter-governmental collaborative networks

General	Basic information	Donor	Objectives
		Recipient	Strategy
		Innovation transfer	Mission
			Legal framework
	Contextual distance [43]	• Cultural	• Knowledge
		• Intention	• Relational
		• Physical	• Technical
		• Political	• Resource
Membership	Participants [17]	• International organization	• Local government
		• National government	• Agencies
		• Citizens	• NGOs
	Participant status [17]	• Equal	• Unequal
Structure	Collaboration type [35]	• Public-public	• Public-non-profit
		• Public-private	
	Promotes cooperation [17]	• Yes	• No
	Individual behavior [17]	• Trust	• Experience

(continued)

Table 1. (*continued*)

	Institutional design [22]	• Level of centrality: low, middle, high	
		• Assigned organizational structures: yes/no	
		• Management practices: yes/no	
		• Inclusion criteria	• Exclusion criteria
	Managerial tasks [32]	• Activating	• Framing
		• Mobilizing	• Synthesizing
	Managerial roles [32]	• International organization	• National government
		• Local government	• Agencies
		• Citizens	• NGOs
	Roles [17]	• Individuals	• Groups
		• Business units	• Organizations
	Decision making [22]	• International organization	• National government
		• Local government	• Agencies
		• Citizens	• NGOs
Operation	Incentives [35]	• Technical	• Organizational
		• Political	
	Incentive type [35]	• Positive (outcome)	• Negative (conflict)
	Transactions [17]	• Individual – group	• Group – business unit
		• Unit – organization	
	Trade flows [17]	• Goods	• People
		• Investments	
	Deliverables [17]	• Tangible	• Intangible
	Policy adjustments [17]	• International	• Regional
		• State	• National
		• Local	
	Legal adjustment [17]	• International	• Regional
		• National	• Local
	Information integration [17]	• Yes	• No

4   Case Studies

This section presents four case studies of inter-governmental collaborative networks, and conducts cross-case analysis. All case studies identify a donor country with mature digital government and related international innovation transfer, and one instance of such transfer from the donor to recipient country. Each case study presents the organization responsible for international dissemination of the donor country's digital government innovations, and analyzes one example of innovation transfer from to a third country using the framework in Table 1. The case studies are presented in

Sect. 4.1 (Estonia), Sect. 4.2 (Republic of Korea), Sect. 4.3 (Singapore) and Sect. 4.4 (USA). Section 4.5 includes cross-case analysis.

4.1 Estonia – e-Governance Academy

Estonian e-Governance Academy was established in 2002 as a non-profit think tank and consultancy organization aimed to help "governments increase their governance efficiency and improve their democratic processes" [44]. In 2015, Tunisia joined the Estonian development cooperation project, managed by e-Governance Academy, to develop the legal and organizational framework for e-governance and look into the possibilities of having a single identifier for Tunisian citizens.

Five contextual distances were identified between donor and recipient countries: cultural, organizational, knowledge, resource and technical. The cultural distance results from differences in national cultures, particularly the rights of citizens to privacy and freedom of expression. Due to previous Tunisian institutional experience in digital government assistance, this distance tends to shrink, establishing an adequate level of trust to build working relations. The organizational distance refers to the constituted independence of each government agency in Tunisia, resulting in the lack of unique identification. The knowledge distance was estimated as appropriate for knowledge transfer. The resource distance is expressed by the level of funding from the Estonia to support the Tunisia project. The technical distance is primarily due to the lack of data integration and information sharing between Tunisian agencies.

The project realizes public-public collaboration. Structural and individual behavior enhanced inter-governmental collaboration by promotion of cooperation and acclamation of trust and institutional experience. We could not identify inclusion or exclusion criteria within this project, or explicitly assigned organizational structure. However, project management was performed by the Academy including activating, framing, mobilizing and synthesizing tasks. The roles were assigned to individuals and organization. The project features positive incentives, and lack of negative ones.

4.2 South Korea – e-Government Cooperation Center

Republic of Korea shares its best practices in public administration with countries around the world through its official development assistance program. The aim is "to contribute to the advancement of the global community as a pioneer in administrative innovation" [45]. The organization responsible for international cooperation in digital government is e-Government Cooperation Center (eGCC). eGCC selects a recipient country using existing cooperative relationships, willingness of the partner country, etc. The cooperation is launched through a high-level dialogue with the recipient. eGCC Committee is established with experts from both countries to decide on the content of cooperation, and to execute managerial tasks. Each cooperation program is aligned to trade flows where Korean government provides USD 1 million and the recipient country provide additional funds subject to negotiation. In the operation phase, e-government experts are dispatched to provide training, consulting, etc.

In 2017, the eGCC cooperation was established between South Korea and Kenya with the aim to: materialize governmental e-offices, share residential ID experiences, provide consultations, and plan the national information infrastructure. Tangible and intangible deliverables, e.g. ICT infrastructure or knowledge sharing, were produced. This cooperation also forced Kenya to adjust its legal frameworks.

The eGCC cooperation type is public-public, enforced by structural and individual behavior. Contextual distances include: organizational distance – related to structure and processes, relational distance – establishing previous positive ties, resource distance – lack of funding and qualified staff, physical distance – geography, and technical distance – low information sharing between agencies.

4.3 Singapore – Infocomm Development Authority International

Countries interested in importing Singapore's digital government technology could turn to IDA International, a subsidiary of Infocomm Development Authority of Singapore (IDA). Established in 2008, IDA International served as the execution arm of public service infocomm collaborations between Singapore and governments around the world [46], focused on delivering public infocomm services, including digital government consultancy, master planning, national infocomm planning, industry and cluster development, and program management.

In 2007, IDA and the Information Technology Authority of Oman signed a MoU to facilitate the use of ICT in government and various economic sectors of Oman. In particular, the transfer was about developing the urban portal, a new service delivery platform for connecting government and citizens. This public-private collaboration joined government agencies and private organizations. Four contextual distances were identified: cultural, political, relational, and knowledge. Unfortunately, the official websites of the Singapore and Oman governments do not provide further information as to the operation, inclusion criteria, and the structure of the collaborative network.

4.4 USA – USAID Global Development Lab

The United States Agency for International Development (USAID) supports intergovernmental collaboration on digital government to strengthen democratic governance through open, responsive, and accountable institutions and processes that serve the needs and preferences of the public. The USAID Global Development Lab is an innovation hub that works external partners to produce innovations and to open development to people. The Lab works with impact investors to catalyze private capital for businesses and to strengthen the environment for entrepreneurship.

The Digital Liberia Electronic Government activity is a one year program funded by the USAID Global Development Lab with the aim to improve Liberian Government's performance through sustainable utilization of ICT-related systems, processes, and procedures at targeted ministries, agencies and commissions. Technology transfer aims to improve government management and decision-making by introducing the Integrated Financial Management System, Asset Management Information System and e-services for the Revenue Authority [47].

The collaboration type is public-non-profit and public-private. Structural and individual behavior are identified as positive. Contextual distances comprise: knowledge, technical, physical, resource and cultural distances. The USAID Global

Development Lab executes managerial tasks. Transactions occur between individual, groups and business units. Project deliverables are both tangible – ICT infrastructure and systems, and intangible – knowledge sharing. The project is funded by the U.S.

4.5   Cross-Case Analysis

This section provides a cross analysis of the four case studies documented in Sects. 4.1 to 4.4, guided by the framework from Table 1.

General: The objectives of technology transfer vary, e.g. the transfer from Estonia and Tunisia is aimed at developing legal and operational frameworks for digital government, while from Singapore to Oman at deploying technical solutions within the Omani infrastructure. All cases address the needs of developing countries or countries with low digital government maturity. Due to this, the donor's and recipient's status is unequal, and except for Singapore, all donors support innovation transfer financially. Except Singapore, all cases have explicit strategies and mission statements for international partnership in the digital government space.

Structure: The cases provide information on the legal frameworks underpinning collaboration. Korea established a comprehensive legal framework for importing its digital government technology. Semi-structured legal frameworks are provided by Estonia and the US. In each case, the collaboration is outsourced to a government subsidiary which hosts the responsibility for managerial coordination and operation. The legal frameworks influence collaboration types, institutional design, managerial tasks, roles, transactions, and trade flows between donor and recipient countries. Contextual distances include knowledge and resource distances.

Membership: Only Korea identified inclusion criteria, conditioning collaboration on shared values and willingness. Both legal framework and project type influence the membership. Two members are constant – national government and agencies. The participation of businesses and NGOs is related to the project's types and objectives. Except the US, all cases represent the public-public type of collaboration. In cases of Estonia and Korea, there is clear acclamation of trust between donor and recipient parties. In every case, donors are assessing the recipient's institutional experience to adjust operations to the recipient's institutional and organizational environment.

Operations: Each case provides group transactions. Managerial tasks are assigned to the governmental subsidiary. Strategic decision-making is assigned to government entities and operational decision-making to agency or businesses. Except Singapore, positive incentives are offered in official announcements. Funding and people flows are common. Project deliverables are tangible when the transfer concerns technical solution deployment, and intangible when the transfer concerns knowledge sharing. Trust among donors and recipients is fundamental. The transfer is not only to promote own digital solutions or industries, but also to build trust between parties. Lack of clear inclusion criteria allows for subjective selection of recipients, becoming an instrument in the donor's economic expansion towards developing countries' markets.

5   Discussion

This study provides an analysis of inter-governmental collaboration networks for digital government innovation transfer. A literature review was conducted on technology transfer, collaborative networks and inter-governmental collaboration for technology transfer. On this basis, we developed a framework that aggregates various models, concepts, definitions and factors related to such networks.

We applied this framework to develop four case studies of donor-driven networks: Estonia, Korea, Singapore and the US. The data highlights various approaches to activating, framing, mobilizing and synthesizing interactions adopted by the donors. Despite all donors establishing purposeful agencies to handle innovation transfer, only Korea offers institutional collaboration framework. None of the cases formulates exclusion membership criteria but only Korea formulates inclusion criteria. Individual recipient's behavior, particularly acclamation of trust and experience is important. All cases established public-public collaborations, except public-non-profit by the US. Each case clearly assigns roles to participants. Given the resource-type contextual distance and the donors' financial support, participant status is unequal. Two participant types are engaged – national government and agencies.

Finally, although selected donors are well-established digital government adopters, only Estonia and Republic of Korea are transparent about undertaken activities. We met substantive difficulties in accessing information on bilateral cooperation on digital government from Singapore, and minor difficulties from the US.

6   Conclusions

Inter-governmental collaborative networks illustrate the importance of partnerships in the global economy. International digital government innovation transfer projects feature effective partnerships, trustful relationships focused on common goals and risk sharing, and access to resource and benefits attained by all parties.

As such, four major points emerge from this work: (1) inter-governmental trust and collaboration in technology transfer should be supported by institutional arrangements and established organizational structures; (2) digital government collaboration open a door to building wider bilateral partnerships; (3) inter-governmental cooperation is based on inclusion criteria which are in turn based on shared values and trust; and 4) the proposed framework has proven itself as a useful research tool.

This research has some limitations. The first is small number of case studies. The second is limited data collected on the Singapore and US cases, due to the difficulties in accessing public information. The third is partial coverage of the studied phenomena, and the consequent difficulties in generalizing the findings. The fourth is that the case studies only cover asymmetric donor-recipient relationships.

Follow up research is to address these limitations and focus on institutional frameworks and their influence on the donor, recipient and network performance. We also plan to develop case studies that represent symmetric peer-peer donor-recipient relationships, more common for North-North and South-South innovation transfer.

References

1. United Nations E-Government Survey 2018. Gearing e-government to support transformation towards sustainable and resilient societies, New York (2018)
2. Kettani, D., Moulin, B.: E-Government for Good Governance in Developing Countries. Anthem Press, London (2014)
3. Gilbert, D., Balestrini, P., Littleboy, D.: Barriers and benefits in the adoption of e-government. Int. J. Public Sect. Manag. **17**, 286–301 (2004). https://doi.org/10.1108/09513550410539794
4. Alawadhi, S., Scholl, H.J.: Smart governance: a cross-case analysis of smart city initiatives. In: Proceedings of the Annual Hawaii International Conference on System Sciences, pp. 2953–2963 (2016). https://doi.org/10.1109/HICSS.2016.370
5. Gil-Garcia, J.R.: Towards a smart state? Inter-agency collaboration, information integration, and beyond. Inf. Polity **17**, 269–280 (2012). https://doi.org/10.3233/IP-2012-000287
6. Gil-García, J.R., Pardo, T.A.: E-government success factors: mapping practical tools to theoretical foundations. Gov. Inf. Q. **22**, 187–216 (2005). https://doi.org/10.1016/J.GIQ.2005.02.001
7. Dawes, S.S.: Interagency information sharing: expected benefits, manageable risks. J. Policy Anal. Manag. (1996). https://doi.org/10.1002/(SICI)1520-6688(199622)15:3<377::AID-PAM3>3.0.CO;2-F
8. Yang, T.-M., Pardo, T., Wu, Y.-J.: How is information shared across the boundaries of government agencies? An e-Government case study. Gov. Inf. Q. **31**, 637–652 (2014)
9. Webster, J., Watson, R.T.: Analyzing the past to prepare for the future: writing a literature review. MIS Q. (2002). https://doi.org/1210112213
10. Janowski, T., Pardo, T., Davies, J.: Government information networks - mapping electronic governance cases through public administration concepts. Gov. Inf. Q. **29**, S1–S10 (2012). https://doi.org/10.1016/j.giq.2011.11.003
11. Janowski, T.: Digital government evolution: from transformation to contextualization. Gov. Inf. Q. **32**, 221–236 (2015). https://doi.org/10.1016/j.giq.2015.07.001
12. Marcuzzo do Canto Cavalheiro, G., Joia, L.A.: Towards a heuristic frame for transferring e-government technology. Gov. Inf. Q. **31**, 195–207 (2014). https://doi.org/10.1016/j.giq.2013.09.005
13. Dawes, S., Gharawi, M., Burke, G.B.: Transnational public sector knowledge networks: knowledge and information sharing in a multi-dimensional context. Gov. Inf. Q. **29**, 112–120 (2012)
14. Heeks, R.: Information systems and developing countries: failure, success, and local improvisations. Inf. Soc. (2002). https://doi.org/10.1080/01972240290075039
15. Korteland, E., Bekkers, V.: Diffusion of E-government innovations in the Dutch public sector: the case of digital community policing. In: Wimmer, M.A., Scholl, J., Grönlund, Å. (eds.) EGOV 2007. LNCS, vol. 4656, pp. 252–264. Springer, Heidelberg (2007). https://doi.org/10.1007/978-3-540-74444-3_22
16. Stanforth, C.: Using actor-network theory to implementation in developing countries. Inf. Technol. Int. Dev. (2007). https://doi.org/10.1162/itid.2007.3.3.35
17. Navarrete, C., Gil-Garcia, J.R., Mellouli, S., Pardo, T.A., Scholl, J.: Multinational e-government collaboration, information sharing, and interoperability: an integrative model. In: Proceedings of Annual Hawaii International Conference on Systems Sciences (2010). https://doi.org/10.1109/HICSS.2010.282

18. Janowski, T.: Implementing sustainable development goals with digital government – aspiration-capacity gap. Gov. Inf. Q. **33**, 603–613 (2016). https://doi.org/10.1016/j.giq.2016.12.001

19. Teece, D.J.: Technology transfer by multinational firms: the resource cost of transferring technological know-how. Econ. J. (2006). https://doi.org/10.2307/2232084

20. Rogers, E.: Diffusion of Innovation, 5th edn. (2003). https://doi.org/10.1080/13506285.2017.1297339

21. Avgerou, C., Walsham, G.: Information Technology in Context: Implementing Systems in the Developing World. Ashgate Publishing, Brookfield (2000)

22. Holsapple, C., Yang, Z.: Influence structure and inter-group learning. In: AMCIS 2013 Proceedings (2013)

23. Gupta, A.K., Govindarajan, V.: Knowledge flows within multinational corporations. Strateg. Manag. J. (2000). https://doi.org/10.1002/(SICI)1097-0266(200004)21:4<473::AID-SMJ84>3.0.CO;2-I

24. Choi, H.J.: Technology transfer issues and a new technology transfer model. J. Technol. Stud. (2016). https://doi.org/10.21061/jots.v35i1.a.7

25. Akubue, A.I.: Technology transfer: a third world perspective. J. Technol. Stud. (2016). https://doi.org/10.21061/jots.v28i1.a.3

26. Nhampossa, J.L.: Re-thinking technology transfer as technology translation: a case study of Health Information Systems in Mozambique (2005)

27. Kasimin, H., Ibrahim, H.: Managing multi-organizational interaction issues: a case study of information technology transfer in public sector of Malaysia. In: Actor-Network Theory and Technology Innovation: Advancements and New Concepts (2010). https://doi.org/10.4018/978-1-60960-197-3.ch013

28. Camarinha-Matos, L.M., Afsarmanesh, H.: Collaborative networks: a new scientific discipline. Virtual Organ. Syst. Pract., 73–80 (2005). https://doi.org/10.1007/0-387-23757-7_6

29. Luna-Reyes, L.F., Picazo-Vela, S., Luna, D.E., Gil-Garcia, J.R.: Creating public value through digital government: lessons on inter-organizational collaboration and information technologies. In: Proceedings of the Annual Hawaii International Conference on System Sciences (2016). https://doi.org/10.1109/HICSS.2016.356

30. Mandell, M.P., Keast, R.: Evaluating the effectiveness of interorganizational relations through networks. Public Manag. Rev. (2008). https://doi.org/10.1080/14719030802423079

31. Zhang, J., Dawes, S.S.: Expectations and perceptions of benefits, barriers, and success in public sector knowledge networks. Public Perform. Manag. Rev. **29**, 433–466 (2006)

32. Agranoff, R., McGuire, M.: Big questions in public network management research. J. Public Adm. Res. Theory (2001). https://doi.org/10.1093/oxfordjournals.jpart.a003504

33. Ku, M., Gil-Garcia, J.R., Zhang, J.: The emergence and evolution of cross-boundary research collaborations: an explanatory study of social dynamics in a digital government working group. Gov. Inf. Q. **33**, 796–806 (2016). https://doi.org/10.1016/j.giq.2016.07.005

34. Powell, W.W.: Neither market nor hierarchy: the sociology of organizations: classic, contemporary, and critical readings. Res. Organ. Behav. **12**, 295–336 (1990)

35. Dawes, S.S., Pardo, T.A.: Building Collaborative Digital Government Systems: Systemic Constraints and Effective Practices. In: McIver, W.J., Elmagarmid, A.K. (eds.) Advances in Digital Government. Advances in Database Systems, vol. 26, pp. 259–273. Springer, Boston (2002). https://doi.org/10.1007/0-306-47374-7_16

36. Luna-Reyes, L.F., Gil-Garcia, J.R., Cruz, C.B.: Collaborative digital government in Mexico: some lessons from federal Web-based interorganizational information integration initiatives. Gov. Inf. Q. (2007). https://doi.org/10.1016/j.giq.2007.04.003

37. Coleman, J.S.: Social capital in the creation of human capital. Am. J. Sociol. (1988). https://doi.org/10.1086/228943

38. Argote, L.: Organizational Learning: Creating, Retaining and Transferring Knowledge. Springer, Heidelberg (2013). https://doi.org/10.1007/978-1-4614-5251-5

39. Uzzi, B.: The sources and consequences of embeddedness for the economic performance of organizations: the network effect. Am. Sociol. Rev. (2006). https://doi.org/10.2307/2096399

40. O'Toole, L.J.: Implementing public innovations in network settings. Adm. Soc. (1997). https://doi.org/10.1177/009539979702900201

41. Yin, R.K.: Case Study Research: Design and Methods. Sage Publications Ltd., London (1994)

42. Eisenhardt, K.M.: Building theories from case study research (1989)

43. Betsill, M.M., Bulkeley, H.: Transnational networks and global environmental governance. Int. Stud. Q. **48**, 471–493 (2004)

44. e-Governance Academy: About Us – e-Governance Academy. https://ega.ee/about-us/

45. South Korea Ministry of the Interior and Safety: International Cooperation in Good Governance. https://www.mois.go.kr/eng/sub/a03/GoodGovernance/screen.do

46. Infocomm Media Development Authority: IDA International to spearhead the export of public sector infocomm expertise. https://www.imda.gov.sg

47. USAID: Digital Liberia and Electronic Government Activity (2016)

Where Are Females in OSS Projects? Socio Technical Interactions

Ikram El Asri[✉] and Noureddine Kerzazi

National Higher School for Computer Science and System Analysis (ENSIAS),
Mohammed V University, Rabat, Morocco
{ikram.asri, n.kerzazi}@um5s.net.ma

Abstract. Recent researches provide evidence that women are underrepresented in the field of computer science. It has been reported that less than 10% of Open Source Software (OSS) contributors in GitHub are women. Although related qualitative and quantitative studies point out the gender gap, the technical and social interaction of females within OSS still remain unexplored and largely misunderstood. As a first step towards proposing articulated actions towards diversity and inclusion, we need first to explore the gender gap in terms of activities and interactions. Thus, we propose to answer the questions: *where are females in OSS projects? How they evolve? and How they contribute to the sustainability of the OSS social capital?*. We particularly focus on building socio-technical networks and analyze them to explain how females contribute and interact in practice. We reflect on interactions' graphs and examine through a preliminary study, using data from six OSS projects, possible links between existing findings and the directions we suggest for more gender diversity. We found that females are extremely underrepresented within OSS communities, but when they participate they are productive just as males, they evolve following relatively the same patterns than males and remain more involved in projects than males.

Keywords: Gender · Diversity · Open Source Software ·
Social Network Analysis · Socio-Technical interactions

1 Introduction

Women are underrepresented in the software development industry and particularly within OSS communities [1–5]. In the software industry, females only account for 21% of the whole software development workforce and earn on average $22,251 less than their male peers [6]. In GitHub[1], a well-known open-source platform, the annual diversity report on OSS communities reported that the overall number of females decreased from 37% in 2017 to 33% in 2018. Repository data from GitHub projects provide an interesting source of information which, under appropriate analysis, may reveal facts related to females' activities and their dynamic interactions in a collaborative development environment. To this end, we undertake a socio-technical analysis

---

[1] https://github.com/about/diversity.

© IFIP International Federation for Information Processing 2019
Published by Springer Nature Switzerland AG 2019
L. M. Camarinha-Matos et al. (Eds.): PRO-VE 2019, IFIP AICT 568, pp. 308–319, 2019.
https://doi.org/10.1007/978-3-030-28464-0_27

to get more insights into females' involvement in OSS projects. More specifically, we seek to answer the questions: Where Are Females in OSS Projects? How They Evolve? And How they contribute to the sustainability of the OSS social capital?

Why Diversity Matters? Diversity in the workplace including diversity of gender, ethnicity, and even religion has been shown to improve retention and reduce the costs associated with employee turnover [4, 7–9]. In a diverse workplace, employees are more likely to remain loyal when they feel respected and valued for their unique contribution [10]. That said, while GitHub is supposed to be a meritocracy based platform and free of gender barriers [11], the situation of females involvement is below the expectations [6] which limits the workforce required for communities growth. To benefit from gender diversity, OSS communities should lower barriers for female developers' self-guided personal development, which is crucial for them to achieve their own technical distinctions.

In order to support gender diversity within GitHub communities, we should understand how members, especially women, interact in these community environments. Understanding social interaction of female's collaboration could reveal insights not only about the structure of collaboration but also how productive are cross-gender collaboration: we know who contributed on what and when by examining historical data from GitHub. From there, we can build a social network of contributors (for both males and females) who have collaborated on the same source code files. Social Network Analysis (SNA) provides a class of metrics known as "centrality" metrics that provide a useful abstraction of the gender interaction information. Thus, we analyze and compare activity data (i.e., #commits, #comments, #fileModified, and code churn) between genders. Then we analyze SNA metrics of interactions (i.e., Female-Female, F-M, and M-M).

In particular, we answer the three following research questions:

RQ1: Where are females in OSS projects?
RQ2: How the top females' performers evolved over time?
RQ3: What is the role of females in building a sustainable collaborative social capital?

Paper Structure. We first discuss related work in Sect. 2. Then we present our methodology in Sect. 3 including data collection and gender detection approach. Section 4 introduces the basic terminology and concepts needed to comprehend how we built social networks, while Sect. 5 offers an overview of our findings along with discussion. In Sect. 6 we discuss possible threats to validity. Finally, Sect. 7 concludes and outlooks future work.

2   Related Work

The study by Vasilescu et al. [4] is the one that shares objectives closest to ours. The authors acknowledge the importance of gender diversity and explored how diverse are online teams with respect to gender and tenure based on the findings of a survey of GitHub contributors. Authors point out that when forming or recruiting a software team, increased gender and tenure diversity are associated with greater productivity. Similarly, James et al. [12] studied the perception, performance, team dynamics, and opportunities using a survey targeting software professionals and reported that there is no significant difference between genders. Medenz et al. [13] investigated a gender inclusive method and how it can help increase gender inclusiveness in the tools that are used by OSS communities.

Wang et al. [11] discussed the existence of the competence-confidence gap. Authors developed a theoretical explanation for female developers' low rate of initiating a pull request in OSS projects arguing that it is not easy for female developers to directly translate competence to confidence [11]. Similarly, Terrell [14] compared acceptance rates of contributions from men and women in an open-source software community and finds that, in overall, women's contributions tend to be accepted more often than men's - but when a woman's gender is identifiable, her Pull requests are rejected more often.

In this study, we investigate the socio-technical interactions of females in OSS communities using SNA. We leverage on the historical data of six projects from GitHub. The benefit of assessing females' position in the overall collaborative networks is that it does not require qualitative information that can only be provided by contributors, such as questions about what they have done before. Analyzing networks of collaboration such as file co-edition, comments, pull requests offer opportunities for understanding the value provided by women in software development and help other researchers recommending improvements.

3   Methodology

3.1   Data Collection

The primary goal of our study is to understand how females interact and evolve within OSS communities. To this end, we performed a preliminary analysis of socio-technical interactions on publicly available historical data from six open source projects, mined from GitHub: *Angular.js, Moby, Rails, Tensorflow, Django, Elasticsearch*. We selected these well-known OSS projects because they are long-lived with more than a thousand contributors, and under diverse programming languages. Table 1 shows descriptive statistics regarding the studied projects.

In order to understand the female's distribution along with their activities within OSS projects, we first extracted information for each commit including the login of contributors, Timestamp of the commit, number of files modified, and code churn information (i.e., quantification of the commit size). Next, we used a Rest GitHub API[2] to extract detailed information of the contributor for each commit. For instance, the HTTP GET request "https://api.github.com/users/Narretz" sends back available details of the account including contributor's name "*Martin Staffa*". However, users registered in GitHub can choose to disclose their names in their profiles, so that out of the six projects studied, 1059 contributor names were missing. To discover as many of the

---

[2] https://api.github.com/users/.

missing names as possible, the GitHub API provides access to user's public events which list all public events performed by a user on the site. This list provides another way to view the personal information associated with GitHub data. For instance, calling "https://api.github.com/users/bumbu/events/public" returns a Json object that includes a full name associated with the user and commits 'Alex Bumbu'. Using this method, we were able to detect 155 names from the missing list since GitHub users can upgrade their privacy settings to hide personal information[3]. We verified that less than 10% of contributors' names are missing for each project. Unknown names in the profile cannot be used to identify genders, we ignored them in our analysis.

Table 1. Quantification of activities by gender. (1) unknown gender is filtered out; (2) numbers are normalized by the number of contributors for each gender.

Project	Lang	Contrib	Commits	%Females	%Males	Commits F(%)	Commits M(%)	Comments F(%)	Comments M(%)	Edited Files F(%)	Edited Files M(%)	Code Churn F(%)	Code Churn M(%)	p_value (F vs M commits)
Angular.js	JavaScript	1601	8897	3.4	76.1	2.79	5.86	0.18	0.94	7.62	20.37	291.5	1162.13	0.17
Moby	Go	1824	36007	3.5	88.1	20.08*	18.73*	0.01	0.19	131.6	93.69	7051.97	5612.75	0.2
Rails	Ruby	3723	70762	4.2	91	8.07	19.21	0.73	4.63	29.62	70.25	77.94	1912.8	0.79
Django	Python	1672	26283	5.3	88	5.51	16.43	0.11	0.84	17.34	70.05	271.48	3467.39	0.09
Elasticsearch	Java	1127	42702	4.2	86.1	25.45	42.24	0.04	0.56	166.08	481.9	6839.1	27271.75	0.43
TensorFlow	C++	1735	44132	5.8	80.7	17.92	25.65	0.09	0.21	131.23	258.34	19601.38	43082.54	0.14

3.2 Gender Detection

GitHub does not store information about contributors' gender identification. There are few approaches to automatically infer a contributor's gender [4, 14, 15]. Vasilescu et al. [4] used first name and country to infer a user's gender. Terrell et al. [14] suggested a method using email to link a user to her Linkedin profiles which contains rich information. Although this method shows a high precision, the recall is not good, especially for female developers from East Asian countries where the usage of Linkedin is not that high. However, these heuristics have not been empirically validated with GitHub data. To alleviate issues related to previous approaches, we used the commercial tool called Namsor API[4]. Table 1 shows a comparison of females and males percentage distributions.

4   Social Network Representation

Social Network Analysis (SNA) is the process of investigating social structures through the use of networks and graph theory [16]. In network analysis, we have nodes (i.e., contributors) which represent vertices of a graph and connections which represent edges (i.e., a type of interaction). An interaction occurs when two developers modify the same source code file or comment on the same topic.

---

[3] https://medium.freecodecamp.org/github-privacy-101-how-to-remove-personal-emails-from-your-public-repos-58347b06a508.

[4] http:/blog.namsor.com/api.

SNA Metrics. Metrics that measure a node's direct connections to other nodes are connectivity metrics. The first metric is the **density** of a network which captures the number of actual connections between members divided by the number of possible connections, as depicted in Fig. 1. Density values range from [0 to 1], a higher density indicates that network nodes have tighter connections with each other. Second, connectivity metric is the **degree centrality** of a node which represents the number of connections incident on a node. Each time two contributors change the same file or comment on the same topic we have one non-weighted connection (i.e., a link). In contrast, a node is considered disconnected if it has no edges with other nodes meaning no interactions with other contributors. Centrality metrics quantify how closely contributors are indirectly connected to other contributors in the network. We consider two metrics: closeness and betweenness. **Closeness** stands for the average number of steps required to go from the current node to all other nodes. Closeness measures the distance between each participant and all other participants (i.e., is a participant connected directly to all other participants, or would information need to pass through several other participants to reach that individual?). **Betweenness** stands for the average number of shortest paths between pairs of other nodes that run through the node. Betweenness is used to measure the extent to which a node lies between other nodes. More shortest paths run through a node, more likely important this node is. **Clustering Coefficient** is calculated as the probability that any two neighbors of the current node are connected. In our study, the clustering coefficient measures the collective collaboration of contributors from different genders.

We used SNA metrics to explore diversity of interactions of Female-Female (**F-F**), Female-Male (**F-M**), and Male-Male (**M-M**) using files co-edition networks from six GitHub projects.

5   Results

RQ1. Where Are Females in OSS Projects?

Motivation. Social capital of open source software needs gender diversity among other diversities (i.e., cultural, ethnic, etc.), to be sustainable [17]. Gender diversity demands coordinated and delicate interactions [4]. Unfortunately, little is known about how females behave and interact within OSS communities, comprehensive view is rarely discussed at least to understand what would be specific for females to ease their integration within OSS communities.

Approach. We first extract historical data of Commits, Comments, and Pull Requests from GitHub with their respective authors similarly to the approach provided by Joblin et al. [18]. After identifying the gender of each contributor, we focused on three groups of interactions cross-gender F-F, M-M, and F-M. Thus, for each project, we built a social network, along with subnetworks regarding the three groups, related to contributors' interactions for the six studied projects. More precisely, by interactions we mean the relation by which two or more contributors collaborate with each other through an activity such as working on the same source code file (i.e., co-edition) or commenting on the same commit. We tracked back this information by looking at the version change history and other elements provided by the GitHub platform.

Results. Figure 1 shows social networks related to contributors' interactions for the six studied projects. Nodes represented in red color point out males and yellow ones highlight the position of females within the overall network. Visually, as shown in Fig. 1, females are distributed throughout the overall network. They are positioned within the Core as well as Peripheral members and are interacting with both genders. Furthermore, to examine interactions regarding gender, we calculate the SNA metrics of three sub-networks Fig. 2: *(i)* interactions between females F-F, *(ii)* interactions between males M-M, and *(iii)* interactions with the opposite gender F-M. Table 2 reports the averages distribution of the most important SNA metrics cross-networks.

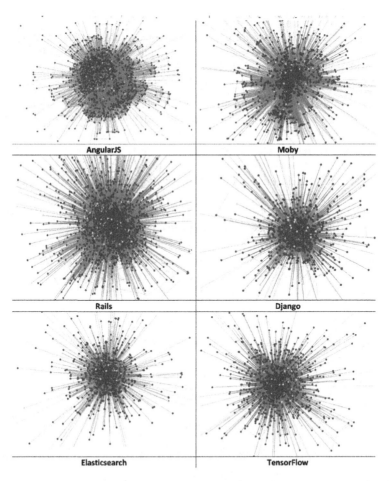

Fig. 1. Social position of females within the socio-technical network (females are represented in yellow). (Color figure online)

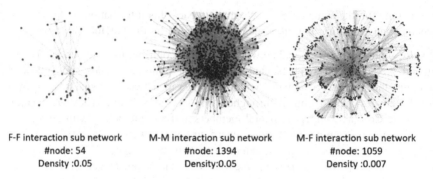

F-F interaction sub network	M-M interaction sub network	M-F interaction sub network
#node: 54	#node: 1394	#node: 1059
Density :0.05	Density:0.05	Density :0.007

Fig. 2. Sub networks representing cross-gender interactions.

For all projects, F-F interactions are as dense as M-M and F-M interactions are less dense meaning that there are more interactions between contributors within the same gender group than the opposite gender. For example, within Angular.JS project, the two networks F-F and M-M have the same density equal to 0.05, however, the density of cross-gender interactions network M-F is very low (=0.007).

The *Avg. degree* metric for the sub-networks F-F is extremely low compared to M-M meaning that females are less directly connected to other females (*2.7* for Angular.js) and also less connected to males (7.05). We hypothesize that this result is skewed because of the unbalanced numbers of contributors for each gender.

The *Avg.ClusCoef* related to the sub-network M-M is much higher than F-F meaning that there are established groups of collaboration (for Angular.js, Avg.Clus-Coef = *0.89* between males (M-M) against *0.46* for F-F) co-editing the same components for a long time. While Avg.ClusCoef value close to 0 for the sub-networks M-F suggesting that there are few cross-gender interactions.

Closeness metric is roughly similar cross-gender meaning that gender has no effect on the proximity of members with other members of the community and how fast the members interact with each other (i.e., fewer steps to reach other nodes).

Betweenness metric has a very small value suggesting that nodes are not that much connected (value = 1 means a hub node and value = 0 means a disconnected node). For instance, in Angular.js project, the average Betweenness for the network F-F equal to 0.02, while it is equal to 6e-4 for the sub-network M-M.

Table 2. Summary of the most important SNA metrics using sub-networks related to gender.

Project	Density			Avg.degree			Avg.ClustCoef			Avg.ClosCentrality			Avg.BetwCentrality		
	F-F	M-M	M-F	F-F	M-M	M-F	F-F	M-M	M-F	F-F	M-M	M-F	F-F	M-M	M-F
Angular.js	0.05	0.05	0.007	2.7	69.58	7.05	0.46	0.89	0	0.41	0.51	0.37	0.02	6 E-04	1 E-03
Moby	0.07	0.05	0.008	6.24	85.03	11.34	0.54	0.87	0	0.41	0.51	0.41	0.01	6 E-04	1 E-03
Rails	0.05	0.06	0.006	8.34	230.67	19.83	0.63	0.85	0	0.42	0.51	0.42	E-03	2 E-04	4 E-04
Django	0.09	0.1	0.014	8.5	161.45	19.37	0.65	0.84	0	0.42	0.53	0.4	0.013	5 E-04	1 E-03
Elasticsearch	0.04	0.05	0.008	2.08	49.31	5.85	0.29	0.89	0	0.31	0.5	0.4	0.029	1 E-03	2 E-03
TensorFlow	0.08	0.07	0.014	7.91	117.38	17.95	0.53	0.89	0	0.42	0.52	0.39	0.01	6 E-04	1 E-03

Also, as one can see in the subnetwork M-F in Fig. 2, females can play a broker role ensuring the communication between sub groups, which can decrease the centralization of the OSS community and increase communication between Core (i.e., experts) and Peripheral members (i.e., casual contributors) [19].

> **Where are females in OSS projects?**
> Although females are underrepresented within OSS communities, we found them in the Core teams as well as in Peripheral. Women are more likely than men to interact with other contributors. However, the density of cross-gender interactions network M-F is very low (=0.007) with less established groups of females (0.46) compared to males (0.89).

RQ2. How the top females' performers evolved over time?

Motivation. A common problem that OSS communities face is the high instability of their contributors [20]. This problem is even amplified by the fact that females are underrepresented, their permanence is also an open issue. We sought to gain more understanding of the evolvement of female contributors over time and to learn from the experience of the top performers.

Approach. For each project, we have retrieved the third quartile (i.e., upper quartile that has the top 25% above it) of the female developers that contribute the most according to the: number of commits, comments, and Pull Requests. From it, we calculate the performance for each contributor according to the following formula.

$$Performance(C_i) = \frac{1}{Total\_activity}[date\_lastActivity(C_i) - date\_firstActivity(C_i)]$$

Results. Figure 3 shows the distribution of performance between males and females. We performed Mann-Whitney-Wilcoxon statistical tests, with a confidence level of alpha = 0.05. We found that for all projects except Moby the tests were not statistically significant (p > 0.05) suggesting that there is no statistical difference of the performance cross-gender except for the project Moby as reported in Table 3.

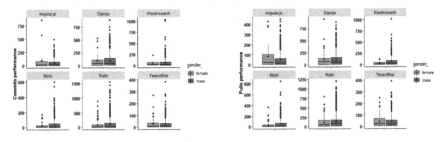

Fig. 3. Comparison of the gender performance

Table 3. ManWhitney significance test

Project	p-value(commits)	p-value(PullRequests)
Angular.js	0.74	0.23
Moby	0.37	0.14
Rails	**0.02**	0.2
Django	0.49	0.6
Elasticsearch	0.78	0.11
Tensorflow	0.72	0.73

How the top females' performers evolved over time?
Females evolve just as males within OSS projects. There is no statistical difference of the performance cross-gender except for the project Moby.

RQ3. What is the role of females in building a sustainable collaborative social capital?

Motivation. Sustained participation in crucial for successful OSS project [19]. We expect that the more often individuals participate in OSS, the higher their chance of prolonged engagement.

Results. Table 1 summarizes the involvement of females in OSS projects. The percentage of females range from *3.4%* to *5.8%* which is drastically less than the average numbers presented in the annual report of GitHub [6]. When normalizing these numbers by genders, we noticed that women contribute slightly less than men except for the Moby project where women outperform (*20.08%* vs. *18.73%* for men). Apparently, in the Angular.js project, the productivity of men is two times higher than women in terms of commits (*2.79%* vs. *5.86%*). Similarly, we report on the difference of productivity for other projects (Moby = *0.9*; Rails = *2.3*; Django = *2.9*; ElasticSearch = *1.6*; TenserFlow = *1.4*).

Moreover, Table 4 shows the evolution of the activity related to both genders (due to lack of space, we report data only for Angular.js). Although OSS projects keep attracting both genders, the number of active contributors (i.e., committing and commenting) decreases proportionally for both genders.

Table 4. Activity evolution. Example of Angulat.Js project.

Year	Contributors		Commits		Edited Files		Code Churn		Comments	
	F	M	F	M	F	M	F	M	F	M
2010	0	6	0	6 → 581	6 → 2687	6 → 175340	0	2 → 4	0	0
2011	0	20	0	17 → 811	17 → 4095	17 → 249305	0	6 → 20	0	0
2012	2	97	↑ 2 → 2	84 → 754	2 → 4	84 → 2848	2 → 24	84 → 124359	0	18 → 32
2013	17	511	↑ 16 → 29	436 → 1503	16 → 16	436 → 4460	16 → 1309	436 → 209275	1 → 1	135 → 276
2014	34	965	↑ 20 → 72	517 → 2131	20 → 230	57 → 6111	20 → 4354	516 → 263323	3 → 4	166 → 525
2015	45	1179	↓ 14 → 34	270 → 960	14 → 50	270 → 3079	14 → 9914	270 → 138804	2 → 3	79 → 229
2016	47	1335	↓ 5 → 5	184 → 879	5 → 5	184 → 3343	5 → 14	184 → 351669	1 → 2	37 → 163
2017	52	1338	↑ 6 → 6	65 → 305	6 → 79	65 → 1254	5 → 68	65 → 75817	0	14 → 32
2018	54	1395	↓ 3 → 3	24 → 252	3 → 5	24 → 548	3 → 58	24 → 33280	0	17 → 35

> **What is the role of females in building a sustainable social capital?**
> Even if females are underrepresented in OSS communities, they contribute in building a sustainable social capital for open software.

6 Threats to Validity

This section discusses the threats that might have affected our findings, and how we have alleviated these threats.

Threats to *Internal Validity* concern alternative factors that could have influenced our results. This exploratory study might suffer from at least the similar threats that other studies using GitHub Data do [21] related to possible issues with data gathering and the missing of validation. We believe that using a large amount of data mitigates this threat. Another threat relates to the accuracy of gender prediction. Various approaches and tools to infer gender based on names and countries have been proposed in the literature [4, 22, 23]. Most of these tools rely on English names stored in databases. However, these heuristics have not been yet empirically validated with GitHub data. We tried three tools [4, 14, 15], and found that each has strengths and drawbacks. We used *Namsor*, a commercial tool with the assumption that it provide the most accurate results. We also assume the gender is a binary attribute.

Threats to *construct validity* consider the agreement between a theoretical concept and a specific measuring procedure. One threat considers the intrinsic blind spots when investigating consecutive snapshots of a dynamic social network over time-stamps (years). Indeed, there is no way to ensure that years are the "optimal" time-stamps to represent the snapshots of our social networks in order to capture the evolvement and interaction between nodes (contributors). Therefore, tracking a community evolution in such a constraint can yield evolving observations in a non-consecutive way. Furthermore, some important events (e.g., major releases, vision changes, etc.) that communities may undergo across time-stamps will not be detected and will be difficult to predict.

Threats to *external validity* relate to the generalization of our findings. We only considered six OSS projects from GitHub. Thus, we cannot assume a generalization to all projects hosted on GitHub or other platforms such as GitLab and Bitbucket, even though there is no inherent reason why they would be biased.

7   Conclusion

We have used SNA approach to study gender diversity within six GitHub communities. We first examined the position of both genders within social networks and their interactions and found that females are spread over the overall network including Core and Peripheral members. Next, we tracked back the evolvement of the upper quartile of the female developers that contribute the most according to the: number of commits, comments, and Pull Request. We found that there is no statistical difference regarding the performance cross-gender except for the project Moby. Finally, even if females are underrepresented in OSS communities, they contribute in building a sustainable collaborative social capital for open software.

The results of this study motivate further fine-grained analysis of female's implication in OSS that will (*i*) investigate the quality of work in terms of introduced bugs or complexity; (*ii*) explore further socio-technical interactions of women to understand the value of their contributions; (*iii*) characterize projects attractiveness for women.

References

1. Feller, J., Fitzgerald, B.: A framework analysis of the open source software development paradigm (2000)
2. Nafus, D.: 'Patches don't have gender': what is not open in open source software. New Media Soc. **14**(4), 669–683 (2012)
3. Steinmacher, I., Chaves, A.P., Conte, T.U., et al.: Preliminary empirical identification of barriers faced by newcomers to Open Source Software projects, pp. 51–60 (2014)
4. Vasilescu, B., Posnett, D., Ray, B., et al.: Gender and tenure diversity in GitHub teams. In: Proceedings of the 33rd Annual ACM Conference on Human Factors in Computing Systems, CHI 2015, pp. 3789–3798 (2015)
5. Filippova, A., Trainer, E., Herbsleb, J.D.: From diversity by numbers to diversity as process: supporting inclusiveness in software development teams with brainstorming, pp. 152–163 (2017). %@ 1538638681
6. Datausa.io. Demographics of Software Developers
7. Hui, J.S., Farnham, S.D.: Designing for inclusion: supporting gender diversity in independent innovation teams, pp. 71–85 (2016)
8. Imtiaz, N., Middleton, J., Chakraborty, J., et al.: Investigating the effects of gender bias on GitHub (2019)
9. Foucault, M., Palyart, M., Blanc, X., et al.: Impact of developer turnover on quality in open-source software, pp. 829–841 (2015)
10. O'Reilly Iii, C.A., Caldwell, D.F., Barnett, W.P.: Work group demography, social integration, and turnover. Adm. Sci. Q., 21–37 (1989)

11. Wang, Z., Wang, Y., Redmiles, D.: Competence-confidence gap. In: Proceedings of the 40th International Conference on Software Engineering Software Engineering in Society, ICSE-SEIS 2018, pp. 81–90 (2018)

12. James, T., Galster, M., Blincoe, K., et al.: What is the perception of female and male software professionals on performance, team dynamics and job satisfaction?: insights from the trenches, pp. 13–22 (2017)

13. Mendez, C., Sarma, A., Burnett, M.: Gender in open source software: what the tools tell, pp. 21–24 (2018)

14. Terrell, J., Kofink, A., Middleton, J., et al.: Gender differences and bias in open source: pull request acceptance of women versus men. PeerJ Comput. Sci. **3**, e111 (2017)

15. Vasilescu, B., Capiluppi, A., Serebrenik, A.: Gender, representation and online participation: a quantitative study of stackoverflow, pp. 332–338 (2012)

16. Zhang, W., Nie, L., Jiang, H., et al.: Developer social networks in software engineering: construction, analysis, and applications. Sci. China Inf. Sci. **57**(12), 1–23 (2014)

17. Dabbish, L., Stuart, C., Tsay, J., et al.: Social coding in GitHub: transparency and collaboration in an open software repository. In: The conference on Computer Supported Cooperative Work, Seattle, WA, USA, pp. 1277–1286 (2012)

18. Joblin, M., Apel, S., Mauerer, W.: Evolutionary trends of developer coordination: a network approach. Empirical Softw. Eng. **22**(4), 2050–2094 (2016)

19. Toral, S.L., Martínez-Torres, M.R., Barrero, F.: Analysis of virtual communities supporting OSS projects using social network analysis. Inf. Softw. Technol. **52**(3), 296–303 (2010)

20. Robles, G., Gonzalez-Barahona, J.M., Herraiz, I.: Evolution of the core team of developers in libre software projects. In: 2009 6th IEEE International Working Conference on Mining Software Repositories, pp. 167–170 (2009)

21. Kalliamvakou, E., Gousios, G., Blincoe, K., et al.: The promises and perils of mining GitHub, pp. 92–101 (2014)

22. Lin, B., Serebrenik, A.: Recognizing gender of stack overflow users, pp. 425–429 (2016)

23. Karimi, F., Wagner, C., Lemmerich, F., et al.: Inferring gender from names on the web: a comparative evaluation of gender detection methods, pp. 53–54 (2016)

Digital Transformation of Supply Chain

A Digital Platform Architecture to Support Multi-dimensional Surplus Capacity Sharing

Henrique Diogo Silva[1(✉)], António Lucas Soares[1,2], Andrea Bettoni[3],
Andrea Barni Francesco[3], and Serena Albertario[4]

[1] INESC TEC, Porto, Portugal
{henrique.d.silva,asoares}@inesctec.pt
[2] University of Porto, Porto, Portugal
[3] SUPSI, Manno, Switzerland
{andrea.bettoni,andrea.barni}@supsi.ch
[4] Holonix Srl, Meda, Italy
serena.albertario@holonix.it

Abstract. The highly disruptive transformation that digital platforms are imposing on entire sectors of the economy, along with the broad digitalization of industrial business processes, is having an impact on supply chains around the world. To take advantage of this new aggregated market paradigm new business models with a heavy focus on servitization are changing the value proposition of businesses. In this paper, we describe a reference architectural framework designed to support a digital platform fostering the optimization of supply chains by the pairing of unused industrial capacity with production demand. This framework aims at harmonizing stakeholder requirements with specifications of different levels in order to set up a coherent reference blueprint that serves as a starting point for development activities. A four-layer approach is used to articulate between technical components, with the data and tools layers, and the ecosystem, with the business and interfaces layers. The overall architecture and component description is presented as extensions of the initial set of affordances.

Keywords: Digital platforms · Digital platform architecture · Manufacturing as a service

1 Introduction

One of the more prevalent effects of the platform paradigm in the economy is the separation of physical assets from the value they create, the separation of function from the form [22]. In the industrial sector, this switch is evidenced by the widespread shift of income generation from the sale of physical products to the charging of customers for the availability of functionalities of a product [31]. From the perspective of companies that chose to invest on hefty fixed assets like top-of-the-line laser cutting machines or a 5-axis CNC machine this selling of capacity allows for better resource distribution while for other businesses it provides facilitated access to costly equipment that can help in alleviating initial costs of business or even the ability to meet seasonal

© IFIP International Federation for Information Processing 2019
Published by Springer Nature Switzerland AG 2019
L. M. Camarinha-Matos et al. (Eds.): PRO-VE 2019, IFIP AICT 568, pp. 323–334, 2019.
https://doi.org/10.1007/978-3-030-28464-0_28

peak demands. The growing willingness of companies to both buy and sell manu-facturing capacity has precipitated the development of the Manufacturing as a Service (MaaS) paradigm [4] that both boosts and leverages the platform economy.

The explosion of the platform business has had a profound impact on businesses structures. The traditional pipeline perspective where processes were arranged step-by-step with producers at one end and consumers at the other has given way to new platform mediated structures [22]. In this new paradigm, the linearity of the value chain is twisted and tangled to the point where the boundaries of user and producer are regularly crossed or in some cases inexistent.

Having this landscape as the starting point, and taking digital platforms as stimu-lants for the transition of industry businesses towards service-oriented approaches [7, 12, 19, 32] it becomes clear that a platform centered ecosystem is needed in order to further advance the MaaS business model. In [4] authors lay out their vision for a digital platform in the MaaS realm that leverages this disruption of the value chain and fluidity of user roles. By adopting a holistic perspective of the value network, and going beyond the simple matchmaking of manufacturing resources, the sharing potential is extended to the whole manufacturing ecosystem network. The fulfillment of this vision, in turn, requires a platform that can establish the bridge between the expected affor-dances of digital platforms and the cross-sectoral environment, in an ecosystem able to generate added value to its users. By bringing together tools and ecosystem, we are promoting a better and more sustainable use of resources, the reintegration in the loop of unused manufacturing capacity, leading to the creation of local, more efficient value networks, and the seamless involvement of different actors along the value network for cross-fertilization of product-service solutions and underlying technologies.

Leveraging the ensued entanglement of the value chain, this paper aims at describing the design approach and resulting core components that will constitute the backbone architecture of a MaaS platform. The paper is divided into a first section that puts into perspective the manufacturing domain that will represent the platform's ecosystem, as well as the features the platform is expected to support, followed by the core section where the components that make up each one of the four layers are described in detail.

2 The Manufacturing Digital Platform Landscape

2.1 Digital Platform Affordances

The development of the sharing economy is a clear example of how digital platforms have played a fundamental role in the development of the market [29]. Scholars point to six crucial affordances that stride the balance between the rigidity of the techno-logical and the human components of platform ecosystems [23]: (1) generation of flexibility; (2) matchmaking; (3) scale and reach extension; (4) transaction manage-ment; (5) trust building; and (6) community creation support.

Digital platforms have the capacity to generate flexibility, not only in how and when users can interact with the platforms [15]. The fluidity between user roles within the platform has also shown a measurable impact in the interactions and consumption habits. Authors such as [8] and [24] point to ability to regularly access sharing economy platforms as an essential component of its success as a business model, while [2] show how the ability to easily change roles within the platform between client and producer has the beneficial effect of incentivizing the engagement on different levels.

The matching of users, along with pulling them to the platform and facilitating their actions and interactions, are some of the main functions of a digital platforms [22]. The ability to perform matchmaking based on a set of attributes then becomes a fundamental function of digital platforms [3, 25]. Different mechanisms for matchmaking currently exist based on algorithmic assignment and powerful searching and sorting tools [29]. This automation of processes then becoming the entire value proposition of many platforms. For industry-focused platforms, perspectives like the one presented by [4] are starting to rethink this process beyond the matching of manufacturing resources to the whole manufacturing ecosystem value network.

The scale and reach brought about by the facilitated access to an extensive network of organizations, consumers, and resources that compose a platform's ecosystem is also one of its main competitive advantages [9]. By striking the balance between the benefits of network externalities and the automation capabilities, made possible by its technological constructs, platforms are able to create a scaling loop that, after crossing the initial hurdle of the point of critical mass, have the potential to grow indefinitely [5, 10, 14].

The management of the transactions involved in the transmission and securing of goods, information or labor is another widespread functionality of sharing economy platforms [30]. In this sense, platforms double up as marketplace and bookkeeper by bringing both parties together while also keeping records of all transactions, ensuring the validity of all the exchanges [6, 33].

Trust and trustworthiness are a contested point in the digital realm. Where anonymity has always been an obstacle in the conduction of transactions through this medium [16], and in-person meetings made for the more trustworthy method, in the last decades the advent of several trust-based mechanisms has started to invert this trend. The popularization of features like user profiles as extensions of resumes [20, 27], the utilization of subjective and non-subjective user reviews system [13] along with the implementation of more strict governance directives for the management of platform's communities [18, 26] have tipped the scales in favor of the digital. When thinking about the impact of trust in digital platforms it's also essential to distinguish between trust between users of the ecosystem and the trust users deposit in the platform itself, as both play an essential role when it comes to the adoption of these systems.

The human component of digital platforms is what truly elevates them to the status of sociotechnical constructs [1, 28]. Community building structures that serve as venues for community interactions and participation play an import role in onboarding new users and the facilitation of new relationships between them [21]. This is a crucial aspect to keep in mind at the platform design stage as previous studies suggest that, for sharing economy platforms, not only economic profit but also community involvement play a critical role as motivators in platform adoption [6, 11], even in platforms with minimal community interaction capabilities.

3   A MaaS Platform Supporting Sharing of Unused Resources

3.1   The MANU-SQUARE Platform

Building on the MaaS concept, the MANU-SQUARE project [4] aims at establishing a European ecosystem of organizations and other relevant stakeholders that, in a marketplace environment, can act as both supplier and client. Through this approach, the platform moves available capacity closer to production demand, further disrupting the traditional linear value network, allowing for the rapid and efficient creation of local value networks for innovative providers of products and services and the optimization and reintroduction in the loop of unused capacity that would otherwise be lost.

The MANU-SQUARE platform goes far beyond the partner search and matching, and supply-chain/virtual enterprises formation proposed in the last 20 years of virtual enterprise literature in three crucial points: (1) extending the sharing potential to the whole manufacturing ecosystem value network; (2) by focusing on surplus capacity; while (3) adopting a multi-dimensional and cross-sectoral vision of capacity.

Current approaches to the sharing of manufacturing capacity have narrowed down their scope to both specific sectors of the industrial ecosystem, and the sharing of unused production resources. This limited view of surplus capacity leaves out, however, much of the wealth that the European industry has been building through the years. Our perspective scopes this vision back up to not only include all the actors that make up the European manufacturing value chain, such as manufacturing organizations, knowledge providers, innovation facilitators, etc. but also to enlarge the concept of capacity beyond production to surplus know-how, technology, and by-products.

This broader scope carries with it the necessity of an architecture able to cope with an increasingly nuanced system. To answer these demands, tried and true standards, such as semantic infrastructures, need to be articulated with state-of-the-art technologies like distributed ledger systems, to produce new and better trust-based, platforms for negotiation, networking and community building.

In this sense, the value proposition of the platform becomes: (1) from a user's perspective, be able to, among a European-wide pool, quickly find trustworthy suppliers according to a set of requirements. This matchmaking would help to manage fluctuating production demand or build/extend production capacity without owning production means relying on a structured RFQ and information sharing system and a transaction management system. (2) From a supplier's perspective, access to a broader cross-sectorial market becomes the main value proposition. This wider access gets complemented by the ability to sell unused capacity, access to up-to-date client information, structured and trustworthy processes for the dissemination of documentation such as RFQs, plus reputation management, and transaction management systems.

3.2 Stakeholders and Functionalities

The vast literature on stakeholder analysis has yet to catch up with the platform reality. Very much focused on stakeholders for small and medium enterprises (SMEs), [34] define five stakeholders roles: Innovation Commercialiser; Innovation Funder; Innovation Generator; End User; and Platform Operator. On a 2017 report, the World Economic Forum divides the roles in a platform ecosystem into four, non-mutually exclusive, categories: Orchestrator; Producer; Consumer; or Infrastructure provider.

From this theoretical underpinning, and supported by interviews and workshops with industry players, eight stakeholder typologies were identified. **Manufacturing** organizations, consisting of producers of products, components, and technology, are the leading stakeholder group. A second group of stakeholders consists of **Service and knowledge providers**, ranging from IT Laboratories, legal and consultancy organizations to research institutes and universities. By integrating joint research projects and offering their services through the platform, these stakeholders become critical in the development of new and improved value chains. In this same vein, **start-ups** and **innovation facilitators** also become essential users of the platform by bringing together innovation/technology hubs that facilitate and promote innovation.

In order to build self-sustaining, thriving communities of both customers and suppliers on the platform, achieving a critical mass of users is essential. This continuous task of community building is supported by two stakeholder roles: **multipliers** and **investors**. Clusters and sectorial network organizations, industry associations and investors that are looking for new business and investment ideas are essential elements in enabling access to larger a pool of ideas and business opportunities.

Also, in supporting roles of the central platform functionalities, **auditors and regulators**, plus **consumers** are relevant stakeholder groups. Regulatory compliance and audit authorities place complex sets of constraints on organizations. With these supervisory bodies as platform stakeholders, organizations can take advantage of the privileged contact in order to facilitate compliance, that can even lead to added value for customers in the case of certifications. On the other hand, the presence of consumers in the platform becomes relevant for the development or improvement of products and services.

Based on the defined stakeholders, a set of base 14 functionalities are described in Table 1. Table 2 maps the relationships of each functionality to the relevant affordance.

Table 1. Platform functionalities

Functionality	Description
Matching	
Production capacity matching	Matchmaking between suppliers of available manufacturing capacity and customers that aims to exploit that capacity. The platform recommends potential compliant suppliers, filtering them according to user selected parameters
Know-how capability matching	Matchmaking among suppliers of available knowledge and customers that require support in the related field of expertise
By-product matching	Matchmaking between companies whose manufacturing processes generate one or more by-products, and customers that can exploit these by-products as an input resource
Optimization	
Sustainability assessment	The platform supports the optimization of matchings according to an environmental sustainability assessment
Ecosystem optimization	The platform supports the ecosystem optimization, ranking suppliers and suggesting the most sustainable matchings
Management	
User profile management	The platform supports each user in the development of its profile
Reputation management	The platform allows for both user subjective and quantitative, KPI based evaluations of involved parties in transactions, for establishing a reputation level of users
Certifications management	The platform allows Auditors and Regulators to certify players through a verified and secure certifications management system
Trust management	The functionality supports the management of information across the platform giving users the right to define the level of accessibility to provide to their information
Communication support	The platform supports communication among platform users, streamlining connections and mediating the interactions among parties
Innovation management	Starting from a user introduced idea, different users can provide tracked and structured contributions. The platform administrates the flow of contributions
RFQ management	The platform provides the infrastructure to enable the definition and management of quotations, managing the level of visibility of the quotations and partners exchanging requests and transactions
Transactions management	The platform supports the creation of traceable transactions across the platform value network
Platform expansion	The platform supports the expansibility of its core functionalities through a complete expansion SKD

Table 2. Mapping of functionalities and relevant affordances.

	Generation of flexibility	Matchmaking	Scale and reach extension	Transaction management	Trust building	Community creation support
Production capacity matching		•	•			
Know-how capability matching		•	•			
By-product matching		•				
Sustainability assessment		•	•			
Ecosystem optimization			•			
User profile management					•	
Reputation management					•	•
Certifications management					•	
Trust management					•	•
Communication support			•			•
Innovation management			•			•
RFQ management	•			•		
Transactions management	•			•		
Platform expansion	•					

3.3   Platform Architecture

Given the socio-technical nature of digital platforms, the architecture design process needs to take into account not only all the technological underpinnings that serve as a platform infrastructure but also all the social and business elements that eventually will develop into the ecosystem. In many ways we may akin the process of platform design to city planning: infrastructure is an intrinsic and essential component of the project, but if focused to the detriment of other components, it may give way to problematic cities. Expansion, of both population and industry/services, equal distribution of services and natural resources and the development of functional transportation networks, are some of the challenges that can be exacerbated by this lack of human perspective.

The adopted four-layer architecture, shown in Fig. 1, can further be divided into two groups. A first group, consisting of the Data and Tools layers, corresponds the technological, infrastructure backbone of the platform, while a second group, corresponding of the Business and Web Portal players, are responsible for the ecosystem management, the human and business component of the platform. Each of these four layers houses components that, through their interplay, allow for all the functionalities of the platform.

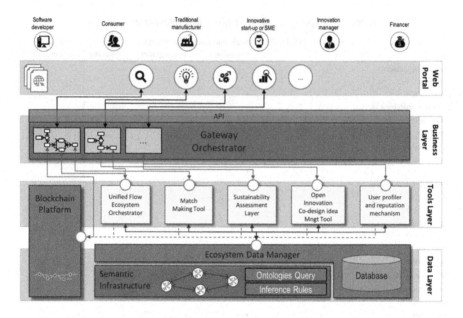

Fig. 1. Low-level platform architecture

The Data layer sits at the heart of any information system. Where more traditional paradigms of data storage/management were static abstractions where value was derived from the read/write logic, with the development of technologies like the semantic-WEB and distributed ledger systems, in between reads and writes we can gather context, inferences, and accountability. Through this layer, we leverage a semantically described ecosystem of actors, interactions and resources flow to feed an inference reasoning engine capable of uncovering non-trivial and previously unknown opportunities. The developed MANU-SQUARE core ontology, presented by [17], acts as the first step in the description of a MaaS ecosystem and along with standard services and interface options such as an RDF data store and a SPARQL endpoint, it will feed other platform tools with rich data for other functionalities.

The Blockchain platform, although still part of the Data layer, spills into the tools layer, due to its very nature. At a high level, this component works to ensure provenance, immutability, and finality of data, by guaranteeing that only mutually agreed upon transactions become part of a consensual and cryptographically secure shared ledger. Features like these make blockchain, and distributed ledger technologies in general, an ideal fit for digital platforms where affordances as trust and trustworthiness are a must, even more, when considering how they can be articulated with other components. Acting as the single point of trust for the ecosystem, from simple operations such as logging user access or storing stakeholder's reputation data in a immutable manner, to automating complex transactional operations that involve the exchange of sensitive information, the integration of the blockchain platform will help to fill trust building, transaction management and flexibility generation functionalities.

Given the modular architecture of the platform and both the data persistence methods previously presented, an extra abstraction to facilitate the access to information independently of its location is needed. By abstracting all the underlying data structures, the ecosystem data manager becomes the data broker for the platform and, by exposing a structured API to other components, allows for ubiquitous access to data, regardless of storage infrastructure, while preserving all of the inherent benefits of each storage method. Because this makes the ecosystem data manager aware of all the data flows within the platform, it will work in conjunction with the blockchain platform as a control point for data access.

The tools layer houses the modular tools that will provide many of the core services of the MANU-SQUARE platform. In an on-demand perspective, these services will be in constant communication with both the data layer and the business layer to fulfill many of the functionalities proposed in Table 1 and cover affordances presented in Sect. 2.1. The five tools that make up this layer are: (1) The Unified Flow Ecosystem Orchestrator that provides functionalities to analyze the needs of the different companies to propose ecosystem (re-)configurations that better link availability of resources with their optimal environmental performance, working closely together with the matchmaking mechanism; (2) the Matchmaking Tool that provides the production, know-how and by-product capacity matching functionalities. Feeding off of all the stakeholder profiling information, this tool is responsible for the optimal pairing of user's needs with available resources in the ecosystem; (3) the Sustainability Assessment Layer that provides functionalities to support the evaluation of the environmental impact of new chains established through the platform; (4) the Open innovation & Co-design Idea Management Tool provides the Innovation Management functionality by leveraging the open innovation paradigm; and (5) the user profiler and reputation mechanism that provide the user profile management, reputation management, and certifications management functionalities. Because establishing trust and trustworthiness between organizations is a complex, time and resource intensive process, by integrating blockchain-controlled transactions to keep track of quantitative KPIs such as on-time delivery and quality of products, beside qualitative platform user feedback, based on the perceived quality of interactions with other actors of the ecosystem, we can strike the balance between the technological with the human components of trust.

The business layer, standing between the user-facing interfaces and the core services of the platform is responsible for the orchestration between tools and the complex set of functionalities. Composed by a combination of the gateway orchestrator and a set of outward facing APIs, this engine is responsible for the implementation of business processes relevant the platform's stakeholders through the use of the tools from the Tools Layer. From a modular architecture standpoint, this layer is essential in realizing the full potential of the ecosystem as it alights the flexibility provided by the decoupling of services with the flexibility in the reorganization of services to better fit different business process needs. At its heart, the gateway orchestrator is powered by decision automation software that can interpret business processes codified in standard business process modeling notation (BPMN) and, according to the services offered by the platform, provide users with the optimal experience.

The web portal directly provides the platform expansion functionality and empowers all the remaining by representing the primary interface through which users will interact with the platform. Leveraging the ubiquitous and flexibility of the WEB platform, this layer provides both general graphical interfaces in the form of web pages as well as platform expansion points for external tools. This layer, in direct contact with the gateway orchestrator, will be able to trigger different business processes and run users through the involved tasks.

4   Conclusions and Next Steps

In this paper, a description of the underlying, layered architecture that serves as the backbone of a MaaS platform has been presented. An initial six affordances, drawn from the gig/sharing economy paradigm, were transposed to the industrial sector and served as guiding principles for the definition of a core set of functionalities required for the introduction of digital platforms as added value tools for the MaaS paradigm. With the actualized architecture, composed by four different layers and eighth individual tools, this framework retains the flexibility of its modular design for the application in different manufacturing sectors, business processes or use cases, all the while maintaining its reliability through the use of state-of-the-art trust-based information technologies in conjunction with tried and true standards.

Next steps will consider the development and integration of the software tools, followed by an iterative approach to the demonstration pilots made possible by the development of the architecture alongside the MANU-SQUARE project.

Acknowledgments. The work presented here was part of the project "MANU-SQUARE - MANUfacturing ecoSystem of QUAlified Resources Exchange" and received funding from the European Union's Horizon 2020 research and innovation programme under grant agreements No. 761145.

References

1. Barnes, S.J., Mattsson, J.: Building tribal communities in the collaborative economy: an innovation framework. Prometheus **34**(2), 95–113 (2016). https://doi.org/10.1080/08109028.2017.1279875
2. Bauer, R.M., Gegenhuber, T.: Crowdsourcing: global search and the twisted roles of consumers and producers. Organization **22**(5), 661–681 (2015). https://doi.org/10.1177/1350508415585030
3. Benoit, S., et al.: A triadic framework for collaborative consumption (CC): motives, activities and resources & capabilities of actors. J. Bus. Res. **79**, 219–227 (2017). https://doi.org/10.1016/j.jbusres.2017.05.004
4. Bettoni, A., et al.: Multi-sided digital manufacturing platform supporting exchange of unused company potential (2018). https://doi.org/10.1109/ICE.2018.8436294
5. Botsman, R., Rogers, R.: What's Mine Is Yours - How Collaborative Consumption is Changing the Way we live (2010). https://doi.org/10.1016/S0168-9525(00)00086-X

6. Carroll, J.M., Bellotti, V.: Creating value together: the emerging design space of peer-to-peer currency and exchange. In: Proceedings of the 18th ACM Conference on Computer Supported Cooperative Work & Social Computing, pp. 1500–1510. ACM, New York (2015). https://doi.org/10.1145/2675133.2675270

7. Cenamor, J., et al.: Adopting a platform approach in servitization: leveraging the value of digitalization. Int. J. Prod. Econ. **192**, 54–65 (2017). https://doi.org/10.1016/j.ijpe.2016.12.033

8. Cheng, M.: Sharing economy: a review and agenda for future research. Int. J. Hosp. Manag. **57**, 60–70 (2016). https://doi.org/10.1016/j.ijhm.2016.06.003

9. Cohen, B., Kietzmann, J.: Ride on! Mobility business models for the sharing economy. Organ. Environ. **27**(3), 279–296 (2014). https://doi.org/10.1177/1086026614546199

10. Cusumano, M.A.: How traditional firms must compete in the sharing economy. Commun. ACM **58**(1), 32–34 (2014). https://doi.org/10.1145/2688487

11. Hamari, J., et al.: The sharing economy: why people participate in collaborative consumption. J. Assoc. Inf. Sci. Technol. **67**(9), 2047–2059 (2016). https://doi.org/10.1002/asi.23552

12. Ian Barrett, M., et al.: Service innovation in the digital age: key contributions and future directions (2015). https://doi.org/10.25300/MISQ/2015/39:1.03

13. Ikkala, T., Lampinen, A.: Monetizing network hospitality. In: Proceedings of the 18th ACM Conference on Computer Supported Cooperative Work & Social Computing, CSCW 2015, pp. 1033–1044. ACM Press, New York (2015). https://doi.org/10.1145/2675133.2675274

14. Irani, L.: The cultural work of microwork. New Media Soc. **17**(5), 720–739 (2013). https://doi.org/10.1177/1461444813511926

15. Ke, Q.: Service providers of the sharing economy: who joins and who benefits? Proc. ACM Hum.-Comput. Interact. **1**(CSCW), 57:1–57:17 (2017). https://doi.org/10.1145/3134692

16. Kim, J., et al.: Why people participate in the sharing economy: a social exchange perspective. In: PACIS, p. 76 (2015)

17. Landolfi, G., et al.: An ontology based semantic data model supporting a MaaS digital platform. In: 2018 9th international Conference on Intelligent Systems (2018)

18. Lee, K., et al.: Characterizing and automatically detecting crowdturfing in Fiverr and Twitter. Soc. Netw. Anal. Min. **5**(1), 2 (2015). https://doi.org/10.1007/s13278-014-0241-1

19. Lenka, S., et al.: Digitalization capabilities as enablers of value co-creation in servitizing firms. Psychol. Mark. **34**(1), 92–100 (2017). https://doi.org/10.1002/mar.20975

20. Ma, X., et al.: Self-disclosure and perceived trustworthiness of Airbnb host profiles. In: Proceedings of the 2017 ACM Conference on Computer Supported Cooperative Work and Social Computing, CSCW 2017, pp. 2397–2409. ACM Press, New York (2017). https://doi.org/10.1145/2998181.2998269

21. Moser, C., et al.: Community commerce: facilitating trust in mom-to-mom sale groups on Facebook. In: Proceedings of the 2017 CHI Conference on Human Factors in Computing Systems, pp. 4344–4357. ACM, New York (2017). https://doi.org/10.1145/3025453.3025550

22. Parker, G., et al.: Platform Revolution. W. W. Norton & Company Inc., New York (2016)

23. Pee, L.G.: Affordances for sharing domain-specific and complex knowledge on enterprise social media. Int. J. Inf. Manag. **43**, 25–37 (2018). https://doi.org/10.1016/j.ijinfomgt.2018.05.006

24. Philip, H.E., et al.: Examining temporary disposition and acquisition in peer-to-peer renting. J. Mark. Manag. **31**(11–12), 1310–1332 (2015). https://doi.org/10.1080/0267257X.2015.1013490

25. Puschmann, T., Alt, R.: Sharing economy. Bus. Inf. Syst. Eng. **58**(1), 93–99 (2016). https://doi.org/10.1007/s12599-015-0420-2

26. Rosenblat, A., Stark, L.: Algorithmic labor and information asymmetries: a case study of Uber's drivers (2016)
27. Sarasua, C., Thimm, M.: Microtask available, Send us your CV! In: 2013 International Conference on Cloud and Green Computing, pp. 521–524 (2013). https://doi.org/10.1109/CGC.2013.87
28. Sutherland, W., Jarrahi, M.H.: The gig economy and information infrastructure. Proc. ACM Hum.-Comput. Interact. 1(CSCW), 1–24 (2017). https://doi.org/10.1145/3134732
29. Sutherland, W., Jarrahi, M.H.: The sharing economy and digital platforms: a review and research agenda. Int. J. Inf. Manag. 43, 328–341 (2018). https://doi.org/10.1016/j.ijinfomgt.2018.07.004
30. Täuscher, K., Laudien, S.M.: Understanding platform business models: a mixed methods study of marketplaces. Eur. Manag. J. 36(3), 319–329 (2018). https://doi.org/10.1016/j.emj.2017.06.005
31. Vargo, S.L., et al.: On value and value co-creation: a service systems and service logic perspective. Eur. Manag. J. 26(3), 145–152 (2008). https://doi.org/10.1016/j.emj.2008.04.003
32. Vendrell-Herrero, F., et al.: Servitization, digitization and supply chain interdependency. Ind. Mark. Manag. 60, 69–81 (2017). https://doi.org/10.1016/j.indmarman.2016.06.013
33. Weber, T.A.: Intermediation in a sharing economy: insurance, moral hazard, and rent extraction. J. Manag. Inf. Syst. 31(3), 35–71 (2014). https://doi.org/10.1080/07421222.2014.995520
34. Zibuschka, J., Laufs, U., Engelbach, W.: Stakeholder analysis of a platform and ecosystem for open innovation in SMEs. In: Camarinha-Matos, L.M., Boucher, X., Afsarmanesh, H. (eds.) PRO-VE 2010. IAICT, vol. 336, pp. 110–116. Springer, Heidelberg (2010). https://doi.org/10.1007/978-3-642-15961-9_12

Investigating Supply Chains Models and Enabling Technologies Towards Collaborative Networks

Elena Pessot[1]([⊠]), Andrea Zangiacomi[1], Frank Berkers[2],
David Hidalgo-Carvajal[3], Ron Weerdmeester[4],
and Rosanna Fornasiero[1]

[1] Institute of Intelligent Industrial Technologies and Systems for Advanced
Manufacturing, National Research Council of Italy, via Alfonso Corti 12,
20133 Milan, Italy
{elena.pessot,andrea.zangiacomi,
rosanna.fornasiero}@stiima.cnr.it
[2] TNO, Schoemakerstraat 97, 2628 VK Delft, The Netherlands
frank.berkers@tno.nl
[3] GCLOG Program MIT SCALE Network,
Massachusetts Institute of Technology,
1 Amherst Street, Cambridge, MA 02142, USA
hidalgod@mit.edu
[4] PNO Consultants, Blijde Inkomstlaan 1, 1040 Brussels, Belgium
ron.weerdmeester@pnoconsultants.com

Abstract. This research employs an extensive multiple case studies analysis to identify the most important business models affecting supply chain configurations and related enabling technologies towards the creation of collaborative networks. The results obtained from the investigation of 24 companies of manufacturing and process industry, informed by literature, identify four 'design principles' of business models, i.e. Personalized production, Servitization, Decentralized and modular production, and Recycle, Re-use and Sustainability. Each model is further described and discussed at the interplay between digitalization and collaborative network practices at supply chain level, showing that adopting one or a combination of the four design principles allows to actuate some of the most important features of collaboration like Vertical integration or networking of smart production systems, Horizontal integration through global value chain networks, Through-engineering across the entire value chain, Acceleration of manufacturing and Digitalization of products and services.

Keywords: Business models · Collaborative practice · Value chain · Digitalization · Supply chain

1 Introduction

Companies need to promote an efficient and sustainable production of high added value goods to remain competitive in global markets and respond to the demanding requirements of consumers [1]. The market dynamics require companies to adapt their

© IFIP International Federation for Information Processing 2019
Published by Springer Nature Switzerland AG 2019
L. M. Camarinha-Matos et al. (Eds.): PRO-VE 2019, IFIP AICT 568, pp. 335–343, 2019.
https://doi.org/10.1007/978-3-030-28464-0_29

business and links within the existing supply chains towards new reconfigured network collaborations and business models that shift from cost competitiveness to cooperative efforts for a higher added value of the supply chain as a whole [2, 3]. A greater vertical and horizontal integration between the involved actors should favor flexible, collaborative and interconnected networks of factories able to manage shorter cycles life of products while maintaining high levels of quality and resource efficiency [4]. Within this context, the digital technologies play a key role in enhancing the collaboration at value chain level and the integration of manufacturing and process sectors by improving flexibility and delivery of added value [4, 5]. Supply chain models are thus evolving in order to benefit from technological innovation (and digitalization), with advantages in promoting a higher focus on customer requirements, improving efficiency in resource utilization, enhancing modularization of products and services [1, 5]. Indeed, the mega-trends identified in literature as reshaping the process and manufacturing sectors are digitalization, customization, resources optimization, servitization and modularization. Nevertheless, companies are still struggling to leverage or react to the shifts characterizing the actual competitive landscape and the way they do their business, and further research is required.

According to the depicted context, the aim of this study is to investigate the enabling technologies and main practices fostering collaboration at supply chain level, basing on the exploration of current practices of companies at the intersection of digitalization and collaborative networks (as in [2]). With this goal, the unit of analysis is represented by the business models emerging from the current trends and consequent opportunities leveraged by companies in their business. Specifically, design principles of business models have been identified and characterized in terms of main features, impacts on supply chain (supply and demand side), technologies and types of collaboration and integration towards digitalization.

2 Methodology

Aiming to perform an exploratory qualitative research, a multiple case study design [6] has been employed. We purposefully selected 24 among leading European companies of high value-added goods demonstrating to leverage on at least one of the main trends identified (i.e. digitalization, customization, resources optimization, servitization and modularization) as the base for the "design principles" to be followed in shaping their business model. A stratified sampling has been adopted in order to have a set of cases including different kinds of value chain partners (i.e. raw material providers, manufacturers, logistics providers, clients), types of manufacturing (process/discrete) and flexibility (e.g. capacity, product, location), sectors, to conduct a cross-sectorial and holistic investigation.

Table 1 provides an overview of cases basing on the integration of these variables.

Data collection was based on semi-structured interviews and secondary data (publicly available and internal documentation provide by interviewees), also for triangulation purposes [6, 7]. Interviews have been conducted by the research team at company site or via Skype call and were based on a common protocol. Questions aimed at assessing the emerging supply chain configurations and business models basing on the combination of several dimensions of analysis: enabling technologies (with related readiness and impact on business model change), coordination and collaboration mechanisms along the supply chain, flexibility parameters to optimize flows in the value chain process, key activities involved in the delivery of value offer. Both multiple-choice (e.g. with provision of the list of technologies) and open questions were included, in order to enhance a further exploration of the real industrial cases. One to two respondents per each case were involved in the different interview meetings among the key roles in the digitalization, supply chain flows or strategy of their respective companies, e.g. CEOs, innovation, supply chain and operations managers.

Table 1. Overview of selected case studies.

Case	Brief description of company main activity and industry
C1	Leather fabrics supplier for customized consumer goods
C2	Flexible manufacturer of customized shoes
C3	Provider of rapid/additive manufactured components
C4	Steel machineries manufacturer for customized small scale batches
C5	Implantable drug delivery devices manufacturer
C6	REE logistics provider for industrial symbiosis
C7	Service provider for recycling tasks in chemicals
C8	Recyclable packaging manufacturer
C9	Aluminum printing plates provider, involved in recycle process
C10	Polymers supplier, focused on sustainability
C11	Mobile industrial processing of biomass
C12	Water utilities provider, involved in re-use process
C13	Processing of biomass flows into bio-based aromatics
C14	Logistics provider of post-consumer textile waste
C15	Pipeline transportation provider re-using residual gasses
C16	Energy- and feedstock intensive company involved in industrial symbiosis
C17	Metal and textile cleaning service provider
C18	Provider of chemical leasing for metal cleaning
C19	Remote chemical production control devices manufacturer
C20	Provider of data analytics software for integrated plant-wide scheduling and control
C21	Biopharmaceutical company developing transportable plants
C22	Food company with flexible modular factory
C23	Provider of equipment for container-based chemical manufacturing
C24	Functional molecule production manufacturer with modular factory

The collected data were qualitatively analyzed and coded independently by the researchers to identify common patterns and elements in the supply chain models, practices and enabling technologies. Emerging results were then compared until reaching agreement among researchers, and further presented and discussed in a workshop with experts from academic and industrial fields, aiming to assess their accuracy and significance for literature on collaborative network practices, digitalization and design principles of business models in a supply chain perspective.

3 Results

Results from pattern-matching and cross-case analysis [6, 7], informed by current literature (e.g. [3, 5]) allowed to identify four main design principles of business models to frame the investigation: Personalized production, Servitization, Decentralized and modular production, Recycle, Re-use and Sustainability (RR&S). These business models are not completely independent from each other and are able to capture the majority of megatrends considered in the study even if they are addressing one of them in a more significant way than the others. This section includes the description of main features, involved value chain actors, type of collaborations and enabling technologies to activate each design principle of business model emerging from the analysis of the cases and the current trends in manufacturing and process industry.

A further analysis of the results, building on the work by [2], allowed to identify how the digital technologies adopted in the implementation of the four models enable the key features of collaborative models at the interplay with digitalization, i.e. Vertical integration or networking of smart production systems, Horizontal integration through global value chain networks, Through-engineering across the entire value chain, Acceleration of manufacturing and Digitalization of products and services.

3.1 Personalized Production

Customization has emerged over the past two decades as one of the strategies that allows companies to differentiate their offer through innovative products, where added value is given by meeting the specific needs of a customer or a target group of customers thanks to highly flexible manufacturing systems [8, 9]. The shift towards personalization is reinforced by new manufacturing technology developments, e.g. in advanced robotics, additive manufacturing and advanced digital simulation of manufacturing processes, enabling shorter production runs and more one-of-a-kind products [5]. Supply chains for personalized products enhance consumers to have products with a unique design and style, along with functional and comfort-related aspects, even in the more traditional sectors, and to make a choice in terms of value, functionality and performance [3].

Enabling Technologies for Personalized Production. Enabling technologies include: 3D scanning, additive manufacturing (as 3D printing) and multi-purpose and hybrid processes for the production of customized components or products; virtual and augmented reality for supporting sales processes; modelling and simulation, business intelligence and sensors to enable changes in product and processes and reconfiguration of production networks; big data to optimize data driven manufacturing, better management of the innovation and the definition and analysis of the effects of location of the supply chain.

Collaborative Practices for Personalized Production. In the attempt to rapidly reconfigure to satisfy custom requirements, the manufacturing systems should develop a high level of integration with customers/users, who become the main creators of the solution produced. For example, C2 developed direct customer relations by avoiding intermediaries as retailers and using on-line channels and platform strategy. Some technologies are also changing the relationships between business partners, as smart materials for C2: material suppliers are becoming technology providers, subject to strict selection and performance evaluation. Therefore, companies along the supply chain need to develop new business models and flexible manufacturing systems capable of producing relatively small batches of customized products at competitive costs, as C4, which outsourced both design and production of part of components to reduce complexity.

Basing on the analysis of the enabling technologies and practices, we can argue that the activation of the Personalized production model allows to realize the dimension of Horizontal integration through value chain, especially with customers for collecting their needs and integrate design activities through 3D scanning and big data analytics; the Through-engineering across the entire value chain thanks to collaborative product design and configuration, also with the use of smart materials; the digitalization of products and services through the use of Virtual reality and Internet of Things in supporting sales channels and design process.

3.2 Servitization

As more companies and industries in the world are increasingly adding value to their products by including additional services [10], the need for a clear business model becomes more relevant. This provides the opportunity for the development of servitization (also known as Product Service System (PSS) [11]) as a design principle that significantly changes the dynamics in a typical value chain, also in terms of services that could be oriented to the product, user, or result [12]. Companies are deciding to offer a broader set of products, ranging from mere products, to bundles of product-services and finally experience-based products and services [13, 14]. Indeed, servitization leads the shift from a traditional linear supply chain centered on the product to a supply chain that increases the relevance of the services around the product, with key differences in terms of risks, responsibilities, ownership shared among the PSS provider and its partners in a value chain.

Enabling Technologies for Servitization. The technologies that have the largest impact in this model are focused on information sharing, monitoring and diagnostic, prognostic analysis and decision-support and include big data and big data analytics (with descriptive, predictive and prescriptive purposes), cloud computing and mobile platforms for customer communication and data access, IoT to enable automatic monitoring along the overall value chain, 3D printing for refurbishing, telemedicine and 360-degree medical data for the e-health services.

Collaborative Practices for Servitization. This design principle creates new relationships between a "supplier" and a "user/buyer", transforming the interaction usually based on single transactions into a long-term ongoing relationship, which can include the delivery of services, goods, management and knowledge. For example, C18 developed result-oriented servitization whereby the supplier and buyer collaborate in a form of payment called "paid per service unit", while reducing production costs and environmental impacts, improving expertise of both parts and optimizing processes.

Beyond the strategy of the single company, the collaboration along the overall supply chain need to become more flexible and agile to incorporate a reconfiguration of the relationship between the manufacturer and the customer. C5 improved customer intimacy to grow trust, understanding of customer needs and faster achievement of outcomes through virtual communications.

It is possible to infer that the implementation of new technologies in this design principle will lead to develop of new services and complement current product offering, towards the dimension of Digitalization of products and services. Moreover, available technologies (Big data, Artificial intelligence, Automation, etc.) are becoming increasingly useful as they generate valuable information to the provider and generate an opportunity for a closer relationship with customer and for the dimension of Horizontal integration along product life-cycle, proving to be a key component in the introduction of new services.

3.3 Decentralized and Modular Production

Companies decentralizing their manufacturing split the production processes into smaller plants to produce in different locations or regions. Decentralized and modular production has effects on the organizational structure of companies, which can be more effective by focusing on their core activity, and on the value chain, which is broken down over more decision-making units that may be outsourced or procured at different locations. This shift leads to supply chains based on economies of scale and customer-specific, from process optimization to agile and distributed processing needs [15].

Enabling Technologies for Decentralized and Modular Production. Enabling technologies for this design principle need to support modularity, ICT for control, electrification, equipment manufacturing referred to novel inexpensive mass production technologies, process intensification and continuous processing and recovery/work-up. These include electrically powered chemical technologies, 3D printing and automated process control for manufacturing, and big data, skid based designs and plate based equipment for engineering.

Collaborative Practices for Decentralized and Modular Production. The business case of small-scale production is mainly focused on locating the production facility closer to the customer. For example, C21 is developing plants consisting of modular building blocks that can be easily extended to address increase in market demand or even adapted to fit in a container, to be easily transportable close to customer location. This changes a pivotal part of the supply chain in the manufacturing and sourcing stages. Also the container-base manufacturing in the value chain of C23 allows for local production and direct use of equipment and produced goods, with transportation discarded from the supply chain and consequent less impact on price volatility. Moreover, the decentralized supply chain is not fixed and can change based on the specific case at hand, with the large scale producer elements that can either be bypassed or integrated in the new supply chain.

Basing on the analysis of the enabling technologies and practices, we can argue that the activation of the Decentralized and modular production model allows to realize the dimension of Vertical integration, with the collaboration among small scale platforms, and the Acceleration of manufacturing, thanks to the increased use of technologies as electrically powered chemical technologies and multilayer disposable plants for small scale production.

3.4   Recycle, Re-use and Sustainability (RR&S)

RR&S business model is based on the principle of Circular Economy, where resource input and waste, emission, and energy leakage are reduced by slowing, closing, and narrowing material and energy loops [16]. The introduction of such a model has impact on both upstream (changed collaboration with raw material suppliers), downstream (collection of waste) and side stream (industrial symbiosis) value chain partners as well as on the value proposition (e.g. new recycling, extended producer responsibility or industrial symbiosis services), with closed material loops [17]. For example, C6 is creating new feedstock types based on waste, contributing to feedstock flexibility as well as environmental benefits with reduced impacts by providing alternative added value.

Enabling Technologies for RR&S. Recycling refers to technologies that aim to recover materials from end-of-life products as disassembly and separation techniques. Technologies and solutions for industrial symbiosis represent an important area of development. Optimization of material use will increasingly see a combination of recyclability and biodegradable materials (e.g. in packaging). Novel "repair technologies" for industrial processes, such as 3D printing enable remanufacturing and repair. Key information and telecommunication technologies support the mapping, tracking and matching of materials throughout the supply chain. Moreover, data driven simulation of business model, product-ageing and reverse supply chain support decision making in the development and design of Circular Economy operations and organizations.

Collaborative Practices for RR&S. The RR&S supply chain requires significant built of trust and collaboration among partners, from design for recycling up to dismantle for recycling (so called "reverse logistics"), from the planning and coordination of the circular supply chain to decision making in terms of remanufacturing, refurbishing and repair. It hence requires solutions that favor value chain coordination from end-of-life collection, treatment and re-introduction as a resource in the primary production process. For example, C13 is innovating the process to be more efficient, introducing new actors in the value chain, reinforcing relationships with neighboring industries and redefining capacity, location and feedstock flexibility for maximizing sustainability and recycling opportunities.

It is possible to infer that the implementation of an RR&S business model allows to enable more than one dimension of collaborative networks, i.e. Horizontal integration, also thanks the adoption of trusted cloud based platforms, e.g. for waste value chain management, the Vertical integration through product-ageing simulation, and Acceleration of manufacturing through selective separation technologies and automated disassembly.

4 Discussion and Conclusions

This study performed a broad investigation of 24 companies of manufacturing and process industry to identify the most important business model affecting supply chain configurations and related enabling technologies towards the creation of collaborative networks. Basing on this analysis, we can argue that the four design principles analyzed enable all the characteristics of collaborative networks for the digitalization of the overall value chain, i.e. Vertical integration or networking of smart production systems, Horizontal integration through global value chain networks, Through-engineering across the entire value chain, Acceleration of manufacturing and Digitalization of products and services, and the integration of the manufacturing and process industry. Design principles are addressed to any type of collaborative network described in [2], i.e. one business model (design principle) does not preclude the implementation of one collaborative network or another. Moreover, the enabling technologies should be targeted for sustaining specific collaborative practices, but also developed in a systemic perspective for enhancing the overall supply chain performance.

Obtained results contribute to advance knowledge in the research on digitalization and collaborative networks by adopting a perspective integrating business model design principles, enabling technologies and collaborative practices implemented at the value chain level. Managers should develop one or a combination of these design principles on the basis of company's competitive priorities, while considering the value chain perspective, in order to foster practices with downstream and upstream actors enabling the digitalization and the implementation of a holistic collaborative network approach. Even if design principles identified in the empirical investigation are not completely new, the originality of the paper consists in providing industry practitioners with examples that can be considered and configured in their own contexts as a sort of 'working ingredients' clustered around the design principles identified. An expected impact is a wider adoption of the business models guiding supply chains configurations towards collaborative networks, in order to improve competitiveness and resilience of European industry in dealing with major industrial challenges.

A recognized limitation of the study concerns the methodology and the sampling adopted that can pre-determine to some extent the emerging patterns of design principles. Nevertheless, the focus is on the exploration of the design principles at the base of supply chains configuration to foster their adoption towards collaborative networks, rather than the identification of the principles themselves.

Acknowledgments. This research has been conducted as part of the INSPIRE project, which has received funding from the European Union's Horizon 2020 Research and Innovation program under Grant Agreement n°723748. The authors wish to acknowledge their appreciation to the European Commission for their support and to all the project team for their contribution during the development of this research.

References

1. Ben-Daya, M., Hassini, E., Bahroun, Z.: Internet of things and supply chain management: a literature review. Int. J. Prod. Res. (2017). https://doi.org/10.1080/00207543.2017.1402140
2. Camarinha-Matos, L.M., Fornasiero, R., Afsarmanesh, H.: Collaborative networks as a core enabler of industry 4.0. In: Camarinha-Matos, L.M., Afsarmanesh, H., Fornasiero, R. (eds.) PRO-VE 2017. IAICT, vol. 506, pp. 3–17. Springer, Cham (2017). https://doi.org/10.1007/978-3-319-65151-4_1
3. Fornasiero, R., Zangiacomi, A., Franchini, V., Bastos, J., Azevedo, A., Vinelli, A.: Implementation of customisation strategies in collaborative networks through an innovative Reference Framework. Prod. Plan. Control 27(14), 1158–1170 (2016)
4. Büyüközkan, G., Göçer, F.: Digital supply chain: literature review and a proposed framework for future research. Comput. Ind. 97, 157–177 (2018)
5. Ivanov, D., Dolgui, A., Sokolov, B.: The impact of digital technology and Industry 4.0 on the ripple effect and supply chain risk analytics. Int. J. Prod. Res. (2018). https://doi.org/10.1080/00207543.2018.1488086
6. Yin, R.K.: Case Study Research: Design and Methods, 5th edn. SAGE Publications, Thousand Oaks (2013)
7. Voss, C., Tsikriktsis, N., Frohlich, M.: Case research in operations management. Int. J. Oper. Prod. Manag. 22(2), 195–219 (2002)
8. Ivanov, D., Das, A., Choi, T.M.: New flexibility drivers for manufacturing, supply chain and service operations. Int. J. Prod. Res. 56(10), 3359–3368 (2018)
9. Montalto, A., Graziosi, S., Bordegoni, M., Di Landro, L., van Tooren, M.J.L..: An approach to design reconfigurable manufacturing tools to manage product variability: the mass customisation of eyewear. J. Int. Manuf. 1–16 (2018). https://doi.org/10.1007/s10845-018-1436-5
10. Vandermerwe, S., Rada, J.: Servitization of business: adding value by adding services. Eur. Manag. J. 6(4), 314–324 (1988)
11. Goedkoop, M.J., van Halen, C.J., te Riele, H.R., Rommens, P.J.: Product Service systems, Ecological and Economic Basics. PRE consultants, Amersfoort (1999)
12. Reim, W., Parida, V., Örtqvist, D.: Product-Service Systems (PSS) business models and tactics – a systematic literature review. J. Clean. Prod. 97, 61–75 (2015)
13. Hassenzahl, M., Diefenbach, S., Göritz, A.: Needs, affect, and interactive products – facets of user experience. Interact. Comput. 22(5), 353–362 (2010)
14. Kimbell, L.: Designing for service as one way of designing services. Int. J. Des. 5(2), 41–52 (2011)
15. Srai, J.S., Kumar, M., Graham, G., et al.: Distributed manufacturing: scope, challenges and opportunities. Int. J. Prod. Res. 54, 6917–6935 (2016)
16. Witjes, S., Lozanoa, R.: Towards a more circular economy: proposing a framework linking sustainable public procurement and sustainable business models. Res. Conserv. Recycl. 112, 37–44 (2016)
17. Bocken, N.M.P., de Pauw, I., Bakker, C., van der Grinten, B.: Product design and business model strategies for a circular economy. J. Ind. Prod. Eng. 33(5), 308–320 (2016)

Toward an Agile Adaptation of Supply Chain Planning: A Situational Use Case

Sanaa Tiss[1(✉)], Caroline Thierry[2], Jacques Lamothe[1],
and Christophe Rousse[3]

[1] Universite de Toulouse, Centre Génie Industriel, IMT Mines Albi, Albi, France
sanaa.tiss@mines-albi.fr
[2] Universite de Toulouse, IRIT, Université Toulouse Jean Jaurès,
Toulouse, France
[3] Supply Chain Direction Pierre Fabre Dermo-Cosmetics, Lavaur, France

Abstract. The project CAASC "Cloud Adaptation for an Agile Supply Chain" (French ANR project) aims to develop monitoring services in multi actors supply chain, by integrating uncertainties in supply chain planning and developing adaptation functions to environment changes.

In this paper we present a use case in the form of a serious game that aim to emerge and validate the required functionalities for the project. The game simulates a collaborative rolling horizon mid-term planning process. By analyzing its processes and results, we identify the central role of deviations analysis of plans to qualify uncertainties, assess robustness and propose response strategies.

Keywords: Collaborative supply chain planning ·
Uncertainties and robustness · Serious game

1 Toward an Agile Supply Chain

The CAASC "Cloud Adaptation for an Agile Supply Chain" project considers a supply chain composed of a set of entities that collaborate in the planning of flows of products, services, and finance. Each entity organizes manufacturing and distribution activities using plans managed by several decision-making centers (multi-actors). CAASC is focusing on coordination problems related to mid-term rolling horizon planning decisions across an internal supply chain.

CAASC takes advantage of three main services developed in a monitoring perspective of supply chain mid-term plans during the H2020-FoF project called C2NET "Cloud Collaborative Manufacturing Networks" [1]: (i) the modeling service which uses collected data (current plans for demand, production, supply, distribution and inventories) to maintain a model of a supply chain according to a reference meta-model. (ii) the detection of deviations service which compares the supply chain status model to the model expressed from the originally validated plans, and therefore detects deviations that are changing the validated plans. (iii) the adaptation service which is a rule-based system that proposes adaptation processes according to some business rules and deviations characteristics.

L. M. Camarinha-Matos et al. (Eds.): PRO-VE 2019, IFIP AICT 568, pp. 344–354, 2019.
https://doi.org/10.1007/978-3-030-28464-0_30

Still focusing on the monitoring services, CAASC aims at developing new features in order to develop robustness as well as agility of the solution while taking advantage of some results of C2NET. Moreover, we are interested in deviation measurement and the interpretation of these movements to quantify and qualify uncertainties.

From a decision maker point of view, uncertainty in the uncontrollable variables of supply chain planning can induce deviations; therefore, increase the nervousness of the plans [2–4].

Different approaches in planning uncertainty modelling are proposed in the literature. Uncertainty in the considered uncontrollable variables can be described mainly by intervals [5], probability distribution [6, 7] or fuzzy sets [8–11].

Using uncertainty modeling, we aim to assess the robustness of plans, enhance anticipation and create a tradeoff between robustness [12] and agility of supply chain planning. However, the project partners belong to different domains (industrial, software developers, supply chain or artificial intelligence researchers) and they do not necessarily know totally interpret the consequences of rolling horizon planning and its related constraints. Thus, before even considering the complexity of integrating uncertainties in collaborative rolling horizon planning, an As-Is emulation was used in a deterministic context to share a user experience. We chose the serious game method for this emulation.

Serious games are known for their use in higher education [13, 14]. Furthermore, many famous serious games are used in trainings. For instance, serious games such as "Beer Game" [15] or "The Fresh Connection" [16] are a supply chain simulation game where the main functions of the company are represented. Serious game has also been used to analyze the dynamic decision-making process in supply [17].

In our case, we chose the serious game method for other reasons, mainly to:

- enable industrial partners to validate a use representative case situation,
- frame the research topic and identify the problems related to the collaborative planning within a rolling horizon process,
- share competences and points of view of the different users,
- allow partners to project themselves into decision-making and validate needs and specifications in terms of agility and robustness evaluation,
- formalize a use case that can be retested to assess the proposed functionalities.

A collaborative approach with the partners of the project (end user, software company, research laboratories) has been adopted to design the serious game. Starting by an industrial interview and a survey on APICS as a reference of planning processes modeling, the collaborative mid-term planning processes was modelled. Then, were defined the components of the game simulating the dynamic of those processes and the physical flow related to the game. After that, in a prepared environment the game was run, and results were collected. Finally, the results issued from the game were analyzed and the main problems and requirement were identified in terms of agility and CAASC functionalities development.

2 Process Under Study

2.1 Industrial Case and APICS Process

The project will provide use cases that come from an analysis of Pierre Fabre Dermo Cosmetics (PFDC) company processes. A series of interviews took place in order to understand the actual process of planning and collaboration between different partners in the supply chain (Fig. 1).

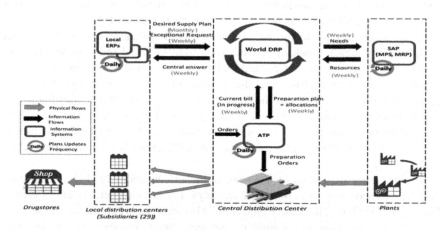

Fig. 1. PFDC supply chain (tactical level).

PFDC supply chain is composed of the following stakeholders: suppliers, manufacturing plants (in France), Central Distribution Centre (in France), local subsidiaries or partners and final customers (drugstores) all over the world [18].

Within CAASC, PFDC supply chain supported by a cloud platform links its various actors. The supply chain is a collaborative network of actors that use the platform in order to perform their collaborative planning process.

Production is stored in a central warehouse in France before being distributed to subsidiaries and partners. PFDC is always trying to improve its performances in terms of service. Aligning the plans of the supply chain partners, agile deployment of stocks and the optimization of the distribution of inventories among the subsidiaries are the primary objectives.

In the context of this industrial case, APICS [19] is our reference to model a generic collaborative planning process.

Considering the supply chain described in the Fig. 1, subsidiaries planners, a supply planner and a production planner are the partners collaborating in the supply chain planning. The master plans exchanged between partners are mainly: Sales and Operations plans, Distribution Requirement planning, Master Production Scheduling [19].

Planning changes are limited by the time fences and delivery time. "Changes that are far off on the planning horizon can be made with little or no cost or disruption to manufacturing, but the nearer to delivery date, the more disruptive and costly changes will be" [19].

In the frozen zone, planning changes are not allowed and required the approval of the decision maker in case of emergency. The slushy zone is a tradeoffs zone, downward demand (conv. Upward production) request is automatically accepted while the upward demand (conv. Downward production) must be confirmed by decision makers. Finally, in the liquid zone the changes are automatically accepted and usually done by the computer within the defined limits of the plans.

2.2   Collaborative Planning Process

The Fig. 2 below details the inputs and outputs (decisions) of every planning related to each partner in the supply chain and for each level of planning. Four steps are identified in the planning process and three different decision makers are concerned:

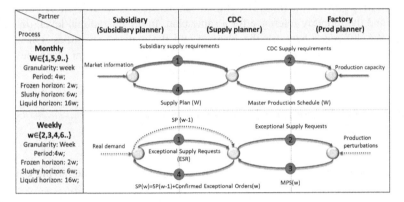

Fig. 2. Collaborative supply chain planning process

Each subsidiary elaborates its sales forecast and define its supply requirements. The confirmed requirements present the desired supply plan from the Central Distribution Center. Each subsidiary order on its own without regard for the available inventory of the distribution center neither the requirements of other subsidiaries nor the pro-duction schedule. However, the supply planner in the CDC has the richest view on all the independent supply chain system (SAP, world DRP) due to his position as coordinator and CDC resource manager in the supply chain.

We make the difference between two levels of planning process. The monthly planning process and the weekly one.

Monthly, in the first week of the month, the requirements of the different subsidiaries are consolidated to become the base of supply chain resources dimensioning for the current month. The resulted plans of this process are the reference of the rest of the month.

Every week, the DRP and MPS master plans are reviewed and can be changed in case of perturbations. We consider perturbations related to the occurrence of a set of events mainly: Demand variation (real sales); Subsidiaries exceptional requests (promotion, shortage…); Quality control problem (rejection of products, high control time…); Operational production problem (breakdowns, closure, schedule changes, order splitting or aggregation, …); Transportation problems (lost products, customs delay).

Regarding time fences, it was identified a planning horizon of 24 weeks including a frozen horizon of 2 weeks plus delivery time, slushy horizon of 6 weeks and liquid horizon of 16 weeks.

2.3   Supply Chain Planning Process Analysis

A deterministic supply chain planning is considered. The variables of supply chain planning such as lead time, costs and other system parameters, are considered known with certainty. In a decision process (weekly or monthly), depending on his role, each decision maker receives, decides and sends plans (forecast, requirement, supply, capacity). The received plans are uncontrollable variables on which uncertainty could be modelled. Conversely, the sent plans become uncontrollable variables for other deciders.

In a rolling horizon planning context, deviations are a set of differences between the weekly and the monthly reference for a same plan. In the operational level, deviations present the difference between the planned and the realized quantities. On received plans deviations enable to qualify uncertainty. On decided and sent plans, deviations enable to qualify robustness of service rate and nervousness.

3   A Serious Game as a Proof of Concept

3.1   Game Description

To best simulate the modelled supply chain planning process while having consistent results, the serious game was sized as follow (Figs. 3 and 4):

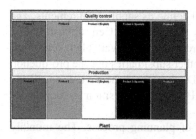

Fig. 3. Plant game board

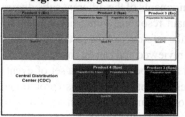

Fig. 4. CDC game board

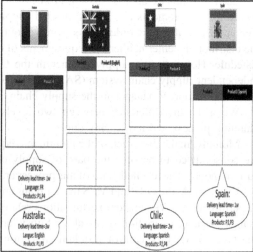

Fig. 5. Subsidiaries game board

- 4 subsidiaries (France, Australia, Spain, Chile); 1 CDC; 1 factory.
- 5 Products: P1 (English), P2 (Spanish), P3 (Spanish), P3 (English), P4 (English). Products are different according to the packaging language. French is a default language in packaging. In order to avoid a shortage, P3 (Spanish) can be sent to Australia and conversely P3 (English) to Spain or Chile.

The game board is designed as shown in Figs. 5, 6 and 7.

In addition to the board game, Excel sheets have been designed as a planning decision support enabling to keep a written record of the game. These sheets are shared on a platform allowing the simultaneous modification of the data. Each decision view is a worksheet [20].

Product code	Process type	Semaine	WD	M1	M2	M3	M4	M5	M6	M7	M8	M9	M10	M11
1134	Monthly;Computer;Decision 2: W1	France Supply Requirements(W1)		30	70	60	50	50	50	50	50	50	50	50
1134		Australia Supply Requirements(W1)		20	50	50	50	50	50	50	50	50	60	68
1134		Objective stock		230	210	200	200	200	200	200	210	228	238	240
1134		MPS(W0)		110	100	100	100	100	100	100	110	118	120	120
1134		CDC Supply Requirement		110	100	100	100	100	100	100	110	118	120	120
1134		Projected stock	170	230	210	200	200	200	200	200	210	228	238	240
1134	Monthly;Decision 3: W1	MPS (W1)		110	100	100	100	100	100	100	110	118	120	120
1134		Projected stock_MPS(W1)	170	230	210	200	200	200	200	200	210	228	238	240
1134		Supply Plan_France (W0)		30	70	60	50	50	50	50	50	50	50	50
1134	Monthly;Decision 4: W1	Supply Plan_France(W1)		30	70	60	50	50	50	50	50	50	50	50
1134		France Project Stock(W1)	140	140	160	110	100	130	110	100	100	100	100	100
1134		Supply Plan_Australia (W0)		20	50	50	50	50	50	50	50	50	60	68
1134		Supply Plan-Australia(W1)		20	50	50	50	50	50	50	50	50	60	68
1134		Australia Project Stock(W1)	140	110	90	70	40	30	70	100	100	100	100	100
1134		Supply Plan(W1)		50	120	110	100	100	100	100	100	100	110	118
1134		Stock CDC_proj. Supply Plan(W1)	170	230	210	200	200	200	200	200	210	228	238	240
1134	Weekly;Computer;Decision 2 :w2	Supply Plan_France (W1)		70	60	50	50	50	50	50	50	50	50	50
1134		Except. Supply Requirement_France (W2)		0	0	0	0	0	0	0	0	0	0	0
1134		Supply Plan_Australia (W1)		50	50	50	50	50	50	50	50	50	60	68
1134		except. Supply Requirement_Australia (W2)		0	0	0	0	0	0	0	0	0	0	0
1134		MPS (W1)		100	100	100	100	100	100	110	118	120	120	
1134		Except. CDC Supply Requirement (W2)		0	0	0	0	0	0	0	0	0	0	
1134	Weekly;Decision 3:W2	CDC projected stock	230	210	200	200	200	200	200	210	228	238	240	
1134		MPS (W2)		100	100	100	100	100	100	110	118	120	120	
1134		Stock_CDC proj. MPS(W2)	230	210	200	200	200	200	200	210	228	238	240	
1134		ESR_France		0	0	0	0	0	0	0	0	0	0	
1134		Supply Plan_France(W2)		70	60	50	50	50	50	50	50	50	50	
1134	Weekly;Decision 4: w2	France projected stock(s)	140	160	110	100	130	110	100	100	100	100	100	
1134		ESR-Australia		0	0	0	0	0	0	0	0	0	0	
1134		Supply Plan-Australia(W2)		50	50	50	50	50	50	50	50	60	68	
1134		Australia projected stock(W2)	110	90	70	40	30	70	100	100	100	100	100	
1134		Supply Plan(W2)		120	110	100	100	100	100	100	100	110	118	
1134		Stock CDC_proj. Supply Plan(W2)	230	210	200	200	200	200	200	210	228	238	240	

| Computer Calculation | System status | Decision | Data (previous plans,other partners decisions) | Frozen zone | Slusy zone | Liquid zone |

Fig. 6. Extraction from the supply planner view (planning of week1 and 2) (Color figure online)

Every decision view is enriched by a set of the decision support tools. They are as follows:

- The projected stock presents the impacts of every decision on stocks with significant colors: Orange in case of a planned consumption of the objective stock and red in case of a planned shortage.
- The previous plans and the current ones can be compared to highlight the deviations and the executed modifications.
- The proposed plans are automatically calculated from the available data.

In accordance to the supply chain planning process, a role sheet exists for each player (Subsidiary planner, supply planner, production planner). Furthermore, a game master has been designated to manage the time of the game and the stocks of other subsidiaries (other than France) and to announce predefined disturbance cards for other players Finally, a test session has been conducted with CAASC project partners. The processes (Figs. 7 and 8) below describe how the session unfolds:

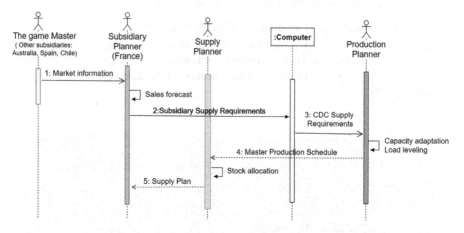

Fig. 7. Decisions flow: monthly supply chain process

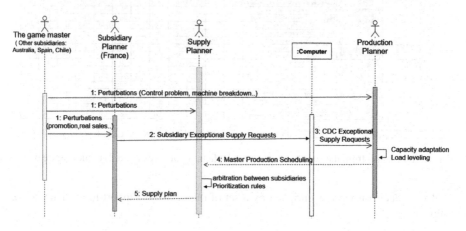

Fig. 8. Decisions flow: weekly supply chain process

3.2   Game Analysis

The game was played once for one supply chain. Authors played the role of the game master and informed subsidiary players about real demand, market changes and production perturbations.

By the end of the game session, two types of analysis of plans on the rolling horizon are performed: (i) The plan deviation measures the difference two successive plans; (ii) the planning error measure the difference between the planned and real (demanded or delivered) quantities.

In the following, the analysis focuses on the relation between one subsidiary (France) and the Central Distribution Center (CDC) and product P1.

Table 1. Scenario of the game for product P1

Week	Network echelon	Scenario (perturbations)
1	No one	Everything is normal and in line with the forecast
2	Subsidiary	Sales vary from ±10 compared to forecasts
3	Subsidiary	Registered sales compared to forecasts: Australia (−10 P1), France (+20 P1)
4	Subsidiary	Registered sales compared to forecasts: Australia (+10 P1), France (−40 P1)
5	Subsidiary	In France: promotion on product P1 on weeks 10 to 14. A doubling of sales is planned on the period. 80% of the sales increase are an anticipation of sales originally forecasted on weeks 15 to 20

Table 2. Deviations of **S**upply **R**equirements (France;P1) = **SR**[w](t) − **SR**[w − 1](t).

Week	t2	t3	t4	t5	t6	t7	t8	t9	t10	t11	t12	t13	t14	t15	t16	t17	t18
w2	0	0	0	0	0	0	0	0	0	0	0	0	0	0	0	0	0
w3		10	0	0	0	0	0	0	0	0	0	0	0	0	0	0	0
w4			20	20	0	0	10	0	0	0	0	0	0	0	0	0	0
w5				-10	30	100	40	50	50	-30	-30	-20	-10	-10	0	0	0
w6					-30	0	40	0	0	0	0	0	0	0	0	0	0

Table 3. Deviations of **S**upply **P**lans (France;P1) = **SP**[w](t) − **SP**[w − 1](t).

Week	t2	t3	t4	t5	t6	t7	t8	t9	t10	t11	t12	t13	t14	t15	t16	t17	t18	t19
w2	0	0	0	0	0	0	0	0	0	0	0	0	0	0	0	0	0	0
w3		0	0	0	0	0	10	0	0	0	0	0	0	0	0	0	0	0
w4			0	0	0	0	0	0	0	0	0	0	0	0	0	0	0	0
w5				0	0	100	40	50	50	-30	-30	-20	-10	-10	0	0	0	0
w6					0	0	40	0	0	0	0	0	0	0	0	0	0	0

Table 4. Supply Requirements Error = $SR[w](t) - SR[t](t)$.

Week	t2	t3	t4	t5	t6
w1	0	-10	-20	-10	0
w2	0	-10	-20	-10	0
w3		0	-20	-10	0
w4			0	10	0
w5				0	30
w6					0

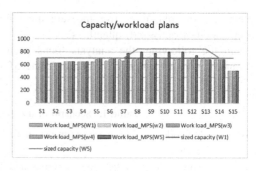

Fig. 9. Production capacity/workload analysis

In Tables 2 and 3, the deviation on Supply Requirements (request from subsidiary) and on Supply plan (answer of CDC) make easier the analysis of the propagation of information within the supply chain. In yellow, appear the Supply Requirement deviations that are requested by the subsidiary within the frozen horizon and not accepted by the CDC. These requests appear to mitigate errors between the subsidiary last forecast and the real customer demand he faces. In week 5, the subsidiary is informed of a promotion (see Table 1). In orange in Tables 2 and 3, appear the impact of the promotion information on the supply requirements.

In red in Tables 2 and 3, appear the process of request and acceptance of a change: it is first requested on week 3 on period t3 in SR, accepted in week 3 on t8 in SP, and maintained at week 4 on t8 in SR.

In Fig. 9, the propagation of the above variation till the factory is depicted. The initial sized capacity was 700 products per week, the amount requirements received from the CDC increase the workload, and the production planner decide to resize the capacity in the week 5 (first week of the second month) to become 850 for the weeks 8 to 12.

In Table 4, the supply Requirement error is shown for weeks 2 to 6. This error can hardly be interpreted according to the game scenario. But it shows the imprecision of the plan.

This user experience enabled to validate the following requirements for the uncertainty integration:

- characterization of the uncertainties undergone by a decision-maker by analyzing deviations and variations in deterministic plans along a rolling horizon. Machine learning tools will be used to well characterize this uncertainty from data collected from the industrial case,
- categorization of products according to the type of uncertainty,
- consideration of uncertainties in the uncontrollable variables to develop and enrich a user decision support interface,
- evaluation of user decisions (plans) in terms of robustness and stability against different disruption scenarios.

4   Conclusion and Future Works

The game simulates the production and distribution of cosmetics supply chain reproducing the current functioning of PFDC planning. It reproduces 2 planning processes: a monthly that starts from sales forecasts to size the resources of the supply chain and a weekly process to adjust plans based on requests in case of perturbation. This version will allow us in the future to implement the complete Serious Game, confronting this time the current and future processes that integrate the functionalities of the project CAASC while considering uncertainty in planning parameters.

The planning errors (difference between scheduled quantities and the real demand (or the real deliveries)) will be the basis for characterizing uncertainties. Otherwise, the plans deviations through the rolling horizon (deviations between successive plans) allow to better isolate the perturbations and their propagation in the supply chain which will enable to make the uncertainties explainable.

The serious game session, as a user experience, enabled partners to validate the required functionalities for the project in terms of uncertainty modelling and integration of uncertainty models in the user decision support interface.

Acknowledgement. Authors want to acknowledge ANR for the funding of the CAASC project.

References

1. Jiang, Z., Lamothe, J., Bénaben, F.: Meta-modeling of collaborative supply chain. In: Mertins, K., Jardim-Gonçalves, R., Popplewell, K., Mendonça, J.P. (eds.) Enterprise Interoperability VII. PIC, vol. 8, pp. 307–320. Springer, Cham (2016). https://doi.org/10.1007/978-3-319-30957-6_25
2. van Donselaar, K., van den Nieuwenhof, J., Visschers, J.: The impact of material coordination concepts on planning stability in supply chains. Int. J. Prod. Econ. **68**, 169–176 (2000)
3. Kadipasaoglu, S.N., Sridharan, V.: Alternative approaches for reducing schedule instability in multistage manufacturing under demand uncertainty. J. Oper. Manag. **13**, 193–211 (1995)
4. Koca, E., Yaman, H., Aktürk, M.S.: Stochastic lot sizing problem with nervousness considerations. Comput. Oper. Res. **94**, 23–37 (2018)
5. Guillaume, R., Thierry, C., Zieliński, P.: Robust material requirement planning with cumulative demand under uncertainty. Int. J. Prod. Res. **55**, 6824–6845 (2017)
6. Birge, J.R., Louveaux, F.: Introduction to Stochastic Programming. Springer, New York (2011). https://doi.org/10.1007/978-1-4614-0237-4
7. Gholamian, N., Mahdavi, I., Tavakkoli-Moghaddam, R.: Multi-objective multi-product multi-site aggregate production planning in a supply chain under uncertainty: fuzzy multi-objective optimisation. Int. J. Comput. Integr. Manuf. **29**, 149–165 (2016)
8. Dubois, D., Prade, H.: Representation and combination of uncertainty with belief functions and possibility measures. Comput. Intell. **4**, 244–264 (1988)
9. Fargier, H., Thierry, C.: The use of possibilistic decision theory in manufacturing planning and control: recent results in fuzzy master production scheduling, p. 15
10. Grabot, B., Geneste, L., Reynoso-Castillo, G., Vérot, S.: Integration of uncertain and imprecise orders in the MRP method. J. Intell. Manuf. **16**, 215–234 (2005)

11. Sun, G., Liu, Y., Lan, Y.: Fuzzy two-stage material procurement planning problem. J. Intell. Manuf. **22**, 319–331 (2011)
12. Genin, P., Thomas, A., Lamouri, S.: How to manage robust tactical planning with an APS (Advanced Planning Systems). J. Intell. Manuf. **18**, 209–221 (2007)
13. Hauge, J.B., Tundys, B., Rzeczycki, A., Lim, T.: Deploying serious games for supply chain management: lessons learned and good practices, p. 18 (2016)
14. Muratet, M., Torguet, P., Jessel, J.-P., Viallet, F.: Towards a serious game to help students learn computer programming. Int. J. Comput. Games Technol. **2009**, 1–12 (2009)
15. Kaminsky, P.: A new computerized beer game: a tool for teaching the value of integrated supply chain management, p. 19
16. The Fresh Connection: the ultimate value experience. http://www.advents.fr/le-blog-des-advengers/the-fresh-connection-le-serious-game-reference-en-supply-chain/
17. Nonaka, T., Miki, K., Odajima, R., Mizuyama, H.: Analysis of dynamic decision-making underpinning supply chain resilience: a serious game approach. IFAC-PapersOnLine. **49**, 474–479 (2016)
18. Hauser, F., Pomponne, V., Jiang, Z., Lamothe, J., Benaben, F.: Processes orchestration for preventing and managing shortages in a supply chain a dermo-cosmetics use case. In: 2017 International Conference on Engineering, Technology and Innovation (ICE/ITMC), pp. 1227–1234 (2017)
19. Chapman, C.: Introduction to Materials Management. Pearson India (2007)
20. Link to the Google sheet of the serious game: https://docs.google.com/spreadsheets/d/1lHfaGeZig1LF7b4NYztoCK9atcsa7MdQgTG_mK7X5CU/edit#gid=319101243

Managing Logistics in Collaborative Manufacturing: The Integration Services for an Automotive Application

Nicola Mincuzzi[1], Mohammadtaghi Falsafi[2,3(✉)],
Gianfranco E. Modoni[1], Marco Sacco[3], and Rosanna Fornasiero[3]

[1] STIIMA-CNR, Via Lembo 38F, 70124 Bari, Italy
{nicola.mincuzzi,gianfranco.modoni}@stiima.cnr.it
[2] Department of Mechanical Engineering, Politecnico di Milano,
Via la Masa 1, 20157 Milan, Italy
[3] STIIMA-CNR, Via Corti 12, 20133 Milan, Italy
{mohammadtaghi.falsafi,marco.sacco,
rosanna.fornasiero}@stiima.cnr.it

Abstract. The critical success factor of the supply chain management process in a modern manufacturing company consists in the company's capability to exploit the data produced by a growing number of different sources. The latter include a network of collaborative sensors, digital tools, and services, made available to suppliers and other involved supply chain actors by the recent advancements in digitalization. The collected data can be processed and analyzed in near real time to extract significant information useful for the company to take some relevant decisions. However, these data are typically produced under the form of heterogeneous formats, as they arrive from different types of sources. This is the reason why the real challenge is finding valid solutions that support the data integration. In this regard, this paper investigates the potential of a solution for data integration that allows supporting a set of interacting decision-support tools within the inbound logistics of the automotive manufacturing. This solution is based on a message-oriented middleware which enables a collaborative approach where suppliers, trucks, dock managers and production plants can share information about their own status for the optimization of the overall system.

Keywords: Inbound logistics · Interoperability · Data integration ·
Middleware · Dock re-scheduling · Optimization

1 Introduction

In the era of modern manufacturing supply chain management (SCM) is becoming more and more complex [1]. Main reasons for this growing complexity are the geographical expansion of the supply chain networks, a huge amount of data (e.g. produced from tracing) which affects the supply chain decisions (e.g. how to manage an anomaly), and the need to increase the speed of decision-making tools due to the advancements of just-in-time delivery practices [2]. In addition, some of the traditional

L. M. Camarinha-Matos et al. (Eds.): PRO-VE 2019, IFIP AICT 568, pp. 355–362, 2019.
https://doi.org/10.1007/978-3-030-28464-0_31

challenges in the SCM still persist and are more emphasized due to the mentioned advancements. One of these challenges is the transportation cost which is increased by the geographical complexity and extensive networks as well as sustainability concerns [3]. Another traditional challenge is the scheduling of orders, transport modes, and unloading points in the inbound and outbound supply chains. This challenge is in particular evident in large industries with a lot of inbound and outbound flows where it is difficult to schedule and re-schedule the plans in case of unexpected disruption events. In order to better address the mentioned challenges, the modern factories are transforming their logistics in a collaborative network where suppliers, trucks, dock managers and production plants share information about the status of the inbound resources for the optimization of the overall system [4]. Such a strong collaborative network is crucial for companies willing to respond to the challenges posed by the globalization [5, 6]. In particular, it allows to quickly take decisions along the whole value chain, thus contributing to a more and more highly dynamic supply chain which in turn is a key factor for the I4.0 logistics [7].

This collaborative network can be realized in its full potential only if it is supported by digital tools capable to exchange and share information among each-other [8]. However, the traditional manufacturing tools are typically based on specific data model and the heterogeneity (also called variety) of these models hinders the tools interoperability, i.e. their capability to exchange information, thus also jeopardizing the cooperation of the involved resources within the overall network [9]. In addition, it is still open so far the debate on which kind of data integration can enhance performance of the supply chain [10]. In order to overcome the issue of data heterogeneity, this paper aims at the development of an experimental platform for integration between traceability systems and management tools and optimization tools within the inbound logistics of automotive assembly plant. The platform leverages the use of a messages-oriented middleware for integration of tracking components with decision-support tools. Thus, thanks to middleware, an optimization tool can exchange significant information with other factory's digital tools (e.g. for production simulation and optimization), thus allowing to re-schedule (e.g. when a disruption event happens) the inbound dock plans and select the best transport modes from the supplier to the docks of the assembly plant.

The remainder of the paper is structured as follows. Section 2 introduces the case study and its problem of interoperability. Section 3 presents the approach and its validation. Section 4 describes the results obtained leveraging the proposed approach. Finally, Sect. 5 draws the conclusions and summarizes the main outcomes.

2 The Case Study

The case study is set in an automotive assembly plant and it focuses on the management of inbound logistics whenever a disruption occurs. The latter could happen in the supplier's side, in the transport modes, and in the unloading docks. In case of any of these disruption events, the manager of the supply chain needs to make recovery decisions to reduce the adverse effects of the delay. In addition, the disruptions that happen in the production could have an impact on the decisions in the inbound logistics and therefore, these disruptions should also be considered. The problem that must be faced consists of two main decisions in the inbound logistics of the assembly plant:

1. Dock re-scheduling;
2. Transportation mode selection.

Before a disruption event happens, a dock schedule exists where a set of trucks are assigned to a set of docks for a specific planning horizon. As a result of a disruption event, it is needed to take a decision to re-schedule the assignments, while the second decision considers the possibility of changing the transport mode of the delayed orders with faster modes. The two decisions are interconnected in the way that the arrival time of the orders to the docks changes by influencing the change of the transport modes. The final decision on the dock re-scheduling and transport selection depends on the trade-off between different costs. Transport cost is the cost of using alternative transport modes. Dock setup cost is the cost of employing additional docks. Buffer cost is the cost of using internal transport means for transferring the specific components (part numbers) from the docks to the assembly line. Extra resource cost is the cost of using more resources than the available ones at the docks. Truck waiting cost is the cost of waiting truck in the dockyard when there are no free docks. Finally, the cost of production re-scheduling is the cost when a part number is not available in the assembly line in the planned time, and therefore, a re-scheduling in the production is necessary. The desired solution is a re-scheduled dock plan and transport plan where the sum of all the costs is minimized.

The solution for this problem proposed within the European research project DISRUPT [11] is to use an optimization model for the inbound logistics where the objective function is the minimization of all the costs as follows [12]:

Minimize (Additional costs caused by the disruption events) = Minimize (Transport cost + Dock setup cost + Buffer cost + Extra resource cost).

The input data for the optimization model are the data related to the inbound logistics combined with data resulting of the analysis of other tools. To handle the disruption and its impact on the inbound logistics decisions, three tools collaborate and propose the final solution as follows:

1. Simulation tool;
2. Optimization tool of the inbound logistics;
3. Optimization tool of production scheduling.

The Simulation tool is first applied to quantify the effects of the disruption on the Key Performance Indicators (KPIs). The most important KPI is Job per Hour (JPH). If the impact of disruption on the JPH is negligible, this is considered as the outcome of the analysis. No further analysis is needed in this case. Otherwise, if the effect is not negligible, the optimization tools are required to minimize the negative consequences of the disruption on the JPH. Generally, two scenarios for inbound logistics tool are possible based on the disruption type as follows (Fig. 1):

1. *The disruption is in the production process (e.g., machine failure).* In this case, if the disruption can be managed by the optimization tool of the production schedule,

it is not needed to apply the inbound logistics optimizer. The outcome is the updated production schedule. If the disruption is not manageable solely by production scheduling tool, Inbound logistics tool should be used. Apart from the other input data, the re-scheduling cost is obtained by the communication of different alternative dock schedules with the production scheduling tool.

2. *The disruption is in the inbound logistics (e.g., the accident of the transport mode).* In this case, the disruption should be managed directly by the inbound logistics tool with the communication of data with the production scheduling tool.

Finally, an optimized dock schedule and transport plan are provided to the supply chain manager who is the final decision maker of the inbound logistics. Behind each state of the workflow, there are different modules, performing different functions. The interactions among different digital tools and software applications are essential to the efficient solution of the optimization model.

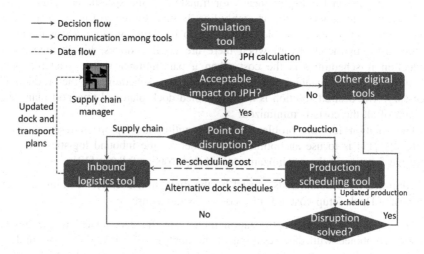

Fig. 1. Application of inbound logistics tool in different disruption events

3   An Overview of the Platform Architecture

In order to overcome the problem of the interoperability, this section investigates the potential of a solution based on a three layers architecture, where the layers are the following (Fig. 2):

- Real Factory;
- DISRUPT Platform Cloud;
- Virtual Factory Tools.

The *Real Factory* comprises the world of the factory, including all aspects inherent the logistic of the fleet of the trucks and the plant production. The *DISRUPT Platform Cloud*, which is one of the main outcomes of the DISRUPT project [13], is the middle-tier of entire system which aims at the integration of all the factory's tools data. In particular, it contains two macro-modules (*Event Dispatcher* and *Digital Twin*) that allow to integrate the data generated by the layer of the *Real Factory* under the form of data streams (*Factory Telemetry*) [14]. Specifically, the *Digital Twin* is a virtual model which represents a faithful mirror of the *Real Factory*, persisted on two structured databases: *Event Disrupt Database* (containing the logic to raise the events) and *Synchro Factory Database* (containing the information related to the supply chain management) [15]. On the base of the information included in the Digital Twin, the *Event Dispatcher* raises the events in case of scheduling delays and forward them to upper Layer. The *Event Dispatcher* leverages a messages-oriented middleware which acts as a glue among the various connected digital tools [16]. Under these conditions, these tools can also run on different platforms and operating systems, as the interoperability is guaranteed by the middleware. Finally, on the top of the architecture, the layer of the *Virtual Factory Tools* comprises various Factory decision-support tools including an *Optimizer for Inbound Logistics* and an *Optimizer for the production scheduling* which leverage the events triggered by *Event Dispatcher*.

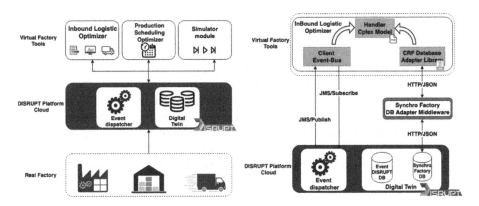

Fig. 2. The architecture of the platform   **Fig. 3.** Inbound Logistic Optimizer software architecture

3.1 An Example of the Use of the Platform

In order to illustrate, through an example, the use of the above described platform to integrate a specific tool within the collaborative network, this section focuses on the *Inbound Logistics Optimizer* tool. As described previously, this tool is an optimization model which aims to re-schedule the inbound dock plans and select the best transport modes from the supplier to the docks of the assembly plant when a disruption event happens. The *Inbound Logistics Optimizer* software architecture is designed foreseeing both a synchronous and asynchronous (or event base) communication with the virtual model of the *Real Factory*. In addition, it includes a model handler, which represents the core mathematical model of the whole *Inbound Logistics Optimizer* tool.

In particular, such tool is composed by the following modules (Fig. 3): (1) *Handler Cplex Model*, described through the software application *Cplex Optimizer*[1], which represents the optimization model based on the current status of the factory. By extracting the updated input parameters, this model finds a solution pool with alternative updated dock schedules and transport plans. Afterwards, based on the related decision variables, it calculates the KPIs for each alternative solution. (2) *Synchro Factory Database Adapter Library* (written in Java), which provides a set of different REST API Web services. In particular, the latter enables the *Inbound Logistics Optimizer* tool to communicate with the DISRUPT Platform Cloud and to use the CRUD (Create, Read, Update, Delete) operations in order to interact with the databases to create, read, update and delete the static and dynamic data, stored on Cloud platform. (3) *Client Event-Bus* (written in Java), which represents the module needed to provide information consistency among the different tools that compose the Virtual Factory Tools layer. The Client Event-Bus[2] is based on the Publish/Subscribe messaging pattern, in which a message is delivered from a producer to any number of consumers. Messages are delivered to the queue destination, and then to all active consumers who have subscribed to this queue.

4 Results

In the proposed approach, through the middleware, a set of input parameters and disruptions are communicated to the Inbound Logistics Optimizer. The optimizer solves the problem by proposing a set of re-scheduled dock plans with the minimum cost as well as the related KPIs. These outcomes are in turn communicated to the middleware, which transmits them to other modules. Exploiting this integration, a set of feasible solutions is provided to the decision-maker in an efficient way. In particular, the results of the inbound logistics optimizer can be divided into three parts as follows:

1. Updated dock schedule
2. Transport selection
3. KPIs.

Figure 4 represents an overview of the results. Alternative solutions are provided to allow the decision maker to choose among the solution alternatives (sub-optimal solutions) which are not satisfied in the optimum solution, based on different cost types. The KPIs are the costs of extra dock setup (DSC), truck waiting (WC), buffer (BC1, BC2), extra resource (ARC) and transportation (TC).

---

[1] https://www.ibm.com/it-it/analytics/cplex-optimizer.

[2] http://um.terracotta.org/.

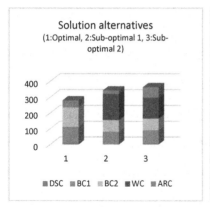 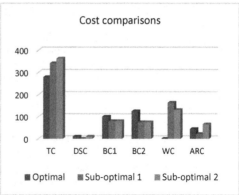

TC: Transport cost ; DSC: Dock setup cost ; BC1: Buffer cost – strategy 1 ; BC2: Buffer cost – strategy 2 ; WC: Truck waiting cost ; ARC: Extra resource cost

Fig. 4. Representation of KPIs for alternative solutions of the inbound logistics optimizer (Optimal: best result with the minimum cost, sub-optimal: alternative results with higher costs)

5 Conclusion

The potential of an approach based on a message-oriented middleware was investigated in this paper to enhance cooperation and collaboration of digital tools supporting logistics within a manufacturing company. The evaluation of the approach in a test environment has demonstrated its validity.

Future works will address the deployment of the proposed solution within the production environment where all the digital tools are deployed and can interact each other. The production environment will give the opportunity to verify the approach under real condition. As the project is still ongoing, the idea is addressing these works in the future months, before the end of the project. Another aspect that must be investigated in the future is the evaluation of the proposed approach within other case studies. It is expected an easy transfer technology from one case study to another thanks to the integration capability of the adopted middleware.

Acknowledgment. The work on this paper is funded mainly by the European Commission through the DISRUPT project H2020 FOF-11-2016, RIA project n. 723541, 20162018). The authors would like to thank the contributions of the different partners of the DISRUPT project.

References

1. Bode, C., Wagner, S.M.: Structural drivers of upstream supply chain complexity and the frequency of supply chain disruptions. J. Oper. Manag. **36**, 215–228 (2015)
2. Hofmann, E., Rüsch, M.: Industry 4.0 and the current status as well as future prospects on logistics. Comput. Ind. **89**, 23–34 (2017)

3. Yu, F., Xue, L., Sun, C., Zhang, C.: Product transportation distance based supplier selection in sustainable supply chain network. J. Cleaner Prod. **137**, 29–39 (2016)
4. Terkaj, W., Tolio, T.: The Italian flagship project: factories of the future. In: Tolio, T., Copani, G., Terkaj, W. (eds.) Factories of the Future, pp. 3–35. Springer, Cham (2019). https://doi.org/10.1007/978-3-319-94358-9_1
5. Macchion, L., Marchiori, I., Vinelli, A., Fornasiero, R.: Proposing a tool for supply chain configuration: an application to customised production. In: Tolio, T., Copani, G., Terkaj, W. (eds.) Factories of the Future, pp. 217–231. Springer, Cham (2019). https://doi.org/10.1007/978-3-319-94358-9_10
6. Macchion, L., Fornasiero, R., Danese, P., Vinelli, A.: The effects of personalization on collaborative production networks location. In: Afsarmanesh, H., Camarinha-Matos, L., Lucas Soares, A. (eds.) Collaboration in a Hyperconnected World. PRO-VE 2016. IFIP Advances in Information and Communication Technology, vol. 480, pp. 433–440. Springer, Cham (2016). https://doi.org/10.1007/978-3-319-45390-3_37
7. Camarinha-Matos, L.M., Fornasiero, R., Afsarmanesh, H.: Collaborative networks as a core enabler of industry 40. In: Camarinha-Matos, L., Afsarmanesh, H., Fornasiero, R. (eds.) Collaboration in a Data-Rich World, PRO-VE 2017. IFIP Advances in Information and Communication Technology, vol. 506, pp. 3–17. Springer, Cham (2017). https://doi.org/10.1007/978-3-319-65151-4_1
8. Koçoğlu, İ., İmamoğlu, S.Z., İnce, H., Keskin, H.: The effect of supply chain integration on information sharing: enhancing the supply chain performance. Proc.-Soc. Behav. Sci. **24**, 1630–1649 (2011)
9. Modoni, G.E., Doukas, M., Terkaj, W., Sacco, M., Mourtzis, D.: Enhancing factory data integration through the development of an ontology: from the reference models reuse to the semantic conversion of the legacy models. Int. J. Comput. Integr. Manuf. **30**(10), 1043–1059 (2017)
10. Kumar, V., Chibuzo, E.N., Garza-Reyes, J.A., Kumari, A., Rocha-Lona, L., Lopez-Torres, G.C.: The impact of supply chain integration on performance: evidence from the UK food sector. Proc. Manuf. **11**, 814–821 (2017)
11. DISRUPT project. http://www.disrupt-project.eu/
12. Falsafi, M., Marchiori, I., Fornasiero, R.: Managing disruptions in inbound logistics of the automotive sector. IFAC-PapersOnLine **51**(11), 376–381 (2018)
13. Tountopoulos, V., Kavakli, E., Sakellariou, R.: Towards a cloud-based controller for data-driven service orchestration in smart manufacturing. In: 2018 Sixth International Conference on Enterprise Systems (ES), pp. 96–99. IEEE, October 2018
14. Modoni, G.E., Sacco, M., Terkaj, W.: A telemetry-driven approach to simulate data-intensive manufacturing processes. Proc. CIRP **57**, 281–285 (2016)
15. Modoni, G.E., Caldarola, E.G., Sacco, M., Terkaj, W.: Synchronizing physical and digital factory: benefits and technical challenges. Proc. CIRP **79**, 472–477 (2019)
16. Modoni, G.E., Trombetta, A., Veniero, M., Sacco, M., Mourtzis, D.: An event-driven integrative framework enabling information notification among manufacturing resources. Int. J. Comput. Integr. Manuf. **32**(3), 241–252 (2019)

Collaborative Services for Digital Transformation

Evaluating the Applicability and Utility of an Elderly Care Ecosystem

Thais A. Baldissera[1,2(✉)] and Luis M. Camarinha-Matos[1]

[1] Faculty of Science and Technology and UNINOVA-CTS,
NOVA University of Lisbon, Campus de Caparica, 2829-516 Caparica, Portugal
{tab, cam}@uninova.pt
[2] Instituto Federal Farroupilha, Santa Maria, RS 97050-685, Brazil

Abstract. The improvement of life expectancy and the decline of total fertility rate worldwide have been key factors for the increasing percentage of the elderly population in the society. Aging comes with several personal needs, which require multiple care services specially tailored (personalized) for each individual. As these needs change throughout life, current services need to adapt (evolve) to reflect new requirements. Advances on collaborative networks for elderly care suggest the integration of services from multiple providers, encouraging collaboration as a way to provide better personalized and evolutionary services. This approach requires a support system to manage the personalized and evolving services for elderly care. In this paper, we present the *Elderly Care Ecosystem* (ECE) framework. ECE is a system designed to support the personalization and evolution of elderly care services following the principles of collaborative networks. To show the feasibility of our approach, we developed a prototype of ECE and evaluated it empirically using the technology acceptance model. Evaluation results are then presented and discussed.

Keywords: Collaborative business services · ICT and ageing ·
Elderly Care Ecosystem · Technology acceptance model

1 Introduction

Society is getting older due to the increase in average life expectancy from 62 to 74 years. This age group represents a bigger slice in the total number of the population. This situation also can be noticed with the increase of the world average age, from 24 years old in 1950 to 29 in 2010, 32 in 2025 and 36 in 2050 [1]. This poses tough challenges to the society on how to provide effective care services that fit the needs of each individual and adjust to the evolution of those needs.

To cope with the needs of this new context, a collaborative Elderly Care Ecosystem (ECE) based in the Collaborative Networks Discipline [4] and following a user-centric perspective, is proposed and briefly presented. ECE involves four main elements (customer, care needs, service, and service provider), four subsystems (ECE Manager, ECE Information, ECE Personalization and ECE evolution) and it is operationalized into three phases (Preparation, Execution, and Monitoring).

© IFIP International Federation for Information Processing 2019
Published by Springer Nature Switzerland AG 2019
L. M. Camarinha-Matos et al. (Eds.): PRO-VE 2019, IFIP AICT 568, pp. 365–378, 2019.
https://doi.org/10.1007/978-3-030-28464-0_32

In this paper, an implementation prototype is described and the evaluation of the ECE framework is performed using an adapted version of the Technology Acceptance Model (TAM).

The remainder of this article is organized as follows: the adopted research method is introduced in Sect. 2; the Elderly Care Ecosystem and its methods for service personalization and evolution are introduced in Sect. 3; Sect. 4 presents the developed ECE software prototype; the conceptual framework evaluation by the adapted TAM is introduced in Sect. 5. Finally, the conclusions and future work are presented in Sect. 6.

2 Adopted Research Method

Frequently, a mix of methods is used to validate the expected results of a research work [2]. In particular, the Constructive Research method [3] can help validating applied research in the area of design science. Validation in design science is performed by building one or more artefacts that solve a domain problem, in order to create knowledge on how the problem can be solved, and show how the solution is new or better than the previous ones.

The ECE framework and methods are evaluated in terms of their applicability and utility considering an adaptation of the Technology Acceptance Model (TAM) methodology [5]. TAM is focused on the intention to use a new technology or innovation and was specifically developed to explain and predict the acceptance of information and communication technologies by potential users.

The evaluation of the perceived utility and applicability of our approach is done through a survey with professional experts in the health and elderly care areas. The interviews were structured in face-to-face meetings following four steps:

1. Introduction: a brief presentation was given to the participants to explain the goals of the research and its details, including the underlying PhD research project and the protocol involving the survey.
2. ECE tutorial: participants watched a brief video tutorial describing the main features of the ECE (personalization and evolution processes) and applications of the ECE using different illustrative examples.
3. Demonstration of the ECE prototype: a brief overview of the prototype was shown to the participants, showing its main functionalities.
4. Survey application: the participants were invited to respond to the survey, which was elaborated according to TAM.

3 Elderly Care Ecosystem Conceptual Framework

An Elderly Care Ecosystem represents a particular case of a Collaborative Business Ecosystem. Our concept characterizes an ECE as an "Elderly Care Collaborative Network" which involves four main elements (more detailed in [6]): Customers (CU): representing the seniors that consume the services provided by virtual organizations (Vos) of providers in ECE. Care needs (CA): representing the care needs of seniors;

these care needs are organized on a taxonomy of care need goals used in a specific ECE. Services (SE): representing the group of services available in ECE. Service Providers (SP): representing a set of organizations (virtual or physical) that provide ECE care services. The ECE environment domain diagram (presented in Fig. 1) highlights the ECE subsystems:

The ECE Manager System (ECE$_{ms}$) represents the component that administers the ECE environment comprising management entities of ECE in the collaborative network environment. The main elements involve the roles of manager, broker, virtual organizations (VO), coordinator and planer of Vos. The ECE Information System (ECE$_{IS}$) is the component that maintains the ECE entities and objects, namely service providers, services, care needs and taxonomy, and customers. The ECE Personalization System (ECE$_{PS}$) involves the personalization subsystem that identifies the customer profile and ranks potential solutions (services and respective service providers) to attend the requirements. The Service Composition and Personalization Environment (SCoPE) method is presented in Sect. 3.1. ECE Evolution System (ECE$_{EV}$) identifies opportunities for service evolution to a new context and supports that evolution (SEvol method), which is briefly presented in Sect. 3.2.

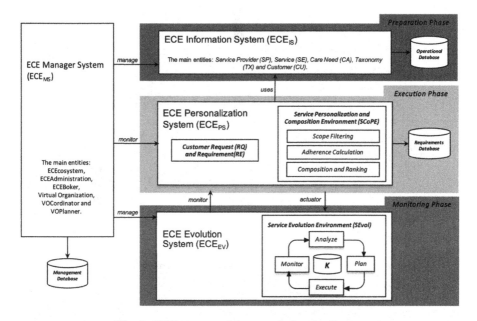

Fig. 1. ECE conceptual framework domain diagram

Considering ECE operationalization, three phases are performed: Preparation, which is responsible for the ECE creation and definition of its rules and functionalities. Execution, which identifies the customer request and its requirements, and the process of composition and personalization of ECE care services are executed. Monitoring, which supports the ECE care service evolution and monitoring in the personalized solution.

3.1   Service Composition and Personalization Environment (SCoPE) Method

The SCoPE method comprises three steps: (1) Scope Filtering, (2) Service Adherence Calculation, and (3) Service Composition and Ranking. Figure 2 shows the SCoPE general approach and these steps.

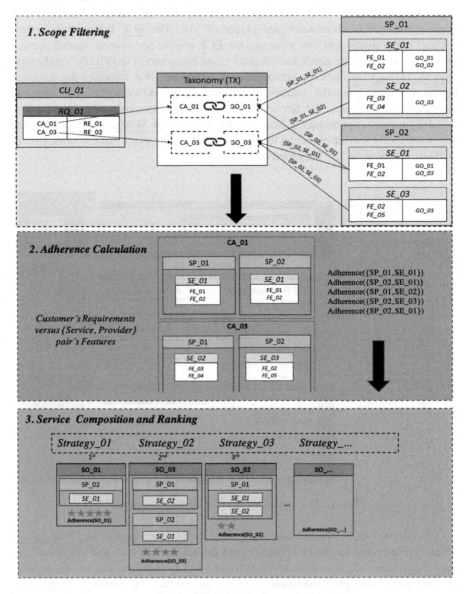

Fig. 2. SCoPE method overview

The first step (*Scope Filtering*) of the algorithm is intended to make a first approach, selecting only the pairs {service, service provider} that provide a valid answer to the customer's needs and requirements.

The second step of the algorithm is the *Adherence Calculation*, which is meant to determine a compatibility index relating the customer's profile, requirements and priorities to the provider's characteristics and care services features. The concept of adherence intends to provide a combined view of how good the match between the service and the need is. The larger the adherence is, the more appropriate the service is for a given customer's profile (and thus the smaller is the probability of obtaining a mismatch).

The adherence is calculated for each pair of service and service provider that will be a possible solution for the customer's care need and it is calculated by estimating three coefficients: Closeness (CL), Partial Adherence (PA), and Adherence (AD).

Since it is aimed to provide the best possible service personalization and adaptability for each customer, particular consideration is put on comparing solutions with the customer's profile and requests. To find the solution that has the best adherence, the assessment is based on each customer's requirement. CL considers how far apart are customer's requirements and the related features of the pair {service, service provider}. The larger the distance is, the smaller the CL is. As each customer has different needs/requirements, the same service and provider fragment can have a different closeness to each customer.

The second calculated coefficient is the partial adherence. It starts with the calculation of G, which is the average of the closeness of all care needs. It then combines G with the comparison of the service coverage level (CO) with the customer's care needs relevance (RL). For each care need a different value of partial adherence is calculated. The CO is defined when a service is registered in the ECE and it is associated with a care need. The RL is defined by the customer when the care need is requested, meaning that he will define how vital is the care need for him. CO and RL coefficients are expressed in a fuzzy scale. However, they are often checked and adjusted at any time, if necessary.

At the end, the vector PA is calculated in which the number of elements correspond to the number of customer's care needs, and afterwards the adherence will be calculated as an average of the PA's of each care need (adherence AD).

In this final step (*Service Composition and Ranking*), the {service, provider} pairs that have been evaluated and which adherences were calculated are rated and there is a suggestion of composition of services based on selected strategies. The solution is presented in terms of lower cost, better cost/benefit ratio and minimization of the number of providers. More details about the SCoPE algorithm and application cases can be found in [7].

3.2 Service Evolution (SEvol) Method

Following the adaptive systems approach, the SEvol method is based on a control loop composed of four main phases: (1) *Monitor:* monitoring events that occur in the surrounding physical and social context; (2) *Analyze*: analyzing monitored data against solution requirements to identify need of adaptation; (3) *Plan*: devising an evolution strategy that reconciles current solution with a new customer's context; and (4) *Execute*: enacting such strategy while minimizing disturbances caused by suggested solutions. These phases are showed and exemplified in Fig. 3.

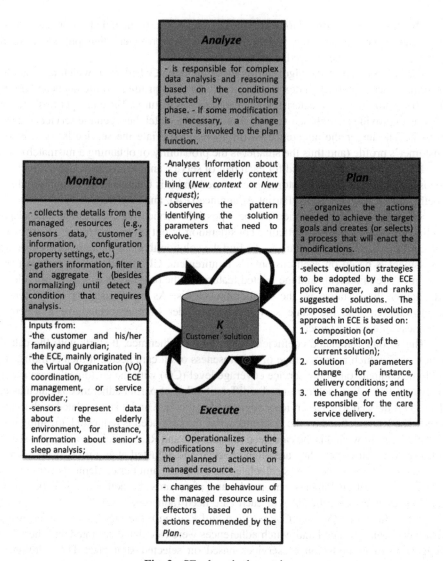

Fig. 3. SEvol method overview

4   ECE Software Prototype

An ECE software prototype was implemented with the necessary information to demonstrate basic operations of the ECE (inclusion, exclusion, customer search, care needs, services, services providers) and the process of personalization and evolution of care services.

The programming language environment used to develop the ECE prototype was *PHP* by *Laravel* Framework and *Laragon* web service [8]. Laravel is a free, open-source *PHP* web framework intended for web app development that follows the model-view-controller (MVC) architectural pattern. Some features of Laravel are a modular packaging system with a dedicated dependency manager, different ways for accessing relational databases, utilities that aid in application deployment and maintenance, and its orientation toward syntactic sugar [8]. *Laragon* is aimed at building and managing web applications and it is focused on performance [8].

4.1   Preparation Phase: ECE Setup and Configuration

Figure 4 presents the use case diagram of the main actors and processes of the prototype setup and configuration involving the ECE$_{ms}$ and ECE$_{IS}$. In this stage, the validation of the elements to start the execution process is done. There is at least one item in each profile (customer, taxonomy, service provider, and service) that must be registered.

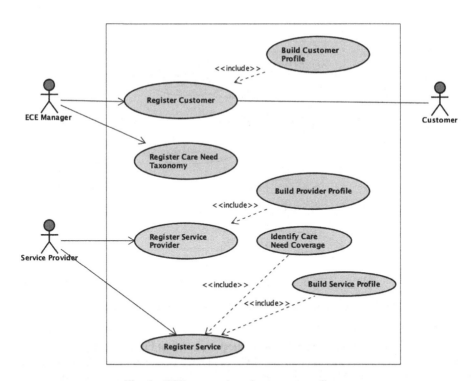

Fig. 4. ECE preparation phase use case diagram

The taxonomy (TX) is registered by the ECE Manager (*Register Care Need Taxonomy*). Only one instance of the taxonomy exists for each ECE. The taxonomy evolves over time and new nodes can be added, updated or deleted. The customer (*Register Customer*), service provider (*Register Service Provider*), and service profile (*Register Service*) are registered through predefined templates. More details about these ECE profile templates can be seen in [6].

4.2 Execution Phase: Customer Request and SCoPE Algorithm Execution

The ECE execution phase covers the following main activities: Customer request, and SCoPE algorithm execution. Figure 5 presents a partial use case diagram of this phase. The ECE Manager selects the customer (*Select Customer*) and registers her/his request (*Register Customer Request*). The personalization algorithm (SCoPE) is executed (*Execute Personalization Algorithm*) by the *Solution Processor* and a list of solutions are presented to the customer (*List Solution*). The customer chooses the best solution for her/him (*Solution Validation*).

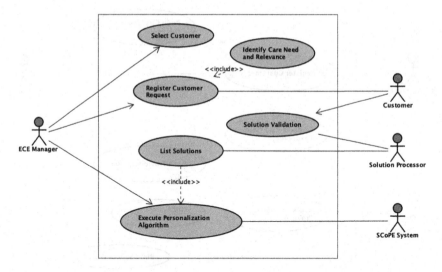

Fig. 5. Customer request and algorithm execution use case diagram

An example of customer profile and request is shown in Fig. 6, where the customer *Beth Maria Santos* is inserted in the ECE with her personal data, limitations and resources, and life style characteristics (part of ECE customer profile template).

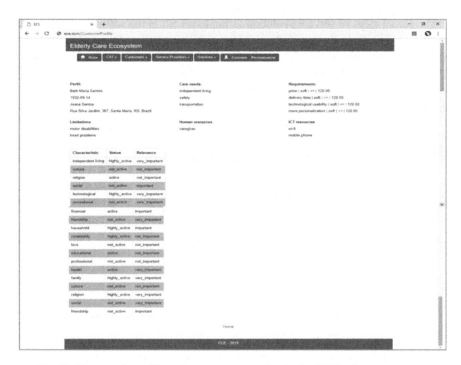

Fig. 6. Customer's profile and request presentation in the ECE software prototype

4.3 Monitoring Phase: SEvol Algorithm Execution

The ECE monitoring phase covers the following main activities (see Fig. 7): *Receive Inputs* including update of customer request (*Customer Request Update*), *Evolution Algorithm Execution* (SEvol), resulting in the new solution (*Evolutionary Solution*), and validation of the evolved solution by the customer (*Solution Validation*).

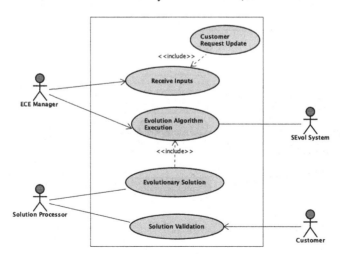

Fig. 7. Monitoring phase partial use case diagram

The partial steps of service evolution as implemented in the software prototype are presented in Fig. 8. In this example, the care need *independent living* is removed and the new care need *recreational activities* is added with *high* relevance. The evolution algorithm is executed, and the solution is presented for customer validation. More details about SEvol algorithm execution can be seen in [9] and [10].

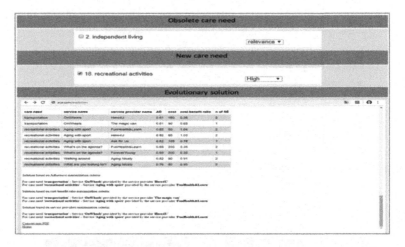

Fig. 8. Evolutionary solution partial steps (in the software prototype)

5   ECE Framework Evaluation

The statements presented in the survey belong to eight dimensions (four originating from TAM and four created for our work) organized in three contexts (built for our evaluation area) that we want to assess: technological context, organization context, and collaborative environment context. Figure 9 shows the proposed model with the corresponding contexts and dimensions.

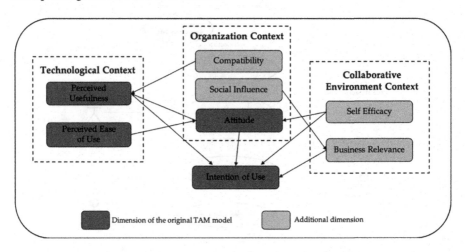

Fig. 9. Extended TAM model

The *Technological Context* includes the dimension *Perceived Usefulness* and *Perceived Ease of Use* from the TAM methodology. The *Organizational Context*, encompasses the dimensions *Attitude*, *Compatibility*, and *Social Influence*. *Attitude* can be defined as the perception by an individual of the positive or negative consequences related to adopting the technology. *Compatibility* refers to the degree of correspondence between an innovation and existing values, past experiences, and needs of potential adopters. *Social Influence* assesses the extent to which an individual believes that stakeholders who are important to him/her will approve his/her adoption of a particular behaviour.

Finally, the *Collaborative Environment Context has two* dimensions to be assessed: *Self Efficacy* and *Business Relevance*. *Self Efficacy* refers to the degree to which an individual believes that an organizational and technical infrastructure exists to support the use of the system. *Business Relevance* represents the influence that innovation can bring to the business. *Self Efficacy* and *Business Relevance* express the needed features/characteristics for participation in a collaborative environment.

Four items about each variable dimension are collected in the survey, totalling thirty-two items. The questions belonging to the various dimensions appear mixed to mitigate any bias in the responses.

Considering the elderly care domain and its business environment, a set of service providers and experts of different type of business are identified: public, philanthropic, private, and mixed organizations. All selected organizations operate in Brazil, at different levels with local, regional, and national market influence.

5.1 Survey Application and Results Analysis

The questionnaire was tested with 95 elderly care professionals belonging to 17 distinct companies. Respondents answered the questionnaire by rating each item on a 5-point Likert scale [11] ranging from "totally disagree" to "totally agree." Scores were developed by computing the mean of all the items that constitute each dimension. Additionally, respondents had to provide information about their age, gender, nationality, background area, number of years in the company, experience in the elderly care domain and in the collaborative networks, and the highest educational grade obtained.

The internal consistency of the instrument was assessed by calculating the Cronbach alpha [12] values for each variable. The construct validity of the model was evaluated using interitem correlation analysis. Cronbach alpha values were acceptably high (>0.7 by [13]) for the remaining theoretical constructs (see Table 1).

Among the 95 elderly care professionals who participated of the experiment, 31 individuals work as administrative staff, 36 are caregivers, and 28 are managers. Most of these individuals act as caregiver as well. More than 76% of the respondents were women, and 60.4% work in the health care domain. Nearly 56,8% were under 30 years old, 44.3% were between the ages of 30 and 60, and only 1.1% were over 60 years old. Almost 42 respondents have technical education, 48 a bachelor or master degree, and 5 a PhD degree.

Table 1. Sample item and Cronbach α by dimensions (translated to English)

Dimension	Sample item	Cronbach α
D1: Perceived Usefulness	ECE can facilitate the service personalization and evolution to my customers	0.81
D2: Perceived Ease of Use	I think that I could easily learn how to use the ECE	0.79
D3: Compatibility	The customer data profile used by ECE is appropriated to my business strategy	0.75
D4: Social Influence	Most of my customer will welcome the fact that I use the ECE	0.82
D5: Attitude	In my opinion, the use of ECE' profiles (service, service provider, customer, and care need) will have a positive impact for service provision	0.81
D6: Self Efficacy*	I would use ECE if I receive appropriate training and the necessary technical assistance	0.78*
D7: Business Relevance*	I believe that the ECE represents a competitive advantage in a fierce market	0.82*
D8: Intention of Use	I intend to use the ECE in my organization when it becomes available	0.90

*considered only for those who work with collaborative networks.

Around 60.1% of the interviewees work exclusively with seniors for a maximum of 3 years, demonstrating that elderly care caregiver represents a promising profession. Relating to the collaborative network area, only approximately 26% work in a collaborative environment, identifying that the area is considered a challenge and not fully consolidated yet.

The results of items and related dimensions are summarized in Fig. 10.

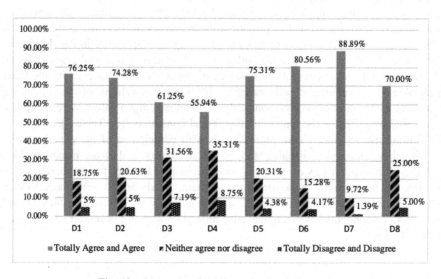

Fig. 10. Summary of results and related dimension

In general, all dimensions had a high acceptance. The two dimensions that were below 70% were D3 and D4. In both, there is a high index of neither disagreement nor agreement. In *Compatibility*, an identified outline refers the absence of the use of an ecosystem to service personalization and evolution (none of the companies we visited has a system for recommendation service; this task is still a human decision).

Relating to *Social Influence,* the participants believe that the customers may not accept being monitored for fear of losing their privacy, and the ECE members may not provide complete data because they feel unsafe and fear disclosure of sensitive information to their competitors (now partners in ECE). With the large data handled by ECE, a reliable information security policy should be implemented to manage the uncertainties which might affect the security of their organization´s information over time, and privacy namely in accordance to GDPR rules. It is demanding proper investment and business adaptation for participating of the ECE.

5.2   Study Limitations

The results of our study should be interpreted in the light of some limitations. First, the same questionnaire was used for staff, caregivers and managers. If we did one for each type of entity, we might get more real data per actuation area. Second, we identified that the concept of collaborative networks is often confused with "cooperatives" in Brazil. Thus, we are not sure that the participants who stated that they work with collaborative networks really do, since they also do not have a computer-based collaboration system. Considering that the dimensions *Self-Efficacy* and Business *Relevance* were evaluated by workers in collaborative environments, the results may not reliably reflect the reality.

A third aspect to consider is that our theoretical model involves additional constructs in relation to the original TAM methodology. It would be interesting to test this model in a future work and add other potentially important variables to improve the predictive power of the theoretical model. Finally, the technology may be a barrier to understanding the proposed concept because most caregivers do not use technologies to provide a service.

6   Conclusions and Future Work

In this paper, we presented an overview and a prototype of an Elderly Care Ecosystem. The main focus of this work contemplates the ECE software prototype implementation and the ECE conceptual framework evaluation based on a survey following a modified TAM. The prototype is presented based on the main functions and steps to algorithm execution. With the demonstration and survey application, the ECE utility and applicability test with partners and related stakeholders (caregivers and elderly care enterprises) is done. The results analysis is presented and in general, all dimensions had a high acceptance. Moreover, the current understanding of the links among collaborative networks, care ecosystems, and personalized and evolutionary services provision, is new and not fully consolidated, representing a challenge.

Acknowledgements. The authors acknowledge the contributions of the Portuguese FCT-Strategic program UID/EEA/00066/2019 for providing partial financial support for this work.

References

1. Bureau PR: 2018 World Population Data 2018 12/04/2019. http://www.worldpopdata.org/index.php/map
2. Pedersen, K., Emblemsvag, J., Bailey, R., Allen, J.K., Mistree, F.: Validating design methods and research: the validation square. In: ASME Design Theory and Methodology Conference, New York (2000)
3. Kasanen, E., Lukha, K., Siitonen, A.: The constructive approach in management accounting research. J. Manag. Account. Res. **5**, 245–266 (1993)
4. Camarinha-Matos, L.M., Afsarmanesh, H.: Collaborative Networks: Reference Modeling. Springer, Heidelberg (2008)
5. Davis, F.D., Bagozzi, R.P., Warshaw, P.R.: User acceptance of computer technology: a comparison of two theoretical models. Manage. Sci. **35**(8), 982–1003 (1989)
6. Baldissera, T.A., Camarinha Matos, L.M., DeFaveri, C.: Designing elderly care ecosystem in collaborative networks environment. In: International Conference on Computing, Networking and Informatics. IEEE, Ota (2017)
7. Baldissera, T.A., Camarinha-Matos, L.M.: SCoPE: service composition and personalization environment. Appl. Sci. **8**(11), 2297 (2018)
8. He, R.Y.: Design and implementation of web based on Laravel framework. In: 2014 International Conference on Computer Science and Electronic Technology (ICCSET 2014). Atlantis Press (2014)
9. Baldissera, T.A., Camarinha-Matos, L.M.: Services evolution in elderly care ecosystems. In: Camarinha-Matos, L.M., Afsarmanesh, H., Rezgui, Y. (eds.) PRO-VE 2018. IAICT, vol. 534, pp. 417–429. Springer, Cham (2018). https://doi.org/10.1007/978-3-319-99127-6_36
10. Baldissera, T.A., Camarinha-Matos, L.M.: Evolutionary and adaptive elderly care ecosystem. In: Misra, S., et al. (eds.) Computational Science and Its Applications – ICCSA 2019. Lecture Notes in Computer Science, vol. 11623, pp. 290–305. Springer, Cham (2019). https://doi.org/10.1007/978-3-030-24308-1_24
11. Likert, R.: A technique for the measurement of attitudes. Arch. Psychol. **22**, 140–155 (1932)
12. Cronbach, L.J.: Coefficient alpha and the internal structure of tests. Psychometrika **16**(3), 297–334 (1951)
13. Nunnally, J.: Psychometric Methods. McGraw-Hill, New York (1978)

Towards a Mobility Payment Service Based on Collaborative Open Systems

A. Luis Osório[1(✉)], Luis M. Camarinha-Matos[2],
Hamideh Afsarmanesh[3], and Adam Belloum[3]

[1] ISEL - Instituto Superior de Engenharia de Lisboa,
Instituto Politécnico de Lisboa and POLITEC&ID, Lisbon, Portugal
lo@isel.ipl.pt
[2] Faculty of Sciences and Technology,
NOVA University of Lisbon and CTS-UNINOVA, Caparica, Portugal
cam@uninova.pt
[3] University of Amsterdam (UvA), Amsterdam, The Netherlands
{h.afsarmanesh,a.belloum}@uva.nl

Abstract. There is a need for a new strategy and approach to effectively develop mobility services in Europe. These services should be seen by customers as integrated services which are offered by a payment service provider using direct debit payments as established by the European Central Bank. The mobility service would enable a citizen to use multimodal transportation means including public transportation, tolling, parking lots, bicycle rental, etc. in Europe under a single contract. Competing mobility service providers need to be trusted and supervised by authorities based on digital supervision and auditing processes. Digital platforms need to smoothly deal with heterogeneous infrastructures of the different operators which validate utilizations using a variety of means such as card, mobile phone, or automatic vehicle identification systems. All transportation-related events need to be reliably communicated to the payment service providers. Detected failures need a clear and easy to follow resolution procedure. The variety of existing technologies and methodologies to develop informatics systems and processes automation make it difficult to reach such objectives and also an obstacle for authorities to effectively supervise the processes. An open system of systems framework approach combined with a collaborative network support infrastructure to facilitate information exchange and coordination among all involved stakeholders is proposed as a promising way to address these challenges. This paper further develops previous research in this area, better clarifying the challenges, and recommending a development strategy which has been proved in a number of partial implementations.

Keywords: Complex informatics systems · Distributed systems ·
Collaborative networks · Integrated mobility services ·
Integrated system of systems

1 Introduction

Digital transformation is likely to have a profound impact in the mobility sector, leading to better services to the citizen. Initial ideas for a European-wide payment system for collaborative multimodal mobility services were introduced in [13]. The

© IFIP International Federation for Information Processing 2019
Published by Springer Nature Switzerland AG 2019
L. M. Camarinha-Matos et al. (Eds.): PRO-VE 2019, IFIP AICT 568, pp. 379–392, 2019.
https://doi.org/10.1007/978-3-030-28464-0_33

base concept relies on a payment service covering public transportation, tolling in highways and bridges, parking lots, bicycle rental, and fuel payment, all under a single contract involving direct bank debit. A new type of operator, the Collaborative Mobility Service Provider (CMSP) emerges as the entity that offers integrated services to the customer and ensures that providers of individual services follow the contractual provisions. The technological support to such services requires an open complex informatics systems of systems (ISoS) [7].

Many existing approaches throughout Europe, such as the model recently adopted in Lisbon and Porto, offer a partial solution (e.g. an intermodal transportation pass for citizens against the payment of a monthly fixed fee). However, such approaches are typically limited to a regional level, are not comprehensive enough in terms of the offered services, and the infrastructure operators maintain control of their clients. Such partial adoption is as an intermediate step for the proposed service mobility model, but further research towards a European unified mobility service is needed.

Progressing towards more integrated mobility services is aligned with a number of general policies aims at European level:

- Improving quality of service, namely in terms of convenience and experience, without geographical borders, can contribute to re-enforce a European identity.
- Facilitation of mobility policies, facilitating different business models, e.g. discounts above certain level of usage, variable prices depending on the period of the day, reduced prices for seniors and students.
- Facilitate increased use of public transportation through smooth integration with tolling and parking payment services.
- Contributing to SEPA vision (Single Euro Payments Area) and cost reduction through increased openness to more operators.
- Contributing to the European ICT industry by actively promoting "replaceability" of systems/sub-systems/services. By eliminating vendor lock-in constraints, this strategy also reduces the risks of adopting solutions from smaller companies, thus facilitating their access to this market.

One important challenge relates to the implementation of an accreditation framework:

- Payment services need that the corresponding providers are accredited/recognized by regulating authorities, namely in order to provide guarantees to the customer.
- Considering wide geographical spaces, involves large numbers of customers and transactions, which represents a significant level of complexity.
- The whole mobility services provision requires supervision and auditing mechanisms to be performed digitally by regulators. This is particularly challenging in case of a large diversity and heterogeneity of technological infrastructures. Adherence to an open reference infrastructure model could thus be a crucial facilitator and a requirement for the process of operators' certification by authorities.
- The need for an open reference infrastructure comes also from the need for collaboration among the various service providers, which use different infrastructures and different identification mechanisms (cards, mobile phones, car identification devices, automatic car plate identification, etc.). All mobility service usage events

need to the properly communicated to the payment service operators. Detected failures need a clear and easy to apply resolution procedure, while conflicts can be mediated by authorities if access to real data can be guaranteed. Furthermore, a distributed responsibility among operators/service providers also needs to rely on an open infrastructure framework.

This context requires a high-level of automation and thus a collaboration among technological sub-systems of the different stakeholders, which should interact without or reduced human intervention.

Currently, regulators/supervision authorities face big obstacles as it is not easy for them to cope with a large diversity of infrastructures and implementations. Changes in policies may also lead to an increasing dependency on a few stakeholders that can afford large investments.

The maturing of the digital networked society requires that technology artifacts are developed and managed under unified frameworks and regulated public policies. However, the state of legacy and current implementations often establishes dependencies from single-vendor or single integrator. Public European decision-makers too often apply "exceptions" to the public tendering, which leads to continuously contracting the same supplier with the argument that assets are not replaceable by competing alternatives. Such (over)used exceptions motivate our research for agile vendor-agnostic distributed infrastructures, which should be simple to develop, to maintain, and evolve. The notion of "openness" is used as a principle that any technological artifact, being a system or an element of a system, must be replaceable [7] under a safe migration process preserving the underlying responsibility. Open also means that in the limit, any European public tender shall be free to decide among competing products (technology artifacts or services).

As shown by previous research, the "imposition" of an open technology framework proved to be a mechanism to reduce costs resulting from an increase in competition. This was observed, for instance, in the Brisa case which adopted a service-oriented electronic toll collection such that roadside equipment elements no longer were depending on a single provider [11].

In this paper we farther discuss an approach for the service payment provider model by adopting and extending previous research contributions considering two main dimensions: (i) structuring the intra-organization infrastructure by adopting the ISoS framework [7], and (ii) pursuing the collaborative networked perspective by adopting Enterprise Collaborative Network (ECoNet) [15].

In the next section, we briefly present and discuss the difficulty of realizing innovation under a philosophy of replaceable technical systems. The difficulties are discussed considering both scientific research and industry contributions towards vendor agnostic solutions. In Sect. 3 we revisit previous research on the Model-driven Engineering Open Systems (MDEOS) initiative and in particular the ISoS (organization) and ECoNet (networked organizations) frameworks, which provide the base for the proposed approach. In Sect. 4 we discuss the proposed paradigm shift from a software engineering to a systems engineering thinking when addressing complex application problems. Section 5 summarizes the discussion and presents further research needs.

2 Brief Overview of Industry Trends

There is increasing awareness about liability, security, and even brand image risks associated to the development of integrated informatics solutions for complex application domains. Given the lack of vendor-neutral development and operation frameworks, most existing technology landscapes are maintained and evolved under proprietary technology setups. The frequent need for unplanned changes as a consequence urgent business challenges is a reason for deepening specificities and therefore dependencies. Furthermore, the trend for establishing collaborative networks also contributes for an additional complexity. For both dimensions, there is a need for reference models on how to structure the involved integration. Additionally, there is a difficulty associated with the adoption of innovations supported by unique "opportunity windows" since "technology and its context of use tend to congeal" [18]. The question is thus: how to elaborate in advance a suitable mobility service provider model that can guide a strategy to generate opportunities for the European industry by "imposing" an open digital technology framework led by the need of collaboration, digital auditing and service quality enforcement?

It seems that in this sector we are facing an opportunity similar to that of the Korean leapfrog on digital TV and mobile phones that happened when the government "imposed" a digital communication standard [6]. The leadership role of public investment seems the key, not only through investing in R&D but also by "imposing" the public interest towards valuing a potential competing industry.

The acquisition of technology companies by major organizations as a strategy to address the development of such complex composites of technology artifacts is an indicator of the problem. The recent decision of Ikea [2], a large ready-to-assemble furniture retailer, of buying the innovative software development TaskRabbit is paradigmatic. This acquisition results from the need to develop a new concept of managing professional services to guarantee quality craft in assembling products. The relationship started with an initial subcontract to develop a mobile application with augmented reality for clients to match products in client's homes. The problem, in this case, is the difficulty of developing a call for tenders since the vision exists but not complete specifications and technical decisions. Technical decisions are not easy to make in advance since they depend on the technological culture of the contractor. The Brisa case we have been following for years [11] followed a similar approach, in this case through the creation of a technology company, Brisa Innovation and Technology (BIT, now A-To-Be). But in spite of their investment in R&D and innovation, and its commitment to MDEOS [12] initiative, current BIT products still do not follow-up any open source software dynamics.

Other approaches exist, like the inference of complex development patterns from analysis of change in logs, as proposed in [3]. Research on modularity dates back to 1970's with a work about software complexity questioning how to modularize software making components testable and maintainable [8]. Despite important developments for about half a century, this and other questions concerning how to structure software developments remain an issue. In [9] it was recognized some years ago that "with respect to current large software-intensive systems, our aspiration to establish *software development as an engineering discipline is, to a significant extent, still an aspiration*". This book discusses the need for abstraction mechanisms, modularity, and composition as a strategy to cope with large software systems. Another example, [16] discusses a component strategy to cope with resilience but without exploring the computing system part. However, along the discussion, terms such as system, dependable system, resilient system, operating system, and distributed system, are used without a clear definition.

It seems that an abstract (implementation independent) conceptual framework, able to cope with the growing networked complexity and following an independent vendor framework, is still a need.

3 Revisiting ISoS, ECoNet and CEDE Concepts

3.1 Base Concepts

The example of developing a mobile service provider concept as discussed in [13] provides a promising endeavor for progressively aggregating research contributions involving technology, engineering, business, economic, and sociological viewpoints. The approach considers the development of replaceable informatics systems (Isystems) as a target goal. As an underlying initiative, the Model Driven Engineering of Open Systems (MDEOS) is a coordinated effort focusing both an open structuration for the computing-related artifacts (ISoS) and some "unification" or alignment of the development "culture" (CEDE), as depicted in Fig. 1.

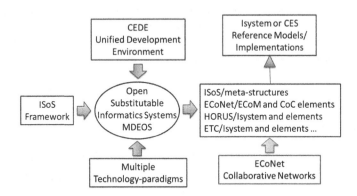

Fig. 1. Open Replaceable Informatics Systems in MDEOS framework

The mobility service provider case is an opportunity to "impose" convergence mechanisms, led by European authorities, in order to facilitate the development and adoption of novel smart solutions, contributing to value creation. As initially proposed in [13], the Collaborative Mobility Service Provider concept foresees a pan-European payment of mobility services. This case offers interesting research challenges considering the multidimensional risks involved in materializing the single euro payment area and the direct debits scheme for the collaborative service provision model. To bring further clarification, the initial formulation in [13] can be expanded by considering the following additional challenges:

- The mobility service provider needs to consider collaboration with complementary industry or services sectors and its standardization dynamics: banks, payment mediation providers, transports and mobility, and government (regulation authorities);
- The need for reducing mediation, as stated by the single European payment initiative, which is hampered by technology interoperation difficulties and debt risks associated with direct interactions between service providers and banks;
- The diversity of infrastructure operators across Europe, which requires to find common mechanisms to make clients perform the payment of mobility related infrastructures. Validation and enforcement mechanisms need to be designed to cope with the diversity of cases, from small transport companies in a small village, to large transport systems in large cities;
- Involved stakeholders need to be prepared to scale up and to manage failure situations since the reliance on the overall solution depends on its availability and recovery mechanisms. For instance, an attendance help-desk mechanism is needed for clients with difficulty in using the service;
- Considering the inhabitants of the EU-28, 509.4 million[1], as potential service users, just one percent share represents five million clients, and if in average a client makes five transactions a day, a service provider must manage 25 million transactions (utilization events) a day. The corresponding technological solution thus needs to scale up, maintaining the quality of services.

The proposed mobility service provider scenario is thus a complex engineering system of systems. The stakeholders, service provider, infrastructure operators, mobility and bank authorities, as depicted in Fig. 2, involve complex distributed collaborative services, which are operationalized through complex collaborative business

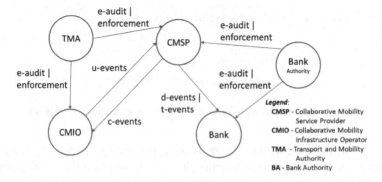

Fig. 2. Collaborative Networked Stakeholders in the mobility service provision case

---

[1] Source: https://ec.europa.eu/eurostat/statistics-explained.

processes [14]. The transport and mobility authorities should be able to interact through auditing events (a-events) with the infrastructure operator and mobility service provider. The infrastructure operator and service provider interact through usage events (u-events). The mobility service provider interacts with banks through debit and transfer events (d-events or t-events). The bank authorities interact with this environment through electronic auditing events (e-audit), a form of "digital auditing".

3.2   Common Organization's Technology Framework

The mobility service provider case requires the participating stakeholders to implement common auditing and enforcement services. The propose ISoS framework, depicted in Fig. 3 considers the organization's computing landscape formed by one or more Isystems.

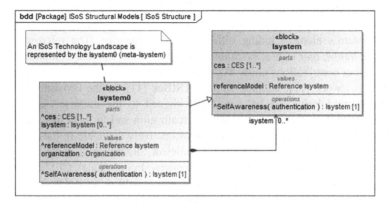

Fig. 3. The SysML model of the ISoS Isystem concept

The ISoS framework suggests the need to develop reference models validated through reference implementations, which contribute to make Isystems replaceable. The development of reference models follows the proposed Reference Implementation concept of the FIWARE framework [20]. The ISoS framework facilitates the investment on reference models and respective validation implementations since formal technology independence is guaranteed through the Cooperation Enabled Services (CES) concept [10]. An Isystem is a composite of one or more CES, as depicted in Fig. 4. The CES abstraction is a composite of one or more services and like an Isystem can also have an associated Reference Model to support replaceability.

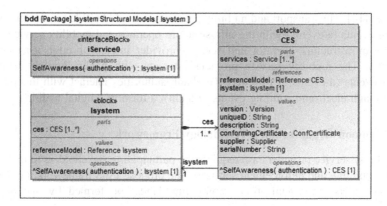

Fig. 4. The SysML model of Isystem and its relation to CES

The CES composite is the atomic concept to cope with legacy or novel technologies. CES follows the new trend of microservices while elementary functionalities and as Isystem's element hiding different implementations. The microservices [1] *"emphasize lightweight virtual machines"* and point to autonomous computing entities. There are other contributions under SOA very similar to microservices. The example of the JINI framework [19], adopted by the ITSIBus [11], in the construction of open autonomous modularity can be considered aligned to the microservices trend. As discussed in [1], the fast-growing role of virtualization and in particular the approach followed by docker, reusing an old mechanism natively available in the Linux kernel (cgroups and namespaces), establishing efficient, lightweight, isolated execution environments [17], is already used in SOA contexts. In our model, CES's services can deploy to a lightweight container and, in this way, establish an isolated, autonomous computing entity. CES is, therefore, a composite of one or more Services, as depicted in Fig. 5. Like an Isystem, also a CES can have a Reference Model, making it a replaceable implementation. The key feature of an ISoS Service that makes it different from related works is the independence from a specific technology.

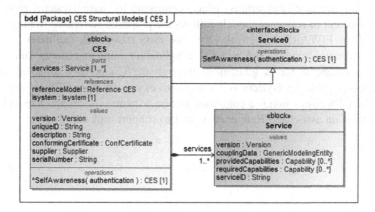

Fig. 5. The SysML model of CES and composite services

As depicted in Fig. 5, by calling the CES selfAwareness() method, the set of implemented Services are obtained, beyond other attributes. Each Service has an associated couplingData, represented by the Generic Modeling Entity (GME) type. GME abstracts specificities of the Service implementation. The decoding of the couplingData content depends on the MIME-Type tag, as depicted in Fig. 6.

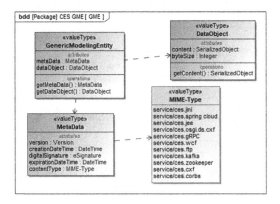

Fig. 6. The SysML model of the Service Generic Modeling Entity (GME)

The MIME-Type uses the Multipurpose Internet Mail Extensions (MIME) concept, an IETF standard used here to discriminate available technology implementations. The MIME-Type values classify (identify) specific technology implementation as a pre-established convention for the model of the dataObject attribute, an instance of the GME entity. Beyond the contentType and other attributes, the metaData object also contains a digitalSignature to trust the Service through some certifying organization. For security and responsibility reasons, it is important to guarantee the integrity of the adopted Service implementation. As the model is applied in products developments by the industry, further open specifications are expected to be detailed or proposed.

After establishing the organization's technology framework based on Isystem/CES/service and the selfAwareness() method of both Isystem and CES, which we designate by Adaptive Coupling Infrastructure (OACI) [7], the next section discusses the interaction between Isystems in the Collaborative Networks context.

3.3   Collaborative Networked Organizations Technology Framework

The ECoNet framework and platform [15] is proposed as a contribution to structure the underlying collaborative environment and make it easier for an organization to get prepared to join a collaborative network. An issue is the diversity of adapters that nowadays are necessary to establish interactions between Isystems of different organizations as discussed in [13]. In this paper, we detail the ECoNet framework and the proposed ECoM as the Isystem that into each networked organization is responsible for managing business exchanges between Isystems of different Organizations. To discuss the need of the ECoNet for the mobility service provider, we revise the ECoNet architecture based on its SysML model as depicted in Fig. 7.

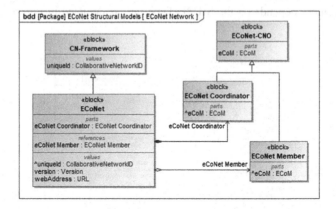

Fig. 7. The SysML model of the ECoNet organization's network

Each service provider stakeholder needs to install an ECoM Isystem obtained from the ECoNet coordination. As proposed in [15], an organization can register at ECoNet coordinator and select a business provider of a supported ECoM implementation. With an ECoM Isystem, specialized in managing collaborative network interactions, a service provider stakeholder is prepared to interact with business partners, based on the required Collaboration Contexts (CoC). Any organization's Isystem can integrate with the ECoM through the ISoS logical integration bus [7], i.e., through the CoC selfAwareness() method since a Collaborative Context is, in fact, a CES composed of the Services necessary to operate and manage the required business exchanges. Figure 8 depicts the SysML model of the ECoM Isystem.

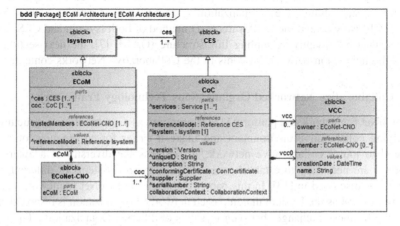

Fig. 8. The SysML model of the ECoM Isystem

A collaboration context is equivalent to the existing adapters used to manage specific interactions between Isystems of business partners. However, by adopting ECoNet, i.e., by installing an ECoM, the adapters are wrapped into services of a collaboration context (CoC). A specific collaboration context establishes a virtual collaboration context with virtually all business partners that join a specific collaboration context. The Virtula Collaboration Context zero (VCC_0) is a kind of shared space among all organizations sharing a common collaboration context. Any business partner can create its own VCC and invite business partners to join the created virtual collaboration context. Each VCC establishes a multi-tenant secure collaboration space. The services implemented by the collaboration context establish the interaction mechanisms to be accessed by the organization's Isystems that need to exchange data or coordination information among ECoNet nodes.

4 From Software to System's Paradigm Shift

Computer science and engineering need to evolve from a software to a systems-centric approach. Even if the SCRUM methodologies [5] are important in organizing software development, the diversity of computing paradigm used by different organizations establishes complex interdependencies difficult to manage. Such complexity suggests the term software system can be abstracted by the informatics system (Isystem) concept, which combines ideas from areas like information systems, distributed systems, database systems, operating systems, web systems, and so forth. In our formulation, the notion of informatics system is central in abstracting computing related paradigms under a unified approach. It establishes a responsibility centered on computing elements, but it can include other specializations or elements from other knowledge bodies. Therefore, by adopting the Isystem concept a move from software to system's thinking is promoted in mapping business requirements and formal high-level concepts with clear responsibility boundaries. Systems thinking is considered a key approach to the study and development of System of Systems and SoS Engineering where interactions among system elements are of paramount importance [4]. Developing complex and reliable systems is difficult since dependencies among a large number of software modules without formal isolation mechanisms make difficult the identification of potential problems.

Moreover, there is a recurrent difficulty in making a clear separation between (business) processes or the "what" is intended, and the structuration of the technology landscape or the "how" to proceed. The difficulty results from the lack of a general framework able to cope with the complex interdependencies among the required computing elements.

The mobility service context requires an automated organization where persons and technology fit well under pleasant and cost-effective (sustainable) symbiosis. An approach where any person "sees" the mechanisms he/she need to fulfill social and professional activities and be manageable under a sustainable model. User's expectation is to hold the right tools and facilities to pursue activities under "perfect" operation and fulfillment. However, the problem is that existing technology artifacts have been evolving, pushed by fierce market competition and without a well-defined open and independent supplier model able to position each artifact independently of its dimension/complexity in cooperation and under a unified managed (coordinated) technology landscape.

To the question if state of the art is ready for the mobility service provider challenge, the answer is no. However, if the question is about the readiness of technology the answer would be yes. The difference is that with state of the art the approach to such a mobility service provider challenge would follow proprietary approaches and a suite of adapters to integrate the participating technology systems. Following the MDEOS strategy, both ISoS and ECoNet have been evolving, under an open specification and co-financed by projects with the industry and Public Authorities (Brisa/A-To-Be, Galp, BP, Road Authority, Ports Authority) converging smoothly for adoption in production.

We argue that the European Public interest, represented by the mobility and bank authorities, shall lead a project to support the mobility service provider vision based on a strong commitment from the research community, and with the participation of interested companies. It is of paramount importance the establishment of ontologies establishing reference models based on standard Isystem or CES in promoting multiple supplying. The social value by pushing the multi-supplier paradigm based on the replaceability principle shall be the investment motivation. From the cases studied in previous research leading to the proposed framework, a recurrent result was the cost reduction resulting from the promotion of market competition [7, 13].

5 Conclusions and Further Research

This paper further explores previous research on ISoS and ECoNet frameworks to support a collaborative mobility service provider. This involved detailing the strategy to develop open reference models, guided by digital auditing from transport and mobility and bank authorities. The potential failure and performance (scalability) risks of current distributed computing technology systems suggest the adoption of an independent technology approach. The proposed ISoS framework was demonstrated in various projects to make viable the adoption of different technology paradigms. The proposed Isystem, CES, and Service concepts make it possible to develop adaptive modular informatics systems and, in this way, offer promising solutions for the identified business processes. For the networked dimension, the ECoNet platform is proposed to unify collaborative business exchanges of both data and control. The collaborative contexts and virtual Collaborative Contexts, managed by the ECoM Isystem, are part of a unified strategy to manage business interactions under a common framework. The organization's Isystems integrate with ECoM to automate collaboration processes and, in the mobility service provider case, to establish the base for a common digital auditing strategy for both transport and mobility and bank authorities.

The complexity of the discussed endeavor requires further research answering several open questions, namely, how to:

i. Implement fault tolerance mechanisms for interactions mediated by a collaboration context (a CoC of the ECoM Isystem);

ii. Coordinate monitoring systems responsible for the generation of explanations for complex exceptions and errors that might happen;

iii. Maintain and evolve the proposed MDEOS open specifications, and reference implementations on the assumption that operational and business risks need to be assumed by a clear leadership; and

iv. Balance the pressure of innovation, frequently led by the market motivated by the advantage to maintain a "windows of opportunity" [18], and the need to converge for replaceable solutions or parts of solutions.

Acknowledgments. Special thanks to Paulo Borges, as a research fellow leading the development of ISoS in a pre-stage for an open specifications and open source initiative under SOCOLNET scientific network and its ARCON-ACM initiative. This work has been partially supported by BP Portugal through the research project HORUS, by the A-to-Be (Brisa Innovation and Technology) with MOBICS/CITS project and SITL-IoT a PT-2020 Research Project with FORDESI Isystems and services development company. Partial support also from the Center of Technology and Systems – UNINOVA, and the Portuguese FCT-PEST program UID/EEA/00066/2019.

References

1. Cerny, T., Donahoo, M.J., Trnka, M.: Contextual understanding of microservice architecture: current and future directions. SIGAPP Appl. Comput. Rev. **17**(4), 29–45 (2018)

2. Daugherty, P., Carrel-Billiard, M.: The post-digital era is upon us are you ready for what's next. Technical report, Accenture Technology Vision 2019 (2019)

3. Hassan, A.E., Holt, R.C.: The chaos of software development. In: Proceedings of the 6th International Workshop on Principles of Software Evolution, IWPSE 2003, 84 p. IEEE Computer Society, Washington, DC (2003)

4. Keating, C.B., Gheorghe, A.V.: Systems thinking: foundations for enhancing system of systems engineering. In: 2016 11th System of Systems Engineering Conference (SoSE), pp. 1–6, June 2016

5. Kuhrmann, M., et al.: Software and system development in practice: waterfall, scrum, and beyond, July 2017

6. Lee, K., Lim, C., Song, W.: Emerging digital technology as a window of opportunity and technological leapfrogging: Catch-up in digital TV by the Korean firms. Int. J. Technol. Manag. **29**, 01 (2005)

7. Osório, A.L., Belloum, A., Afsarmanesh, H., Camarinha-Matos, L.M.: Agnostic informatics system of systems: the open ISoS services framework. In: Camarinha-Matos, L.M., Afsarmanesh, H., Fornasiero, R. (eds.) PRO-VE 2017. IAICT, vol. 506, pp. 407–420. Springer, Cham (2017). https://doi.org/10.1007/978-3-319-65151-4_37

8. McCabe, T.J.: A complexity measure. In: Proceedings of the 2nd International Conference on Software Engineering, ICSE 1976, p. 407. IEEE Computer Society Press, Los Alamitos (1976)

9. Northrop, L., et al.: Ultra-large-scale systems - the software challenge of the future. Technical report, Software Engineering Institute, Carnegie Mellon, June 2006

10. Osório, A.L., Camarinha-Matos, L.M., Afsarmanesh, H.: Cooperation enabled systems for collaborative networks. In: Camarinha-Matos, L.M., Pereira-Klen, A., Afsarmanesh, H. (eds.) PRO-VE 2011. IAICT, vol. 362, pp. 400–409. Springer, Heidelberg (2011). https://doi.org/10.1007/978-3-642-23330-2_44

11. Osório, A.L., et al.: Open multi-technology service oriented architecture for "its" business models: the ITSIBus Etoll services. In: Camarinha-Matos, L.M., Afsarmanesh, H., Ortiz, A. (eds.) PRO-VE 2005. ITIFIP, vol. 186, pp. 439–446. Springer, Boston, MA (2005). https://doi.org/10.1007/0-387-29360-4_46

12. Osório, A.L.: Towards vendor-agnostic IT-system of IT-systems with the CEDE platform. In: Afsarmanesh, H., Camarinha-Matos, L.M., Lucas Soares, A. (eds.) PRO-VE 2016. IAICT, vol. 480, pp. 494–505. Springer, Cham (2016). https://doi.org/10.1007/978-3-319-45390-3_42

13. Osório, A.L., Camarinha-Matos, L.M., Afsarmanesh, H., Belloum, A.: On reliable collaborative mobility services. In: Camarinha-Matos, L.M., Afsarmanesh, H., Rezgui, Y. (eds.) PRO-VE 2018. IAICT, vol. 534, pp. 297–311. Springer, Cham (2018). https://doi.org/10.1007/978-3-319-99127-6_26

14. Osorio, L.A., Camarinha-Matos, L.M.: Distributed process execution in collaborative networks. J. Rob. Comput. Integr. Manuf. 24(5), 647–655 (2008)

15. Osório, L.A., Camarinha-Matos, L.M., Afsarmanesh, H.: ECoNet platform for collaborative logistics and transport. In: Camarinha-Matos, L.M., Bénaben, F., Picard, W. (eds.) PRO-VE 2015. IAICT, vol. 463, pp. 265–276. Springer, Cham (2015). https://doi.org/10.1007/978-3-319-24141-8_24

16. Stoicescu, M., Fabre, J.-C., Roy, M.: Architecting resilient computing systems: a component-based approach for adaptive fault tolerance. J. Syst. Architect. 73, 6–16 (2017). Special Issue on Reliable Software Technologies for Dependable Distributed Systems

17. Thalheim, J., Bhatotia, P., Fonseca, P., Kasikci, B.: Cntr: lightweight OS containers. In: 2018 USENIX Annual Technical Conference (USENIX ATC 2018), pp. 199–212. USENIX Association, Boston (2018)

18. Tyre, M.J., Orlikowski, W.J.: Windows of opportunity: temporal patterns of technological adaptation in organizations. Organ. Sci. 5(1), 98–118 (1994)

19. Waldo, J.: Alive and well: Jini technology today. IEEE Comput. 33(6), 107–109 (2000)

20. Zahariadis, T., et al.: FIWARE lab: managing resources and services in a cloud federation supporting future internet applications. In: Proceedings of the 2014 IEEE/ACM 7th International Conference on Utility and Cloud Computing, UCC 2014, pp. 792–799. IEEE Computer Society, Washington, DC (2014)

Value-Added Services, Virtual Enterprises and Data Spaces Inspired Enterprise Architecture for Smart Cities

Sobah Abbas Petersen[1(✉)], Zohreh Pourzolfaghar[2], Iyas Alloush[2],
Dirk Ahlers[3], John Krogstie[1], and Markus Helfert[2]

[1] Department of Computer Science,
Norwegian University of Science and Technology, Trondheim, Norway
{sap,krogstie}@ntnu.no
[2] Lero - The Irish Software Research Centre, School of Computing,
Dublin City University, Dublin, Ireland
{Zohreh.Pourzolfaghar,iyas.alloush,
markus.helfert}@dcu.ie
[3] Department of Architecture and Planning,
Norwegian University of Science and Technology, Trondheim, Norway
Dirk.ahlers@ntnu.no

Abstract. As a part of their digital transformation, municipalities across Europe have taken initiatives to support Open Data platforms and provide services leveraging on data. This challenges the traditional business driven IT strategy promoted by several Enterprise Architecture methodologies, which are designed to operate within a single enterprise that has a complete overview of its data and ICT systems. We envisage scenarios where public and private collaborative networks provide value added services to its citizens by leveraging on data. In this paper, we propose an Enterprise Architecture Framework for Cities to support them maneuvre smartly within their data space to create value added services through a variety of collaborative networks or Virtual Enterprises that bridge organisational boundaries. The novel elements of this Enterprise Architecture Framework are a DataxChange, the Value-Added Services and Virtual Enterprise layers. This work has been conducted within the EU H2020 Smart City project +CityxChange.

Keywords: Data Spaces · Enterprise Architecture Framework · Smart Cities · Collaborative networks · Positive Energy Blocks

1 Introduction

Sustainability and digital transformation and are two of the main driving forces for cities and municipalities today. Current Smart City approaches have advanced from monitoring various aspects of a city through sensor and other data to providing services to its citizens in more collaborative ways [1, 2]. We adopt the view of a smart city that integrates people, technology and information to create a sustainable and resilient infrastructure that provides high quality services for its citizens [3]. The data that is

© IFIP International Federation for Information Processing 2019
Published by Springer Nature Switzerland AG 2019
L. M. Camarinha-Matos et al. (Eds.): PRO-VE 2019, IFIP AICT 568, pp. 393–402, 2019.
https://doi.org/10.1007/978-3-030-28464-0_34

gathered through sensors and/or other sources are central to developing value added services for the citizens. We envisage scenarios where public and private collaborative networks (CNs) provide value added services to its citizens by leveraging on data and systems that bridge different organisations.

The work reported in this paper is motivated the EU H2020 project +CityxChange, which focuses on Positive Energy Blocks (PEBs) to reduce emissions in cities and communities towards reaching the Paris Climate Goals [4]. Taking a broad perspective of cities and communities in the light of UN's Sustainable Development Goals (SDG); in particular SDGs 7, 11 and 13 (Affordable Clean Energy, Sustainable Cities and Societies and Climate action respectively), there is a need to engage citizens and to develop a portfolio of value added services that will enable citizens to increase their awareness about environmental sustainability and to help them make better choices. Furthermore, cities are motivated to engage their private businesses and other stake-holders in novel and innovative partnerships to provide value added services to the citizens.

One of challenges faced by cities and service providers is the lack of access to relevant data or indeed an overview of available data and relevant actors. Enterprise Architecture (EA) used initially in the business world to bridge between the business needs and the ICT strategy of a company has been used in Smart City contexts to bridge the needs of a city with ICT, resulting in a number of Smart City Enterprise Architecture Frameworks (EAFs). Our review of several EAFs from Smart City projects show that while several of them identify the need for services, the emphasis on the role of data is not so evident. We argue that the role of data must be a central component of a Smart City EAF, to support the drive for digital transformation as well as the effective use of available data.

In this paper, we propose a layered EAF for +CityxChange and Smart Cities in general where a DataxChange lies at the heart of the EAF. The DataxChange bridges the technology layers and the higher layers of the architecture, such as the business collaborations and value added services. The proposed architecture builds upon existing work, and complements them by emphasising the novel elements, which are the DataxChange, the Value-Added Services and the Virtual Enterprise (VE) layers to support CNs.

This paper is structured as follows: Sect. 2 describes the +CityxChange project; Sect. 3 describes our vision for a Smart City EAF; Sect. 4 describes the +CityxChange EAF to realise such a vision; Sect. 5 illustrates how value added services can be supported by EAF; Sect. 6 gives an overview of related work and Sect. 7 summarises the paper and provides an outline of the future work.

2   +CityxChange Project

The background and motivation for this paper is the EU H2020 funded +CityxChange project [5] that aims to develop PEBs in smart cities and communities as part of emission reductions to reach the Paris Climate Goals [4]. It is a Lighthouse project, where Trondheim, Norway, and Limerick, Ireland, are the lighthouse cities, and five follower cities showcase replication. The consortium of 32 partners include universities, municipalities, utility and infrastructure providers and other private entrepreneurs. It follows an integrative approach with a strong focus on city integration, open innovation and replicability. The approach combines:

- Integrated Planning and Design of cities;
- Creation and Enabling of a Common Energy Market;
- A CommunityxChange with all stakeholders of the city to create connected and engaged communities.

The project focuses on the technical solutions as well as the interactions and integration between buildings, users, cities and the energy system. It also focuses on the implications and impact on city planning, city systems, energy trading, citizen involvement, policies and regulations, data and digitalisation and socio-economic issues. A Positive Energy Blocks (PEB) is defined by the EU as several buildings that actively manage their energy consumption and the energy flow between them and the wider energy system[1]. They achieve an annual positive energy balance through use, optimization and integration of advanced materials, energy reduction, local renewable energy production and storage, smart energy grids, demand-response, energy management of electricity, heating and cooling, user involvement. PEBs or Positive Energy Districts (PEDs) are designed as an integral part of the district energy system. They should be intrinsically scalable up to positive energy districts and cities and are well embedded in the spatial, economic, technical, environmental and social contexts.

New forms of integrated spatial, social, political, economic, regulatory, legal and technological innovations are envisaged to deliver citizen observatories, innovation playgrounds and regulatory sandboxes linked to Urban Living Labs. Municipalities will develop Bold City Visions to engage civil society, local authorities, industry and Research and Technology Organisations to scale up from PEBs to PEDs or Positive Energy Cities, supported by a distributed and modular energy system architecture.

The ICT related challenges faced by the +CityxChange project include the lack of a means or forum for discovering existing and available data and services and indeed accessing and retrieving relevant data from available data sources [6], for use in developing value added services. ICT is envisaged to play a central role as an enabler for innovative value added services, stimulating new collaborations and in achieving PEBs and scaling up to the district and city levels. Similarly, ICT will provide support for the replication of solutions from the Lighthouse cities to the follower cities [4, 6].

3 Vision

Our vision for an EAF to support the +CityxChange project and Smart Cities in general is driven by the need and availability of data and systems and the central role that data plays in today's cities and how the data could be leveraged to provide value-added services to the citizens. Many Smart City concepts are inherently multi-disciplinary and

---

[1] https://ec.europa.eu/info/funding-tenders/opportunities/portal/screen/opportunities/topic-details/lc-sc3-scc-1-2018-2019-2020.

need the collaboration of various stakeholders from different domains, including cities and citizens [7]. New and innovative value added services could be provided by diverse constellations of CNs or VEs, which are a group of partners that collaborate to achieve a specific goal [8]. Our vision will address some of the shortcoming of existing EAFs to meet the needs of smart cities.

We believe that data can play a central role in bridging the technology aspects to the strategic and business aspects of an enterprise, such as the business collaborations and value added services. The central role of data and its value to an organisation has been discussed in many contexts, such as Industry 4.0 [9]. The need for supporting collaborative data analysis and processing and enhancing collaboration support among the data owners, data scientists and indeed service providers have received attention [10]. Examples of leveraging on data in the context of smart cities have appeared recently in the literature; in Helsinki, the city has been considered as a Living Lab and the data that is collected has been used to develop services as mobile applications [11]. The need for easy discovery of existing and available data and services and indeed accessing and retrieving relevant data is increasing and is one of the main challenges in the +CityxChange project. Thus, an EAF that supports an overview of data and the meta-data related will be an important asset to the creation and operation of value-added services in a smart city. If the stakeholders of a smart city have an overview of data that is potentially accessible and available for them to leverage on, the potential of value added services for the citizens can be enhanced.

CNs and VEs have long been discussed as means and drivers for value creation [12]. More recently, they have been discussed as an important mechanism in the context of leveraging on the vast amounts of data that are available in many contexts; e.g. [13]. Bringing these concepts to the heart of an EAF is essential in supporting the creation of innovative and value added services in the context of smart cities. This can facilitate the integration of services vertically within a city such as technological support, data processing as well as operational services, and connecting them to a clearly identified value to the city and citizens. Similarly, it can ensure the integration of the processes horizontally across the value chain around data, such as the data owners, processors and data consumers. Furthermore, this can support empowerment not only of the citizens, but provide opportunities for project partners to collaborate in new and innovative CNs, VEs and business models.

4   +CityxChange Enterprise Architecture Framework

Based on the literature and the smart city EAFs developed in relevant EU projects, such as the Smart City project SmartEnCity [2] and the standardisation efforts in ESPRESSO [1], we propose a layered EAF for the +CityxChange project, as illustrated in Fig. 1. The main driver for the EA is the "service-based ecosystem", identified as an objective for the EA in the +CityxChange project [6]. The scenarios envisaged for the project span many application domains (or silos) such as energy, transport, IoT, built environment and governance. An example of a value added service considered in the project that spans several application domains is eMobility as a service, across energy, transport and urban planning domain.

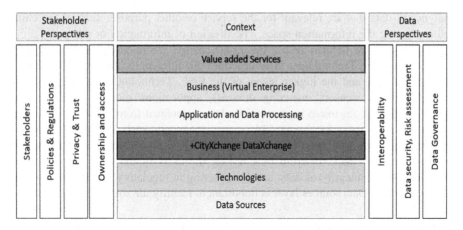

Fig. 1. +CityxChange enterprise architecture framework

Several horizontal layers are defined in the EAF to support value added services, which utilise data and are provided by collaborations among two or more enterprises; i.e. by a VE. The thinking behind the layered approach is that each layer supports the layer above it. Thus, the value-added services are supported by one or more businesses or a VE, which are supported by one or many applications, which use data from the +CityxChange DataxChange layer. The +CityxChange DataxChange is supported by technologies and finally, the data is obtained from data sources.

The +CityxChange DataxChange is at the heart of the EAF, where this layer provides an overview of all available data and systems and relevant information about the data that is required for creating value added services. Relevant information about the data will include the owner of the data, how the data may be accessed and the conditions and criteria that may be necessary to access or use the data. The DataXchange plays a central role in providing a comprehensive overview of the available data, providing the support that the various service providers need. Indeed, it should provide information about the relevant and potential collaboration partners that could participate in providing value added services to citizens, leveraging the data. The DataXchange provides a means to bridge the lower levels of the EAF, such as supporting technologies, and the higher levels of the EAF, such as the value added services. Furthermore, this layer will also serve as a common "platform" for the lower layers to facilitate access to data for the higher layers. Together with the Business Layer, this layer is designed to support concepts such as data markets and data as a commodity in the near future.

The highest layer of the EA is the context layer, which drives the services and the business context. Value added services are created to meet the needs of the citizens or to affect and change their behaviour to meet the strategy of the city or some business actor. The Value added Service layer is below the Context layer, which both offers services to and uses data and applications from the different application domains and involves one or more actors. The Application and Data Processing Layer describes the different applications that support the services. Applications may support processing or analytics of data that are relevant for the service or other purposes such as searching and navigating the information space, visualisation of information or other.

Two layers are defined below the DataXchange: Technologies layer and Data Sources layer. The Technologies layer describes the different technologies that support the DataXchange and the higher layers of the EAF. Technologies include hardware (e.g. servers and sensors, metering devices), applications such as databases and infrastructure, e.g. for micro payments. As data is obtained from a variety of sources such as IoT, sensors or local renewable energy production such solar panels mounted on private property, the origin of the data is essential for data governance; for ensuring the quality of the data, fostering trust among the users of the data, for supporting transparency and integrity of data, and for adhering to regulatory frameworks such as GDPR. Thus the Data sources layer is important to identify the sources that provide the data.

Related to the horizontal layers, we have two perspectives: (i) Stakeholder perspective to highlight the different stakeholders, their roles and perspectives; and (ii) Data perspective to address the specific principles and guidelines that are relevant in data-rich environments. These perspectives apply to all or most levels of the EAF as shown in Fig. 1. A number of high level principles were identified for the +CityxxChange EAF in [6]. These perspectives provide a means of structuring and contextualising guidelines and principles for using the +CityxChange EAF. A detailed description of principles and guidelines are provided in [14].

4.1 Stakeholder Perspectives

The +CityxChange project has a citizen focussed approach with several tasks dedicated to citizen engagement. Similarly, the service-based ecosystem and the participation of several public and private entities call for close attention to the diverse stakeholders that are a part of the city-wide or +CityxChange-wide EA space. Stakeholders describe the various entities involved in the city-wide EA space, which include citizens, service providers and consumers, who develop service to create added value. Stakeholders also include data owners, providers, processors and consumers of data, public authorities, private enterprises, researchers and various communities (e.g. a local housing complex).

Privacy and Trust describes the relevant principles and guidelines that need to be followed not only to respect and protect the privacy of individual people and organisations, but also support a network of trust among the various stakeholders of the +CityxChange DataxChange and value added services. Given the focus on stakeholders and the protection of individuals through the recent EU GDRP regulations, we have chosen to separate privacy and trust from data security (although they are dependent on one another). An EAF for a smart city spans beyond organisational boundaries and consequently the potential of sharing privacy-related data among stakeholders and data processors from a number of different organisations can be envisaged. Thus, the need to increase awareness of privacy-related issues and designing to ensure privacy and trust and compliance to regulations, in particular with respect to the use of stored data for multiple purposes, increases.

Policies and regulations describe the regulatory stakeholders that are involved in the project, the influencers and stakeholders and services that are affected by the specific policies and regulations. Ownership and access describe the relationships between the stakeholders and the entities that will be represented in the layers of the EAF. The scenarios envisaged in the project highlight that the relationships between the data and other entities or the ownership or accessibility models for data elements are not simple, uniform or trivial.

4.2 Data Perspectives

The +CityxChange project envisages value added services that leverage on data and system integration that is available through the +CityxChange DataxChange or indeed Open Data. Thus, there is a data perspective related to all layers of the EAF, from the data sources to the value added services. This raises a need to address the data perspectives.

Interoperability addresses how entities, through all the layers in the EAF, could be brought together in a cohesive way to provide the value added services. Interoperability applies to all the levels of the EAF.

Data security and risk assessment apply to all the layers of the EAF to ensure that the data is handled in a secure and reliable manner. The security of data is not a static state; i.e. data that is secure at any time may not be secure at a future time, and thus requires regular assessments of risks and threats to the security of the data.

Data Governance ensures proper data management and ownership processes and data quality and encompasses people, organisations and processes. Data governance ensures that data is consistent, available and useable.

5 Value Added Services

One or more value added services (example services A, B and X) could be created by using the data available from the +CityxChange DataxChange, as shown in Fig. 2.

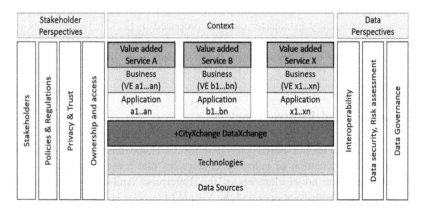

Fig. 2. Value added services as an instance in the +CityxChange EAF

Each of the services are likely delivered by collaboration among one or more organisations; any organisation may participate in the delivery of one or more services and participate in one or more VEs. For example, the municipality of a specific city may be a part of a VE that provides both the Services A and B. Similarly, the same municipality may also play a role in Service X, perhaps different to that for the Services A and B. This simple example illustrates that several elements (data/services) from the DataxChange may be used by one or more services.

Based on the scenarios envisaged for the +CityxChange project and the visions of the Lighthouse cities that have been shared and integrated so far, we see the need to support such value added services and the need to share data and the ability to incorporate new data that is generated through the value added services. The +CityxChange DataxChange is designed to facilitate such activities.

6   Related Work

EA concerns the overall ICT landscape and alignment of the business strategy and its ICT implementation. Several EAFs have been proposed for Smart Cities. Based on the leading EAF in the industry [15], The Open Group's EA, TOGAF [16], several Smart City EAFs are based on a multi-tier or layered approach proposed; e.g. [1, 17–20]. The notion of services is identified explicitly in some of the EAFs [1, 2, 19, 21]. The service layer identifies the business and the stakeholder perspectives, often considered as services offered by municipalities or the cities.

Of particular interest to our work is the Intelligent Data Spaces Reference Architecture Model (IDS-RAM), proposed by the German Fraunhofer Institute and the International Data Spaces Initiative [9]. They describe an Industrial Data Space as a "virtual data space leveraging existing standards and technologies as well as accepted governance models for the data economy, to facilitate the secure and standardized exchange and easy linkage of data in a trusted business ecosystem". Similar to other EAFs, IDS-RAM also takes a layered approach. However, a few things distinguish it from the other frameworks and methodologies; e.g. it focuses on the Industrial Data Space and it takes a data-centric approach and thus supports both top-down and bottom-up approaches. A framework which describes foundation and principles for Information Technology in smarter cities is proposed in [22]. It incorporates instrumented data from sensors, Integration of data and intelligent inclusion of complex analytics, modelling and optimization, and visualization in operational business processes.

7   Summary and Future Work

An EAF to support a service-based ecosystem for the +CitxChange project is proposed, which supports the creation of value added services that leverage available data and services/systems. The novel elements of this Enterprise Architecture are the DataxChange, the Value-Added Services and the Virtual Enterprise layers. A DataxChange is at the heart of this architecture, which we argue is an essential part of a Smart

City EAF, and which will bring together all available data and relevant information about the data to support the creation of value added services, by collaborative networks of partners from public private and research sectors. The DataXchange layer provides a bridge between the lower levels of the EAF, such as supporting technologies and data sources, and the higher levels of the EAF, such as the value added services.

The proposed architecture is work in progress and we are working on refining this EAF by applying it to describe the different services that will be developed in the project. Furthermore, this EAF is envisaged as a support in reaching out to the partners who will participate in the VEs providing the value added services, and in driving the dialogue in the iterative definitions of the value added services. As such, it can also support many of the collaborative relationships within a complex project and provide additional technical frameworks and collaboration spaces, based on a joint understanding of the ICT relationships and networks within the project. These should also support easier communication, information access, and knowledge finding and sharing within the project. Our next steps are to describe a few scenarios and services using this EAF and facilitate the service description process, while refining the EAF based on the feedback.

Acknowledgements. +CityxChange is a smart city project under the Smart Cities and Communities topic that is funded by the European Union's Horizon 2020 Research and Innovation programme under Grant Agreement No. 824260. The authors would like to thank the project partners from Trondheim Municipality, Limerick City Council and the participants of work packages 1 and 2 as well as the whole project team.

References

1. ESPRESSO project (systEmic Standardization apPRoach to Empower Smart citieS and cOmmunities): Deliverable D4.2 – Definition of Smart City Reference Architecture (2016)
2. SmartEnCity: Deliverable 6.3: Data Model Architecture Implementation (2017)
3. Villanueva-Rosales, N., et al.: A collaborative, interdisciplinary initiative for a smart cities innovation network. In: EEE First International Smart Cities Conference (ISC2), pp. 25–28. IEEE, Guadalajara, October 2015
4. United Nations Climate Change: What is the Paris Agreement? https://unfccc.int/process-and-meetings/the-paris-agreement/what-is-the-paris-agreement. Accessed 20 May 2019
5. +CityXChange: Positive Energy Blocks (2019). http://cityxchange.eu/. Accessed 19 May 2019
6. Ahlers, D., Wienhofen, L.W.M., Petersen, S.A., Anvaari, M.: A smart city ecosystem enabling open innovation. In: 19th International Conference Innovations for Community Services (I4CS), Wolfsburg, Germany (2019)
7. Ahlers, D., Driscoll, P., Löfström, E., Krogstie, J., Wyckmans, A.: Understanding smart cities as social machines. In: Workshop on the Theory and Practice of Social Machines @ WWW 2016, IW3C2 2016 (2016)
8. Petersen, S.A.: Virtual enterprise formation and partner selection: an analysis using case studies. Int. J. Netw. Virtual Organ. **4**(2), 201–215 (2007)
9. Otto, B., Lohmann, S., Steinbuß, S., Teuscher, A.: IDS reference architecture model, industrial data space, version 2.0. In: International Data Spaces Association & Fraunhofer (2018)

10. Park, K., Nguyen, M.C., Won, H.: Web-based collaborative big data analytics on big data as a service platform. In: 17th International Conference on Advanced Communication Technology (ICACT). IEEE (2015)
11. Hielkem, H., Hongisto, P.: Developing the Helsinki smart city: the role of competitions for open data applications. J. Knowl. Econ. **4**(2), 190–204 (2013)
12. Camarinha-Matos, L.M., Afsarmanesh, H.: Collaborative networks. In: Wang, K., Kovacs, G.L., Wozny, M., Fang, M. (eds.) PROLAMAT 2006. IIFIP, vol. 207, pp. 26–40. Springer, Boston, MA (2006). https://doi.org/10.1007/0-387-34403-9_4
13. Camarinha-Matos, L.M., Fornasiero, R., Afsarmanesh, H.: Collaborative networks as a core enabler of industry 4.0. In: Camarinha-Matos, L.M., Afsarmanesh, H., Fornasiero, R. (eds.) PRO-VE 2017. IAICT, vol. 506, pp. 3–17. Springer, Cham (2017). https://doi.org/10.1007/978-3-319-65151-4_1
14. Petersen, S.A., Alloush, I., Pourzolfaghar, Z., Helfert, M.: +CityxChange - D1.2 Report on the Architecture for the ICT Ecosystem - Initial Version (2019)
15. Cameron, B.H., McMillan, E.: Analyzing the current trends in enterprise architecture frameworks. J. Enterp. Archit. **9**(1), 60–71 (2013)
16. The Open Group: The Open Group Architecture Framework TOGAF Version 9.1 (2011)
17. Harrison, C., Donnelly, I.A.: A theory of smart citie. In: Proceedings of the 55th Annual Meeting of the ISSS-2011. Hull (2011)
18. IEC International Electrotechnical Commission: ISO/IEC JTC 1 Information technology, WG11 on Smart Cities (2019). https://www.iec.ch/dyn/www/f?p=103:14:34897880612264::::FSP_ORG_ID,FSP_LANG_ID:12973,25. Accessed 29 Apr 2019
19. Pourzolfaghar, Z., Bastidas, V., Helfert, M.: Standardisation of enterprise architecture development for smart cities. J. Knowl. Econ. (2019, under publication)
20. Winter, R., Fischer, R.: Essential layers, artifacts, and dependencies of enterprise architecture. J. Enterp. Archit. (2007)
21. Ferguson, D., Sairamesh, J., Feldman, S.: Open frameworks for information cities. Commun. ACM **47**(2), 45–49 (2004)
22. Harrison, C., et al.: Foundations for smarter cities. IBM J. Res. & Dev. **54**(4), 1–16 (2010)

Collaborative Building Ecosystems

Outlining a New Collaborative Business Model as a Result of the Green Building Information Modelling Impact in the AEC Supply Chain

João Vilas-Boas[1,2(✉)], Vahid Mirnoori[2], Alim Razy[2], and Agostinho Silva[3]

[1] Instituto Universitário de Lisboa (ISCTE-IUL), Lisbon, Portugal
jmvbs@iscte-iul.pt
[2] Business Research Unit (BRU-IUL), Lisbon, Portugal
{svmid,alim.al.razy}@iscte-iul.pt
[3] CEI – Companhia de Equipamentos Industriais, Lda.,
São João da Madeira, Portugal
a.silva@zipor.com

Abstract. BIM (Building Information Modelling) technological push has enabled to integrate the design/construction outcomes of 3D-CAD along the product/service AEC (Architecture, Engineering and Construction) SC (supply chain) through an intelligent DMS (Data Management System) based on standard and interoperable data formats. The proposed end-to-end approach overcomes a typical AEC gap, enables the operationalisation of the sustainable/green building LCA (Life Cycle Assessment) and puts together new collaborative relationships with the owner, among SC stakeholders and with new forms of BIM procurement. The outlined collaborative business model is based on the Quality Control and Assurance framework and provides conceptual consistency to the reintroduction of the owner concerns/satisfaction in the SC, as well as enables consistent and accountable relationships between (smart)materials procurement and building specification. An expert's focus group carried out a preliminary check of the model's interest/applicability, resulting in recommendations for its further detailing and for propositions development into a systematic enquiring process.

Keywords: Collaboration in the AEC supply chain ·
Collaborative business model for green BIM · Green BIM procurement ·
Collaborative customer relationships · Quality conformance in built assets

1 Introduction

Higher uncertainty in customized products demand, product range broadening, increasing product complexity, higher quality needs, shorter product life cycles, increasing green requirements, decreasing revenue margins, investment in Advanced Manufacturing Technology (AMT) are illustrative of current competitive challenges. These have been introducing requirements for: new organizational structures and, new business models, theories, processes and technologies, which, in turn, should allow companies to create innovative operations paradigms to face them [1].

© IFIP International Federation for Information Processing 2019
Published by Springer Nature Switzerland AG 2019
L. M. Camarinha-Matos et al. (Eds.): PRO-VE 2019, IFIP AICT 568, pp. 405–417, 2019.
https://doi.org/10.1007/978-3-030-28464-0_35

The proactive adoption of BIM by the AEC Industry has resulted from environmental, social and economic concerns and pressures that also foster the development of sustainable services and manufacturing processes [2, 3]. Moreover, Europe is going to adopt BIM for public contracting as promoted by the European Union Public Procurement Directive [4].

On the other hand, the lean paradigm aims also provide a basis for improving sustainability practices. These aims are, as follows: using fewer resources, improving quality and, reducing rework and waste and so, pollution. In turn, reducing rework and waste also supports a variety of lean transformation objectives [5] in a circular way. Moreover, it is possible to reduce waste and energy consumption, and to improve construction quality by using BIM [6]. In fact, BIM might significantly impact the business by promoting a technological push concerning: (i) the functional integration along the supply chain, which is not yet fully explored [7]; (ii) the data standardization that defines the information formats, geometry, behaviour and so, the presentation of BIM smart objects; for instance, the Industry Foundation Class (IFC) format maximizes consistency, efficiency and interoperability across the construction industry [8]; (iii) the data interoperable usability [9]; (iv) the inclusion of Information and Communication Technology (ICT) frameworks and technologies that support stakeholders' collaboration over projects life-cycle [10]; (v) the cloud-based sharing of the lists of products and materials with Building Product Manufacturers [11] and, (vi) a positive impact on materials conformance by assuring the improvement of consistency, quality and compatibility of BIM smart objects. Therefore, the need for consistent and available data, as well as for more precise and reliable procedures to effectively work with BIM is imperative [4]. While for design disciplines, BIM is an extension to CAD, for non-design disciplines, such as contractors and project managers, BIM is more like an intelligent Data Management System (DMS). These data management tools can quickly and directly take off data from CAD packages [12], despite both BIM and these applications are becoming more and more integrated. In fact, BIM objects operate in a Common Data Environment (CDE). Thus, through the use of a common standard, the integration of building and materials information, becomes possible leading to a more effective use of materials [8].

In classical Design-Bid-Build (DBB) project delivery there is a poor understanding between owner and users that together with the used architect milestones both generate large planning periods, lack of proper coordination and no collaboration. This results into late identification of excessive costs, nonconformance, too much reaction in control (no dependability), lead time increase, due date missing and contractual penalties [13, 14]. By replacing DBB, the use of BIM to provide data for the *earlier* evaluation of both energy performance and sustainability has been a cornerstone of the Green BIM definition; leading design organizations are adopting this approach to enable integrated design, construction and maintenance towards Net Zero Energy buildings. Green BIM includes Building Energy Modelling (BEM) dealing with project energy performance to identify better options to optimise building energy efficiency during the life cycle [4]. Within a DBB context, the energy analysis packages, when used, provide late feedback to the designers, just regarding how much energy the building will use, what are the anticipated CO_2 emissions and if the built asset will pass performance criteria (such as, LEED or BREEAM). In addition, materials decisions are usually based on cost minimisation and enter in the process too late, missing their critical role in the building envelope, specially the external walls [15]. However, BIM applications for energy analysis (BEM) have been introducing this discussion at earlier stages of the design stage [10]. Thus, shortcomings in materials' decisions could also be eliminated by an integrate project delivery approach [13] that might also change the owner participation role and promote active collaboration among stakeholders.

Therefore, in the following section of this paper, it is reported a unique conceptual merge between technical and management knowledge that will address a relevant gap that has been a missing link of building sustainability. In fact, there is an emerging need for a conformance correlation between the customer/owner dynamic priorities or expectations and the built asset. The use of conforming materials operationalised within the conceptual positioning on an end-to-end collaborative green model supported by BIM procurement was identified as a possible way to address the problem-situation. Reddy and Jagadish [16] confirm the interest of this gap concluding that material selection greatly contributes to the reduction of operational energy and emissions, in a separated way from the effects on embodied energy consumption. Moreover, Hardin and McCool [17] also position material selection and use among the three main areas of sustainable design that have a direct relationship to BIM.

So, in Sect. 2, a new innovative conceptual model focusing on the energy used by buildings during its operation will be deductively outlined from an in-depth literature review. Section 3 explains the adopted methodology. In Sect. 4, the empirical findings coming from a focus group of three experts are communicated and discussed to prepare this preliminary proposal for future adjustments and confirmation. Finally, in the conclusions section, the paper is closed over the research question, by considering the empirical findings. Recommendations for further developing the outlined conceptual model towards a process of enquiry are also made.

2   Outlining a Conceptual Model

Buildings account for a substantial proportion of global energy consumption [18]. The building sector is responsible for about 40% of the energy demand worldwide, 32% of CO_2 emissions, and about 24% of raw materials extraction [19, 20], which makes the AEC sector a major target for environmental improvement [21]. So, Bynum et al. [22] consider that global warming threats puts pressure on the construction industry to address more seriously the need for energy efficient buildings. Therefore, sustainability, in general, and energy efficiency, in particular, have become a key measure of building performance [10]. In fact, the main objective of sustainable design is to create buildings in sustainable cities that are livable, comfortable and safe. On the other hand, BIM does have the potential to aid designers to select the right type of materials during the early design stage and to make vital decisions that have great impacts on the life cycle of sustainable buildings [23].

This investigation is only going to focus on the energy used by buildings during its operation, which has been a major research trend [24] in green buildings. In fact, the operational stage consumes a bigger proportion of energy than all the other stages, over the lifecycle of buildings. These stages have been described as raw materials extraction and materials manufacturing (*initial embodied energy*, as defined by Yohanis and Norton [25]), construction and maintenance (*recurring embodied energy* as defined by Cole and Kernan [26] and, Ibn-Mohammed et al. [27]) and end of life (demolition and disposal) [28].

In fact, embodied energy can represent approximately 10 to 20% of the life cycle energy of a conventional building [29], which might be considered negligible. However, in some low-energy buildings, embodied energy contributes to more than 60% of life cycle energy [30, 31]. During the construction and demolition of the buildings, transportation is responsible for about 10 to 40% of the embodied energy demand and nearly 2% of the embodied carbon emissions [32–34]. Recent studies reveal that energy use for on-site construction makes only a marginal contribution to the building life cycle energy and emissions, which is made up of about 6.5% of embodied energy, 8% of embodied SO_2, 12% of embodied NO_x and 8% of embodied CO_2 [35, 36]. Therefore, in some studies energy use and emissions during on-site construction were also excluded from modelling and measurements [33, 37].

So, the energy performance of the building envelope and its components (external walls, roofs, windows etc.) can be critical in determining how much energy is required internally [38]. Popovic and Arnold [39] also consider that a properly designed and constructed envelope should be considered in the construction of a building façade. In addition to aesthetics, façades have an important role in affecting energy savings. However, façade failures are also originated by deficiencies caused by lack of quality control and supervision in design, construction, and maintenance [40]. Hence, this research is going to focus on the role of the external walls in the thermal balance of the building during its operation. So, the materials to be addressed concern the ones required to build adequate façades/external walls in thermal terms.

Within this context, and by following Garvin [41] guidance, a non-defective built asset, as regards operational energy performance, must conform with its Thermal Specification, which is a Design Outcome. In addition, the Design Outcome should conform with the Product Requirements Document, i.e. the Customer Expectations Outcomes (Fig. 1a). This approach eliminates a major gap pointed out by Naoum and Egbu [42], which concerns the separation of design from construction. Furthermore, the explicit inclusion of the customer (owner) priorities and expectations in the business process, also enables to overcome another gap concerning the lack of dynamic adjustments, by formally introducing them (also Naoum and Egbu, [42]). This is in line with the findings of Grilo et al. [43] that suggest that the role of the building owner is changing. They also identified requirements for a more open collaborative network, where specialised and integrated agents increase end-user interactions with users, flexibility and iterative facilities design. This organizational design is required to satisfy the social behaviour adequate to the operationalisation of the outlined model. In addition, a non-defective built asset must use materials with characteristics conforming the required building thermal specification. Thus, the materials SPEC should match its required thermal performance defined by their thermal requirements previously expressed in the Building Thermal Specification (Fig. 1b). This is the way that this descriptive conceptual model operationalises the material fitness for use as defined by Juran and Gryna [44].

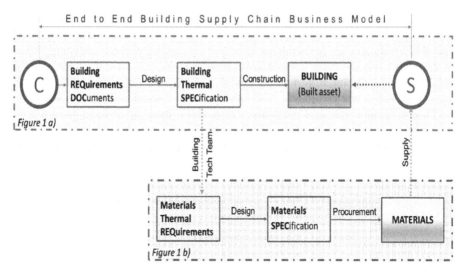

Fig. 1. Root definitions of a collaborative end-to-end business model to guarantee materials conforming to the building owner expectations

A collaborative end to end business model guided by the Quality Control and Assurance (QCA) principles is outlined, in Fig. 1. It is expected that it might guarantee that the chosen materials are adequate to the customer expectations for the building. Quality control and quality assurance are two terms that are often used interchangeably. Quality has been defined as fitness for use, conformance to requirements, and the pursuit of excellence [45]. The use of the QCA body of knowledge enabled the establishment of a direct link between the materials employed and the fulfilment of the building owner expectations by using a relevant objective criteria, i.e. the expected building energy performance. It might be argued that the quality control process might support a different customer requirements (CR) reasoning and a different type of procurement, i.e. BIM procurement (Fig. 1). In fact, QCA together with 3D CAD enables the energy analysis modules (BEM) to be run at early stages of the specification, on the top of the virtual building generated by BIM. So, the owner might be involved in the technical decision making process required to adjust the SPEC to the energy requirements of a green building taking visual advantage of a powerful Graphic Unit Interface (GUI). Moreover, using smart objects from electronic databases means the powerful ability to automatically adjust the building specification, if the material definition parameters are changed, e.g. to cope with changed owner requirements.

BIM includes a technical, an organisational and a social dimension. In this context, Singh et al. [12] consider that should include a concern with collaboration because AEC projects are mostly multi-organizational and multi-disciplinary. Thus, the success of BIM depends on its collective adoption by the professional users that are expected to participate in the collaboration activities. Moreover, the collaboration requirements would vary from project to project, and, hence, collaboration should be an integral part of the BIM development to better facilitate the adoption of the new technologies, leading to more intelligent automation in the AEC Industry. This collaborative social behaviour is the *glue* required to operationalise an integrated end to end approach to the AEC Supply Chain (AEC SC), i.e. from the building owner to the constructor, if a built asset that fits the use is expected to be delivered. Accordingly, cloud computing – i.e., an innovative way to access information in real time [46] and share it via internet – is identified as a relevant ICT missing link that is required to enable *seamless* data interchange across the end-to-end AEC SC in a *quasi*-integrated data approach [47].

To sum up, the outline of the conceptual model is made up of three parts. Firstly, the graphical representation of the idea was depicted. Secondly, a supported explanation of the assumptions, models and concepts is provided and, then, a supported description of the main elements and relationships of the model draft is made. Finally, a research question is formulated, as follows:

Which type of collaborative relationships might arise along the AEC supply chain powered by BIM procurement within the green building scope?

3 Methodology

When approaching a problem-situation we may take several types of world views – *Weltanschauung* [48]. While the specialists' one favours the detail, others might broaden the scope by enabling fresh insights from the chosen areas of knowledge. The latter also increase the complexity, but bring in a richer picture of the problem-situation, which is useful when the social component is relevant, in addition to the technical one [49]. Our choice was to include, in the root definitions of the problem [50], recognised knowledge such as Quality, Supply Chain Management, Sustainability, Collaborative Relationships and IS/IT in response to the repeated claims of the authors in the area. These were pointing out the same flaws for several years without a sufficient reaction from the specialists. So, the generic knowledge of these areas was first considered in the outline of a model to reposition the problem-situation and to structure it after an interdisciplinary approach. This aims at merging the views from technical, social and organizational backgrounds by offering the potential to structure the problem-situation in a different way that includes several relevant points of view, in addition to the specialists' one, i.e. Design-Bid-Build, BIM, BEM and BIM procurement, usually the ones strictly considered in the AEC Industry.

As this is an innovative approach, it was decided to run an exploratory qualitative research, which was conducted by putting together a focus group of specialists that were carefully chosen and so, by asking about their perceptions, opinions, beliefs, and attitudes towards the presented ideas. Three engineers were participating. They were chosen because of their technical, social and organizational competencies, as follows: (i) in AEC Industry and BIM (2 out of 3); (ii) in IS/IT and Customer Requirements (1); (iii) in CAD (3); (ii) in Collaborative Operations, Supply Chain, Procurement, Quality and Change Intervention Programmes (1); (iv) in Energy Balances and Sustainability (1). Topics were defined as clear and precise as possible, in an iterative way. There was a focus on enabling and taking notes about the outcomes of the interactive discussions between participants. The participants had both interest and characteristics related to the topics being discussed and they were encouraged to share their points of view without any pressure to reach a consensus.

These discussions were run several times, for 2 h each time, with similar participants. The group met on a regular weekly basis to discuss on going progress, during 4 months (February–May). Progress and adjustments were always emerging from the focus group meetings, in terms of the clarification of topics relevance, theories, concepts and their relationships. The results were also analysed together with the INOVSTONE® 4.0 Project Chief, in three occasions within this 5 month time horizon, to collect some feedback, guidance and validation. Data were treated and processed according to adequate techniques that are usually used to process text (i.e. the focus group notes) in qualitative analysis, i.e. contents analysis [51].

Moreover, issues to be discussed were generated from the literature review, which configures a hypothetical-deductive approach. The kick off question concerned the impact on the owners' role of new customer requirements arising from BIM procurement and green concerns in the AEC; then, a collaborative customer-centric view was developed; papers from a specialist background providing a clear picture of the status of the art in the AEC Industry were further read and discussed (main outcomes: need for quality procedures, unifying a split SC, green building and energy issues); so, the topic of Green Building related to lifecycle analysis and the identification of the building operation energy as critical, have showed up as the next tip to be followed; then, the impact of BIM in the project delivery and the comparison with the DBB approach brought in the BEM issue were the topics on demand; finally, the idea was to put together generic established knowledge like Quality, end-to-end Supply Chain, and Collaboration with the BIM integrated project delivery, in the scope of a relevant energy analysis considering the building LCA. The outline of the conceptual model (Fig. 1) was the resulting summary of all the relationships found.

To sum up, this exploratory assignment collected feedback from experts aiming at progressing towards a detailed conceptual model [52], in the future. Then, the emerging propositions will support the definition of questions for fine tuning a questionnaire to support semi-structured interviews taking place as further work.

4   Empirical Findings and Discussion

This section will report the preliminary findings coming from the focus group and run a first cross check with what some fellow researchers and authors in the addressed domains are saying from the same topics.

4.1   Conceptual Model Positioning After Quality Control and Assurance Guidance

The experts considered that the use of the quality Body of Knowledge (BoK) [e.g. 45], a well-established domain in the scientific community, provides a robust embedding for the descriptive model of the problem-situation (Fig. 1). The Quality BoK has being been sharply developed since the 1970s, when The British standard BS 5750 was first published, in 1979, despite many isolated but important occurrences might be traced back to earlier times [53]. In fact, by setting a credible, well-defined, relevant, clear and supported relationship between the building owner requirements and the physical materials to be procured and incorporated in construction appears to be an attractive idea, given the AEC problems. This would merge several knowledge areas under the umbrella of quality. Garvin [41] is very clear on identifying several definitions and a multi-dimension model to define and position quality. So, in the proposed conceptual model (Fig. 1), the following dimensions were used: (i) *product-based*, since a precise way to assess and link procured materials to building specification was outlined; (ii) *user-based*, since the building owner expectations/requirements were reintroduced in the end-to-end SC approach that supported the conceptual operationalisation of the QCA framework; this also satisfies a concern from the Service Science domain [54], which brings in services to the outlined model equation, in addition to the built asset as the physical product; (iii) *manufacturing-based* approach, since the concerns of manufacturing and procurement sides are included in the outlined model (Fig. 1); (iv) *value-based*, since value is about tangible and intangible benefits for the stakeholders and so, both the effort done to achieve them and the inclusion of owner view brings in to the equation the redefinition of the customer/owner requirements within a holistic context; BIM procurement is also addressed as a collaborative and empowered approach to the traditionally fragmented AEC SC; moreover, by the use of digital technologies all the AEC SC will be leveraged, from customer to materials suppliers. In this way, it is argued that the outlined model enables the conceptual design of an interdisciplinary rich picture (as defined *in* Silva, [55]) of the AEC SC. Still according with the specialists, this contextualization fits very well the needs of a holistic end-to-end approach to the supply chain that copes with many pointed out structural problems [e.g. 42, 56], in an innovative but supported way.

4.2 Impact of Building Information Modelling

Secondary data [51] coming from checking a practitioner' site [11] confirmed the experts' opinion that BIM as an intelligent cloud based collaborative Data Management System (DMS) is a *sine qua non* condition to create and share design, bill of materials, tenders, bids and direct orders seamlessly and so, overcome the AEC weakness concerning the split between design and construction [e.g. 42, 56]. In fact, allowing the automation of several procurement processes, diminishing the probability of errors and processes duration are expected direct results of the BIM procurement DMS component [57]. Moreover, data interoperability and standardization are required to do a comparison of the products supplied by different suppliers [58] and so, increase visibility, transparency and fairness through BIM procurement. In addition, collaborative processes in procurement arise primarily from buying requirements through the specification development process, using real-time communication and exchange of information [59], which confirms the DMS need *ab initio*. Therefore, a collaborative environment is possible to develop in BIM procurement, instead of confrontational attitudes between client, contractors and consultants under the traditional procurement arrangement [42].

The specialists went further on by considering that the requirements for Digital Technologies have to match the DMS base together with the reinforced CAD functionalities of modern BIM to support different functional or simulation systems and, massive real world data gathering and communication, which is corroborated by the findings of buildingSMART® [60]. According to them, BIM implementation should be done before any requirements or expectations concerning further processing by many other different systems (e.g. Digital Business Platforms, e-procurement, engineering packages, etc.), information/data broadcasting, sensory systems to collect real world data, big data analytics, augmented/virtual reality technologies, cyber physical systems, etc. For instance, an improved coordination among appliances to optimize the usage of room allocated to maintenance accesses or, the use utilisation of augmented reality to follow/detect pipes embodied in the walls are just two examples of innovative functionalities enabled by BIM reinforced CAD functionalities that were mentioned by the experts. Many examples supporting more types of new functionalities coming from 4D CAD are also mentioned in the literature. For instance, the combination of 3D CAD and 4D animations can dramatically improve communication, coordination, and planning of construction projects, while reducing risks and costs [13].

4.3 Sustainable Collaborative Supply Chain

The focus group participants also agreed that the expected supply chain view is not always pursued in practice [e.g. 42, 56] and, also, that it should be expanded to include not only the design/built asset relationship, but also the customer/building owner expectations/requirements, as well [44]. This is a holistic end-to-end SC approach that is also required by LCA, which is a core concept in green building [28]. The general feeling is that addressing the whole supply chain from the building-owner to the materials supplier, under a collaborative approach supported by a BIM platform using interoperable data, promotes more transparent and fairer design and construction processes with an expected improvement in terms of product conformance, timings and costs [e.g. 60]. Moreover, the experts are quite confident that involving the owner/customer with the building specification and construction, by assuring a more reliable, participative and objective collaborative partnership, should generate visibility, transparency, full traceability and higher fulfilment of its expectations. In some way, this will soften the ownership of many technical decisions that used to be exclusively made by the building technical team, by co-creation with the customer [54]. One of the participants even commented that this is a similar process of the one supporting the House of Quality technique [61], where the technical decisions are related to the customer (in this context, the owner) requirements (customer-centric). Therefore, the decisions might be more humanized, perhaps more driven towards a broader sustainable interest and not focusing exclusively on short term costs [23], as many times happens, accordingly to the experts' opinion. Still, according to them, the current stricter unidimensional focus was advanced as one major reason why the last part of the LCA concerning maintenance and demolition is ignored, exactly as suggested by Vigovskaya et al. [62].

5 Conclusions

Revisiting both the formulated research question and the experts' opinions, one might conclude that there are relevant positive correlations and synergies among the involvement of the built assets owner (i.e. a customer-centric approach), internal collaborative works (including all the involved professionals) and the BIM procurement process. In fact, evolving information technologies applied to innovative integrated project delivery approaches have shown up as powerful drivers to outline a new conceptual business model for the AEC SC context. So, the implementation of a new information paradigm for the AEC sector (BIM) is expected to leverage the whole supply chain performance under a quality umbrella that links the owner expectations to the procurement of smart materials. Guided by BEM, sustainable operations are pushed towards LCA, which is a core concept for green building ratings. Therefore, the expected resulting reduction in energy consumption during the total operational life of the building represents a relevant positive impact on the environment, which is an important contribution to the practice and society in general [*vide* 63]. In addition, the outlined model enables the practitioner to benefit from the possibility to specify and procure materials for the external walls that are in conformance with the built asset thermal specification. So, there appears to be a relevant research contribution of this business model concept that enables a different decision making support to materials procurement, when compared with the consultants prescriptions based on their unsupported and many times biased opinion. At last, it is argued for the outlined conceptual model as being innovative because it adds value to the AEC sector by working on the boundaries of several areas of knowledge, promoting their merge towards a relevant collaborative proposal for the construction industry.

However, a research limitation was recognized as regards the empirical part of the exploratory study, which was purposefully designed to preliminarily check the feasibility and interest of the presented approach. In order to overcome it, in the sequence of this paper, our research line has been cross-investigating if the BIM authoring tools are complying with the generic expectations that were introduced by the outlined model. So, the innovative contribution to theory is the operationalisation of a richer picture of the problem-situation by expanding its root definitions, during the structuring of the real world situation (unstructured). This includes knowledge areas that could provide a more complete response to the recurrent criticism of the authors from an AEC background. This is neither the best, nor the unique answer, but a relevant innovative one, because it is unique and supported on knowledge accepted by the scientific community.

As a recommendation for future work, the grounded knowledge generated by the preliminary empirical discussion of this model might support an extension to the in depth literature review towards establishing robust innovative propositions that further detail it. These propositions would generate questions for a process of inquiry [55] to be operationalised by semi-structured interviews that would gather the empirical data required to a more robust confirmation of the model. Moreover, the introduced customer centric approach leading to co-design and co-creation should be further discussed under the umbrella of adequate management theories that concern how well the representing actors (agents) match the ones that are being represented (principals).

Acknowledgements. This research is supported by the INOVSTONE® 4.0 Project, which is funded by *Portugal 2020*, within the scope of *Programa Operacional Competitividade e Internacionalização e Programa Operacional Regional de Lisboa*.

References

1. Camarinha-Matos, L.M., Afsarmanesh, H., Galeano, N., Molina, A.: Collaborative networked organizations-concepts and practice in manufacturing enterprises. J. Comput. Ind. Eng. **57**(1), 46–60 (2009)
2. Sacks, R., Koskela, L., Dave, B., Owen, R.: Interaction of lean and BIM in construction. J. Constr. Eng. Manag. **136**(9), 968–980 (2010)
3. Arayici, Y., Coates, P., Koskela, L., Kagioglou, M., Usher, C., O'reilly, K.: Technology adoption in the BIM implementation for lean architectural practice. J. Autom. Constr. **20**(2), 189–195 (2011)
4. Maltese, S., Tagliabue, L.C., Cecconi, F.R., Pasini, D., Manfren, M., Ciribini, A.L.: Sustainability assessment through green BIM for environmental, social and economic efficiency. Proc. Eng. **180**, 520–530 (2017)
5. Piercy, N., Rich, N.: The relationship between lean operations and sustainable operations. J. Oper. Prod. Manag. **35**(2), 282–315 (2015)
6. Bonenberg, W., Wei, X.: Green BIM in sustainable infrastructure. Proc. Manuf. **3**, 1654–1659 (2015)
7. Papadonikolaki, E., Vrijhoef, R., Wamelink, H.: The interdependences of BIM and SC partnering. J. Architect. Eng. Design Manag. **12**(6), 476–494 (2016)
8. NBS National BIM Library - BIM Object Standard nbs-bim-object-standard/scope-and-purpose. https://www.nationalbimlibrary.com/en/. Accessed Mar 2019
9. Lee, G., Sacks, R., Eastman, C.M.: Specifying parametric building object behavior (BOB) for a BIM system. J. Autom. Constr. **15**(6), 758–776 (2006)
10. Motawa, I., Carter, K.: Sustainable BIM-based evaluation of buildings. J. Proc.-Soc. Behav. Sci. **74**, 419–428 (2013)
11. BIM Object - BIM Supply. https://www.bimobject.com. Accessed Mar 2019
12. Singh, V., Gu, N., Wang, X.: A theoretical framework of a bim-based multi-disciplinary collaboration platform. J. Autom. Constr. **20**(2), 134–144 (2011)
13. Kymmell, W.: Building Information Modeling: Planning and Managing Construction Projects with 4D CAD and Simulations. McGraw Hill Professional, New York (2008)
14. Eastman, C., Teicholz, P., Sacks, R., Liston, K.: BIM handbook: A guide to Building Information Modeling for Owners, Managers, Designers Engineers and Contractors. Wiley, Hoboken (2011)
15. Röck, M., Hollberg, A., Habert, G., Passer, A.: LCA and BIM: visualization of environmental potentials in building construction at early design stages. J. Build. Environ. **140**, 153–161 (2018)
16. Reddy, B.V., Jagadish, K.S.: Embodied energy of common and alternative building materials and technologies. J. Energy Build. **35**(2), 129–137 (2003)
17. Hardin, B., McCool, D.: BIM and Construction Management: Proven Tools, Methods, and Workflows. Wiley, Indianapolis, Indiana (2015)
18. Recast, E.P.B.D.: Directive 2010/31/EU of the European Parliament and of the Council of 19 May 2010 on the energy performance of buildings (recast). J. EU. **18**(06), 13–35 (2010)
19. Ardente, F., Beccali, M., Cellura, M., Mistretta, M.: Building energy performance: a LCA case study of kenaf-fibres insulation board. J. Energy Build. **40**(1), 1–10 (2008)

20. Schlueter, A., Thesseling, F.: Building information model based (En/Ex)ergy performance assessment in early design stages. J. Autom. Constr. **18**(2), 153–163 (2009)
21. Bribián, I.Z., Usón, A.A., Scarpellini, S.: Life cycle assessment in buildings: state-of-the-art and simplified LCA methodology as a complement for building certification. J. Build. Environ. **44**(12), 2510–2520 (2009)
22. Bynum, P., Issa, R.R., Olbina, S.: Building information modeling in support of sustainable design and construction. J. Constr. Eng. Manag. **139**(1), 24–34 (2012)
23. Jalaei, F., Jrade, A.: Integrating BIM and LEED system at the conceptual design stage of sustainable buildings. J. Sustain. Cities Soc. **18**, 95–107 (2015)
24. Saadah, Y., AbuHijleh, B.: Decreasing CO2 emissions and embodied energy during the construction phase using sustainable building materials. J. Sustain. Build. Technol. Urban Develop. **1**(2), 115–120 (2010)
25. Yohanis, Y.G., Norton, B.: Life-cycle operational and embodied energy for a generic single-storey office building in the UK. J. Energy. **27**(1), 77–92 (2002)
26. Cole, R.J., Kernan, P.C.: Life-cycle energy use in office buildings. J. Build. Environ. **31**(4), 307–317 (1996)
27. Ibn-Mohammed, T., Greenough, R., Taylor, S., Ozawa-Meida, L., Acquaye, A.: Operational vs. embodied emissions in buildings—a review of current trends. J. Energy Build. **66**, 232–245 (2013)
28. Ajayi, S., Oyedele, L., Ceranic, B., Gallanagh, M., Kadiri, K.: Life cycle environmental performance of material specification: a BIM-enhanced comparative assessment. J. Sustain. Build. Technol. Urban Develop. **6**(1), 14–24 (2015)
29. Dixit, M., Fernández-Solís, J., Lavy, S., Culp, C.: Identification of parameters for embodied energy measurement: a literature review. J. Energy Build. **42**(8), 1238–1247 (2010)
30. Sartori, I., Hestnes, A.G.: Energy use in the life cycle of conventional and low-energy buildings: a review article. J. Energy Build. **39**(3), 249–257 (2007)
31. Karimpour, M., Belusko, M., Xing, K., Bruno, F.: Minimising the life cycle energy of buildings: review and analysis. J. Build. Environ. **73**, 106–114 (2014)
32. Ramesh, T., Prakash, R., Shukla, K.K.: Life cycle energy analysis of buildings: an overview. J. Energy and Buildings. **42**(10), 1592–1600 (2010)
33. Monahan, J., Powell, J.C.: An embodied carbon and energy analysis of modern methods of construction in housing: a case study using a lifecycle assessment framework. J. Energy Build. **43**(1), 179–188 (2011)
34. Chang, Y., Ries, R.J., Lei, S.: The embodied energy and emissions of a high-rise education building: a quantification using process-based hybrid life cycle inventory Model. J. Energy Build. **55**, 790–798 (2012)
35. Pullen, S.F.: Energy used in the construction and operation of houses. J. Architect. Sci. Rev. **43**(2), 87–94 (2000)
36. Nässén, J., Holmberg, J., Wadeskog, A., Nyman, M.: Direct and indirect energy use and carbon emissions in the production phase of buildings. J. Energy **32**(9), 1593–1602 (2007)
37. Gustavsson, L., Sathre, R.: Variability in energy and carbon dioxide balances of wood and concrete building materials. J. Build. Environ. **41**(7), 940–951 (2006)
38. Abanda, F.H., Byers, L.: An investigation of the impact of building orientation on energy consumption in a domestic building using emerging bim (building information modelling). J. Energy **97**, 517–527 (2016)
39. Popovic, P.L., Arnold, R.C.: Preventing failures of precast concrete facade panels and their connections. In: 2nd Forensic Engineering, pp. 532–539. ASCE, San Juan (2000)
40. Moghtadernejad, S., Mirza, S.: Performance of building facades. In: 4th Structural Specialty, Canadian Society for Civil Engineers (CSCE), Halifax (2014)
41. Garvin, D.A.: What does "product quality" really mean? Sloan Manag. Rev. Fall, 25–43 (1984)

42. Naoum, S., Egbu, C.: Critical review of procurement method research in construction journals. J. Proc. Econ. Finance **21**, 6–13 (2015)
43. Grilo, A., Zutshi, A., Jardim-Goncalves, R., Steiger-Garcao, A.: Construction collaborative networks: the case study of a building information modelling-based office building project. J. Comput. Integr. Manuf. **26**(1–2), 152–165 (2013)
44. Juran, J.M., Gryna, F.M.: Quality Planning and Analysis. McGraw-Hill, London (1993)
45. Vanlande, R., Nicolle, C., Cruz, C.: IFC and building lifecycle management. J. Autom. Constr. **18**(1), 70–78 (2008)
46. Rüßmann, M., et al.: Industry 4.0: the future of productivity and growth in manufacturing industries. Boston Consult. Group. **9**(1), 54–89 (2015)
47. Hemanth, G., Sidhartha, C., Jain, S., Saihanish, P., Rohit, V.: AHP analysis for using cloud computing in supply chain management in the construction industry. In: 2nd International Conference for Convergence in Technology (I2CT), pp. 1228–1233. IEEE, Mumbai (2017)
48. Checkland, P.: Systems Thinking, Systems Practice. John Wiley & Sons Ltd., England (1994)
49. Checkland, P.B.: OR and social science: fundamental thoughts. In: Jackson, M.C., Keys, P., Cropper, S.A. (eds.) Operational Research and the Social Sciences, pp. 35–41. Springer, Boston (1989). https://doi.org/10.1007/978-1-4613-0789-1_4
50. Vilas-Boas da Silva, J.M.: Validation of a conceptual model to find adequate organisational structures. In: 14th International Annual Conference of the EurOMA, Chalmers University of Technology, Göteborg (2009)
51. Bell, E., Bryman, A., Harley, B.: Business Research Methods. Oxford University Press, Oxford (2018)
52. Geissdoerfer, M., Savaget, P., Evans, S.: The cambridge business model innovation process. J. Proc. Manuf. **8**, 262–269 (2017)
53. Fortune, J.: Quality Improvement (T831). The Open University, Milton Keynes (1992)
54. Vargo, S.L., Lusch, R.F.: Institutions and axioms: an extension and update of service-dominant logic. J. Acad. Mark. Sci. **44**(1), 5–23 (2016)
55. Silva, J.M.: Development and testing of a process of enquiry to identify relevant production planning and control procedures. Ph.D. dissertation, Cranfield University (2002)
56. Forgues, D., Koskela, L.: The influence of a collaborative procurement approach using integrated design in construction on project team performance. J. Manag. Projects Bus. **2**(3), 370–385 (2009)
57. Costa, A., Grilo, A.: BIM-based e-procurement: an innovative approach to construction e-procurement. J. Sci. World J. **2015**, 1–15 (2015)
58. Empirica GmbH.: The European e-Business Report: A Portrait of e-Business in 10 Sectors of the EU Economy. Technical report, European Commission (2007)
59. Presutti Jr., W.D.: Supply management and e-procurement: creating value added in the supply chain. J. Ind. Mark. Manag. **32**(3), 219–226 (2003)
60. buildingSMART®. https://www.buildingsmart.org. Accessed Mar (2019)
61. Hauser, J.R., Clausing, D.: The house of quality. Harvard Bus. Rev. **66**(3), 63–73 (1988)
62. Vigovskaya, A., Aleksandrova, O., Bulgakov, B.: LCA in building materials industry. In: MATEC Web of Conferences, vol. 106, EDP Sciences, Les Ulis (2017)
63. United Nations sustainable Development Goals. https://www.un.org/sustainabledevelopment/cities/. Accessed Mar 2019

Development of a Conceptual Architecture for the Energy Management of Building Ecosystems

Filipa Ferrada[1,2(✉)], Ana Inês Oliveira[1,2], João Rosas[1,2],
Patrícia Macedo[2,3], Ricardo Almeida[1,2],
and Luis M. Camarinha-Matos[1,2]

[1] Faculty of Sciences and Technology, Nova University of Lisbon,
Caparica, Portugal
[2] Uninova Institute, Centre of Technology and Systems (CTS),
Caparica, Portugal
{faf,aio,jrosas,cam}@uninova.pt,
rdl.almeida@campus.fct.unl.pt
[3] ESTSetúbal, Polytechnic Institute of Setúbal, Setúbal, Portugal
patricia.macedo@estsetubal.ips.pt

Abstract. The current environmental, social, and political pressure for more efficient use of energy led to the emergence of new legislation and directives both at National and European levels and, as a consequence, to the creation of various focused technological initiatives. In this line, several developments are being carried out to increase energy efficiency by reducing the energy consumption of buildings, costs, and carbon emissions, while providing adequate levels of comfort to the building's occupants. This work intends to contribute to this area, by proposing a conceptual architecture, based on collaborative networks of physical components/devices virtualized as services to compute and communicate information to support efficient energy management of building ecosystems. The architecture is designed considering the functional requirements, the most relevant technological challenges, and the implementation strategies.

Keywords: Energy efficiency of buildings · Conceptual architecture · Building ecosystem

1 Introduction

One of the current topics of attention in our society is the large energy consumption and its self-sustainability, making it clear that it is necessary to increase energy efficiency, reducing energy consumption and carbon emissions in this sector [1, 2]. In this context, it becomes essential to address these problems in industry and service buildings (public and private), checking the main energy efficiency gaps, and intervening to rectify the main issues in building's equipment that contribute to inadequate energy consumptions.

© IFIP International Federation for Information Processing 2019
Published by Springer Nature Switzerland AG 2019
L. M. Camarinha-Matos et al. (Eds.): PRO-VE 2019, IFIP AICT 568, pp. 418–430, 2019.
https://doi.org/10.1007/978-3-030-28464-0_36

On the other hand, the need for environmental comfort in buildings often comes into conflict with the awareness of reducing energy consumption, creating the need to find solutions that integrate the comfort of the occupants, the indoor air quality (IAQ) and efficient energy management, and consequently, the level of carbon emissions. Some building energy management systems (BEMS) already consider these issues, nevertheless the costs for implementing such systems are still quite high and with no capacity to scale or adapt. Environmental comfort in buildings requires a transformation of BEMS to accomplish some objectives, namely, energy efficiency and occupants' comfort, scalability and interoperability of systems, and reduced cost of implementation. In addition, as sub-systems/components become more intelligent, embedding higher computational power, a promising approach is to consider the building as an ecosystem of collaborative sub-systems.

In this context, a conceptual architecture for building energy management with low implementation cost, high adaptability, versatility, and easy maintenance is proposed and described. This architecture, which is based on collaborative networks of smart physical components/devices, considers the management and implementation of a set of previously defined environmental quality parameters and energy performance indicators which, in conjunction with machine learning capabilities, supports efficient energy decision-making leading to effective energy management. The approach corresponds to a case of collaborative cyber-physical system and is aligned with the premises of Industry 4.0.

This work is developed in the context of the project AMBIOSENSING – Autonomous and Intelligent Systems for Energy Saving,

The remainder of this paper is structured as follows: Sect. 2 presents the current research trends in the energy efficiency area; in Sect. 3 an overview of business requirements of the system is presented with the identified functional and non-functional requirements along with a use case diagram; Sect. 4 presents the proposed conceptual architecture; in Sect. 5 a discussion regarding the implementation aspects is provided, and finally Sect. 6 concludes and highlights future work.

2   Energy Efficiency Research Challenges

2.1   Regulatory Framework

The topic of energy efficiency has become increasingly relevant in Europe and its Member States, which have been working on updating and harmonizing the main European policy instruments in this area. The buildings sector in Europe accounts for around 40% of total energy consumption [3]. However, it is estimated that more than 50% of this consumption can be reduced by implementing energy efficiency measures, which can represent an annual reduction of CO_2 emissions to the atmosphere of around 400 million tons. This represents almost the whole of the European Union's (EU) commitment under the Kyoto Protocol [4, 5]. One of the short-term measures to put in practice the reduction of energy consumption relies on renovating existing buildings. Annual investments in building renovation will have to triple to reach the 32.5% energy efficiency target by 2030.

In addition, energy efficiency is one of the most cost-effective means of supporting the transition to a carbon-neutral economy and a key policy for implementing the Paris Agreement [6] to try to limit GHG emissions to a level that limits global temperature increase to less than 1.5 °C and preventing catastrophic and irreparable effects on ecosystems. While environmental commitments are being met, energy efficiency also reduces energy bills and import dependency.

Energy efficiency is thus one of the pillars of carbon neutrality strategies of the European Union. In this context, the European Commission (EC) adopted on 28 November 2018 its strategic vision for surpassing the 2030 climate target and to set eyes on achieving a net zero carbon economy by 2050, through what it called a fair transition involving all sectors of the economy [7]. The transition to a carbon-neutral economy is possible from a technological, economic and social points of view, but requires a profound societal and economic transformation within a generation.

In this context, the Directive (EU) 2018/844 of the European Parliament and of the Council [8] establishes a set of measures and guidelines, some of which are briefly highlighted here:

- Promote research and testing of new solutions to improve the energy performance of buildings;
- Consider the installation of self-regulating devices in existing buildings;
- Use of smart readiness indicators for intelligent technologies, namely in measuring the capacity of buildings to use information and communication technologies and electronic systems to adapt the operation of buildings to the needs of the occupants;
- Provide effective inspections of the central heating systems and air-conditioning systems, including those which are combined with ventilation systems, to obtain better energy efficiency results;
- Provide new buildings with self-regulating devices to be able to regulate the comfort conditions in each room of buildings and facilities, autonomously.

The architecture proposed in this work takes the above policies and measures into consideration.

2.2 Building Energy Management Systems

The building energy management systems (BEMS) are responsible for monitoring and controlling the environment in commercial, industrial and institutional facilities, ensuring operational performance as well as the comfort and safety of buildings' occupants. These systems usually use computer networks to monitor and control the energy of services and equipment in buildings, such as Heating, Ventilation, and Air Conditioning (HVAC) systems, lighting systems, energy systems, pumping systems, among others [9].

BEMS are often confused with Building Management Systems (BMS) and Building Automation and Control Systems (BACS), however, in practice they are not the same. BMSs can be used to monitor and control a wide range of existing building systems including fire, smoke detection, alarms, CCTV, security and access control, elevators, among others, while the BACS focus on management and control and automation processes. On its turn, BEMS are specifically related to energy systems.

They can, however, be connected to one or both systems if necessary. BEMS can combine data from all systems to provide better and more accurate visualization of energy use and consumption.

BEMSs provides real-time remote monitoring and integrated control of a wide range of connected systems and devices, providing information on modes of operation, energy use, environmental conditions, maintenance, among others, including measurement, notification trend and diagnosis of unnecessary energy use; performance optimization by setting operating hours, set-points, among others; preventive and corrective actions and building comfort [8]. BEMSs also allow the recording of performance history, enabling performance benchmarking about other buildings or locations. The best energy and comfort management systems in buildings should also add external information such as service's billing, electricity network, and meteorological data.

Energy Monitoring Systems. These are systems capable of measuring the consumption of one or more electrical equipment in a building. They emerge from the need to reduce unnecessary energy consumption to achieve better energy efficiency. These systems quantify and identify the consumption of energy in real time of an area or location and determine the associated economic impact. They also provide the identification of abnormal consumption, facilitating its correction.

There are several energy consumption monitoring systems on the market, each with its characteristics, but not all of them respond to the same type of needs. Some are more dedicated to the analysis of electrical parameters while others are limited to reading remote data. Table 1 presents a comparison of various monitoring systems according to the identified characteristics.

Table 1. Comparison of various energy monitoring systems

	ViGIE 2.0 [10]	Wi-LEM [11]	SiteSage [12]	Optimal monitoring system [13]	EMC [14]	BeEnergy [15]
Automation functionality	✓		✓			✓
Multi-parameters monitoring	✓	✓	✓	✓	✓	✓
Reporting	✓			✓	✓	
Cost and consumption detailed analysis	✓		✓	✓	✓	✓
Wi-Fi communication	✓	✓	✓	✓	✓	✓
Alerts generation	✓		✓	✓	✓	
Use of energy in multiple sites benchmarking			✓		✓	
Historical data		✓	✓	✓	✓	
Centralized management		✓		✓	✓	✓
Proprietary (integration only with own equipment)	✓	✓		✓	✓	

Control and Automation Systems in Buildings. Also known as building automation systems, these systems have undoubtedly led to the general specifications of monitoring and measurement systems. These control systems are generally centralized and integrate software and hardware networks that monitor and control indoor weather conditions. The operational performance of buildings, as well as the safety and comfort of occupants, is usually ensured by these control systems.

Existing building control systems can be roughly categorized as conventional controllers and intelligent controllers. The conventional ones focus essentially on energy consumption, being the best known the on/off controllers (better known as thermostats), and the P, PI and PID controllers [10, 11, 16]. On its turn, the intelligent controllers besides the energy consumption, also consider the comfort of the occupants in buildings. Examples of intelligent controllers are: methods based on learning that include artificial intelligence, fuzzy systems and systems of neural-fuzzy networks with conventional controllers, adaptive neural-fuzzy inference systems (ex. ANFIS - Adaptative Neural Fuzzy Inference System), etc. [8, 12]; models based on predictive control techniques (MPC), which follow the principles of classical controllers [13–15]; and control models based on agents [17, 18].

A more in-depth analysis has been carried out about the products supplied by various manufacturers. This study was done by selecting the products that have functionalities relevant to energy efficiency. The information was obtained online, through the manufacturer's commercial web pages, as well as from product/solution brochures, when available. This was a difficult task given the natural and understandable resistance from the manufacturers to reveal the most technical details of their products. In this sense, some technical information may be omitted due to lack of available information. Nevertheless, the solutions and products analyzed provide a wide range of alternatives for the control and energy optimization of buildings. Due to space constraints, the detailed analysis is not presented. However, it can be said that the predictive control models have gained popularity, especially in recent works, being the most common model used by most of the reviewed products and literature. Predictive control can be explained having into account that this type of model, grouped under the name of Model Predictive Control (MPC), consistently have better performance levels than other optimization and control algorithms. These models have proved their value with their ability to adapt to: *(i)* unpredictable disturbances or errors in prediction; *(ii)* exploration of the thermal mass of a building; *(iii)* consideration for variable energy prices, and; *(iv)* ability to protect the load against voltage peaks. New generations of intelligent buildings should not only take into account aspects such as space occupation prediction and meteorological conditions but also be sufficiently adaptable to maximize the use of renewable energy sources, energy storage units and program their consumption around periods of low energy cost [19].

Currently, some commercial building energy management systems [20, 21] already started to cover some of the intelligent aspects described above, nevertheless, they are still in an embryonic stage. Moreover, the costs associated to these systems are still quite high and with no capacity to scale or adapt. In this line, the proposed architecture aims to cover intelligent techniques aspects, such as optimization algorithms, with low implementation cost, high adaptability and scalability, and easy maintenance.

3   Requirements in Energy Management of Building Ecosystem

The identification of requirements, from the end user's point of view, is a key point in the process of design and development of a system. For the specific case, to identify the main functionalities that the system should provide, a set of potential usage scenario have been foreseen for its usage, namely: a factory of cosmetic production, a green-house for flower production, an anchor store, and a call center. Table 2 presents the identification of the main functional requirements of the system, while Table 3 shows the main non-functional requirements.

Table 2. Identification of the main functional requirements of the system

Functional requirements (FR) [requirements related to technical functionalities or system performance]	
FR1	The system must be able to define the environmental variables to be controlled: CO_2, Humidity, Temperature, Particles, COV, and Brightness, etc.
FR2	The system shall allow the configuration of several sensors and the connection of the sensors to environmental variables
FR3	The system must allow configuration and connections of actuators and actuation systems (valves, switches, blades, etc.)
FR4	The system must allow integrated control of environmental variables
FR5	The system must allow the replacement of sensors or actuators while the system is running
FR6	The system must allow energy usage profiles to be defined and its control should be adjusted accordingly
FR7	The system shall withstand operation in automatic mode and manual mode. In manual mode, the energy profile is selected manually (RF6), in automatic mode, the profile is automatically selected by the system to optimize its performance
FR8	The system should allow the simulation of different energy profiles by creating scenarios
FR9	The system must allow remote supervision, supporting real-time monitoring and alarm configuration
FR10	The system must support behavioral analysis
FR11	The system must allow historical data consultation
FR12	The system must support the generation of reports on its performance

Table 3. Identification of the main non-functional requirements of the system

Non-functional requirements (NFR) [requirements related to the description of system performance].	
NFR1	Availability: The system must be operational at least 90% of the time
NFR2	Accessibility: The system must provide user interfaces for mobile and non-mobile devices
NFR3	Performance: the system should allow efficient intelligent supervision and optimization of energy efficiency considering the comfort of the occupants
NFR4	Performance: the system must efficiently support the management of large and complex data sets
NFR5	Maintenance: the system must have a set of processes to allow real-time monitoring, with mechanisms to recover from failures/errors, such as data loss and communication failures
NFR6	Scalability: the system must allow the introduction and removal of new measurement devices and actuation systems
NFR7	Interoperability: the system must support the integration of heterogeneous systems (e.g., IoT solutions, legacy systems, etc.), with different degrees of intelligence/autonomy
NFR8	Storage: the system must allow the storage of a large volume of information
NFR9	Cost: the implemented solution must use non-proprietary and freeware software and equipment, throughout its life cycle

Given the heterogeneity of all the elements in terms of energy management resources and services, the architecture for such a system should leverage solutions that enable these elements to be organized into collaborative ecosystems [23] in which they can understand each other, exchange information, and collaborate. Therefore, there are two main phases for such a system, including the installation and exploitation.

For the installation phase, the main user of the system is an *Installer*, who will perform the entire configuration of the energy management system. There is another user, the *Administrator*, that is present in the whole life cycle of the system and is in charge of making the registration of all users.

In the exploration phase, different profiles of System Users can exist, namely: the *Administrator*, the *Technical Manager,* and the *Occupant* of the installations. The Administrator is allowed to register *users* and has access to the functionalities that allow global analysis of the Energy Management System (generation of reports, consultation of historical data, simulations, etc.), but also has access to all functionalities of the System available to the *Technical Manager*. The *Technical Manager* is the *user* responsible for daily operation and maintenance, being able to monitor all the controlled environmental variables and associated equipment and change the basic configurations of the energy control. The *Occupant* can introduce preferences into the System, as well as report his/her degree of satisfaction regarding environmental comfort. The main use cases for the exploitation phase are illustrated in Fig. 1.

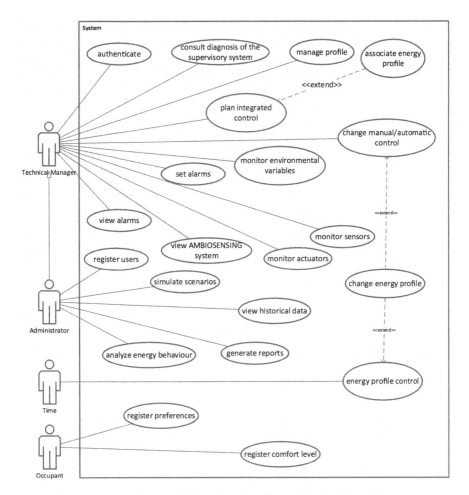

Fig. 1. Use case diagram of the exploration phase of the Ambiosensing system

4   Conceptual Architecture

The conceptual architecture (or high-level view) aims to show succinctly, the main elements and functionalities that make up the system architecture, regardless of any technological specificity. Based on the specification of the use cases, a conceptual architecture for the Ambiosensing system was developed as illustrated in Fig. 2. A layered architecture is proposed to identify and separate the different levels of interaction and to better manage dependencies. Each layer has a specific responsibility, being the upper layers able to use services from the lower layers, but not the opposite. Thus, in the case of the Ambiosensing System, three layers have been defined as follows below.

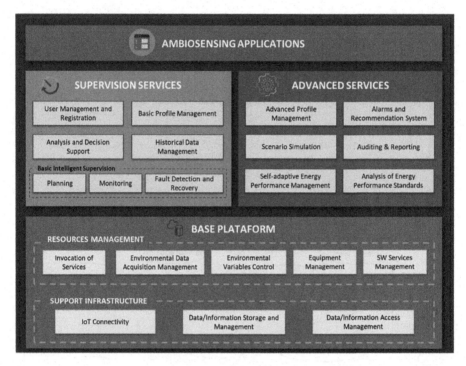

Fig. 2. Detailed diagram of the Ambiosensing architecture.

Base Platform Layer, which is composed of two sub-layers: the Support Infrastructure Layer and the Resource Management Layer. The main objective is to provide cloud services to support the development and management of IoT functionalities (intelligent networks of sensors and/or remote devices, actuators, devices, automation mechanisms, etc.), materializing digital twins, and the necessary functionalities of the Ambiosensing system. Specifically, it aims to support: the installation of sensors and actuators via standard communication protocols and their representation as digital twins; and management services for the processing of large volumes of data from multiple sensors and actuators of various types, such as variable speed drives, luminosity sensors, presence, etc., being all these devices modeled as software service. This layer is also intended to support the storage and management of data/information inherent to the Ambiosensing system as well as access mechanisms to them. The invocation and composition of software services, as well as data collection, control of environmental variables, management of equipment and devices and also the management of existing software services in the Ambiosensing environment, is also included. Through this platform, the various physical components are seen as a community of collaborative digital twins (a kind of collaborative cyber-physical system) [24], which are abstracted through the services they provide and their collaboration capabilities. Figure 3, illustrates a building floor scenario where several sensor units (assuming that sensors are not intelligent) are physically connected to a single board computer (Ambiosensing intends to adopt the Raspberry Pi model for prototyping) which on its turn makes part of a collaborative network of single board computers which operate in a coordinate way in order to collaboratively compute and communicate raw and/or processed data to the Ambiosensing IoT based platform. Ambiosensing can thus be seen as a collaborative cyber-physical system [25].

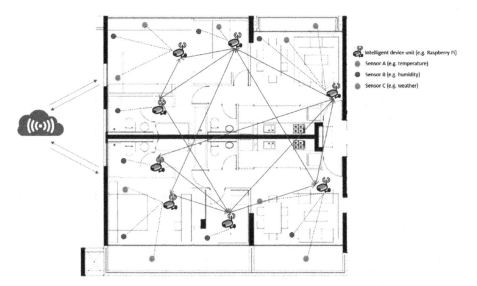

Fig. 3. An illustration of a collaborative network of intelligent devices of a building floor.

Service Layer, which is composed of two sub-layers at the same conceptual level: the Supervision Services Layer and the Advanced Services Layer. The first aims at providing support services for supervision, analysis and decision support to allow the correct operation of the Ambiosensing system by its users. It must also allow, through basic management, the configuration and parameterization of the desired operating profiles. To accomplish this objective, the supervision services shall be capable of monitoring, interpreting and analyzing the correct operation of the Ambiosensing system, considering the normal operating parameters. These parameters must consider the operating profile desired by its users. Authorized users shall be provided with tools to support analysis and decision support considering instantaneous monitoring results and historical data. The advanced services sub-layer has the main objective to provide advanced monitoring and decision-making support services that enhance the proper functioning of the Ambiosensing system, taking into account the composition of the underlying digital twins ecosystem. Based on the acquisition of information, it should be possible to extract knowledge about the proper functioning of space with the Ambiosensing system and adapt its functioning within desirable parameters. To this end, services capable of interpreting the information extracted from the operation of a space with an Ambiosensing system should be developed, verifying its operation and analyzing consumption. Techniques and methodologies of machine learning should be used for the analysis of usage patterns to adapt to the general functioning of the building to improve its efficiency. For this purpose, information visualization mechanisms based on simulation of scenarios may be considered.

Ambiosensing Applications Layer: Including interaction applications with the various stakeholders that allow the execution of the use cases previously identified in this paper.

5 Implementation Aspects

The proposed architecture presents a set of important aspects that should be highlighted. Such elements are relevant for future instantiations of this architecture and cover three dimensions, namely, (1) technological, (2) strategic, and (3) regulatory and social. For this paper purpose, only a rough description of the technical aspects is explored.

Typically, an energy management ecosystem involves a variety of different technologies. To deal with the inherent complexity, a service-oriented approach (SOA) should be adopted to maintain the desired level of abstraction of the use of functionalities versus their respective implementations. In this way, platforms should, as far as possible, be agnostic about the technologies used.

This heterogeneity of technologies imposes major challenges in terms of interoperability. Typically, in this kind of systems, elements need to work together to be able to satisfy their functionalities, and a good amount of effort is put into programming appropriate interaction mechanisms. Alternatively, to deal with this complexity, it is suggested the development and use of ontologies [22]. Ontologies allow the various elements, involved in an energy efficiency scenario, to share a standardized set of terms for referencing the equipment and its respective control, including the interactions performed by and between the respective services, thus facilitating collaboration among digital twins. Having the services of a platform developed with these ontologies as a reference, any management element in the layer above should be able to interact with the elements below, achieving in this way a level of integration and quasi-agnostic interoperability. For instance, it is intended that regardless of its manufacturer, a climate control service will be able to interact with any type of temperature sensor.

The current stage of this ongoing project was validated by our industrial partners and considering its compliance with the identified target application scenarios.

6 Conclusions and Future Work

Throughout this work, a description of the proposed conceptual architecture for the energy management of building ecosystems was carried out. This architecture emerges as a response to several factors which are considered simultaneously, namely, the diversity of technological resources that are typically used in efficient energy management systems, the need for these resources to exchange information and the need to work together. Other considered important factors are the challenges underlying the legislation recently approved by the EU in terms of energy efficiency management.

In terms of the developed work, an exhaustive survey of functional requirements was initially carried out, which is briefly represented in the use-case diagram. The proposed architecture is composed of a significant number of elements distributed over three layers, namely, the base platform layer, the services layer, and the application layer.

The architecture elements aim to cope with the functional and non-functional requirements as well as with the EU directives and policies in the area of energy efficiency. For instance, the "Self-adaptive Energy Performance Management" block meets one of the guidelines approved in the EU. The strategy consists in being able to adapt the operating conditions through intelligent services that identify specific circumstances in building divisions and react to them. In this way, the system will be able to adapt and update its operating energy profile to the circumstances detected. Another aspect that is taken into consideration is the current technological trends, such as industry 4.0. In this line, a simulation element is considered [23, 24] due to its potential to, among others, study/anticipate the behavior of simulated systems. The proposed architecture includes an element for the simulation of scenarios, to anticipate the effects of certain management strategies and assess their quality.

The concept of collaborative business ecosystem [23] and the notion of digital twins [24, 25], to represent the physical systems in the cyber space give the base conceptual framework for the proposed system.

As future work, it is intended to instantiate the architecture in collaboration with our industrial partners, building a platform that will be used and tested in a controlled environment for proof of concept of operation of the system.

Acknowledgments. This work was funded in part by the Project AMBIOSENSING - Autonomous & Intelligent Systems for Energy Saving – nº. 038253, within the specific scope of the Incentive Scheme for Research and Development - PORTUGAL 2020 - launched by Nº 01/SI/2018. Partial support also comes from the Portuguese FCT Strategic program UID/EEA/00066/2019.

References

1. J.B./ DGEG: Estratégia para a Eficiencia Energética nos edificios Públicos (2015). http://www.lneg.pt/download/10887/DGEG_REPublic_ZEB11dez2015.pdf
2. DGEG: Balanço Energético, sintético (2016). http://www.dgeg.gov.pt/
3. Masson-Delmotte, V., et al.: Global Warming of 1.5°C. An IPCC Special Report on the impacts of global warming of 1.5°C above pre-industrial levels and related global greenhouse gas emission pathways, in the context of strengthening the global response to the threat of climate change, sustainable development, and efforts to eradicate poverty. IPCC (2018, in press)
4. Council of the European Union: Energy efficient buildings – Presidency secures provisional deal with European Parliament (2017)
5. European Commission: Clean Energy for All Europeans," European Commission, pp. 1–13 (2016)
6. United Nations: Paris Agreement (2015)
7. European Commission: Our Vision for A Clean Planet for All, November 2018

8. European Parliament: Directive (EU) 2018/844 of the European Parliament and of the Council of 20 May 2018 amending Directive 2010/31/EU on the energy performance of buildings and Directive 2012/27/EU on energy efficiency," Off. J. Eur. Union, vol. L156, 19 June 2018, pp. 75–91 (2018)
9. Gromicho, I.: Protocolo de Quioto continua a ser essencial para países reduzirem emissões. Ambiente Magazine, 16 Nov 2017
10. V. Solutions: ViGIE 2.0. https://www.vigiesolutions.com/wp-content/uploads/2017/09/vigie_pt.pdf
11. LEM: Wi-LEM (2018). https://www.lem.com/en/wilem
12. Energy Circle: SiteSage (Previously eMonitor) Energy Monitor (2016). https://www.energycircle.com/energy-monitors/sitesage-previously-emonitor-energy-monitor
13. Optimal Monitoring: Features of the Optimal Energy Monitoring Software System (2016). http://www.optimalmonitoring.com/system-features/#toggle-id-3-closed
14. Siemens: Energy Monitoring & Controlling Solution (EMC) (2011). https://www.downloads.siemens.com/download-center/Download.aspx?pos=download&fct=getasset&id1=A6V10328881
15. Novalec: BeEnergy - Monitorização de energia (2017). http://www.novalec.pt/1255/beenergy—monitorizacao-de-energia.htm
16. Manic, M., Wijayasekara, D., Amarasinghe, K., Rodriguez-Andina, J.J.: Building energy management systems: the age of intelligent and adaptive buildings. IEEE Ind. Electron. Mag. **10** 25–39 (2016)
17. European Commission: Smart Finance for Smart Buildings Investment Facility (2018). https://ec.europa.eu/clima/sites/clima/files/docs/pages/initiative_7_smart_en.pdf
18. Levermore, G.J.: Building Energy Management Systems: An Application to Heating and Control. E & FN Spon, London (1992)
19. Shaikh, P.H., Nor, N.B.M., Nallagownden, P., Elamvazuthi, I., Ibrahim, T.: A review on optimized control systems for building energy and comfort management of smart sustainable buildings. Renew. Sustain. Energy Rev. **34**, 409–429 (2014)
20. Vishwanath, A., Chandan, V., Saurav, K.: An IoT based data driven pre-cooling solution for electricity cost savings in commercial buildings. IEEE Internet Things J. (2019). https://doi.org/10.1109/JIOT.2019.2897988
21. General Electrics: Control Systems (2018). https://www.geautomation.com/products/control-systems
22. Zhou, X., Wu, Z., Yin, A., Wu, L., Fan, W., Zhang, R.: Ontology development for unified traditional Chinese medical language system. Artif. Intell. Med. **32**(1), 15–27 (2004)
23. Brettel, M., Friederichsen, N., Keller, M., Rosenberg, M.: How virtualization, decentralization and network building change the manufacturing landscape: an industry 4.0 perspective. Int. J. Mech. Ind. Sci. Eng. **8**(1), 37–44 (2014)
24. Rodič, B.: Industry 4.0 and the new simulation modelling paradigm. Organizacija **50**(3), 193–207 (2017)
25. Nazarenko, A.A., Camarinha-Matos, L.M.: Basis for an approach to design collaborative cyber-physical systems. In: Camarinha-Matos, L.M., Almeida, R., Oliveira, J. (eds.) DoCEIS 2019. IAICT, vol. 553, pp. 193–205. Springer, Cham (2019). https://doi.org/10.1007/978-3-030-17771-3_16

Collaborative Safe Escape in Digital Transformation

Ana Inês Oliveira[1,2(✉)], Pedro Pereira[1,2], and Javad Jassbi[1,2]

[1] Faculty of Sciences and Technology, Nova University of Lisbon,
Caparica, Portugal
pmrp@fct.unl.pt
[2] Uninova Institute, Centre of Technology and Systems (CTS),
Caparica, Portugal
{aio,j.jassbi}@uninova.pt

Abstract. Hazards are part of human life and every year thousands of people are affected by different types of natural or human provoked disasters. The evacuation is a crucial part of any rescue plan and there are many procedures and standards to support the process. Nevertheless, traditional methods and procedures need radical changes according to the "4.0" Paradigm. The rate of growth, penetration, and development of technology and more specifically what is known as emerging technologies, changing the norms and routines, and Cyber-physical systems bring intelligent to our life where Hazard Management is no exception. In this paper, a model based on emerging paradigms, called "Collaborative Safe Escape" is proposed for indoor evacuation process. This environment is based on four collaborative networks where evacuee network is a temporary network which would be created in the field when required, while the other are long-term networks with the aim to collaborate in case of hazards to assist the potential victims. The technology and the collaboration between networks create a dynamic connected environment to support the decision of potential victims. In the proposed model, smart buildings including all sensors and devices could provide rich information to be analyzed both by evacuee and rescue team. The Smart Application will keep the people involved in hazards updated by supportive information either by the rescue team or by analyzing the ambient intelligent information. The proposed idea is a future model of Safe Escape Systems in the era of Collaborative Networks and digital transformation.

Keywords: Collaborative Safe Escape · Collaborative Networks ·
Intelligent buildings · Cyber-physical systems · Evacuation process ·
Evacuee decision process

1 Introduction

Dealing with disasters is part of human life since the beginning. In history, many approaches and solutions could be found, and all efforts were simply targeting the life of the impacted people. This is a multidisciplinary subject while most of the works could be categorized into three classes, before, during and after disasters. As this is not a new subject, there is a rich tradition and deep knowledge and experience while emerging technologies and disruptive approaches could help and support the idea in a different

© IFIP International Federation for Information Processing 2019
Published by Springer Nature Switzerland AG 2019
L. M. Camarinha-Matos et al. (Eds.): PRO-VE 2019, IFIP AICT 568, pp. 431–444, 2019.
https://doi.org/10.1007/978-3-030-28464-0_37

way comparing with existing solutions. Regardless of all efforts, nobody could claim that the probability of disasters, either natural or human-provoked, is decreasing while forecasting techniques help us to manage the situations and reduce the consequences but still many people lose their lives or will be affected each year. This paper is focused on a very common problem which is safe escape in indoors situation in case of any hazard, with the aim to employ new concepts to assist the involved people in making the best decisions during the time of the escape process. The proposed concept is based on two fundamental pillars: Intelligent connected building, focusing on cyber-physical systems, and collaborative networks. Intelligent connected Building is simply the future of buildings while the building included all things such as furniture and materials could be a "Cyber Physical System" where everything is connected and could collect data, process and share the relevant information. The second key issue is Collaborative Networks which could be considered a key enabler to transit collective behaviour and information to decisive information based on technological solutions. Collaborative Safe Escape using new technologies addressed by IoT, IoP, Bigdata and many other emerging technologies is a new approach to save lives and reduce injuries caused by unpredictable events. The main objective of this paper is to introduce and discuss ae new paradigm of evacuation process based on the latest emerging technologies. This does not mean Smart Building or Connected Devices are new but trying to employ these technologies in a collaborative way and formalize the concept as an innovative operational model to be used in disasters is the goal of this paper. The paper is organized as follow: In the next section, the related trends and challenges are discussed. In section three, the new concept based on four Collaborative Networks is proposed, while section four is dealing with the information flow and decision process of the introduced model. Finally, section five wrap up the final remarks, conclusion and future works.

2   Trends and Challenges in Digital Safe Escape

A safe escape planning is very challenging due to the disordered and unorganized situation occurring in a crisis situation. Regrettably, decision makers often have an incomplete picture of hazards and potential escape opportunities. The situation turns out to be more complex due to the fact that people affected are sometimes left alone without any support that could be provided by a rescue team [1]. Without any doubt, decision-making in crises situations needs to be made in the shortest time in order to minimize the potential risk or threat.

Considering the technological evolution and digital transformation that the various contexts of our society have been undergoing, there are certainly several areas of work and research in which new methodologies can be provided in order to support emergency teams and the traditional models of evacuation, naturally aligned with all the inherent legal and social constraints. In the scenario of a panic situation, it is difficult for affected people to determine what are the best decisions in an escape situation. This makes escape planning particularly difficult [3, 4]. On the other hand, this also opens the door to new challenges, that must be tackled, aiming a more efficient escape under a disaster scenario, reducing its consequences (material or human). Therefore, such an environment should include decision systems to enable the choice of the best way to escape, and simulation models to assist in the selection of the fastest and safest escape strategy. These models can use techniques based on agents and artificial intelligence, as is the case of the proposal of the intelligent system for disaster management [2]. In Fig. 1 is shown what Authors identified as relevant areas that when combined, perform a collaborative environment, are the key for an effective safe escape.

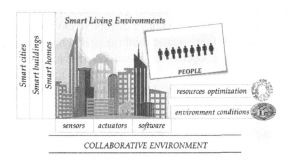

Fig. 1. Relevant contributing areas.

Several management system proposals are based on the use of intelligent Augmented Reality (AR) models in order to suggest guiding ways which allows rescue teams to quickly reach building occupants [5], for example in case of fire. To this end, a relationship of the physical virtual domain in the building is important.

There are some works and prototypes with the aim to perform tasks automatically after emergency situations. An example is the case of active disaster response system (ADRS) [6], which acts automatically after the occurrence of an earthquake. Types of action of this type of system can be for example the opening of doors and windows, cutting water and gas pipes.

To deal with location issues, there are also several works and technological proposals to leverage and streamline solutions for a fast and efficient response in case of disasters [7]. A safe evacuation system by using roads, when a natural disaster occurred, is analyzed and highlighted in [8]. If under such kind of disaster some roads cannot be used, or are blocked, evacuees cannot follow the evacuation procedures by just using default maps after disaster. A safety route guidance system, by using participatory sensing, that uses GPS data and accelerometer data from pedestrians' smartphone, was proposed in [8]. However, the system relies on information that cannot be guaranteed, as is the case of evacuees' smartphone. On the other hand, for indoor issues, there are studies [9] that point out that it is important to know the internal structures and the magnetic fields that buildings can generate, to be able to recognize sources of location. Related to issues of indoor location, there are numerous works that mention vast applications of fingerprint techniques [7, 10, 11]. Moreover, in the context of indoor spaces, WiFi connections are so widespread that internal location based on WiFi has attracted many research efforts. Since fingerprint techniques are considered simple and highly compatible with the hardware that exists in the interior contexts of buildings, the intersection is natural. However, due to unexpected environmental changes, the existing fingerprint location algorithms may not work as expected. There is research suggesting that it is possible, through offline mechanisms and voting systems, to improve the accuracy of the location, when effectively compared with the existing fingerprint location algorithms [10]. Other works suggests algorithms that improve received signal strength indication (RSSI) [12, 13], or use Bluetooth Low Energy positioning methods based on the fingerprint technique, according to Wi-Fi location techniques [14]. These localization mechanisms are used in various contexts, such as location (non-evasive) of the elderly [14], nonetheless, they can be used or adapted for use in emergency situations or in disruptive environments.

In [15] is reported a firefighting scenario, affirming that most fire departments make judgments during fire rescue operations based on previous acquired knowledge, without a path-planning system that is capable of real-time information. An evacuation architecture supported by multi-agents that collects information from evacuees and from sensors in a real-time basis, aims to provide the safest and fastest escape route for different groups inside the same building, is propose in [16].

Several works on Crowd Behaviour Analysis Technology for Disaster Management [17–20] have been performed and are useful in this type of situations where an inherent characteristic is the behavioural analysis of the occupants of spaces to be evacuated. In this type of situations, however, there should be a collaborative support so that the various entities related to the situation that is occurring can intervene. As so, with a support that makes these entities more prepared to collaborate in cases of incidents, their intervention can become faster and more effective. There are studies to create working models for complex emergency situations, with support in multi-risk analysis [21] to explore different courses of action, using a Cross Impact Analysis and Interpretative Structural Modeling (CIA-ISM) [22, 23] methodology to support group collaboration. In order to select collaboration partners and tasks during the formation of the collaborative crisis response network, it is necessary that various requirements are considered and parameterized [24]. There are projects, such as the SoKNOS project [25] to develop and test required concepts to support government, private and non-profit organizations involved in public security issues that include Human-Computer Interaction (HCI). It can also be considered systems that can help people, especially those with sensory impairments (visual or hearing) [26].

Fig. 2. Structure diagram for a Safe Escape.

Empowering such a Safe Escape system requires a cyber-physical infrastructure that combines new software platforms with very challenging requirements related with safety, security and privacy. Additionally, the system must be able to collect, manage and process a massive amount of data. Today's standard is the use of a cloud platform in which most data is stored, and several real-time applications are continuously running, although issues regarding data security and data protection are still quite demanding. At this point it is worth to highlight that from the Authors point of view a Safe Escape relies in a "system" that comprises different stages: data collection, processing, decision-making and actions; as depicted in Fig. 2.

A proper understanding of both "cyber" and "physical" components that considers the importance of privacy, security and safety, allied with the diverse nature of data collection, and consequently the actuation procedures that should occur, is required. One of the main challenges that must be tackled is the integration of a widely sort of distributed devices into a common framework. For instance, the different type of sensors, such as cameras, temperature, smoke, crack detection, among many others, that could be installed in a certain building, must be able to communicate/interact with each other, as well as with building occupants through smartphones, tablets, laptops and, of course, servers. From Authors' perspective, several reported works are too focused in proposing a solution at a physical layer level, sometimes forgetting the social and collaborative behaviour of evacuees. Thus, it is our understanding that a safe escape should consider: (1) aggregate data from different sources (sensors, historical data, among others), (2) new but also mature technologies in order to increase the system resilience, (3) interaction between different players, as networks, for instance building managers, and local teams, rescue teams including firefighters, police, etc., creating a collaborative ecosystem, and (4) cooperation/ collaboration between cyber physical systems and smart social environment, and dynamic decision-making platforms.

3   Towards a Conceptual Model for Collaborative Escape

In order to achieve an environment to become more effective for all parties involved in the escape process, a solution based on the collaboration of all stakeholders and making use of an appropriated infrastructure is proposed. In this direction, it is aimed to achieve an environment that creates disaster awareness and support in situations of need, based on the combination of cyber-physical systems and collaborative networks paradigms (Fig. 3). On one hand, the Collaborative Networks [27] paradigm can provide appropriate mechanisms, adding value to the logical collaboration between rescue entities, but also between all other parties involved, including the local spaces from where the escape needs to take place, to the users of the spaces themselves. On the other hand, the cyber-physical systems can deal with the integration of computation, networking and physical processes.

In this context, it is possible to foresee distinct types of network, namely: rescue network, local network, evacuees network, and a network of cyber-physical systems existing in the corresponding spaces. A brief description of these networks is included in Table 1.

Fig. 3. Disaster awareness and support environment bases.

Figure 4 shows the concept of the proposed model and the flow of information among the four networks in Safe Escape. There is an evident combination of characteristics among these networks, starting from their duration, that can be long or short term, to their membership, that can include or not members from other networks. Therefore, to have a clearer understanding of these networks, tables below include their characterization using the ARCON Framework [28].

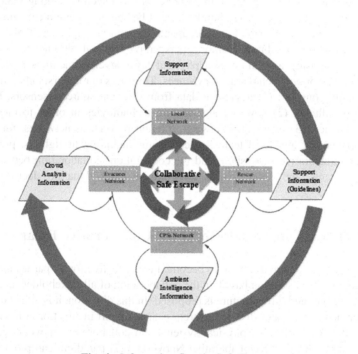

Fig. 4. Information flow in Safe Escape.

Being the focus, a general representation of concepts and related relationships, the ARCON's Model Intent general representation layer [28] is used, converging on the description of the main elements of the endogenous and exogenous perspectives (namely on the structural and componential endogenous perspective and support and societal exogenous perspective). This characterization considers the operation stage of the lifecycle of the identified networks. The other stages, namely formation, dissolution and evolution are out of scope of the work presented in this paper and will be characterized in further works (Tables 2, 3, 4 and 5).

Table 1. Description of involved collaborative networks.

Network	Description
Rescue network	Long-term alliance that involves different types of rescue entities, that must collaborate in a disaster situation
Local network	Long-term strategic network to provide support to local places or spaces in case of disaster. Places can differ in their nature, from a shopping center, to a hotel or any other indoor environment. This network includes the owner of the space, the managers, employees, etc.
Evacuees network	Temporary virtual organization involved in the rescue process and involving the occupants of the corresponding indoor contexts. The created consortium typically dissolves after the resolution of the hazard
Cyber-physical systems network	Network of intelligent physical and software entities that are present in the local places

Table 2. Characterization of rescue network.

Rescue network	
Endogenous Elements	
Subspace: Structural – Structure and composition of the network constituting elements, as well as the roles performed by those actors	
Roles	**Administrator** can be performed by an entity responsible for all rescue network stage. All **members** can be any organization with its own competences and can actively contribute. The **potential customers** are among those interested in having collaboration in rescue situations
Relations	**Control Supervision** is ensured by the administrator to enforce coordination and collaboration principles and agreements. All members are responsible for **cooperation and collaboration, and exchange and sharing** of information and resources. Also, it is essential to continuously increase the **levels of trustworthiness**
Network	Long-term alliance that involves different types of rescue entities, that must collaborate in a disaster situation
Subspace: Componential – Individual/ tangible elements of the network	
ICT Resources	A software platform to support the rescue network management and collaboration among the network members
Human Resources	Individuals within an organization/entity member of the rescue network
Knowledge Resources	Detailed profile of members; information about potential customers; network profile data; main common ontologies for common understanding; shared resources repository; value system; governance principles; etc.
Exogenous Interactions	
Subspace: Support – Issues related to support services provided by third party institutions	
Network Identity	**Social Nature** with non-for-Profit oriented organization
Interaction parties	Insurance entities; certification entities; etc.
Interactions	**Services Acquisition** by the rescue network, such as insurance services, financial services, technical services, etc.; **Agreements Establishment** through protocols and actions involved in the establishment of agreements with third parties
Subspace: Societal – Issues related to interaction between the network and the society	
Network Identity	Defining the **legal status** of the rescue network; Defining the **values and principles** that characterize the identity the rescue network
Interaction parties	Identifying the **governmental organizations** and **associations** that interact with the rescue network; Identifying the public or private entities (**Regulatory Bodies**) that issue regulations and standards
Interactions	**Political Relations:** defining with which parties there are political interactions established; **Information Transfer**: defining the information that is transferred between the rescue network and each third party

Table 3. Characterization of local network.

Local network	
Endogenous Elements	
Subspace: Structural – Structure and composition of the network constituting elements, as well as the roles performed by those actors	
Roles	**Administrator** is the responsible to administrate all phases of the local network. The **Members** are all the relevant participants that whose activity take place in the context of the local infrastructure. The **potential customers** are the clients of the local spaces
Relations	**Control Supervision** is ensured by the administrator to enforce coordination and collaboration principles and agreements. All members are responsible for **cooperation and collaboration, and exchange and sharing** of information and resources. The continuous **trusting** among members is vital
Network	Long-term strategic network to provide support to local places in case of disaster. Places can differ in their nature, from a shopping center, to a hotel or any other indoor environment. This network includes the owner of the space, the managers, employees, etc.
Subspace: Componential – Individual/ tangible elements of the network	
ICT Resources	A software platform to support the local network management and collaboration among the local network members
Human Resources	Individuals within the entity members of the local network
Knowledge Resources	Detailed profile of members; information about potential customers; network profile data; main common ontologies for common understanding; shared resources repository; value system; governance principles; etc.
Exogenous Interactions	
Subspace: Support – Issues related to support services provided by third party institutions	
Network Identity	**Social Nature** with for-Profit oriented organization
Interaction parties	Insurance entities; certification entities, etc.
Interactions	**Services Acquisition** by the local network, such as insurance services, financial services, technical services, etc.; **Agreements Establishment** through protocols and actions involved in the establishment of agreements with third parties
Subspace: Societal – Issues related to interaction between the network and the society	
Network Identity	Defining the **legal status** of the local network; Defining the **values and principles** that characterize the identity the local network
Interaction parties	Identifying the **governmental organizations** and **associations** that interact with the local network; Identifying the public or private entities (**Regulatory Bodies**) that issue regulations and standards
Interactions	**Political Relations:** defining with which parties there are political interactions established; **Information Transfer**: defining the information that is transferred between the local network and each third party

Table 4. Characterization of evacuees network.

Evacuees network	
Endogenous elements	
Subspace: Structural – Structure and composition of the network constituting elements, as well as the roles performed by those actors	
Roles	**Planner** is responsible for the formation of the evacuees network, typically some member of local network; the **Coordinator** is responsible for the coordination of the evacuees network during its duration; the **Partner** represents all the involved actors within the collaborative space of evacuees
Relations	**Control Supervision** under the responsibility of the Coordinator; **Collaboration, Exchanging and Sharing** between all partners; The continuous **trusting** among members is vital
Network	Temporary virtual organization involved in the rescue process and involving the occupants of the corresponding indoor contexts. The created consortium typically dissolves after the resolution of the hazard
Subspace: Componential – Individual/ tangible elements of the network	
ICT Resources	A software platform to support the formation and the management of the evacuees network. This platform is typically part of the platform used by the local network
Human Resources	Different partners can be assigned to specific tasks of the evacuees network; Specific individuals can contribute
Knowledge Resources	Local network Shared Resources; Templates with models or reference documents to be instantiated for a specific use case; Main common ontologies used to facilitate the common understanding among the network partners; etc.

Table 5. Characterization of cyber-physical systems network.

Cyber-physical systems network	
Endogenous Elements	
Subspace: Structural – Structure and composition of the network constituting elements, as well as the roles performed by those actors	
Roles	Due to the different nature of this network, namely its partners, the defined roles and corresponding relations have to be defined and configured according to the nature of the corresponding environment context
Relations	
Network	Network of intelligent physical and software entities that are present in the local places
Subspace: Componential – Individual/ tangible elements of the network	
ICT Resources	A software platform to support the formation and the management all the devices that can be part of the cyber-physical systems network. This platform is typically part of the platform used by the local network or by the rescue network
Human Resources	N/A
Knowledge Resources	Local network Shared Resources; relational and no relational databases, etc.

Needless to say that the core communication channel in Collaborative Safe Network is based on technology and there is always the risk of collapsing infrastructure which causes all centralized systems to stop working. That's why it is important to make sure the system is being developed based on a modular approach and with peer to peer strategy. This can help in case of degradation and collapse of technological infrastructure to continue the support of the evacuees. Most people could use their smartphones and if it could not be connected to any central network, they could connect to each other and exchange information to support the decisions for a safe escape. Also, using temporary technological solutions such as mobile autonomous robots that could help to bring back temporary network or connect to smartphones, analyze the information and exchange messages as alternative solutions. Moreover, it is important to have different protocols and strategies to make sure collaborative networks could continue working on different occasions.

4 Dynamic Decision Model in Collaborative Escape

The main idea of the proposed model in this paper is based on the simple fact that the most important issue in the time of disasters is to make the right decisions at the right time. This means both efficiency and effectiveness are important and time is crucial. Not only because each second could save a life but due to the dynamism of the problem and rapid changes which could happen. For example, if the static maps show the exit path and even it was the best solution in the initial stage of the hazard, due to many factors such as the effect of infrastructure or behavior of the people, it could change from time to time. Collaborative Escape is a solution to keep the evacuees updated online and help them for the best decisions.

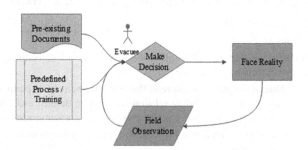

Fig. 5. Simple decision-making process of evacuee.

Figures 5 and 6 compare the decision making process of evacuees in the current situation and in the ideal situation which we call "Collaborative Safe Escape". As it could be seen, in the classic model, in the best scenario, the potential victim has the regular information, know the process and could follow the pre-existing signs and guidelines while the field observation is the only way to receive feedback. This means s/he could change his/her strategy only when could feel something is wrong which could be sometimes too late. In the proposing model, not only the smart Building as a CPS, but the cumulative behaviour of the evacuee and the information from the local network could help the rescue team and the evacuee to manage the situation. All information, considering different types of data sources, would be analyzed and different scenarios would be simulated to give the best and last guidelines to the people who are trying to escape from danger. As illustrated in Fig. 6, a variety of information and data sources and the technologies could help the evacuees to make a better decision and avoid common pitfalls such as following wrong dominant behaviour or failing by running to trap. There is no doubt that creating a Safe Escape Collaborative Network is not just technology, but a conceptual model based on CNs paradigm to employ emerging technologies in an efficient and effective way. The goal is to develop a system which could be active in case of any disaster. Smart Building as a CPSs and AI to analyze and simulate the crowd behaviour and Big data to enhance the level of services which could be provided in evacuation process in disasters to save more lives and reduce the negative impact of hazards.

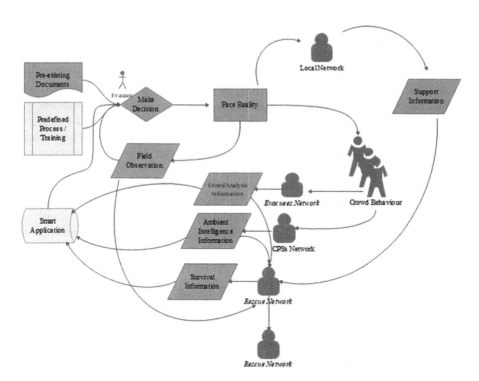

Fig. 6. Decision making process of evacuee in Safe Escape.

5   Final Remarks

Dealing with disasters is part of human life, nonetheless, several approaches and solutions have been proposed to minimize its impacts on citizens daily life. As shown, this is a multidisciplinary topic, thus can only be handled by multidisciplinary teams. In this work, Authors tried to show that smart buildings, which includes not only all things (equipment or materials) inside it, but also people, can be seen as a CPS, where everything is connected. The information management system should be able to collect data from different sources, process it and share significant information. Additionally, in a higher layer, a collaborative network should be considered as a key enabler in order to translate collective behaviour and information into decisive information thanks to technological solutions. Collaborative Safe Escape using new technologies is a new approach, that must be tackled, aiming a more efficient escape, reducing its consequences (material or human) due to unpredictable events. The characterization of the different networks presented in Sect. 3, shall be further detailed including the specification of the functional and behavioural, and market and constituency dimensions of the endogenous and exogenous perspectives, respectively, in the Model Intent general representation layer of the ARCON reference model. Furthermore, in this work only the operation stage of the networks is characterized, thus the complete lifecycle shall be characterized in latter works. Finally, in Sect. 4, the proposed model is discussed from the perspective of the decision-making process while the evacuee, as a potential victim, is considered as a decision maker. The combination of data sources from the networks and technologies could support the decision process and in a smart online platform, the evacuee could receive supportive information to find the best personalized solution to escape from the danger. Being this work still ongoing, it is expected that its content can provide decision-makers, as well as building owners, with supportive guidelines and directions for achieving effective and efficient safe escape.

In conclusion, this paper proposes a conceptual model which could be a revolutionary strategy to change the evacuation process in disasters. However, further research is required in areas which can be considered as interesting directions, such as: challenge of communication between the evacuees and the collaborative networks as peer to peer system; distributed computing system to keep the system running in case of failure of central infrastructure; modeling the processes and procedure in CNs and between CNs to understand the needs and to improve the efficiency according to the goals in the evacuation process; simulation of the evacuation process using the proposed model to see the weaknesses, disadvantages in practice and try to find solutions to improve it; blockchain technology to improve communications security in order to improve cybersecurity, avoiding cyberattacks aiming to create panic due to false disaster alert; Artificial Intelligence and Machine Learning can be used to improve facial recognition algorithms, which can be used to identify evacuees; etc.

Acknowledgments. This work was funded in part by the Portuguese FCT Strategic program UID/EEA/00066/2019.

References

1. Goodwin, M., Granmo, O.-C., Radianti, J., Sarshar, P., Glimsdal, S.: Ant colony optimisation for planning safe escape routes. In: Ali, M., Bosse, T., Hindriks, K.V., Hoogendoorn, M., Jonker, C.M., Treur, J. (eds.) IEA/AIE 2013. LNCS (LNAI), vol. 7906, pp. 53–62. Springer, Heidelberg (2013). https://doi.org/10.1007/978-3-642-38577-3_6
2. Mirahadi, F., McCabe, B., Shahi, A.: Smart disaster management system for tall buildings. In: Canadian Society for Civil Engineering (CSCE) Annual Conference (2017)
3. Li, Q., Rus, D.: Navigation protocols in sensor networks. ACM Trans. Sens. Netw. (TOSN) 1(1), 3–35 (2005)
4. Li, Q., De Rosa, M., Rus, D.: Distributed algorithms for guiding navigation across a sensor network. In: Proceedings of the 9th Annual International Conference on Mobile Computing and Networking, pp. 313–325. ACM (2003)
5. Park, S., et al.: Design and implementation of a smart IoT based building and town disaster management system in smart city infrastructure. Appl. Sci. 8(11), 1–27 (2018)
6. Lin, C., Chu, E.T., Ku, L., Liu, J.W.: Active disaster response system for a smart building. Sensors 14, 17451–17470 (2014)
7. Wenge, T., Chew, M.T., Alam, F., Gupta, G.S.: Implementation of a visible light based indoor localization system. In: IEEE Sensors Applications Symposium (SAS) (2018)
8. Ikeda, Y., Inoue, M.: An evacuation route planning for safety route guidance system after natural disaster using multi-objective genetic algorithm. Proc. Comput. Sci. 96, 1323–1331 (2016)
9. Kwak, M., Park, Y., Kim, J., Han, J., Kwon, T.: An Energy-efficient and lightweight indoor localization system for Internet-of-Things (IoT) environments. Proc. ACM Interact. Mobile. Wearable Ubiquit. Technol. 2(1), 1–28 (2018)
10. Luo, J., Yin, X., Zheng, Y., Wang, C.: Secure indoor localization based on extracting trusted fingerprint. Sensors 18(2), 1–23 (2018)
11. Félix, G., Siller, M., Álvarez, E.N.: A fingerprinting indoor localization algorithm based deep learning. In: Eighth International Conference on Ubiquitous and Future Networks (ICUFN), pp. 1006–1011 (2016)
12. Xue, W., Qiu, W., Hua, X., Yu, K.: Improved Wi-Fi RSSI measurement for indoor localization. IEEE Sens. J. 17(7), 2224–2230 (2017)
13. Xue, W., et al.: A new weighted algorithm based on the uneven spatial resolution of RSSI for indoor localization. IEEE Access 6, 26588–26595 (2018)
14. Longo, A., et al.: Localization and monitoring system based on BLE fingerprint method. In: Proceedings of the Workshop on Artificial Intelligence with Application in Health (WAIAH), 1982, pp. 25–32 (2017)
15. Chou, J.-S., Cheng, M.-Y., Hsieh, Y.-M., Yang, I.-T., Hsu, H.-T.: Optimal path planning in real time for dynamic building fire rescue operations using wireless sensors and visual guidance. J. Autom. Constr. 99, 1–17 (2019)
16. Khalid, Q., Fernández, A., Lujak, M., Doniec, A.: A group evacuation method for smart buildings. In: Camarinha-Matos, L.M., Almeida, R., Oliveira, J. (eds.) DoCEIS 2019. IAICT, vol. 553, pp. 206–213. Springer, Cham (2019). https://doi.org/10.1007/978-3-030-17771-3_17
17. Integrating Physical and Cyber Security for Safer Cities (A Frost & Sullivan White Paper). https://dkf1ato8y5dsg.cloudfront.net/uploads/5/82/nec-integratingphysicalandcybersecurityforsafercities.pdf
18. Taking of with Digital Identity – How a single ID will transform air travel. https://dkf1ato8y5dsg.cloudfront.net/uploads/5/82/2.pdf

19. Securing Experiences via Digital Identity (A Frost & Sullivan Executive Briefing Paper). https://dkf1ato8y5dsg.cloudfront.net/uploads/5/82/nec-securingexperiences-executivevriefingpaper.pdf
20. Ensuring Digital Safety with Robust Cyber Security (NEC public safety white paper). https://dkf1ato8y5dsg.cloudfront.net/uploads/5/82/nec-ensuring-digital-safety.pdf
21. Bañuls, V.A., Turoff, M., Hiltz, S.R.: Collaborative scenario modeling in emergency management through cross-impact. Technol. Forecast. Soc. Chang. **80**(9), 1756–1774 (2013)
22. Turoff, M., Bañuls, V.A., Plotnick, L., Hiltz, S.R., Huerga, M.R.: Collaborative evolution of a dynamic scenario model for the interaction of critical infrastructures. In: Proceedings of the International Conference on Information Systems for Crisis Response and Management (ISCRAM) (2015)
23. Turoff, M., Bañuls, V.A., Plotnick, L., Hiltz, S.R., Huerga, M.R.: A collaborative dynamic scenario model for the interaction of critical infrastructures. Futures **84**(A), 23–42 (2016)
24. Bodinab, Ö., Nohrstedtc, D.: Formation and performance of collaborative disaster management networks: evidence from a Swedish wildfire response. Glob. Environ. Change **41**, 183–194 (2016)
25. Flentge, F., Weber, S.G., Behring, A., Ziegert, T.: Designing context-aware HCI for collaborative emergency management. In: International Workshop on HCI for Emergencies (2008)
26. Baudoin, G., Venard, O.: Information, communication and localization environment for travelers with sensory disabilities in public transports. In: 5th International ICST Conference on Communications and Networking, pp. 1–7 (2010)
27. Camarinha-Matos, L.M., Afsarmanesh, H.: Collaborative networks: a new scientific discipline. J. Intell. Manuf. **16**(4–5), 439–452 (2005)
28. Camarinha-Matos, L.M., Afsarmanesh, H., Ermilova, E., Ferrada, F., Klen, A., Jarimo, T.: ARCON reference models for collaborative networks. In: Camarinha-Matos, L.M., Afsarmanesh, H. (eds.) Collaborative Networks Reference Modeling, pp. 83–112. Springer, Boston (2008). https://doi.org/10.1007/978-0-387-79426-6_8

Data Semantics in Food and Agribusiness

Semantic Support for Scenarios to Improve Communication in Agribusiness

Leandro Antonelli[1(✉)], Diego Torres[1,2,3], Mariángeles Hozikian[1], and Jorge E. Hernandez[4,5]

[1] Lifia – Facultad de Informatica, Universidad Nacional de La Plata,
La Plata, Argentina
{leandro.antonelli,diego.torres,
marian.hozikian}@lifia.info.unlp.edu.ar
[2] CICPBA – Comision de Investigaciones Cientificas de la Provincia de BsAs,
Tolosa, Argentina
[3] Departamento de Ciencia y Tecnologia, Universidad de Nacional de Quilmes,
Bernal, Argentina
[4] School of Management, University of Liverpool, Liverpool, United Kingdom
J.E.Hernandez@liverpool.ac.uk
[5] Universidad de La Frontera, Temuco, Chile

Abstract. Organizations produce and exchange a huge amount of critical information, which main purpose is to obtain acceptable results. Hence, the trend is by considering integrated systems that can be easily adapted to several domains, especially when they need to exchange information. In this context, the agribusiness sector is a good example where massive data is generated, which implies the need for information sharing and collaboration, where the great challenged is support and understand the colliding context. However, every software system relies on its context, with its own rules, dynamism, and languages. Hence, it implies a significant effort to have a complete understanding of the composed domain. For this purpose, scenarios are well-known tools to describe dynamic domains and are commonly described under text-based context. When different stakeholders build Scenarios, it is essential to review them in order to unify their description. Thus, Scenarios under this unified perspective will better support the analysis and identification of relationship between two or more domains. This analysis is the key to design mechanisms to exchange information. Therefore, in the light of this, this paper proposes a semantic definition of Scenarios and a set of queries to identify issues in the Scenarios and improve their quality. In addition to this, a wiki platform to implement the semantic support and the queries is also provided.

Keywords:: Agribusiness · Requirements · Scenarios · Ontologies

1 Introduction

Nowadays, there is a huge level of integration between different software systems. Everyone produces a big amount of data and different organizations share this information to improve their results [5]. Collaboration is needed in every sector. Food and

L. M. Camarinha-Matos et al. (Eds.): PRO-VE 2019, IFIP AICT 568, pp. 447–456, 2019.
https://doi.org/10.1007/978-3-030-28464-0_38

agribusiness are not an exception. Their supply chains are pioneers in the use of massive data, sometimes due to rigorous legislation that force to trace lots of variables along the supply chain [14]. Scenarios are well-known tools to describe situations of the domain [2]. They can be used to capture the context of different applications to identify their relationship. Thus, it is possible to establish a mechanism to make the applications to exchange information.

Nevertheless, it is not an easy task to design a mechanism to interoperate two different applications already developed [5]. Every software system relies on its context, with its rules, dynamic, and language. Scenarios should use the language of the stakeholders since the stakeholders are the ones that describe them. Thus, Scenarios need to be described with narrative text [7]. However, it can be hard to identify joints points in Scenarios that are described by two different groups of stakeholders that belong to two different contexts [11].

There are some quality attributes that good specification must satisfy: completeness, consistency, unambiguity, and correctness [6]. Completeness means that no piece of a specification can be missed because some absence can lead to suppositions. Consistency means that the different points of view should provide a unified description. Unambiguous is related to the use of terms and expressions that should be carefully chosen in order to avoid misunderstanding. Finally, correctness is related to assure that the description satisfy the reality. That is, there is no gap between the intended meaning and the specification.

Scenarios are used to understand the context of the application since they promote communication when there is a great variety of experts [2, 10]. Scenarios should be written carefully in order to satisfy the quality attributes. Nevertheless, it is challenging to achieve this goal [12]. Scenarios have been historically described by only one person, the requirements engineer who elicited the knowledge, organized it and produced a homogenous specification [7]. This classical view is being replaced by a collaborative model, where every stakeholder contributes directly to the specification [4]. Let us consider the expression "cultural labor". In the agricultural domain, it refers to some task (labor) to take care of the plants (cultures). Nevertheless, the expression can also refer to some artistic (cultural) activity (labor).

A semantic support helps to improve the quality of narrative descriptions [3]. An ontology description is a semantic mechanism that relates every relevant syntactic element (for example, nouns and verbs) to a semantic element [13]. For example, a homonym could be related to two different ontology elements. Thus consistency and unambiguity can be improved [1, 15]. Moreover, ontologies can be described in semantic tools that make possible automatic processing to infer conclusions. For example, let consider the following sentences: "A tomato is a vegetable" and "Any vegetable needs irrigation." A semantic query can conclude that "A tomato needs irrigation."

Different approaches use ontologies as a body of knowledge to create scenarios in many domains. To our knowledge, there are no approaches that create ontologies from narrative scenarios to improve their quality. In this paper, we propose a semantic description of the Scenarios, a set of semantic queries, and a tool support for them. This contribution provides an automatic processing of the Scenarios to help to improve their quality regarding consistency, ambiguity, completeness and correctness. The proposal identifies issues in the description of the Scenarios while stakeholders are describing them. Thus, the stakeholders alerted by the tool can discuss the issues among them in order to improve their shared knowledge and consolidate it in the Scenarios.

This knowledge makes possible the analysis of the colliding areas captured in Scenarios to design an interoperation mechanism. This paper only focuses on identifying issues to improve the quality of the Scenarios. Nevertheless, this is a crucial step to design an interoperation mechanism. Commonly, every organization has its own culture (language, techniques, and process). Thus, when two organization need to interoperate, they need to share the same culture. It is important to mention, that it is also needed in differents working group in the same organization. The rest of the paper is organized in the following way. Section 2 describes the template of the Scenario. Section 3 presents the semantic definition. Section 4 proposes semantic queries to identify issues. Section 5 describes the tool. Section 6 discusses some conclusions.

2 Scenario Template

Leite [7] defines a Scenario with the following attributes: (i) a title that identifies the Scenario; (ii) a goal to be reached through the execution of the episodes; (iii) a context that sets the starting point to reach the goal; (iv) the resources, relevant physical objects or information that must be available, (v) the actors, agents that perform the actions, and (vi) the set of episodes, smaller task (that could also be described as a Scenario) to accomplish the goal

Listing 1 and 2 provide examples. The domain used is a farm that grows vegetables, but it also breeds animals in order to be ecologically self-sufficient as well as profitable. The goat milking Scenario (Listing 1), describes some basic steps to obtain milk from the goats. The actors and resources attributes should be used in the episodes, although it is possible that episodes mention actors and resources not mentioned in these both attributes due to the iterative construction of the Scenarios. That is, in a first step, some stakeholder identifies a Scenario describing its title, then other stakeholders describe the main actors and resources, and finally some other with more knowledge describes the set of episodes. The Cheesemaking Scenario (Listing 2) is related to the Goat milking Scenario because the milk obtained with the first Scenario is used to produce cheese. This relation is showed in the context of the Scenario Cheesemaking and the goal of the Scenario Goat Milking.

3 Semantic Definition of the Scenarios

This section describes the ontology designed for providing a semantic description of the Scenarios. Using the proposed ontology, stakeholders can keep using an iterative and incremental approach to describe the Scenarios, but the ontology will provide support to identify inconsistencies.

The description uses the main principles of the OWL language [8]. We defined six main semantic concepts that are described as classes. The first one is the Scenario. Then, some attributes of the Scenario are also classes: Actor, Resource, and Episodes.

Finally, there are two different attributes (Goal and Context) that are described with the same class: Condition. Each of the class concepts has the following intent:

Scenario: It is the core conceptualization in the ontology. It has a title, a data property defined as a string. Additionally, Scenario includes a Goal and a Context, both of them are Conditions. The Context is the pre-condition to perform the Scenario while the Goal is the postcondition. The Scenario also contains actor, resources, and episodes, steps that could be atomic actions represented by Episodes, or more complex ones, described as Scenarios.

Condition: It represents a situation, and it is used to describe goals (the desired situation to achieve) and context (needed situation to allow the execution of the Scenario).

Actor: It represents the subject that is in charge of the Episodes actions and the owner of the scenarios.

Resource: It represents the resources that are used in the episodes by the actors.

Episode: It represents each task that the actor performs with some resource. Thus, the episode is related to an actor, a resource and a verb. Moreover, the episode is related to a previous episode that must be completed.

Action: It represents the main action of an episode. It is important to mention, that the semantic representation of the action not only consider a verb, but it could also be a more complex expression that provides an accurate description of the domain.

Scenario: Goat Milking
Goal: The goat milk is stored in a refrigerated tank.
Context: Goats located at the extraction facility
Resources: goats, refrigerated tanks, milking machine
Actors: farmer
Episodes:
The farmer sets the goat in the milking machine
The farmer extracts milk with the milking machine.
The farmer conducts the milk to a refrigerated tank.
Listing 1. Goat milking Scenario

Scenario: Cheesemaking
Goal: To have cheese to sell and obtain money to run the farm
Context: The goat milk is stored in a refrigerated tank.
Resources: Milk
Actors: Cheesemaker
Episodes:
The cheesemaker curdles the milk with lactic ferments
The cheesemaker adds rennet to the milk
The cheesemaker drains the milk in mussels
The cheesemaker salts the milk
The cheesemaker leaves the milk to refine for 24 h
Listing 2. Cheesemaking Scenario

Figure 1 shows the different classes and the dependencies between them. The figure uses the Scenarios described in Listing 1 and 2. The Scenario Goat Milking (Listing 1) is completely described, while the figure only describes the elements of the Scenario Cheesemaking (Listing 2) that are related to the first one. That is the case of the condition "The goat milk is stored in a refrigerator tank", shared as a goal and a context. Then, it is important to mention that the actions are complex expressions, for example: "conducts the milk to," instead of referring only to a verb.

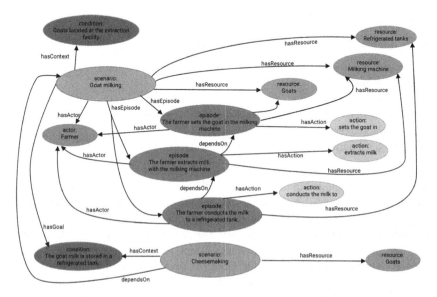

Fig. 1. Classes and dependencies

4   Semantic Queries to Identify Issues

This section describes the semantic artifacts that allow the stakeholders to check requirements quality attributes as completeness and consistency. These queries should be checked constantly along with the collaborative definition of Scenarios. Thus, when some issue is identified, an alert is shown explaining the issue, so that it can be fixed. The rest of this section describes five semantic queries conceptually and we also present a SPARQL query definition.

Query 1. Consistency between actors and episodes
All the actors included in the attribute actor of the scenario should be mentioned in at least one of the episodes. That is, if an actor a belongs to the scenario s, there should be an episode (or scenario which is an episode of s) that refers to the actor a. Because of the iterative and incremental description of the Scenarios, it is not necessary to check that all the actor mentioned in the episodes should be listed in the attribute actor. The SPARQL query detailed in Listing 3 shows the list of actors that are inconsistent for the <scenario>. If the query returns an empty list, it represents the lack of actors and episodes inconsistency.

For example, Listing 4 shows a new version of the Cheesemaking Scenario (partially described) that has actors and episodes inconsistency because the actor farmer is not mentioned in any episode. The query applied to the example will return a list with farmer.

```
1. SELECT ?actors WHERE {
2. {<scenario> hasActor ?actor}
3. MINUS{
4. <scenario> hasEpisode ?episode.
5. ?episode hasActor ?actor.}}
```

Listing 3. SPARQL query to detect inconsistency between actors and episodes.

Scenario: Cheesemaking
Actors: farmer
Episodes:
The cheesemaker curdles the milk with lactic ferments
The cheesemaker adds rennet to the milk

Listing 4. A scenario with inconsistency between actors and episodes

Query 2. Consistency between resources and episodes
All the resources included in the attribute resource of the scenario should be mentioned in at least one of the episodes. That is, if a resource r belongs to the scenario s, there should be an episode (or scenario which is an episode of s) that refers to the resource s. This query is similar to the previous one. The SPARQL query detailed in Listing 5 shows the list of resources that are inconsistent for the <scenario>. For example, Listing 6 shows a new version of the Goat Milking Scenario that has resources and episodes inconsistency because the resource horses is not mentioned in any episode. The query applied to the example will return a list with horses.

```
1. SELECT ?resources WHERE {
2. <scenario> hasResource ?resource}
3. MINUS{
4. <scenario> hasEpisode ?episode.
5. ?episode hasResource ?resource.}}
```

Listing 5. SPARQL query to detect inconsistency between resources and episodes.

Scenario: Goat Milking
Resources: goats, refrigerated tanks, milking machine, horses
Episodes:
The farmer sets the goat in the milking machine
The farmer extracts milk with the milking machine.
The farmer conducts the milk to a refrigerated tank.

Listing 6. A scenario with inconsistency with a resource

Query 3. Completeness with the satisfaction of contexts by goals

A scenario s can be performed if all its conditions described in the context attribute are contained in the union of the conditions described in the goal of other scenarios. Goals describe the intended situation (final states, postconditions) while contexts describe the starting point situations (initial states, preconditions). Thus, the context of a Scenario should be satisfied with the goals of other Scenarios, in order to be performed. The SPARQL query detailed in Listing 7 shows the list of conditions (contexts) for the <scenario> that are not satisfied by any other Scenario. For example, Listing 2 describes the Cheesemaking Scenario, where its context is satisfied by the goal of the Goat Milking Scenario described in Listing 1. Nevertheless, the context of the Goat Milking Scenario, is not satisfied with the goal of Cheesemaking Scenario.

```
1. SELECT ?contextCondition WHERE {
2. <scenario> hascontext ?contextCondition.}
3. MINUS{
4. ?otherScenario a Scenario.
5. ?otherScenario hasGoal ?contextCondition.}}
```

Listing 7. SPARQL query to detect context and goals completeness.

Query 4. Consistency in the sequence of the Scenarios

A scenario s can be performed if all its conditions described in the context attribute are contained in the union of the conditions described in the goal of the depending on scenarios. This query is a complement of the previous query that only checks if some goal can satisfy a context, while this query checks that a previous Scenario is the one that should satisfy the goal. The SPARQL query detailed in Listing 8 shows the list of conditions (contexts) for the <scenario> that are not satisfied by any depending on Scenario. For example, Figure 1 shows a dependency between Cheesemaking Scenario on Goat milking Scenario. This dependency is based on some stakeholders who stated that Goat milking should be done first and after that can be done Cheesemaking. Considering this dependency, this query tests if the Cheesemaking Scenario context is satisfied by the goal of the Goat Milking Scenario described.

```
1. SELECT ?contextCondition WHERE {
2. <scenario> hascontext ?contextCondition.}
3. MINUS{
4. ?otherScenario a Scenario.
6. <scenario> dependsOn ?otherScenario.
7. ?otherScenario hasGoal ?contextCondition.}}
```

Listing 8. SPARQL query to detect consistency in the sequence of the Scenarios.

Query 5. Completeness in the redundancy of goals

Some scenarios s1 and s2 have the same goal, thus, they should be refined in order to have different and specifics goals. When a group of stakeholders is collaboratively describing Scenarios, it is difficult that all of them have a complete understanding of the whole domain. Thus, when Scenarios with duplicated goals are identified it means that two overlapping scenarios are described. The SPARQL query detailed in Listing 9 shows the list of Scenarios that has a duplicated goal with the <scenario>. For example, Listing 10 and 11 shows a new version of the Goat milking and Cheesemaking Scenarios. This new version has the same goal because both scenarios are overlapped. The last episode of the Goat Milking Scenario overlaps Cheesemaking Scenario, and the first episode of the Cheesemaking Scenario overlaps with the GoatMilking Scenario.

```
1.SELECT ?scenarios ?goal WHERE {
2. ?scenario a Scenario.
3. <current> hasGoal ?goal.
4. ?scenario hasGoal ?goal.
5. FILTER(?scenario <> <current>).}
```

Listing 9. SPARQL query to detect redundancy of goals.

Scenario: Goat Milking
Goal: Obtain cheese from the goats
Episodes:
The farmer sets the goat in the milking machine
The farmer extracts milk with the milking machine.
The farmer conducts the milk to a refrigerated tank.
The cheesemaker producer makes cheese.

Listing 10. Goat milking Scenario overlapped with Cheesemaking Scenario

Scenario: Cheesemaking
Goal: Obtain cheese from the goats
Episodes:
The farmer do goat milking.
The cheesmaker curdles the milk with lactic ferments
The cheesmaker adds rennet to the milk
The cheesmaker drains the milk in mussels
The cheesmaker salts the milk
The cheesmaker leaves the milk to refine for 24 h

Listing 11. Cheesemaking Scenario overlapped with Goat milking Scenario

5   Tool Support

We developed a Media Wiki [9] based application to support the semantic representation of the Scenarios and the queries to identify issues. Media Wiki is an open source implementation written in PHP that uses the MySql database engine. Wikipedia and other projects of Wikimedia use Media Wiki. We have added two extensions: (i) an ad-hoc collaborative catalog and editor, and (ii) a semantic Media Wiki. Since it relies on the wikitext format, users with no knowledge of HTML or CSS can easily edit the pages and the result looks like web pages that users are familiar to. Media Wiki stores in a database all the different versions of each page, in a collaborative environment could be necessary to access a previous version. Another advantage of Media Wiki is the management of the links between pages. Although the destination of a link does not exist, the link can also be written and Media Wiki shows it anyway, when the user clicks the link, Media Wiki allow to create the page. It is a useful feature to connect Scenarios while they are being described. Figure 2 shows a screenshot of the Goat Milking Scenario with some report about an inconsistency detected with actors.

Fig. 2. Goat milking Scenario without any reported issue

6 Conclusions

We have presented a semantic description of Scenarios and a set of semantic queries, both things implemented in a semantic Media Wiki in order to support the collaborative description of Scenario. This proposal contributes to identify issues that arise because of the collaborative nature of the construction. Moreover, the agricultural domain is very specific because practices vary between different regions as well as their language. Thus, in order to communicate and interoperate different software systems, it is necessary to unify the knowledge of the different domains. We claim that our proposal provides an approach to capture the knowledge from different stakeholders and obtain a shared knowledge through an iterative and incremental process of checking and improving. This work is supported by the RUC APS project, in which three different groups of teams participate: IT experts, agricultural engineers and business specialist. We are using Scenarios and preliminary results are satisfactory. We plan to improve the scenarios verification developing more complex queries to check internal consistency between scenarios and we are also working in comparing scenarios with other sources of knowledge.

Acknowledgement. This research is supported by Agroknowledge and Ruc-Aps, a H2020 RISE-2015 project, aiming at Enhancing and implementing Knowledge based ICT solutions within high Risk and Uncertain Conditions for Agriculture Production Systems.

References

1. Bhatia, M.P.S., Kumar, A., Beniwal, R.: Ontology based framework for detecting ambiguities in software requirements specification. In: 3rd INDIACom, New Delhi. pp. 3572–3575 (2016)
2. Carroll, J.M.: Five reasons for scenario-based design. In: Interacting with Computers, vol. 13, no. 1. pp. 43–60 (2000). https://doi.org/10.1016/s0953-5438(00)00023-0
3. Dzung, D.V., Ohnishi, A.: Improvement of quality of software requirements with requirements ontology. In: 9th ICQS, Jeju, pp. 284–289 (2009). https://doi.org/10.1109/qsic.2009.44
4. Ge, C., Yu, S., Yang, G., Wang, W.: A collaborative requirements elicitation approach based on scenario. In: 10th International Conference on Computer-Aided Industrial Design & Conceptual Design, Wenzhou, pp. 2213–2216 (2009). https://doi.org/10.1109/caidcd.2009.5375171
5. Ilyas, M., Khan, S.U.: An empirical investigation of the software integration success factors in GSD environment. In 15th SERA, London, pp. 255–262 (2017)
6. Kummler, P.S., Vernisse, L., Fromm, H.: How good are my requirements?: A new perspective on the quality measurement of textual requirements. In: 11th QUATIC, Coimbra, pp. 156–159 (2018). https://doi.org/10.1109/quatic.2018.00031
7. do Prado Leite, J.C., et al.: Enhancing a requirements baseline with scenarios. Requirements Eng. **2**(4) 184–198 (1997). https://doi.org/10.1109/isre.1997.566841
8. McGuinness, D.L., Van Harmelen, F.: OWL web ontology language overview. W3C Recommendation **10**(10) (2004). http://www.w3.org/TR/owl-features/
9. Media Wiki. https://www.mediawiki.org
10. Potts, C.: Using schematic scenarios to understand user needs. In: 1st Conference on Designing Interactive Systems: Processes, Practices, Methods, & Techniques (1995)
11. Ramasubbu, N., Kemerer, C.F.: Managing technical debt in enterprise software packages. IEEE Trans. Softw. Eng. **40–8**, 758–772 (2014)
12. Sarmiento, E., do Prado Leite, J.C., Almentero, E.: Using correctness, consistency, and completeness patterns for automated scenarios verification. In: 5th RePa, pp. 47–54 (2015)
13. Shunxin, L., Leijun, S.: Requirements engineering based on domain ontology. In: 2010 International Conference of Information Science and Management Engineering, Xi'an, pp. 120–122 (2010). https://doi.org/10.1109/isme.2010.110
14. Tan, L., Haley, R., Wortman, R., Zhang, Q.: An extensible and integrated software architecture for data analysis and visualization in precision agriculture. In: 13th IRI, Las Vegas, NV, pp. 271–278 (2012). https://doi.org/10.1109/iri.2012.6303020
15. Zait, F., Zarour, N.: Addressing lexical and semantic ambiguity in natural language requirements. In: Fifth ISIICT, Amman. pp. 1–7 (2018). https://doi.org/10.1109/isiict.2018.8613726

Collaboration Networks for Information Empowerment of Food Consumers

Antonio Palmiro Volpentesta, Alberto Michele Felicetti[✉],
and Nicola Frega

Department of Mechanical Energy and Management Engineering,
University of Calabria, Via P. Bucci, 87036 Rende, CS, Italy
{antonio.volpentesta, alberto.felicetti,
nicola.frega}@unical.it

Abstract. The growing popularity of social networking platforms and recent advances in the internet of "things for food" open the way to conceive new information solutions to assist food consumers in their consumption activities. This paper deals with an egalitarian and bottom-up approach, where food consumers and stakeholders of the food supply chain interact to create and share valuable and reliable food information possibly coming from food instrumental measurements performed by consumers via smart food things. In particular, we propose a model of a collaborative network where members manage food information in a collective and distributed way (in terms of information generation, validation and delivery). Moreover, we highlight the outcome value of this new collaborative way of food information management under a consumer perspective.

Keywords: Food information · Food consumer's empowerment ·
Internet-of-food · Collective awareness · Consumer's perceived value

1 Introduction

Today's food consumers need more reliable food information to be aware of the consequences of choices that they make along their food consumption activities.

Food information is traditionally provided by food producers and/or distributors through mass media and labels on-package. This way of food information provision is producer-centered since it tends to satisfy companies marketing-related objective, rather than consumers' information needs.

On the other hand, food consumers are increasingly demanding high-quality, safe and healthy food [1], as they are more and more engaged in food related discussions in social networks with other consumers. Moreover, they interact with food related business (food producers, distributors, third parties) in loose, open and flexible ways, continuously searching for food information transparency along food supply chains.

Recently, the convergence between "Social Networking Platforms" and "Internet of things" opened the way for a new generation of context-aware systems [2]. The increasing availability of sensors and mobile devices represent the technological layer

L. M. Camarinha-Matos et al. (Eds.): PRO-VE 2019, IFIP AICT 568, pp. 457–466, 2019.
https://doi.org/10.1007/978-3-030-28464-0_39

of a cyber-physical system that is able to provide context-based services to people in a smart environment [3].

New smart food applications and devices (e.g. "food scanner" or "food sniffer" for food analysis) suggest that the time is ripe to conceive new approaches to food information management that would empower consumers and be more responsive to their information needs.

The main challenge is to exploit the potential of collaboration through ICT networks to create a collective intelligence [4]. The basic assumption is that "a large number of individuals tied in a social network can provide more accurate answers to complex problems than a single individual or a small group" [5]. Collective knowledge represents an interesting issue that has been addressed in many research fields [6, 7]. The food sector represents another promising application field. In fact, technological advances in the so-called Internet of Food (IoF), make possible the development of a new generation of intelligent food services [8] able to provide context-based food information to consumers. In particular, IoF can be viewed as a network of food smart object augmented with sensing, computing (e.g. time-temperature indicators, sensors to detect food spoilage or bacterial infection, and so on), allowing a fast analysis of food items.

The consumer's opportunity to access to more food information and the capability to exchange opinions and information with other consumers, are gradually shifting the balance of the competition. The chance to collect more information makes consumers more powerful, giving them the opportunity to be aware of their food-related choices. In particular, consumers' information empowerment, i.e. the consumers' improved capability to access, process and share food information [8], is gaining more and more importance. In fact, the possibility for consumers of "being in control" and "of being smarter" is crucial to carry out better food-related decisions during their food consumption activities.

This "consumer-centric" perspective of food information management (FIM) opens new ways in offering value to food consumers, driving some tech companies to enter the food information market at full steam. These companies offer the opportunity to exploit benefits new technologies, providing consumers to manage food information more responsive to their requests for information. In particular, these emerging trends make possible to design new collaboration networks where consumers and stakeholders of the food supply chain interact to create and share valuable and reliable food information.

This work aims to propose a model of a collaborative network where members manage food information in a collective and distributed way (in terms of information generation, validation and delivery), leveraging on open food data, IoF-based devices, and cloud/app-based solution. The model is a tool for researchers and practitioners, to explore a pathway towards collective food knowledge and information empowerment for a food consumer community.

Moreover, we propose an analysis of the outcome value of this new collaborative process of FIM under a consumer perspective that considers an evaluation of benefits and costs a consumer perceives as the result of the collaborative process when compared with other available FIM processes.

2   Modeling Food Information Empowerment Network

In a consumer-centric perspective of food information management, we envisage a new form of collaboration as letting consumers to be more aware during their food consumption activities. This collaboration can leverage on both potentialities of new smart-food technologies in determining food properties (from a physical, biochemical, and microbiological point of view), and a cooperative process in fostering collective food knowledge awareness. The rationale is to let a consumers' community have the opportunity to create and share reliable information about food.

In the emerging network, called Food Information Empowerment Network (FIEN), empowered food consumers collectively manage (generate, verify/validate, and distribute) information about several aspects (e.g. safety, quality) of food products and processes. In what follows, we view a FIEN as a collaboration network and we model it by describing its main endogenous dimensions, as suggested in [9].

2.1   Structural Dimension

This dimension deals with the composition of a FIEN in terms of its constituting elements and roles performed by these elements.

We identify the following actors and roles in a FIEN:

- *Simple Consumer (SC)*: a community member requesting for information about a specific food item performance [10].
- *Empowered consumer (EC)*: a community member who provides (in an implicit or explicit way) some measurements of food item characteristics by means of a smart food thing (i.e. a device able to catch some signals from food, like infrared emission, volatile compounds, etc.) and other descriptive data about a food item (e.g., date and place of production, batch number)
- *Information Broker (IB)*: an intermediate agent that processes requests from SCs, receives and controls data acquired by ECs and provide SCs with understandable (i.e. human-readable) food information.
- *Food Analyzer (FA):* an agent able to perform a diagnosis on a food item. It could be assisted by a software tool applying some intelligent methods (e.g. statistical methods, machine-learning based techniques) to determine food item characteristics.
- *Food Ledger Manager (FLM)*: a food database manager that receives and organizes data that comes from the Food Analyzer. Moreover, it provides results to query formulated by a Collective Challenge Solver.
- *Collective Challenge Solver (CCS)*: an agent playing the fundamental role in the collective process to generate reliable food information. It leverages on a food knowledge base and collectively reliable criteria to find the value of the food performance p shared by all food items that possess the same identity properties i.
- *Network Authority (NA)*: an entity that is in charge to manage the governance of the FIEN. Referring to the collaborative process, it sets and manages the criteria adopted by the Collective Challenge Solver to generate food information. These

criteria are based on a collective interpretation of food item characteristics, in order to determine to what extent information on food performances are reliable.

2.2 Functional Dimension

This dimension addresses the flows of operations (procedures, processes and methods) dealing with the operational phase of a FIEN. In particular, we focus on a collaborative process that allows the consumer community of a FIEN to create and share information on food performances related to some food items that belong to the same food class. The assumption that underpins the process model is that the reliability of food performance information can be derived from a collective interpretation of food characteristics information coming from measurements performed by smart food things.

The process consists of the following activities:

A.0.1 Collective Criteria Definition: *NA* defines the rules (e.g. methods, threshold values) for collective interpretation of food items' characteristics.

A.1.1 Request formulation: *SC* needs for reliable information about a specific performance *p* of a food item. *SC* makes a request *r(i, p)* to *IB*, where *i* is referred to a set of identity property values (food item descriptive data), while *p* represents a specific a performance SC wants to know (e.g. safety). *SC* transmits request data to *IB* through his/her own handheld device.

A.1.2 Request Acquisition: *IB* verifies if the request can be instantly satisfied by querying a database containing data on challenges already solved. Otherwise, *IB* send a new challenge to the *CCS*.

A.1.3 Challenge formulation: Do food items with the same identity value *i* have the same value of performance *p*? *CCS* identifies food characteristics that are needed to determine *p*, by leveraging on a a food knowledge base. CCS formulates the query *q(i, c)* to *FLM* in order to retrieve values related to food items sharing the same identity value *i*.

A.1.4 Ledger Answer: *FLM* also provides results to the query *q(i, c)* formulated by *CCS*. Query results consist in a set of values of characteristics *c* for food items sharing the same identity value *i*;

A.1.5 Challenge Solution: *CCS* analyzes data provided by *FLM* and verifies whether the value of *p* can be calculated by leveraging on collectively reliable criteria established by the *NA*. If so, CCS determines *p*. Ther result is sent to FIB that is in charge to set-up the solution in a format understandable for *R*. Moreover, the result is stored in the solved challenge database. Otherwise, it notifies to *IB* that the challenge could not be resolved.

A.1.6 Results provision: *IB* receives challenge results from the CCS and provides results to *SC* in a human-readable form.

A.1.7 Results acquisition: *SC* receives Food information.

A.2.1 Food Data Acquisition: *EC* scans a food item by using his/her smart devices in order to acquire food properties data. In addition to these data, EB also provides descriptive data on food identity (*id*)

A.2.2 Food Data Validation: *IB* acquires and verifies food data as well as other interaction context data catched through environmental sensors. It passes the whole data to *FA*.

A.2.3 Food Data Analysis: *FA* performs a diagnosis of the food item in order to determine the value *c* of some food characteristics. In particular, it applies some intelligent methods (e.g. statistical methods and machine learning-based approaches) able to deduce food characteristics. The pair (*id, c*) is sent to *FLM*.

A.2.4 Food Data Storaging: *FLM* collects and organizes data, namely the pair (*id, c*), in a database.

In Fig. 1, we provide a BPMN representation of the collaborative process, highlighting the contact points between consumers and the back-end process.

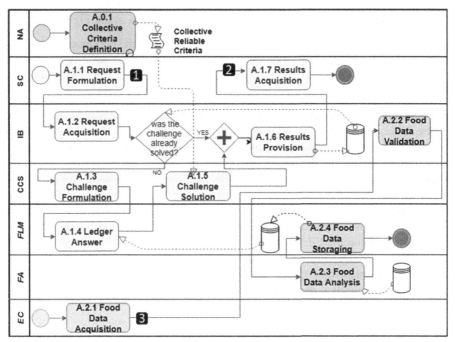

1 2   points where the SC and the back-end process interact
3   point where the EC and the back-end process interact

Fig. 1. A BPMN representation of a collaborative process in a FIEN.

2.3 Componental Dimension

Intangible and tangible resources of a FIEN (e.g. information, knowledge, software, hardware) are taken into account by this dimension. In [11] a three-tier conceptual architecture for the FIEN has been proposed. This architecture consists of: (1) an interface layer that enables the user to entry, fetch and process food data; (2) a logic tier for food data computation and analysis; and (3) a storage layer concerning with food information storage and retrieval. More details about a FIEN technological are provided in [11].

2.4 Behavioral Dimension

Along this dimension, the focus is onh policies, principles and governance rules influencing the behavior of the FIEN members. The *NA* has a crucial role in managing network members' behavior. In particular, the *NA* plays a dual role as:

- *technological intermediary*, whose role is to provide the ICT platform including, front-end and back-end software, security and communication;
- *guarantee authority*, that is responsible for the "ethical code" and "behavioural rules" for FIEN members. Moreover, it has an important role in attracting and selecting new members of the FIEN. It provides a comprehensive governance role, ensuring behavioural correctness of members' interactions in the FIEN.

In a FIEN, food information trustworthiness depends on the consumers' reliability on instrumental measurement, food data analysis techniques and security of information flows. The *NA* takes on the burden of building consumers' trust by defining the following aspects:

- *cooperation agreements*: the *NA* must guarantee the effectiveness and correctness of the measuring instruments adopted by the *ECs*. Therefore it should make collaboration agreements with smart things producers in order to define a set of certified and guaranteed FIEN platform tools.
- *obligatory behavior*: define rules and principles that are mandatory to be followed inside the FIEN. This comprises the definition of the collectively reliable criteria that are applicable to generate new food information, the definition of authorization profiles within the platform as well the definition of operational and managerial processes within the FIEN.
- *constraints and conditions*: ensuring transparency throughout the whole process of generation and sharing of food information and define the degree of restriction on the use of intellectual property of FIEN.

3 Consumers' Value of FIM

The multifaceted nature of food consumption makes the outcome of a FIM process extremely valuable to a consumer [1]. From a consumer perspective, the FIM outcome value is the ultimate trade-off between benefits and costs a consumer perceives as the result of his/her interaction with the FIM process and the involved community. Benefit/cost assessment varies from a consumer to another as it is affected by consumer's attributes (knowledge, food related values, experiences, attitudes). In what follows, we present a FIM outcome value framework consisting of the following factors and components:

Utility Benefits. They refer to the overall utility of the information that a consumer acquires when interacting with a FIM process. Here, we refer to this utility as a measure of the impact on consumer's food-related decision-making, brought about by the variation that occurs in consumer's assessment of a food product/service, because the interaction with the FIM process. Two entities play a crucial role in determining utility benefits:

(a) *Content*: a set of information 'cues' that are exchanged between the consumer and the FIM process during the interaction. They may be declarative, as they describe and specify food quality attributes, or procedural, as they concern with food consumption activities. The main value factor is the **content relevance** that establishes how much impact the "what" is exchanged has on a consumer's food decision process. Content relevance sub factors are topicality, accuracy, depth, scope, clarity, organization, and format of the information exchanged [12].

(b) *External Context:* a set of characteristics of the situation (food presence, place, time, food consumption activity, social relations, etc.) in which the consumer interacts with the FIM process. The main value factor is **situation relevance** that establishes how much impact the "how", "when", and "where" of the interaction has on a consumer's food decision process [8]. It may be defined as the extent to which information content is required to be specified to practical matters of the current situation.

Sociocultural Benefits. They concern with the satisfaction of consumer's sociocultural needs through the consumer participation at the FIM community formed by other consumers and food chain stakeholders. Participation at the community brings a wealth of food cultural knowledge (including beliefs or practices), social norms, food literacy, as well as challenges that occur in consumer daily lives, e.g. credibility of food information sources. Main value factors are:

(a) *Sociability* of the FIM community. It affects satisfaction of consumer needs of personal connectedness and relationships with other consumers and food chain stakeholders;

(b) *Trustworthiness* of information sources in the FIM community. It affects consumer assessment of the reliability of the information content that FIM provides;

(c) *Transparency* of the FIM process. It affects satisfaction of consumer needs of information empowerment and information asymmetry reduction [13].

Costs. They refer to consumer's physical and cognitive efforts that a consumer needs to interact with the FIM process or community, such as time, inconvenience and comprehension of food information. These efforts may be of two types:

• *Personal burden.* It refers to the amount of efforts a consumer has to put into interacting with a FIM process to get food information for personal use;

• *Collaborative burden.* It is the overload of efforts due to the participation to a collaborative FIM process.

In what follows, we apply the above framework to highlight main factors of the outcome value of FIM processes belonging to three broad classes: conventional FIM, social FIM, and collaborative FIM based on a FIEN.

In conventional FIM, consumers obtain food information through traditional channels like labels, radio, newspapers and television. The information content provided is:

- *massive and generic,* i.e., unable to meet specific consumer needs,
- *limited,* in terms of information amount and time-space availability,
- *biased,* as it is often directly provided by manufacturers or sellers who might emphasize some food properties, due to business oriented purposed.

As a result, consumers are sceptical, and they often ignore the information provided or perceive it as misleading. Moreover, they express concern about the information truthfulness and do not perceive any social benefits [14].

Social FIM uses internet-based technologies (the so-called web 2.0, including mobile apps and social media) for sharing information and overcoming some limitations of conventional channels [15, 16]. In social FIM, consumers group together in communities around a collective goal and contribute to the creation and distribution of food information, but they rely on third parties (e.g., forum moderators, food bloggers, recommender systems) that control the FIM process [17]. Consumers may access:

- *a larger amount of information;*
- *tailored information,* according with consumer's profile and use;
- *in-time and in-place information.*

However, beyond these advantages, utility and sociocultural benefits remain limited by the lack of a verification and validation of the food information shared by consumers [18].

In collaborative FIEN-based FIM, social and IoF technologies enable a cooperative process focused on promoting collective food knowledge and awareness. Through such a process, food consumers may share food information originated from scientific instrument measurement of food properties. This type of FIM is still to come and it has been envisaged in this paper.

Even if it results in collaborative costs, as it engages a consumer in providing or validating information, collaborative FIEN-based FIM provides significant utility and social benefits. Food information based on scientific data, coming from in-context smart food things, could assure higher accuracy and depth, more correct scope, and specified for in-context food items. In addition to that, the collective validation process could enhance consumer trust in food information sources.

Table 1 summarizes significant characteristics affecting the consumer's value of the three types of FIM above discussed.

Table 1. FIM valuable components to assess the consumer's value of three types of FIM.

Valuable components	Conventional FIM	Social-based FIM	Collaborative-based FIM
Content information	- Static, limited in amount, massive, and generic	- Consumer tailored	-Consumer tailored -Based on scientific data
Contextualized provision	- No contextualization	- In-time and in-place	- In-time and in-place - Tailored on consumer's food activity - Specific for in-context food items
Community engagement	- Consumer's information understanding and contextualizing	- Seeking and evaluating channels and sources -Contextualization efforts - Reduced cognitive effort for consumer's tailored information	- IoF device interaction - Reduced cognitive effort for consumer's tailored information - Reduced cognitive effort for context tailored information
Personal burden	- Passive receptivity of contents - Information source limited to producers and distributors	- Strengthening social relationships - Information flows controlled by third parties - No verification process	- Strengthening social relationships - Consumer empowerment - Information based on scientific evidences - Information collectively validated
Collaborative burden	- No costs	- Participation in community activities	- Participation in providing and validating food data

4   Conclusions

Conventional ways to provide food information have proved to be inadequate to satisfy today's food consumers' needs. In this direction, we have introduced a collaborative approach that offers to food consumers the opportunity to be more food aware and to carry-out more informed food-related decisions. This approach relies on a collaboration network where consumers manage food information in a collective and distributed way. The resulting collective food awareness would contribute to make vanish many "problems" linked-up with information asymmetries, driving consumers towards a greater consciousness about environmental, social and health-related issues.

Moreover, we highlighted the consumer's value of this new way of food information management by making a comparison with current ways of food information provision to consumers.

References

1. Volpentesta, A.P., Felicetti, A.M.: Research investigation on food information user's behaviour. In: Camarinha-Matos, Luis M., Afsarmanesh, H., Rezgui, Y. (eds.) PRO-VE 2018. IAICT, vol. 534, pp. 190–202. Springer, Cham (2018). https://doi.org/10.1007/978-3-319-99127-6_17

2. Atzori, L., Iera, A., Morabito, G., Nitti, M.: The social internet of things (SIoT)–when social networks meet the internet of things: concept, architecture and network characterization. Comput. Netw. **56**(16), 3594–3608 (2012)

3. Ammirato, S., Sofo, F., Felicetti, A.M., Raso, C.: Bank branches as smart environments: introducing a cognitive protection system to manage security and safety. In: Camarinha-Matos, Luis M., Afsarmanesh, H., Rezgui, Y. (eds.) PRO-VE 2018. IAICT, vol. 534, pp. 61–73. Springer, Cham (2018). https://doi.org/10.1007/978-3-319-99127-6_6

4. Volpentesta, A.P., Muzzupappa, M., Ammirato, S.: Critical thinking and concept design generation in a collaborative network. In: Camarinha-Matos, L.M., Picard, W. (eds.) PRO-VE 2008. ITIFIP, vol. 283, pp. 157–164. Springer, Boston, MA (2008). https://doi.org/10.1007/978-0-387-84837-2_16

5. Surowiecki, J.: The Wisdom of Crowds. Doubleday, New York (2004)

6. Ammirato, S., Sofo, F., Felicetti, A.M., Raso, C.: A methodology to support the adoption of IoT innovation and its application to the Italian bank branch security context. Eur. J. Innov. Manag. **22**(1), 146–174 (2019)

7. Yang, X.S., Karamanoglu, M.: Swarm intelligence and bio-inspired computation: an overview. In: Swarm Intelligence and Bio-Inspired Computation, pp. 3–23 (2013)

8. Volpentesta, A.P., Felicetti, A.M., Ammirato, S.: Intelligent food information provision to consumers in an internet of food era. In: Camarinha-Matos, Luis M., Afsarmanesh, H., Fornasiero, R. (eds.) PRO-VE 2017. IAICT, vol. 506, pp. 725–736. Springer, Cham (2017). https://doi.org/10.1007/978-3-319-65151-4_65

9. Camarinha-Matos, Luis M., Afsarmanesh, H.: A modeling framework for collaborative networked organizations. PRO-VE 2006. IIFIP, vol. 224, pp. 3–14. Springer, Boston, MA (2006). https://doi.org/10.1007/978-0-387-38269-2_1

10. Peri, C.: The universe of food quality. Food Qual. Prefer. **17**(1/2), 3–8 (2006)

11. Volpentesta, A.P., Felicetti, A.M., Frega, N.: Organizational and technological aspects of a platform for collective food awareness. Adv. Hum.-Comput. Interact. **2018**, 16 p. (2018). Article ID 8608407

12. Nocella, G., Romano, D., Stefani, G.: Consumers' attitudes, trust and willingness to pay for food information. Int. J. Consum. Stud. **38**(2), 153–165 (2014)

13. Verbeke, W.: Impact of communication on consumers' food choices. Proc. Nutr. Soc. **67**(3), 281–288 (2008)

14. Fenko, A., Kersten, L., Bialkova, S.: Overcoming consumer scepticism toward food labels: the role of multisensory experience. Food Qual. Prefer. **48**, 81–92 (2016)

15. Wendel, S., Dellaert, B.G.: Situation variation in consumers' media channel consideration. J. Acad. Mark. Sci. **33**(4), 575–584 (2005)

16. Corvello, V., Felicetti, A.M.: Factors affecting the utilization of knowledge acquired by researchers from scientific social networks: an empirical analysis. Knowl. Manag. **13**(3), 15–26 (2014)

17. Bialkova, S., Grunert, K.G., Van Trijp, H.: Standing out in the crowd: the effect of information clutter on consumer attention for front-of-pack nutrition labels. Food Policy **41**, 65–74 (2013)

18. Saracevic, T.: Relevance: a review of the literature and a framework for thinking on the notion in information science. Part III: behavior and effects of relevance. J. Am. Soc. Inf. Sci. Technol. **58**(13), 2126–2144 (2007)

Big Data Transformation in Agriculture: From Precision Agriculture Towards Smart Farming

María Angeles Rodríguez, Llanos Cuenca[(⊠)], and Ángel Ortiz

Research Centre on Production Management and Engineering (CIGIP),
Universitat Politècnica de València, Camino de Vera S/N, 46002 València, Spain
{marodsa4, llcuenca, aortiz}@cigip.upv.es

Abstract. Big data is a concept that has changed the way to analyse data and information in different environments such as industry and recently, in agriculture. It is used to describe a large volume of data (structured or unstructured data), which are difficult to obtain, process or parse using conventional technologies and tools like relational databases or conventional statistics, in a reasonable time for their insight. However, Big Data is applied differently in each area to take advantage of its potential and capabilities. Specially in agriculture that presents more demanding conditions due to its inherent uncertainty, so Big Data methods and models from other environments cannot be used straight away in this area. In this paper, we present a review/update of term Big Data and analyse the evolution and the role of Big Data in agriculture outlined the element of collaboration.

Keywords: Big Data · Smart Farming · Precision Agriculture

1 Introduction

Agriculture has been a sector with few influences of new technologies, such as Internet of Things (IoT), Cloud Computing or Big Data. Indeed, advanced technologies for data like Big Data or Advanced Data Analysis have not been used until the last decade, although it has always been an area focused on the use and exploitation of data (manual data management in its origins).

Recently, the modern technologies have been introduced in agriculture and it raised new concepts such as Smart Farming. This new concept has burst in to stay and banish old terms like Precision Agriculture. Also, these technologies make the old procedures (re)adapt and new automatized procedures emerge for improve daily management farming and increase collaborative networks between stakeholders.

Therefore, the main contributions of this paper are: the literature update of term Big Data, the proposal of an actual review of Big Data in Agriculture, a description of evolution of Big Data from its origins towards nowadays, and the role of Big Data in collaborative networks.

In order to write this paper, we searched well-known databases, such as Scopus or Elsevier. Searching has focused on most relevant articles to the area of Agriculture

L. M. Camarinha-Matos et al. (Eds.): PRO-VE 2019, IFIP AICT 568, pp. 467–474, 2019.
https://doi.org/10.1007/978-3-030-28464-0_40

research describing or using Big Data. In this way, we used the following search keywords: ["Precision Agriculture" OR "Smart Agriculture" OR "Precision Farming" OR "Smart Farming"] AND ["Big Data"] Also, the research has been carried out since the year 1980–1990, when the terminology of old term (Precision Agriculture) is already used, until now, when the use of new term (Smart Farming) has spread. Our analysis is divided in two stages: (1) providing a review and an update of term Big Data, and (2) summarizing evolution of Big Data in Agriculture highlighting the aspect of collaboration. Therefore, this paper is organized as follows. In Sect. 2, a review of overview in Big Data are detailed. An evolution of Big Data from Precision Agriculture towards Smart Farming and its implications are described in Sect. 3. Finally, in Sect. 4 conclusions of this paper are exposed.

2   Big Data: An Overview

The term Big Data was coined by Cox and Ellsworth in 1997 [1]. And that term was used to describe a problem they observed: *"data sets are generally quite large, taxing the capacities of main memory, local disk, and even remote disk"*. The supercomputer they used for their Computational Fluid Dynamics research often generated large amounts of data (could exceed 100 Gbytes) that could not visualize or process.

However, the concept Big Data does not refer only to the amount of data. As can be seen in his characterization in 2001, Laney [2] provided Big Data with 3 dimensions:

- *high* Volume (V1): *Size of data*. The important increase in data size.
- *high* Velocity (V2): *Real-Time data*. It has also increased the speed of data generation. This means that their access and analysis must be within a reasonable time to take advantage of this data. That is to say, the data not only must be available immediately, moreover data must be analyzed while data is useful and relevant.
- *high* Variety (V3): *Muti-source*. There is a wide variety of structured or unstructured data sources.

These three dimensions are focused on the storage and processing of data, but there is a lack of analyze the data. Subsequently, in 2012 Laney [3] added two dimensions:

- Value (V4): *Insight*. Extract knowledge from the data.
- Veracity (V5): *High Quality*. The data must be reliable.

The Table 1 quantifies in numerical data the meaning of the 5 V's. In the table it can be noticed that Big Data is more than huge data, also it is different kinds of data, streaming data and data quality. Standing out the significance of last two V's, because they play an important role in decrement corporate earnings due to, for instance, the expenditures for poor data quality and its inadequate management. Specially veracity, because without it; Big Data is less accurate, confidence, consistent or reliable. By this way, inconsistent and unreliable data sets will result in inconsistent and unreliable knowledge [4].

Table 1. Quantification of meaning of the 5 V's [5]

Volume *Size of data*	Variety *Multi-source*	Velocity *Real-time data*	Value and veracity *Insight and high quality*
90% of today data has been created in last 2 years Every day we create 2.5 quintibillion bytes of data Facebook has 1 petta bytes of storage	90% of generate data is unstructured 80% of data is video, images and documents	216.000 Instagram posts/every 60 s 204.000.000 email sent/every 60 s 50.000 GB/s is the estimated rate of global Internet traffic	Poor data quality cost business 600 billion a year 30% of data collected by marketers are not usable

Therefore, as Laney indicates: "*Big data is high volume, high velocity, and/or high variety information assets that require new forms of processing to enable enhanced decision making, insight discovery and process optimization*".

After Laney, the definition of Big Data was unified and most used the characterization of Big Data in dimensions to define it. Such is the case of NIST [6], IBM [7] and Oracle [8]; which uses 5 V's, only uses 3 V's, and focuses on the challenge of traditional databases, respectively. According to this, the authors' definition is, *Big Data is an effective way to store, process and analyse large amounts of data that are generated nowadays according to business needs.*

The Big Data applications are many, such as healthcare [9] to provide better medical attention to the patient; governments organization [10] to controlled governance dynamics, industry [11] to opens a bright perspective for smart manufacturing or agriculture [4] to improve the productivity in farms or crops.

3 Evolution of Big Data in Agriculture

Agriculture sector was delayed in introducing new technologies such as IoT or Big Data. The IoT concept in agriculture appears for the first time in studies dating from 2010 [12] and it is described as a wireless automation system by monitoring crop and farm data [13]. And Big Data concept in agriculture appears in decade of 2010s and it is described using characterization of 5 V's [14]. Agriculture has always been focused on data. In fact, farmers have always collected amounts of data on their crops and soils for its daily management. That data collection was initially manual and, later, it was automated, until our days is fully automated thanks to the IoT [15].

The use of new technologies in any area, is associated with the appearance of new terms, and in the case of agriculture, two terms must be highlighted: *Precision Agriculture* and *Smart Farming*.

3.1   Precision Agriculture

This concept is special, because over the years it has undergone a change in its meaning and use. Precision Agriculture was presented for the first time in the late 1980s [16], when new Information and Communications Technology (ICT) in agriculture were not yet developed. But it was not until 1990s, when the application of this term began to appear in scientific studies.

At the beginning, in mid 1990s, Precision Agriculture was based as the management of crop, for instance, targeting of fertilizers and herbicides, according to locally determined ('meter-by-meter') requirements, that is to say, precision refers on geolocated data of soil and crop parameters [17]. After ten years, in 2000s, farmer was used complex data such as images or photographs. Detailed spatial information like digitized aerial photographs on crop is needed for controlling crop operations. In this case, Precision Agriculture refers to the application of geospatial technologies (like Geographic Information System, GIS) that allowing farmers access and visualize to images that influence their decisions for the purpose of improving crop performance [18]. Finally, in decade of 2010, as a result to the emergence of IoT and Big Data, everything was based on monitoring data in real time and management of large amount of data that it generates. Furthermore, the concept of Precision Agriculture that is known and used nowadays, is defined as management of agricultural plot by monitoring, data processing and intervention of crops to optimize the consumption of resources and provides the farmers an added value of decision making for exploitation daily operations and management. [19].

The Fig. 1 below, shows the evolution of concept Precision Agriculture over the years. As times goes by, it can be observed that in decade of 2000 in agriculture only 2 of the 3 dimensions that were characterized at that time were used. Volume (V1) and Variety (V3) were being used with the introduction of the use of images, because it was possible to have data sources of different types and, in addition, a large size of data was collected. However, Velocity (V2) was not achieved, because data not collected in real time, although sending of the complex data like images were faster than in previous times, it was collected quasi real time not full real time. In fact, it was not until the year 2010, when the Velocity (V2) was achieved, thanks to the monitoring with sensors the sending and acquisition of data in real time.

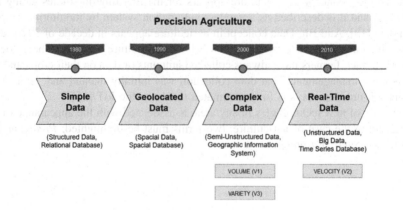

Fig. 1. Evolution of Precision Agriculture

3.2   Smart Farming (Smart Agriculture)

Recently, we have get used to see word *Smart* associate to other words like city (*Smart City*), industry (*Smart Industry*), health *(Smart Health)*, etc. The fast proliferation of Smart applications in multiple sectors, is mainly due to the existence of calls for proposals of European Union's Research and Innovation funding programme such as *FP7* (first *Smart* was *Smart City*) or current programme *Horizon 2020 (Smart Transport, Smart Energy, Smart Farming, Smart Agri-food, etc.)*.

The term Smart Farming emerges after the concept Precision Agriculture and both are inherently related. At the beginning of 2010s, the term Smart Farming [20] began to be used to refer to that new advanced definition of Precision Agriculture. The aspect of precision (location/geolocation data sent by satellites) disappears, and it materializes on aspect of *Smart* (real-time data sent by smart sensors - IoT architecture, which highlighted for their ability to communicate its data). In agriculture sector, many Smart Farming applications supports a large amount of heterogeneous real-time data sent by sensors. [21] This kind of data is considered Big Data with 5 V's, because the term Smart assumes the challenges of last two V's: insight and high-quality.

Another aspect relevant in this new term is collaboration. In Precision Agriculture farmer is the main figure or responsible of data and has his own local database system (1980–2000) that he does not share with other farmers, suppliers, etc. New technologies as a Big Data, IoT and Cloud Computing (after 2000), have been able to increase collaboration quickly, because the data is in cloud database systems that can be shared and this real-time data that help to accelerate decisions making. Consequently, decision making be able to include more interlocutors. Everyone can visualize the same data (although each kind of stakeholder sees the information in a different way according to their knowledge). In addition to collaborating in decision making, the information runs between all of them in a connected way, that is, the isolated farm becomes a *connected farm* [22]. The idea of connected farm that appears in Smart Farming, is the fundamental vision of collaborative systems in agriculture. The role played by Big Data in the connected farm is of vital importance and, as already mentioned, it has to assume the challenge of the last two V's. Both daily decisions and strategic decisions of the farm, it is necessary to have adequate information extracted from the data (remember that depending on the stakeholder the information must be presented in a different way) - this is provided by Value; and also, the information has to be of quality (poor data can cost wrong decisions) - this is provided by Veracity. And, the role played by IoT in the connected farm is also relevant, mentioned in [15], for instance, FIspace [23] (European business-to-business collaboration IoT platform – belongs to *FP7*) can exchange data or use shared and customizing solutions with minimal costs to help small or medium sized companies.

The Fig. 2 below, adds the evolution of concept Smart Farming in Fig. 1 previous. It can be observed that in decade of 2010 Smart Farming consumes Precision Agriculture, and it incorporates the last two V's (Value and Veracity). Moreover, this aspect of the transition makes it enhancer faster the collaboration between stakeholders.

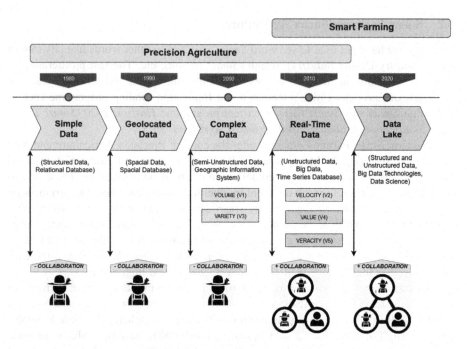

Fig. 2. Evolution of Smart Farming

As an example of Smart Farming application is Agricolus. This system uses IoT (crop and soil monitoring), Cloud Computing (process data in cloud), and Big Data (farm management and decision support system for treatments and fertilizers) [24]. And data process of solution is similar to Big Data process. In Big Data, the first step is to capture and save the data - V1, V2 and V3 - (in Agricolus the recollected data provided by sensors), the second step is to prepare and transform data - V5 - (in Agricolus the store data is converted in data quality) and, finally, the third step is to analyze the data and act (in Agricolus the data is analyzed and visualized in application to support decisions about agricultural operations). Each of the phases of Big Data process presents challenges, mainly the second step (data preparation and transformation). For instance, this step requires 80% of effort and time, due to the particularities of any dataset (different formats, missing values, duplication of data, …) and its subsequent cleaning, selection and transformation to value data [25]. To reduce this time, could automate data preparation in field of agriculture with a tool such as START (Soil daTA Retrieval Tool) [26]. It was designed to automated preparation of soil input data files for multiple crop models. This tool consumed about 33% of time compared with 80% of time in manual preparation. However, they do not mention that automatization must be without lost data quality - V5.

4 Conclusions

This paper has defined Big Data for characterization of 5 V's (Volume, Velocity, Variety, Value, Veracity) and we have provided a more up-to-date and simple definition of the term. Also, we have updated concepts of Big Data in agriculture, for that purpose we have explained the evolution of new technologies focused on data in agriculture. Finally, we have described collaboration as another aspect of Big Data application.

Without being aware of it, the Big Data approach has always been present in this sector. On a daily basis, large amounts of data are collected and analysed in crops or soils. Before the arrival of digital transformation and TICs, many of these procedures were done manually and only the farmer was responsible for the data and decisions. But nowadays, everything is automated, and the farmer is part of a collaborative network. Moreover, agriculture is to be congratulated, research and innovation in this field is being encouraged from the EU Framework Program called Horizon 2020. For instance, IoF2020 explores the potential of IoT for food and farming industry [27].

To conclude, we have observed that Smart Farming is more collaborative than Precision Agriculture, and only with new technologies as Big Data (5 V's) and IoT, connected farms is a reality. In addition, the future with automatized tools for data preparation or new concept Data Lakes (repository of structured and unstructured big data) present new challenges such as quality and ethics in data and overload of information.

Acknowledgments. All authors acknowledge the partial support of Project 691249, RUC-APS: Enhancing and implementing Knowledge based ICT solutions within high Risk and Uncertain Conditions for Agriculture Production Systems, funded by the EU under its funding scheme H2020-MSCA-RISE-2015; and the project "Development of an integrated maturity model for agility, resilience and gender perspective in supply chains (MoMARGE). Application to the agricultural sector." Ref. GV/2017/025 funded by the Generalitat Valenciana. This first author was supported by the Aid Programme of Research and Development of Universitat Politècnica de València [PAID-01-18].

References

1. Cox, M., Ellsworth, D.: Application-controlled demand paging for out-of-core visualization. In: Proceedings of the 8th Conference on Visualization 1997, p. 235. IEEE Computer Society Press (1997)
2. Laney, D.: 3D data management: controlling data volume, velocity and variety. META Group Res. Note **6**, 1 (2001)
3. Beyer, M.A., Laney, D.: The Importance of "Big Data": A Definition. Gartner, Stamford (2012)
4. Kamilaris, A., et al.: A review on the practice of big data analysis in agriculture. Computers and Electronics in Agriculture **143**(C), 23–37 (2017)
5. Marr, B.: How Much Data Do We Create Every Day? The Mind-Blowing Stats Everyone Should Read (2019). https://www.forbes.com/sites/bernardmarr/2018/05/21/how-much-data-do-we-create-every-day-the-mind-blowing-stats-everyone-should-read/#5671a61d60ba

6. NIST. The definition of Big Data. https://bigdatawg.nist.gov/home.php
7. IBM. The definition of Big Data. https://www.ibm.com/analytics/hadoop/big-data-analytics
8. Oracle. The definition of Big Data. https://www.oracle.com/big-data/guide/what-is-big-data. html
9. Shahbaz, M., Gao, Ch., Zhai, L., Shahzad, F., Hu, Y.: Investigating the adoption of big data analytics in healthcare: the moderating role of resistance to change. J. Big Data 6 (2019). https://doi.org/10.1186/s40537-019-0170-y
10. Trom, L., Cronje, J.: Analysis of data governance implications on big data. In: Arai, K., Bhatia, R. (eds.) FICC 2019. LNNS, vol. 69, pp. 645–654. Springer, Cham (2020). https:// doi.org/10.1007/978-3-030-12388-8_45
11. Tao, F., et al.: A field programmable gate array implemented fibre channel switch for big data communication towards smart manufacturing. Robotics and Computer Integrated Manufacturing 57, 166–181 (2019)
12. Lu, Y., Li, X., Zhong, J., Xiong, Y.: Research on the innovation of strategic business model in green agricultural products based on Internet of Things (IOT) - May 2010 (2010)
13. Zhao, L., Yin, S., Liu, L., Zhang, Z., Wei, S.: A crop monitoring system based on wireless sensor network - December 2011 (2011)
14. Chi, M., Plaza, A., Benediktsson, J.A., Sun, Z., Shen, J., Zhu, Y.: Big data for remote sensing: challenges and opportunities. Proc. IEEE 104(11), 2207–2219 (2016) https://doi. org/10.1109/jproc.2016.2598228
15. Rodriguez, M.A., Cuenca, L., Bas, A.: FIWARE open source standard platform in smart farming - a review. In: Proceedings of the 19th IFIP WG 5.5 Working Conference on Virtual Enterprises, PRO-VE 2018, Cardiff, UK, 17–19 September 2018 (2018). https://doi.org/10. 1007/978-3-319-99127-6_50
16. Stafford, J., LeBars, J.: A GPS backpack system for mapping soil and crop parameters in agricultural fields. J. Navig. 49(1), 9–21 (1996)
17. Robert, P.C.: Precision agriculture: research needs and status in the USA. In: Stafford, J.V. (ed.) Proceedings of the 2nd European Conference on Precision Agriculture, Part 1, pp. 19– 33. Academic Press, SCI/Sheffield (1999)
18. Long, D.S., Nielsen, G.A., Henry, M.P., Westcott, M.P.: Remote sensing for northern plains precision agriculture. In: Paper Presented at the Space 2000, pp. 208–214 (2000)
19. Ge, Y., Thomasson, J.A., Sui, R.: Remote sensing of soil properties in precision agriculture: a review. Front. Earth Sci. 5(3), 229–238 (2011)
20. Sundmaeker, H., Verdouw, C., Wolfert, S., Pérez L.: Internet of food and farm 2020. In: Paper presented at Digitising the Industry - Internet of Things Connecting Physical, Digital and Virtual Worlds, River Publishers, Gistrup/Delft, pp. 129–151 (2016)
21. Barmpounakis, S., et al.: Management and control applications in agriculture domain via a FI Business-to-Business platform. Inf. Process. Agric. 2(1), 51–63 (2015)
22. Musat, G., et al.: Advanced services for efficient management of smart farms. J. Parallel Distrib. Comput. 116, 3–17 (2018)
23. FIspace. https://www.fispace.eu/whatisfispace.html
24. Agricolus (2019). https://www.agricolus.com/
25. Paton, N.W.: Automating data preparation: can we? Should we? Must we? In: CEUR Workshop Proceedings, p. 2324 (2019)
26. Kim, K.S., Yoo, B.H., Shelia, V., Porter, C.H., Hoogenboom, G.: START: a data preparation tool for crop simulation models using web-based soil databases. Comput. Electron. Agric. 154, 256–264 (2018). https://doi.org/10.1016/j.compag.2018.08.023
27. IoF2020 (2019). https://www.iof2020.eu/

Digital Transformation in Food and Agribusiness

Servitization of Biomass Processing for a Virtual Biorefinery: Application to the Lignocellulosic Biomass in a French Local Territory

Michelle Houngbé[(✉)], Anne-Marie Barthe-Delanoë, and Stéphane Négny

Laboratoire de Génie Chimique, Université de Toulouse, CNRS, INPT, UPS, Toulouse, France
michelle.houngbe@inp-toulouse.fr,
{annemarie.barthe,stephane.negny}@ensiacet.fr

Abstract. Processing biomass requires four major steps (pretreatment, fermentation, separation and purification) achieved by dedicated plants called biorefineries. These highly specialized structures cannot cope with the high variability of the whole biomass supply chain. Thus, providing agility to biorefineries is a key challenge to foster biomass processing. The goal is to design a virtual biorefinery as a collective network supported by the servitization of unit operations and the reuse of existing devices. In this regard, the first step described in this paper aims to gather and organize knowledge about a given local area (stakeholders, services) and the existing transformation process operations (inputs, outputs) through a framework. To this end, two metamodels are proposed: one to collect and structure the required information about the local area; one to organize the knowledge about the transformation processes. Their use is illustrated by a use case provided by a municipalities community located in South-West France.

Keywords: Servitization · Biomass · Collaborative network modeling · Collaborative process · Industry 4.0

1 Introduction

Biomass requires dedicated transformation processes, depending on the biomass type, quality, purity (and even quantity) and also on the targeted bioproduct. These processes operate under high-specialized conditions, where each process step requires specific equipment (specific operating methods and specific unit operations). At the plant level, biorefineries are standalone plants dedicated to a specific biomass transformation process. Thus, biorefineries are not able to face the variabilities regarding supply and demand as well as the biomass variety. The challenge, as underlined in [1], is to bring agility to the biorefinery system to foster biomass processing.

In this sense, the research works presented in [2] aim to decentralize the biomass process through a virtual biorefinery. The virtual biorefinery concept lies on the short-

© IFIP International Federation for Information Processing 2019
Published by Springer Nature Switzerland AG 2019
L. M. Camarinha-Matos et al. (Eds.): PRO-VE 2019, IFIP AICT 568, pp. 477–486, 2019.
https://doi.org/10.1007/978-3-030-28464-0_41

term collaboration of different stakeholders, each one achieving one or several steps of the transformation process. This collaboration enables low coupling among the process steps in order to adapt the biomass processing when a change occurs (supply, demand etc.). Besides, leaning on the reuse of existing equipment and/or plants would avoid investments into physical structures dedicated to a given process. To achieve this goal, a servitization framework is required to help the stakeholders to describe their activities with a product-service strategy. This paper focus on the developed approach to support the servitization of the stakeholders involved into this collaborative biomass processing.

The paper is structured as follows: the next section highlights the state of art of servitization for biorefineries. Section 3 describes our proposal to support the servitization of biomass processing stakeholders (farmers, chemical plants, etc.). Section 4 illustrates the proposed servitization framework with a use case provided by a municipalities community located in South-West France, before addressing the further work to be done and concluding.

2 State of the Art of Servitization in Biorefineries

The servitization concept emerged in the late 1980s under an uncertain industrial context marked by: a strong competition between companies in the global market place; a raise of product customization to satisfy customers changeable needs; the constant evolution of technologies. Since its first definition as "bundles' consisting of customer-focused combinations of goods, services, support, self-service, and knowledge" [3], it has been a growing interest for this topic, for the researchers and the industrials [4]. By adding different levels of services such as base (spare parts), intermediate (maintenance, training) and advanced (contract) to an initial physical product, servitization affects the whole industry from the marketing department to the production workshop.

The description of the actors' services is part of a Product-Service System (PSS) strategy. As a servitization specification, the PSS differs by taking into consideration the life cycle of the integrated product and service offering. [5] classifies the PSSs into eight categories according to four main dimensions: market value for the user, costs for the provider, capital needs, and ability to sustain value in the future. Based on this classification, the agile biorefinery tends to be close to the result-oriented category of PSSs (within the functional result subcategory). Indeed, this is the capability (the capabilities) (i.e. one or more services) proposed by each actor into the collaboration that is (are) involved to fulfill one (or more) step(s) of the biomass transformation according to the targeted objective. However, the PSS was determined for the manufacturing sector by focusing how the company creates added value. In this approach, the transformation process of the matter with all its constraints is not taken into account. Therefore, it has to be adapted in the context of a biorefinery.

As mentioned earlier, this paper focuses on the servitization to support the collaboration which is the core concept of the virtual biorefinery. Regarding the domain of virtual enterprises, that are defined by [6] as "temporary consortium of enterprises that join skills and resources, supported by computer networks, to better respond to a business opportunity", they lean on existing frameworks to implement servitization. [7] 's studies have developed a methodology based on Model Driven Service, which is based on Model Driven Engineering, that contains all the phases of the service life cycle (requirements, design, testing and implementation). This approach aims to support the shift from a production focused on the product towards a production focused on a service-oriented strategy for virtual manufacturing environment. Besides, [8] propose a framework organized along three dimensions: extended product, service typology and service innovation organization. Combined together, they help companies to determine their servitization position. This framework was tested in several companies, which want to move towards the service-oriented virtual enterprise: a machine tool manufacturer, a TV manufacturer and a clothing manufacturer. These frameworks apply particularly to manufacturing companies.

Regarding the chemical industry, there are fewer examples of servitization compared to the manufacturing domain. But it is important to note that the ongoing trend in the chemical industry area is to shift from a high volume in mass production towards custom products. This customization trend changes the companies' business models to more innovative ones. [9] show that three types of business models encourage servitization in chemical industries. Chemical Product Services (CPS) gives priority to the sale/use of chemical product-service bundles. Chemical Management Services (CMS) leans on long-term contract policy between customers and suppliers. For instance, PPG, a company specialized in wastewater treatment, is paid according to the amount of cleaned water. Chemical Leasing makes available chemicals for service and ensure their maintenance instead of selling them. Among these three business models promoting servitization, the most widespread is CMS [9].

It is interesting to underline that in the literature related to this business area, servitization is studied from the company strategy point of view (macro scale). There is a lack of framework to support and guide servitization of the transformation process (meso scale), especially for biomass transformation process. The next section presents a proposal of such a framework.

3 A Framework to Support Servitization of Biomass Transformation Processes

3.1 Collaborative Situation Characterization

The first step is to define the collaborative situation: stakeholders, targeted bioproduct, available biomass, etc. To this end, a meta-model structuring the knowledge is necessary, as detailed in [2]. This meta-model dedicated to the biorefinery is based on the CORE meta-model [10]. This meta-model is structured around four families of concepts: the *context* (the environment of the collaboration), the *actors* (the partners of collaboration), the *objectives* (the purpose of the collaboration) and the *performance* (assessment of the collaboration based on Key Performance Indicators). An enhanced version of the concepts of the first version of the virtual biorefinery meta-model is proposed here (Fig. 1).

In the context package, the *deposit* concept is crucial. It complies with a sector logic as wood sector, agricultural sector, etc. It takes into account the *biomass* which is characterized by its intrinsic *physical and biochemical properties*, by a *seasonality* and by a *crop rotation*. Besides, the geographical *area* where the deposit is located has a specific *pedology*, *topography* and *climate* where a type of *production* (intensive, extensive, organic) is realized. Finally, the deposit concept integrates the *goods* concept that includes the *roadways* to access to the deposit. Finally, *people* and *institutions* concerned by its exploitation are also considered.

In the objective package, the *biomass processing* is the main goal to reach. It produces bioproducts and have to meet *market opportunities*. However, *impact factors* about *technology*, *finance*, *society* or *environment* can affect positively or negatively the main goal.

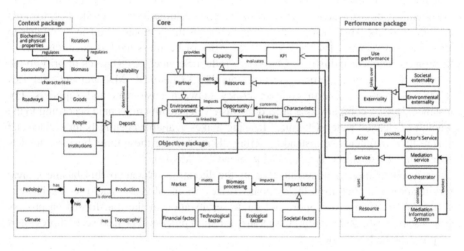

Fig. 1. Meta-model of collaborative situation for the virtual biorefinery.

In the partner package, each stakeholder of the collaboration is called an *actor*. She/he provides one or several *services* that requires *resources*. The whole collaboration is orchestrated by a Mediation Information System (MIS).

The performance package consists on assessing the collaboration, thanks to *Key Performance Indicators* (KPI). Relevant KPI lean for instance on the sale of use performance for each actor and the overall performance. The services generate externalities, positive or negative for the environment (e.g. pollution, reforestation) and the society (e.g. job creation, economic decline).

Thus, the meta-model contains concepts about the whole collaborative situation. The instantiation of the meta-model into a model is made with data about the stakeholders, the availability of biomass on the studied territory or the targeted bioproduct, etc. All of these data can be gathered either manually or automatically. Indeed, in the area of Agriculture 4.0, the amount of emitted data regarding farms, weather conditions, crops, etc. is exploding. Based on these data, information regarding (for example) the biomass valorization opportunities can be inferred based on weather conditions, etc. to feed the model of the virtual biorefinery.

This gathered knowledge about the collaborative situation is essential to define the collaborative transformation process, that will be performed by the virtual biorefinery. Nevertheless, additional knowledge is required in order to choose the relevant transformation process (from a chemical point of view), given the biomass characteristics and the bioproduct identified through the virtual biorefinery model.

3.2   Biomass Processing Knowledge Organization

The second step of this servitization framework aims to structure the knowledge required to identify the chemical process involved into the biomass processing.

Lignocellulosic biomass processing can be seen as a four major step process: (i) pretreatment; (ii) conversion; (iii) separation; (iv) purification. Biomass pretreatment is crucial for the next process phases. Indeed, in this step the structure of the biomass is modified to make sugar accessible from lignin, cellulose and hemicellulose. The next phase is the biomass conversion into building blocks (C2 to C6 sugars). It can be achieved in different ways: chemical, bio chemical, thermochemical. These building blocks are the bases to design bioproducts, bioenergy and biofuel. Finally, separation and purification refine the output to fit with the customer's requirements. Each major step is composed of sub-process or unit operations which are specified according to the input biomass characteristics and the targeted bioproducts.

Given this background, the minimal required knowledge about the chemical process is, for each major step (respectively each sub-process or unit-operation): input (biomass, intermediate products; output (intermediate product, final product); operating conditions. As there is no knowledge base organizing the knowledge about existing processes for biomass transformation at the required level of abstraction, an additional meta-model is proposed to this end, based on the SADT-IDFE0 diagram notation. SADT-IDEF0 offers a degree of details which is relevant regarding the above-mentioned needs. An example of such a model is detailed in Sect. 4.3.

This knowledge base can also embed additional knowledge regarding the matching between the services proposed by the actors and the required process steps (sub-process, unit operation), as Montarnal et al. [11] propose in their research work regarding the manufacturing industries. Each process, sub-process and unit operation is therefore seen as an objective that an actor service (or a set of actors' services) will fulfill. This way, the required knowledge about services is structured and ready to be used to deduce a relevant collaborative transformation process.

4 Case Study

4.1 Case Study Presentation

Two municipalities communities from the French department of the Landes (Communauté de Communes Coeur Haute Lande, and Communauté de Communes de Mimizan) look for solutions to recycle green waste. The lignocellulosic biomass is abundant and diversified within their territory. The characterization of these two local territories using the presented framework will support the identification of the existing stakeholders and of their related services to meet these opportunities to valorize local biomass. Besides, this knowledge will also be used to design the collaborative process treatment, performed by the virtual biorefinery.

4.2 Instantiation of the Metamodel for Collaborative Situation

To instantiate the metamodel, stakeholders able to play a role in the biomass processing were identified. Then, semi-directive interviews were organized according to an interview guide. These interviews focused on the following topics: business environment, role in green waste processing, existing or possible partnership with a company inside or outside the territory, positive impact of the activity (for the stakeholder, for the territory). The objective is to understand the environment in which these actors of the biomass area evolve. These interviews also helped to determine the existing constraints.

4.2.1 Instantiation of the Context Package
The instantiation of the context (Fig. 2) reveals that on these local territories the green waste deposit involves two parts of green waste: woody and non-woody. Each of them owns a specific density, humidity and seasonality.

About 15,000 tons of green waste are available in these territories. Different institutions (cities, local authorities, consular organizations) are involved in this recycling initiative as well as the citizen association "SAS Energie Citoyenne Haute Lande".

4.2.2 Instantiation of the Partner Package
Different types of actor (public entity, farmer, environment service provider) are able to provide services to perform a step of the transformation process. The instantiation of the partner concept shows that a process activity can be realized by different actors, such as the composting step that can be performed by the Communauté de Communes Coeur Haute Lande, Mimizan, VEOLIA or RTE (Electricity Transmission Network) (Fig. 3) or such as the shearing (performed by citizens or the local authority).

Resource used by the actor will differentiate the actor's service. But it will be necessary to define functional and non-functional requirement (price, delay, reputation) to sort services in case of competition.

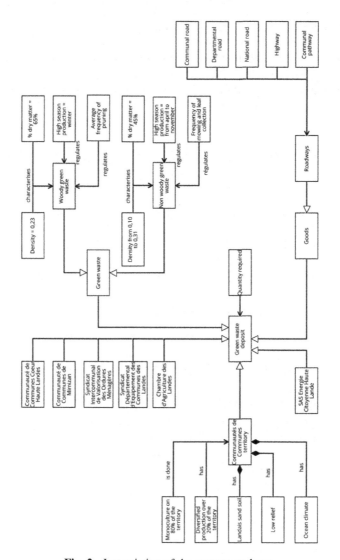

Fig. 2. Instantiation of the context package.

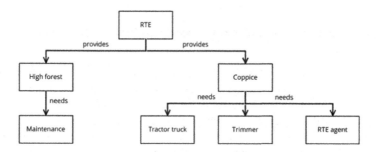

Fig. 3. Instantiation of the partner package: example of the RTE actor.

4.2.3   Instantiation of the Objective Package

Regarding the instantiation of the objective package concepts, Fig. 4 highlights that the main objective 'composting biomass' meets different opportunities, which represents sub-objectives. The main objective (i.e. the targeted bioproduct) is "biogas fuel" and "standard compost". In this study case, the identified impact factors have a positive impact on the collaboration objective.

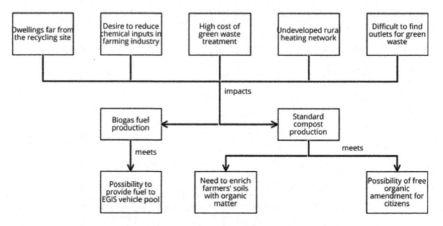

Fig. 4. Instantiation of the objective package.

4.2.4   Instantiation of the Performance Package

The performance to be reached by some stakeholders as the SIVOM (Fig. 5) and the farmers is determined by contract. These services generate positive externalities as job creation (the creation of a new job for compost quality control), or additional revenues linked to the compost sale.

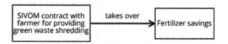

Fig. 5. Instantiation of the performance package: example of the SIVOM contract.

4.3   Knowledge Base for Chemical Process Involved in the Composting Processing

In addition to the model representing the knowledge about the collaborative situation, it is now necessary to collect and organize additional knowledge about the composting process and the matching services. To gather knowledge about the generic composting process, we leaned on dedicated handbooks, such as [12]. The model obtained in the Fig. 6 represents both the composting process as (sub-)objectives, and the proposed actors' services matching these (sub-)objectives.

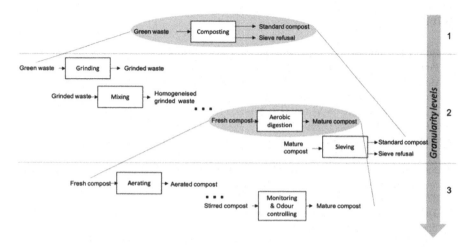

Fig. 6. Composting process description using a SADT-IDEF0 inspired meta-model.

5   Perspectives and Conclusion

Biomass processing is subject to several constraints to the structural level (i.e. biorefinery) and to the process level generating high variability in biomass supply and bioproduct production. This is the reason why it is necessary to bring agility to the entire system in order to improve the biomass transformation process. In this perspective, the "virtual biorefinery" concept enables the collaboration between the stakeholders of the biomass processing. It is based on services provided by the actors to fulfill one or more steps of the process biomass treatment. Thus, this paper presents a servitization framework composed by two meta-models. The first meta-model aims to characterize and structure the knowledge about the collaborative situation according to the environment, the partners, the objective(s) and the performance, with data collected manually or with sensors. It is coupled with a second meta-model to structure the additional knowledge about the biomass transformation processes. As presented in the case study, the instantiation of these two meta-models provides the necessary knowledge to establish a collaborative biomass transformation process. On a short-term perspective, the next step of these works is to choose and implement the algorithm to design the collaborative transformation process. The competition among several services fulfilling the same objective has to be considered: the use of functional and non-functional criteria may provide a way to choose the most relevant option.

Acknowledgments. These research works are funded by the French Research Agency (ANR) regarding the research project ARBRE [Grant number ANR-17-CE10-0006], 2017-2021. The authors would like to thank the project partners for their advice and comments regarding this work.

References

1. European Commission: Innovating for Sustainable Growth - A bioeconomy for Europe. Publications Office of the European Union, Luxembourg (2012)
2. Houngbé, M., Barthe-Delanoë, A.-M., Négny, S.: Towards virtual biorefineries. In: Proceedings of the Collaborative Networks of Cognitive Systems - 19th IFIP WG 5.5 Working Conference on Virtual Enterprises, PRO-VE 2018, Cardiff, UK, 17–19 September 2018, vol. 534, pp. 571–580 (2018)
3. Vandermerwe, S., Rada, J.: Servitization of business: adding value by adding services. Eur. Manag. J. 6(4), 314–324 (1988)
4. Baines, T., Ziaee Bigdeli, A., Bustinza, O.F., Shi, V.G., Baldwin, J., Ridgway, K.: Servitization: revisiting the state-of-the-art and research priorities. Int. J. Oper. Prod. Manag. 37(2), 256–278 (2017)
5. Tukker, A.: Eight types of product–service system: eight ways to sustainability? Experiences from SusProNet. Bus. Strat. Environ. 13(4), 246–260 (2004)
6. Camarinha-Matos, L.M., Afsarmanesh, H.: Collaborative networks: a new scientific discipline. J. Intell. Manuf. 16(4–5), 439–452 (2005)
7. Ducq, Y., Chen, D., Alix, T.: Principles of servitization and definition of an architecture for model driven service system engineering. In: van Sinderen, M., Johnson, P., Xu, X., Doumeingts, G. (eds.) IWEI 2012. LNBIP, vol. 122, pp. 117–128. Springer, Heidelberg (2012). https://doi.org/10.1007/978-3-642-33068-1_12
8. Chen, D., Cusmeroli, S.: Framework for manufacturing servitization in virtual enterprise environment and ecosystem. IFAC-PapersOnLine 48(3), 2244–2249 (2015)
9. Buschak, D., Lay, G.: Chemical industry: servitization in niches. In: Lay, G. (ed.) Servitization in Industry, pp. 131–150. Springer, Cham (2014). https://doi.org/10.1007/978-3-319-06935-7_8
10. Bénaben, F., Lauras, M., Truptil, S., Salatgé, N.: A metamodel for knowledge management in crisis management. In: Proceedings of the 49th Hawaii International Conference on System Sciences (HICSS 2016) (2016)
11. Montarnal, A., Mu, W., Benaben, F., Lamothe, J., Lauras, M., Salatge, N.: Automated deduction of cross-organizational collaborative business processes. Inf. Sci. 453, 30–49 (2018)
12. Willson, G.B., Van de Kamp, M., Rynk, R.: Northeast regional agricultural engineering service. In: On-Farm Composting Handbook (1992)

Collaborative, Distributed Simulations of Agri-Food Supply Chains. Analysis on How Linking Theory and Practice by Using Multi-agent Structures

Alejandro Fernandez[1(✉)], Jorge E. Hernandez[2,3], Shaofeng Liu[4], Hervé Panetto[5], Matías Nahuel Pankow[1], and Esteban Sanchez[1]

[1] LIFIA, CIC/Faculty of Informatics, National University of La Plata, La Plata, Argentina
Alejandro.Fernandez@lifia.info.unlp.edu.ar
[2] Management School, The University of Liverpool, Liverpool, UK
[3] Universidad de La Frontera, Temuco, Chile
[4] Plymouth Business School, Plymouth University, Plymouth, UK
[5] CRAN Université de Lorraine, CNRS, Villers-lès-Nancy, France

Abstract. Simulations help to understand and predict the behaviour of complex phenomena's, likewise distributed socio-technical systems or how stakeholders interacts in complex domains. Such domains are normally based on networked based interaction, where information, product and decision flows comes in to play, especially under the well-known supply chains structures. Although tools exist to simulate supply chains, they do not adequately support multiple stakeholders to collaboratively create and explore a variety of decision-making scenarios. Hence, in order to provide a preliminary understanding on how these interaction affects stakeholders decision-making, this research presents an study, analysis and proposal development of robust platform to collaboratively build and simulate communication among supply chain. Since realistic supply chain behaviours are complex, a multi-agent approach was selected in order to represent such complexities in a standardised manner. The platform provides agent behaviours for common agent patterns. It provides extension hotspots to implement more specific agent behaviour for expert users (that requires programming). Therefore, as key contribution, technical aspects of the platform are presented, and also the role of multi-level supply chain scenario simulation is discussed and analysed, especially under de context of digital supply chain transformation in the agri-food context. Finally, we discuss lessons learned from early tests with the reference implementation of the platform.

Keywords: Digital transformation · Supply chain · Simulations

1 Introduction

In the last two decades, companies of all sizes have realized the importance of collaboration with suppliers and customers [1]. Supply chain collaboration can be defined as "long-term relationships where participants generally cooperate, share information,

© IFIP International Federation for Information Processing 2019
Published by Springer Nature Switzerland AG 2019
L. M. Camarinha-Matos et al. (Eds.): PRO-VE 2019, IFIP AICT 568, pp. 487–495, 2019.
https://doi.org/10.1007/978-3-030-28464-0_42

and work together to plan and even modify their business practices to improve joint performance" [2]. Despite the existence of abundant literature (as a recent literature review on supply chain collaboration [3] shows) organizations still have problems understanding how collaboration can impact their performance, and they are consequently reluctant to explore it.

ANONYMOUS is multidisciplinary, collaborative project whose goal is help agri-food value chains deal with risk and uncertainty. Researchers that participate in the project understand the importance of value chain collaboration. They regularly meet with different actors of the value chain, in an attempt to understand to what extent collaboration takes place, and to foster collaboration. In doing so, they must cross multiple knowledge boundaries. There are knowledge boundaries among organizations in the value chain, and there are knowledge boundaries among researchers and practitioners. Researchers understand they need to act as boundary spanners [4] (helping cross knowledge boundaries) and for that they need support.

Simulations have long been used as a means to understand and predict complex phenomena. The complexity can be understood as the variety of nodes and alternatives that exist in order to reach a solution, but, and more importantly, how protocols, hardware and software platforms are able to interact in order to provide the right recommendation, in the right time with the right quality. Thus, these kind of complex interactions are mostly found in supply chain domains, where resources, information, products and decision flows are required to commit to the end-customer requirement. Therefore, by the use of these simulations, what-if analysis are considered to help stakeholders and to understand the benefits and issues from co-operative environment rather than playing a pure transaction role with others [5, 6]. In the line of this, but specially to provide a deep understanding and analysis about the relevance of such collaborations, this research work is committed to propose a platform that simulate communications and interaction based behaviours amongst supply chain stakeholders, which are represented by using agents. For this purpose, and based on the current analysis from [7], the main agri-food challenges and complexities are considered, this within the purpose of driving the supply chain agent-based structure. These aspects are: (a) complexity of interactions across agricultural value chain; (b) understands decision-makers challenge to build the solution; (c) Quantification of factors to generate desired solution; and (d) understand the whole-of-chain practical problem, especially when social, environmental and technological are the key drivers. Hence, this platform, which also consider the work from [6] as starting point, is oriented ease the creation, deployment, exercising and analysis of distributed supply chains within an agri-food view. This is achieved via the simplicity, standardization, scalability, collaboration of its main components. We argue that it offers adequate to support the task of boundary spanners looking to disseminate the benefits of collaboration in value chains.

2 Approach Overview

Multiple platforms exist to create multi-agent systems. In the context of agri-food, as [8] analysed, agent based model has been dominated by the following characteristics: single echelon supply chains; cases in high and middle income countries; unprocessed food products; use of empirical data; decisions related to production planning and investment; and the use of black box validation. Moreover, from technical point view validation, JADE [9], for example, is a well-known framework and supporting tools that aims at supporting the creation of multi-agent, peer-to-peer systems. It is domain independent, which is JADE, makes no assumptions regarding the behaviour of agents and the rules for the interaction. This makes JADE powerful, and consequently complex. A supply chain is a particular case of multi-agent system. Conversations follow certain specific conversation patterns (e.g., call for proposal, proposal, accept proposal). Existing agent platforms are rich and powerful but consequently difficult to use. Ad-hoc simulation tools are simpler to use, but limited to the features provided by its creators. We aim at something midway from both extremes. Instead of providing simulation authors with a full-fledge agent systems such as JADE, we have chosen to hide those fixed patterns behind an object-oriented framework. The framework captures common aspects of all supply-chain-simulations and implements then in a robust design. The platform, that we named **Sim-a-chain** currently focuses on demand-offer negotiations, similar to what occurs in agri-food domains.

Thus, The Foundation for Intelligent Physical Agents (FIPA) proposed a series of standards for the definition of agent systems, namely FIPA's Contract Net Interaction Protocol Specification and ACL Message Structure Specification[1]. The standards cover aspects such as inter-agent communication, agent management across and within agent platforms, and the transport and representation of messages between agents. Sim-a-chains adopts FIPA's proposals for message transport and representation of messages. For the content of a message (e.g., an offer), we looked at a newer development in the web; the Schema.org vocabularies [10]. These vocabularies have become a standard to represent certain types of objects in the web, in particular *products, offers, and demands* (which are the key elements in a supply chain conversation).

Existing agent platforms, and agent simulations platforms, requires users to deploy an agent execution engine to a server. Preparing and maintaining these servers (operating systems, security, updates, etc.) is only worth if simulations will be created and run frequently. A way to reduce the effort of server maintenance is virtualization. Sadly, traditional server virtualization does not help get rid of the cost of idle servers (when no simulation run, the server is still running). Moreover, when simulations grow in number of agents and computation needs, servers need to be provisioned. Recent developments in serverless [11] computing reduce the effort and cost of server maintenance, automate scalability, and remove the need to pay for idle time. Sim-a-chain has been built as serverless.

3   Sim-a-Chain's Abstract Model

The core-modelling concept in Sim-a-chain is the Supply Chain Agent environment. Agents have a unique identifier, a short descriptive name, a list of products they can offer, an internal memory, and a behaviour. Agents have a messaging inbox. An agent's

---

[1] FIPA specifications - http://www.fipa.org/specs/ - Last accessed on June 2019.

behaviour depends on its type (e.g., a raw materials producer, a factory, a storage facility, a distributor, etc.). In this model, an agent's behaviour is determined by the way the agent reacts to messages from other agents.

Agent are normally dormant (idle). When an agent receives a message, it wakes up and reacts by activating the part of its behaviour that corresponds to the message type (e.g., a Call for Proposals). It accesses its internal memory, which holds information about available stock, or a list of suppliers. If necessary, the agent can send messages to other agents, including the sender of the message that activated it in the first place. After this, the agent goes back to idle state.

Messages in this model reflect what was proposed by FIPA's Contract Net Inter-action Protocol Specification. From the protocol specification, we take only the proposal negotiation part, and leave out the contract fulfilment part.

A conversation among two agents starts when an *initiator* agent sends a cfp (call for proposal) message to another agent (the *participant*). In response to a cfp, the participant can send a propose message (if it can satisfy the call), or a refuse message to the initiator. When the initiator receives a propose message, it can accept the proposal, and consequently send an accept-proposal message to the participant. A proposal can also be rejected by sending a reject-proposal message to the particip-ant. Upon receiving a reject-proposal message, the participant can try with a new proposal, or desist. A conversation among two agents reaches a (local) finish state when a cfp message is refused, when a propose message is accepted, or when a propose message is rejected and the sender of the proposal desists. In response to a cfp, an agent can in turn send cfp messages to its suppliers thus involving these agents into the conversation. A conversation reaches a (global) finish state when it reaches local finish state for all pairs of two agents involved in it.

When the first cfp of a conversation is created, a unique, global conversation-id is generated. This id will identify all messages that derive from the first call. In order to pair responses to requests, messages include a replay-with and in-reply-to attributes.

Agents live in "nodes". A node is a computing infrastructure that offers storage, computing, and communication facilities to agents. Within nodes, agents can be organized in collections. Nodes and collections are not to be confused with Supply Chains. A Supply Chain in this model is an abstraction that emerges from the dependencies and interactions among agents. Upstream connections in a chain are the result of agents knowing other agents as their suppliers. Downstream connections are the result of agents receiving call for proposal messages from other agents. Chains, therefore, span collections and even nodes. In this model, supply chains are not explicitly modelled. They are the result of the creations of multiple, potentially dis-tributed, agent authors.

4   Reference Implementation

We have implemented platform model version on the basis of modern digital web standards. At the centre of our approach lies an extensible object-oriented framework that simplifies development of new agent types and simulation models, and fosters extensibility. Nodes, the execution environment for agents, are implemented as serverless functions with minimal deployment requirements. Communication among agents is implemented via REST requests. Messaging protocol follows the FIPA standard, and message content adopts semantic web principles in the form of the Schema.org vocabulary. Collaboration among simulation authors occurs when agents in nodes under the control of different institutions/persons talk to each other. Usable editor tools lower the barrier for non-expert simulation editors. Following, we discuss each of these claims in more detail.

4.1 Serveless Architecture

Serverless is a new systems architecture approach that removes the requirement of provisioning and maintenances of servers. Applications are implemented as a series of functions that can be activated by a variety of events such as HTTP requests, or database triggers. Serverless platform providers, such as Amazon, Google and Microsoft, take care of provisioning the resources necessary for functions to execute. Platform users are only charged for the resources used by functions (and only when they execute). In our case, this means no servers to provision and administer; no maintenance cost when no simulation is running; automated scaling of resources in response to simulation needs; and high availability and fault tolerance.

For the reference implementation of the Nodes element of the proposed platform we have selected AWS Lambda (Amazon Web Services implementation of serverless functions), and AWS DynamoDB for persistence. It can be ported with minimal effort to other platforms.

Communication among agents is implemented via HTTP REST requests. Communications is asynchronous. This means that a response to a message (e.g., a **propose** that responds to a **cfp**) will take place as an independent and asynchronous REST request.

The FIPA standard for the structure of ACL messages proposes various alternatives for the content of messages. Three attributes of a message describe its content: language, encoding, and ontology. In the case of framework messages are encoded following the mime-type "application/json". As for the ontology, we have decided to use a selection of elements from the Schema.org vocabulary. In particular, we use the class http://schema.org/Demand and its properties for the content of **cfp** messages, and the class http://schema.org/Offer and its properties for the content of **propose** messages.

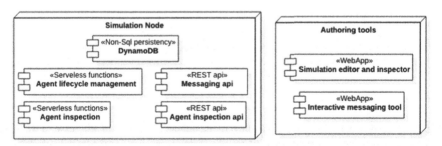

Fig. 1. Overall architecture implemented in the framework. Authoring tools connect to simulation nodes to create and interact with simulations. All communication occurs via REST protocols.

492   A. Fernandez et al.

4.2   Object Oriented, Supply Chain Simulations Framework

An object-oriented framework [12] captures key knowledge of a domain, offering a well-tested, robust implementation for a family of applications in the domain. It hides the complexity of the implementation of the common parts of all applications in the family (frozen-spots), while providing extension points (hot-spots) for applications developers to introduce variability. An object-oriented framework for supply chain simulations materializes the abstract model presented in previous sections. Figure 1 provides an overview of the architecture of the framework and supporting tools.

The sequence diagram in Fig. 2 depicts how incoming messages are handled by the framework. The diagram shows the particular case of a call for proposal (cfp) message. The *messageReceived()* serverless function is activated by a REST request to a URL that represents the messaging inbox of an agent in a node. The framework retrieves the agent from the persistent storage, and delegates to it the processing of the Call for Proposals message. A hierarchy of classes model all possible types of messages (following the FIPA ontology as discussed in the previous section). Message classes offer utility methods to create message templates from them (thus reducing the room for configuration errors). In this case, a propose message template is created from the cfp message. The fields conversationId, inReplyTo, sender and receiver are set accordingly to match those of the original message. The content of the propose message depends on the specific behavior of the agent class and its internal state. The Agent class is an extension point (a hotspot) which means that simulation authors with programming skills can define subclasses that implement specific behavior for processing messages. Once the agent finished processing the message, any queued messages are delivered, the agent (its conversations included) is saved, and the *messageReceived()* function deactivates until a new message arrives.

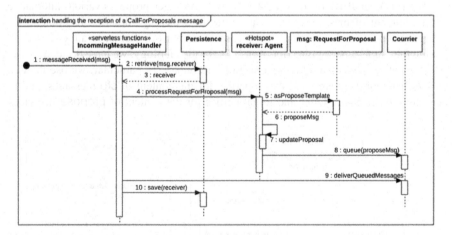

Fig. 2. Sequence diagram for the handling of incoming messages. In this case, a Call for Proposal message. This interaction constitutes one of the frozen-spots of the framework (adapted from [6]).

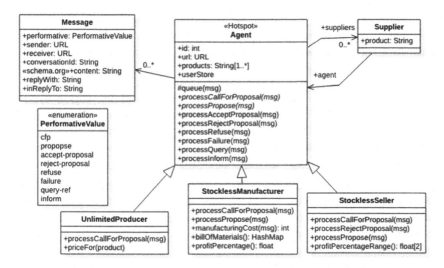

Fig. 3. UML class diagram showing the Agent class hotspot. Subclasses of the abstract agent class implement variability in agent behaviour. The message class with the possible values for its "performative" attribute constitute a frozen-spot (non-variable aspect) of the framework.

The (abstract) Agent class and its subclasses implement the most important hotspot offered by the framework. Each possible activation event of an agent (i.e., the reception of a different type of message) is implemented as a hook method that subclasses can override. The UML class diagram in Fig. 3 shows three example subclasses of agent, implementing specific behavior. The UnlimitedProducer agent class, for example, will answer to a cfp (call for proposals) with a propose if the product of the call matches one of those offered by the agent, regardless of the quantity requested (thus the "Unlimited" name) of the call. The userStore property of a UnlimitedProducer agent stores pricing information for each product.

The framework hides the complexity of inter-agent communication from simulation authors. It provides out of the box agent behaviour for common agent patterns. It provides extension hot-pots to implement more specific agent behaviour for expert users (that requires programming).

5 Preliminary Evaluation

In order to obtain a preliminary evaluation of the applicability of the approach we conducted two pilots. Asking a software developer to create new agent types using the framework, and presenting the platform to an expert on value chains (with experience in simulations) to obtain feedback.

The Framework Developer: A skilled software developer was tasked to use the framework to build new agents. He first received training in the hotspots and frozen spots of the framework. Then, a description of the desired agent behaviour was provided. He used one of the scripts provided with the framework to generate a stub agent class (JavaScript). Then, he modified the generated until de desired agent behaviour was obtained. For this, he had to iterate multiple time in a cycle: program - build simulation - run simulation - program. The following paragraphs summarize the findings. He concluded that the tool in fact allows the agent developer to abstract from agent life-cycle management, packaging of messages, and agent persistency. However, he noticed that with the current capabilities, the program-model-run-program cycle was too time demanding. There is currently no provision for isolated agent testing (alike Unit Testing). Moreover, bugs in agent code were hard to track as error reports intertwined framework and agent code.

The Value-Chain Simulation Expert: The platform (from the perspective of the simulation authoring tools) was presented to an expert on value chains. He had, in the past, built agent simulations using JADE. His opinion was that the general idea (as explained to him), and the reference implementation adequately captured the needs he had to create simulations of value chains. He was able to propose new agent behaviours that matched the capabilities and philosophy of the framework. In particular, he highlighted the improvement that this approach offered (as opposed to JADE) in terms of distribution of agents and collaboration among agent authors. He criticized the inability of the tools to graphically visualize (animate) message exchange in real time. He stressed the importance of making it possible to define agent behaviour as calls to external systems. This made sense, as many experts in value chain simulation frequently have programming skills, but not in JavaScript (or have already programmed an agent's behaviour that they may want in to integrate in a simulation).

6 Conclusions and Future Work

Simulations are a valuable tool to understand and explore value chains. As already exposed by [6], supply chain complexities are certainly a source of limitations for collaboration. In the agri-food world, stakeholders are getting involved in not only one supply chain, but also in several. This necessarily implies multiple relationships, which turns even more complex the management of decision-making process. Hence, a high volume of experiments and scenarios are required to understand and mitigate agri-food complexities. In this context, using general-purpose agent platforms to create value chain simulations involves programming boilerplate code that does not add value to the simulation (e.g., checking the validity of messages, packaging message content, delivering, etc.). For that, a dedicated framework and supporting tools is a valuable contribution. Thus, Sim-a-chain, as an abstract model and a reference implementation has made visible the fact that a key area for future development is support to speed up the agent development cycle, supporting other programming languages and integration with existing systems. As further research, real-based evaluation will be performed to test and evaluate the usability and applicability of the simulation authoring tools to support value-chains decision-making for several types of food products.

Acknowledgement. This research is supported by Ruc-Aps, a H2020 RISE-2015 project, aiming at Enhancing and implementing Knowledge based ICT solutions within high Risk and Uncertain Conditions for Agriculture Production Systems.

References

1. Hieber, R.: Supply Chain Management. A Collaborative Performance Measurement Approach. vdf Hochschulverlag AG, Zurich (2002)
2. Whipple, J.M., Lynch, D.F., Nyaga, G.N.: A buyer's perspective on collaborative versus transactional relationships. Ind. Mark. Manag. (2010). https://doi.org/10.1016/j.indmarman.2008.11.008
3. Ralston, P.M., Richey, R.G., Grawe, S.J.: The past and future of supply chain collaboration: a literature synthesis and call for research. Int. J. Logist. Manag. **28**, 508–530 (2017). https://doi.org/10.1108/IJLM-09-2015-0175
4. Keszey, T.: Boundary spanners' knowledge sharing for innovation success in turbulent times. J. Knowl. Manag. **22**, 1061–1081 (2018). https://doi.org/10.1108/JKM-01-2017-0033
5. Hernández, J.E., Lyons, A.C., Mula, J., Poler, R., Ismail, H.: Supporting the collaborative decision-making process in an automotive supply chain with a multi-agent system. Prod. Plan. Control. (2014). https://doi.org/10.1080/09537287.2013.798086
6. Hernández, J.E., Lyons, A.C., Poler, R., Mula, J., Goncalves, R.: A reference architecture for the collaborative planning modelling process in multi-tier supply chain networks: a Zachman-based approach. Prod. Plan. Control. (2014). https://doi.org/10.1080/09537287.2013.808842
7. Higgins, A.J., Miller, C.J., Archer, A.A., Ton, T., Fletcher, C.S., McAllister, R.R.J.: Challenges of operations research practice in agricultural value chains. J. Oper. Res. Soc. (2010). https://doi.org/10.1057/jors.2009.57
8. Utomo, D.S., Onggo, B.S., Eldridge, S.: Applications of agent-based modelling and simulation in the agri-food supply chains (2018). https://doi.org/10.1016/j.ejor.2017.10.041
9. Moraitis, P., Spanoudakis, N.: The Gaia2JADE process for multi-agent systems development. Appl. Artif. Intell. (2006). https://doi.org/10.1080/08839510500484249
10. Guha, R.V., Brickley, D., Macbeth, S.: Schema.org. Commun. ACM. **59**, 44–51 (2016). https://doi.org/10.1145/2844544
11. Hendrickson, S., Sturdevant, S., Harter, T., Venkataramani, V., Arpaci-Dusseau, A.C., Arpaci-Dusseau, R.H.: Serverless Computation with OpenLambda. In: 8th {USENIX} Workshop on Hot Topics in Cloud Computing (HotCloud 2016). {USENIX} Association, Denver, CO (2016)
12. Fayad, M., Schmidt, D.C.: Object-oriented application frameworks (1997). https://doi.org/10.1145/262793.262798

Enhancing the Sustainability Performance of Agri-Food Supply Chains by Implementing Industry 4.0

David Pérez Perales, María-José Verdecho[✉],
and Faustino Alarcón-Valero

Research Centre on Production Management and Engineering,
Universitat Politècnica de València, Camino de Vera s/n, 46022 Valencia, Spain
{dapepe,mverdecho,faualva}@omp.upv.es

Abstract. In order to enhance the sustainability in the supply chain, its members should define and pursue common objectives in the three dimensions of the sustainability (economic, environmental and social). The Agri-Food Supply Chain (AFSC) is a network of different members such as farmers (producers), processors and distributors (wholesales, retailers…), etc.. In order to achieve the performance objectives of the AFSC, Industry 4.0 technologies can be implemented. The aim of this paper is to present a classification of these technologies according to two criteria: objective to be achieved (environmental or social) specified in the main issues to be covered in each objective and member of the AFSC supply chain where it is implemented. In this work, we focus on technologies that deal with environmental and social sustainability because economic sustainability will depend on the specific characteristics of the business (a supply chain using a specific Industry 4.0 technology may be profitable while others do not).

Keywords: Sustainability · Performance · Agri-food supply chains · Industry 4.0

1 Introduction

As [1] point out, Industry 4.0 has become an "integration factor" for various new technologies towards a new generation of more efficient, agile, and sustainable industrial systems where collaboration issues are at the heart of most challenges of this movement. Collaborative networks community is a field for the analysis and development of Industry 4.0 knowledge [1, 2]. The term "Industry 4.0" comprises several technologies as Internet of Things (IoT), Big Data, Artificial Intelligence, Virtual Reality, 3D Printing, Cyber Security, etc. [3].

On the other hand, Sustainable supply chain management is defined by [4] as *'the management of material, information and capital flows as well as cooperation among companies along the supply chain while taking goals from all three dimensions of sustainable development, i.e., economic, environmental and social into account which are derived from customer and stakeholder requirements'*. Thus, the supply chain members should define and pursue common objectives in the three dimensions of the

© IFIP International Federation for Information Processing 2019
Published by Springer Nature Switzerland AG 2019
L. M. Camarinha-Matos et al. (Eds.): PRO-VE 2019, IFIP AICT 568, pp. 496–503, 2019.
https://doi.org/10.1007/978-3-030-28464-0_43

sustainability. The sustainability performance of the supply chain will be monitored by the achievement of all these objectives.

The Agri-Food Supply Chain (AFSC), as any other supply chain, is a network of different actors working together in different processes and activities in order to bring products and services to the market, with the purpose of satisfying customers' demands [5]. Different actors can be considered depending of the AFSC type. The most complex AFSC would include farmers (producers), processors and different tiers of distributors (wholesales, retailers…). Simpler AFSC would substitute the processors by different types of traders. These actors perform different activities, such as growing, harvesting, storaging, processing, washing, sorting, grading, packaging, labeling and distributing, etc. However, AFSCs hold some relevant characteristics that characterize them [6]: limited shelf-life, high levels of uncertainty and increasing awareness in environmental and social aspects.

In order to achieve the performance objectives of the AFSC, Industry 4.0 technologies can be implemented. The aim of this paper is to present a classification of these technologies according to two criteria: objective to be achieved (environmental or social) specified in the main issues to be covered in each objective and member of the AFSC supply chain where it is implemented.

The paper is structured as follows. Section 2 presents the background. Section 3 presents the main issues of environmental sustainability in AFSC and Industry 4.0 main technologies to enhance its performance. Section 4 presents the main issues of social sustainability in AFSC and Industry 4.0 main technologies to enhance its performance. Finally, in the last section, conclusions are exposed.

2   Background

Industry 4.0 is a field of growing interest at both practitioner and academic levels but is still in its initial stage of development and implementation. Previous literature reviews propose different classification frameworks. [7] expose a literature review on Industry 4.0 technologies for manufacturing processes to identify theoretical and methodological approaches. Some recent literature reviews link Industry 4.0 and sustainability concepts. [8] present a review of works that assess the relation between Industry 4.0 and specific objectives of the three dimensions of sustainability (economic, environmental or social). [9] analyze the environmental impact and challenges of Industry 4.0 from four different scenarios: deployment, operation and technologies, integration and compliance with the sustainable development goals, and long-run scenario. [10] develop a review of works to show the impact of Industry 4.0 technologies on environmental sustainability but limited to waste collection issue. Other related works are [11–13]. In these works, it is observed that there is a lack of studies focusing on providing a framework addressing the intersection of the following components in AFSC: AFSC members, environmental and social sustainability issues, and Industry 4.0-based technologies. Therefore, the aim of our work is to focus on how these technologies can enhance AFSC environmental and social issues, respectively, depending on the AFSC main actors (farmers, processors and distributors). Due to space limitations, social issues will be more extensively deployed than the environmental ones.

3 Industry 4.0-Based Technologies for Environmental Sustainability

Environmental sustainability performance is approached in various ways in the literature. Some authors distinguish between input and output oriented indicators. Others classify them into different categories such as procurement, internal operation and product development. Using the works [14–17], we consider as the most relevant environmental sustainability issues: soil management, crop protection, water management, animal welfare, energy efficiency, waste control and pollution control.

Table 1 shows how Industry 4.0-related technologies can enhance soil and waste management issues. Table 1 is an adaptation from [18].

Table 1. Industry 4.0-based technologies for environmental sustainability of soil and waste management (adapted from [18])

Soil Management		
REF	Farmers	
[19-21]	(1) **Aerial drones** to map weeds, yield and soil variation; (2) **Performance maps** that allow to know the performance of the soil in a certain area thanks to **georeferenced images** of the soil; (3) **Robots** capable of microdot application of fertilizer; (4) **Smart tractors GPS controlled** steering and optimized route planning to diminish soil erosion and saving fuel costs	
Waste Management		
REF	Farmers	Processors	Distributors
[22-24]	(1) **ICT** to the deployment of "production on demand" business models; (2) **Precision agriculture leveraging technologies** for decisions related to planting and harvesting time	(1) **Intelligent equipment** enables quality detections in the process, reducing the number of failures and material consumption; (2) **Cloud computing** platform to share data with suppliers to synchronize orders and shipments and reducing stock	(1) **Artificial intelligence** applied to consumers trends to reduce waste; (2) **Automatic control** of temperature to reduce product spoilage; (3) **Point of sale applications** that collect and transmit information at the point of sale in real time by reading their respective barcodes

4 Industry 4.0-Based Technologies for Social Sustainability

Social sustainability performance is also approached in various ways in the literature. Although social standards such as ISO 260000 and Social Accountability SA8000 are well-known among companies, there is a wide spectrum about the different issues that must be taken into consideration to manage and measure this social performance, mainly due to their intangible nature. Using the works ([6, 25–27]) we use as the most relevant social sustainability issues: employment, work conditions, safety, health, nutrition, traceability and community engagement. Table 2 shows how Industry 4.0-related technologies can enhance each one of the previous issues, affecting the overall social sustainability performance of a generic AFSC. It has to be noted that the literature regarding social sustainability technologies so far is not so extent as the literature dealing with environmental technologies.

Table 2. Industry 4.0-based technologies for social sustainability

REF	Farmers	Processors	Distributors
Employment			
[28, 29]	(1) Cooperatively used **farm-monitoring technology** of agriculture might influence employment opportunities and job profiles of farmers and farming related professionals	(1) **Digital technologies** to automate some tasks where labor is difficult to hire	(1) **ICTs** for better employee education, integration and inclusion, work enrichment, and better work-life balance
Work conditions			
[30]	(1) **ICT tools** to lower administrative workload, enhance regulatory laws, allow "hands-free" reporting automation and make work/life balance for farmers easier; (2) **"Farmer-friendly" technologies** designed taking into account the final client	(1) **Intelligent assistance systems** can simplify some tasks providing some previously unknown information (f.e. **augmented reality glasses**); (2) **Intelligent assistance systems**, such as **Learn instruments**, can make work more ergonomic simplifying it	(1) **ICT application** in non-automated transportation activities can provide digital information that can help to make more ergonomic and safer labour conditions by optimizing loading-related tasks
Safety			
[31–33]	(1) **Smart Devices** implemented in tractors that send alerts when they detect immediate overturning risks; (2). **Drones** used in the fields, enabling farmers to control growth in a comfortable and safety manner	(1) **Intelligent Manufacturing equipment** in processes controlled by **ICT** to reduce pollutants and noise	(1) **Intelligent tachograph** that allows the driver to book parking, cancel telematics tolls in advance and helps reduce unnecessary stops by traffic agencies; (2) **GPS** that allows trucks drivers remote access to data (speed, distance…) on work time, avoiding delays and helping to meet the delivery time

(*continued*)

Table 2. (*continued*)

REF	Farmers	Processors	Distributors
Health			
[34, 35]	(1) **ICT** tools to make farmers more aware about consumer eating habits, and how their sold products are perceived and performed in the market-place; (2) The use of the **IoT** to maintain healthier crops and optimize the use of fertilizers and pesticides	(1) **Automated machines** to perform dangerous, dirty and demanding tasks previously manually managed	(1) **Intelligent packaging** that has sensors in each package for sending real-time data on the status of the products via cellular network or wifi to a platform for processing and analysis; (2) **Intelligent processing tools** for making consumer habits more understandable and having a better feedback from them
Nutrition			
[36, 37]	(1) Application of **genetic modified crops** to improve food production and nutrients	(1) Use of **High Intensity Ultra-Sound technology** to induce some changes in the nutritional profile of some beverages	(1) **Food testing devices and freshness sensors** to supervise and prevent products to loss their nutrients
Traceability			
[38–40]	(1) **Geographic information systems (GIS), global positioning systems (GPS) and remote sensing (RS)** integration to allow site-specific agriculture and obtain agriculture products-related data on the farm	(1) **Life-cycle improvement technology** and food processing technology	(1) **Logistics tracking software;** (2) **ICT tools** providing consumers with more complete, transparent and reliable information **on** food composition, origin and health-related issues (f.e. intolerances)
Community engagement			
[41, 42]	(1) **Blockchain technologies** to check sustainable performance indicators such as the resources origin or child labour conditions; (2) **Online networks** to facilitate direct delivery between farmers and market place points (f.e Food-hub.org and LocalHarvest.org programs)		(1) **ICT-based business models** to encourage engagement among regional supply chains (e.g. online shopping)

5   Conclusions

Sustainability in the supply chain is a topic of high interest in business and academic literature. Sustainability is composed of three dimensions: economic, environmental and social sustainability. Supply chains pursuing sustainability must define common objectives (in these three dimensions) to be reached by the different members.

The accomplishment of these objectives in AFSCs can be supported by the introduction of Industry 4.0 technologies. Specifically, different Industry 4.0 technologies can be used to support specific issues within sustainability dimensions. In this work, on the one hand, we have selected as environmental issues: soil management, crop protection, water management, animal welfare, energy efficiency, waste control and pollution control. On the other hand, we have defined as social issues: employment, work conditions, safety, health, nutrition, traceability and community engagement. It has to be noted that in this work, we focus on technologies that deal with environmental and social sustainability because economic sustainability will depend on the specific characteristics of the business. Once the environmental and social issues have been defined, the different Industry 4.0 technologies have been associated to each issue and to the different members (farmers, processors and distributors) of the supply chain.

In the literature, there are less Industry 4.0-related technologies explicitly reported for dealing with social sustainability issues than in the environmental case, probably due to the different nature. There is still a need to develop further both environmental and, especially, social technologies that improve the sustainability performance of AFSCs in order to improve efficiency and competitiveness.

Acknowledgements. This work has been funded by the Project GV/2017/065 "Development of a decision support tool for the management and improvement of sustainability in supply chains" funded by the Regional Government of Valencia. Authors also acknowledge the Project 691249, RUC-APS: Enhancing and implementing Knowledge based ICT solutions within high Risk and Uncertain Conditions for Agriculture Production Systems.

References

1. Camarinha-Matos, L.M., Fornasiero, R., Afsarmanesh, H.: Collaborative networks as a core enabler of Industry 4.0. In: Camarinha-Matos, L.M., Afsarmanesh, H., Fornasiero, R. (eds.) PRO-VE 2017. IAICT, vol. 506, pp. 3–17. Springer, Cham (2017). https://doi.org/10.1007/978-3-319-65151-4_1
2. Stich, V., Gudergan, G., Zeller, V.: Need and solution to transform the manufacturing industry in the age of Industry 4.0 – a capability maturity index approach. In: Camarinha-Matos, L.M., Afsarmanesh, H., Rezgui, Y. (eds.) PRO-VE 2018. IAICT, vol. 534, pp. 33–42. Springer, Cham (2018). https://doi.org/10.1007/978-3-319-99127-6_3
3. Flores, M., Maklin, D., Golob, M., Al-Ashaab, A., Tucci, C.: Awareness towards Industry 4.0: key enablers and applications for internet of things and big data. In: Camarinha-Matos, L.M., Afsarmanesh, H., Rezgui, Y. (eds.) PRO-VE 2018. IAICT, vol. 534, pp. 377–386. Springer, Cham (2018). https://doi.org/10.1007/978-3-319-99127-6_32
4. Seuring, S., Müller, M.: From a literature review to a conceptual framework for sustainable supply chain management. J. Clean. Prod. **16**, 1699–1710 (2008)

5. Prima, W.A., Xing, K., Amer, Y.: Collaboration and sustainable agri-food supply chain: a literature review. In: MATEC (2016). https://doi.org/10.1051/matecconf/20165802004

6. Pérez Perales, D., Alarcón Valero, F., Drummond, C., Ortiz, Á.: Towards a sustainable agri-food supply chain model. The case of LEAF. In: Ortiz, Á., Andrés Romano, C., Poler, R., García-Sabater, J.-P. (eds.) Engineering Digital Transformation. LNMIE, pp. 333–341. Springer, Cham (2019). https://doi.org/10.1007/978-3-319-96005-0_40

7. Savastano, M., Amendola, C., Bellini, F., D'Ascenzo, F.: Contextual impacts on industrial processes brought by the digital transformation of manufacturing: a systematic review. Sustainability **11**, 891 (2019)

8. Varela, L., Araújo, A., Ávila, P., Castro, H., Putnik, G.: Evaluation of the relation between lean manufacturing, Industry 4.0, and sustainability. Sustainability **11**, 1439 (2019)

9. Bonilla, S.H., Silva, H.R.O., da Silva, M.T., Gonçalves, R.F., Sacomano, J.B.: Industry 4.0 and sustainability implications: a scenario-based analysis of the impacts and challenges. Sustainability **10**, 3740 (2018)

10. Bányai, T., Tamás, P., Illés, B., Stankeviciute, Z., Bányai, A.: Optimization of municipal waste collection routing: impact of Industry 4.0 technologies on environmental awareness and sustainability. Int. J. Environ. Res. Public Health. **16**, 634 (2019)

11. Lin, K.C., Shyu, J.Z., Ding, K.: A cross-strait comparison of innovation policy under Industry 4.0 and sustainability development transition. Sustainability **9**, 786 (2017)

12. Kamble, S.: Sustainable Industry 4.0 framework: a systematic literature review identifying the current trends and future perspectives. In: Process Safety and Environmental Protection Transactions of the Institution of Chemical Engineers, Part B, vol. 117, pp. 408–25. Institution of Chemical Engineers (2018)

13. Franciosi, C., Iung, B., Miranda, S., Riemma, S.: Maintenance for sustainability in the Industry 4.0 context: a scoping literature review. IFAC-Pap. Online **51**(11), 903–908 (2018)

14. Bocken, N.M.P., Short, S.W., Rana, P., Evans, S.: A literature and practice review to develop sustainable business model archetypes. J. Clean. Prod. **65**, 42–56 (2014)

15. Bourlakis, M., Maglaras, G., Aktas, E., Gallear, D., Fotopoulos, C.: Firm size and sustainable performance in food supply chains: insights from Greek SMEs. Int. J. Prod. Econ. **152**, 112–130 (2014)

16. Garbie, I.H.: An analytical technique to model and assess sustainable development index in manufacturing enterprises. Int. J. Prod. Res. **52**(16), 4876–4915 (2014)

17. Beier, G., Niehoff, S., Ziems, T., Xue, B.: Sustainability aspects of a digitalized industry - a comparative study from China and Germany. Int. J. Precis. Eng. Manuf. Green Technol. **4**, 227–234 (2017)

18. Pérez, D., Verdecho, M.J., Alarcón, F: Industry 4.0 for the development of more sustainable decision support tools for agri-food supply chain management. In: 13rd International Conference on Industrial Engineering and Industrial Management, XXIII, Gijón, Spain (2019)

19. Xiaolin, L., Linnan, Y., Lin, P., Wengfeng, L., Limin, Z.: Procedia engineering county soil fertility information management system based on embedded GIS. Procedia Eng. **29**, 2388–2392 (2012)

20. Satyanarayana, G.V.: Wireless sensor based remote monitoring system for agriculture using ZigBee and GPS. In: 2013 (CAC2S), pp. 110–114 (2013)

21. Phillips, A.J., Newlands, N.K., Liang, S.H.L., Ellert, B.H.: Integrated sensing of soil moisture at the field-scale: measuring, modeling and sharing for improved agricultural decision support. Comput. Electron. Agric. **107**, 73–88 (2014)

22. Liopa-tsakalidi, A., Tsolis, D., Barouchas, P.: Application of mobile technologies through an integrated management system for agricultural production. Procedia Technol. **8**, 165–170 (2013). (Haicta)

23. Yerpude, S., Singhal, T.K.: Impact of Internet of Things (IoT) data on demand forecasting. Indian J. Sci. Technol. **10**, 5 (2017)
24. Wolfert, S., Ge, L., Verdouw, C., Bogaardt, M.: Big data in smart farming – a review. Agric. Syst. **153**, 69–80 (2017)
25. Castka, P., Balzarova, M.A.: ISO 26000 and supply chains-on the diffusion of the social responsibility standard. Int. J. Prod. Econ. **111**(2), 274–286 (2008)
26. Stock, T., Obenaus, M., Kunz, S., Kohl, H.: Industry 4.0 as enabler for a sustainable development: A qualitative assessment of its ecological and social potential. Process. Saf. Environ. **118**, 254–267 (2018)
27. Verdecho, M.J., Pérez, D., Alarcón F.: Proposal of a customer-oriented sustainable balanced scorecard for agri-food supply chains. In: 12th International Conference on Industrial Engineering and Industrial Management, Girona, Spain, 12–13 July (2018)
28. Valcour, P.M., Hunter, L.W.: Technology, organizations, and work-life integration. In: Kossek, E.E. Lambert, S.J. (eds.), Work and Life Integration: Organizational, Cultural, and Individual Perspectives, pp. 61–84. Lawrence Erlbaum Associates, Mahwah (2005)
29. Arntz, M., Gregory, T., Zierahn, U.: The risk of automation for jobs in OECD countries: a comparative analysis. In: OECD Social, Employment and Migration Working Papers, no. 189. OECD Publishing, Paris (2016)
30. Grubert, J., Langlotz, T., Zollmann, S., Regenbrecht, H.: Towards pervasive augmented reality: context-awareness in augmented reality. IEEE Trans. Vis. Comput. Graph. **23**, 1 (2016)
31. Velthuis, A.G.J.: New Approaches to Food-Safety Economics. Kluwer Academic Publishers, Dordrecht (2003)
32. Sándor, Z.P., Csiszár, C.: Development stages of intelligent parking information systems for trucks. Acta Polytechnica Hungarica **10**(4), 161–174 (2013)
33. Scognamiglio, V., Arduini, F., Palleschi, G., Rea, G.: Biosensing technology for sustainable food safety. Trends Analyt. Chem. **62**, 1–10 (2014)
34. Brynjolfsson, E., McAfee, A.: The Second Machine Age. Work, Progress, and Prosperity in a Time of Brilliant Technologies. W.W. Norton & Company, London (2014)
35. Smith, A., Caiazza, T.: Automation in everyday life (2017). http://assets.pewresearch.org/wpcontent/uploads/sites/14/2017/10/03151500/PI_2017.10.04_Automation_FINAL.pdf
36. Hefferon, K.L.: Nutritionally enhanced food crops; progress and perspectives. Int. J. Mol. Sci. **16**, 3895–3914 (2015)
37. Glass, S., Fanzo, J.: Genetic modification technology for nutrition and improving diets: an ethical perspective. Curr. Opin. Biotech. **44**, 46–51 (2017)
38. Moe, T.: Perspectives on traceability in food manufacture'. Trends Food Sci. Technol. **9**(5), 211–214 (1998)
39. Latino, M., Corallo, A., Menegoli, M.: From Industry 4.0 to Agriculture 4.0: how manage product data in agri-food supply chain for voluntary traceability, a framework proposed. In: 20th International Conference on Food and Environment (ICFE), Rome (2018)
40. Linus, U.O.: Traceability in agriculture and food supply chain: a review of basic concepts, technological implications, and future prospects. J. Food Agric. Environ. **1**(1), 101–106 (2003)
41. Maumbe, B.M., Okello, J.: Uses of information and communication technology (ICT) in agriculture and rural development in Sub-Saharan Africa: experiences from South Africa and Kenya. IJICTRDA **1**(1), 1–22 (2010)
42. Dlodlo, N., Kalezhi, J.: The internet of things in agriculture for sustainable rural development. In: International Conference on Emerging Trends in Networks and Computer Communications (ETNCC) (2015)

Data Management for Collaboration in Value Creation Networks

Data-Driven Pattern-Based Constructs Definition for the Digital Transformation Modelling of Collaborative Networked Manufacturing Enterprises

Concetta Semeraro[1,2,3(✉)], Mario Lezoche[2], Hervé Panetto[2],
Michele Dassisti[1], and Stefano Cafagna[3]

[1] Department of Mechanics, Management and Mathematics,
Polytechnic of Bari, Bari, Italy
concetta.semeraro@poliba.it
[2] Université de Lorraine, CNRS, CRAN, Nancy, France
[3] Master Italy s.r.l, Conversano, Bari, Italy

Abstract. The digital transformation of collaborative networked manufacturing enterprises requires the building and the applying digital models representing the set of resources and processes knowledge. Modelling such digital copy of the physical system to perform real-time validation and optimization is quite complex and thus needs a big amount of data and some modelling patterns representing the operational semantics of the modelled elements. Generally, the modelling action has a specific application type. For this reason, the core challenge of the digital transformation modelling is to create a modular "digital model", namely a decomposable and re-composable model, towards different applications. The authors propose an approach based on the combination of data-driven and model-based approaches, to identify and formalize modelling patterns, that combine for developing a modular executable model of the studied system.

Keywords: Data-driven approaches · Model-based approaches · Modularity · Knowledge Sharing

1 Introduction

In the age of the so-called "Factory of the Future" also named "Industry of the Future" or Industry 4.0 to name only a few of those initiatives, the transformation from an Automated Factory to an Autonomous Factory [1] needs to overcome the information asymmetry amongst technology, processes, people and organizations [2] along the entire system lifecycle. This action requires to create a so-called collaborative network enterprise [3]. The interactions between entities should be supported by computer networks. The collaborative network, in the design phase, guides the designers to interact with customers. Iteratively it lets them adjusting the network according to their expectations, improving the design models and achieving personalized product design [4]. In the production phase, it enables the simulation of the plant in a virtual space,

© IFIP International Federation for Information Processing 2019
Published by Springer Nature Switzerland AG 2019
L. M. Camarinha-Matos et al. (Eds.): PRO-VE 2019, IFIP AICT 568, pp. 507–515, 2019.
https://doi.org/10.1007/978-3-030-28464-0_44

identifying and optimizing the actual production and predicting failures. In the service phase, the collaborative network can provide value-added services with the support of physical simulation and data-driven intelligence [5]. In the context of manufacturing processes, the prerequisite of a manufacturing network collaboration is to share skills and core competencies [6]. A "digitalization" approach enables the virtual replication of the factory to monitor and simulate real time physical processes. It allows to connect the entire value chain [7] by merging sensor data acquired from the physical world into virtual or simulation-based models. It is then necessary to emulate the system behaviour through realistic models. However, with the advent of cyber-physical systems (CPS) [8], it is hard to construct an accurate model by using traditional model-based approaches because of the complexity of the systems. On the other hand, recent advances in sensor technology [9] have enabled significant growth of data collection and analysis, leading researchers to focus on data-driven methods.

The paper proposes the combination of a data-driven approach with a model-based approach [10] in order to help designers to generate models from collected data, based on a set of patterns representing standard functions of the real manufacturing processes. The core elements of a digital model are implemented by the fusion of sensor-based data, physical-based patterns and data-driven models. They enable the creation of a reliable decision making system [11] for a collaborative network. At the same time, a modular approach needs to be developed to improve the efficiency of those digital models.

2 State of Art

The increasing complexity of manufacturing systems requires new approaches to detect production failures and diagnose operating profiles [5]. Model-based and data-driven approaches cope with such issue [10]. The model-based approaches compare simulated results with known information, represented by mathematical or physical equations. The model approach is based on a set of different models to represent the structure, the behaviour and the interactions of a physical system to be monitored or predicted [12]. There are various models focusing on the representation of different characteristics of the reality. Here below a not exhaustive list of the most studied and used:

- A geometric model defines shapes, sizes, positions and it assemblies the relations of machine components [13]. It reflects the geometry, the kinematics, the logic and the interfaces of the real system.
- A physical model analyses the phenomena, such as deformation, cracking and corrosion. It simulates the physical properties (e.g. function/capacity, cutting force, torque and wear) and loads (e.g. stress, resistance and temperature) [14].
- A behaviour model describes the way the physical system is governed by driving factors (e.g. control orders) or disturbing factors (e.g. human interferences).
- A collaborative information model [15] defines how different components interact and simulates the collaborative behaviour among several assets.
- A decision-making model [15] makes the model capable of evaluating, reasoning, and validating. It consists of variable input, algorithms and a collection of constraints and rules. It includes rules of constraints, associations and deductions [12]

and it stores and analyses the running status data, then it makes decisions using machine learning algorithm.

The geometric, physical, behaviour and collaborative models are descriptive models [16], while the decision-making model is an intelligent model [16] and it could be related to data-driven approach. The data-driven approaches refer to models derived from processed data (e.g. sensor/actuator data) which represent the current state of the system [17]. Data-driven models are designed to mine the hidden patterns and knowledge through the analysis of a huge amount of historical data [18]. The patterns mining methods make use of the context data and they unveil the complex coupling relationships. The data-driven approaches can be classified in supervised, unsupervised and reinforcement learning approaches [19]. The supervised learning develops models based on input and output data [10]. The algorithms of this class consist of a target/outcome variable (or dependent variable) which is to be predicted by a given set of predictors (independent variables). This approach enables to classify and determine a list of system's defaults [20] with health indicators for each part of it [21]. The unsupervised learning [22], instead, discovers an internal representation from input data only. It has not any target or outcome variable to predict and estimate and are used to create autonomously clusters for different working regimes and machine conditions [23]. Finally, the reinforcement learning trains the machine to make specific decisions [24]. The machine is exposed to an environment where it trains itself continually using trial and error. Compared to supervised and unsupervised learning methods, the machine learns from past and tries to capture the best possible knowledge to make accurate business decisions [25].

On the one hand, the data-driven approaches allow to integrate parameters across different domains of a collaborative network (e.g. product, process and logistics) into models that would be difficult to build with the traditional model-based modelling approaches [26]. The data-driven, in fact, aim at transforming the data into relevant information but the quality and scope of the data play a critical role [27].

On the other hand, the model-based approaches rely on the use of mathematical models to simulate the systems behaviour in different operating conditions but for complex systems, these models are not easy to develop and keep updated during the system life-cycle [27]. At the same time, a single approach cannot be adapted to all different applications of a collaborative network because of the complexity and the variety that characterize manufacturing systems. Hybrid approaches [10] are been developed to cope with problems such as fault detection and diagnosis [28], prediction or classification accuracy [29] for specific application case. It means that is necessary to develop and standardize modelling patterns to achieve a modular approach. Modularity, in fact, is concerned with shifting from rigid systems and inflexible production models toward an agile system. The modularity is defined as the capability of system components to be separated and combined easily and quickly [30]. For the digital transformation modelling, the modularity is the ability to integrate, to add, and to replace models [31] based on the specific application. The idea behind a modular approach is to use, and especially re-use, predefined functional patterns, that are systematically developed and linked for the configuration of a holistic manufacturing system [32]. The paper presents a modular approach to discover automatically data-driven pattern-based constructs in order to generate semi-automated models.

3 Data-Driven Pattern-Based Constructs Definition

The modular design approach is developed to capture patterns from data and to share and to reuse knowledge encapsulated in a pattern among systems or processes operating in a similar condition. It enables the virtual replication of an enterprise and then monitoring, simulating and predicting failures in manufacturing processes. The idea is to build knowledge-based modelling constructs representing data-driven patterns contextualised in different process' situations.

FCA (Formal Concept Analysis) is a mathematical theory oriented at applications in knowledge representation [33]. It provides tools to group the data and to discover formal patterns by representing it as a hierarchy of formal concepts organised in a semi ordered set named lattice. Given a set of objects, a set of properties, and defined the relations between objects and properties, a formal concept represents a subset of objects sharing the same sub-set of properties. A concept is constituted by two parts: its extension which consists of all objects belonging to the concept, and its intension which comprises all properties shared by those objects. This understanding allows a formal discovering of associations among concepts and consequently recognizing which concepts are closely related based on the set of shared properties. In this context, FCA is applied to discover automatically patterns from data. The patterns generated are selected and evaluated for detecting relationships, associations, and anomalies that characterize the system in analysis. A pattern helps to discover useful knowledge from a collection of data. It can describe recurrent behaviours of the system or it can codify tacit associations that can be used to predict the future behaviour. The patterns discovered are modelled in System Modelling Language (SysML) [34]. SysML provides nine interrelated types of diagrams to describe the function, the structure, the behaviour and the system requirements. It supports the specification, analysis, and verification of systems' models.

The modular approach developed is articulated in four different stages. The first stage is to define the knowledge structure in a data table (Fig. 1a). The data table presents the objects on the rows and the properties on the columns. The cross indicates that exists a relation between an object and an attribute. In second stage, FCA converts automatically the data table into a lattice (Fig. 1b). The lattice presents nodes, connecting line and names. Nodes represent formal concepts and the lines connect objects and attributes belonging to a concept. The name of each objects is noted under nodes instead the name of each property above nodes. The third stage is to evaluate the patterns extracted from the lattice (Fig. 1c) and to detect the behaviours, the associations to model. It is possible also to identify the relationships among patterns. The last stage is to generate the model of the pattern in SysML diagrams (Fig. 1e), based on the features defined in the previous step. The objects are modelled as blocks and the properties as value properties using the block definition diagram (bdd). The behaviour of a pattern is modelled as a set of actions to describe how the inputs are transformed into outputs. In particular, the state diagram (stm) models the behaviour defining states and events of an object during its lifetime. It simulates how the states change based on internal or external events. The parametric diagram (par) models the associations discovered in terms of constraints. Constraints represent physical laws or mathematical and logical operators or decisions that evaluate input parameters to return a result. The modular approach enables to create semi-automated models based on the patterns discovered.

4 Case Study

An Italian SME, the Master Italy s.r.l, that produces small accessories for civil window frames, is here considered to test how to construct data-driven pattern. The process and the product in analysis are respectively the die casting aluminium and the steel corner.

Die casting is a metal casting process that is characterized by forcing molten metal under high pressure into a mould cavity. The injection cycle of die casting aluminium process is composed by four different phases:

1. Melting: the aluminium enters at the solid state and exits at the molten state.
2. Injection: the molten aluminium is injected into the mould, through a plunger.
3. Moulding: the molten aluminium solidifies in the mould cavity.
4. Extraction: an ejection mechanism pushes the casting out of the mould cavity.

The data set presents the injection cycles as objects and technological parameters as properties (Fig. 1a). The technological parameters monitored are: plunger course 'C1'(m),'), 'C2'(m), and time 'T1'(sec) 'T2'(sec), in first and second stage of injection phase, multiplied course 'CC' (m), multiplied pressure 'PM' (bar), cavity pressure 'PS' (bar), clamping force 'FC' (N). The FCA is applied to determine the hierarchical lattice (Fig. 1b). There are five different range of values for each parameter. The first pattern extracted (Fig. 1c) has a set of objects sharing the properties C2-1, T1-2, C2-5, T2-1, PM-1, FC-3. The second pattern (Fig. 1d) instead has the properties C2-1, T1-2, C2-5, T2-1, PM-1, FC-4, PS-2. The objects of the patterns share most of properties (C2-1, T1-2, C2-5, T2-1, PM-1) but FC operates in the range 4 and it depends also on PS-2 in the pattern b). These are two different but correlated patterns. The parameters C1, C2, T1, T2, PM are parameters related to the injection stage, while FC and PS are related to the moulding stage. It means that there are physical equations between the technological parameters of the two phases. Clamping force (FC), in fact, refers to the force applied to a mould by the clamping unit of the injection moulding machine. In order to keep the mould closed, this force must oppose the separating force, caused by the injection parameters (C1, C2, T1, T2, PM). The required clamping force depends on the cavity pressure (PS) inside the mould and the projected area, on which the pressure acts. For this reason, the patterns are respectively the clamping pattern (a) and the pressure control pattern (b). The model of the compression pattern (Fig. 1e) presents the process stage as blocks and the technological parameters as value properties on the block definition diagram. The physical laws are modelled on the parametric diagram. The state diagram can simulate if all injection cycles (objects) of the clamping pattern are conformed to the quality product. In the clamping pattern, all parameters (properties) operate into the defined ranges. In the pression control pattern, the state of the property FC-4 closes out of range. It means that PS can be analysed to detect and to implement a strategy capable of preventing quality defects caused by FC.

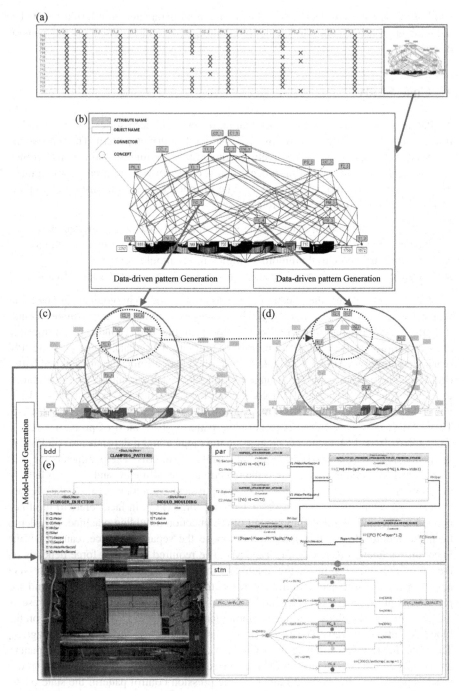

Fig. 1. (a) Data table (b) FCA lattice (c) Clamping pattern (d) Pression control pattern (e) SysML structure and behaviour model of the clamping pattern

5   Conclusions and Future Works

The paper presents how to construct data-driven patterns in order to create a modular approach for digital modelling transformation. The approach defines how to build a semi-automated model based on the patterns discovered automatically in FCA.

The patterns are systematically modelled in SysML and linked for the configuration of a holistic manufacturing system. The approach shows also how it is possible to discover the behaviours and associations from data and how to analyse the relationships between patterns. The goal is to use the same patterns for modelling other systems. The future work is to enrich the pattern' semantics to create a comprehensive library of formalized data-driven patterns. In this way, data-driven patterns can be combined, based on the specific application, to create easily dynamic models. The approach tested is inductive. It means that the data help to design model about the meaning of their content. The idea is to develop also a deductive approach. In this case, the modular design approach can be used also to verify if a certain model (or hypothesis) is consistent with the available data or if it is necessary to implement a monitoring strategy to collect new data. Continued monitoring, data collection and analysis provide up-to-date information about the behaviours of the system in a continuous stream. Those actions enable to collect and convert data in information, share the information acquired, formalize the knowledge, joint performance measurements and leverage the skills and the knowledge. These benefits are in line with the collaboration-associated benefits of a collaborative network.

References

1. Rosen, R., von Wichert, G., Lo, G., Bettenhausen, K.D.: About the importance of autonomy and digital twins for the future of manufacturing. IFAC-Pap. **48**(3), 567–572 (2015)
2. Padovano, A., Longo, F., Nicoletti, L., Mirabelli, G.: A digital twin based service oriented application for a 4.0 knowledge navigation in the smart factory. IFAC-Pap. **51**(11), 631–636 (2018)
3. Camarinha-Matos, L.M., Afsarmanesh, H.: Collaborative networks. In: Wang, K., Kovacs, G.L., Wozny, M., Fang, M. (eds.) PROLAMAT 2006. IIFIP, vol. 207, pp. 26–40. Springer, Boston, MA (2006). https://doi.org/10.1007/0-387-34403-9_4
4. Qi, Q., Tao, F.: Digital twin and big data towards smart manufacturing and Industry 4.0: 360 degree comparison. IEEE Access **6**, 3585–3593 (2018)
5. Wang, J., Ye, L., Gao, R.X., Li, C., Zhang, L.: Digital Twin for rotating machinery fault diagnosis in smart manufacturing. Int. J. Prod. Res. **57**(12), 3920–3934 (2018)
6. Min, S., et al.: Supply chain collaboration: what's happening? Int. J. Logist. Manag. **16**(2), 237–256 (2005)
7. Ghobakhloo, M.: The future of manufacturing industry: a strategic roadmap toward Industry 4.0. J. Manuf. Technol. Manag. **29**(6), 910–936 (2018)
8. Lee, J., Bagheri, B., Kao, H.-A.: A cyber-physical systems architecture for Industry 4.0-based manufacturing systems. Manuf. Lett. **3**, 18–23 (2015)
9. Dassisti, M., et al.: Industry 4.0 paradigm: the viewpoint of the small and medium enterprises. In: 7th International Conference on Information Society and Technology, ICIST 2017, vol. 1, pp. 50–54 (2017)

10. Tidriri, K., Chatti, N., Verron, S., Tiplica, T.: Bridging data-driven and model-based approaches for process fault diagnosis and health monitoring: a review of researches and future challenges. Annu. Rev. Control **42**, 63–81 (2016)
11. Liu, Z., Meyendorf, N., Mrad, N.: The role of data fusion in predictive maintenance using digital twin. In: AIP Conference Proceedings, vol. 1949 (2018)
12. Tao, F., Zhang, M., Liu, Y., Nee, A.Y.C.: Digital twin driven prognostics and health management for complex equipment. CIRP Ann. **37**, 169–172 (2018)
13. Ayani, M., Ganebäck, M., Ng, A.H.C.: Digital twin: applying emulation for machine reconditioning. Procedia CIRP **72**, 243–248 (2018)
14. Post, J., Groen, M., Klaseboer, G.: Physical model based digital twins in manufacturing processes. Opt. Lett. **34**(13), 1982–1984 (2009)
15. Bao, J., Guo, D., Li, J., Zhang, J.: The modelling and operations for the digital twin in the context of manufacturing. Enterp. Inf. Syst. **13**(4), 534–556 (2018)
16. Luo, W., Hu, T., Zhu, W., Tao, F.: Digital twin modeling method for CNC machine tool. In: IEEE 15th International Conference on Networking, Sensing and Control (ICNSC), pp. 1–4 (2018)
17. Talkhestani, B.A., Jazdi, N., Schlögl, W., Weyrich, M.: A concept in synchronization of virtual production system with real factory based on anchor-point method. Procedia CIRP **67**, 13–17 (2018). Presentato al
18. Zhang, Y., Ren, S., Liu, Y., Sakao, T., Huisingh, D.: A framework for big data driven product lifecycle management. J. Clean. Prod. **159**, 229–240 (2017)
19. Jain, S., Shao, G., Shin, S.-J.: Manufacturing data analytics using a virtual factory representation. Int. J. Prod. Res. **55**(18), 5450–5464 (2017)
20. Asimov, R.M., Chernoshey, S.V., Kruse, I., Osipovich, V.S.: Digital twin in the analysis of a big data (2018)
21. Ding, K., Chan, F.T.S., Zhang, X., Zhou, G., Zhang, F.: Defining a digital twin-based cyber-physical production system for autonomous manufacturing in smart shop floors. Int. J. Prod. Res. 1–20 (2019)
22. Sutharssan, T., Stoyanov, S., Bailey, C., Yin, C.: Prognostic and health management for engineering systems: a review of the data-driven approach and algorithms. J. Eng. **2015**(7), 215–222 (2015)
23. Lee, J., Kao, H.-A., Yang, S.: Service innovation and smart analytics for Industry 4.0 and big data environment. Procedia Cirp **16**, 3–8 (2014)
24. Zhou, L., Pan, S., Wang, J., Vasilakos, A.V.: Machine learning on big data: opportunities and challenges. Neurocomputing **237**, 350–361 (2017)
25. van Otterlo, M., Wiering, M.: «Reinforcement learning and markov decision processes». In: Wiering, M., van Otterlo, M. (eds.) Reinforcement learning, pp. 3–42. Springer, Heidelberg (2012). https://doi.org/10.1007/978-3-642-27645-3_1
26. Kusiak, A.: Smart manufacturing. Int. J. Prod. Res. **56**(1–2), 508–517 (2018)
27. Tobon-Mejia, D.A., Medjaher, K., Zerhouni, N., Tripot, G.: A data-driven failure prognostics method based on mixture of Gaussians hidden Markov models. IEEE Trans. Reliab. **61**(2), 491–503 (2012)
28. Zhang, X., Hoo, K.A.: Effective fault detection and isolation using bond graph-based domain decomposition. Comput. Chem. Eng. **35**(1), 132–148 (2011)
29. Ghosh, K., Ng, Y.S., Srinivasan, R.: Evaluation of decision fusion strategies for effective collaboration among heterogeneous fault diagnostic methods. Comput. Chem. Eng. **35**(2), 342–355 (2011)
30. Mabkhot, M., Al-Ahmari, A., Salah, B., Alkhalefah, H.: Requirements of the smart factory system: a survey and perspective. Machines **6**(2), 23 (2018)

31. Schleich, B., Anwer, N., Mathieu, L., Wartzack, S.: Shaping the digital twin for design and production engineering. CIRP Ann. - Manuf. Technol. **66**(1), 141–144 (2017)
32. Guo, J., Zhao, N., Sun, L., Zhang, S.: Modular based flexible digital twin for factory design. J. Ambient Intell. Humaniz. Comput. 1–12 (2018)
33. Ganter, B., Stumme, G., Wille, R.: Formal Concept Analysis: Foundations and Applications, vol. 3626. Springer, Heidelberg (2005). https://doi.org/10.1007/978-3-540-31881-1
34. Friedenthal, S., Moore, A., Steiner, R.: A Practical Guide to SysML: the Systems Modeling Language. Morgan Kaufmann, Burlington (2014)

Data Privacy Concerns Throughout the Customer Journey and Different Service Industries

Marko Mäki[(⊠)] and Ari Alamäki

Haaga-Helia University of Applied Sciences, Helsinki, Finland
{marko.maki,ari.alamaki}@haaga-helia.fi

Abstract. Data privacy concerns play a significant role during collaboration with customers in digital networks. An important element in collaboration between business partners is the utilization of customer data in common offering development, marketing, and service operations. The aim of this paper was to focus on data privacy in the context of the customer journey and in different service industries. Based on empirical survey data (n = 306), our findings highlighted the importance of recognizing phases in the customer journey and have drawn attention to information sensitivity in different service industries. Findings showed that customers' willingness to share data with different industries varied. Moreover, consumers' attitudes towards the use of their personal data varied at different phases of the customer journey. Our findings have emphasized the importance of information sensitivity in different phases of the customer journey, especially when designing a means for effective data utilization in collaborative networks.

Keywords: Data · Privacy concerns · Customer journey · Service industries

1 Introduction

Creating a superior customer experience has become a dominant aim and stream of value chains and ecosystems. One important element in developing new digital services is the utilization of customer data in personalization, online service performance monitoring, and sales and marketing operations improvement [1]. While companies have created multichannel designs for customers and have become more data driven in their daily activities, customers, as the most important actors of business ecosystems, have become increasingly concerned about their privacy. Privacy concerns are prevalent, especially in online environments [2, 3] where customers and service providers interact in collaborative networks.

Many companies have highlighted the importance of customer experience [4]. Customer experience has become an important part of marketing and service development, and it is the basis of the emerging experience economy [see 4]. Successful attempts to build connection with customers and to ensure customer satisfaction and superior customer experience require the use of customer data. There are growing concerns among consumers about revealing personal information, and many are

L. M. Camarinha-Matos et al. (Eds.): PRO-VE 2019, IFIP AICT 568, pp. 516–526, 2019.
https://doi.org/10.1007/978-3-030-28464-0_45

dissatisfied with the way in which some organizations collect and use their information. This may pose a major problem, hampering growth in some areas, such as e-commerce [5]. In general, digital servicescapes and markets pose unique information privacy threats due to two-way communications possibilities [see 5]. Moreover, new General Data Protection Regulation (GDPR) regulations pinpointed data privacy issues when the legislation was enforced within the EU in spring 2018. New regulations have underlined the importance of customer experience in a service context The GDPR regulations has two major aspects related to use of data, the need for permission for the customer data utilization [6] and the more general need for companies to become more customer driven when utilizing data [see 7]. There is an identified research gap concerning to customer preference and choice related to organizational use of their information [3].

The aim of this paper was to focus on data privacy in the context of the customer journey and in different service industries. In this study, data privacy refers to the claim of individuals to determine when, how, and to what extent information about them is communicated to others [see 3]. The research questions were as follows: (1) is there a difference in privacy concerns throughout the phases of the customer journey, and (2) how do different service industries differ in terms of privacy concerns? We also discuss about related data analytics theme. This paper consists of four sections. After this introduction, customer privacy concerns in the context of the customer journey have been discussed. Then, the methodology and survey sample have been defined. In the last two parts of the study, conclusions and implications have been discussed.

2 Data Privacy Throughout the Customer Journey

Digital service environments and digital tools have become widespread in the service industry in recent years. Although these practices have allowed the target group to participate in a branded e-marketplace, consumer advocates have expressed growing concern about the invasion of privacy caused by e-marketers' information collection practices [8]. Customer interaction, which may be one of the most important elements in service delivery [see 4], looks quite different in digital servicescapes than in traditional personal interactions between services clerks and customers. Moreover, the development of marketing and service practices using consumer data and analytics has advanced rapidly in recent years, which has raised data privacy concerns among consumers.

2.1 Privacy Concerns

Previous research [9–11] has shown that privacy concerns affect online customer behavior during the use of digital services. Customers may become concerned if they feel that their privacy has been invaded or threatened in some way [2]. News items about the vulnerability of digital services and stolen private data promote privacy concerns among customers. The vulnerability of digital services also creates potential business risks for companies [12]. Privacy concerns are also directly connected to customers' purchase behavior, as online stores require customers to provide personal information while shopping online [2, 4]. Customers are mindful of privacy concerns while shopping online. However, this may create a competitive advantage for companies who are good at creating online trust between customers and service providers [13]. Previous research has shown that customers felt fewer privacy concerns when they interacted with trusted retailers [9, 10]. Additionally, good control over customers' shared personal information and visible data collection processes have been shown to improve trust [14, 15].

Many factors, including information type, situational factors, the features of service providers, and the individual characteristics of customers have been shown to affect customer's privacy concerns [10, 11]. However, there are differences between individual customers [16], as each observes the potential risks of online shopping for products and services differently [17]. Gender differences and the health of individuals may also influence privacy concerns [11].

2.2   Customer Journey

A customer journey can be defined as 'a description of customer experience where different touchpoints characterize customers interaction with a brand, product, or service of interest' [18]. Følstad and Kvale [19] highlight the processual and experiential aspects of services as seen from the customer's viewpoint. It is described as the repeated interactions between a service provider and the customer within a customer journey. Customers interact with service providers via different digital touchpoints throughout their customer journey [20]. In the omni-channel environment, customer interactions often follow a non-linear structure. Additionally, the critical interaction is with the brand, not with the channel [21]. This scenario is typical in digital platform interactions in general and in the service industry. Customers may use multiple devices in different phases of their customer journey. During the early stages of a customer journey, when contacting a potential customer, search engines, Search Engine Marketing (SEO), Search Engine Marketing (SEM), and display ads play a critical role. For example, search engine results pages present a convenient way for consumers to gather information about service brands [22]. Behavioral targeting connects consumers with brands based on data relating to their past online behaviors. These data could comprise web pages they have visited, the time they spent on each page, and the things they put in their shopping baskets or purchased online [23]. All these actions, which are based on the use of customer data, take place in conversions during a customer journey.

2.3   Service Industries

Service industries differ across many attributes. Early service industry categorization and conceptualization focused on distinguishing the characteristics of service delivery from the sale of physical products [see 24, 25]. Service industry classification has focused on service delivery or encounter-based activities or solutions, including social interaction and perceived risk [26] and service script-based classifications [27]. It has also involved examining the level of emotional attachment or investment a customer has in the customer experience process, for example, a customer is likely to have a lower level of emotional attachment to purchasing fast food compared to having medical treatment [28]. Cheng, Anderson, Zhu, and Choi [22] have enriched the existing literature on service categorization with their explanation of the complex online service environment. In this study, we have analyzed four different industries; Municipal health stations, Private health stations, Insurance companies, Hobby clubs and Grocery stores. The last two industries represent a low level of perceived risk and purchase effort where consumers are thought to have little involvement, while both health station alternatives represent high involvement service consumption situation. In this classification, we followed Stell and Donoho [29] line of thinking. In general, customer involvement varies from passive participation of customer, such as simple physical presence, to a very high degree of user integration as a part of the service process [30].

In general, categorization and classification models and concepts help management understand and learn about service operations in different industries [31]. While service industry characteristics modify service encounters and operations in general, it is likely that customers in different service sectors have different levels of concern related to their data privacy when interacting with a company.

3 Methods

Data were collected from undergraduate students in Finland, who represented customers of healthcare companies. Student samples are often used in academic research. Yavas [32] states that students are appropriate surrogates in studies where e.g. attitude–behavior relationships or orders of attitudes are researched. University students also represent young digital customers in the omni-channel environments. There were 309 responses, of which 306 were valid and were used in this research. Descriptive statistics revealed that the sample was female-dominant; 67% (n = 205) of respondents were female, and 33% (n = 101) were male.

Participants were sent an email that included a web-link to the questionnaire. All participants who answered the questionnaire were invited to participate in a lottery that gave them the chance to win minor gifts. We used the questionnaire to measure privacy concerns using four items adopted from Martin et al. [3]. Tradeoff value questionnaire items were adopted from Martin et al. [3] and information sensitive items from [33]. In the questionnaire, respondents were asked to rate value using a 5- point Likert scale ranging from totally agree (5) to totally disagree (1). Results were analyzed using Statistical Package for the Social Sciences (SPSS) version 25.0.

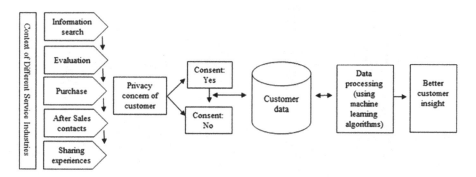

Fig. 1. The relationship of customer journey and industry segments to privacy concern.

In Fig. 1, a conceptual model of the study has been shown. This study examines how privacy concern vary throughout different phases of the customer journey and in different service industries. The prior research [9–11] reveals that privacy concerns affect online customer behaviors. Additionally, information type, situational factors, the features of service providers have been shown to affect customer's privacy concerns [10, 11]. The individual characteristics of customers also affect to privacy concerns indicating that there are differences between individuals [16]. Furthermore, differences between the phases of customer journey and service industries may be related to information sensitivity, as context and situation affect the behavior of customers. From an interactional psychology perspective, situational factors influence customer behavior and vice versa [34]. Thus, a customer may more easily give their consent to use his or her personal data during different phases of the customer journey and in the context of different service industries. This has significant implications for the digitalization projects of companies and for collaborations with customers in different business ecosystems.

4   Results

Data Privacy Throughout the Customer Journey

We analyzed respondents' willingness to share information at different phases of the customer journey. The journey process consisted of information search, alternative evaluation, purchase, after sales contact, and the sharing of information, such as customer experiences and reviews. The model was adopted from Solomon et al.'s [35] customer journey process model (Table 1).

Table 1. Respondents' willingness to share their data at different phases of the customer journey.

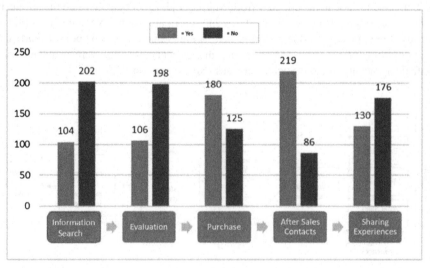

Findings indicated that respondents were more willing to share their data when they were "in buying mode" and actually in the process of buying a product or service. On the other hand, respondents had data privacy concerns at the beginning of their customer journeys. These results challenged current marketing practices, such as re- targeting, which is typically done in a digital environment. We further analyzed the sample according to gender, and there were some indications that female respondents were more willing to interact with the company during the after-purchase phase, but differences were not statistically significant.

Data Privacy Within Different Service Industries
We asked respondents how willing they would be to disclose personal information in five different service industry cases (Table 2).

Table 2. Respondents' willingness to disclose personal information in different service industries (n = 306)

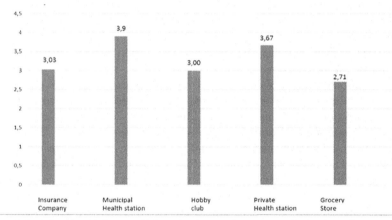

"I do not feel comfortable with the type of information that (service x) requests from me" (totally agree = 1, ..., totally disagree = 5)

Both private and municipal health stations were examples of services that respondents access with high levels of emotional attachment and cognitive processing, while a grocery store was a service environment in which the role of service encounters was smaller.

Findings indicated that respondents were more willing to disclose their personal data in service settings where they were more involved. Here, involvement referred to consumers' motivation to process product related information at a given point in time [see 35]. The definition also consisted of a person's perceptions of the relevance of an object. We assumed that municipal and private health stations represented service situations where more cognitive processing is likely to take place during a customer journey; hence, the relevance of these settings was higher than in other examples.

We tested our sample with a t-test to explore gender differences in data privacy concerns in different industries. In all industries, female respondents were more willing to share their private information with a company than male respondents. The t-test for equality of means indicated that this difference was statistically significant in insurance company services ($p = 0.02$) and private healthcare stations ($p = 0.04$).

5 Discussion

The first research question in this study concerned differences in privacy concerns related to the phases of the customer journey. Findings revealed that respondents (72%) were most willing to share personal data with service providers after their purchase. Of the total sample, 59% were willing to share their personal data while completing their purchase. Respondents were least willing to share their personal data during the information search (34%) and evaluation (35%) phases. Respondents were more willing to share personal data when they were already customers of service providers or when they were purchasing products and services. In these cases, they would have built a relationship with service providers. Respondents had privacy concerns at the beginning of their customer journey, when they would not have developed a formal relationship with service providers.

The second research question concerned differences in privacy concerns across service industries. Results suggested that healthcare information was more sensitive than information concerning purchases from grocery stores, hobby organizations, or insurance companies. Information sensitivity varied across service sectors. Different value chains and business networks deal with different types of information, which may affect the same customer differently. Moreover, our findings indicated that female customers were more willing to interact with companies than male customers.

There is little previous research on privacy concerns throughout the customer journey and in different service industries. This study filled this research gap by exploring personal data disclosure throughout the customer journey and in different service industries. Respondents seemed to focus constantly on information sensitivity and the value that they would receive if they provided personal information. We concluded that at the heart of most privacy concerns is a trade-off between the costs and benefits of the disclosure of personal information. This aligned with prior research suggesting that customers evaluate the pros and cons of a behavior before acting (see, for example, Lanier and Saini [36].

The current study has contributed to data privacy and service marketing practices in different service industries. Our study supported the personalization-privacy paradox [37], which suggests that personalization can both enhance and diminish customer engagement with the firm. That is, targeted offerings generated by customer data analysis may enhance the customer experience, but they may also raise privacy concerns among customers. The critical issue here appears to be the phase of customer journey. Our findings indicated that the best times for businesses to use customized communication is close to when the consumer actually makes a purchase and right after the purchase. This raises concerns over cookie remarketing activities that are typically conducted according to potential customers' browsing behavior. If personalized messages and actions trigger customers' privacy concerns about how the firm is using their personal information, then these may lead to decreased engagement [37 p. 98]. Privacy concerns among customers may increase skepticism toward and avoidance of advertising and can prompt negative actions. All these reactions may reduce overall marketing effectiveness [37 p. 99] and harm customer experience. In general, customer experience may be good (enjoyable) or bad (unenjoyable), leading to positive or negative customer response with regard to value, image, quality, patronage, loyalty, satisfaction, recommendations, and purchase intentions [38, p. 655.].

Today's companies operate in collaborative networks that utilize computer networks [39]. Collaborative networks are also becoming data-rich environments [39, 40] and it raises issues such as the privacy concern of customers. Service ecosystems based on collaborative networks include new platform ecosystems who compete in service offering without ownership to a subject [see 41]. They collect and manage data to operate their business ecosystem and several companies participate value creation in different phases of value chains Thus, data sources that are needed to serve and build customer relationships and operative processes are located in collaborative networks of customers, partners, and service providers. From the customer's viewpoint, privacy issues are related to all phases of a customer journey, as each phase is often served and operated by different service providers. For example, search history and marketing relate to marketers, such as Google and advertisement agents, while purchase and payment data are collected by platform owners and payment operators, and service providers deal with usage and customer satisfaction data. Hence, throughout their customer journey, customers interact with many service providers, providing or withholding consent for each to collect their personal data. Data privacy is not a single point event but is a key question in the operations of collaborative networks.

The findings provide new knowledge for marketers about the respondents' information sensitivity concerning different industry segments and privacy concern relating to the phases of customer journey. Privacy concern in different phases of the customer journey often reflects to the different roles of service providers in the value chain of service ecosystems. Marketers should pay attention to these differences in planning data collection and motivating customers to provide consent for the use of their private data in managing omni-channel operations. From the perspective of collaborative networks literature, the findings contribute to the processes of collaborative networks [42], especially to the management and governance of omni-channel service ecosystems.

6 Conclusions

This study showed that companies and business networks should consider privacy concerns when planning and designing new digital services. Privacy concerns are closely related to data analytics, which are crucial in digital service delivery. Findings suggested that businesses should focus customer engagement actions close to the actual buying phase and that information sensitivity across different service sectors varied. During the early stages of the customer journey, companies should focus on offering and brand development and possibly SEO activities, which may draw a customer's attention without provoking data privacy concerns. Additionally, companies should give special attention to the visibility of data usage at the beginning of a buying journey.

The basic limitation of this study is its quite small target group consisting of student sample. It limits the generalizability of the results, and this study increases only understanding about the factors that affect the respondents' online behavior. Finally, this study suggested that respecting customers and their data privacy is an investment in relationship building. The results of this study have suggested that researchers should explore privacy concern empirically, especially in the context of value chains and networks, as customers deal with several actors throughout their journey. Additionally, the different types of information in different customer journeys merit further research.

Acknowledgments. The authors would like to thank the Big Data–Big Business (BIG) Project, all parties behind the project, and Business Finland (the Finnish innovation funding, trade, investment, and travel promotion organization) for their support of this study.

References

1. Alamäki, A., Rantala, T., Valkokari, K., Palomäki, K.: Business roles in creating value from data in collaborative networks. In: Camarinha-Matos, L.M., Afsarmanesh, H., Rezgui, Y. (eds.) PRO-VE 2018. IAICT, vol. 534, pp. 612–622. Springer, Cham (2018). https://doi.org/10.1007/978-3-319-99127-6_53
2. Ackerman, M.S., Cranor, L.F., Reagle, J.: Privacy in E-commerce: examining user scenarios and privacy preferences. In: Proceedings of the 1st ACM Conference on Electronic Commerce, pp. 1–8. ACM (1999)
3. Martin, K.D., Murphy, P.E.: The role of data privacy in marketing. J. Acad. Mark. Sci. **45** (2), 135–155 (2017)
4. Walter, U., Edvardsson, B., Öström, Å.: Drivers of customers' service experiences: a study in the restaurant industry. Manag. Serv. Qual. **20**(3), 236–258 (2010)
5. Malhotra, N.K., Kim, S.S., Agarwal, J.: Internet users' information privacy concerns (IUIPC): the construct, the scale, and a causal model. Inf. Syst. Res. **15**(4), 336–355 (2004)
6. Kolah, A., Foss, B.: Unlocking the power of data under the new EU general data protection regulation. J. Direct Data Digital Mark. Pract. **16**(4), 270–274 (2015)
7. Mitchell, A.: GDPR: evolutionary or revolutionary? J. Direct Data Digital Mark. Pract. **17** (4), 217–221 (2016)
8. Youn, S.: Determinants of online privacy concern and its influence on privacy protection behaviors among young adolescents. J. Consum. Aff. **43**(3), 389–418 (2009)
9. Chellappa, R.K., Sin, R.G.: Personalization versus privacy: an empirical examination of the online consumer's Dilemma. Inf. Technol. Manag. **6**(2–3), 181–202 (2005)
10. Bleier, A., Eisenbeiss, M.: The importance of trust for personalized online advertising. J. Retail. **91**(3), 390–409 (2015)
11. Wilkowska, W., Ziefle, M.: Privacy and data security in E-health: requirements from the user's perspective. Health Inf. J. **18**(3), 191–201 (2012)
12. Martin, K.D., Borah, A., Palmatier, R.W.: Data privacy: effects on customer and firm performance. J. Mark. **81**(1), 36–58 (2017)

13. Bart, Y., Shankar, V., Sultan, F., Urban, G.L.: Are the drivers and role of online trust the same for all web sites and consumers? A large-scale exploratory empirical study. J. Mark. **69** (4), 133–152 (2005)
14. Culnan, M.J., Armstrong, P.K.: Information privacy concerns, procedural fairness, and impersonal trust: an empirical investigation. Organ. Sci. **10**(1), 104–115 (1999)
15. Phelps, J., Nowak, G., Ferrell, E.: Privacy concerns and consumer willingness to provide personal information. J. Public Policy Mark. **19**(1), 27–41 (2000)
16. Sjöberg, L.: Factors in risk perception. Risk Anal.: Int. J. **20**(1), 1–12 (2000)
17. Nordin, F., Kowalkowski, C.: Solutions offerings: a critical review and reconceptualisation. J. Serv. Manag. **21**(4), 441–459 (2010)
18. Wolny, J., Charoensuksai, N.: Mapping customer journeys in multichannel decision-making. J. Direct Data Digital Mark. Pract. **15**(4), 317–326 (2014)
19. Følstad, A., Kvale, K.: Customer journeys: a systematic literature review. J. Serv. Theory Pract. **28**(2), 196–227 (2018)
20. Hallikainen, H., Alamäki, A., Laukkanen, T.: Individual preferences of digital touchpoints: a latent class analysis. J. Retail. Consum. Serv. **50**, 386–393 (2018). (Advanced online publication)
21. Elizabeth, M.P., Peltier, J.W., Barger, V.A.: Omni-channel marketing, integrated marketing communications, and consumer engagement. J. Res. Interact. Mark. **11**(2), 185–197 (2017)
22. Cheng, M., Anderson, C.K., Zhu, Z., Choi, S.C.: Service online search ads: from a consumer journey view. J. Serv. Mark. **32**(2), 126–141 (2018)
23. Yu, S., Hudders, L., Cauberghe, V.: Targeting the luxury consumer. J. Fash. Mark. Manag. **21**(2), 187–205 (2017)
24. Brown, S.W., Fisk, R.P., Bitner, M.J.: The development and emergence of services marketing thought. Int. J. Serv. Ind. Manag. **5**(1), 21–48 (1994)
25. Grönroos, C.: Service Management and Marketing: A Customer Relationship Management Approach. Wiley, Hoboken (2001)
26. Johnston, R., Clark, G.: Service Operations Management. Pearson Education, London (2001)
27. Shoemaker, S.: Scripts: precursor of consumer expectations. Cornell Hotel Restaurant Adm. Q. **3**(1), 42–53 (1996)
28. Bolton, R.N., Gustafsson, A., McColl-Kennedy, J.R., Sirianni, N.J., Tse, D.K.: Small details that make big differences: a radical approach to consumption experience as a firm's differentiating strategy. J. Serv. Manag. **25**(2), 253–274 (2014)
29. Stell, R., Donoho, C.L.: Classifying services from a consumer perspective. J. Serv. Mark. **10** (6), 33–44 (1996)
30. Dadfar, H., Brege, S., Sedigheh Sarah, E.S.: Customer involvement in service production, delivery and quality: the challenges and opportunities. Int. J. Qual. Serv. Sci. **5**(1), 46–65 (2013)
31. Payane, A.: The Essence of Services Marketing. Prentice-Hall, Upper Saddle River (1993)
32. Yavas, U.: Research note: students as subjects in advertising and marketing research. Int. Mark. Rev. **11**(4), 35–43 (1994)
33. Dinev, T., Xu, H., Smith, J.H., Hart, P.: Information privacy and correlates: an empirical attempt to bridge and distinguish privacy-related concepts. Eur. J. Inf. Syst. **22**(3), 295–316 (2013)
34. Terborg, J.R.: Interactional psychology and research on human behavior in organizations. Acad. Manag. Rev. **6**(4), 569–576 (1981)
35. Solomon, R.M., Bamossy, G.S., Askegaard, R., Hogg, M.K.: Consumer Behaviour – A European Perspective. Prentice-Hall, Upper Saddle River (2016)

36. Lanier, C.D., Saini, A.: Understanding consumer privacy: a review and future directions. Acad. Mark. Sci. Rev. **12**(2), 1–48 (2008)
37. Aguirre, E., Roggeveen, A.L., Grewal, D., Wetzels, M.: The personalization-privacy paradox: implications for new media. J. Consum. Mark. **33**(2), 98–110 (2016)
38. Jain, R., Aagja, J., Bagdare, S.: Customer experience - a review and research agenda. J. Serv. Theory Pract. **27**(3), 642–662 (2017)
39. Camarinha-Matos, L.M., Fornasiero, R., Afsarmanesh, H.: Collaborative networks as a core enabler of Industry 4.0. In: Camarinha-Matos, L.M., Afsarmanesh, H., Fornasiero, R. (eds.) PRO-VE 2017. IAICT, vol. 506, pp. 3–17. Springer, Cham (2017). https://doi.org/10.1007/978-3-319-65151-4_1
40. Bruno, G., Antonelli, D., Villa, A.: A reference ontology to support product lifecycle management. Procedia CIRP **33**, 41–46 (2015)
41. Appio, F.P., Martini, A., Massa, S., Testa, S.: Collaborative network of firms: antecedents and state-of-the-art properties. Int. J. Prod. Res. **55**(7), 2121–2134 (2017)
42. Barile, S., Lusch, R., Reynoso, J., Saviano, M., Spohrer, J.: Systems, networks, and ecosystems in service research. J. Serv. Manag. **27**(4), 652–674 (2016)

Connected and Multimodal Passenger Transport Through Big Data Analytics: Case Tampere City Region, Finland

Riku Viri[1]([⊠]), Lili Aunimo[2], and Heli Aramo-Immonen[3]

[1] Tampere University, Transport Research Centre Verne,
P.O. Box 600, 33014 Tampere, Finland
riku.viri@tuni.fi
[2] Haaga-Helia University of Applied Sciences, Ratapihantie 13,
00520 Helsinki, Finland
lili.aunimo@haaga-helia.fi
[3] Örebro University, Business School, Fakultetsgatan 1, 701 82 Örebro, Sweden
heli.aramo-immonen@oru.se

Abstract. Passenger transport is becoming more and more connected and multimodal. Instead of just taking a series of vehicles to complete a journey, the passenger is actually interacting with a connected cyber-physical social (CPS) transport system. In this study, we present a case study where big data from various sources is combined and analyzed to support and enhance the transport system in the Tampere region. Different types of static and real-time data sources and transportation related APIs are investigated. The goal is to find ways in which big data and collaborative networks can be used to improve the CPS transport system itself and the passenger satisfaction related to it. The study shows that even though the exploitation of big data does not directly improve the state of the physical transport infrastructure, it helps in utilizing more of its capacity. Secondly, the use of big data makes it more attractive to passengers.

Keywords: Big data · Analytics · Collaborative network · API ·
Cyber-physical social system · Passenger transport · Mobility · Open data

1 Introduction

Passenger transport is becoming more and more connected and multimodal. Instead of just purchasing a ticket to a single means of transportation, the future passenger will purchase a mobility service that will take him from the point of departure to the point of arrival. A multimodal transport service combines several different ways of transport – such as bus, train and a bicycle ride - under a single transport service. This multimodal and connected transport service is regarded a MaaS (Mobility as a Service) if the following requirements are met: (1) the physical transport service is augmented with other services such as trip planning, reservations and payments, (2) the services can be used through a single interface, and (3) the services are packaged into a tailored mobility package similar to a monthly mobile phone contract [1]. ABI Research [2]

© IFIP International Federation for Information Processing 2019
Published by Springer Nature Switzerland AG 2019
L. M. Camarinha-Matos et al. (Eds.): PRO-VE 2019, IFIP AICT 568, pp. 527–538, 2019.
https://doi.org/10.1007/978-3-030-28464-0_46

estimates that MaaS revenues will exceed \$1 trillion by 2030 and customers' mindset is moving towards buying a service instead owning.

Currently, during the journey, the passenger will typically use several different means of transportation and hopefully receive timely information concerning his itinerary. Ticket purchases, information seeking and sharing as well as real-time communications regarding the purchased journey will all performed using a digital application. Thus, instead of just taking a series of vehicles to complete a journey, the passenger will actually be interacting with a connected cyber-physical [see e.g. 3] social (CPS) transport system. The system is constantly producing stream data, such as IoT data from the vehicles, mobility data of the passengers and interaction data created by passengers and transport service providers. When all this data is combined with static and standardized data such as public transport trajectory, ticket fare, service provider and geographic data, we have a big data landscape on which the connected CPS transport ecosystem can be built. The different layers of a CPS transport system are illustrated in Fig. 1.

PASSENGER ACTION	CYBER	PHYSICAL	SOCIAL
Control the system	Personalize the user interface based on user data (also accessibility issues such as speech user interfaces).	Priority in traffic lights based on personal mobility data.	Ride sharing based on crowd sourced information on future rides by private people.
Reservations and payments	MaaS plan consisting of a service level and a monthly fee.	A ticket containing the journey from door-to-door and including several modalities.	Digital payment applications enabling exchange of mobility services between private people.
Passive consumption of information	Timetables and trajectories in a digital application.	Real-time location, timetable and availability of places – information on physical screens.	Crowd-sourced real-time information about disruptions and tips on trajectories.

Fig. 1. The CPS transport system divided into three layers from the point of view of the passenger interacting with the system. Each layer and dimension of the CPS transport system is illustrated with an example.

The research on multimodal collaborative CPS transport systems is scant. There are existing models for dealing with some aspects of the multimodal collaborative transport systems. One example is the proposal for a common architecture for payments handling in such a system [4]. However, there is no systematic study about all aspects of a multimodal collaborative CPS transport system. In this paper, we study through a case study the data-architecture of a multimodal collaborative CPS transport system in the Tampere city region. Special attention is given to all available open data – stream and static as well as to open interfaces that can be used to control the system (such as the traffic light API) as well as to how passengers interact with the data using digital applications. Based on this, a novel data architecture for a big data driven multimodal and connected CPS transport system is developed.

There are currently several initiatives that foster the advent of transport 4.0. Transport 4.0 means that different and previously disconnected forms of transportation are being integrated into one single passenger interaction that combines several modalities of transport and that takes the passenger from door-to-door. In this paper, we adhere to the general definition of Industrie 4.0 [5] from which the concept of Transport 4.0 is derived. We also regard MaaS as a business model that implements the concept on Transport 4.0. The initiatives towards Transport 4.0 are related to either legislation or availability and standardization of transportation related data and application programming interfaces (APIs) or both. One example of such an initiative of the level of the European Union is the first phase of National Access Point (NAP) system which will become mandatory by the end of 2019. The NAP system has to be implemented in every member state. It contains the essential information about every national mobility service provider with more detailed information coming in subsequent phases scheduled in December 2020 and 2021 [6].

Currently there are multiple sources of transport related open data. Most common are SIRI and GTFS - APIs that are used in public transport. SIRI is standardized in Europe and it is used in several cities and regions to offer real-time location data on public transport [7]. GTFS is a globally used specification used to publish bus routes and timetables for journey planning [8]. It was originally created for Google Maps, but now days majority of big public transport operators in Europe provide GTFS formatted timetables. GTFS has also been extended to support real-time fleet updates [9].

In this study we present how big data and analytics can produce value to transport organizations, cities and end users. In addition, a data-architecture derived from the case study is presented. The goal of the study was twofold. Firstly, it aimed to find ways in which big data and different interfaces can be used to improve the multimodal and collaborative CPS transport system itself and the passenger satisfaction. Secondly, the study aimed to illustrate the data-architecture of such a system. The study contributes to the big data, transportation 4.0 and CPS transport systems debate where various types of data is collected from several actors participating in the collaborative network. The paper is organized as follows: First, we review the fundamental concepts behind the study, namely: (1) Big data analytics for decision makers, (2) Big data in MaaS and (3) Collaborative networks in passenger transport. In Sect. 3, we present both the research methodology used and the case of Tampere City region in Finland. Sections 4 and 5 present the system architecture and results through example cases. Section 6 includes a discussion on the significance and contribution of the results.

2 Big Data and Connected Multimodal Passenger Transport Systems

The expected impacts of big data analytics in passenger transportation are related to both the assistance of decision makers and to the development of new data-driven services for passengers. Big data also serves as a technological enabler for new business models and for a new platform economy.

2.1 Big Data Analytics for Decision Makers

Decision makers at different levels of public administration as well as in the wide industry of passenger transportation and travel benefit from convenient tools for strategic planning like feasibility studies, environmental, competitor, and trend analyses. Analyzed big data gives keys to follow and understand consumer and traveler behavior better, but also in some cases to upgrade customer service through optimization. The taxi business provides a good example of this. Several studies show how passengers' travel trajectories and city structure have been mined from taxi ride data [10, 11]. This information may be used in order to understand passenger behavior and in transport planning. In addition to this, the taxi business may also use taxi ride data for optimizing its business [12, 13]. Typical optimization cases in the taxi business include optimizing the location of idle taxis at a given point in time and optimizing the trajectory of a taxi that has a passenger at a given moment. This contributes to the goal of more sustainable cities as the existing resources (taxis and routes) can be exploited in an optimal manner and the need for new resources may be decreased.

In addition to being able to optimize the usage of resources, it is also very important to provide fast reaction to changes in traffic flows. Examples of events that produce changes are mass events, sudden malfunction in some part of the transport system and changes in weather. To be able to react to these events timely, real-time or near real-time information as well as information about the future - such as upcoming events and weather forecasts - are needed. This kind of data is readily available e.g. from devices that are located in vehicles, but also from passengers' devices such as mobile phone location data and smart card data. Chen et al. [14] have performed human mobility pattern mining on mobile phone data and Tao et al. [15] have used smart card data in passenger transport related case studies.

In addition to the above-mentioned proprietary data sources, freely available open data sources and open interfaces for retrieving the data are a very important source of transportation-related data. Open datasets have been used e.g. in data driven customer demand prediction and dynamic pricing [16]. Pereira et al. [17] use freely available event data from the Internet to predict public transport rides in the City of Singapore.

Big data analytics supports transport companies as well as public communal, local district and governmental partners and planning associations in their strategic decisions. It also complements the decision process with data for potential assessment, different studies, and analyses. Big Data analytics contributes to itinerary and route planning of transportation companies (e.g. coach/bus and car rental companies), but probably also to tour operators, incoming agencies and travel management departments in private companies and public institutions including fleet management.

Big data analytics tools can inform mobility center how they can include the data in their day-to-day-work for example. Big data analytics allows to improve the customer service of travel intermediaries and travel service suppliers by allowing to react faster e.g. in strikes and/or unpredictable occurrence of traffic disruptions.

In order to fully utilize big data analytics in passenger transportation EU-wide guidelines and recommendations regarding the integration of new data sources as well as a novel data formats are needed. Furthermore, existing privacy and legislation frameworks need to be noted. For example, in Europe, the GDPR (General Data Privacy Regulation) [18] has to be taken into account when dealing with data that may contain privacy issues. Only data that has been properly anonymized is free from regulations concerning privacy. In turn, big data analytics provides an infrastructure and analytical functionality enabling the prediction of mobility and congestion hotspots.

2.2 Big Data in Multimodal Transport Services

Multimodal transport services mean that the passenger only purchases one ticket from the point of departure A to the point of arrival B. The journey from A to B typically involves several modalities of transport, such as airplane, ship, train, tram, bus, car sharing, taxi and/or bicycle. The transportation service providers that offer different modalities of transport are an example of a collaborative network. A collaborative network (CN) is a network of largely autonomous, geographically distributed, and heterogeneous organizations that collaborate to better achieve common goals, and whose interactions are supported by a computer network [19]. The modalities may change dynamically during the journey due to traffic incidents, weather or traffic conditions, among others. An important part of the multimodal transport service is the application that is used to communicate between the collaborative network of service providers and the passenger.

The MaaS business model is an example of an implementation of a multimodal transportation service where the digital applications related to it are an important part of the service. These digital applications are typically are to route planning, payments and communicating timely information from the transport provider to the passenger.

The tools used in big data analytics enhances opportunities also for start-ups and other companies to innovate new mobility services and enable new business models such as new platforms, interfaces and APIs for example. All this is possible given that the MaaS companies adhere to the local privacy regulations. One good solution for sharing mobility data containing personal identifiers between organizations is to anonymize it. It is important to choose the correct level of anonymization so that the data still has value.

Big data analytics could be integrated in existing mobility services like Moovel, Switch and Whim. However, also completely new mobile service possibilities will appear in connection to analyzed data available. Big data analytics also contributes to the emerging MaaS business model that many of the new start-ups have adopted.

2.3 Collaborative Networks in Passenger Transport

The collaborative network of multimodal transport service providers presented in the previous section is just one example of the existing and future networks in passenger transport. There are several other examples of collaborative networks in transport. Most of them involve organizations, but some also involve passengers in an active role. Crowdsourcing and sharing economy are typical examples of collaborative networks in transport. The use of open data also calls for collaborative networks because the producers and users of open data seldom are those who build the applications,

Crowdsourcing and social transportation offer new possibilities for passengers to organize their journeys [20]. Crowdsourcing may also be used in cases of traffic disruption where the official travel service providers fail to deliver accurate and on-time information. Crowdsourcing is a sourcing model in which individuals or organizations obtain goods and services, including ideas, from a large, relatively open and often rapidly evolving group of internet users. This type of group can be called collaborative network. Crowdsourcing divides work between participants to achieve a cumulative result. [e.g. 21, 22]

Sharing economy - also called collaborative economy - is a mode of consumption where goods and services are not owned by a single user, but temporarily accessed by members of a collaborative network with or without charge. Sharing economy can refer to social peer-to-peer processes that include sharing of access to goods and services [23], or any rental transaction facilitated by a two-sided market, sometimes also including business to consumer (B2C) [24].

3   Method and Case Description

In this study, we firstly have a review in conceptual part of the paper. Secondly, we picked a case region to support our findings on what kind of open data platforms and APIs there are and what is already being implemented on top of the APIs to make the stakeholders benefit from the data. Since the value from the data for the citizens using the services cannot be presented using a numerical method, we use a set of case examples to illustrate how the solutions built upon the data generate benefits to different stakeholders. Both pilots and known products are considered. The region chosen is the Tampere Region, which is the second largest metropolitan area in Finland with about 385 000 inhabitants. The city center of Tampere is located between two lakes limiting the connection possibilities through the city. Thus, it is important to develop a system that exploits the currently existing physical infrastructure and uses it as efficiently as possible.

On national level, Finland moved towards new legislation about mobility services, which aimed to unify all transport regulations into one code. A large part of the changes in new act was to achieve cost savings in transportation due to information system development and new open data interfaces. One of main targets was to open all the essential data of transportation services to public and to define the provisions of more unified ticket and payment systems, which would allow better combination of different service providers and forms of transportation [25]. Finland as a country has also been early adopter of new data interfaces, such as Digiroad and Digitraffic [26, 27]. Therefore, many of Finland's largest cities have some similar APIs and sources freely available compared to Tampere. To simplify the results, the paper is chosen to use one case area, in this case, Tampere, which is familiar to the writers and is one of the cities having the most data and APIs available. The city also has a program to create new smart city solutions in cooperation with local research facilities and businesses.

On top the Finnish data, the City of Tampere has also multiple data sources that support the mobility development. Some of the APIs are only in use in the City of Tampere but some also cover the whole region. Examples of different APIs, in addition to already mentioned GTFS- and SIRI-APIs, available consist for example for traffic lights, route planning (for different modes), parking and incidents and roadworks [28].

A large part of the APIs are available freely, though some special information is available upon agreement. For example open parking API gives basic information, but fares and exact capacities are in closed API [29]. Different sources of both national and regional data can be seen in Fig. 2. The Figure also shows examples of amount of regional data provided.

Examples of different data sources – Case Tampere Region

	NATIONAL SOURCES	REGIONAL SOURCES	EXAMPLES OF DATA PROVIDED
maps & roads	Digiroad National maps from different government bodies	Local maps for different transport modes More specific POIs (for example status of parking areas in addition to location)	Road and mapping data is derived from national sources 21 parking facilities around city provide status information about their capacity
routes	Digiroad Digitransit	API for journey planning per different transport modes GTFS and SIRI for public transport	GTFS inludes information of all public transport in region SIRI curretly has location data of about 75% of buses in use. Some regional routes do not have the equipment. The ongoing system renewal may also affect the share of buses visible on system currently.
traffic volumes & incidents	Digitraffic (for example national TMS data, incident reports and roadworks on national road network and positions and status of trains on rail network)	Own calculation points and sensors (for example traffic light sensors)	All city's 173 traffic lights deliver real-time information about traffic volume and congestion based on the detectors.
other	Weather information and forecasts	Noise and pollution measurements around city	Noise is measured every 5 years (both day and night) and modeled for whole city area and forecasted to year 2040

Fig. 2. Examples of different data sources – Case Tampere Region [29–33]

National data sources include for example different official platforms, like Digiroad, Digitransit and Digitraffic. Even though shown separated in Fig. 2, most of the data sources are linked together. For example, Digiroad and national maps provide basis to local mapping solutions and Digitransit combines regional GTFS-data to build national data [34]. It should also be noted that these services itself rely on different global data sources, like Digitransit uses OpenStreetMap-data based mapping solution [34].

The City of Tampere is also focused on collaboration in mobility area to create new solutions and pilots. ITS Factory is a network that consist of the city and local authorities, local businesses and research facilities. The main concept of the network is to connect different stakeholders. The city provides different test areas and opens new mobility data sources to allow companies to pilot and develop new services and products. Different research facilities are closely connected in the process as a part of development and pilot phases. The City of Tampere also hosts test sites to pilot for example 5G networking, autonomous cars in everyday traffic and indoor positioning.

4   Results

Based on the case study of the Tampere region mobility services and on the different information sources in use, the authors propose a novel data architecture for digital services that enable MaaS. This architecture is depicted in Fig. 3.

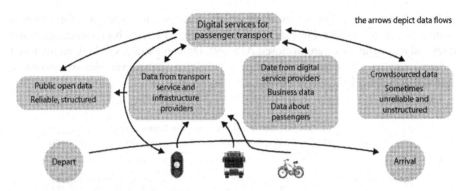

Fig. 3. The data architecture for a MaaS service. The journey of the passenger starts with a bus and ends with a bicycle ride. The bottom layer illustrates the physical dimension of the system. It could consist of any combination and number of transport modes operated by different service providers as well as of physical infrastructure that is connected to the network. In this figure, the traffic lights are connected to the data repository as well as to the digital services.

As can be observed from the Fig. 3, there is a collaborative network of organizations and end users that all contribute to creating the big data that is the fuel of the MaaS solutions. In the bottom layer of the picture, we can observe that there is IoT data generated from the vehicles. This may be real-time location data as well as real-time occupation rate data. Special sensors may also measure the availability of wheelchair, children's buggy and luggage slots, for example. The middle layer of the image consists of the big data collected by different organizations of the collaborative network. The leftmost data source contains open data such as the data available through the NAP-interface or SIRI and GTFS data regarding timetables and trajectories. The transport and infrastructure providers create this data and it is reliable and well structured.

The next data source is created or obtained from sensors from the transport service or infrastructure providers. Typical transport infrastructure providers are route keepers and parking facility businesses. In addition to the data collected from the first layer, this layer contains mobility data from the passengers and business data.

The third data source contains data from digital services for passenger transport. In addition to business data, this data contains significant quantities of usage data from passengers. This data includes data such as all saved trajectories, paid trips and performed searches for each user of the service.

The last data source contains crowdsourced data, which is created by passengers and it may sometimes be unreliable and unstructured. It contains data such as ratings of service providers and services as well as real-time information about traffic disruptions and about shared transportation resources such as ride sharing.

5 Discussion

In our case area Tampere region, multiple different APIs are used to serve as a backbone of providing new services creating value through data; these include for example real-time location of city busses and congestion data of road network through the city's traffic lights. Nowadays, different public transport and routing APIs can be seen presumable to support. It should still be remembered that it is just a start when the data is open and accessible. The key of creating value from the data is to make different solutions and applications that the end-user uses and benefits from. In this study, examples on what kind of different benefits are found from APIs and big data in our case region and how they affect users, organizations or the city, are given.

For the user, value can mean many things. It is normal to assume that different apps can show possible routes around city or that public transport timetables can be found digitally, which doesn't make the user consider it as a benefit. Same applies to accident reports and basic traffic flow information that are provided in many areas around the world. In our case area traffic flow can be better estimated through traffic lights that share the traffic volume and wait time information through the API [35]. Same API can also be used to check the status of a specific light (green/amber/red). The status itself doesn't necessarily give any value to the user, but there are different pilots that use the connected traffic lights. For example, mobile app GLOSA aims to read the status of next set of traffic lights and then show the car driver the desired speed to approach so that no stop on red lights would be necessary [36]. Currently, the pilot runs on 16 of the city's 173 traffic lights [37]. For traffic light junctions with pedestrian and cyclist crossing button, CrossCycle is a mobile app, which tracks the route of the cyclist and reserves the green light in advance, turning it green when the cyclist arrives. The app is supported in 36 light guided junctions around the main cycle paths heading city center [38]. Added value for user can also be seen in arrival guidance to parking areas, which can be implemented in current navigation applications. Since the status and current capacity of the area can be queried beforehand, the user can be automatically routed to a location that will have free spaces [29] and be also given extra information about parking fares and different services, like EV charging.

For different infrastructure users, the value can be defined more easily. For transport providers, the better the information about delays and accidents, the better it is to minimize delays of own fleet and to calculate new routes when needed. For example, the public transport operator can get an priority in the connected traffic lights through the public transport information systems, which can be used to improve the punctuality and shorten the journey times [39]. In a study conducted in Helsinki, it was noted that there is no common results of the effects of these benefits. They ran a pilot by removing priority from public transport for a day. As a result, the punctuality dropped on average by 3%, but the results were largely route dependent. It was also noted that the main effect of these benefits is to improve the punctuality and not to shorten the actual journey time [40]. In Tampere, 118 traffic light junctions support the public transport priority, which covers practically the areas where public transport is widely used [41]. Through an own system, also emergency vehicles can be given priority on junctions to make the traffic flow in the desired direction [42].

The city can also benefit from the different services build on top of data. Different routing solutions that take the congestion into account can separate the traffic flow into different paths, which generates virtually more capacity, since infrastructure is better used. Different applications that create value to the user can also collect information to the city, which gets information about the routes and choices that users normally take.

The different solutions build on mobility data and APIs can also help to reach different sustainability targets. Different routing applications, which all rely on public APIs to gather information, can be used to promote new methods of transport and make them more attractive to the user by for example showing different recommendations for walking (interesting and walkable) and cycling (avoids large ascents) directions. This can promote modal shift towards sustainable modes of transport. Big data and analytics give possibility to route passengers and transport more efficiently and thus lower congestion and emission in cities. Better traffic management will allow greater capacity for passengers and goods allowing present infrastructure to be used more efficiently and therefore resources to be used more effectively.

6 Conclusion

Big data analytics offers new opportunities for both decision makers and new businesses as well as for passengers. Many of the new opportunities contribute also to sustainable development – from an environmental or from a social perspective. Open data and APIs have a key role since they allow to seamlessly connect different services, and in this case transport modes, into one easy-to-use solution for the passenger, who does not have to be aware on what is happening in the background. The system would also work in case of different incidents and congestion situations, since all this data would be available for the CPS transport platform that handles the journeys of users.

The study showed that even though the exploitation of big data does not directly improve the state of the physical transport infrastructure itself, it helps in utilizing more of its capacity. In the Tampere region case analyzed in this study, this means for example that the existing road network can be used more efficiently as transport service providers and individual drivers can plan their itineraries to avoid traffic congestions due to mobility data available from the road network. Another result of the study was that the use of big data makes the CPS transport system more attractive to passengers. An example of this is that displaying the real-time locations of the fleet to the passengers typically does improve passenger satisfaction with the system. This applies especially in cases where there is delay in the public transportation timetables.

In the future, new sensors and IoT could allow entirely new ways to collect and provide data to users. For example, IoT-sensors would allow to track the current occupancy rate of different public transport services and all the data could be integrated into new services. Data from different transport modalities is already available. However, the collaborative network is the core for the functioning CPS transport system. Via collaboration such as sharing and sourcing data and services within the network, the connected multimodal passenger transport systems are completed.

Interesting further research questions could relate to new business model possibilities in collaborative networks and transport systems. Another line of future research could relate to the usability of the CPS transport system by different passenger groups, since sustainable mobility is not just about improving transport infrastructure and services, but also about overcoming socio, economic, political and physical challenges. It would be important to study which passenger segments have a risk of being excluded from new digital mobility services. The CPS transport system requires different skills and attitudes from the passengers than a very traditional transport system that only has a physical dimension. Even though big data, open APIs and collaborative networks do provide significant improvements to the CPS transport system, the most important factor remains the usability of the system. Even the most intelligent system provides only very little value if it is not being used by the passengers.

References

1. Jittrapirom, P., Caiati, V., Feneri, A.M., Ebrahimigharehbaghi, S., Alonso González, M.J., Narayan, J.: Mobility as a service: a critical review of definitions, assessments of schemes, and key challenges. In: Rasouli, S., Timmermans, H., Yang, D. (eds.) Smart Cities—Infrastructure and Information (2017)
2. ABI Research forecasts global mobility as a service revenues to exceed $1 trillion by 2030. https://www.abiresearch.com/press/abi-research-forecasts-global-mobility-service-rev/
3. Lee, E.A.: Cyber physical systems: design challenges. In: 11th IEEE (ISORC), pp. 363–369. IEEE (2008)
4. Osório, A.L., Camarinha-Matos, L.M., Afsarmanesh, H., Belloum, A.: On reliable collaborative mobility services. In: Camarinha-Matos, L.M., Afsarmanesh, H., Rezgui, Y. (eds.) PRO-VE 2018. IAICT, vol. 534, pp. 297–311. Springer, Cham (2018). https://doi.org/10.1007/978-3-319-99127-6_26
5. Hermann, M., Tobias, P., Boris, O.: Design principles for Industrie 4.0 scenarios. In: 2016 49th Hawaii International Conference on System Sciences (HICSS). IEEE (2016)
6. Commission Delegated Regulation (EU) 2017/1926 of 31 May 2017 supplementing Directive 2010/40/EU of the European Parliament and of the Council with regard to the provision of EU-wide multimodal travel information services. Document 32017R1926. EUR-Lex (2017)
7. CEN/TC 278 - Intelligent transport systems. CEN (2015)
8. GTFS Static Overview. Google Developers. https://developers.google.com/transit/gtfs/
9. GTFS Realtime Overview. Google Developers. https://developers.google.com/transit/gtfs-realtime/
10. Ferreira, N., Poco, J., Vo, H.T., Freire, J., Silva, C.T.: Visual exploration of big spatio-temporal urban data: a study of New York City taxi trips. IEEE Trans. Vis. Comput. Graph. **19**(12), 2149–2158 (2013)
11. Tang, J., Liu, F., Wang, Y., Wang, H.: Uncovering urban human mobility from large scale taxi GPS data. Physica A: Stat. Mech. Appl. **438**, 140–153 (2015)
12. Zhao, K., Khryashchev, D., Freire, J., Silva, C., Vo, H.: Predicting taxi demand at high spatial resolution: approaching the limit of predictability. In: 2016 IEEE International Conference on Big Data (Big Data), Washington, D.C. 2016, pp. 833–842 (2016)
13. Xu, M., Wang, D., Li, J.: DESTPRE: a data-driven approach to destination prediction for taxi rides. In: UbiComp Proceedings of the 2016 ACM International Joint Conference on Pervasive and Ubiquitous Computing, Heidelberg, Germany, pp. 729–739 (2016)

14. Chen, C., Ma, J., Susilo, Y., Liu, Y., Wang, M.: The promises of big data and small data for travel behavior (aka human mobility) analysis. Transp. Res. Part C: Emerg. Technol. **68** (Suppl. C), 285–299 (2016)

15. Tao, S., Corcoran, J., Mateo-Babiano, I., Rohde, D.: Exploring bus rapid transit passenger travel behaviour using big data. Appl. Geogr. **53**(Suppl. C), 90–104 (2014)

16. Noulas, A., Salnikov, V., Lambiotte, R., Mascolo, C.: Mining open datasets for transparency in taxi transport in metropolitan environments. EPJ Data Sci. **4**(1), 23 (2015)

17. Pereira, F.C., Rodrigues, F., Ben-Akiva, M.: Using data from the web to predict public transport arrivals under special events scenarios. J. Intell. Transp. Syst. **19**(3), 273–288 (2015)

18. Regulation (EU) 2016/679 of the European parliament and of the council of 27 April 2016. European Union (2016)

19. Camarinha-Matos, L.M., Afsarmanesh, H.: Collaborative networks: a new scientific discipline. J. Intell. Manuf. **16**(4–5), 439–452 (2005)

20. Zheng, X., et al.: Big data for social transportation. IEEE Trans. Intell. Transp. Syst. **17**(3), 620–630 (2016)

21. Brabham, D.C.: Crowdsourcing. The MIT Press, Cambridge (2013)

22. Estellés-Arolas, E., González-Ladrón-de-Guevara, F.: Towards an integrated crowdsourcing definition. J. Inf. Sci. **38**(2), 189–200 (2012)

23. Hamari, J., Sjöklint, M., Ukkonen, A.: The sharing economy: why people participate in collaborative consumption. JASIST **67**(9), 2047–2059 (2016)

24. Eckhardt, G.M., Bardhi, F.: The sharing economy isn't about sharing at all. Harvard Bus. Rev. **28** (2015)

25. Hallituksen esitys liikenteen palveluista annetun lain muuttamiseksi, III vaihe. Finnish Government

26. Digiroad - National Road and Street Database, Finnish Transport Infrastructure Agency. https://vayla.fi/web/en/open-data/digiroad

27. Digitraffic. Finnish Transport Infrastructure Agency. https://vayla.fi/web/en/open-data/digitraffic

28. ITS Factory Wiki. http://wiki.itsfactory.fi/index.php/ITS_Factory_Developer_Wiki

29. Tampere Parking DATEX2. ITS Factory (2015)

30. Digitraffic. Traffic Management Finland. https://www.digitraffic.fi/

31. Tampere Public Transport timetables and routes (GTFS). (CC Attribution 4.0). https://data.tampere.fi/

32. Tampere Traffic Monitoring (2019). https://lissu.tampere.fi. Accessed 13 June 2019

33. Tampere Noise Pollution Analysis 2017. (CC Attribution 4.0) (2017). https://data.tampere.fi/

34. Digitransit. HSL. https://digitransit.fi/

35. Trafficlightdata Service: User documentation (ver 1.2). Infotripla & Dynniq 14 p. (2017)

36. Liikennevalot kommunikoivat entistä monipuolisemmin kuljettajan kanssa Tampereella. The City of Tampere (2017)

37. Dynniq Finland: Map of traffic lights supporting GLOSA (2017)

38. Pyöräilijälle vihreää valoa ja etuisuutta 36 liittymässä mobiilisovelluksella. The City of Tampere (2019)

39. Tampereen seudun joukkoliikenteen tietojärjestelmiä uudistetaan. The City of Tampere (2017)

40. Hillo, K.: Joukkoliikenteen reaaliaikadatan hyödyntäminen suunnittelussa. Väylät & Liikenne 2018 esitelmät, pp. 144–147 (2018)

41. Traffic light controlled intersections in Tampere. From data.tampere.fi (CC Attribution 4.0)

42. HALI - tavoitteena kansallinen standardi. The Association of Finnish Local and Regional Authorities (2018)

Collaborative Decision-Making in Value Creation Networks

Framework to Model PSS Collaborative Value Networks and Assess Uncertainty of Their Economic Models

Xavier Boucher[1(✉)], Khaled Medini[1], and Camilo Murillo Coba[1,2]

[1] Mines Saint-Etienne, Université Clermont Auvergne, CNRS, UMR 6158, LIMOS-Institut Fayol, 158 Cours Fauriel, 42023 Saint-Etienne, France
{xavier.boucher,khaled.medini,
camilo.murillocoba}@mines-stetienne.fr
[2] e.l.m. leblanc SAS, Bosch-Thermotechnology, 126 rue de Stalingrad, 93 705 Drancy Cedex, France

Abstract. This paper presents a framework for addressing the challenge of economic value sharing among actors of Product-Service value networks. More specifically the framework is dedicated to the assessment of alternative collaborative value networks and their associated economic models, at the time of designing a product-service system (PSS). The framework includes three main components: modelling, simulation and uncertainty assessment. The framework is briefly presented as parts of its components were discussed in previous research. The paper provides an illustration with a design project of a PSS solution in the agro-alimentary industry, requiring a balanced configuration of collaborative value network.

Keywords: Product service systems · Value network · Economic models

1 Introduction

Innovation on Product-Service-Systems generated a rather large background of scientific advances on supporting their design and engineering processes over the last decade. However, their concrete operationalization remains confronted to key challenges, notably concerning the balance of multi-actor collaboration within PSS value chains. The mix among products and services open new profit opportunities and, consequently, a strong need to regulate economic value sharing among collaborative actors. This paper tackles this challenge by proposing an integrated framework to assess economic models of PSS collaborative delivery networks. The framework is based on three key components: modelling, simulation and uncertainty assessment.

The paper is structured according to these three dimensions: modelling, simulation and uncertainty assessment of collaborative PSS value networks, with a state of the art (Sect. 2) introducing these three aspects, a conceptual contribution highlighted in Sect. 3, and a case study in the agro-alimentary industry in Sect. 4. This case study puts forth a multi-actor value network, emphasizing the economic-sharing issues.

L. M. Camarinha-Matos et al. (Eds.): PRO-VE 2019, IFIP AICT 568, pp. 541–551, 2019.
https://doi.org/10.1007/978-3-030-28464-0_47

2 Modelling and Evaluation of PSS Collaborative Value Networks

2.1 Modelling of PSS Value Networks

Over the last decade, key advances were developed in the field of PSS Modelling [1] to support the integration of products and services models. This section is focused on papers about modelling PSS value network to support their economic assessment. A first set of models support an explicit representation of actor networks, which can be extended to stakeholders. The research works from [2] model the value flows of a PSS offer through a generic formalism of Receiver/Provider actors, using a mathematical representation. Lindahl goes one step forward by considering the various types of PSS network actors and establishing a qualitative approach to model the service-based or product-based value flows among them [3]. An approach where actor networks are represented through value creation scenarios is proposed in [4] and the sustainability of alternative value proposition scenarios is addressed in [5]. In these 2 last works, the final objective is a performance assessment, however the quantitative assessment process are not developed. This first set of works provide advances for qualitative modelling, but do not address economic evaluation.

Complementarily, in the field of strategic network analysis, stakeholder value network has been developed to assess value flows among stakeholders and identify dependency or power relationships [6]. Until now, this approach has not been applied specifically to PSS. In the field of PSS, the PRO-VA approach provides a seminal work for multidimensional value assessment [7]. The authors build a clear contribution to assess both monetary and non-monetary value. However the approach only focuses on the provider's point of view and on PSS components: it does not assess the value network in itself. This second set of modelling work provides important insights on value exchange assessment, however they do not make possible an explicit and sharable representation of alternative scenarios of collaborative value networks and do not analyse precisely the economic flows among actors.

2.2 Simulation of PSS Value Networks

Simulation methods offer quantitative assessment solutions, with a direct focus on value network modelling: based on process-oriented models, all activities required for PSS delivery are modelled and their integrated performance can be simulated. Typical of this orientation, is the work from Bosch-Mauchand et al. [number] using discrete simulation to assess value criteria in terms of cost, risk, product conformity, time and function satisfaction [8]. The authors compare value creation scenarios according to the point of view of the various actors of the network. However, this approach remains only product-oriented. In the field of PSS, some contributions conceptualize the basis for generic PSS simulation platform [9, 10], by integrating both service and product dimensions. A service-oriented performance simulation method is developed in this general perspective in [11]. Simulation models for PSS business is proposed for specific application areas and decisional objectives in [12]. Such works provide concrete advances for quantitative evaluation, however the alternative value network models are not explicitly represented, and a domain-independent platform for PSS value network is still missing.

2.3   PSS Uncertainty Analysis for PSS Economic Assessment

Uncertainty management is a key issue for PSS design. In the field of PSS uncertainty propagation was applied to some PSS concrete cases [13, 14] for economic evaluation. An uncertainty diagnosis approach, integrating both qualitative and quantitative methods, was applied in the PSS context in [13, 15]. Wang and Durugbo [16] define a set of uncertainty metrics evaluated by applying fuzzy-based techniques. However, these advances on uncertainty in PSS context mainly focus on cost of service delivery and market conditions. Revenues or other dimensions of economic models are not considered. Additionally, current contributions mainly emphasize on the provider point of view, without considering all stakeholder's impacts.

3   A Framework for PSS Value Network Modelling and Evaluation

The following sections present a modelling and assessment framework for PSS, as an integrated approach to tackle the key issues identified previously: (i) provide an explicit and sharable representation of the diversity of collaborative value networks at the time of PSS solution design; (ii) support a multi-actor simulation of PSS value network economic models; (iii) assess the impact of distinct types of uncertainties for various stakeholders. Three integrated components of the framework are introduced (Fig. 1): modelling, simulation, uncertainty assessment. PSS value networks are constituted by collaborative sets of companies contributing to PSS delivery, including PSS user when necessary. By hypothesis, the approach only deals with BtoB PSS context and the value network assessment only considers economic dimension of value exchanges.

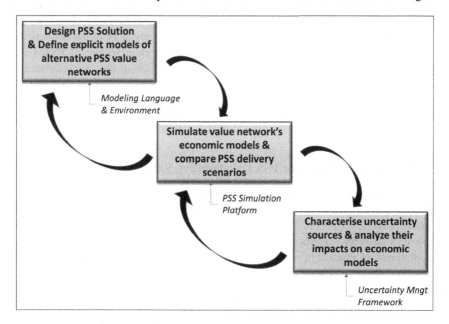

Fig. 1. Overview of the overall framework

3.1   A Modelling Language for Value Network Representation

The modelling component was developed on a conceptual level as a modelling language dedicated to PSS models and, on a pragmatic level, as a computer-based modelling tool called PS3M (PSS Scenario Modeler). PS3M offers 9 complementary views to support PSS design process [17, 18]. The so-called '*Scenario view*' is dedicated to model PSS collaborative value networks, using three major modelling constructs:

- *PSS Offer:* each alternative value network is associated to a specific *Offer*, including the specification of PSS components together with the characterization of PSS selling contract (The *Offer view* further details the precise elements of the offer).
- *Actor Roles:* each value network gathers a set of *Roles*, with the *Role* specifying the responsibilities and activities taken in charge by some actor of the value network. The delimitation of the roles is specific to each value network configuration. Performance indicators can also be associated to *Roles*, to characterize performance expectations.
- *Organizational Actors* represent the various companies/organizations involved in the value creation network. They can be assigned to the various *Roles* within the value network depending on their organizational capabilities and on the designer decisions.

With this three modelling concept several alternative value networks can be defined, each specified by a specific offer, a set of roles necessary to deliver all the components of this PSS offer and the assignment of organizational actors to these roles.

Figure 3 of the case study illustrates the graphical representation of the PS3M Scenario View. The modelling language presents the advantage of an explicit representation of the alternative options of collaborative value networks for PSS delivery, using a graphical representation easily understandable by any actor of the network, thus facilitating collaborative decision-making. Another important feature of PS3M modelling language also consists in supporting the identification of the characteristics and parameters of the economic models under study. This economic data is captured from the actors of the network, then gathered throughout the nine views of the modelling language, helping the subsequent step about economic model evaluation through simulation (see next section).

3.2   Simulation Platform for PSS Collaborative Value Networks

The simulation component has been developed as a reconfigurable PSS Economic model simulator called PS3A (PSS Scenario Analyzer). The objective of the platform is to make possible to generate a reliable cost/revenue simulation of the various alternative PSS delivery scenarios defined via the previous PS3M modelling component. The platform is consistent with a multi-actor perspective, by providing economic results (costs/revenues/profits) for each of the actors of the collaborative PSS delivery network.

The economic calculation model follows an activity cost/revenue assessment approach applied both to manufacturing and service processes, with the formalized model and algorithms detailed in [19]. The costs of each actor within the PSS network are the aggregate manufacturing and service activities assigned to each of those actors. Revenues are derived from the costs using manufacturing or service margin rates. The calculations are executed for a given demand profile representing the yearly number of contracts [19].

The platform is reconfigurable, in the sense that the internal economic calculations provided by the simulator are precisely customizable for each PSS case study. A technological interoperability between PS3M (modelling component) and PS3A (simulation component) was implemented in order to accelerate the customization of the simulation platform for each case study and ensure a higher level a reliability for the economic outputs generated.

3.3   Uncertainty Propagation and Analysis Procedure

The simulation platform ensures reliable economic outputs to compare alternative PSS value networks. However, managing uncertainty requires embedding the simulator within a consistent uncertainty management framework. As presented in [20], this Framework results from the integration of qualitative and quantitative methods for uncertainty analysis and management. It includes the four main steps underlined by Fig. 2: step 1 consists in defining, characterizing and classifying the potential sources of uncertainty; step 2 consists in formalizing a mathematical representation of uncertain parameters; step 3 consists in propagating uncertainties through the PSS economic model calculator (presented in Sect. 3.2) using Monte Carlo simulations, to support a sensitivity analysis; step 4 consists in interpreting the outputs from this sensitivity analysis to look for action plan reducing uncertainty impacts (mitigation strategies).

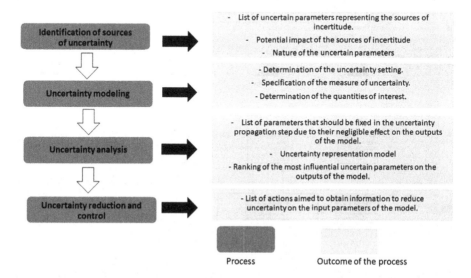

Fig. 2. Overview of the uncertainty management process

4   Case Study in the Field of Industrial Robotics

The case study concerns the development of a PSS solution for the meat industry (agro-alimentary sector). The PSS offer envisioned offer is a robotic solution for easy cleaning of the fridges, where the meat undergoes the transformation process. The current cleaning activities interfere with the production, leading to higher cost and lower cleaning quality. The innovative offer entails an autonomous cleaning robot with specific moving and cleaning abilities dedicated to meat environment, and a set of services to ensure the availability and performance of the robot, reduce the production interferences and improve the cleaning frequency and quality. The PSS collaborative value network involves three stakeholders: (E1) a small-sized manufacturing company that designs and assembles special machines including robots as customized solutions, (E2) a small-sized manufacturing company that provides batteries for the robot and (E3) a medium-sized company from the meat transformation industry as the client of the offer. A fourth stakeholder (E4) is considered in some of the configurations: a service provider that assumes the role of PSS solution provider. The application of the framework helps configuring the collaboration among stakeholders, by supporting the design of alternative value chains and by the analysis of the potential economic results through the simulation and uncertainty approach, as presented in the next sections.

4.1   Key Results Concerning PSS Value Network Modelling

The PSS modelling language introduced in Sect. 3.1, was implemented on the ADOXX enterprise modelling platform (open meta-modelling platform supported by the Open Models Laboratory initiative - OMiLAB). The resulting PS3M modelling

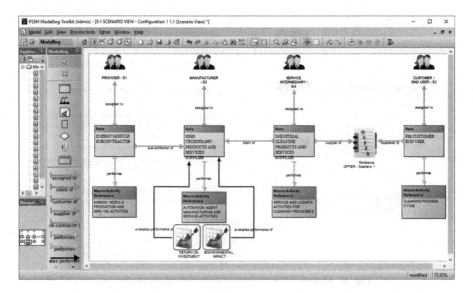

Fig. 3. Example of PSS value chain, modelled through PS3M modelling component

environment (Fig. 3) is utilized in order to build consistent models of the alternative PSS value networks, which are associated to distinct potential economic models.

Typically, for the Clean Robot case study, the value network could be implemented following the usual product-, use- or result-oriented PSS economic models. The structure of the value network strongly depends on these economic schemes: the content of the 'offer', the roles in the value network and the organizational actors, considering their internal economic parameters. Figure 3 shows a PSS value network for a use-oriented contract offer with roles assigned to the 4 actors: the customer E3 takes in charge the cleaning activity, the service intermediary E4 manages the contractualization, the manufacturer E1 provides the robot and technology-oriented services, and the battery provider E2 ensures specific maintenance tasks. Economic analysis discussed in next section only focuses on the three main alternative scenarios described in Table 1.

Table 1. Three alternative PSS scenarios, for further economic analysis

Actors	S1 – Product oriented PSS	S2 – Use oriented PSS	S3 – Result oriented PSS
E1	Sells the robot and services to E3	Provides the robot and services on an availability basis	Takes over the cleaning of E3 fridges
E2	Sells the battery system to E1	Sells the battery system to E1	Sells the battery system to E1
E3	Purchase and use the robot for cleaning the fridges	Purchase and use the robot for cleaning the fridges	Pays for the cleaning service

4.2   Key Results Concerning PSS Economic Model Simulation

The modelling presented in the previous section supported the definition of the required data for the simulation. This latter is performed following the algorithmic approach and the model presented in [19]. The simulation model is implemented in web-based platform allowing a quick modelling and simulation process. The output is a set of cost and revenue indicators for different actors involved in the designed offer. The simulations show a significant increase in E1 net profit when moving towards a more service-oriented offer (Fig. 4). Unsurprisingly, E2 profit remains stable over the three scenarios as it is only a supplier of the battery system. Scenario S2 referring to a use-oriented offer brings an additional revenue stream coming from the monthly rent of the robot and most importantly maintenance services. The net profit is doubled from S1 to S2. For the customer E3, this increase in costs is compensated by more availability of the equipment and thus better cleaning performance. E1 profit increase is more significant when it comes to the result-oriented scenario as the profit increases with almost 260% compared to S2. This is explained by the big share of cleaning service in the profit: this service is delivered by A1 in S3, instead of the customer in S2. From a mere economic point of view, this shows that the profit generated by delivering the cleaning process outranks the one from the initially designed PSS. However, in practice, this

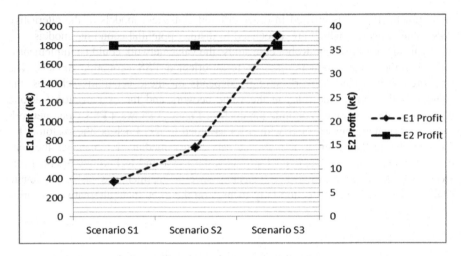

Fig. 4. Economic assessment results

scenario is hindered by organisational issues linked to service capabilities of E1 and business competition of the cleaning market: the final decision regarding the most appropriate scenario belongs to the project consortium.

4.3 Key Results Concerning Uncertainty Propagation and Analysis

The goal in this stage is to identify the parameters of the economic model that have the largest influence on the variability of the profits for the actors of the value chain. These analyses were applied to the use-oriented scenario (S2), considered as the more interesting for the industrial actors.

First, a One-at-a Time (OAT) sensitivity analysis was performed on a set of parameters: contract length, number of contracts initiated each year, lease amount, robot lifetime, frequency of services, number of robots, robot payback period and contract type. Then, tornado diagrams were plotted to visualize the influence of these key parameters on the variability of the revenues for E1, the Original Equipment Manufacturer (OEM) (Fig. 5). A base scenario with a set of parameters was defined, and then two other scenarios with 'extreme' values were specified. Due to the large influence of the demand on the variability, three diagrams with different values of initiated contracts per year were plotted. The use of these tornado diagrams enabled to visualize the negligible impact on the variable of interest of varying the values of robot lifetime and frequency of services. This result led to the decision of not including these two parameters in the uncertainty propagation step.

In order to include the effects of the interactions among uncertainty parameters, a scenario decomposition was applied, and then, the finite change sensitivity indices were calculated [20]. This sensitivity analysis set the parameters for the next step of uncertainty propagation step: another two parameters were considered to have a negligible effect on the simulated revenues: number of operating robots and robot payback period. Next, the economic model was run 1000 times while variating the values of the

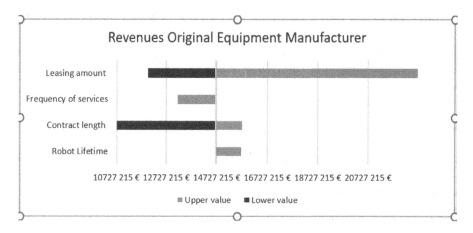

Fig. 5. Example of a tornado diagramme used in the uncertainty analysis

contract length, the number of contracts initiated per year, the lease amount and the robot lifetime.

The outputs of the simulations were analysed by using scatterplots and Pearson correlation coefficients (Fig. 6) [20]. Scatterplots assist in screening the degree of sensitivity between a parameter and the variable of interest. From the resulting scatterplots, it was concluded that the main parameter having high sensitivity to the simulated revenues for the OEM and the battery supplier was the number of ongoing contracts per year. This conclusion was drawn from the presence of a pattern in the chart. This finding was confirmed by the computation of the Pearson correlation coefficients. On the contrary, the remaining charts displayed points uniformly scattered; which indicated low sensitivity to the expected revenues (Fig. 6).

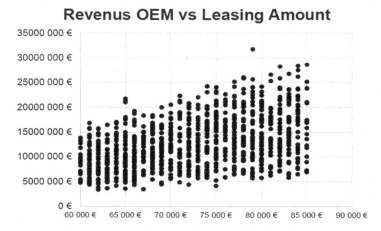

Fig. 6. Example of a scatterplot used in the uncertainty analysis

This analysis led to the conclusion that demand for robotic industrial cleaning solutions represented the largest uncertainty source in the economic model. The increasing variation of the lease amount and contract length showed to have also a positive effect on the profits, when Robot lifetime demonstrated to have a negligible effect.

5 Conclusions

The industrial case study illustrates how the modelling, simulation and uncertainty components of the framework help industrial consortiums to identify and characterize, alternative economic models available to implement collaborative PSS delivery networks and, then, evaluate and confront them to uncertainty. Thus, the framework supports a decision-making process which, first, makes explicit alternative economic value sharing scenarios, second helps selecting the best scenarios by a comparative analysis of economic results, then assesses the sensibility of these results to uncertainty factors. An important perspective under development is the genericity of the approach, to cope with the variability of potential PSS economic models.

References

1. Qu, M., Yu, S., Chen, D., Chu, J., Tian, B.: State-of-the-art of design, evaluation, and operation methodologies in PSS. Comput. Ind. **77**, 1–14 (2016)
2. Sakao, T., Sundin, E., Lindahl, M., Shimomura, Y.: A methodology for designing services: a modeling method, design method, CAD tool and Their industrial Applications. In: Salvendy, G., Karwowski, W. (eds.) Service Engineering, pp. 269–293. Wiley, Hoboken (2010)
3. Lindahl, M., Sakao, T., Carlsson, E.: Actor's and system maps for integrated product service offerings - practical experience from two companies. Procedia CIRP **16**, 320–325 (2016)
4. Medini, K., Moreau, V., Peillon, S., Boucher, X.: Transition to product service systems: methodology based on scenarios identification, modelling and evaluation. In: Proceedings PROVE 2014, Amsterdam, Netherlands, 6–8 October 2014 (2014)
5. Neubert, G., Lambey-Checchin, C.: The sustainable value proposition of PSSs: the case of ECOBEL "Shower head". Procedia CIRP **47**, 12–17 (2016)
6. Reed, M., Graves, A., Dandy, N., Posthumus, H.: Who's in and why? A typology of stakeholder analysis methods for natural resource management. J. Environ. **90**, 1933–1949 (2009)
7. Matschewskya, J., Sakao, T., Lindahl, M.: ProVa – provider value evaluation for integrated product service offerings. Procedia CIRP **30**, 305–310 (2015)
8. Mauchand, M., Siadat, A., Perry, N., Bernard, A.: VCS: value chains simulator, a tool for value analysis of manufacturing enterprise processes. J. Intell. Manuf. **23**, 1389–1402 (2012)
9. Phumbua, S., Tjahjono, B.: Towards product-service systems modelling: a quest for dynamic behaviour and model parameters. IJPR **50**(2), 425–442 (2012)
10. Garetti, M., Rosa, P., Terzi, S.: Life cycle simulation for the design of product-service systems. Comput. Ind. **63**, 361–369 (2012)
11. Pezzotta, G., Pinto, R., Pirola, F., Ouertani, M.Z.: Balancing product-service provider's performance and customer's value: the SErvice engineering methodology (SEEM). Procedia CIRP **16**, 50–55 (2014)

12. Alfian, G., Rhee, J., Yoon, B.: A simulation tool for prioritizing product-service system models in a carsharing service. Comput. Ind. Eng. **70**, 59–73 (2014)
13. Erkoyuncu, J.A., Roy, R., Shehab, E., Cheruvu, K.: Understanding service uncertainties in industrial PSS cost estimation. IJAMT **52**(9–12), 1223–1238 (2011)
14. Lanza, G., Rühl, J.: Simulation of service costs throughout the life cycle of production facilities. CIRP JMST **1**(4), 247–253 (2009)
15. Durugbo, C., Erkoyuncu, J.A., Tiwari, A., Alcock, J.R., Roy, R., Shehab, E.: Data uncertainty assessment and information flow analysis for product-service systems in a library case. IJSOI **5**(4), 330–350 (2010)
16. Wang, X., Durugbo, C.: Analysing network uncertainty for industrial product-service delivery: hybrid fuzzy approach. Expert Syst. Appl. **40**(11), 4621–4636 (2013)
17. Boucher, X., Medini, K., Vaillant, H.: PS3M: integrative modelling environment to support PSS design. Procedia CIRP **73**, 73–78 (2018)
18. Medini, K., Boucher, X.: Specifying a modelling language for PSS engineering – a development method and an operational tool. Comput. Ind. **108**, 89–103 (2019)
19. Medini, K., Boucher, X., Peillon, S., Vaillant, H.: Economic assessment of customer driven value networks for PSS delivery. In: International Conference on Advances in Production Management Systems, Seoul, Korea (2018)
20. Murillo-Coba, C., Boucher, X., Medini, M., Gonzalez Feliu, J.: Simulation-based approach to apply uncertainty evaluation framework for PSS economic models. In: 11th CIRP Conference on Industrial Product-Service Systems, IPS2 2019, Zhuhai, China, May 2019 (2019)

A Business Model Assessment and Evaluation Framework for City Logistics Collaborative Strategic Decision Support

Giovanni Zenezini[1(✉)], Jesus Gonzalez-Feliu[2], Giulio Mangano[1], and Laura Palacios-Arguello[2]

[1] Department of Management and Production Engineering,
Politecnico di Torino, Turin, Italy
{giovanni.zenezini,giulio.mangano}@polito.it
[2] Henri Fayol Institute, Ecole de Mines de St. Etienne, Saint-Étienne, France
{jesus.gonzalez-feliu,laura.palacios}@emse.fr

Abstract. Several City Logistics (CL) initiatives have emerged in the last two decades with the aim to reduce the negative externalities of freight distribution in urban areas. Such initiatives can be public and/or private but need to not break or impeach current operations efficiency so to not hinder their profitability. In order to provide business value to CL initiatives and thus fostering their long-term success, it is necessary to understand the decision-making of private companies operating in the urban freight ecosystem. This paper proposes an ex-ante assessment and evaluation framework built around the concept of an ecosystem business modelling that includes the decision-making by CL stakeholders. A theoretical framework previously developed is extended to evaluate a collaborative business model of an Urban Consolidation Centre (UCC). Cost-Benefit analysis (CBA is used estimate the impact of the business model configuration. Finally, research and practice implications are also addressed.

Keywords: City logistics · Business model · Cost-Benefit analysis · Consolidation Centre

1 Introduction

Collaboration among various stakeholders is a crucial subject in operations, business and logistics management. In urban logistics, the issue of identifying stakeholders and examining the most suitable ways of collaboration among them has started to be addressed, mainly in the form of optimization models or in a qualitative way. However, the key of success of such collaboration is strongly related to reaching a solid business model. Designing and assessing a solid long-term collaborative business model is therefore of vital importance for closing this gap and turn CL innovative solutions into sustainable, large-scale endeavors.

When dealing with cutting-edge innovations business models need to be assessed, both qualitatively (to identify levers and limits) and quantitatively (to examine their economic viability). Although business model deployment is popular in logistics and starts being applied to CL [1, 2], they are far to propose a systematic, unified approach

© IFIP International Federation for Information Processing 2019
Published by Springer Nature Switzerland AG 2019
L. M. Camarinha-Matos et al. (Eds.): PRO-VE 2019, IFIP AICT 568, pp. 552–561, 2019.
https://doi.org/10.1007/978-3-030-28464-0_48

that would address the collaboration issues. Furthermore, its assessment remains little done as existing works make it either on a qualitative or quantitative way only, without combining both approaches [3, 4].

The aim of this paper is thus to propose a methodological framework to analyze the potential BM in collaborative CL; being able to identify stakeholders, key elements and cost-benefit issues to develop and assess a suitable business model for city logistics collaboration. First, the background and literature related to that subject, i.e. urban logistics assessment and evaluation, stakeholder collaboration and business model assessment are presented. Then, the methodological frameworks is presented. After that, an example of application is presented via a case study for a university collaborative consolidation center for B2C flows. Finally, as a conclusion, research and practice implications are presented.

2 Research Background and Theoretical Framework

The literature section provides the theoretical background upon which the assessment framework is built. In the first section the most important aspects of collaboration in logistics are explored, in order to define the nature of such collaboration. Business modelling in CL context is explored in the following section, focusing on the potential case application and the shortcomings that convey the need for an innovative approach for CL evaluation. Finally, the Cost-Benefit Analysis (CBA) method is explained in Sect. 2.3.

2.1 Stakeholders' Collaboration in Logistics

In city logistics, the subject of multi-stakeholder collaboration has been widely addressed by various authors [5]. Given the multiple stakeholders involved in urban logistics, the collaboration among them can be of different nature (public-public, public-private or private-private), and arise at different level (transactional, informational, decisional, i.e. dealing with strategic, tactical or operational planning [6]). Logistics collaboration can be observed from different viewpoints:

- By its object, the collaboration can be informational, infrastructure-based, based on purchases or vehicle-based [7].
- By the organizational aspects, which are closely related to the functions of the supply chain that are shared [8]: longitudinal collaboration, which takes place between complementary actors in the same logistics chain; and transversal collaboration, often takes place between actors at the same level but not necessarily in the same supply chain.

In both cases, collaboration can be formal (on the basis of contracts [9]) or informal (without a legal base) but supposes important organizational, technological and cultural changes, which can impact the business model of the supply chain or proposed solutions.

Various authors have studied public-private collaboration, on a wide viewpoint [10], concluding on the need of assessing the value of those partnerships and the need of collaboration to establish them in a sustainable way. That can be done via the definition of business models [11] that can support the consensus search procedures [7], but to make final choices, decision support methods are required, as shown in the conceptual framework proposed by [12].

2.2 Business Model Theory and Usage in CL Context

The concept of Business Modelling (BM) relates to theoretical frameworks able to assess the potential economic value that an organization can create by selling a product or service [13]. [14] center their business model framework proposition on four different components, namely customer value proposition, profit, key resources, and key process. Hence, in summary a business model includes the following components: a value proposition and a revenue model adopted to gain a share of the value created [15]; a value chain including key resources, key processes and key partners; and finally a cost structure.

The business model approach has been applied so far by few CL scholars. [2] assessed an automated parcel lockers (APL) solution by means of the Business Model Canvas (BMC), one of the most used BM framework proposed by Osterwalder and Pigneur [16]. Through the BM framework, the authors highlight the value proposition offered to both customers and society, in addition to constructing a business case according to different business model scenario. According to [17], the value proposition of a last-mile service aggregates different components such as price, order lead-time, service quality, scope of service, sustainability and other benefits including cost reduction convenience or flexibility of service. The BMC has been also used by [1] to assess the feasibility of an investment in a shared, multi-stakeholder digital platform for CL management. However, [18] argue that accounting for the different goals of CL stakeholders is out of the scope of the BMC, which thus shows some shortcomings in terms of assessing the overall feasibility of a CL solution.

2.3 Ex-Ante Evaluation of CL with CBA

To evaluate the suitability of business models, it is important to assess the costs and benefits generated by it, and find the economic equilibrium and potential monetary gains/losses [3]. One of the most used technique in transport infrastructure or passenger transport systems long-term assessment is Cost-Benefit analysis (CBA). However, CBA was very little used in city logistics until 2012 [4], but is starting to be generalized since then. It has been used to evaluate if the benefits delivered by a new transportation infrastructure exceed the costs and determined an efficient allocation of resources [19]. CBA has mainly been applied to assess the economic viability of urban consolidation centers, to define suitable fees for new urban logistics systems or also to define an economically viable urban freight railway system, among others [4, 20], and also to obtain the suitable value of fees for the use of technology-based city logistics services [3]. Main works on CBA deal with investment-based methods, but also operational planning methods, based on marginal cost analysis, have been seen in CL [12].

3 Methodology

The tenets of the proposed methodology are as follows. First, CL systems are interpreted as business ecosystems, characterized by the interplay between stakeholders' activities, decisions and objectives. In order to respond to this challenge we propose a classification of CL stakeholders according to the main activities performed or space they occupy in the ecosystem [12, 17]:

- The first group includes the transport demand generators, who generate demand and use the transport and logistics services (e.g. citizens, local retailers and shippers);
- The second group includes the service providers, or transport operators, who are appointed by shippers or receivers to deliver parcels and other goods (e.g. express couriers such as DHL and the like, small city transport companies);
- The third group comprise those stakeholders who are in charge of coordinating the network, or interface roles. Usually transport providers provide coordination services but, in some cases, intermediary platforms or public authorities can take on this role.
- The fourth and last group includes the stakeholders who manage and plan the logistics space, or space organizers. They comprise public authorities in charge of land use planning and real estate facility managers aiming to increase the quality of life of their employees or tenants.

The categories identified aggregate functions and activities necessary in a CL business ecosystem, and can be defined as roles [17].

The second tenet of the proposed framework ensues as a consequence of the first one: the same CL solution can be implemented through different business model configurations where stakeholders take up different roles and exchange different value propositions. A specific business model configuration determines which stakeholder takes certain decisions and invest in resources, as well as the collaboration links between stakeholders. In turn, the business model configuration chosen has an impact on activity execution and the success of the collaboration between the stakeholders measured via proper metrics. Table 1 summarizes the main elements of a collaborative CL business ecosystem.

Table 1. Main components of a CL business ecosystem

Component	Operational description
Resource	They are owned by stakeholders
Activity	Activities are performed to offer services, and consume resources
Metric	KPIs measure the business objects (e.g. activities, value proposition)
Decision	Stakeholders make decisions in the fulfilment of their roles, based on a set of constraints, variables, decision parameters
Service	Aggregation of activities that use resources and are role-based

The next step of the methodology is the assessment of the business model, or the quantification of the effects on all stakeholders of the business ecosystem role-playing and linkages between the stakeholders themselves. A suitable method to validate a Business Model is the Cost-Benefit Analysis [3]. For an exploratory approach, instead of using long-term IRR-based (internal return rate) frameworks [3], we propose a cashflow analysis, which is widely used in business research and presents a more aggregated vision than marginal cost analyses [12] making it suitable for strategic/tactical planning purposes [21]. In the proposed framework, costs and benefits are calculated in a monetary value (€) and only real, and direct monetary cashflows are estimated. More precisely, costs are accrued by the stakeholders according to the activities they perform as well as the investment committed to acquire the resources they use. Benefits are instead represented through the exchange of value proposition among the stakeholders, expressed in monetary terms, and the actual inflow of revenues. The cashflow analysis estimated then the monetary values, in a 1-year horizon, for each quarter. Then, each quarter's net cashflow is calculated, to examine its evolution. The proposed methodology for designing and assessing a CL business ecosystem business model is shown in Fig. 1.

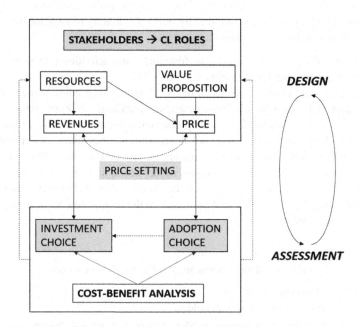

Fig. 1. Methodology for designing and assessing a CL business ecosystem business model

4   Case Study

The proposed case study hinges on an internal consolidation center, sized approximately 20 m^2, located in the Politecnico di Torino, the technical university of Turin, Italy. The center's operations are subcontracted to an external logistics service provider

(LSP), and is focused on receiving deliveries for all employees (about 2000 people) and sorting them to the university departments.

4.1 Business and Operational Model

The center handles two different kinds of deliveries: the institutional ones refer to work-related purchases and are delivered from the center to the departments, and the private ones. For the latter, the employees must go to the center for the picking. In the center, one employee works full time, flanked by two part- time workers in the morning. Even though there are 8 LSPs serving the consolidation center, each LSP typically associate the same driver to the route that includes the center. For most LSPs, the drivers are employees of local freight operators who the LSPs sub-contract the last-mile of the delivery. All the parcels accepted are identified via QR system, and the software automatically sends an e-mail to the final receiver through the internal e-mail system. When he/she arrives in the consolidation center, thorough a digital signature the final delivery is registered and it is traced by the software.

By delivering to an operated consolidation center, the LSPs are sure that the deliveries will not fail, and at the same time, the employees have the whole working day available for the picking. Moreover, LSPs can optimize their routing by consolidating more deliveries in a lower number of stop and thus can increase their routing efficiency. Finally, final customers (or end-consumers) simply update the delivery location to the center and thus do not incur in extra costs with the inclusion of the new platform. Table 2 summarizes the main roles played by the stakeholders in this CL ecosystem, and highlights that all costs are borne by the employer (i.e. the university) while all potential benefits are scattered across the whole ecosystem.

Table 2. Stakeholders, roles, costs and benefits for the pickup point solution, compared with the status quo (without the pickup point)

Stakeholders	Role(s)	Costs	Benefits
Consolidation center operator	Receiver Network Coordination	One full-time and three part-time employees Mobile terminal for delivery management	Subcontracting fee
Employer	Real Estate management	Investment in logistics spaces and equipment Subcontracting fee	Less congestion More attractive environment Employees' satisfaction
Express couriers	Logistics service provider	No change from the status quo	Increase in routing efficiency
Local carriers	City delivery	No change from the status quo	Better working condition for drivers
Online retailers	User of logistics service	No change from the status quo	Certainty of delivery to final customer
Employees	User of logistics service	No change from the status quo	Certainty of receiving the ordered items

The proposed case study shows an interesting example of informational collaboration. As shown, a central stakeholder, the university, proposes an infrastructure assuming the costs and subcontracting a logistics service provider to manage the consolidation center, however for its operational planning a real informational collaboration system is established. Indeed, delivery companies arrive to the consolidation center and rely on the university's employees for steering and operating the system. For that reason, a strong communication among each delivery company and the users is required. In this regard,, receiving the same driver for each LSP every day helps the relationship between the drivers and the employees of the consolidation centers and thus improves the quality of the working conditions for both parties. Delivery companies organize their delivery schedules in relation to free space and customers' uses. For that reasons, an optimal use of the facility would require a more reactive and integrated information system.

4.2   Collaboration Risks

In order to enhance that collaboration, a traceability or availability information system would support that informational collaboration. However, some risks ensue from this kind of collaboration [6].

For this particular logistics collaboration, we do not presume significant technological risks. This consideration is due to the use of well-consolidated mobile terminal technology deployed by the Consolidation center operator for the Delivery Management. In fact, the process of receiving the parcel involves only reading the parcel barcode and updating automatically the information on a spreadsheet. This technology moreover does not depend on the extant information systems of logistics service providers, which will manage their own information flow embedded in the delivery process and transmit the information up to the shipper. Hence, the final recipient will receive a double notification of the delivery i.e. from their shipper and from the consolidation center operator. Some risks on the other hand might arise from the management of the resources, since at least three employees are needed at any time from the consolidation center. If, by any chance, the operator would not be able to provide enough human resources the center could not be operated. Should the operator not inform the LSPs of its disruption in the service then the LSP would waste time by stopping at the University. This risk is then correlated to the process-related risks, in the sense that LSPs permanently changed their routing after the introduction of the center. As a consequence, not informing them of the disruption will end up in a failed delivery (and consequently a return to the LSP's warehouse), and a longer delivery tour. The center operator must then collaborate closely with the LSP and inform them of any disruption or change in the service in order to assure the success of the collaboration.

4.3   Cost-Benefit Analysis Results

To propose a first step into the CBA application via cashflow analysis, we aim to identify the costs and earnings of the proposed collaborative urban logistics space. For that analysis, we need first to identify the cost structure for each of the stakeholders whose cashflows are affected by the center, namely:

1. Logistics providers, for which no new incoming flows are expected, but whose outcoming flows can vary (mainly decrease) because of an efficiency improvement due to the use of the platform; that improvement (in terms of distances, times and vehicle use) will be modeled using the flow estimation approach shown in [12];
2. The host institution of the platform, here Politecnico di Torino, who operates the center through the subcontractor and whose costs are estimated to be around 450€ (on the basis of an empirical calculation based on local manpower and rental costs).

We take into account that the only costs related to transport that need to be calculated are those of logistics providers. Using the general framework of flow estimation (via analytical models) of [22], we estimate the number of end-consumers not visited at home and consolidated into the platform, and the resulting changes on transport flows. The platform receives an average number of 150 deliveries/day, which are then split according to each LSP's national market share [23]. Moreover, we assume an average number of 45 deliveries per vehicle per day (for classical B2C deliveries) and a total capacity of about 100 deliveries per vehicle per route [12]. Then, using the costs of transport in the geodelivery-Territoire Platform[1], we estimate the main unitary costs, and then estimate the main transport costs of routes.

We observe, for each carrier, a gain of 10 to 45 km/day, which, when converted into cost (and then taking into account manpower and time-based costs), leads to a decrease of outcoming cashflows of 30 to 140€/day, with a total outcoming cashflow gain of 545€. It is important to note that for 7 of the 8 carriers, the demand of the platform does not allow to dedicate a specific vehicle, and for one of them the reorganization allows to have a dedicated vehicle with a potential gain of 140€/day. As shown above, although the platform manages a small amount of deliveries nowadays (about 0.3% of total deliveries for Turin's area), cost gains of that re-organization are not negligible for carriers, and would increase widely if the number of deliveries increase or a network organization (for this type of platforms) is deployed.

5   Discussion and Conclusion

The proposed methodology aims to provide a framework for designing, assessing and validating the business model of a CL innovation from a multi-stakeholder's perspective. The framework is used to design a systemic business model taking into consideration a collaborative network of stakeholders, and then validate each stakeholder's business model by means of a cost-benefit analysis. Therefore, the framework allows designing different business model configurations while demonstrating the economic "winners" and "losers". The framework thus enables to propose a correct allocation of resources and benefits so to increase the chance of a widespread diffusion. The framework has been applied to a consolidation center operated by a northern Italian university, which allows its employees to pickup their e-commerce deliveries at the more convenient times and benefits the route optimization of LSPs. The CBA calculation have indeed proven that LSPs reduce their operating costs, and thus

---

[1] https://territoire.emse.fr/solutions/?type=geodelivery.

proposed methodology enables to shed light on an apparent opportunism of LSPs and final customers alike, who reap the benefits and do not share the costs. On the other hand, those costs are all borne by the University.

The main research and practical implications are the following. First, the framework is able to identify stakeholders, their roles and their relations, as well as to define the main investment and adoption choices. This will lead to a unified tool to assess the suitability of business models and support consensus search. Moreover, this case study serves as a testbed for the assessment methodology, which will be used for other collaborative logistics case studies in the future. Nevertheless, it might provide a best practice not only for other universities but also for other publicly-operated facilities (e.g. hospitals, central administration offices, ministries etc.) which account for a significant share of employment and could improve last-mile systems.

However, the framework is at a preliminary stage and needs an in-depth investigation of cost structures and cost-benefit assessment elements that will be done in a further research. The main goal of future research will be directed towards making the framework as a decision-making support tool for both private and public CL stakeholders.

References

1. De Marco, A., et al.: Business modeling of a city logistics ICT platform. In: 41st Annual IEEE Computer Software and Applications Conference (COMPSAC), pp. 783–789. IEEE (2017). https://doi.org/10.1109/COMPSAC.2017.76
2. Quak, H., Balm, S., Posthumus, B.: Evaluation of city logistics solutions with business model analysis. Procedia - Soc. Behav. Sci. 125, 111–124 (2014). https://doi.org/10.1016/j.sbspro.2014.01.1460
3. Gonzalez-Feliu, J., Basck, P., Morganti, E.: Urban logistics solutions and financing mechanisms: a scenario assessment analysis. Eur. Transp. Eur. 54, 1–16 (2013)
4. van Duin, J.H.R., Quak, H., Muñuzuri, J.: Revival of cost benefit analysis for evaluating the city distribution center concept. In: Innovations in City Logistics, pp. 97–114. Nova Science, New York (2008)
5. Lindawati, van Schagen, J., Goh, M., de Souza, R.: Collaboration in urban logistics: motivations and barriers. Int. J. Urban Sci. 18, 278–290 (2014)
6. Gonzalez-Feliu, J., Morana, J.: Collaborative transportation sharing: from theory to practice via a case study from France. In: Technologies for Supporting Reasoning Communities and Collaborative Decision Making: Cooperative Approaches, pp. 252–271. IGI Global, Hershey (2011)
7. Gonzalez-Feliu, J., Morana, J., Grau, J.-M.S., Ma, T.-Y.: Design and scenario assessment for collaborative logistics and freight transport systems. Int. J. Transp. Econ. (internazionale di Econ. dei Trasp.) 40, 207–240 (2013)
8. Pan, S., Ballot, E., Fontane, F.: The reduction of greenhouse gas emissions from freight transport by pooling supply chains. Int. J. Prod. Econ. 143, 86–94 (2013)
9. Lambert, D.M., Emmelhainz, M.A., Gardner, J.T.: Developing and implementing supply chain partnerships. Int. J. Logist. Manag. 7, 1–18 (1996)
10. Quak, H., Lindholm, M., Tavasszy, L., Browne, M.: From freight partnerships to city logistics living labs–giving meaning to the elusive concept of living labs. Transp. Res. Procedia. 12, 461–473 (2016)

11. Macário, R., Galelo, A., Martins, P.M.: Business models in urban logistics. Ing. y Desarro. **24**, 77–96 (2008)
12. Gonzalez-Feliu, J.: Sustainable Urban Logistics: Planning and Evaluation. Wiley, Hoboken (2018)
13. Afuah, A.: Business Models: A Strategic Management Approach. McGraw-Hill/Irwin, New York (2004)
14. Johnson, M.W., Christensen, C.M., Kagermann, H.: Reinventing your business model. Harv. Bus. Rev. **86** (2008). https://doi.org/10.1111/j.0955-6419.2005.00347.x
15. Amit, R., Zott, C.: Value creation in e-business. Strateg. Manag. J. **22**, 493–520 (2001). https://doi.org/10.1002/smj.187
16. Osterwalder, A., Pigneur, Y.: Business Model Generation: A Handbook for Visionaries, Game Changers, and Challengers. Wiley, New York (2010). https://doi.org/10.1523/JNEUROSCI.0307-10.2010
17. Zenezini, G.: A new evaluation approach to city logistics projects - a business-oriented agent-based model (2018)
18. Cagliano, A.C., De Marco, A., Mangano, G., Zenezini, G.: Assessing city logistics projects: a business-oriented approach. In: Proceedings of the Summer School Francesco Turco, Napoli, Italy, 13–15 September 2016 (2016)
19. Suksri, J., Raicu, R.: Developing a conceptual framework for the evaluation of urban freight distribution initiatives. In: Procedia - Social and Behavioral Sciences Seventh International Conference on City Logististics which was held 7–9 June 2011, Mallorca, Spain, vol. 39, pp. 321–332 (2012). https://doi.org/10.1016/j.sbspro.2012.03.111
20. Gonzalez-Feliu, J.: A joint freight catchment and cost benefit analysis to assess rail urban logistics scenarios. In: Temponi, C., Vandaele, N. (eds.) ILS 2016. LNBIP, vol. 262, pp. 14–27. Springer, Cham (2018). https://doi.org/10.1007/978-3-319-73758-4_2
21. Dixon, T.: Computer software availability for valuation (property valuation, development appraisal and portfolio analysis). J. Valuat. **4**, 21–32 (1986)
22. Gonzalez-Feliu, J.: Sustainable Urban Logistics. Wiley, Hoboken (2018). https://doi.org/10.1002/9781119421948
23. AGCOM: Servizio Economico Statistico (2018)

Assessment of Failures in Collaborative Human-Robot Assembly Workcells

Domenico A. Maisano, Dario Antonelli$^{(\boxtimes)}$,
and Fiorenzo Franceschini

DIGEP (Department of Management and Production Engineering),
Politecnico di Torino, Corso Duca degli Abruzzi 24, 10129 Turin, Italy
{domenico.maisano,dario.antonelli,
fiorenzo.franceschini}@polito.it

Abstract. Collaborative Human-Robot workcells introduce robot-assisted operations in small-volume production or assembly processes, where conventional automation is noncompetitive. Unfortunately, the collaborative work of humans and robots sharing the same work area and/or working on the same assembly operation may pose unprecedented problems and failure risks. *Failure Mode, Effects and Criticality Analysis* (FMECA) is a popular tool to design reliable processes, which investigates the potential failure modes from the perspective of *severity*, *occurrence* and *detection*. The traditional FMECA approach requires the assessment of failure modes to be carried out collectively by a group of experts. Nevertheless, in the field of Human-Robot collaboration, experts are often unlikely to agree in their judgements, due to the almost inexistent historical records. Additionally, the traditional approach is not appropriate for decentralized production/assembly processes.

The paper revisits the traditional approach and integrates it with the ZM_{II}-technique – i.e., a recent aggregation technique developed by the authors – which overcomes some limitations, including but not limited to: (i) arbitrary categorization and questionable aggregation of the expert judgments, (ii) disregarding the variability in these judgments, and (iii) disregarding the result uncertainty. The description is supported by a real-life application example.

Keywords: FMECA · Distributed manufacturing systems ·
Human-Robot collaboration · Failure-mode assessment

1 Introduction and Literature Review

Human-Robot Collaboration (HRC) is one of the more significant enabling technologies in the Industry 4.0 framework. Several countries adopt supporting policies to boost the upgrade of existing machine tools and robots with new collaborative models compliant with Industry 4.0 guidelines [1].

The technical issues raised by the introduction of humans and robots in the same workspace have been solved by robot manufacturers. Safety standards specific for HRC have been defined (ISO/TS 10218 and ISO/TS 15066) [18, 19]. Precision, accuracy and repeatability of HRC are in line with most industrial requirements [2].

© IFIP International Federation for Information Processing 2019
Published by Springer Nature Switzerland AG 2019
L. M. Camarinha-Matos et al. (Eds.): PRO-VE 2019, IFIP AICT 568, pp. 562–571, 2019.
https://doi.org/10.1007/978-3-030-28464-0_49

Nevertheless, there are still some unsolved problems that are strictly linked to the concept of HRC. First, there is a diffuse lack of confidence in the robot as a teammate. Furthermore, mistakes in the communication between human and robot may represent an unprecedented source of problems and failure risks for the process. It is therefore necessary to develop proofing methods that neutralize the most critical problems.

Common risk analysis methods applied to robotic workcells are *Fault Tree Analysis* (FTA) and *Failure Mode and Effects and Criticality Analysis* (FMECA) [3]. There is consensus among authors that both of them are not immediately applicable because the information of the risks cannot be estimated at this stage. Additionally, FTA can only be applied with the support of history of preceding similar processes. This is not the case of the study, as HRC is a new process non-experimented before.

This paper focuses on the FMECA, which is a very popular technique to improve the reliability of products, services and manufacturing processes, by analyzing failure scenarios before they have occurred and preventing the occurrence of causes or mechanisms of failures [4]. Applied to manufacturing processes, the FMECA is very useful to improve reliability and safety and provide a useful basis for planning the corresponding predictive maintenance [5].

The FMECA is carried out by a cross-functional and multidisciplinary team of experts (typically composed of engineers and technicians specialized in design, testing, reliability, quality, maintenance, manufacturing, safety, etc.), coordinated by a team leader. The experts must overcome conflicting situations and converge towards a shared agreement.

The most critical activity is concerned with the priority assessment of failure modes/causes, based on the *Risk Priority Number* (*RPN*), which is a composite indicator given by the product of the three dimensions of *occurrence* (*O*), *severity* (*S*), and *detection* (*D*). Each of these dimensions is determined by collective judgment, using a conventional ordinal scale from 1 to 10. The failure modes with higher *RPN*s are considered more critical and deserve priority for the implementation of risk mitigation actions: since the resources (time and money) available for corrective actions are (by definition) limited, it is reasonable to concentrate them where they are most needed, tolerating the minor failure modes.

The traditional method for prioritizing failure modes shows important shortcomings, extensively debated in the scientific literature [6–8]; including but not limited to:

- Use of arbitrary reference tables for assigning scores to the three dimensions *S*, *O* and *D*.
- The three dimensions *S*, *O* and *D* are arbitrarily considered as equally important.
- Since *S*, *O* and *D* are evaluated using ordinal scales, their product is not a meaningful measure according to the measurement theory [9].
- The degree of disagreement among the team members in formulating collective judgments is not taken into account.

It is particularly challenging to assess the role of FMECA in the current globalised scenario, which is increasingly characterised by *distributed manufacturing processes* i.e., a form of decentralized manufacturing practiced by enterprises, using a network of geographically dispersed facilities that are supposed to be flexible, reconfigurable and coordinated through information technology. Unfortunately, decentralized production in some ways hampers the application of the traditional FMECA. Firstly, the fact that experts are numerous may increase the chances of conflicts [10]. Secondly, only few of them generally have competence on HRC. Thirdly, there is not a great deal of experience on which to rely on.

The purpose of this paper is to revisit the traditional FMECA approach, making it reliable also when there is a substantial disagreement among experts on the potential problems and failure risks of a process. The revisited approach allows the aggregation of individual judgments by experts, through a recent aggregation technique – called ZM_{II} – which combines the Thurstone's *Law of Comparative Judgment* (LCJ) and the *Generalized Least Squares* (GLS) method [11–13].

The remainder of the paper is organized into four sections. Section 2 introduces a real-life case study that will accompany the explanation of the proposed approach. Section 3 briefly recalls the ZM_{II}-technique. Section 4 illustrates the proposed methodology in detail, exemplifying its application to the above case study. Finally, Sect. 5 summarizes the original contributions of this paper, its practical implications, limitations and suggestions for future research.

2 Case Study

An important multinational company (anonymous for reasons of confidentiality) designs, develops, manufactures and markets seats for a number of applications, ranging from cars to aircrafts. Since the relevant assembly operations are complex and require a relatively high level of dexterity, they are largely manual. To support operators in critical manual tasks, reducing the possibility of error, collaborative robots are introduced. The case study is the assembly of a seat-frame component, which consists of fixing different flanges on a common base. Figure 1a shows the flowchart of human and robot interaction through a Human Robot Interaction System (HRIS). In Fig. 1b a simplified part is designed for sake of laboratory tests. The most frequent collaborative task is when the robot holds a flange in position and the operator fixes it with screws; this operation is performed collaboratively, as illustrated in Fig. 1c.

The company carries out this manufacturing process in four worldwide plants located in four countries (i.e., Germany, Poland, United States and China). Since, the employed equipment is almost equivalent, it is reasonable to expect that equivalent processes are likely to be subject to the same failure modes/causes. Following this reasoning, it would be appropriate to share the experience accumulated in the various production facilities.

The above four processes are managed by twenty total engineers/technicians, hereinafter referred to as "experts". Given the great difficulty in bringing together all the experts and making them interact to reach shared decisions, the traditional FMECA approach would be extremely difficult to manage, especially with reference to activities concerning the formulation of collective judgments.

The initial activities of data collection, process analysis and determination of failure modes/causes are coordinated by a team leader, who collects information and technical indications received from other experts, processing and organizing them appropriately.

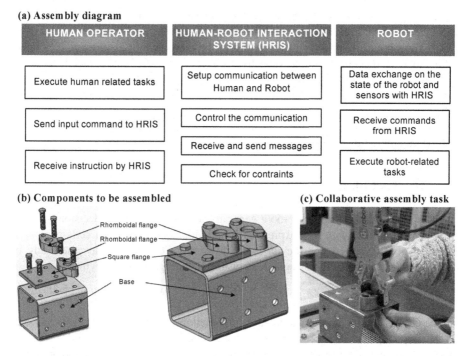

(a) Assembly diagram

HUMAN OPERATOR	HUMAN-ROBOT INTERACTION SYSTEM (HRIS)	ROBOT
Execute human related tasks	Setup communication between Human and Robot	Data exchange on the state of the robot and sensors with HRIS
Send input command to HRIS	Control the communication	Receive commands from HRIS
	Receive and send messages	
Receive instruction by HRIS	Check for contraints	Execute robot-related tasks

(b) Components to be assembled

Rhomboidal flange
Rhomboidal flange
Square flange
Base

(c) Collaborative assembly task

Fig. 1. Synthetic description of a sub-process of collaborative Human-Robot assembly: (a) assembly diagram, (b) drawing of the components to be assembled, and (c) example of assembly task performed collaboratively.

Function	Failure modes	Potential effects	(S) Sever.	Failure causes	(O) Occurr.	Current process control(s)	(D) Detect.	Failure mode-cause abbreviation	RPN
A - Picking and positioning flanges	A.1 - Non-starting of the assembly cycle	Assembly process delay		A.1.1 - Incorrect reception of the voice command		Notification of the received voice command		f_1	
				A.1.2 - Wrong voice command by the operator		None		f_2	
	A.2 - Flange failure to pick up	Assembly process interruption		A.2.1 - Empty flange buffer		Operator visual control		f_3	
				A.2.2 - Robot does not clamp the flange		None		f_4	
	A.3 - Flange drop	Flange damage and assembly process slowdown		A.3.1 - Defective grasp of the end robot gripper		Operator visual control		f_5	
	A.4 - Incorrect positioning of the flange on the base	Assembly process slowdown		A.4.1 - Incomplete removal of flange packaging		Operator visual control		f_6	
				A.4.2 - Flange unloaded inaccurately (spatially and/or temporally).		Operator visual control		f_7	
	A.5 - Collision between robot and operator	Assembly process slowdown and (minor) injuries to the operator		A.5.1 - Wrong operator position		None		f_8	
				A.5.2 - Malfunctioning of robot collision-avoidance sensor		None		f_9	
B - Fixing flanges to the base	B.1 - Unstable robot while keeping the flange in position	Slight slowdown of the assembly process		B.1.1 - Malfunctioning of robot position sensor		Operator visual control		f_{10}	
	B.2 - Picking the wrong screw	Slowdown of the assembly process		B.2.1 - Human error in the choice of the correct screw		Poka-yoke		f_{11}	
	B.3 - Screw stripping	Non-conformity of the assembled part and slowdown of the assembly process		B.3.1 - Excessive tightening torque		None		f_{12}	

Fig. 2. (Incomplete) FMECA table related to a Human-Robot collaborative assembly process of a seat frame.

The results of the initial activities are summarised in the (incomplete) FMECA table in Fig. 2, in which twelve failure mode-cause combinations have been determined (f_1 to f_{12}), which should be prioritized according to the three factors of interest. It is interesting to note that the potential (negative) effects of failure modes mainly concern interruptions/slowdowns in assembly operations, with no real safety risks. This is no longer surprising, given the relatively stringent safety standards of collaborative robots [19].

Collective assignments of the S, O and D scores and their aggregation through RPN will be completed using the new revisited FMECA.

3 ZM_{II}-Technique

The ZM_{II}-technique can be used more generally for any large group-decision problem in which a number of *judges* express their individual judgments on certain *objects*, based on the degree of specific *attributes* [14, 16]. Considering the case study in Sect. 2, we can identify three separate decision-making problems in which:

- the judges are the twenty experts (e_1 to e_{20}) affiliated to four production plants of the company of interest.
- the objects are the failure mode-cause combinations (f_1 to f_{12}) in Fig. 2; for the sake of simplicity, these objects will be hereafter referred to as "failure modes".
- the attributes are respectively S for the first problem, O for the second problem, and D for the third problem.

The ZM_{II}-technique can be seen as a black box transforming some specific *input* data – i.e., judgments on n failure modes, formulated by m experts – into some specific *output* data – i.e., *ratio* scaling of the failure modes, with a relevant uncertainty estimation. Precisely, for each (i-th) failure mode, the ZM_{II}-technique produces an estimate of (1) the (mean) ratio-scale value y_i and (2) the corresponding standard deviation σ_{y_i}.

A prerequisite of the ZM_{II}-technique is that each expert formulates a ranking of the failure modes – i.e., an ordered sequence of them, with those having the highest grade of the attribute in the top positions and those having the lowest grade of the attribute in the bottom ones. E.g., considering the case study in Sect. 2, the failure modes are supposed to be ranked according to the degree of each of the dimensions of interest (i.e., S, O or D).

Apart from the *regular* failure modes, experts may also include two (fictitious) *dummy* failure modes in their rankings: i.e., one (f_Z) corresponding to the *absence* of the attribute of interest, and one (f_M) corresponding to the *maximum-imaginable* degree of the attribute. Referring to the case study, f_Z corresponds to a fictitious failure mode of absent severity/occurrence/detection (e.g., a failure mode associated with the score $S = 1/O = 1/D = 1$ [15]), while f_M corresponds to a fictitious failure mode of the maximum-imaginable severity (e.g., a failure mode associated with the score $S = 10/O = 10/D = 10$).

In the best cases, experts formulate *complete* rankings, characterised by relationships of *strict dominance* (e.g., "$f_i > f_j$") or *indifference* (e.g., "$f_i \sim f_j$") among the possible pairs of failure modes [17]. The formulation of these rankings may be problematic when the number of failure modes is large. To overcome this obstacle, a flexible response mode that tolerates *incomplete* rankings can be adopted.

Returning to the case study, each of the experts formulates his/her own three distinct (subjective) rankings of the failure modes, based on the three dimensions S, O and D; results are shown in Fig. 3. It can be noted that most of the experts have opted for the formulation of incomplete rankings, probably because they are simpler and faster. This kind of response mode may also favour data reliability since, in case of indecision, experts are not necessarily forced to provide complete and falsely precise responses [17].

Rankings indicate a significant inter-expert disagreement; e.g., while several experts place the failure mode f_5 among the top positions of their S-rankings, others place it among the bottom positions. This reflects the actual difficulty of experts to converge towards a collective judgement.

The mathematical formalization of the problem relies on the postulates and simplifying assumptions of the *Law of Comparative Judgment* (LCJ) by Thurstone [11], who postulated the existence of a *psychological continuum*, i.e., an abstract and unknown unidimensional scale, in which objects are positioned depending on the degree of a certain attribute. The position of a generic i-th object (f_i) is postulated to be distributed normally, in order to reflect the intrinsic expert-to-expert variability: $f_i \sim N(x_i, \sigma_i^2)$, where x_i and σ_i^2 are the unknown mean value and variance related to the degree of the attribute of that object.

Considering two generic objects, f_i and f_j, and having introduced further simplifying hypotheses [4] (e.g., lack of correlation, $\sigma_i^2 = \sigma^2 \ \forall i, \ldots$), it can be asserted that:

$$p_{ij} = P\left[(f_i - f_j) > 0\right] = 1 - \Phi[-(x_i - x_j)] \tag{1}$$

Extending the reasoning to all possible pairs of objects, an over-determined system of equations (similar to that in Eq. 1) can be obtained and solved by applying the *Generalized Least Squares* (GLS) method [12], which allows to obtain an estimate of the mean value of the degree of the attribute of each failure mode: $X = [\ldots, x_i, \ldots]^T$, which is expressed on an arbitrary *interval* scale, with a relevant dispersion estimation.

Process	Expert	Ranking type	Manage f_Z/f_M?	t/b value	Order t/b-objects?	Dimension	Ranking
						S	$(f_M \sim f_8)>f_3>(f_1 \sim f_9)>(f_2 \sim f_{12})>f_4>f_{11}>(f_5 \sim f_{10})>f_6>(f_7 \sim f_Z)$
	e_1	Complete	Yes	N/A	N/A	O	$f_M>f_3>f_8>(f_4 \sim f_7 \sim f_1 \sim f_{11})>(f_6 \sim f_2)>f_{10}>f_{12}>f_5>(f_9 \sim f_Z)$
						D	$(f_M \sim f_9 \sim f_{10} \sim f_{12})>f_6>f_7>f_4>(f_8 \sim f_2)>(f_{11} \sim f_3)>f_1>f_5>f_Z$
						S	$\{f_M \Vert f_5 \Vert f_9\}>\{f_Z \Vert f_1 \Vert f_2 \Vert f_3 \Vert f_4 \Vert f_6 \Vert f_7 \Vert f_8 \Vert f_{10} \Vert f_{11} \Vert f_{12}\}$
	e_2	Type-t	N/A	2	No	O	$\{f_M \Vert f_3 \Vert f_{11}\}>\{f_Z \Vert f_1 \Vert f_2 \Vert f_4 \Vert f_5 \Vert f_6 \Vert f_7 \Vert f_8 \Vert f_9 \Vert f_{10} \Vert f_{12}\}$
						D	$\{f_M \Vert f_6 \Vert f_{10}\}>\{f_Z \Vert f_1 \Vert f_2 \Vert f_3 \Vert f_4 \Vert f_5 \Vert f_7 \Vert f_8 \Vert f_9 \Vert f_{11} \Vert f_{12}\}$
						S	$\{f_M \Vert f_1 \Vert f_2 \Vert f_5 \Vert f_8 \Vert f_9\}>\{f_3 \Vert f_4 \Vert f_{10} \Vert f_{12}\}>\{f_Z \Vert f_6 \Vert f_7 \Vert f_{11}\}$
	e_3	Type-t&b	N/A	3	No	O	$\{f_M \Vert f_2 \Vert f_6 \Vert f_{12}\}>\{f_1 \Vert f_3 \Vert f_4 \Vert f_7 \Vert f_{10} \Vert f_{11}\}>\{f_Z \Vert f_5 \Vert f_8 \Vert f_9\}$
						D	$\{f_M \Vert f_7 \Vert f_{10} \Vert f_{12}\}>\{f_1 \Vert f_2 \Vert f_4 \Vert f_5 \Vert f_6 \Vert f_9\}>\{f_Z \Vert f_3 \Vert f_8 \Vert f_{11}\}$
						S	$\{f_M \Vert f_3 \Vert f_8\}>\{f_2 \Vert f_4 \Vert f_6 \Vert f_7 \Vert f_9 \Vert f_{12}\}>\{f_Z \Vert f_1 \Vert f_5 \Vert f_{10} \Vert f_{11}\}$
1.GER	e_4	Type-t&b	N/A	2	No	O	$\{f_M \Vert f_5 \Vert f_7 \Vert f_{11} \Vert f_{12}\}>\{f_2 \Vert f_3 \Vert f_4 \Vert f_6\}>\{f_Z \Vert f_1 \Vert f_8 \Vert f_9 \Vert f_{10}\}$
						D	$\{f_M \Vert f_6 \Vert f_9\}>\{f_1 \Vert f_2 \Vert f_3 \Vert f_4 \Vert f_5 \Vert f_{10} \Vert f_{11} \Vert f_{12}\}>\{f_Z \Vert f_7 \Vert f_8\}$
						S	$\{f_M \Vert (f_2 \sim f_9)\}>(f_8 \sim f_1)>(f_5 \sim f_6 \sim f_{10} \sim f_{12})>(f_4 \sim f_7 \sim f_3)>\{f_Z \Vert f_{11}\}$
	e_5	Quasi-complete	No	N/A	N/A	O	$\{f_M \Vert (f_3 \sim f_{11} \sim f_{12})\}>f_2>(f_1 \sim f_6)>f_{10}>f_5>f_8>\{f_Z \Vert (f_9 \sim f_4 \sim f_7)\}$
						D	$\{f_M \Vert (f_5 \sim f_6 \sim f_9)\}>f_{12}>f_3>f_{11}>f_2>f_{10}>f_4>f_8>f_7>\{f_Z \Vert f_1\}$
						S	$\{f_M \Vert f_3 \Vert f_8 \Vert f_9\}>\{f_Z \Vert f_1 \Vert f_2 \Vert f_4 \Vert f_5 \Vert f_6 \Vert f_7 \Vert f_{10} \Vert f_{11} \Vert f_{12}\}$
	e_6	Type-t	N/A	3	No	O	$\{f_M \Vert f_3 \Vert f_6 \Vert f_{12}\}>\{f_Z \Vert f_1 \Vert f_2 \Vert f_4 \Vert f_5 \Vert f_7 \Vert f_8 \Vert f_9 \Vert f_{10} \Vert f_{11}\}$
						D	$\{f_M \Vert f_5 \Vert f_{10} \Vert f_{12}\}>\{f_Z \Vert f_1 \Vert f_2 \Vert f_3 \Vert f_4 \Vert f_6 \Vert f_7 \Vert f_8 \Vert f_9 \Vert f_{11}\}$
						S	$\{f_M \Vert f_2 \Vert f_8\}>\{f_1 \Vert f_5 \Vert f_7 \Vert f_9 \Vert f_{10} \Vert f_{11} \Vert f_{12}\}>\{f_Z \Vert f_3 \Vert f_4 \Vert f_6\}$
	e_7	Type-t&b	N/A	2	No	O	$\{f_M \Vert f_2 \Vert f_3 \Vert f_5 \Vert f_{12}\}>\{f_1 \Vert f_8 \Vert f_{10} \Vert f_{11}\}>\{f_Z \Vert f_4 \Vert f_6 \Vert f_7 \Vert f_9\}$
						D	$\{f_M \Vert f_5 \Vert f_9\}>\{f_3 \Vert f_6 \Vert f_7 \Vert f_8 \Vert f_{10} \Vert f_{11} \Vert f_{12}\}>\{f_Z \Vert f_1 \Vert f_2 \Vert f_4\}$
						S	$(f_M \sim f_8)>(f_5 \sim f_1)>\{f_Z \Vert f_2 \Vert f_3 \Vert f_4 \Vert f_6 \Vert f_7 \Vert f_9 \Vert f_{10} \Vert f_{11} \Vert f_{12}\}$
	e_8	Type-t	Yes	3	Yes	O	$(f_M \sim f_3)>f_6>(f_2 \sim f_8)>\{f_Z \Vert f_1 \Vert f_4 \Vert f_5 \Vert f_7 \Vert f_9 \Vert f_{10} \Vert f_{11} \Vert f_{12}\}$
						D	$(f_M \sim f_9)>f_{10}>f_3>\{f_Z \Vert f_1 \Vert f_2 \Vert f_4 \Vert f_5 \Vert f_6 \Vert f_7 \Vert f_8 \Vert f_{11} \Vert f_{12}\}$
						S	$(f_M \sim f_4 \sim f_8)>f_3>\{f_1 \Vert f_2 \Vert f_5 \Vert f_6 \Vert f_9 \Vert f_{11}\}>(f_7 \sim f_{10} \sim f_Z \sim f_{12})$
	e_9	Type-t&b	Yes	3	Yes	O	$(f_M \sim f_2)>f_6>f_{10}>\{f_1 \Vert f_3 \Vert f_5 \Vert f_7 \Vert f_{11} \Vert f_{12}\}>(f_9 \sim f_4 \sim f_Z \sim f_8)$
						D	$(f_M \sim f_5 \sim f_9)>f_4>\{f_3 \Vert f_7 \Vert f_8 \Vert f_{10} \Vert f_{12}\}>(f_{11} \sim f_6)>f_1>(f_Z \sim f_2)$
2.POL						S	$\{f_M \Vert f_5 \Vert f_9\}>\{f_Z \Vert f_1 \Vert f_2 \Vert f_3 \Vert f_4 \Vert f_6 \Vert f_7 \Vert f_8 \Vert f_{10} \Vert f_{11} \Vert f_{12}\}$
	e_{10}	Type-t	N/A	2	No	O	$\{f_M \Vert f_3 \Vert f_{12}\}>\{f_Z \Vert f_1 \Vert f_2 \Vert f_4 \Vert f_5 \Vert f_6 \Vert f_7 \Vert f_8 \Vert f_9 \Vert f_{10} \Vert f_{11}\}$
						D	$\{f_M \Vert f_3 \Vert f_4 \Vert f_{12}\}>\{f_Z \Vert f_1 \Vert f_2 \Vert f_5 \Vert f_6 \Vert f_7 \Vert f_8 \Vert f_9 \Vert f_{10} \Vert f_{11}\}$
						S	$\{f_M \Vert f_5 \Vert f_8 \Vert f_9 \Vert f_{12}\}>\{f_1 \Vert f_3 \Vert f_4 \Vert f_6 \Vert f_{11}\}>\{f_Z \Vert f_2 \Vert f_7 \Vert f_{10}\}$
	e_{11}	Type-t&b	N/A	3	No	O	$\{f_M \Vert f_3 \Vert f_{10} \Vert f_{11}\}>\{f_1 \Vert f_4 \Vert f_5 \Vert f_6 \Vert f_7 \Vert f_{12}\}>\{f_Z \Vert f_2 \Vert f_8 \Vert f_9\}$
						D	$\{f_M \Vert f_3 \Vert f_4 \Vert f_9\}>\{f_5 \Vert f_6 \Vert f_7 \Vert f_{10} \Vert f_{11} \Vert f_{12}\}>\{f_Z \Vert f_1 \Vert f_2 \Vert f_8\}$
						S	$(f_M \sim f_5)>f_3>\{f_Z \Vert f_1 \Vert f_2 \Vert f_4 \Vert f_6 \Vert f_7 \Vert f_8 \Vert f_9 \Vert f_{10} \Vert f_{11} \Vert f_{12}\}$
	e_{12}	Type-t	Yes	2	Yes	O	$f_M>f_6>(f_2 \sim f_1 \sim f_{11})>\{f_Z \Vert f_3 \Vert f_4 \Vert f_5 \Vert f_7 \Vert f_8 \Vert f_9 \Vert f_{10} \Vert f_{12}\}$
						D	$(f_M \sim f_{10} \sim f_{12})>\{f_Z \Vert f_1 \Vert f_2 \Vert f_3 \Vert f_4 \Vert f_5 \Vert f_6 \Vert f_7 \Vert f_8 \Vert f_9 \Vert f_{11}\}$
						S	$f_M>f_8>(f_4 \sim f_{12})>\{f_1 \Vert f_2 \Vert f_3 \Vert f_5 \Vert f_7 \Vert f_9 \Vert f_{11}\}>(f_6 \sim f_{10})>f_Z$
	e_{13}	Type-t&b	Yes	2	Yes	O	$f_M>(f_3 \sim f_6)>\{f_1 \Vert f_2 \Vert f_4 \Vert f_7 \Vert f_8 \Vert f_{11} \Vert f_{12}\}>(f_9 \sim f_{10} \sim f_5 \sim f_Z)$
						D	$(f_M \sim f_9 \sim f_{12})>\{f_2 \Vert f_3 \Vert f_4 \Vert f_5 \Vert f_6 \Vert f_8 \Vert f_{10} \Vert f_{11}\}>f_7>(f_1 \sim f_Z)$
3.USA						S	$\{f_M \Vert f_3 \Vert f_5 \Vert f_9\}>\{f_Z \Vert f_1 \Vert f_2 \Vert f_4 \Vert f_6 \Vert f_7 \Vert f_8 \Vert f_{10} \Vert f_{11} \Vert f_{12}\}$
	e_{14}	Type-t	N/A	3	No	O	$\{f_M \Vert f_3 \Vert f_5 \Vert f_{11}\}>\{f_Z \Vert f_1 \Vert f_2 \Vert f_4 \Vert f_6 \Vert f_7 \Vert f_8 \Vert f_9 \Vert f_{10} \Vert f_{12}\}$
						D	$\{f_M \Vert f_2 \Vert f_{10} \Vert f_{11} \Vert f_{12}\}>\{f_Z \Vert f_1 \Vert f_3 \Vert f_4 \Vert f_5 \Vert f_6 \Vert f_7 \Vert f_8 \Vert f_9\}$
						S	$\{f_M \Vert f_8\}>f_3>\{f_1 \Vert f_4 \Vert f_5 \Vert f_6 \Vert f_7 \Vert f_9 \Vert f_{11} \Vert f_{12}\}>f_2>\{f_Z \Vert f_{10}\}$
	e_{15}	Type-t&b	No	2	Yes	O	$\{f_M \Vert f_{12}\}>(f_6 \sim f_5)>\{f_1 \Vert f_2 \Vert f_3 \Vert f_4 \Vert f_7 \Vert f_{11}\}>\{f_Z \Vert (f_9 \sim f_{10} \sim f_8)\}$
						D	$\{f_M \Vert (f_9 \sim f_{12})\}>\{f_2 \Vert f_3 \Vert f_4 \Vert f_5 \Vert f_6 \Vert f_8 \Vert f_{10}\}>(f_{11} \sim f_7)>\{f_Z \Vert f_1\}$
						S	$(f_M \sim f_8)>\{f_Z \Vert f_1 \Vert f_2 \Vert f_3 \Vert f_4 \Vert f_5 \Vert f_6 \Vert f_7 \Vert f_9 \Vert f_{10} \Vert f_{11} \Vert f_{12}\}$
	e_{16}	Type-t	Yes	1	Yes	O	$(f_M \sim f_2)>\{f_Z \Vert f_1 \Vert f_3 \Vert f_4 \Vert f_5 \Vert f_6 \Vert f_7 \Vert f_8 \Vert f_9 \Vert f_{10} \Vert f_{11} \Vert f_{12}\}$
						D	$(f_M \sim f_{10} \sim f_{12})>\{f_Z \Vert f_1 \Vert f_2 \Vert f_3 \Vert f_4 \Vert f_5 \Vert f_6 \Vert f_7 \Vert f_8 \Vert f_9 \Vert f_{11}\}$
						S	$\{f_M \Vert (f_8 \sim f_9)\}>(f_3 \sim f_7)>\{f_1 \Vert f_2 \Vert f_{12}\}>(f_5 \sim f_6 \sim f_{10} \sim f_4)>\{f_Z \Vert f_{11}\}$
	e_{17}	Type-t&b	No	3	Yes	O	$\{f_M \Vert f_{11}\}>f_{12}>f_3>\{f_1 \Vert f_2 \Vert f_4 \Vert f_7 \Vert f_8\}>(f_5 \sim f_6)>\{f_Z \Vert (f_{10} \sim f_9)\}$
						D	$\{f_M \Vert f_{12}\}>(f_{10} \sim f_9)>\{f_2 \Vert f_4 \Vert f_5 \Vert f_6 \Vert f_7 \Vert f_8\}>\{f_Z \Vert (f_3 \sim f_1 \sim f_{11})\}$
						S	$\{f_M \Vert (f_4 \sim f_8)\}>\{f_Z \Vert f_1 \Vert f_2 \Vert f_3 \Vert f_5 \Vert f_6 \Vert f_7 \Vert f_9 \Vert f_{10} \Vert f_{11} \Vert f_{12}\}$
4.CHN	e_{18}	Type-t	No	2	Yes	O	$\{f_M \Vert f_3\}>(f_2 \sim f_7 \sim f_8)>\{f_Z \Vert f_1 \Vert f_4 \Vert f_5 \Vert f_6 \Vert f_9 \Vert f_{10} \Vert f_{11} \Vert f_{12}\}$
						D	$\{f_M \Vert f_{12}\}>(f_{10} \sim f_3)>\{f_Z \Vert f_1 \Vert f_2 \Vert f_4 \Vert f_5 \Vert f_6 \Vert f_7 \Vert f_8 \Vert f_9 \Vert f_{11}\}$
						S	$(f_M \sim f_8)>\{f_1 \Vert f_2 \Vert f_3 \Vert f_4 \Vert f_5 \Vert f_6 \Vert f_9 \Vert f_{10} \Vert f_{12}\}>(f_Z \sim f_{11} \sim f_7)$
	e_{19}	Type-t&b	Yes	1	Yes	O	$(f_M \sim f_3)>\{f_1 \Vert f_2 \Vert f_5 \Vert f_6 \Vert f_7 \Vert f_8 \Vert f_{11} \Vert f_{12}\}>(f_9 \sim f_{10} \sim f_Z \sim f_4)$
						D	$(f_M \sim f_{10})>\{f_2 \Vert f_3 \Vert f_4 \Vert f_5 \Vert f_6 \Vert f_7 \Vert f_8 \Vert f_9 \Vert f_{11} \Vert f_{12}\}>(f_1 \sim f_Z)$
						S	$\{f_M \Vert (f_8 \sim f_9)\}>(f_1 \sim f_5)>\{f_Z \Vert f_2 \Vert f_3 \Vert f_4 \Vert f_6 \Vert f_7 \Vert f_{10} \Vert f_{11} \Vert f_{12}\}$
	e_{20}	Type-t	No	3	Yes	O	$\{f_M \Vert f_1\}>f_5>f_{12}>\{f_Z \Vert f_2 \Vert f_3 \Vert f_4 \Vert f_6 \Vert f_7 \Vert f_8 \Vert f_9 \Vert f_{10} \Vert f_{11}\}$
						D	$\{f_M \Vert f_9\}>f_6>(f_7 \sim f_4)>\{f_Z \Vert f_1 \Vert f_2 \Vert f_3 \Vert f_5 \Vert f_8 \Vert f_{10} \Vert f_{11} \Vert f_{12}\}$

Fig. 3. Rankings of failure modes, formulated by the experts for each of the three dimensions (*S*, *O* and *D*). The failure modes identified directly by the experts are marked in black, while the reconstructed parts are marked in red. (Color figure online)

4 Proposed Methodology

The experts' rankings related to a certain dimension (*S*, *O* and *D*) are aggregated through the application of the ZM_{II}-technique. For a generic (*i*-th) failure mode, the aggregation can be performed through the classic multiplicative model of the *RPN* [4].

The uncertainty related to the RPN_i values can be determined by applying *delta method*, also referred as *law of propagation of uncertainty* or *error transmission formula* [17]. It is thus obtained:

$$\sigma_{RPN_i} = \sqrt{(O_i \cdot D_i)^2 \cdot \sigma_{S_i}^2 + (S_i \cdot D_i)^2 \cdot \sigma_{O_i}^2 + (S_i \cdot O_i)^2 \cdot \sigma_{D_i}^2}, \qquad (2)$$

where $\sigma_{S_i}^2$, $\sigma_{O_i}^2$ and $\sigma_{D_i}^2$ are the variances associated with the S_i, O_i and the D_i values related to the i-th failure mode.

The results of the application of the proposed methodology to the case study are shown in Table 1 and synthetically represented in the Pareto chart of Fig. 4. The most critical failure modes are those with higher RPN_i values. The relatively wide uncertainty bands (depicting the expanded-uncertainty values $\pm 2 \cdot \sigma_{RPN_i}$) indicate that the RPN_i alone is a "myopic" indicator, since it may perform differentiations that are unfounded from a statistical point of view. For instance, while it makes sense to say that f_3 is more critical than f_{10} or f_{11} (being the uncertainty band not superimposed), it can not necessarily be said that f_{10} deserves priority over f_{11}. These considerations give the team a few more degrees of freedom in the choice of corrective actions, perhaps taking into account other external constraints (such as cost, technical difficulty, time required, etc.).

Finally, we note that failure causes with higher RPN_i values tend to have higher dispersion. This sort of *heteroschedasticity* depends on the multiplicative aggregation model of S, O and D. The model could be replaced by other models (e.g. additive ones), in which appropriate weights could be introduced for weighing the three dimensions.

Table 1. Results of the analysis in terms of mean value and standard deviation of the S_i, O_i, D_i values and corresponding RPN_i values.

	S_i values		O_i values		D_i values		RPN_i values		
	Mean	St.dev.	Mean	St.dev.	Mean	St.dev.	Mean	St.dev.	U_{RPN_i}
f_1	5.35	0.54	4.81	0.53	1.05	0.67	235.9	36.1	70.7
f_2	4.68	0.54	5.91	0.49	3.55	0.56	222.8	33.2	65.1
f_3	5.92	0.50	7.57	0.53	4.97	0.50	138.3	23.8	46.6
f_4	4.63	0.52	2.80	0.56	5.18	0.52	98.1	20.9	40.9
f_5	6.00	0.49	4.34	0.50	5.32	0.51	89.4	24.3	47.7
f_6	2.71	0.60	5.71	0.50	5.78	0.51	89.4	22.7	44.5
f_7	2.57	0.57	4.17	0.54	3.79	0.54	67.3	16.9	33.1
f_8	8.78	0.56	3.64	0.53	2.80	0.62	50.3	16.3	32.0
f_9	7.53	0.56	0.19	0.71	7.78	0.50	45.8	15.6	30.5
f_{10}	2.33	0.60	2.92	0.54	7.40	0.48	40.6	11.9	23.3
f_{11}	2.21	0.62	6.28	0.52	3.31	0.57	26.9	17.7	34.7
f_{12}	4.76	0.54	6.33	0.51	7.83	0.49	11.3	41.8	81.9

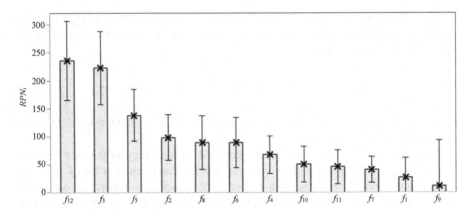

Fig. 4. Pareto chart of the failure modes based on RPN_i values and relevant expanded-uncertainty bands ($\pm 2 \cdot \sigma_{RPN_i}$).

5 Conclusions

The paper illustrated an innovative approach for FMECA, when applied to HRC in distributed manufacturing environments. This approach has important implications that make it more suitable than the traditional FMECA for this practical context, characterised by the greater difficulty of experts in converging towards a collective decision.

Among the advantages: the method does not require experts to meet physically and make collective decisions; it includes a flexible response mode; it provides an estimation of the uncertainty of the results.

Although there is no absolute reference ("gold standard") to evaluate the validity of the proposed approach with respect to the traditional one, we believe that it is superior from the conceptual point of view as it overcomes some widely debated shortcomings of the classic FMECA (e.g., it does not require the use of arbitrary reference tables for S, O and D and it does not introduce any unduly "promotion" of the judgment scales).

Among the limitations: the proposed response mode, although being flexible, represents a novelty that could create some problems, especially for more experienced users that are accustomed to the traditional procedure; like the traditional procedure, the three dimensions S, O and D were considered as equally important.

Regarding the future, we plan to replace the classic multiplicative model of the RPN with a new one that allows (1) to weigh the contributions of S, O and D and (2) to visualize their uncertainty contribution on the resulting RPN values.

References

1. Almada-Lobo, F.: The industry 4.0 revolution and the future of manufacturing execution systems (MES). J. Innov. Manag. **3**(4), 16–21 (2016)
2. Antonelli, D., Astanin, S.: Qualification of a collaborative human-robot welding cell. Procedia CIRP **41**, 352–357 (2016)

3. Gopinath, V., Johansen, K.: Risk assessment process for collaborative assembly – a job safety analysis approach. Procedia CIRP **44**, 199–203 (2016)
4. Stamatis, D.H.: Failure Mode and Effect Analysis: FMECA from Theory to Execution. ASQ Quality Press, Milwaukee (2003)
5. Johnson, K.G., Khan, M.K.: A study into the use of the process failure mode and effects analysis (FMECA) in the automotive industry in the UK. J. Mater. Process. Technol. **139** (1–3), 348–356 (2003)
6. Certa, A., Hopps, F., Inghilleri, R., La Fata, C.M.: A Dempster-Shafer theory-based approach to the failure mode, effects and criticality analysis (FMECA) under epistemic uncertainty: application to the propulsion system of a fishing vessel. Reliab. Eng. Syst. Saf. **159**, 69–79 (2017)
7. Liu, H.C., You, J.X., Shan, M.M., Su, Q.: Systematic failure mode and effect analysis using a hybrid multiple criteria decision-making approach. Tot. Qual. Manag. Bus. Excellence **30** (5–6), 537–564 (2019)
8. Das Adhikary, D., Kumar Bose, G., Bose, D., Mitra, S.: Multi criteria FMECA for coal-fired thermal power plants using COPRAS-G. Int. J. Qual. Reliab. Manag. **31**(5), 601–614 (2014)
9. Franceschini, F., Galetto, M., Maisano, D.: Designing Performance Measurement Systems: Theory and Practice of Key Performance Indicators. Management for Professionals. Springer, Berlin (2019). https://doi.org/10.1007/978-3-030-01192-5
10. Cai, C.G., Xu, X.H., Wang, P., Chen, X.H.: A multi-stage conflict style large group emergency decision-making method. Soft. Comput. **21**(19), 5765–5778 (2017)
11. Thurstone, L.L.: A law of comparative judgment. Psychol. Rev. **34**(4), 273 (1927)
12. Kariya, T., Kurata, H.: Generalized Least Squares. Wiley, New York (2004)
13. Franceschini, F., Maisano, D.: Fusion of partial orderings for decision problems in quality management. In: Proceedings of ICQEM 2018, Barcelona, 11–13 July 2018 (2018)
14. Franceschini, F., Maisano, D.: Fusing incomplete preference rankings in design for manufacturing applications through the ZMII-technique. Int. J. Comput. Integr. Manuf. (2019, to appear). https://doi.org/10.1007/s00170-019-03675-5
15. AIAG (Automotive Industry Action Group) and VDA (Verband der Automobilindustrie): Failure Mode and Effects Analysis – Design FMECA and Process FMECA Handbook, Southfield, MI (2019)
16. JCGM 100:2008: Evaluation of Measurement Data - Guide to the Expression of Uncertainty in Measurement. BIPM, Paris (2008)
17. Franceschini, F., Galetto, M.: A new approach for evaluation of risk priorities of failure modes in FMECA. Int. J. Prod. Res. **39**(13), 2991–3002 (2001)
18. ISO 10218:2011: Robots and Robotic Devices – Safety Requirements for Industrial Robots. ISO, Geneva (2011)
19. ISO/TS 15066:2016: Robots and Robotic Devices – Collaborative Robots. ISO, Geneva (2016)

Discrete Event Simulation as a Support in the Decision Making to Improve Product and Process in the Automotive Industry - A Fuel Pump Component Case Study

Luis E. Villagomez[1(✉)], Daniel Cortés[1], José Ramírez[1],
Alejandro Álvarez[1], Rafael Batres[1], Ivann Reyes[2], Germán Esparza[3],
Nancy Cruz[3], and Arturo Molina[1]

[1] School of Engineering and Sciences, Tecnologico de Monterrey,
14380 Mexico City, Mexico
{levg, a01655708, a00995924, a01421567,
rafael.batres, armolina}@tec.mx
[2] Grupo Dinamex, S.A. Technical Support, Mexico,
52976 Lopez Mateos, Mexico
ireyes@dinamex.com.mx
[3] Siemens PLM Mesoamerica, Mexico City, Mexico
{german.esparza, nancy.cruz}@siemens.com

Abstract. In Mexico, the automotive sector is one of the most profitable industrial activities as it contributes 2.9% of the national GDP [1]. However, there still exist facilities that are in transit of manufacturing processes improvement. In recent years, the adoption of emergent technologies, practices and tools that lead into the Industry 4.0, has been a parameter to compete and remain competitive in the global market. Upgrading all the processes is not always a viable solution. Thus, companies must identify the optimal solution to increase their productivity. Numerous technologies are available to facilitate this migration. This paper aims to show how discrete event simulation with an action research cycle supports the decision making in process improvement aided by the information collected in Collaborative Networks. A case study is shown in the automotive sector to validate changes in processes based on estimated energy consumption, maintenance strategies, process time reduction and the implementation of state-of-the-art sustainable processes.

Keywords: Automotive industry · Discrete event simulation ·
Plant Simulation · Plasma nitriding · Modeling and simulation ·
Collaborative Networks

1 Introduction

In recent years, Industry 4.0 has been a parameter of progress among the developing countries [2–4]. The adoption of new information technologies and techniques can promote sustainable motives [5] within a circular economy [6], with an integral society [7] and environmental benefits [8, 9]. According to Stock and Seliger [10], sustainability

© IFIP International Federation for Information Processing 2019
Published by Springer Nature Switzerland AG 2019
L. M. Camarinha-Matos et al. (Eds.): PRO-VE 2019, IFIP AICT 568, pp. 572–581, 2019.
https://doi.org/10.1007/978-3-030-28464-0_50

trends are based on macro perspectives, such as value creation networks and business models but also on a micro perspective such as improvements in product, process, manufacturing equipment, organization optimization and better management of human resources, through end-to-end engineering, vertical and horizontal integration. This interconnectivity allows for the creation of smart factories that implement the emergent technologies, practices and tools to create environments where hardware and software interact in real-time and enable manufacturing information flow. Interconnection, information transparency and decentralised decisions are the principles that promote manufacturing firms into Industry 4.0 [11]. In fact, the natural way to migrate from a traditional manufacturing firm into sensing, smart and sustainable firm system. This can be achieved by implementing Collaborative Networks (CN), which in turn enable those principles as a native evolution. CN not only allows the relationship among different areas of the manufacturing firm but also delivers information flow about the individual processes along all the productive line giving information that can be used to perform improvements. In this way, process optimisation can be monitored and reduced using adequated technology that can be rapidly assessed using CN. A commonly resource subject to optimisation among industries is energy consumption. For this, Otis et al. [12] establishes a relationship on the reduction of energy consumption with the improvement of manufacturing process plans, such as reduction of start-up times, execution of preventive maintenance, proper planning of the master production program and materials.

Within a manufacturing complex, there exist many entities where either big or small adjustments could be carried out to improve the production process [13], however, it identifies the changes that result in better economic and sustainable outcomes. Decision-making practices driven by CN and based on knowledge to improve the quality of processes and the use of technological tools like Tecnomatix Plant Simulation software allow to visualise and evaluate in detail the effects of such decisions on the plant layout to find the optimal results. This paper focuses on a simulation-based and CN approach applied to a production system to assess the advantages of migrating to sustainable technology. This system is owned by a Mexican company, which is dedicated to aftermarket spare parts. A CN was used to link information related to manufacturing into the decision-making process and pursue the motives of a manufacturing firm in the automotive sector. In Sect. 2, presents a brief introduction of how Discrete Event Simulation (DES) can be used to model complex production systems. Then, in Sect. 3, Action Research is described. Subsequently, in Sect. 4, the authors explain the use of DES to the creation of a collaborative network. Furthermore, in Sect. 5, discusses the results obtained with a case study. Finally, in Sect. 6 presents the conclusions and future work.

2   Discrete Event Simulation

Computer simulation is described as an attempt to model a real or hypothetical situation. Computational simulation is divided into continuous simulation and discrete event simulation (DES). DES tracks the changes in the components of a model when they occur. Unlike a continuous simulation, where the clock runs constantly, DES clock jumps from one event to the next, showing only the state changes of the model components at certain moments. Negahban and Smith [14] showed that DES is an effective tool to assist the plant design and operation but recognised that there is still the need of supporting with more efficient techniques to deal with the complexity of manufacturing systems. DES has been adopted as an instrument from Industry 4.0 [15–17] to analyse and optimise decisions ranging from production decisions to supply chain management. It provides the ability to visualise changes in specific variables, relevant aspects for the stakeholders, supply chain, human safety. In general, scenarios that would prevent costs for the decision makers [18, 19]. Thus, enterprises have been benefited with the introduction of simulation, achieving results in an agile manner. For instance, manufacture in the automotive sector is based on the sequence of operations, known as discrete events [20] which assemble parts from different suppliers into a complete product. For this automotive production, plants could be studied as a discrete event phenomenon that can be easily modelled in DES software.

3   Action Research Cycle

Chavarría-Barrientos et al. [21] proposed a model typology. The model typology is composed of three types of models, namely, black-box model, operation model and integrated operation model, which vary in terms of the level of complexity that is required by the simulation task. A "Black box" (Fig. 1a) represents the main activity of the process which simplifies details about the behaviour of the process components [22]. A black box model is useful for a preliminary estimation of the productive capacity of the integrated activities involving the process. Scenarios with this level of detail can be found in [23, 24]. Aspects such as layout configuration, operator actions, material transport, and operating strategies are not considered.

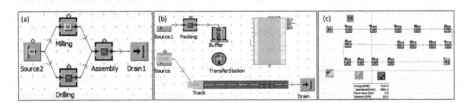

Fig. 1. Model typology from left to right, (a) black box model, (b) operation model and (c) integrated operating model.

An Operation Model (Fig. 1b) is a building block for creating an integrated model of operations. This level of detail is suitable for modelling a specific activity, a workstation or a small process [25]. Benefits reach from a clear understanding of the process to rapid identification of possible problems or improvements. In this case, detailed behavioural aspects of the process are considered (idle times, failures, material transport, parameters, and so on). The Integrated Operating Model (Fig. 1c) is the interaction of operation models blocks and black box models working together. Because of the multiple interactions between models, numerous variables and scenarios can be tested for evaluation of worker efficiency, machine failure, processing times, buffer efficiency, among others. This type of simulation is richer in terms of information processed and enabler to make decisions, however, compared with the black box or operation model, it requires more interaction between all stakeholders to gather information to simulate (i) the real scenario and (ii) optimise multiple alternatives. Chavarría-Barrientos et al. [21] proposed a methodology, based on the Action-Research Cycle (ARC) (See Fig. 2) to develop simulation models.

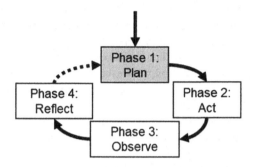

Fig. 2. Action-research cycle.

Thus, to develop a simulation model (See Fig. 3), it is necessary to accomplish the stages described below:

- Plan: define problem, target, objectives, and how objectives might be evaluated. Planning provides information about resources available, time and relevant information for those in charge of the project.
- Act: Determine the type of model according to model typology (Fig. 1), data gathering, develop a model and validate the model. The type of model would impact directly on the information needed to be precise in the simulation model. Permits and key informants are the backbones for a useful simulation.
- Observe: Simulate the model and evaluate the objectives. The objectives proposed in the planning stage must be related to the results obtained from the simulation. Optimisation of the manufacturing process plan is expected with simulation models.
- Reflect: Identify one or more courses of action according to the results of the observing step. Restart the cycle if the objectives are not accomplished in the simulation scenarios. The results obtained from the simulation must provide valuable information for decision-makers.

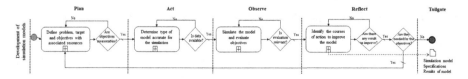

Fig. 3. Development of simulation models. Proposed technique based on ARC

4 DES to Support the Creation of a Collaborative Network

According to Gobbo et al. [26], industrial safety and environmental protection are linked to the concept of Industry 4.0. However, as manufacturing becomes more complex, factories face the challenge to minimise costs, improve processes and reduce the time of implementation deployment and revamping of production lines. These challenges are generally out of the expertise of the self-company; thus, they need to collaborate further with different actors to deal with these problems. Manufacturing firms rely on CN to manage the core processes of the business model, allowing the integration of different actors whose synergy help decision makers to improve and reach a common objective by providing the necessary technologies, practices and tools to solve problems in a shorter period. However, making use of the ARC to simulate different scenarios, guides them into novel practices to optimise resources and improve the productivity of the manufacturing system.

DES simulation is enriched by the information provided by multiple stakeholders. Once identified the main objective to optimise, it becomes a valuable tool as is ubiquitous and allows to make evaluations about the implementation of new technologies through the creation of virtual scenarios in a shorter period. Thus, forecasting a precise result and permitting early identification of opportunity areas by modeling and simulating different scenarios. In this way, the use of resources is reduced compared to commissioning or physical experiments [27]. DES has been widely adopted in the automotive sector, and one of the common uses is the optimisation of raw materials for the creation of parts. Solutions reached by simulation models are compared against the actual production process. DES is a tool to evaluate the ideas generated by the ARC technique with the information provided by CN to generate effective decision making without executing an implementation or generating additional costs by physical tests. All in all, a feasible solution is put in practice into the manufacturing firm (See Fig. 4).

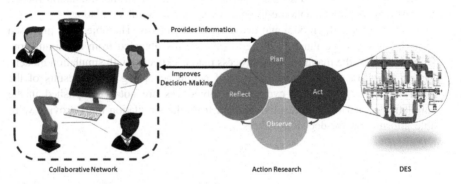

Fig. 4. A proposed framework to aid decision-making in the CN context using DES

5 Case Study

A case study is developed in Grupo Dinamex S.A., a fifty-year-old company, which has a long tradition and expertise in manufacturing processes and distribution of automotive products for the aftermarket. Despite its long presence in the local market, the introduction of low-cost products from Asia motivated it to improve their processes and reduce costs. This work is focused on optimising the production of one of the critical components for an electric fuel pump, which is called the turbine impeller. For the creation of this component (formed by eleven metallic parts), different manufacturing processes are required such as die-cutting, boring, reaming, polishing, lapping, deburring, among others. Components exposed to wear and corrosion are also heat treated in several gas ovens. The heat treatment process was identified as a bottleneck since it cannot maintain the takt time (working time between consecutive units) of the process. This process handled salts that can be harmful to health and the environment. To reduce cost and to improve processing time, plasma nitriding heat treatment is proposed. Pilot testing was run by Termoinnova S.A de C.V, which is a company dedicated to heat treating and surface coating in different materials. The nitrided parts pass the design requirement, and they have a higher ratio between the number of parts produced over the production time than the traditional heat treatment applied in Dinamex. The use of this heat treatment has not been contemplated for the production of media components. To be able to make the collaboration, plasma nitriding application might be justified in terms of improving the process and the product. It was decided to collaborate with Tecnologico de Monterrey. In order to evaluate the plasma nitriding alternative, black box models were developed, and the process was simulated using DES.

5.1 Process Changes and Decision Making

Before making changes in the actual production line, a diagnosis based on the project executed by [28] allowed to know the status of the process's productivity and energy consumption in the production line. DES software (Siemens Plant Simulation) was used to experiment with different scenarios for the evaluation of the current state of the production line to make proposals for improvement in the processes. However, the result had to be evaluated and comply with the economic, personnel and technology restrictions. The simulation structure is carried out using the Action-Research cycle.

5.2 Action Research Cycle

Plan. The objective is to evaluate the feasibility of changing traditional heat treating with a plasma nitriding process. The feasibility is evaluated by energy consumption and processing times of a 1040 steel component.

Act. A black box model [20] is selected from the model typology to represent each of the twenty-four activities of the current process (Fig. 4a). The model was developed in Tecnomatix Plant Simulation. By using this model type, the distance between processes, the number of operators and the time of material transfer between processes were not considered. Only considers the process times, idle time and failures. The process was operated according to a schedule consists of a work shift of nine and a half hours with a break of 30 min and a proposed process line operating only five days a week. Process flow diagrams and the study of process times were gathered during a previous project [28]. On the other hand, energy consumption was estimated by the maintenance team of the company. Energy consumption was calculated by knowing the supply voltage, the current consumed, by the machine in different states and the power factors delivered by the manufacturer or identified on the nameplate of the machine.

Observe. Once the model was created in Plant Simulation, a debugging of possible errors was made, and the simulation was run for an equivalent time of five days. In this way, an estimated production is calculated for a normal work week. The results of the new simulation were compared with the current production data. The simulation of the modified process shows an improvement in the number of produced parts and energy consumption. In this iteration of ARC, the frequency of machine failures was not considered, such as electrical system failures, hydraulic or mechanical system failure as well as failures due to the breaking of cutting tools.

Reflect. With the result of the simulation, it was decided to restart the cycle, modify the model and run additional simulations. This decision was motivated by the difference between simulation and real production statistics.

5.3 Restart the Cycle

In the stage of planning, the objectives and objectives measures are maintained. Meanwhile, new data were collected as indicated by the methodology (Act), such as failure frequency and the time it takes the process to recover from them. It should be noted that initially, a preventive maintenance plan was missing. Only a corrective maintenance program was managed. When the fault's data was introduced into the model, the production system behaviour is like the physical production system (Observe), and data of the current processes was saved for further analysis. A new cycle (Reflect) was required to model and simulate the process improvement options such as the application of new technology and a decrease in the frequency of failures. The introduction of the new heating process results in a modified production system with fewer processes (15 instead of the 24 processes in the original production system). Plasma nitriding removes engineering restrictions to manufacture the product. This situation allows to introduce a set of new processes such as blasting process to remove the burr of the pieces coming from stamping, and the acquisition of a twin head drill to perform simultaneous drilling operations (Fig. 5).

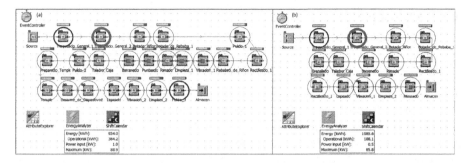

Fig. 5. A black box model of (a) the current metallic turbine impeller processes, (b) the proposed metallic turbine impeller processes including plasma nitriding.

Plasma nitriding allowed the product to incorporate softer materials and give a similar or longer lifetime compared to the original design material selection. With the new heat treatment process, the number of maintenance actions in the dies was reduced due to wear, and it is expected to see a reduction in the frequency of stoppages caused by the tooling failure. On the other hand, the application of preventive maintenance may achieve a reduction in the frequency of failures by 50%.

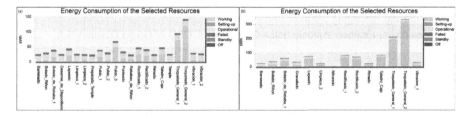

Fig. 6. Energy consumption of (a) the current process for the creation of the turbine impeller, (b) the proposed process for the creation of the turbine impeller.

Applying the methodology by [20], a simulation of the model with the improvements proposed was run, and as shown in Fig. 5b, the model of the production system alternatives has a considerable reduction in the number of processes. This same figure remarks that Stamping 1 and 2 consume most of the energy. However, the energy consumption of the stations when they are in failures or in idle time has a considerable reduction, as can be seen in Fig. 5b. In the simulation of the original process (Fig. 6a) has a consumption of 934 kWh, in 5 days. On the other hand, the simulation with the modified process (Fig. 6b) gives us the consumption of 1,085 kWh. According to this value, the machines are operational longer, instead of waiting. The improved process can deliver 268% more parts in the same period. An equivalent production of the current number of pieces with the modified process, energy consumption will be closed to 400 kWh, and the production line only works a day and a half instead of five days.

6 Conclusions

DES was used as part of the action research cycle to improve decision-making generated with the collected information of a Collaborative Network. CN for this article is comprised of a private industry, academic researchers and different systems connected through the Internet. The framework arose naturally aided by different subsystems which gather and share information. The main motivation for this work was to reduce energy consumption in a manufacturing firm, which is reflected after the implementation of the model. With these applications, considering that the remaining components of the piece belong to the same product family, an 80% reduction in gas consumption of the company is estimated; 46% savings in direct costs, close to 84% of the time of processes and a reduction of more than 50% in energy consumption. Discrete event simulation assists in creating different scenarios, where changes in processes can be properly tested while the processes are kept running daily. For future work, it is planned to create a highly complex simulation, in which a user can make production planning evaluations for multiple products that share similar processes. This new simulation should include the preparation times, the material transfers, the number of operators and a more detailed operation logic.

Acknowledgement. A special mention is made to the company Grupo Dinamex S.A. for allowing us to do this work, giving us the flexibility to obtain the necessary data for the creation and simulation of the model. Termoinnova S.A. de C.V. for nitriding parts and making the product test and measuring hardness in components.

In Memoriam, Engineer Antonio Salim Guraieb Kuri, CEO of Grupo Dinamex S.A.

References

1. AMIA: Boletín de Prensa. Diálogos con la Industria Automotriz (2018). http://www.amia.com.mx/boletin/dlg20182024.pdf
2. Hamzeh, R., Zhong, R., Xu, X.W.: A survey study on industry 4.0 for New Zealand manufacturing. Procedia Manuf. **26**, 49–57 (2018)
3. Santos, C., Mehrsai, A., Barros, A.C., Araújo, M., Ares, E.: Towards industry 4.0: an overview of European strategic roadmaps. Procedia Manuf. **13**, 972–979 (2017)
4. Sung, T.K.: Industry 4.0: a Korea perspective. Technol. Forecast. Soc. Chang. **132**, 40–45 (2018)
5. Weichhart, G., Molina, A., Chen, D., Whitman, L.E., Vernadat, F.: Challenges and current developments for sensing, smart and sustainable enterprise systems. Comput. Ind. **79**, 34–46 (2016)
6. Saidani, M., Yannou, B., Leroy, Y., Cluzel, F., Kendall, A.: A taxonomy of circular economy indicators. J. Clean. Prod. **207**, 542–559 (2019)
7. Stock, T., Obenaus, M., Kunz, S., Kohl, H.: Industry 4.0 as an enabler for a sustainable development: a qualitative assessment of its ecological and social potential. Process Saf. Environ. Prot. **118**, 254–267 (2018)
8. De Sousa Jabbour, A.B.L., Jabbour, C.J.C., Foropon, C., Godinho Filho, M.: When titans meet – can industry 4.0 revolutionise the environmentally-sustainable manufacturing wave? The role of critical success factors. Technol. Forecast. Soc. Chang. **132**, 18–25 (2018)

9. Moktadir, M.A., Ali, S.M., Kusi-Sarpong, S., Shaikh, M.A.A.: Assessing challenges for implementing industry 4.0: implications for process safety and environmental protection. Process Saf. Environ. Prot. **117**, 730–741 (2018)
10. Stock, T., Seliger, G.: Opportunities of sustainable manufacturing in industry 4.0. Procedia CIRP **40**, 536–541 (2016)
11. Hermann, M., Pentek, T., Otto, B.: Design principles for Industrie 4.0 scenarios. Paper presented at the 2016 49th Hawaii International Conference on System Sciences (HICSS), 5–8 Januray 2016 (2016)
12. Otis, P.T., Douglas, H.: Improve production scheduling to increase energy efficiency. CEP Mag. (2017). https://www.aiche.org/resources/publications/cep/2017/march/improve-produc-tion-scheduling-increase-energy-efficiency
13. Singh, J., Singh, H.: Continuous improvement approach: state-of-art review and future implications. Int. J. Lean Six Sigma **3**, 88–111 (2012)
14. Negahban, A., Smith, J.S.: Simulation for manufacturing system design and operation: Literature review and analysis. J. Manuf. Syst. **33**(2), 241–261 (2014)
15. Antonelli, D., Litwin, P., Stadnicka, D.: Multiple system dynamics and discrete event simulation for manufacturing system performance evaluation. Procedia CIRP **78**, 178–183 (2018)
16. Barrera-Diaz, C.A., Oscarsson, J., Lidberg, S., Sellgren, T.: Discrete event simulation output data-handling system in an automotive manufacturing plant. Procedia Manuf. **25**, 23–30 (2018)
17. Guimarães, A.M.C., Leal, J.E., Mendes, P.: Discrete-event simulation software selection for manufacturing based on the maturity model. Comput. Ind. **103**, 14–27 (2018)
18. Benefits of simulation-driven development. World Pumps **2016**(2), 18–20 (2016)
19. Kurkalova, L.A., Carter, L.: Sustainable production: using simulation modelling to identify the benefits of green information systems. Decis. Support Syst. **96**, 83–91 (2017)
20. Silva, M.: On the history of discrete event systems. Annu. Rev. Control **45**, 213–222 (2018)
21. Chavarría-Barrientos, D., et al.: A methodology to support manufacturing system design using digital models and simulations: an automotive supplier case study. IFAC-PapersOnLine **51**(11), 1598–1603 (2018)
22. Schriber, T.J., Brunner, D.T., Smith, J.S.: Inside discrete-event simulation software: how it works and why it matters. In: Proceedings - Winter Simulation Conference (2018)
23. Siderska, J.: Application of Tecnomatix plant simulation for modeling production and logistics processes. Bus. Manag. Educ. **14**(1), 64–73 (2016). ISSN 2029-7491
24. Kliment, M., Popovic, R., Janek, J.: Analysis of the production process in the selected company and proposal a possible model optimization through PLM software module Tecnomatix plant simulation. Procedia Eng. **96**, 221–226 (2014). ISSN 18777058
25. Musil, M., Laskovský, V., Fialek, P.: Analysis of logistic processes using the software Tecnomatix plant simulation. In: International Conference on Industrial Logistics, Zakopane, Poland, pp. 195–200 (2016). ISBN 9788362079063
26. Gobbo, J.A., Busso, C.M., Gobbo, S.C.O., Carreão, H.: Making the links among environmental protection, process safety, and industry 4.0. Process Saf. Environ. Prot. **117**, 372–382 (2018)
27. Ranke, D., Lanza, G.: Planning, evaluation and optimization of product design and manufacturing technology chains for new product and production technologies on the example of additive manufacturing. Procedia CIRP **70**, 108–113 (2018)
28. Reyes, I.V.: Optimización de procesos y recursos en una línea de producción metal mecánica automotriz. Instituto Politécnico Nacional UPIICSA, Ciudad de México (2016)

Virtual Reality in Education for Industry 4.0

Application of Virtual Reality in Designing and Programming of Robotic Stations

Dariusz Szybicki[1(✉)], Krzysztof Kurc[1], Piotr Gierlak[1],
Andrzej Burghardt[1], Magdalena Muszyńska[1], and Marek Uliasz[2]

[1] Rzeszow University of Technology, Rzeszow, Poland
{dszybicki,kkurc,pgierlak,andrzejb,magdaw}@prz.edu.pl
[2] Pratt & Whitney Rzeszow S.A., Rzeszow, Poland
Marek.Uliasz@pwrze.utc.com

Abstract. The article presents the subject of the practical application of virtual reality in the design and programming of robotic stations. Robotic stations designed with the use of virtual reality were created in a collaborative network study consisting of a university, enterprise and government organization - National Centre for Research and Development. An example of a project implemented within the framework described in the collaboration article is the robotisation of the manufacturing processes of aircraft engine components.

Keywords: Virtual reality · Robots · Robotic stations ·
Collaborative network · Design of robotic stations

1 Introduction

The article presents an example of the use of virtual reality in the design of robotic stations. The project was carried out as part of a collaborative network consisting of a university, a company and a government organization – the National Centre for Research and Development (Fig. 1).

The network of cooperating units in question consists of independent institutions that differ in their goals, environment, organization and culture [1, 2]. The company that is included in this network has clearly defined goals. The modern theory of the company is based on the contention that the most important goal in the company is to maximize its market value. Besides this general goal, there are also marketing goals, i.e. a level increase in sales, innovative goals - product innovation, and financial goals - profitability. The aim of the University is to educate students, conduct scientific research and create favourable conditions for innovation. The National Centre for Research and Development (NCRD) established in Poland has the following objectives:

- management and implementation of strategic research and development programs that directly translate into the development of innovation;
- supporting commercialization and other forms of transfer of research results to the economy, management of applied research programs and implementation of projects in the field of defence and state security;

L. M. Camarinha-Matos et al. (Eds.): PRO-VE 2019, IFIP AICT 568, pp. 585–593, 2019.
https://doi.org/10.1007/978-3-030-28464-0_51

- ensuring good conditions for the development of academic staff, implementing, inter alia, international mobility programs for researchers.

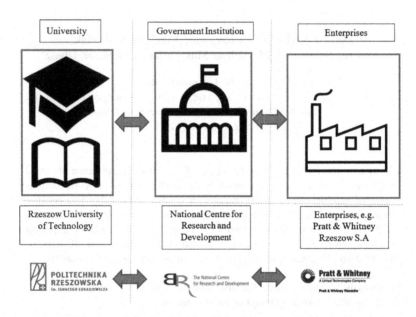

Fig. 1. Diagram of the functioning of the discussed collaborative network

In pursuing these goals, the NCRD ensures that public money spent on research and development work brings the greatest benefits to the Polish economy. Through several dozen programs, the Centre can provide financial support for a project at all levels of technological readiness – from initial industrial research to the development of an innovative product, service or technology. This offer is complemented by programs supporting the financing of international protection of industrial property and foreign expansion of young innovative companies.

The Rzeszow University of Technology, together with industrial partners, has implemented and continues to implement several dozen projects that are co-financed and implemented in cooperation with the NCRD. The team involved in the presented in this work project focuses on the design of advanced robotic stations and robotization of various types of processes in the aviation industry. An example of projects implemented within this collaborative network is the robotic quality control of jet engine components presented in the works [3–5]. Jointly implemented projects also included autodiagnostics of robotic stations and robotic machining processes in the aviation industry which are the subject of publications [6–14].

Functionally, the collaborative network based on NCRD allows companies to implement innovative solutions related to robots, for example, and researchers can conduct advanced research using the latest technologies. Projects implemented thanks to financial and substantive support of the NCRD allow the creation of cooperation networks and the development of the units involved. Patents, scientific articles or PhD theses are often the result of cooperation. Companies thanks to the collaborative network have access to laboratories, substantive support and can acquire students as future employees. The implementation of joint projects is very important for didactics. Students may be familiarized with the work being carried out, and they may also take part in the tasks performed. An example of a project implemented within the discussed collaborative network is the robotization of the manufacturing processes of aircraft engine components. During the design and programming of the station for the machining of aircraft engine components, virtual reality techniques were used.

2 Virtual Reality

Virtual reality (VR) is an artificial image of reality created using information technology. It involves the multimedia creation of a computer visualisation of objects, space and events. It can represent both elements of the real world and completely fictional ones. In virtual reality it is possible to simulate the presence and operation of the user and feedback information is sent to one or more senses in such a way that the user has a sense of immersion in the simulation.

The virtual reality system exposes objects to the user with the help of image, sound and sensory stimuli, and allows interaction, giving the impression of being in a simulation. Sensory feedback provides users with direct sensory information depending on their physical location in a virtual environment. Sensory information is transmitted through synthetic stimuli, that is computer-generated visual, audio or tactile information. Most of the feedback is implemented via visual information, although some environments only use tactile information. In addition to simulation, the virtual reality system requires an interface that allows users to "enter" virtual reality. One of the first such devices was an invention by Morton Heilig, named the Sensorama Simulator from 1962, which was the first video game allowing immersion in virtual reality [15]. The device displayed a colourful, three-dimensional graphic on a stereoscopic display, it was equipped with a stereo sound system, an odour generator, fans that simulated breeze and a movable seat. The game consisted of riding a motorcycle on the streets of New York. The players felt the unevenness of the road, the smells of food from restaurants and the air movement resulting from the movement of the motorcycle. However, it was not possible to interact with the virtual environment objects. Heilig also started work on virtual reality glasses mounted on the head equipped with headphones. He did not complete his invention, but the potential of his solutions was noticed. The development of technology allowed for the construction and improvement of virtual reality interfaces. Nowadays VR devices are widely available and systematically increasing the number of their applications, both commercial and specialist.

One of the most frequently used examples of the practical application of virtual reality are flight simulators [16]. Pilots can practice flying in different conditions, simulate failures and ways of responding to them. Simulators of surgical operations are another important example [17]. An operation is a dangerous situation for the patient, because a single error can lead to his or her death. Following the example of flight simulators, surgical simulators provide a virtual environment in which the surgeon can use realistic touch interfaces (which look like real surgical tools) to perform surgical procedures on various patients. Virtual patients do not necessarily have to be imaginary objects. Modern imaging methods, such as computed tomography, can be used to create a three-dimensional image of the human body. Before a real operation, surgeons can practice on a virtual patient with very similar characteristics to the real patient being prepared for surgery. Surgical simulators have become particularly widespread thanks to the creation of surgical robots that allow the whole operation to be performed using a touch interface and a screen.

In [18] the authors proposed the use of virtual reality to train employees in positions where they cooperate with robots. The reason for this approach was to improve safety. Thanks to VR, an inexperienced employee is able to learn the principles of safe cooperation with machines. The work [19] presents a VR application for training in the field of management of industrial processes, with particular emphasis on pneumatic systems. The virtual application consists of a virtual laboratory and a virtual industrial plant.

3 Design and Software of a Robotic Station Created with the Help of Virtual Reality

For designing and programming a robotic station, it was decided to use currently available tools for designing and programming robots off-line. Off-line programming is recommended for use in the construction and modification of complex robotic systems. The direct benefits of using off-line programming are:

- shortening break times in production;
- automatic generation of NC code;
- numerical (CAD) representation of elements of the position – easier and faster integration of the robotic station;
- use of graphic editor in testing (verification) and optimization of the work program;
- facilitated interchangeability of programs between robots;
- the ability to create complex work programs, complex position logics, and advanced, large sensory systems.

Using modern computer programs for programming industrial robots, fast and accurate generation of control programs can be obtained. It is possible to test various organizational variants of the position and work scenarios while maintaining both easy and quick corrections and the safety of testing (e.g. collision detection) of the program, thanks to simulation in a virtual environment. The design method of advanced robotic stations is shown in Fig. 2.

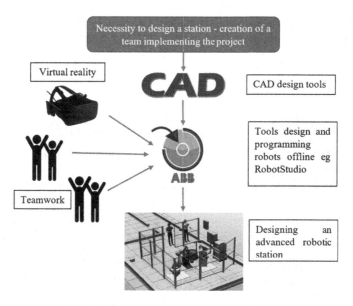

Fig. 2. The design method of robotic stations

After a review of the available solutions for designing and programming a robotic station, the ABB tool, RobotStudio, was chosen (Fig. 3). Earlier, the use of other available off-line programming tools was considered. The possibilities of using virtual reality of RoboGuide software by Fanuc, Kuka Sim Pro by Kuka and K-Roset by Kawasaki were analyzed. Unfortunately, none of these tools has such options.

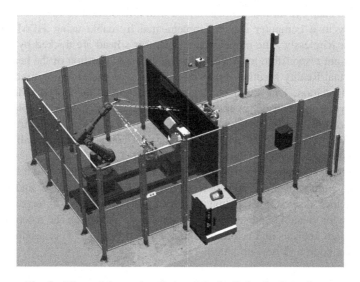

Fig. 3. View of the station designed in the RobotStudio software

RobotStudio versions available since 2017 work with VR glasses, allow the user to design and program robots in the virtual world and interact with its components (Fig. 4).

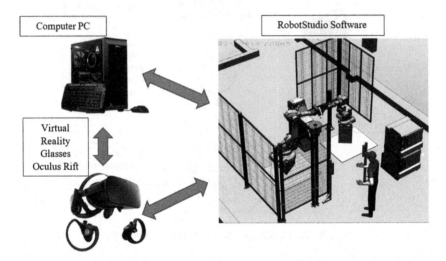

Fig. 4. The concept of cooperation of RobotStudio software with VR tools

A PC with RobotStudio software and VR Oculus Rift glasses were used to design and program the robotic station. After the glasses are put on, they display the image of the computer-generated world in front of the user's eyes. The user can look around in a natural way, moving their head or body. The Oculus Rift model used has a screen displaying to each eye an independent image with a resolution of 1080×1200 pixels. Connectivity to a computer can be implemented by cable using HDMI and USB interfaces or wirelessly. The movements of the user's head are tracked by two sets of sensors that are responsible for tracking the rotation and position of the head in space.

The Virtual Reality Meeting turned out to be a very useful option used during the design of the station. This solution, which is a function of the RobotStudio software, allows a virtual meeting of several people in one robotic station. People can be in different locations, and distance is not important. Thanks to the Virtual Reality Meeting, users can see their avatars in the form of coloured glasses, talk, draw and annotate in a virtual model of a robotic station (Fig. 5).

The RobotStudio application with the Virtual Reality Meeting option allows users to run "live simulations" where robots perform paths, objects move, and the virtual reality provides accurate perception of dimensions. Checking of ergonomics and accessibility for cleaning and servicing equipment are available. The meeting function helps in design analysis and error correction at an early stage. This results in a much shorter installation and start-up phase.

Fig. 5. View of the station designed using Virtual Reality Meeting

An example of a project implemented with the use of the off-line design, virtual reality and Virtual Reality Meeting tools, discussed above, can be seen in a robotic station for machining aircraft engine components. Pratt & Whitney Rzeszow S.A., which is part of UTC, in its operations performs technological operations involving the machining of V2500 engine diffuser castings. One of many technological operations is edge deburring. In the process of making a diffuser, there are a number of edges that require deburring, which is an operation that is carried out manually. As part of a joint venture, coordinated and co-financed by the NCRD, a robotic station for carrying out this process was designed and constructed (Fig. 6).

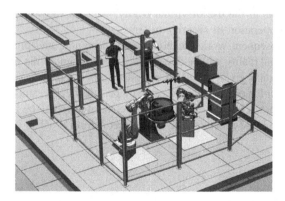

Fig. 6. View of a station designed for machining aircraft engine components

The operation of the station is divided into three stages: removal of oversizes (flash), chamfering and grinding of the machined surfaces. The whole process is performed by the ABB IRB140 robot, and the implementation of subsequent processing stages is possible thanks to the exchange of tools located in a four-position changer.

As part of the work, a precise model of the station was prepared using VR, the location of the station elements and the method of loading the workpieces were discussed with the industrial partner, and scenarios of failures, repairs and service inspections were analysed. Due to the need for meetings with engineers from the USA and Canada, the Virtual Reality Meeting function proved useful.

4   Conclusions

The article presents the available possibilities and an example of the use of virtual reality in the design of robotic stations. This innovative project was created as part of a collaborative network consisting of the Rzeszow University of Technology, the company Pratt & Whitney Rzeszow S.A. and the National Centre for Research and Development. The concept and way of functioning of this network are discussed in the article. The approach based on the cooperation of a technical university and a company, supported by the assistance of a government institution, results in interesting and advanced projects. Thanks to the cooperation of scientists with specialist knowledge and appropriate tools with a company dealing with high technologies, the benefits are shared by both sides and the level of innovation in the state is raised. The method of designing robotic stations shown in the article can be applied in the design of various robotic stations and automated systems. The use of off-line design and programming tools, virtual reality and Virtual Reality Meeting capabilities allows designing and planning in a way that was previously unachievable. The station and similar discussed in the article, developed in cooperation with the industry, are used in the education process. In the case of the station described in the article, students took part in the design of the station elements' layout and prepared some CAD models. In addition, students can see how the design and implementation of the advanced robotic station looked like. Thanks to the use of virtual reality, you can show the way the station is operated and the operation of security systems.

As part of subsequent works, techniques for designing and programming robotic stations using virtual reality will be developed. Improvement of the possibilities of joint and remote work on a given project is intended to be prepared. Advanced avatars of team members implementing the project will be added. The students will be more involved in the project. A base of virtual-interactive objects will be built, from which it will be possible to build more robotic stations as if from blocks.

References

1. Shuman, J., Twombly, J.: Collaborative networks are the organization: an innovation in organization design and management. Vikalpa **35**(1), 1–14 (2010)
2. David, T., Robert, S.: Collaborate and innovate: a new world of sourcing (2007)
3. Burghardt, A., Kurc, K., Szybicki, D., Muszyńska, M., Nawrocki, J.: Robot-operated quality control station based on the UTT method. Open Eng. **7**(1), 37–42 (2017)

4. Burghardt, A., Kurc, K., Szybicki, D., Muszyńska, M., Nawrocki, J.: Software for the robot-operated inspection station for engine guide vanes taking into consideration the geometric variability of parts. Tehnički vjesnik 24(Suppl. 2), 349–353 (2017)

5. Burghardt, A., Kurc, K., Szybicki, D., Muszyńska, M., Szczęch, T.: Robot-operated inspection of aircraft engine turbine rotor guide vane segment geometry. Tehnički vjesnik 24 (Suppl. 2), 345–348 (2017)

6. Burghardt, A., Kurc, K., Szybicki, D., Muszyńska, M., Szczęch, T.: Monitoring the parameters of the robot-operated quality control process. Adv. Sci. Technol.-Res. J. 11(1), 232–236 (2017)

7. Teti, R., Jemielniak, K., O'Donnell, G., Dornfeld, D.: Advanced monitoring of machining operations. CIRP Ann. 59(2), 717–739 (2010)

8. Gierlak, P.: Hybrid position/force control in robotised machining. In: Solid State Phenomena, vol. 210, pp. 192–199. Trans Tech Publications, Switzerland (2014)

9. Barnfather, J.D., Goodfellow, M.J., Abram, T.: A performance evaluation methodology for robotic machine tools used in large volume manufacturing. Robot. CIM-Int. Manuf. 37, 49–56 (2016)

10. Burghardt, A., Szybicki, D., Kurc, K., Muszyńska, M., Mucha, J.: Experimental study of Inconel 718 surface treatment by edge robotic deburring with force control. Strength Mater. 49(4), 594–604 (2017)

11. Kurc, K., Burghardt, A., Gierlak, P., Szybicki, D.: Non-contact robotic measurement of jet engine components with 3D optical scanner and UTT method. In: Hanus, R., Kreischer, C., Mazur, D. (eds.) MSM 2018. LNEE, vol. 548, pp. 151–164. Springer, Cham (2019). https://doi.org/10.1007/978-3-030-11187-8_12

12. Szybicki, D., Burghardt, A., Kurc, K., Pietruś, P.: Calibration and verification of an original module measuring turbojet engine blades geometric parameters. Arch. Mech. Eng. 66, 97–109 (2019)

13. Hui-Ping, L., Dai-Min, C., Miao, Y.: Communication of multi-robot system on the TCP/IP In: International Conference on Mechatronic Science, Electric Engineering and Computer (MEC), pp. 1432–1435. IEEE (2011)

14. Zhsao, P., Shi, Y.: Composite adaptive control of belt polishing force for aero-engine blade. Chin. J. Mech. Eng. 26(5), 988–996 (2013)

15. Burdea, G.C., Coiffet, P.: Virtual Reality Technology. Wiley, Hoboken (2003)

16. Mihelj, M., Novak, D., Beguš, S.: Virtual Reality Technology and Applications. Springer, Dordrecht (2014). https://doi.org/10.1007/978-94-007-6910-6

17. Gallagher, A.G., et al.: Virtual reality simulation for the operating room proficiency-based training as a paradigm shift in surgical skills training. Ann. Surg. 241(2), 364–372 (2005)

18. Koźlak, M., Kurzeja, A., Nawrat, A.: Virtual reality technology for military and industry training programs. In: Nawrat, A., Kuś, Z. (eds.) Vision Based Systems for UAV Applications. Studies in Computational Intelligence, vol. 481, pp. 327–334. Springer, Heidelberg (2013). https://doi.org/10.1007/978-3-319-00369-6_21

19. Ortiz, J.S., et al.: Virtual training for industrial automation processes through pneumatic controls. In: De Paolis, L.T., Bourdot, P. (eds.) AVR 2018. LNCS, vol. 10851, pp. 516–532. Springer, Cham (2018). https://doi.org/10.1007/978-3-319-95282-6_37

Application of Virtual Reality in the Training of Operators and Servicing of Robotic Stations

Magdalena Muszyńska[1]([⊠]), Dariusz Szybicki[1], Piotr Gierlak[1],
Krzysztof Kurc[1], Andrzej Burghardt[1], and Marek Uliasz[2]

[1] Rzeszow University of Technology, Rzeszow, Poland
{magdaw,dszybicki,pgierlak,kkurc,andrzejb}@prz.edu.pl
[2] Pratt & Whitney Rzeszow S.A., Rzeszow, Poland
Marek.Uliasz@pwrze.utc.com

Abstract. The article discusses the subject of the use of virtual reality in training the service and maintenance of robots and robotic stations. The developed trainings use virtual reality, thus they are interactive and allow advanced operations without the risk of damaging expensive equipment. The idea of the training program and the application of virtual reality was based on the collaborative network defined in the article. The individual chapters discuss the idea of virtual reality, tools used to develop the training system and examples of activities carried out. Real tools used to obtain virtual reality are shown. Methods of developing interactive elements necessary in simulations are presented.

Keywords: Virtual reality · Robotic stations · Operator training · Robot service

1 Introduction

The article presents the concept of training operators and service technicians in the support, maintenance and servicing of robotic stations. The training system is implemented as part of a collaborative network consisting of a university and companies forming part of the Aviation Valley Association (Fig. 1). This network consists of autonomous components that vary with respect to the operational environment, social capital and culture [1, 2]. The aim of the university is to conduct scientific research, educate students and influence the technological development of the region. The goals of companies are widely known to be the satisfaction of the needs of other entities of social life through the production of products and services. In the Podkarpackie region of Poland, the Aviation Valley Association was established to strengthen the role of south-eastern Poland as one of the leading regions in the aviation industry in Europe.

The detailed goals of Aviation Valley are:

- The cooperation with universities of technology, which would promote new ideas and scientific research within the aerospace industry.
- The further development of aerospace research, aptitudes and skills.
- The organization and development of a low cost supply chain.

L. M. Camarinha-Matos et al. (Eds.): PRO-VE 2019, IFIP AICT 568, pp. 594–603, 2019.
https://doi.org/10.1007/978-3-030-28464-0_52

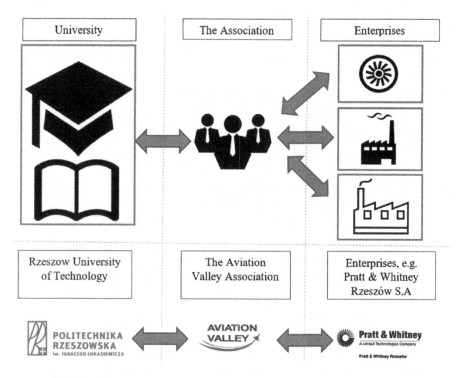

Fig. 1. Diagram of the functioning of the discussed collaborative network.

- The creation of favorable conditions in order to enhance the development of aerospace industry enterprises in this region.
- The protection of enterprise and businesses in the aerospace industry.

Aviation Valley connects over 160 companies from the aviation industry. Cooperation with higher education institutions, especially with the Rzeszow University of Technology, is very important for this association. Joint research projects are carried out as part of this cooperation. An example of cooperation with the companies of Aviation Valley presented in this work focuses on designing advanced robotic stations and robotization of various types of processes. One such jointly developed process is the robotic quality control of jet engine components presented in the works [3–5]. Robotic machining processes in the aviation industry and diagnostics of the components of robotic stations are the subject of publications [6–14]. The existence of this collaborative network allows companies to implement advanced robot-related solutions, and academic staff can co-create and publish interesting works. A very important component of the university's cooperation with companies is the education of students within the so-called dual courses conducted simultaneously at the university and in companies, as well as commissioned work related to training. An example of such work is the training of robotic operators and servicers. The idea of organizing training in the field of robot service and servicing appeared during meetings of the University employees with representatives of associated companies in the Valley. The university has staff specializing in robot programming, designing robotic stations and station servicing. In addition to the staff at the Faculty of Mechanical Engineering and Aeronautics, 10 different types of robots, grouped into dedicated stations, are available (Fig. 2).

Fig. 2. A photograph of one of the robotic stations.

Companies in Aviation Valley are currently investing in robotization, more and more advanced stations are being created, and more processes are becoming robotized and automated. Due to ongoing robotization, training and raising of awareness among staff regarding robots are necessary. After analysing the needs of companies, it was decided to prepare a common training program for robot operators and service technicians. The program has been prepared so that it can also be used in an engineering study program. Market research was carried out and due to the advantage of robotic stations with ABB robots, training related to the company's solutions was prepared. The first training was carried out for Pratt & Whitney Rzeszow S.A. (P&W). After consultation with the company's representatives, analysis of the most frequent support and servicing procedures and review of the types of stations, it was decided to use virtual reality to prepare interactive training. The use of virtual reality made it possible to adapt the training program to specific robots that exist in P & W without interrupting production. It was possible to develop alternative scenarios for support, repairs and maintenance. In addition, in the safe simulation environment operators could perform advanced maintenance activities.

2   Virtual Reality

Virtual reality (VR) is an interactive computer simulation that detects and simulates the presence and actions of the user in a virtual environment and sends sensory feedback to one or more senses in such a way that the user has the feeling of immersion in the simulation [15]. The virtual environment is represented by the description of computer-generated objects in the simulation as well as the principles and relations of managing them. These objects have such physical characteristics as size, shape, colour, mass and behaviour. The features of virtual environment objects depend on the degree of interactivity of a given component and the complexity of the physical model of the virtual environment. For the virtual reality to be realistic, it must react to the user's actions, i.e. be interactive. The user's ability to influence the environments generated by the computer is one of the forms of interaction. Another option is to change the location and orientation from which the user sees the environment. If multiple users can exist in one virtual environment, the virtual reality system should allow interaction between them. Flight training simulators are one of the best examples of the practical application of virtual reality [16]. Pilots can practice flying in different conditions. Flight exercises in difficult weather conditions are particularly beneficial for the training process, and the occurrence of airplane system failures can be simulated. Pilots can thus experience how the machine behaves in certain situations and their errors will not cause a plane crash. Driving simulators have been developed for a similar purpose – they enable safe driving lessons in various conditions (rain, ice, congestion) or tests of new cars [17]. In a virtual environment, you can change any of the car's functions (both aesthetic and functional) and then observe how real drivers react to the changes. The simulation allows to test cars designed before building a prototype.

Thanks to widespread access to VR equipment, new applications using virtual reality are constantly emerging. Scientific institutions also contribute to the development of virtual reality applications. The Fraunhofer Institute for Factory Operation and Automation IFF develops high-level interactive VR environments that can be specifically used in a wide range of industrial training programs [18]. The work [18] presents a methodology for creating an example of a virtual educational platform for operators. Realistic models of components used by the company for which the platform was built were used to build the virtual environment. On the other hand, in [19], a virtual reality system was proposed for training employees of industrial plants on sites where they cooperate with robots. The motivation to build the station was to improve security. Thanks to this, an inexperienced employee will be able to learn the principles of safe cooperation with machines. The work [20] presents the use of VR technology and computer graphics by industry in order to reduce production costs, minimize learning curves and eliminate hazardous situations. In addition, examples of procedural training and VR simulators are shown, as well as their use for military training and support for soldiers. The authors of work [21] built a virtual reality application to teach the management of industrial processes, with particular emphasis on pneumatic systems. The virtual application includes the environment of a virtual laboratory and a virtual industrial plant. The proposed solution allows the participation of multiple users in one virtual environment and interaction between them.

3   Designing of a Training Program and Virtual Robotic Stations

For the construction of a training program together with industrial partners, it was decided to use currently available tools for designing and programming robots off-line. The computer tools offered on the market allow for the three-dimensional design of robotic stations and the creation of simulation models through which the way a new station will look and function can be seen in detail before its launch. Due to the previously accepted assumption that the training is to concern ABB robots, the company's tool, RobotStudio, was used to build virtual stations (Fig. 3).

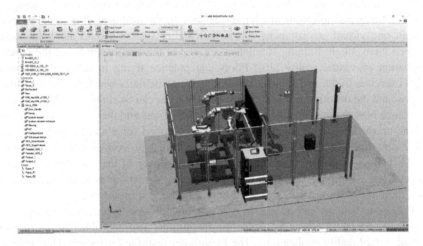

Fig. 3. View of a station designed in the RobotStudio software.

The RobotStudio software from ABB is a robot programming environment. It can be used to build robotic stations and program robots both off-line and on-line. Virtual controller technology is implemented in the environment, allowing for a precise reflection of the actual work of the controller, and hence, among others, accurate determination of the actual work cycles of the device. The latest versions of the software work with VR glasses, allow to program robots in the virtual world and interact with their components (Fig. 4).

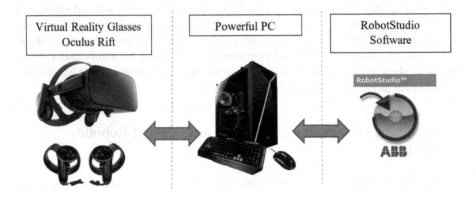

Fig. 4. The concept of cooperation of RobotStudio software with VR tools.

High-performance PCs with RobotStudio software and Oculus Rift glasses were used to build training stations. Oculus Rift is a set of virtual reality goggles. After they are placed on the user's head, they display the image of a computer-generated world or a film recorded in 360°. The user can look around them in a natural way, moving their head or body. The image displayed in front of the eyes is then transformed to create the illusion of being in the virtual world or in the centre of the action taking place in the film. The Oculus Rift version used was equipped with a screen displaying to each eye independent images with a resolution of 1080 × 1200 pixels. Connection with the computer is made by means of HDMI and USB interfaces. The movements of the user's head are tracked by two sets of sensors that are responsible for tracking the rotation and position of the head in space. The idea is that the device should properly interpret both shaking the head from side to side and, for example, leaning it forward.

RobotStudio makes available, for example, three-dimensional models of robots offered or their controllers. Unfortunately, they are not detailed models, there are no components inside; they only show the dimensions and external appearance. For the purpose of the training program, precise, interactive models of components of robotic stations were built. 3D CAD software was used to build the models. Next, the models prepared were exported to the RobotStudio software using the SAT standard (Fig. 5).

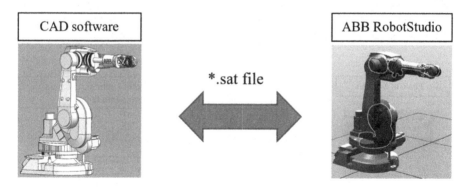

Fig. 5. Diagram of the export of detailed models.

Due to the adopted training program, the focus was on support and servicing of 6-axis robots and the latest IRC5 controller. ABB's technical and service documentation was used for the building of detailed models of station components (Fig. 6).

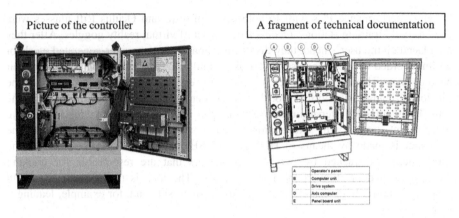

Fig. 6. Construction of the IRC5 controller.

Based on photographs and available units, detailed models of the most important components of the IRC5 controller were built, such as, for example, an axis computer, a main computer and drive controllers. Models of IRC5 components are equipped with interactive components (e.g. LEDs) informing about status, operating mode and failures. The built-in components are connected programmatically with a virtual controller that allows the execution of robot programs. In addition, the models built were equipped with a mechanism that randomly generate failures, display error messages and prompt methods for solving problems. The picture of the upper computer, its model and information displayed using the VR technique is shown in Fig. 7.

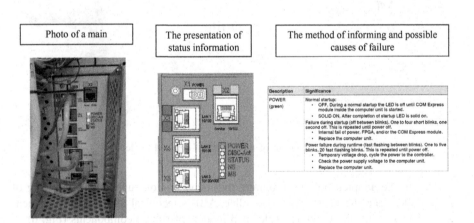

Fig. 7. The idea of building interactive components of a robot controller.

Similarly to the IRC5 controller model, models of the most common robots were built. They are equipped with gears, brakes and components related to the calibration and replacement of oils in the gears (Fig. 8).

A fragment of the virtual environment	Examples of activities performed by the operator

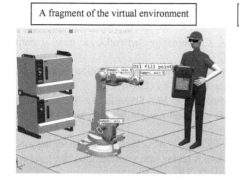

Maintenance activity	Equipment	Interval
Changing	Gearbox oil, axes 5 and 6 IRB1600	20,000 hrs
Changing	Gearbox oil, axes 5-6 IRB1600ID	20,000 hrs
Inspection	Damper axes 2, 3 and 5	20,000 hrs

Fig. 8. A section of the virtual environment developed.

As part of the work, scenarios of failures, repairs and servicing of robotic stations were prepared using VR. The person being trained, equipped with glasses and hand controllers, deals with support and servicing of the station. Their tasks include identification of the type of controller failure based on the symptoms, operation of the robot consisting in the calibration, checking of shock absorbers and the replacement of oil in the gears. The structure of functioning and the components developed allow the training program to be developed in the future.

4   Conclusion

The article presents a developed system of training of operators and service technicians in the field of operation, maintenance and servicing of robotic stations. This system uses virtual reality, thanks to which the training is interactive and allows advanced operations without the risk of damage to expensive equipment. As part of subsequent works, a training program with the use of virtual reality will be expanded. There will be added next activities performed on the robots and the expanded base of possible system failures. The number of stations whose service can be simulated will be increased. The students will be more involved in the project and a database of virtual-interactive objects subject to servicing and service will be built. In subsequent works, we plan to use the augmented reality as an element complementing the training system. The concept and the training program were created thanks to the existence of a collaborative network based on the Aviation Valley Association. At present, no company, university or government has the time or resources for continuous innovation. The global market places higher and higher demands, and there is a tendency towards specialization and continuous development. In the case of the collaborative network discussed, the cooperation of the university, bringing tools and specialist knowledge, with companies, which have experience and high technology, can bring mutual benefits and create new value. The presented cooperation stems from a common belief that together network members can achieve goals that would not be possible to achieve separately or would require more time and resources.

References

1. Camarinha-Matos, L.M., Afsarmanesh, H.: Collaborative networks: a new scientific discipline. J. Intell. Manuf. **16**(4–5), 439–452 (2005)
2. Shuman, J., Twombly, J.: Collaborative networks are the organization: an innovation in organization design and management. Vikalpa **35**(1), 1–14 (2010)
3. Burghardt, A., Kurc, K., Szybicki, D., Muszyńska, M., Szczęch, T.: Robot-operated inspection of aircraft engine turbine rotor guide vane segment geometry. Tehnički vjesnik **24** (Suppl. 2), 345–348 (2017)
4. Burghardt, A., Kurc, K., Szybicki, D., Muszyńska, M., Nawrocki, J.: Software for the robot-operated inspection station for engine guide vanes taking into consideration the geometric variability of parts. Tehnički vjesnik **24**(Suppl. 2), 349–353 (2017)
5. Burghardt, A., Kurc, K., Szybicki, D., Muszyńska, M., Nawrocki, J.: Robot-operated quality control station based on the UTT method. Open Eng. **7**(1), 37–42 (2017)
6. Teti, R., Jemielniak, K., O'Donnell, G., Dornfeld, D.: Advanced monitoring of machining operations. CIRP Ann. **59**(2), 717–739 (2010)
7. Gierlak, P.: Hybrid position/force control in robotised machining. In: Solid State Phenomena, Switzerland, vol. 210, pp. 192–199 (2014)
8. Burghardt, A., Kurc, K., Szybicki, D., Muszyńska, M., Szczęch, T.: Monitoring the parameters of the robot-operated quality control process. Adv. Sci. Technol.-Res. J. **11**(1), 232–236 (2017)
9. Burghardt, A., Szybicki, D., Kurc, K., Muszyńska, M., Mucha, J.: Experimental study of Inconel 718 surface treatment by edge robotic deburring with force control. Strength Mater. **49**(4), 594–604 (2017)
10. Barnfather, J.D., Goodfellow, M.J., Abram, T.: A performance evaluation methodology for robotic machine tools used in large volume manufacturing. Robot. CIM-Int. Manuf. **37**, 49–56 (2016)
11. Kurc, K., Burghardt, A., Gierlak, P., Szybicki, D.: Non-contact robotic measurement of jet engine components with 3D optical scanner and UTT method. In: Hanus, R., Kreischer, C., Mazur, D. (eds.) MSM 2018. LNEE, vol. 548, pp. 151–164. Springer, Cham (2019). https://doi.org/10.1007/978-3-030-11187-8_12
12. Hui-Ping, L., Dai-Min, C., Miao, Y.: Communication of multi-robot system on the TCP/IP In: International Conference on Mechatronic Science, Electric Engineering and Computer (MEC), pp. 1432–1435. IEEE (2011)
13. Szybicki, D., Burghardt, A., Gierlak, P., Kurc, K.: Robot-assisted quality inspection of turbojet engine blades. In: Hanus, R., Kreischer, C., Mazur, D. (eds.) MSM 2018. LNEE, vol. 548, pp. 337–350. Springer, Cham (2019). https://doi.org/10.1007/978-3-030-11187-8_28
14. Szybicki, D., Burghardt, A., Kurc, K., Pietruś, P.: Calibration and verification of an original module measuring turbojet engine blades geometric parameters. Arch. Mech. Eng. **66**, 97–109 (2019)
15. Burdea, G.C., Coiffet, P.: Virtual Reality Technology. Wiley, Hoboken (2003)
16. Shao, F., Robotham, A.J., Hon, K.K.: Development of a 1: 1 scale true perception virtual reality system for design review in automotive industry (2019)
17. Gallagher, A.G., et al.: Virtual reality simulation for the operating room: proficiency-based training as a paradigm shift in surgical skills training. Ann. Surg. **241**(2), 364 (2005)

18. Koźlak, M., Kurzeja, A., Nawrat, A.: Virtual reality technology for military and industry training programs. In: Nawrat, A., Kuś, Z. (eds.) Vision Based Systems for UAV Applications. Studies in Computational Intelligence, vol. 481, pp. 327–334. Springer, Heidelberg (2013). https://doi.org/10.1007/978-3-319-00369-6_21

19. Matsas, E., Vosniakos, G.C.: Design of a virtual reality training system for human–robot collaboration in manufacturing tasks. Int. J. Interact. Des. Manuf. (IJIDeM) 11(2), 139–153 (2017)

20. Ortiz, J.S., et al.: Virtual training for industrial automation processes through pneumatic controls. In: De Paolis, L.T., Bourdot, P. (eds.) AVR 2018. LNCS, vol. 10851, pp. 516–532. Springer, Cham (2018). https://doi.org/10.1007/978-3-319-95282-6_37

21. De Pace, F., Manuri, F., Sanna, A., Zappia, D.: An augmented interface to display industrial robot faults. In: De Paolis, L., Bourdot, P. (eds.) Augmented Reality, Virtual Reality, and Computer Graphics. LNCS, pp. 403–421. Springer, Cham (2018). https://doi.org/10.1007/978-3-319-95282-6_30

VR Training for Security Awareness
in Industrial IoT

Vasiliki Liagkou and Chrysostomos Stylios[(⊠)]

Department of Informatics and Telecommunications, University of Ioannina,
Arta, 47100 Ioannina, Greece
liagkou@kic.uoi.gr, stylios@uoi.gr

Abstract. Virtual Reality technology provides new solutions and more efficient opportunities for a revolutionary new manufacturing training environment. This work focus on presenting a VR training environment on a new and promising IoT communication protocol, the Low-Power Wide-Area Networks (LPWAN). The LP-WAN have recently emerged as a standard IoT communication system that satisfies the challenges of industrial networks by enhancing their reliability and efficiency. The LPWAN is a promising response to the limitations showed by current IoT technologies. Here are exploited the possibilities of the 3D virtual world technology to create experiential learning simulations, which address IoT users' real needs for privacy and security awareness. To this aim, a 3D role playing game is introduced and a group of master students have evaluated its ability to help them for handling the security features of LPWAN.

Keywords: Virtual Reality · VR training · Industry 4.0 · E-learning · Internet of Things · LPWAN

1 Introduction

Nowadays Virtual Reality (VR) is a new pillar for developing training and learning environment for Industry 4.0. VR is able to provide an integrated training environment where users are able to design, test and perform various manufacturing process activities like being on a real workspace. VR has many abilities that make it suitable for a novel manufacturing training environment [1]. Virtual reality applications for training and learning propose have attracted great interest from the research community [2, 3]. VR have proposed to develop various training scenarios mainly based on 3D role playing games. But, only a few VR scenarios are focused on security issues [4, 5]. The majority of simulations and games have been developed in role based use case scenarios and they use two dimensional graphical representations. In this work, we present a 3D training environment on privacy and security issues for an IoT industrial environment.

Collaboration networks [6] can help Industry 4.0 to support several collaboration environments but this collaborative link between enterprises, customers, employees, and systems is vulnerable to cyber-attacks [7]. The security challenge is a crucial requirement for industry 4.0 to realize a reliable, trustful and seamless cooperation between enterprises, employees and customers. The new communication technologies

© IFIP International Federation for Information Processing 2019
Published by Springer Nature Switzerland AG 2019
L. M. Camarinha-Matos et al. (Eds.): PRO-VE 2019, IFIP AICT 568, pp. 604–612, 2019.
https://doi.org/10.1007/978-3-030-28464-0_53

include various security mechanisms that can reduce security risks but enterprises and employees hesitate to use them due to their lack of skills and awareness.

To this direction our work tries to investigate the capabilities of Virtual Reality (VR) technology for familiarizing users with the functionalities of a promising Internet of Things communication system suitable for industrial networks... The authors introduce a VR training scheme that help users to investigate the security mechanisms in Low-Power Wide-Area Networks [8]. The scope of the proposed VR training scheme is to increase user security awareness by helping users to identify the risks and vulnerabilities that they should have in mind when they use an IoT protocol.

The Internet of Things (IoT) is a basic component of the fourth industrial revolution: Industry 4.0. On the other hand, Low-Power Wide-Area Networks (LPWANs) are becoming one promising IoT communication protocol for the Industrial IoT (IoT) ecosystem since it can provide long-range communication at very low speed to an industrial IoT network. The current implementations could replace 2G/3G/4G/5G cellular networks because LPWAN can also increase the transmission range of devices by trading-off data transmission rate while preserving at the same time power consumption at low levels [8]. The Low-Power Wide Area Networks (LPWANs) exploit the abilities of low frequency signals to transmit over any obstacle or using multipath propagation. They are widely used because of their robustness and reliability [9]. LPWAN technology has becoming promising and widely adopted for IoT networks because it supports the connection of IoT devices at a distance. LPWANs main characteristics include energy autonomy for the IoT devices along with low cost, great coverage capabilities that are requirements of the Industry 4.0 applications [10].

1.1 Outline

Our work focus on a new and promising IoT communication protocol, the Low-Power Wide-Area Networks (LPWAN) and it uses a VR training environment for helping users to explore its security mechanisms. The LP-WAN have recently emerged as a hopeful IoT communication system that can satisfy the challenges of industrial networks by enhancing their reliability and efficiency [11]. The LPWAN can be a solution to the limitations showed by current IoT applied approaches, but their implementations were recently introduced, so it will be necessary users to acquaint their self with the provided security services and increase their awareness.

Our envision is that Virtual Reality can help potential users of Industry 4.0 to understand how the security mechanisms that are provided by LPWAN can be integrated through the whole industrial chain.

2 Security Challenge in Industrial IoT

Industrial IoT systems require an interconnected ecosystem that supports on-line access to interdependent and real-sensing data between enterprises in different geographic places, thus these systems are not designed to be protected against a hostile unsecured internet environment. Security is a critical issue for novel Industrial IoT systems because the transmitted real-time data is confidential and its disclosure could cause huge financial loss for the industry. Nowadays, industrial competitors invest on "Industrial Espionage" in order to gain a completive advance e.g. by finding the design of a new product. Unfortunately, several companies spend a lot of effort to gather competitor's critical knowledge about its manufacturing processes, construction techniques, research plans or pricing/binding deals. If a competitor manages to gather any critical inside information, he could also have access to the enterprise's critical knowhow and this fact will cause huge loss of enterprise's intellectual property.

In an IoT industrial system there is a horizontal interaction through the whole value chain from users and partners to customers thus huge amounts of data are being transmitted, audited, aggregated, annotated, stored and processed. If a competitor succeeds to gather a part of these collected data he can use it for creating a competitive advantage and he can also violate company's and customers' privacy [12, 13]. An IoT system must fulfill the security requirements for preserving data's confidentiality, integrity and privacy. Moreover, it is essential to extend the traditional security requirements in order to guarantee the confidentiality of the aggregated data from smart devices, especially when these devises are distributed in open and uncontrolled environments. Inherently, IoT environment is considered as a vulnerable link in an industrial network since they can be attacked by external devices for compromising their data and disrupting their operation. There are several efficient security solutions for IoT environment in the recent literature and the majority of them try to address resources constraints and scalability issues. The authors in [14] present an extended review of the most recent proposed security and privacy solutions in IoT systems.

Here we explore a new IoT communication protocol, the Low-Power Wide-Area Networks (LPWAN). Nevertheless the security remains a challenge that must also be considered in LPWAN [15–17]. The authors in [18] present a set of security issues of LPWAN server that must be solved. An alternative key management scheme suitable for LPWAN is presented in [19]. Here we take a different direction and we try to increase users' security awareness in LPWAN by helping them to exploit the provided security mechanisms.

3   The VR Training Scheme

In this work, we present a Virtual Reality (VR) scheme for training users to the basic security tools of LPWAN. The provided VR scheme help users to exploit the security issues and tools in IoT protocols and to better understand new risks and vulnerabilities that they should consider and address when they use IoT protocol.

Our VR training environment is decomposed in the following four phases that are implemented in VR 3D role based game scenario (see Fig. 1). The user must execute specific actions in order to successfully complete each phase and then he can proceed to the next one.

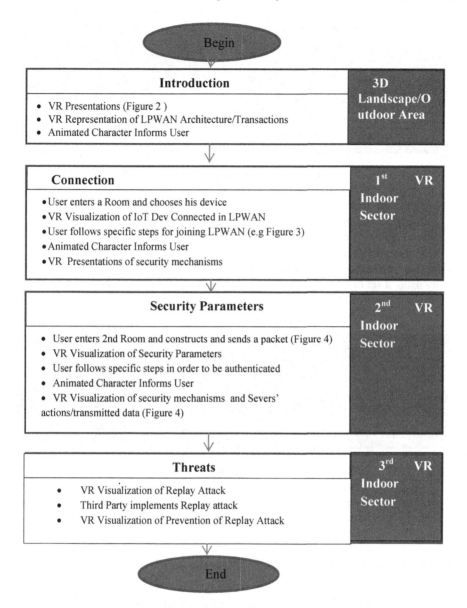

Fig. 1. VR training phases.

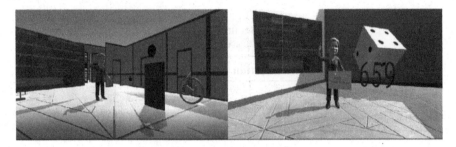

Fig. 2. VR presenter for informing user.

- *Introduction section* includes VR presentations and 3D visualization of the basic architecture and interactions in LPWAN.
- *Connection section* includes specific visualizations and steps so that the user to be able to understand how he can connect various devices in LPWAN. The user thought navigation is able to understand how the LPWAN authenticates his device by using a set of keys. Moreover here the user can select two types of IoT devices by following two distinct paths for joining the LPWAN (see Fig. 3).

Fig. 3. VR for connecting two different IoT devices.

- *Security Parameters section* includes a more detailed description of LPWAN security mechanisms (see Fig. 4). During this phase the user has to complete specific tasks in order to visualize how the network server generates and verifies the message integrity code and the corresponding keys.
- *Threat section*, visualizes how LPWAN tries to prevent replay attack.

Fig. 4. Transmitted package from Network server and Packet Construction

3.1   VR Scheme's Learning Achievements

The presented VR environment improves learning and training processes because it allows capturing attention to IoT users for increasing their awareness of the transmitted data. Our VR training scheme uses a VR character for informing the user about the set of actions that he can make for increase data's confidentiality. Moreover, VR application has included in several points of navigation a VR presenter for familiarizing the user with the available set of actions for protecting his transmitted data. (see Fig. 4). The proposed scheme presents the security features and cryptographic information in a logic and direct way. The utilised VR scenario uses several VR spaces that simulate conventional actions. User's avatar could make specific actions like navigation, interaction with objects, communication and objects creation for gaining a dipper understanding of available security tools of LPWAN.

The provided VR environment helps users to think without being influenced by others and it provides a VR experience for a set of connection activities. LPWAN's security tools need specific actions from the IoT user for connecting his device in LPWAN. It is very difficult and unrealistic for users to execute such privacy policies and complex security mechanism. Our VR scenario trains the user how to connect his device in order to follow the right connecting procedures. We have implemented two different VR scenarios where the user's avatar follows specific steps and takes specific actions for connecting two different types of IoT devices, a refrigerator and a mobile phone (see Fig. 3). The security factors that must be taken into account by an IoT user for connecting a static or mobile IoT device are different. Our VR scheme help users to understand what factors have to consider for joining in LPWAN network. The main goal of the presented VR platform is that gives the opportunity to the users use some security tools and to visualize a set of vulnerabilities. Most of the security and privacy concerns are invoke by misconfiguration of users. Our VR scenario visualizes in various steps of its navigation the potential risks and vulnerabilities that users should consider and address when they use LPWAN protocol. The presented training environment assess users' knowledge about the provided security level for every action their avatar makes and evaluates if they understand the potential security flaws for its actions (see Fig. 4).

Finally the user through his VR navigation can control connection procedures of IoT network. The interconnection and communication among the IoT devices and LPWAN server vary according to the user actions or protocols phase. Our VR model visualize transmitted data packages information and servers' interactions in order the user to understand how security policy of LPWAN works and what are the bounds of the provided security level. The user will be able to develop analytic and problem solving abilities. Our proposed VR scheme simulates experiential real life use case scenarios for solving problems in order users to gain a better comprehension of security risks in LPWAN and to help the to understand the functionalities of security mechanisms. User's avatar can throw a dice for generating a random number or it may pic specific boxes for constructing a network package.

4   VR Exploitation's Security Requirements

In this work, we investigate how VR technology is able to create and evaluate experiential learning simulations that address IoT users' needs for privacy and security awareness. It has presented a 3D role playing game, which was tested by a group of students who evaluated handling the security features of a LPWAN. The majority of IoT Industrial use cases must take a very careful consideration of security requirements and the implemented VR training platform investigate users' awareness to the following privacy and security concerns in IoT networks:

4.1   Confidentiality/Non Leakage of Sensitive Information

Leakage of critical information to unauthorized users or competitors is unacceptable for any industry. Usually, an industrial plan deploys a lot of smart devices that are used for collecting manufacturing processes data. If these devices are hacked by an attacker, then he can monitor all industrial activities and access critical information. To avoid this attack, LPWAN uses symmetric data encryption between gateway and devices. VR users through their navigation to the learning world are able to understand how the encryption of the payload is by default enabled in every transmission in LPWAN. Moreover, VR user understands what information is transmitted by an IoT device thus the VR environment visualizes the contents of every transmitted package by including the information of identifiers and payload data. Complementary LPWAN do not use a specific gateway, thus our scheme visualizes how the data frames do not include any gateway identifier. In this way, user must be aware that it is possible for anyone to receive the encrypted data packets. LPWAN tries to authenticate the IoT device for detecting the unauthorized access. VR training schemes includes two different VR scenarios in order to visualize how the LPWAN network authenticates an IoT device by two different joining methods.

The application data should remain confidential against theft and tampering since application data of IoT could be industrial or enterprise. The VR training scheme shows at different scenes of the navigation that a 128-bit Application Session Key is used to encrypt the data frame between the IoT device and the application server (see Fig. 4).

4.2   Integrity

Preserving the data integrity is one critical requirement, so LPWAN have to include a method for preventing any unauthorized on stored and transferred data. Data integrity in LPWAN can be realized by the computation message authentication code (MAC) functions. The VR training scheme includes a 3D game for visualizing how the message authentication code is produced using the Network Key, which is confirmed by the Network server. It shows at different scenes of the navigation how an IoT device can be authenticated by using the network key. Finally LPWAN also encrypts the transmitted data file.

4.3   Robustness

An industrial IoT network should be shielded against various attacks and threats caused by human factors or natural disasters. LPWAN uses a frame counter for upstream and downstream messages which will block a transmission from being sent more than once. The VR scenario visualizes how this generated number prevents the replay attack.

5 Implementation Details

Here, we have designed, developed and presented a training scenario by using the Unity 3D environment. The Virtual reality application is built in WebGL Unity Project. The WebGL build option allows Unity to publish content as JavaScript programs that use HTML5 technologies and the WebGL rendering. Just a few web browsers support WebGL, and most of the mobile devices are not supported by Unity WebGL. Actually, Mozilla Firefox browser supports all the utilities of WebGL. We have created the 3D objects for the VR training environment via importing collada files, into the Project's asset. The VR training environment is accessed by iframe and when users navigate on a VR training game through the browser. The developed scripts in VR Training environment are created in Unity Project by writing scripts in C# Language.

6 Conclusion and Discussion

This work presents developing and usage a Virtual Reality (VR) training environment that can help potential users of LPWAN to familiarize with the provided security mechanisms by LPWAN and to increase their security awareness. We used a small group of master students in Computer Security theme for training purposes. Most students found the proposed VR scheme useful for exploiting new technologies. In addition, we explored how useful students found the VR technology as a training tool. Whereas 95% of them believe that VR is the easiest and most convenient way to explore IoT system's functionalities. All students strongly agreed that protecting their data in an IoT environment is important to them. Overall, 85% of the students declared that they would prefer the utilized VR scheme to include more entertaining and game role characteristics. We are planning to further update VR model and to redesign the VR use case scenarios in order to provide a more entertaining game-role based experience.

Acknowledgements. This work has been partially supported by the "TIPHYS 4.0- Social Network based doctoral Education on Industry 4.0" project No 2017-1-SE01-KA203-03452 funded by ERASMUS+ of the European Commission.

References

1. Büttner, S., et al.: The design space of augmented and virtual reality applications for assistive environments in manufacturing: a visual approach. In: International Conference on PErvasive Technologies Related to Assistive Environments, pp. 433–440 (2017)
2. Stuchlíková, L., Kósa, A., Benko, P., Juhász, P.: Virtual reality vs. reality in engineering education. In: 15th International Conference on Emerging eLearning Technologies and Applications, pp. 1–6 (2017)

3. Carruth, D.W.: Virtual reality for education and workforce training. In: 15th International Conference on Emerging eLearning Technologies and Applications, pp. 1–6 (2017)

4. Ryoo, J., Techatassanasoontorn, A., Lee, D.: Security education using second life. IEEE Secur. Priv. **7**, 71–74 (2009)

5. Ryoo, J., Techatassanasoontorn, A., Lee, D., Lothian, J.: Game based InfoSec education using OpenSim. In: 15th Colloquium for Information Systems Security Education (2011)

6. Camarinha-Matos, L.M., Fornasiero, R., Afsarmanesh, H.: Collaborative networks as a core enabler of industry 4.0. In: Camarinha-Matos, L.M., Afsarmanesh, H., Fornasiero, R. (eds.) PRO-VE 2017. IAICT, vol. 506, pp. 3–17. Springer, Cham (2017). https://doi.org/10.1007/978-3-319-65151-4_1

7. Ervural, B.C., Ervural, B.: Overview of cyber security in the industry 4.0 era. Industry 4.0: Managing The Digital Transformation. SSAM, pp. 267–284. Springer, Cham (2018). https://doi.org/10.1007/978-3-319-57870-5_16

8. Centenaro, M., Vangelista, L., Zanella, A., Zorzi, M.: Long-range communications in unlicensed bands: the rising stars in the IoT and smart city scenarios. IEEE Wirel. Commun. **23**, 60–67 (2016)

9. Raza, U., Kulkarni, P., Sooriyabandara, M.: Low power wide area networks: an overview. IEEE Commun. Surv. Tutor. **19**, 855–873 (2017)

10. Boulogeorgos, A.-A.A., Diamantoulakis, P.D., Karagiannidis, G.K.: Low power wide area networks (LPWANs) for internet of things (IoT) applications: research challenges and future trends. *CoRR*, vol. abs/1611.07449 (2016). http://arxiv.org/abs/1611.07449

11. Luvisotto, M., Tramarin, F., Vangelista, L., Vitturi, S.: On the use of LoRaWAN for indoor industrial IoT applications. Wirel. Commun. Mob. Comput. **2018**, 11 (2018). https://doi.org/10.1155/2018/3982646

12. Pavlou, P.: State of the information privacy literature: where are we now and where should we go? MIS Q. **35**(4), 977–988 (2011)

13. Price, B.A., Adam, K., Nuseibeh, B.: Keeping ubiquitous computing to yourself: a practical model for user control of privacy. Int. J. Hum.-Comput. Stud. **63**(1), 228–253 (2005)

14. Kouicem, D.E., Bouabdallah, A., Lakhlef, H.: Internet of things security: a top-down survey. Comput. Netw. **141**, 199–221 (2018)

15. Aras, E., Ramachandran, G.S., Lawrence, P., Hughes, D.: Exploring the security vulnerabilities of LoRa. In: 3rd IEEE International Conference on Cybernetics (CYBCONF 2017), pp. 1–6 (2017)

16. Chatzigiannakis, Y., Liagkou, V., Spirakis, P.: Providing end-to-end secure communication in low-power wide area networks (LPWANs). In: 2nd International Symposium on Cyber Security Cryptography and Machine Learning (CSCML 2018) (2018)

17. Emekcan, A., Gowri, R., Piers, L., Danny, H.: Exploring the security vulnerabilities of LoRa. In: 3rd IEEE International Conference on Cybernetics (CYBCONF), vol. 06, pp. 1–6 (2017)

18. Michorius, J.: Whats mine is not yours: LoRa network and privacy of data on publishing devices. In: 25th Twente Student Conference on IT (2016)

19. Naoui, S., Elhdhili, M.E., Saidane, L.A.: Enhancing the security of the IoT LoRaWAN architecture. In: International Conference on Performance Evaluation and Modeling in Wired and Wireless Networks (PEMWN 2016), pp. 1–7 (2016)

Education and Enabling Tools for Industry 4.0

Simulations of Manufacturing Systems: Applications in Achieving the Intended Learning Outcomes

Paweł Litwin, Maksymilian Mądziel, and Dorota Stadnicka[✉]

Faculty of Mechanical Engineering and Aeronautics,
Rzeszow University of Technology, Al. Powstancow Warszawy 12,
35-959 Rzeszow, Poland
{plitwin,mmadziel,dorota.stadnicka}@prz.edu.pl

Abstract. The work describes various problems that can arise in the planning, organization and operation of manufacturing processes. The consequences for the companies resulting from the problems are deliberated together with the proposed remedies. It is important to teach students what kind of problems they may face in their future work and how they can analyze the problems and look for appropriate solutions. The students should also understand how the problems can influence on other companies working in a collaborative network (CN). In the work, the intended learning outcomes that can be achieved are presented. Then, simulations of chosen problems are analyzed and discussed.

Keywords: Industrial problems · Simulations · Intended learning outcomes

1 Introduction

The manufacturing technologies fast development and dissemination enforces a necessity of quick knowledge acquisition by companies current and future employees. Therefore, adequate learning tools and methods such as simulations [1, 2] virtual reality [3] or social networks [4] have to be engaged. For each educational program not only teaching methods but also methods using for students' knowledge verification are important [5]. Also companies adapt different learning means, since their employees' knowledge and skills have to be improved continuously. The employees learn to understand better the problems and to know which tools should be applied to solve the problems.

Manufacturing processes (MPs) planning and organization concern many issues that should be analyzed starting from understanding of customers' requirements and ending with customers' satisfaction assessment. The main goal of MPs is to produce on time the ordered quality products. Low quality or delivery delays can cause collaborators to choose another company, that is able to deliver required products. Additionally, since, the clients' requirements can change in time, the manufacturing lines (MLs) has to be adapted. In a collaborative world the problems, which arise in one company can affect other companies in a network. Since, a CN consists of a variety of entities geographically distributed, operating in different environment, having different

Published by Springer Nature Switzerland AG 2019
L. M. Camarinha-Matos et al. (Eds.): PRO-VE 2019, IFIP AICT 568, pp. 615–623, 2019.
https://doi.org/10.1007/978-3-030-28464-0_54

culture [6], a risk connected with the collaboration can be high. The companies deal with different problems which can influence on a ML operation and potentially on collaborators. Quality issues cause reworking, scraps, delays and waiting and are analyzed with the use of quality tools [7] and six sigma projects [8]. Machine failures cause stoppages, waiting, delays, nonconforming products and can be minimized by TPM implementation [9]. Materials delivery delays cause waiting, high material inventory levels. These causes can be minimized by implementation of supermarkets, Kanban System, Just in Time [10]. Clients' requirements changes cause scraps and technology changes. These negative consequences can be minimized by improvement of communication system. Excessive work in process causes long lead time, what can be minimized by Supermarkets, Kanban System or FIFO implementation [11]. Unfortunately not all of the problems can be eliminated. Therefore, a company, knowing the scale of the problems, can make a manufacturing system resistant to the troubles to protect client.

This paper is focused on simulation applications in educational process concerning problems that can arise in or influence management of MPs and which can potentially influence company's collaborators in a network. The authors propose an approach based on simulations involving a set of steps to analyze the problems. The goal of this approach is to teach effectively students the methods that can be used in such analyses.

2 Simulations Applied in Educational Process

System Dynamics (SD) is a method of modeling and simulation systems containing causal relationships with their logic, time delays and feedback loops. Researchers inspired by successful applications of the SD method in various fields (management, engineering, physics, economy) began to apply the SD approach also in the field of teaching and learning. Students can use SD models to perform experiments, which can be easily repeated using various parameters and alternative scenarios. In many cases, the simulation is the only available way to observe the results of the experiment. The first applications of the method in schools showed that SD, in addition to the benefits of understanding cause-and-effect relationships, helps increase students' involvement in voluntary projects, even after school time [12]. As a result of the positive adoption of the SD method to schools, a number of educational projects have been developed. Jay Forrester indicates the three main benefits that the SD method used in education gives [13]: (1) develops personal skills such as clarity of thought for good communication, courage for having unconventional opinions; (2) shapes an outlook and personality to match the challenges of the 21st century; (3) allows to understand the nature of systems in which we work and live. This paper presents examples of the third benefit, in particular related to the modeling of supply chain (SC).

The use of the SD method for simulation of the SC dates back to the second half of the 20th century. Model of the production and distribution system to which the "Forrester Supply Chain" (FSC) label is attached [14] was the subject of many research works. An overview of research on SC, including, among others, SC design, inventory management, demand amplification, and SC reengineering is presented in [15]. The SD method was also used to study the impact of the information flow model on the level of stocks of enterprises collaborating in the SC [16].

Discrete event simulation (DES) is another commonly used modelling technique [17]. This kind of simulation is an operative research technique that has a great potential to help understand the analyzed system. One of the advantages of using DES over other mathematical models is the simulation capability to model complex flow scenarios [18]. One of the tool which can be applied in DES is Flexim. Flexsim is a virtual mapping of a real system based on real data. It allows to conduct simulation experiments and check different variants of solutions. It is an attractive tool in the student education process because it gives the opportunity to analyze visually modelled object parameters and material flow in real time. Students working in this program may partly feel like in a computer game in which they have a strictly defined goal to achieve. Flexsim software is used for simulation of transport processes, storage and delivery as well as for production-manufacturing purposes [19]. Examples of using the Flexsim program for simulation purposes are widely presented in works [20, 21]. The use of this program in such a number of industries gives a signal to universities to use it also in the process of student education. Flexsim allows to check the results of calculations in simulation, which gives students additional visual control of the correctness of their calculations. An example of works that describe the use of Flexsim software in the field of student education are presented in [22]. The mentioned works justify the simulation application in educational process in the context of collaborative networks analyses.

3   Case Studies

1st Problem Description: In the MP nonconforming products can be identified. It can happen on different stages of a MP. A nonconforming product might be reworked or will be a scrap. Quality level of a MP can be described with the use of First Time Yield (FTY) or First Pass Yield (FPY) [2]. The measures can be calculated on the base of historical data.

Consequences of the 1st Problem: If a product can be reworked, it will go back to the previous process and use additional time for the repeated manufacturing operation. If a product will be a scrap, all previous MPs have to be repeated. It creates additional costs and can lead to delivery delays and clients dissatisfaction what even can lead to exclusion the company from a CN.

Proposed Solutions or Remedies: To improve the quality on a MP TQM can be implemented. The employees can be involved in identification of quality problems and they can propose solutions connected with better work organization, product or process design etc. That can lead to decreasing quality problems.

Proposed Analyses: The analyses proposed for such problems concern assessing how nonconformities can influence on a MP and affect deliveries. For this purpose, DES simulations taking into account FTY and FPY, will be carried out.

Intended Learning Outcomes

ILO1: Identify potential consequences of nonconforming products, which can be reworked or scraps, in a specified processes in a ML.

ILO2: Use standard measures such as FTY and FPY in simulations.

ILO3: Understand how a place (a work stand) in which a nonconforming product is identified influences on lead time increasing.

Case Study Description: The case study presents situation in which a ML consisted of 4 MPs which manufactures three kinds of products operates. In Processes 1, 2 and 3 operators make a quality control after the machining process. Then, after the Process 4 all products go to the control process (Process 5) performed on a coordinate measuring machine (CMM). Initial quality parameters are presented with the use of FTY and FPY. **FTY** is connected with the products which are assessed to be **scraps**. **FPY** is connected with the products which have to be **reworked**. The input data are presented in Table 1. Tact time equals 15 min. The production material is available from the beginning of the simulation and is released every 15 min. First material delivery is realized at time $t = 0$. The ML works for first shift only. Available working time equal 450 min.

Table 1. Data concerning the ML; PT – proc. time, QI – values after quality improvement.

Process	PT [min]	Setup [min]	FTY	FPY	FTY-QI	FPY-QI
Process 1	30	0	0.92	0.95	0.93	0.96
Process 2	30	0	0.95	0.90	0.96	0.91
Process 3	30	0	0.98	0.95	0.99	0.96
Process 4	10	5	0.90	0.88	0.91	0.89
Process 5	5	10	–	–	–	–

The number of products that should be delivered to the customer every day is 30 pcs (10 pcs. of each type). The order of performing different types of products is random. Setups are needed only for Processes 4 and 5 on which all three kinds of products are treated. Processes 1, 2 and 3 are dedicated to one type of the product.

Computer Model Development: Computer model of the ML was developed in Flexim software.

Simulation Scenarios: Students perform simulations for the following scenarios:

Scenario Q1: A simulation under predetermined parameters and ML organization before quality improvement.

Scenario Q2: A simulation in which the ML works also for the second shift, with the same tact time 15 min.

Simulation Results: Simulations allow to obtain the following results (Table 2).

Table 2. DES simulation results – machine load (ML), average inventory level (AIL), product average stay time in input and output inventories of the processes (AST).

Process	ML [%]	AIL [pcs]	AST [min]	ML [%]	AIL [pcs]	AST [min]
	Scenario Q1			Scenario Q2		
Before Process 1	–	3.8	33.2	–	6.4	54
Process 1	100	4.2	82.3	96.6	8.1	82.2
Process 2	100	4.2	82.3	96.6	8.1	82.2
Process 3	80	4.2	82.3	89.9	8.1	82.2
Process 4	62.2	2.3	25.2	64.4	4.9	55.2
Process 5	30	0	0	31.7	0	0

Average Lead Time (ALT) for Q1 equals 203.5 min. A number of good quality products manufactured in a working day (QC) equals 24 pcs. Time required to manufacture 30 pcs (TR) equals 555 min. For Q2 ALT equals 284 min and during 2 shifts 46 pcs of QC are produced.

Discussion and Proposed Solutions: Performed simulations show that the solution that meets the production assumptions (30 pcs) is Scenario Q2, which consisted of extending the work and adding a second shift in production. The Q1 does not meet the production requirement. If the solution with the second shift was to be considered, other pros and cons of this solution should be deliberated, such as economic analysis, etc. This state of affairs also encourages the student to think and search for another effective solution that would fully meet the assumptions of the work task, because the Q2 exceeds the demand for the products. Students are motivated to propose and implement other changes to the ML to see their influence on the results.

2nd Problem Description: Pull systems require feedback between supply and demand for production volume planning, and simulation can be very helpful in these cases [23]. Presented problem concerns parts and products flow between a supplier, a producer, a retailer and a client, and illustrates the formation of so-called bullwhip effect, which consists of transferring reinforced changes in demand through the SC.

Consequences of the 2nd Problem: Relatively small fluctuations in the demand reported by the customers increase as the information is communicated upstream to the producer and further to the supplier. Information transferred in the form of orders through the SC does not actually reflect changes in demand on the retail market, but contains a number of decisions regarding inventories. This can cause excessive stocks in the SC.

Proposed Solutions or Remedies: To deal with this problem the companies can, implement modified replenishment policy or redesign the information flow that will improve inventory management throughout the SC.

Proposed Analyses: The activities proposed for this problem concern the assessment of the impact of demand fluctuations and stock replenishment policies on the volume of stocks in individual parts of the SC.

Intended Learning Outcomes: In simulations students are able to obtain the following intended learning outcomes:

ILO1: Identify potential consequences of bullwhip effect in SC.
ILO2: Assess the impact of demand fluctuations on stock levels in SC.
ILO3: Propose a solution that avoids excessive stock in the SC.

Case Study Description: The case study presents application of SD method for analyzing the stocks in the SC. The supplier is responsible for the delivery of parts to the manufacturer. The producer manufactures finished products using parts from the supplier. These products are transferred to the retailer and then to customer. The customer's task is to generate demand and collect products delivered by the retailer. Variability of demand is considered one of the main factors responsible for the formation of the bullwhip effect. The effect lies in strengthening demand changes carried upstream the SC. The information is falsified: besides the actual changes in demand it includes the replenishment policy decisions. In the analyzed SC model shaping the level of inventories is based on the assumption that the demand in the next period will be the same as demand in the current period.

Replenishment is only carried out when the level of inventory is lower than required. Formula (1) presents the method of determining the amount of the parts order by the producer:

$$po = \text{IF THEN ELSE}((pp < 2 * pq), 2 * pq - pp, 0) \tag{1}$$

where: po - parts ordered, pp - parts stock at producer, pq - production quantity

The advantage of the presented formula is its simplicity, however, it has some drawbacks. The selected inventory replenishment policy assumes demand unchanged. In business practice, this assumption may cause some problems. If the demand in the next period decreases significantly – the result will be an excessive accumulation of goods in the SC, and hence an increase of storage costs. There may also be a situation when the demand for the next period will be much higher than the current demand. The result of such a situation will be extended time of order fulfillment.

Computer Model Development: A modified version of FSC (Fig. 1) contains stocks of supplier, producer retailer and customer. The model shows the impact of the adopted procurement strategy on the levels of stocks of collaborating enterprises.

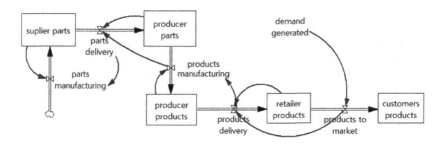

Fig. 1. The structure of the tested SC in Vensim.

This study presents the application of the SD method for analyzing SC stock levels in conditions of constant and variable demand. Inventory levels are analyzed over a period of 250 days.

Simulation Scenarios: In experiments, 3 demand distributions were considered:

Scenario D1 – Constant daily demand of 5 pcs.
Scenario D2 – Random normal distribution (mean – 5 pcs, st. dev. – 1.6 pcs.).
Scenario D3 – Random uniform distribution.

In D2 and D3, integer pseudo-random numbers in the range (0–10) are generated as the demand values. For all scenarios, initial stock levels of 3 pcs. were established.

Simulation Results: After a short period of simulation the levels of all stocks in D1 scenario stabilized at 5 pcs. The longest period of inventory stabilization concerns the supplier's stock and amounts to 6 days. The maximum level of the supplier's inventory (19 pcs.) is achieved on the second and third day of simulation.

In the D2 scenario, the variability of demand caused changes in stocks in individual parts of the SC. Changes in stock of the part supplier were particularly large. The average supplier stock was 16 pcs. and the maximum reach 38 pcs.

The feature of D3 scenario is strongly variable demand. This resulted in a reinforcement of the bullwhip effect. Maximum retailer's stock level was 44 pcs. and the mean value was 25 pcs. (Fig. 2).

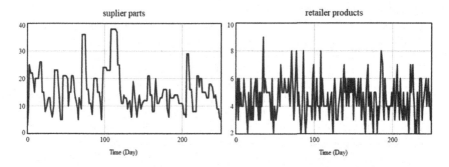

Fig. 2. Stocks of the supplier's and retailer. Random normal demand distribution.

The simulation results indicate that the intensity of the bullwhip effect increases with the increase in demand variability. The presented simulations can be used for educational purposes as an effective tool for demonstrating the bullwhip effect. Additionally, with the ability to modify the model, students can implement other stock replenishment policies and examine their impact on stock levels. Finally, students assisted by the teacher can redefine the way of information flows so that each link in the SC uses data on the current market demand. As demonstrated in [17], this will significantly reduce the bullwhip effect and its impact on stock levels.

4 Summary

The presented work deals with simulations which can be applied in didactic processes to achieve the specified ILOs what is the main paper contributions to the science. The presented approach consisted of a set of steps ensure deep understanding of problem consequences and allow to find the best solution. Additionally, such way of analyses increase students creativity, as they want to check many different solutions, since it is easy to do in computer simulations. Additionally, the students realize that the companies are not the isolated islands and operate in CNs. Being a part of CN gives the company opportunities but also creates responsibilities. The mistakes such as quality issues and delivery delays can cause the company exclusion from a network.

In the future work the authors will also investigate other problems that can be analyzed with the use of simulations and create educational case studies with indicated ILOs. Additionally, in the future works the authors are planning to add another step to the presented approach that is Design of Experiment (DOE), which will allow to look for an optimal solution of an analyzed problem.

Acknowledgments. This work has been partially supported by the "TIPHYS 4.0 – Social Network based doctoral Education on Industry 4.0", project No. 2017-1-SE01-KA203-03452 funded by ERASMUS+ of the European Commission.

References

1. Antonelli, D., et al.: Tiphys: an open networked platform for higher education on Industry 4.0. Procedia CIRP **79**, 706–711 (2019)
2. Stadnicka, D., Litwin, P.: Value stream mapping and system dynamics integration for manufacturing line modelling and analysis. Int. J. Prod. Econ. **208**, 400–411 (2019)
3. Liagkou, V., Salmas, D., Stylios, C.: Realizing virtual reality learning environment for industry 4.0. Procedia CIRP **79**, 712–717 (2019)
4. Putnik, G., Costa, E., Alves, C.F.V., Shah, V.: Analyzing the correlation between social network analysis measures and performance of students in social network-based engineering education. Int. J. Technol. Des. Educ. **26**(3), 413–437 (2016)
5. Stadnicka, D., Litwin, P., Antonelli, D.: Human factor in intelligent manufacturing systems - knowledge acquisition and motivation. Procedia CIRP **79**, 718–723 (2019)
6. Camarinha-Matos, L.M., Afsarmanesh, H.: On reference models for collaborative networked organizations. Int. J. Prod. Res. **46**(9), 2453–2469 (2008)

7. Juran, J.M., Godfrey, A.B.: Total Quality Management. McGraw-Hill Companies, New York (2001)
8. Pande, P.S., Neuman, R.P., Cavanagh, R.: The Six Sigma Way: How to Maximize the Impact of Your Change and Improvement Efforts. McGraw-Hill Education, New York (2014)
9. Nakajima, S.: Introduction to TPM: Total Productive Maintenance. Productivity Press, Cambridge (1988)
10. Liker, J.K., Franz, J.K.: The Toyota Way to Continuous Improvement: Linking Strategy and Operational Excellence to Achieve Superior Performance. McGraw-Hill Education, New York (2011)
11. Feld, W.M.: Lean Manufacturing: Tools, Techniques, and How to Use Them. St. Lucie Press, Boca Raton (2000)
12. Nuhoğlu, H.: The effect of the system dynamics approach on understanding causal relationship skills in science education. Procedia – Soc. Behav. Sci. 2(2), 3614–3618 (2010)
13. Forrester, J.W.: Learning through system dynamics as preparation for the 21st century. Syst. Dyn. Rev. 32(3–4), 187–203 (2016)
14. Forrester, J.W.: Industrial Dynamics. MIT Press, Cambridge (1961)
15. Angerhofer, B.J., Angelides, M.C.: System dynamics modeling in supply chain management: research review. In: Proceedings of the 2000 Winter Simulation Conference, pp. 342–351 (2000)
16. Litwin, P., Jakieła, J., Olech, M.: Dynamic simulation based optimization of information flow in extended enterprise and its impact on business partners production efficiency and stock replenishment. Adv. Manuf. Sci. Technol. 40(1), 33–45 (2016)
17. Robinson, S.: Discrete-event simulation: from the pioneers to the present, what next? J. Oper. Res. Soc. 56(6), 619–629 (2005)
18. Fiallos, A., Ochoa, X.: Discrete event simulation for student flow in academic study periods. In: Twelfth Latin American Conference on Learning Technologies (LACLO) (2017)
19. Gang, L., An, S., Liao, J.: The optimization and simulation of automobile spread production line. Ind. Eng. 11(6), 71–75 (2009)
20. Wu, G., Yao, L., Yu, S.: Simulation and optimization of production line based on FlexSim. In: Chinese Control and Decision Conference (CCDC) (2018)
21. Tokgöz, E.: Industrial engineering and simulation experience using Flexsim software. Comput. Educ. J. 8, 4 (2017)
22. Rostkowska, M.: Simulation of production lines in the education of engineers: how to choose the right software? Manag. Prod. Eng. Rev. 5(4), 53–65 (2014)
23. Holweg, M., Disney, S., Hines, P., Naim, M.: Towards responsive vehicle supply: a simulation-based investigation into automotive scheduling systems. J. Oper. Manag. 23, 507–530 (2005)

Influence of Trust Factors on Shared Laboratory Resources in a Distributed Environment

Jannicke Baalsrud Hauge[1,4(✉)], Valentin Kammerlohr[2],
Barbara Göbl[3], and Heiko Duin[1]

[1] BIBA - Bremer Institut für Produktion und Logistik, Bremen, Germany
baa@biba.uni-bremen.de
[2] Faculty of Surveying, Informatics and Mathematics,
Hochschule für Technik Stuttgart, Stuttgart, Germany
[3] Faculty of Computer Science, University of Vienna, Vienna, Austria
[4] KTH-Royal Institute of Technolgy, Stockholm, Sweden

Abstract. Every collaboration stands on a foundation of mutual trust. This is a pre-requisite for any information sharing as well as the basis to successfully carry out collaborative tasks. This article presents the use case of Open Digital Lab 4you, a digitized laboratory environment, and identifies relevant trust factors based on a literature review and action-based research. In this paper stakeholders' needs and requirements are discussed and these are linked to several, critical aspects of trust when sharing resources among public institutions.

Keywords: Trust · Shared resources ·
Collaboration in distributed environments · Information uncertainty ·
Incentives · Shared laboratory

1 Introduction

During the last decades, new concepts on shared resources have been developed and successfully implemented within the manufacturing industry [1]. As a socio-economic ecosystem, resource sharing involves human and physical resources [2], as well as non-physical resources. The concept and practice of sharing undergoes a transition from its traditional role towards the so called sharing economy; referring to resources as well as collaborative consumption as described in [2–7], all having in common that either individuals or organisations put efforts in jointly utilizing existing resource(s). In this way they will gain benefits in terms of higher utilization of resources, cost benefits, but also through access to knowledge they don't have [1, 2].

The operation of laboratories for educational purposes is an example that might benefit from implementing the concept of shared knowledge, infrastructure and facilities. It is a costly activity for any educational or training institution. Laboratories often require specific and expensive equipment and infrastructure as well as trained and skilled workforce. The utilization of highly specialized laboratories is often low [8] and

© IFIP International Federation for Information Processing 2019
Published by Springer Nature Switzerland AG 2019
L. M. Camarinha-Matos et al. (Eds.): PRO-VE 2019, IFIP AICT 568, pp. 624–634, 2019.
https://doi.org/10.1007/978-3-030-28464-0_55

the access is limited to specific user groups, mostly those working or studying in the institution owning the laboratory.

However, several important questions remain. Under which circumstances is it possible to realise different concepts of shared resources? How should the agreement at inter-, intra and individual level look like and what are the barriers and the drivers? Are they the same for all industries and how much do they vary? Is it possible to implement the same business models in this public environment as within the manufacturing sector? Educational institutions educating engineering students for fulfilling future needs, have a detailed knowledge about such concepts from the industry as well as long experience in working in inter-organisational research collaborations [9]. Therefore, this knowledge can be used as a background for implementing a concept for shared laboratories for providing students, researchers and staff access to a larger variety of technologies and knowledge than within an organisation. From the aforementioned collaboration and experiences it is known that trust is a pre-requisite for any functioning collaboration, we will first look at this aspect for our case study. Back in 1995, Mayer [10] defined trust as a conscious choice to be vulnerable towards another's actions, without any means to control or monitor and thus solely based on the expectation that the other will perform a certain, important action. While the author's research originally focused on trust dynamics within organisations, this definition certainly holds true in inter-organisational relations as well. Trust problems can be attributed to complexities resulting from: structure of the sharing network, uncertainties underlying the logistics processes, and partner behaviour [11].

The two research questions we will address here are therefore:

- RQ1: Which trust factors have an influence on the inter-organisational and individual level related to shared resources
- RQ2: How does the difference in incentives for different stakeholders and roles influence the collaboration among partners and employees?

The paper is structured as follows: Sect. 2 describes the research methodology and is followed by a literature review related to trust factors and frameworks for trust factors. Based on this literature review the first relevant factors are identified and applied in a case study. The relation between the stakeholders' needs and requirements and the different trust factors is discussed in Sect. 5. Section 6 summarises the finding and gives an outlook on next steps.

2   Research Methodology

A mixed method approach was used for the research: a structured literature review and action-based research in combination with brainwriting [12], in this instance a case study. A literature review (LR) in the field of organisational trust in different fields was carried out. It was based upon [13] three step approach: planning a review, conducting a review, and reporting and dissemination. This analysis helped in identifying the key factors influencing the trust relation, the differentiation between static and process-oriented factors and shed some light in which challenges we might face in order to achieve the long-term goal of establishing distributed laboratory environments.

The action-based research according to Sein, Henfridsson et al. [14] was carried out as a case study, investigating the current relations and future needs and requirements among the participating organisations. As basis a workshop was conducted where the method brainwriting [12] was applied, the consortium partners wrote their ideas on paper following an exchange of the written ideas. The approach of the case study was selected as research method, because of its potential to investigate a phenomenon in its context [15].

3 Literature Review

Trust is a diffuse term, and there exist many different definitions [1, 11]. Determinants of trust are elements, behaviour, and criteria or factors, which characterize trust in relationships [16]. Sharing something takes time, it requires to take others' schedules, needs, desires, abilities and safety into account and also to trust (perceived risk) in regard to theft, strangers, and privacy issues [17]. Resource sharing, as we would like to realise, is a challenging activity with many uncertainties. Irrespective of these trust uncertainties, the functioning of collaboration on shared resources in logistics rests on fulfilment of trust-based requirements. Partners involved in the sharing need to know and trust: (1) states (conditions) of shareable assets in regard to capacity, presence and/or (idle time), capability; (2) previous experience in the sharing of same resource; (3) restrictions and compensation; (4) level of behavioural congruence of actors participating in the sharing; (5) regulatory issues and dispute resolution. [2] further clarifies that partners involved in the sharing have to trust that: service will be delivered to a reasonable standard and expectation. Nevertheless, trust is needed to overcome uncertainties in shared information, fairness of incentive schemes, and partner's incongruent behaviours [11]. In order to be able to develop and implement a concept of shared laboratory resources, we need to consider the aforementioned findings in our project's context. Therefore, we have analysed different frameworks aiming at describing trust elements from different perspectives.

Daudi et al. [16] presents a generic trust model in resource sharing and cooperation. It consists of three phases as depicted in Fig. 1. Especially differing between static and dynamic factors seems a promising approach, as process-based trust is often not or only superficially discussed in other literature.

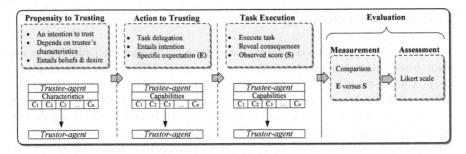

Fig. 1. A generic model of trust mechanisms according to Daudi [16, p. 74]

These generic trust mechanisms are based on a Belief-Desire-Intention model [18], where belief and desire relate to the first phase (propensity to trusting) and intention is related to the second phase (action to trusting). Other approaches take a more specific look at trust between organisations and the mechanism as a function of the collaboration phase. As depicted in Table 1, formal institutions, i.e. law and certification, are most important in the early stages of a business relationship and when swift trust is in demand [19]. In both situations there is usually little knowledge available and a weaker form of trust would normally suffice for a (potential) trustor to take the first step. Here it is the antecedent expectations and behaviours that are formed by potential business partners vis-à-vis such conditions that matter. Reputation, as one form of an informal institutional structure, matters most with regard to swift trust development and situations where the products or services exchanged are characterized by a relatively low level of asset specificity. Community norms, structures and procedures are institutional arrangements which matter specifically in mature industries where the players are few, large and well-known [19].

Table 1. Trust mechanisms and situations according to Bachmann and Inkpen [19, p. 297]

	Legal regulation	Reputation	Certification of exchange partners	Community norms, structures and procedures
Early stages of a relationship	x	(x)	x	
Swift trust	(x)	x	x	
Low asset specificity	(x)	x	(x)	
Mature industries	(x)	(x)		x

x = primary relationship, (x) = secondary relationship

The intended collaboration on shared laboratory resources can be understood as a virtual enterprise defined as: "[…] a special form of a network. Companies are interconnected as a network, for the fulfilment of a concrete task" [20, p. 114]. Regarding trust, [20] identifies different trust relations in virtual enterprises and defines the following main trust decisions that are critical: (1) Trust disposition, (2) Rational calculus, (3) Trust through identification, (4) Positive assessment of abilities, (5) Positive experiences, (6) Transfer of institutional trust and (7) Trust transfer through third parties.

Besides the factors coming into play when considering virtual enterprises, the future cooperation in our remote laboratory environment will be based on roles and less on individuals. It is expected that the sharing of resources will be more a matter of the function and role within an organisation than the personal, individual preference, so that it is matter of role-based trust as defined by [20] and refined by [21, 22] which includes elements of impersonal trust. Nevertheless, Ashnai et al. [23] emphasize that inter-personal trust is a part of inter-organisational trust as well as a predictor. The authors also discuss the impact of opportunistic behaviour on inter-organisational trust and how inter-organisational trust influences information sharing behaviour. Emotion is identified as main source of inter-personal trust, i.e. when a group or person from a company trusts a group or person in a partner company. Rationality, on the other hand, is the key source for inter-organisational trust, i.e. when a company relies on a partner company. Inter-organisational trust, or reliance, is believed to be dependent on factors such as proven capability and expected benefits – hence, objective criteria [25].

Another parallel can be found in service relationships, as discussed by Johnson and Grayson [26]. The authors confirm the importance of the trusting process and summarize four types of trust that play a role of varying importance depending on the stage of the cooperation: (1) Generalized trust; which is based on social norms and refers to a general level of trust in absence of doubt or mistrust. (2) System trust; which is based on rules set by legislative or regulatory authorities as well as on the specific rules and efficiency of enforcement. (3) Process-based trust; which is built on continued interaction in dyadic relationships [27]. This type of trust is based on current and previous behaviour of involved parties and is likely low at the beginning but increases over time. Finally, (4) Personality-based trust depends on the individuals involved and their characteristics. The level of trust is strongly influenced by situational cues. In absence of these cues, personality-based factors become more important. Hence, especially in early stages when situational cues might still be missing, personality-based factors are relevant. Additional to the types of trust, Johnson and Grayson later identify three dimensions, a cognitive, an affective and a behavioural one [28]. The impact of these different dimensions will be investigated at a later stage.

RQ 1 is related to trust in collaborations, and among others [16, 24] have elaborated trust as determinant in collaborations in two different areas: public service and logistics. There are several similarities in their work, so that it can be expected that the identified factors may hold even for the shared laboratory resources which we investigate. For simplification reasons we use the model developed by [16]. Furthermore, Daudi described behavioural elements, as depicted in Fig. 2. It establishes how behavioural factors influence trust and articulates parameters (criteria) which constitute each factor [16]. Additional to the discussed static and process-based factors, several measures can be taken to actively support trust building. The usage of platforms can foster trust in several ways, like by assessing partners before, and ratings once those partners have started using the platform's services [27, 29].

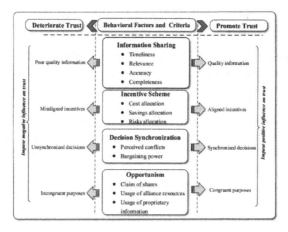

Fig. 2. Behavioural factors and parameters influencing trust in logistic collaboration according to Daudi [16, p. 43]

4   Case Study – The DigiLab4U Project

As described in the introductions, the main purpose of this paper is to understand how different trust factors affect the collaboration climate. In Sect. 3, the factors identified as relevant by reviewing the literature across several sectors were presented. In the next step, it needs to be validated to what extent these also holds for a specific case - an inter-organisational collaboration on shared resources for public organisations. This is the first part of a larger work, and shall lay the foundation for the development of suitable business models.

4.1   The DigiLab4U Project

The cross-institutional Open Digital Lab 4you[1] (brief: DigiLab4U) project intend to offer a digitized laboratory environment that enables cross-site networking of real and virtual laboratory facilities. The project consortium consists of 2 German and 1 Italian Universities as well as a research institute. Three of them offering education and training in logistics and technology implementation and usage. These are supported by stakeholders with special competence in learning analytics and didactic and educational technologies. The goal is to develop an integrated, hybrid learning and research environment consisting of a large variety of learning materials, data and laboratory technologies as a digital educational offering that can be used by any kind of students from bachelor to doctoral students. It is the intention of the project to enable location-independent access to a digitized and networked learning and research environment in such a way that students located in one place can access laboratories in other places.

---

[1] https://digilab4u.com/.

4.2 Identification and Analysis of Factors and the Influence on the Stakeholders

Although resource sharing is beneficial, there are several challenges to overcome before becoming reality. Besides that, the above mentioned goal requires collaboration agreements between the different institutions as well as suitable collaboration models and business models, taking into account the different needs and incentives of all involved stakeholders at organisational level. As described in the previous section, the success of the intended access to shared resources will, therefore, to a large extent depend on the ability to build trust and mutual understanding. As a first step, a workshop was organised with project members. The objectives were the identification of stakeholders and their requirements on distributed networked laboratories. The method used was brainwriting [12]. Each participant wrote the involved stakeholders and their corresponding needs and requirements on cards. These cards were viewed in the group, discussed and grouped at the end. In total 44 stakeholders and 29 needs and requirements have been identified. The main results are summarised in Table 2. How these are related to the trust factors identified in the literature review is described in Sect. 5.

Table 2. Main results of stakeholder and their needs and requirements from the DigiLab4U workshop

Stakeholders	Needs and requirements
(a) Students	**Knowledge acquisition** Individualisation Situated and authentic learning
(b) Professors	*Publications and reputation* ***Knowledge (that has been transferred)*** *Better assessment* *Time savings*
(c) Universities	Innovative teaching strategies *Higher quality of teaching* *Teaching capabilities*
(d) Providers	*Visibility and reputation* Promotion of Products Turnover
(e) Companies (as users)	Cutting costs on learning
(f) Researchers	*Publications and reputation* Data for research **New knowledge (on sharing principles and trust)**

The stakeholders are categorised according to their main usage of the DigiLab4U platform: for training (a, e), teaching (b) and research (f). The Bachelor's or Master's student, a private person or an industrial company use the platform for the purpose of learning (a, e). A professor, a lecturer and/or a teacher will use the platform for purpose of teaching (b). In addition to the learning, an industrial company, researchers or research organisations can also use the platform for research (e, f). The technical operator is usually equated with the provider, but in the context of digitized laboratory environment the provider may be different from the technical operator (d). With respect to DigiLab4U, the providers are the consortium partners, and can be extended by further partners from research and industry. Universities and research institutions, as well as other third parties, may take on the role of sponsor or sales partner, which were eventually added by analysis of the workshop (c).

5 Discussion

The above mentioned approach and analysis of stakeholders as well as their needs and requirements contributes to the research on shared laboratory resources in many ways. In combination with the presented literature review, the analysis in the previous section can help to identify factors which are of special relevance. It is a first step for identifying and understanding the interrelation and the goals of the different stakeholder groups. The description of stakeholders and their motives in itself support a better understanding of involved roles. This enables trust relations to be more easily developed [22]. This is important in remote settings or early stages of a cooperation where hardly any trust based on personal relations has embraced or for organisational trust, where other factors have to support initial trust building [26]. As can be seen above, the need for reputation is a common need for several stakeholder groups. According to Table 1 [7, 9, 11, 19] reputation is heavily linked to trust. As mentioned in Sect. 3, establishing rating systems can serve the trust-building process. These systems seem especially relevant in light of the identified needs, as these ratings can support both initial trust and serve the stakeholder's need for improving their reputation as well. Another interesting factor in this specific setting is information-sharing, identified as a part of process-based trust [16, 26], which may serve both the trust-building process and the need for knowledge acquisition, which is associated with several stakeholders.

The mentioned requirements such as cost savings, promotion of products and turnover, may be linked to the behavioural factors related to incentive scheme as displayed in Fig. 2 [16]. From the business model perspective, the main challenge for the growth of the sharing economy is to establish trust [31] as depicted in [2, 26]. Common market methods compared to physical markets is the possibility of establishing a transparent evaluation system for the quality and reliability of transaction partners, especially providers [23]. [32] describes this as Customer Relationship in the Business Model Canvas, which needs to be taken into account. In the environment of the Shared Laboratory, the relationship and trust concerns are mainly related to the key partners. Therefore, it is important to understand which stakeholders influence the business model, which impact they may have [32].

6 Conclusion and Outlook

This paper presents an overview of trust and determining factors in a setting of shared lab environments. A combination of action-based research and a literature review is used to discuss the importance of these factors. Based on the discussed findings, it can be concluded that further investigation of the interaction between the different trust factors, the stakeholders and needs in collaboration can be carried out for a deeper understanding of the interactions as well as to understand different incentives affect the organisational and individual engagement in the shared resources. As stated in [1, 9] simulations and games used in a workshop setting or as a multi-player game seem to be suitable tools for this purpose. Therefore, the next step will be to develop a serious multi-player game in which the different interactions and relations can be investigated. The game's scenarios, stories and tasks will be based on relevant, collaborative use cases, and the identified trust factors will be integrated into the game's design. Eventually, analysing individual and cooperative game play can help to assess identified trust factors and dependencies. In addition, analysis of the stakeholders through user stories would give a more detailed insight into the respective roles such as administration, marketing, decision makers or data protection officer.

Acknowledgement. This work has been funded by the German Federal Ministry of Education and Research (BMBF) through the project DigiLab4U (No. 16DHB2112/3). The authors wish to acknowledge the BMBF for their support. We also wish to acknowledge our gratitude to all DigiLab4U project partners for their contribution.

Barbara Göbl is supported by a DOC-team fellowship of the Austrian Academy of Sciences.

References

1. Baalsrud Hauge, J., Kalverkamp, M., Forcolin, M., Westerheim, H., Franke, M., Thoben, K.-D.: Collaborative serious games for awareness on shared resources in supply chain management. In: Grabot, B., Vallespir, B., Gomes, S., Bouras, A., Kiritsis, D. (eds.) APMS 2014. IAICT, vol. 439, pp. 491–499. Springer, Heidelberg (2014). https://doi.org/10.1007/978-3-662-44736-9_60

2. Goudin, P.: The Cost of Non-Europe in the Sharing Economy. European Union, Brussels (2016). https://doi.org/10.2861/26238

3. Daudi, M., Hauge, J.B., Thoben, K.-D.: A trust framework for agents' interactions in collaborative logistics. In: Freitag, M., Kotzab, H., Pannek, J. (eds.) Dynamics in Logistics. LNL, pp. 53–63. Springer, Cham (2017). https://doi.org/10.1007/978-3-319-45117-6_5

4. Frenken, K., Schor, J.: Putting the sharing economy into perspective. Environ. Innov. Soc. Transitions **23**, 3–10 (2017). https://doi.org/10.1016/j.eist.2017.01.003

5. Gesing, B.: Sharing economy logistics: rethinking logistics with access over ownership, Troisdorf, Germany (2017). http://www.dhl.com/content/dam/downloads/g0/about_us/logistics_insights/DHLTrend_Report_Sharing_Economy.pdf

6. Schönberger, J., Kopfer, H., Kotzab, H.: A micro- and macroeconomic view on shared resources in logistics. In: Kotzab, H., Pannek, J., Thoben, K.-D. (eds.) Dynamics in Logistics. LNLO, pp. 3–12. Springer, Cham (2016). https://doi.org/10.1007/978-3-319-23512-7_1

7. Tussyadiah, I.P.: An exploratory study on drivers and deterrents of collaborative consumption in travel. In: Tussyadiah, I., Inversini, A. (eds.) Information and Communication Technologies in Tourism 2015, pp. 817–830. Springer, Cham (2015). https://doi.org/10.1007/978-3-319-14343-9_59

8. Heradio, R., et al.: Virtual and remote labs in education: a bibliometric analysis. Comput. Educ. **98**, 14–38 (2016). https://doi.org/10.1016/j.compedu.2016.03.010

9. Thoben, K.-D., et al.: Training through gaming: applying a simulation based business game to train people for collaboration in virtual enterprises. In: Online Educa Berlin 2005, International Conference on Technology Supported Learning and Training (2006)

10. Mayer, R.C.: An integrative model of organisational trust. Acad. Manag. Rev. **20**, 709–734 (1995)

11. Daudi, M., et al.: Behavioral factors influencing partner trust in logistics collaboration: a review. Logist. Res. **9**(1), 19 (2016). https://doi.org/10.1007/s12159-016-0146-7

12. Wilson, C.: Brainstorming and Beyond: A User-Centered Design Method, pp. 43–60. Elsevier Science, Burlington (2013). https://doi.org/10.1016/C2012-0-03533-8

13. Tranfield, D., Denyer, D., Smart, P.: Towards a methodology for developing evidence-informed management knowledge by means of systematic review. Br. J. Manag. **14**(3), 207–222 (2003). https://doi.org/10.1111/1467-8551.00375

14. Sein, M.K., et al.: Action design research. MIS Q. **35**(1), 37–56 (2011). https://doi.org/10.2307/23043488

15. Yin, R.K.: Case Study Research: Design and Methods, 4th edn. SAGE, London (2009)

16. Daudi, M.: Trust in sharing resources in logistics collaboration (2018)

17. Buczynski, B.: Sharing is Good: How to Save Money, Time and Resources through Collaborative Consumption. New Society Publishers, Gabriola Island (2013)

18. Georgeff, M., Pell, B., Pollack, M., Tambe, M., Wooldridge, M.: The belief-desire-intention model of agency. In: Müller, J.P., Rao, A.S., Singh, M.P. (eds.) ATAL 1998. LNCS, vol. 1555, pp. 1–10. Springer, Heidelberg (1999). https://doi.org/10.1007/3-540-49057-4_1

19. Bachmann, R., Inkpen, A.C.: Understanding institutional-based trust building processes in inter-organisational relationships. Organ. Stud. **32**(2), 281–301 (2011). https://doi.org/10.1177/0170840610397477

20. Fladnitzer, M., Grabner-Kräuter, S.: Vertrauen als Erfolgsfaktor virtueller Unternehmen. 1, pp. 188–197. Aufl. s.l.: DUV Deutscher Universitäts-Verlag (2006)

21. Müthel, M.: Erfolgreiche Teamarbeit in deutsch-chinesischen Projekten. Dissertation Universitäit Lüneburg, 2005. Wiesbaden: Deutscher Universitäts-Verlag/GWV Fachverlage GmbH (2006)

22. Zolin, R., et al.: Modeling & monitoring trust in virtual A/E/C teams. Trust in virtual teams. In: CIFE Working Paper #62. Center for Integrated Facility Engineering, Stanford (2000)

23. Ashnai, B., et al.: Inter-personal and inter-organisational trust in business relationships: an attitude–behavior–outcome model. Ind. Mark. Manag. **52**, 128–139 (2016). https://doi.org/10.1016/j.indmarman.2015.05.020

24. Chen, B.: Assessing interorganizational networks for public service delivery: a process-perceived effectiveness framework. Publ. Perform. Manag. Rev. **31**(3), 172–187 (2008)

25. Jiang, Z., Henneberg, S.C., Naudé, P.: The importance of trust vis-à-vis reliance in business relationships: some international findings. Int. Mark. Rev. **28**(4), 318–339 (2011). https://doi.org/10.1108/02651331111149921

26. Johnson, D.S., Grayson, K.: Sources and dimensions of trust in service relation-ships. In: Handbook of Service Relationship, pp. 357–370 (2000)

27. Zucker, L.G.: Production of trust: institutional sources of economic structure, 1840-1920. Res. Organ. Behav. **8**, 53–111 (1986)

28. Johnson, D., Grayson, K.: Cognitive and affective trust in service relationships. J. Bus. Res. **58**(4), 500–507 (2005)

29. Westphal, I., Thoben, K.-D., Seifert, M.: Measuring collaboration performance in virtual organizations. In: Camarinha-Matos, L.M., Afsarmanesh, H., Novais, P., Analide, C. (eds.) PRO-VE 2007. ITIFIP, vol. 243, pp. 33–42. Springer, Boston (2007). https://doi.org/10.1007/978-0-387-73798-0_4

30. Schallmo, D., et al.: Digitale Transformation von Geschäftsmodellen. Grundlagen, Instrumente und Best Practices, p. 194. Springer Fachmedien Wiesbaden, Wiesbaden (2017). https://doi.org/10.1007/978-3-658-12388-8

31. Goudin, P.: The Cost of Non-Europe in the Sharing Economy. Economic, Social and Legal Challenges and Opportunities, p. 22. European Parliamentary Research Service, European Added Value Unit, Brussels (2016)

32. Osterwalder, A., et al.: Business model generation. In: A Handbook for Visionaries, Game Changers, and Challengers, p. 204. Wiley, Hoboken (2010)

Key Performance Indicators Integrating Collaborative and Mobile Robots in the Factory Networks

Khurshid Aliev, Dario Antonelli[(✉)], Ahmed Awouda,
and Paolo Chiabert

Politecnico di Torino, Corso Duca degli Abruzzi 24, 10129 Turin, Italy
{khurshid.aliev,dario.antonelli,ahmed.awouda,
paolo.chiabert}@polito.it

Abstract. Measuring performances of collaborative robots in Industry 4.0 applications is an open research area since the emergence of collaborative and mobile robots as a support for semi-automatic manufacturing processes. A compelling management problem is the definition of convenient performance measures on which to assess the new generation of robots, to improve process performances both at the robotic cell design stage and at the production stage. A consequent problem is to gather the required data to measure performances. Data must be obtained automatically and in real time. Different levels of communication protocols have to be harmonized in order to transfer data from robots and other factory machines to the cloud on the internet and eventually to the production control system. A case study allows to demonstrate the operation of data acquisition system for collaborative and mobile robots and the real–time monitoring dashboard. The outcome of the study is the gathering of data at field level, the evaluation of robot performances at machine level in order to execute the real time production control at factory level.

Keywords: KPI · ISO 22400 · Cobots · Mobile robots ·
Factory network protocols

1 Introduction

Collaborative robots (Cobots) and mobile robots are being introduced massively in the smart factory. Indeed, they have been considered as an advanced manufacturing solution and are an enabling technology in Industry 4.0 (I4.0) [1]. The main reason for their success is the combination of robot strength and endurance with the dexterity and the flexibility of human operator.

Going in detail, there are several assets of Cobots with respect to traditional robots: easy to program, safe interaction with human, possibility to share the workspace with other humans and robots, no need for fixed workplace surrounded by fences. This last feature means that cobots are easily movable, while mobile robots, by design, are able to move in the plant without following fixed trajectories. In the framework for workcell architecture design proposed by [2], this feature addresses specifically the operative perspective.

L. M. Camarinha-Matos et al. (Eds.): PRO-VE 2019, IFIP AICT 568, pp. 635–642, 2019.
https://doi.org/10.1007/978-3-030-28464-0_56

During the operation, it is practice to monitor the Key Performance Indicators (KPIs) of the process. Unfortunately, as the robot is no more constrained to stay in a specific cell, the measure of production performances is made both difficult to execute and to assign to a specific process. The choice of suitable indicators and their monitoring on a mobile robot or on a robot that does not belong to a specific workcell poses new and unprecedented problems [3] that are the target of this paper.

Transfer of robot data from the field level to the factory internet allows to leverage the exploitation of collaborative networks. In this network collaboration is the process of various agents working together on a voluntary basis by respecting a set of behavior rules [16]. Evaluation of Cobots' performance in such a collaborative network (CN) plays significant role in the domain of Industry 4.0 and can be supportive tool for a successful business.

Industrial machines and sensors from different vendors have different standardized protocols which can be challenging for data exchange and to align them in the CN. For that reason, this paper proposes a framework of connecting different robots and sensors with different protocols to increase the overall performance of the CN and to monitor performance of the robots [15].

In Sect. 2, the related literature is presented. In Sect. 3, the implementation of the data transfer in order to measure cobot performance is discussed. In Sect. 4, the KPIs suitable for cobot operations are defined and calculated for the case study of Sect. 5. Eventually, in Sect. 6 the study's outcomes are discussed and the future work is introduced.

2   Related Works

Low cost and precise way of measurement of the machine performance in industry grasped the attention of managers and researchers for many years. The integration of performance monitoring with maintenance systems can assist the manufacturer in achieving the goal of maintaining the performance of machines and support the control strategies [3].

Therefore, there are various proposed frameworks and systems for performance monitoring. Authors of [4] implemented and visualized KPIs according to ISO 22400 standards within a discrete manufacturing web-based interface to monitor and control an assembly line at runtime. In [5] review has been made by focusing on aspects of KPIs management, unification of taxonomy gathers relevant aspect highlighted by the literature and which captures the unique characteristics of KPIs in a more fully way. Observed characteristics can help researchers to decide about the most suitable solution for their requirements. General definition of the KPI scheme for monitoring on-line production process is described with 8-step iterative closed-loop model by authors of [6]. Real time monitoring energy consumption using five selected KPIs of the work cell that composed: robot, cabinet and conveyor successfully implemented in [7]. All above mentioned reviews mainly focused on models and simulations of the models. Moreover, proposed models and frameworks are not low cost which can be suitable for education and Industrial IoT (IIoT) applications. In next sections, we describe the open-source and reduced cost implementation of KPIs for collaborative and mobile robots and sensors within the factory networks.

3 High Level and Low Level Protocols in Factory Networks to Connect Machines into Cloud

Developing Industrial IoT networks which can connect and exchange data between sensors and machines to the backend systems are very challenging. Protocols provide device-to-device or device-to-server communications. There is a big variety of protocols used in today's industrial scene and the choice among these different protocols is application dependent and device specific. Industrial communication protocols are classified as Ethernet and non-Ethernet protocols: Non-Ethernet-Fieldbus protocols (Modbus RTU, Profibus DP), and Industrial Ethernet protocols (such as Modbus TCP and Profinet). Industrial communication protocols are low level or device management protocols. High level open source IoT domain data exchange protocols are Message Queuing Telemetry Transport (MQTT), CoAP (Constrained Application Protocol), Advanced Message Queuing Protocol (AMQP), Extensible Messaging and Presence Protocol (XMPP). In this section the implemented ones are discussed.

Modbus is an application layer protocol that defines the rules for organizing and interpreting data independent of the underlying communication layers and the transmission medium used [8]. *Modbus TCP/IP* is an alternative of the *Modbus* protocol where the message frame is encapsulated in a TCP/IP wrapper. TCP/IP refers to the Transmission Control Protocol and Internet Protocol, which provides the transmission medium for Modbus TCP messaging. The primary function of TCP is to ensure that all packets of data are received correctly, while IP makes sure that messages are correctly addressed and routed.

Modbus TCP combines a physical network (Ethernet), with a networking standard (TCP/IP), and a standard method of representing data which results in Modbus TCP being fully compatible with the already installed Ethernet infrastructure of cables, connectors, network interface cards, hubs, and switches. Simply stated, Modbus TCP shares the same physical and data link layers of traditional IEEE 802.3 Ethernet and uses the same TCP/IP suite of protocols.

Another protocol used in this work and resident to the IOT domain is *MQTT* and *REST*. *Message Queuing Telemetry Transport (MQTT)* is a protocol designed to connect the physical world devices and networks, with applications and middleware to develop Web applications in IT area. It is designed to minimize network bandwidth and device resource requirements whilst also attempting to ensure reliability and some degree of assurance of delivery, also MQTT protocol is a good choice for wireless networks that experience varying levels of latency [9].

MQTT uses the Publish/Subscribe Model which consists of three main components: publishers, subscribers, and a broker. Publishers are the lightweight sensors and devices that connect to the broker to send their data and go back to sleep whenever possible. Subscribers are applications or devices that are interested in a certain topic, or sensory data, so they connect to brokers to be informed whenever new data is received. The brokers classify sensory data in topics and send them to subscribers interested in those topics only. A device can behave as a publisher and a subscriber at the same time by publishing to specific topics and subscribing to others, the term MQTT client is used to distinguish publishers/subscribers from brokers.

Representational State Transfer (REST) or RESTful web services describes a set of architectural principles by which data can be transmitted over a standardized interface such as Hypertext Transfer Protocol (HTTP). REST does not contain an additional messaging layer and focuses on design rules for creating stateless services. A client can access the resource using the unique URI (Uniform Resource Identifier) and a representation of the resource is returned. With each new resource representation, the client is said to transfer state. While accessing RESTful resources with HTTP protocol, the URL of the resource serves as the resource identifier and GET, PUT, DELETE, POST and HEAD are the standard HTTP operations to be performed on that resource.

In next section we describe KPIs and most suitable KPIs for collaborative and mobile robots according to the standards.

4 Selection of KPIs for Cobots and Mobile Robots

Key performance indicators (KPIs) gives possibility to measure the performance and progress of the manufacturing machines and systems. Acquired data from different machines and things in Industry can serve to monitor and visualize energy consumption, planning and scheduling, maintenance, product quality, inventory, machines capability and etc. Standardized KPIs are defined in ISO 22400 and can be used in different fields of industry. On the other hand, implementation of those KPIs in real industrial applications are challenging. The title of the ISO 22400 is "Automation systems and integration—Key performance indicators (KPIs) for manufacturing operations management" that is collection of 34 KPIs. ISO 22400 standards composed of two parts: ISO 22400-1 describes basic overview and terminologies of the KPIs framework in the manufacturing [10]. ISO 22400-2 is dedicated to definitions and descriptions of 34 possible KPIs which can be used in industry [11]. In [12] five top KPIs that can improve the performance of cobots and robots are defined and possible measurement techniques are described. Moreover, importance of standard metrics such as Overall Equipment Effectiveness (OEE) that is standard for measuring manufacturing productivity is explained. Taking account above mentioned standards, following five KPIs has been selected to implement for cobots and mobile robots in our case study:

Cycle time – Summation of the steps time of the robot while executing sequence of tasks

$$Cycle\ time = \sum Time\ to\ execute\ a\ single\ process \tag{1}$$

Cycles completed – increment a variable every time a cycle is completed

$$Cycle\ completed = \sum_{i}^{n} C_i = C_1 + C_2 + C_3 + \cdots + C_n \tag{2}$$

Wait time – percentage of time that the robot is waiting or time that not executing productive tasks. Wait time is defined as sum of all individual wait times:

$$Wait\ time = \sum Robot\ static\ time = Planned\ use\ time - \sum C_i \qquad (3)$$

Planned Use Time is defined from the Cycle Time per unit, multiplying by the number of products that are going to be processed.

Utilization – measures how long a robot is being used compared to how long it could be used. Utilization for robots can be defined as following formula:

$$Utilization = \frac{Total\ Use\ time}{Total\ time} \qquad (4)$$

Efficiency – percentage of time that the robot performs productive work while running a program.

$$Efficiency = \frac{\sum C_i(Total\ Cycle\ Times)}{Total\ Use\ time} \qquad (5)$$

5 Implementation and Application to a Case Study

5.1 Collaborative Network Integrating Data from Cobots and Mobile Robots

The proposed CN to collect data from industrial machines and to transfer them to the cloud is presented in Fig. 1. The framework is composed by three layers. In the bottom layer all industrial machines are located (here the mobile robot MIR100 and the cobotUR3) together with external sensors like temperature, proximity.

Data acquisition from MIR100 and UR3 has been executed using the Modbus TCP/IP protocol where the robots are a Modbus Server and the RPi is a Modbus Client the client sends requests to read specific registers available on the robot's internal memory, the robot responds by providing the value of the requested register. Both UR3 and MIR100 registers can hold discrete variables such as On/Off status. Moreover, UR3 has access to analog values such as joint velocities, angles and also robot temperature and input current. At the same time, it was possible to retrieve battery level, positions, orientation data and control the mobile robot through MODBUS TCP/IP.

The middle layer is responsible for gateway and networking the machines and things using open source hardware and software. Raspberry Pi is used as operating system that runs open source software such as Node-red (used to create and visualize live data on browsers), Mosquitto (massage broker that implements MQTT protocol) and NGROK (reverse proxy software that creates a secure tunnel on a local machine along with a public URL). NGROK is used to allow the Node-Red Dashboard to be accessible via a public URL on the internet. The ESP8266 is Wi-Fi module with a full TCP/IP Stack and microcontroller capability. The module has been operated as an MQTT client that acquires sensor data from the sensors connected to it and then transmits the data to the Raspberry Pi via MQTT protocol.

On the top layer of the framework, all data is transmitted to the Thingspeak platform [13] to store data and perform analytics. Moreover, Node-red dashboard is used to visualize KPIs on the browsers. The implementation and resulting graphs of this component are presented in further sections.

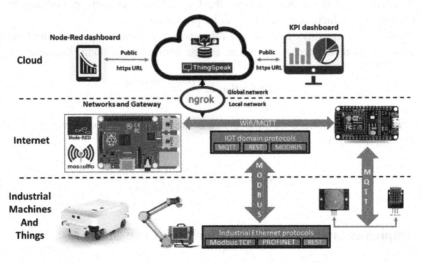

Fig. 1. Architecture of the CN for sharing information among factory machines.

5.2   Calculation KPIs from Robot Data and Their Visualization on the Dashboard

In case study, KPIs of the mobile robot has been evaluated and implemented on the dashboard. KPIs of the mobile robot was implemented for the transportation tasks of the metallic pieces to the UR3 manipulator [14]. Basically, MIR100 has 10 missions to transport metallic piece and the aim of the experiment was to estimate KPIs of the MIR100 in this demonstrator. The sequence of the mission on the dashboard of the MIR100 is shown in Fig. 2.

The experiment was conducted in the following way: to demonstrate KPIs of the MIR100 on the dashboard and on the cloud, we considered that MIR100 was working for an hour. Total time is 60 min but the robot was On for 30.78 min which results in a total use time of 30.78 min. The robot spent 6.3 min to transport all workpieces and completes its task with a total cycle time of 6.3 min. Taking account values coming from MIR100 and using above mentioned KPIs formulas, Utilization and Efficiency of the MIR100 have been estimated as 51% and 20.5% respectively.

$$Utilization = \frac{Total\ Use\ time}{Total\ time} = \frac{30.78\ min}{60\ min} * 100 = 51\%$$

$$Efficiency = \frac{\sum C_i(Total\ Cycle\ Times)}{Total\ Use\ time} = \frac{6.3\ min(378.1\ s)}{30.78\ min} = 20.5\%$$

Cycle time, cycle completed and wait time, utilization and efficiency have been calculated triggering registers of the MIR100 and programmed on the node-red using user defined functions (formulas has been converted into functions) and transferred to the dashboard.

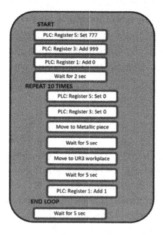

Fig. 2. Sequence of the missions of the mobile robot on the control dashboard.

On the top level of the proposed framework, KPIs are integrated and visualized. KPI formulas are implemented on the Node-red software with user defined functions. Node-red requests necessary data (state, start time, uptime, downtime etc.) through MODBUS TCP/IP to calculate KPIs. Received raw data are converted in human readable data and robot KPIs are calculated. Results are sent to the Node-red dashboard (Fig. 3). Dashboard reports general information (battery level, state of the robot, distance and length of the mission), cycle time (number of CT completed, previous and average cycle time, initial mission time), Supervisory Commands (pause, play, cancel, clear mission queue) and selected KPIs (utilization, efficiency and wait time).

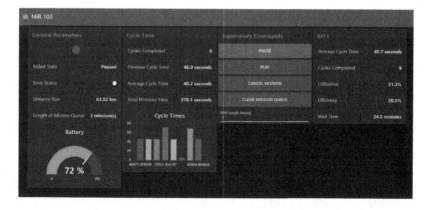

Fig. 3. KPIs of the mobile robot on the Node-red dashboard. (Color figure online)

6 Conclusions and Future Works

The paper demonstrates the practical integration and implementation of KPIs inside a CN by gathering data from field level and using them to measure performance at factory level. Developed system is composed by open access tools and protocols that are a suitable demonstrator of Industry 4.0 for academics and manufacturers. Future work will be the application of the measuring system in an actual industrial contest to assess the robustness of the system in factory conditions.

References

1. Lorenz, M., et al.: Man and Machine in Industry 4.0: How will Technology Transform the Industrial Workforce Through 2025. The Boston Consulting Group, Boston (2015)
2. Djuric, A.M., et al.: A framework for collaborative robot (CoBot) integration in advanced manufacturing systems. SAE Int. J. Mater. Manuf. **9**(2), 457–464 (2016)
3. Weiss, B.A., Qiao, G.: Hierarchical decomposition of a manufacturing work cell to promote monitoring, diagnostics, and prognostics. In: ASME 2017 12th International Manufacturing Science and Engineering Conference. ASME (2017)
4. Ramis Ferrer, B., Muhammad, U., Mohammed, W., Martínez Lastra, J.: Implementing and visualizing ISO 22400 key performance indicators for monitoring discrete manufacturing systems. Machines **6**(3), 39 (2018)
5. Domínguez, E., Pérez, B., Rubio, Á.L., Zapata, M.A.: A taxonomy for key performance indicators management. Comput. Stand. Interfaces **64**, 24–40 (2019)
6. Rakar, A., Zorzut, S., Jovan, V.: Assessment of production performance by means of KPI. In: Proceedings of the Control, pp. 6–9 (2004)
7. Zhang, B., Postelnicu, C., Lastra, J.L.M.: Key performance indicators for energy efficient asset management in a factory automation testbed. In: IEEE 10th International Conference on Industrial Informatics, pp. 391–396. IEEE (2012)
8. Modicon, I.: Modicon Modbus protocol reference guide, pp. 28–29. North Andover, Massachusetts (1996)
9. OASIS Standard: MQTT ver. 3.1.1 (2014). https://docs.oasis-open.org/mqtt/mqtt/v3,1
10. ISO22400-1: Automation systems and integration - key performance indicators (KPIs) for manufacturing operations management - Part 1: overview, concepts and terminology (2014)
11. ISO22400-2: Automation systems and integration - key performance indicators (KPIs) for manufacturing operations management - Part 2: definitions and descriptions (2014)
12. Top 5 Cobot key performance indicators: how to measure and improve the performance of collaborative robots. https://info.universal-robots.com/how-to-measure-you-cobots-performance-cobot-kpi
13. Official website of the Thingspeak platform. https://thingspeak.com/pages/learn_more
14. Aliev, K., Antonelli, D.: Analysis of cooperative industrial task execution by mobile and manipulator robots. In: Trojanowska, J., Ciszak, O., Machado, J.M., Pavlenko, I. (eds.) MANUFACTURING 2019. LNME, pp. 248–260. Springer, Cham (2019). https://doi.org/10.1007/978-3-030-18715-6_21
15. da Piedade Francisco, R., Azevedo, A., Bastos, J., Almeida, A.: Using key alignment indicators for performance evaluation in collaborative networks. In: Camarinha-Matos, L.M., Pereira-Klen, A., Afsarmanesh, H. (eds.) PRO-VE 2011. IAICT, vol. 362, pp. 159–166. Springer, Heidelberg (2011). https://doi.org/10.1007/978-3-642-23330-2_18. (hal-01569982)
16. Talukdar, S.N.: Collaboration rules for autonomous software agents. Decis. Support Syst. **24** (3-4), 269–278 (1999)

Author Index

Abreu, Antonio   115
Afsarmanesh, Hamideh   193, 205, 379
Ahlers, Dirk   393
Alamäki, Ari   173, 516
Alarcón-Valero, Faustino   496
Albertario, Serena   323
Alexandrou, Dimitrios   234
Aliev, Khurshid   635
Alloush, Iyas   393
Almeida, Ricardo   418
Álvarez, Alejandro   572
Anes, Vitor   115
Antonelli, Dario   562, 635
Antonelli, Leandro   447
Aramo-Immonen, Heli   527
Aunimo, Lili   173, 527
Awouda, Ahmed   635

Baalsrud Hauge, Jannicke   624
Bai, Yuewei   259
Baldissera, Thais A.   365
Barata, José   29
Barthe-Delanoë, Anne-Marie   220, 477
Batres, Rafael   572
Belloum, Adam   379
Benaben, Frederick   151, 193
Berkers, Frank   335
Bettoni, Andrea   323
Biliri, Evmorfia   234
Boucher, Xavier   541
Bruno, Giulia   163
Burghardt, Andrzej   585, 594

Cafagna, Stefano   507
Camarinha-Matos, Luis M.   43, 103, 245,
    365, 379, 418
Cao, Tiancheng   220
Cellary, Wojciech   3
Chiabert, Paolo   635
Ciesielska, Magdalena   295
Coba, Camilo Murillo   541
Coche, Julien   151

Cortés, Daniel   572
Cruz, Nancy   572
Cuenca, Llanos   467

Dassisti, Michele   507
de Vrieze, Paul   259
Dias, Tiago   43
Duin, Heiko   624

El Asri, Ikram   308
Esparza, Germán   572

Falsafi, Mohammadtaghi   355
Felicetti, Alberto Michele   457
Fernandez, Alejandro   487
Ferrada, Filipa   418
Fornasiero, Rosanna   335, 355
Franceschini, Fiorenzo   562
Francesco, Andrea Barni   323
Frega, Nicola   457
Friedrich, Julia   128

Gierlak, Piotr   585, 594
Göbl, Barbara   624
Gonzalez-Feliu, Jesus   552
Gou, Juanqiong   193, 205
Graça, Paula   245
Guerrini, Fábio Müller   69

Harder, Philipp   81
Helfert, Markus   393
Hernandez, Jorge E.   447, 487
Hidalgo-Carvajal, David   335
Houngbé, Michelle   477
Hozikian, Mariángeles   447

Janowski, Tomasz   295
Jassbi, Javad   431

Kammerlohr, Valentin   624
Kasse, John Paul   259

Kerzazi, Noureddine   308
Ketamo, Harri   173
Krogstie, John   393
Kurc, Krzysztof   585, 594

Lamothe, Jacques   344
Lampathaki, Fenareti   234
Lezoche, Mario   507
Liagkou, Vasiliki   604
Litwin, Paweł   185, 615
Liu, Qinghua   193
Liu, Shaofeng   487
Lombardi, Franco   163
Luetkehoff, Ben   143

Macedo, Patrícia   418
Mądziel, Maksymilian   615
Maisano, Domenico A.   562
Mäki, Marko   516
Mangano, Giulio   552
Medini, Khaled   541
Mezgár, István   21
Mincuzzi, Nicola   355
Mirnoori, Vahid   405
Modoni, Gianfranco E.   355
Molina, Arturo   572
Montarnal, Aurélie   151, 220
Mu, Wenxin   193, 205, 220
Muszyńska, Magdalena   585, 594

Naudet, Yannick   11
Négny, Stéphane   477
Nikghadam-Hojjati, Sanaz   29

Ojo, Adegboyega   285
Oliveira, Ana Inês   418, 431
Ortiz, Ángel   467
Osório, A. Luis   43, 379

Palacios-Arguello, Laura   552
Panetto, Hervé   11, 487, 507
Pang, Beibei   205
Pankow, Matías Nahuel   487
Parvinen, Lasse   173
Paśko, Łukasz   185

Pereira, Pedro   431
Pérez Perales, David   496
Pertselakis, Minas   234
Pessot, Elena   335
Petersen, Sobah Abbas   393
Phinikettos, Marios   234
Pourzolfaghar, Zohreh   393

Rabelo, Ricardo J.   55
Ramírez, José   572
Razy, Alim   405
Reyes, Ivann   572
Rodríguez, María Angeles   467
Romero, David   55
Rosas, João   103, 271, 418
Rousse, Christophe   344

Sacco, Marco   355
Sanchez, Esteban   487
Santos, Ricardo   115
Schroeter, Moritz   143
Schuh, Günther   81
Semeraro, Concetta   507
Silva, Agostinho   405
Silva, Henrique Diogo   323
Soares, António Lucas   323
Stadnicka, Dorota   615
Steinlein, Felix   143
Stich, Volker   143
Stroh, Max-Ferdinand   81
Stylios, Chrysostomos   604
Szybicki, Dariusz   585, 594

Tapia, Andrea   151
Taurino, Teresa   93
Tavares, José   43
Tenera, Alexandra   103, 271
Thierry, Caroline   344
Tiss, Sanaa   344
Torres, Diego   447
Traini, Emiliano   163

Uliasz, Marek   585, 594
Urze, Paula   103

Verdecho, María-José   496
Vilas-Boas, João   405
Villa, Agostino   93
Villagomez, Luis E.   572
Viri, Riku   527
Volpentesta, Antonio Palmiro   457

Weerdmeester, Ron   335

Xu, Lai   259

Yamanari, Juliana Suemi   69
Yilma, Bereket Abera   11
Ying, Wenchi   193

Zacharias, Marios   234
Zambiasi, Saulo Popov   55
Zangiacomi, Andrea   335
Zeller, Violett   81
Zenezini, Giovanni   552
Zinke-Wehlmann, Christian   128

Printed in the United States
by Baker & Taylor Publisher Services